Taxation

Taxation

Finance Act 2000

Alan Melville

FCA BSc Cert. Ed.

FINANCIAL TIMES

Prentice Hall

An imprint of **Pearson Education**

Harlow, England · London · New York · Reading, Massachusetts · San Francisco · Toronto · Don Mills, Ontario · Sydney
Tokyo · Singapore · Hong Kong · Seoul · Taipei · Cape Town · Madrid · Mexico City · Amsterdam · Munich · Paris · Milan

Pearson Education Limited
Edinburgh Gate
Harlow
Essex CM20 2JE
England

and Associated Companies throughout the world

Visit us on the World Wide Web at:
http://www.pearsoneduc.com

First published 2001

ISBN 0 273 64669 9 PPR

British Library Cataloguing-in-Publication Data
A catalogue record for this book is available from the British Library

10 9 8 7 6 5 4 3 2 1
04 03 02 01

Printed and bound in Great Britain by
Redwood Books Ltd, Trowbridge

Contents

Payments made on termination of employment · The PAYE system ·
Construction industry tax deduction scheme · Employee incentive schemes

Preface

The main aim of this book is to describe the UK taxation system in sufficient depth and with sufficient clarity to meet the needs of those undertaking a first course of study in taxation. The book has not been written with any specific syllabus in mind but is suitable for students who are preparing for any of the following examinations :

Examining body	Level	Examination title
Institute of Chartered Accountants in England and Wales	Professional Stage	Taxation
Association of Chartered Certified Accountants	Certificate Stage	The Tax Framework
Chartered Institute of Management Accountants	Intermediate Level	Business Taxation
Chartered Institute of Public Finance and Accountancy	Professional 2	Public Policy and Taxation
Association of Taxation Technicians	Associateship	Personal and Business Taxation
Association of Accounting Technicians	Technician Stage	Preparing Personal and Business Taxation Computations
Association of Chartered Certified Accountants (Technician qualification)	Level C	Preparing Taxation Computations and Returns
Association of International Accountants	Foundation Stage	Auditing and Taxation
Institute of Company Accountants	Level 2	Taxation 1

The book will also be of value to those studying taxation as part of a university or college course in accounting, finance or business studies and may be used as an introductory text for a study of taxation at an advanced level.

Every effort has been made to explain the tax system as clearly as possible. There are numerous worked examples and each chapter (except Chapter 1) concludes with a set of exercises which thoroughly test the reader's grasp of the new topics introduced in that chapter. The book also contains four sets of review questions which are drawn from the past examination papers of the professional accounting bodies. The solutions to most of the exercises and review questions are to be found at the back of the book but the solutions to those exercises and questions marked with an asterisk (*) are provided in a separate Lecturer's Guide.

This sixth edition incorporates the provisions of the Finance Act 2000.

Alan Melville
June 2000

Capital Allowances

Writing Down Allowance (WDA) per annum:

Plant and machinery	25%
Long-life assets	6%
Industrial buildings acquired after 5/11/62	4%
Agricultural buildings	4%

First Year Allowance (FYA) on qualifying plant and machinery:

Acquired 2 July 1997 to 1 July 1998[†]	50%
Acquired on or after 2 July 1998[†]	40%
Long-life assets acquired 2 July 1997 to 1 July 1998[†]	12%
ICT acquired 1 April 2000 to 31 March 2003[‡]	100%

[†] *Small and medium-sized businesses only.*
[‡] *Small businesses only.*

National Insurance Contributions

	2000/01	1999/00
CLASS 1 (Not contracted out)		
Primary threshold (weekly)	£76	£66
Upper earnings limit (weekly)	£535	£500
Employee contributions[†]		
Rate on earnings between primary threshold and UEL	10%	10%
Employer contributions[‡]		
Secondary threshold (weekly)	£84	£83
Rate on earnings beyond secondary threshold	12.2%	12.2%

[†] *No employee contributions payable if earnings do not exceed primary threshold.*
[‡] *No employer contributions payable if earnings do not exceed secondary threshold.*

	2000/01	1999/00
CLASS 1A		
Rate	12.2%	12.2%
CLASS 2		
Weekly contribution	£2.00	£6.55
Small earnings exemption limit	£3,825	£3,770
CLASS 3		
Weekly contribution	£6.55	£6.45
CLASS 4		
Rate	7%	6%
Lower profits limit	£4,385	£7,530
Upper profits limit	£27,820	£26,000

Capital Gains Tax

	2000/01 £	1999/00 £
Annual exemption - individuals and disabled trusts	7,200	7,100
- other trusts	3,600	3,550
Chattels exemption	6,000	6,000
Retirement relief - upper limit for 100% relief	150,000	200,000
- upper limit for 50% relief	600,000	800,000

Corporation Tax

Year	Starting rate	Small company rate	Full rate	Marginal relief fraction	Starting rate limits		Small company rate limits	
					Lower £	Upper £	Lower £	Upper £
FY1994	-	25%	33%	1/50	-	-	300,000	1,500,000
FY1995	-	25%	33%	1/50	-	-	300,000	1,500,000
FY1996	-	24%	33%	9/400	-	-	300,000	1,500,000
FY1997	-	21%	31%	1/40	-	-	300,000	1,500,000
FY1998	-	21%	31%	1/40	-	-	300,000	1,500,000
FY1999	-	20%	30%	1/40	-	-	300,000	1,500,000
FY2000	10%	20%	30%	1/40	10,000	50,000	300,000	1,500,000

The rate of ACT was 20% for FY1994 through to FY1999 (until 6 April 1999).

Inheritance Tax

Date of transfer	0% Band	Rate on chargeable lifetime transfers	Rate on death
10 March 1992 to 5 April 1995	0 - £150,000	20%	40%
6 April 1995 to 5 April 1996	0 - £154,000	20%	40%
6 April 1996 to 5 April 1997	0 - £200,000	20%	40%
6 April 1997 to 5 April 1998	0 - £215,000	20%	40%
6 April 1998 to 5 April 1999	0 - £223,000	20%	40%
6 April 1999 to 5 April 2000	0 - £231,000	20%	40%
On or after 6 April 2000	0 - £234,000	20%	40%

Value Added Tax

Standard rate (from 1 April 1991)	17.5%
Registration threshold (from 1 April 2000)	£52,000
Deregistration threshold (from 1 April 2000)	£50,000

PART 1
INCOME TAX AND NATIONAL INSURANCE

Chapter 1

Introduction to the UK tax system

Introduction

The purpose of this first chapter is to provide an overview of the UK tax system. The main taxes are introduced, the principal sources of tax law are explained and the structure of the Inland Revenue (the main body concerned with the assessment and collection of tax in the UK) is described. This chapter also outlines the administration system which is used to assess the tax liability of an individual.

UK taxes

The UK taxation system is composed of a number of different taxes, some of which are *direct* taxes and some of which are *indirect* taxes :

(a) Direct taxes are charged on a taxpayer's income, profits or other gains and are often paid by the taxpayer directly to the tax authorities. The main direct taxes are income tax, capital gains tax and inheritance tax (all paid by individuals) and corporation tax (paid by companies). These taxes are administered by the Inland Revenue. National Insurance contributions (which can also be looked upon as a form of direct taxation) are administered by the National Insurance Contributions Office (NICO) of the Inland Revenue.

(b) Indirect taxes are taxes on spending. They are charged when a taxpayer buys an item and are paid to the vendor as part of the purchase price of the item. It is then the vendor's duty to pass the tax on to the tax authorities. The main indirect taxes are value added tax (VAT), customs duties and the excise duties levied on alcohol, tobacco and petrol. The only indirect tax considered in this book is VAT, which is administered by the Customs and Excise.

Sources of tax law

There is no single source of UK tax law. The basic rules are laid down in Acts of Parliament but it is left to the courts to interpret these Acts and to provide much of the detail of the tax system. In addition, the Inland Revenue and the Customs and Excise issue various statements, notices and leaflets which explain how the law is implemented in practice. These statements have no legal backing but they do provide information on the tax authorities' interpretation of the law and will be adhered to unless successfully challenged in the courts.

Statute law

The basic rules of the UK tax system are embodied in a number of tax *statutes* or Acts of Parliament. The main statutes currently in force are as follows :

Tax	*Statute*	*Abbreviation*
Income tax & }	Income and Corporation Taxes Act 1988	ICTA 1988
Corporation tax }	Capital Allowances Act 1990	CAA 1990
Capital gains tax & } Corporation tax }	Taxation of Chargeable Gains Act 1992	TCGA 1992
Inheritance tax	Inheritance Tax Act 1984	IHTA 1984
National Insurance	Social Security Contributions & Benefits Act 1992	SSCBA 1992
Value added tax	Value Added Tax Act 1994	VATA 1994
Administration of direct taxation	Taxes Management Act 1970	TMA 1970
Administration of indirect taxation	Customs and Excise Management Act 1979	CEMA 1979

These statutes are amended and supplemented each year by the annual Finance Act, which is based upon the Budget proposals put forward in March by the Chancellor of the Exchequer. From time to time, all of the statute law relating to a particular tax is consolidated into a new statute. In 1994, for example, the law relating to value added tax (which was previously embodied in VATA 1983, as modified and extended by subsequent Finance Acts) was consolidated into the new VATA 1994.

Some of the tax statutes provide for the making of detailed regulations by *statutory instrument*. A statutory instrument (SI) is a document which is laid before Parliament and which automatically becomes law within a stated period unless any objections are raised to it.

It is worth noting that membership of the European Union involves adherence to EU law and that if there is a conflict between EU law and the law of a member state then EU law will take priority. This applies as much to tax law as to any other category of law and the European influence on UK tax law is likely to increase over time. At present, the main impact is on VAT, where the prevailing legislation takes the form of

EU Directives. These Directives are binding on the UK and dictate the results which the internal legislation of the UK must bring about.

Case law

Over the years, many thousands of tax cases have been brought before the courts and the decisions made by judges in order to resolve these cases form an important part of the tax law of the UK. Some of the more significant cases are referred to in this book.

Statements made by the tax authorities

The main statements and other documents produced by the Inland Revenue as a guide to the law on direct taxation are as follows :

(a) **Statements of Practice**. A Statement of Practice (SP) sets out the Inland Revenue's interpretation of tax legislation and clarifies the way in which the law will be applied in practice. For example, SP 4/97 (the fourth SP issued in 1997) deals with the taxation of commissions, cashbacks and discounts.

(b) **Extra-Statutory Concessions**. An Extra-Statutory Concession (ESC) consists of a relaxation which gives taxpayers a reduction in liability to which they are not entitled under the strict letter of the law. Most ESC's are made so as to resolve anomalies or to relieve hardship. For example, ESC B10 is concerned with the income of contemplative religious communities.

(c) **Press releases**. These are issued throughout the year on a wide variety of tax-related subjects. Of especial interest are the Budget press releases which are issued on Budget day and which provide a detailed explanation of the Budget proposals.

(d) **Internal Guidance Manuals**. The Inland Revenue produces a very comprehensive set of internal tax manuals for the guidance of its own staff. These manuals may be inspected at Inland Revenue Enquiry Centres and are also available for sale.

(e) **Pamphlets**. These are aimed at the general public and explain the tax system in non-technical language. For example, pamphlet IR121 is a guide to income tax for pensioners.

Similarly, the Customs and Excise issues a range of explanatory notices and leaflets on matters relating to VAT.

The tax year

The proposed amendments to the tax system which are put forward in the annual Budget speech are usually intended to take effect as from the beginning of the next tax year, though some of the proposals may have a more immediate effect.

A *tax year* (also known as a "fiscal year" or "year of assessment") runs from 6 April to the following 5 April. For example, the tax year referred to as 1999/00 began on 6 April 1999 and ended on 5 April 2000. This book takes into account the provisions of the Finance Act 2000 (based on the March 2000 Budget proposals) and describes the UK tax system for tax year 2000/01.

It is worth noting that the tax year for corporation tax purposes is slightly different from the fiscal year. A corporation tax *financial year* runs from 1 April in one year to 31 March in the following year and is identified by the year in which it begins. This book describes the corporation tax system for Financial Year 2000, which runs from 1 April 2000 to 31 March 2001 inclusive.

Structure of the Inland Revenue

The structure of the Inland Revenue, which is responsible for the administration of the direct tax system, is described below. The structure of the Customs and Excise, which has responsibility for the indirect tax system, is described in Chapter 30.

The Inland Revenue is a large body of civil servants headed by the *Commissioners of Inland Revenue* (CIR). The Commissioners, who are known collectively as the *Board of Inland Revenue*, are appointed by the *Treasury*. This Government department is managed by the *Chancellor of the Exchequer* and has overall responsibility for the public finances of the UK. The main duties of the Commissioners of Inland Revenue are as follows :

(a) to implement the statute law relating to direct taxation

(b) to provide advice to the Chancellor of the Exchequer on direct tax matters

(c) to administer the many divisions and offices into which the Inland Revenue is organised.

The Inland Revenue has specialist offices which deal with such matters as pension schemes, oil taxation, share valuations etc. but most of the day-to-day work of the Inland Revenue is carried out by *Inspectors of Taxes*, whose function is to calculate or "assess" a taxpayer's tax liability, and *Collectors of Taxes*, whose function is to collect the tax due. Under the Self Assessment system (see below) each taxpayer is given the opportunity of calculating his or her own tax liability, in which case it is the Inspector's responsibility to check the taxpayer's "self-assessment".

For many years, Her Majesty's Inspectors of Taxes (HMIT) have been organised into several hundred local district offices, each managed by a district Inspector with the assistance of other Inspectors and clerical staff. The Collectors of Taxes have worked from entirely separate district offices with much of the routine collection work being performed by centralised accounts offices.

This traditional separation of assessment and collection inevitably gives rise to communication problems and seems to possess few virtues. In consequence, the Inland Revenue has embarked upon a programme of internal reorganisation. Many of the old district offices have now been replaced by :

(a) **Enquiry Centres**. These centres deal with taxpayers' general queries and carry stocks of tax forms and pamphlets.

(b) **Service Offices**. These offices are responsible for most of the routine assessment and collection work.

(c) **District Offices**. These offices concentrate mainly on compliance work (checking that taxpayers have complied with tax regulations).

When this reorganisation is complete, the functions of assessment and collection will merge and the terms "Inspector" and "Collector" will be replaced by the term "Officer of the Board".

Administration of the tax system

The remainder of this chapter describes the system which is used each year to assess an individual's liability to income tax and to capital gains tax. Later chapters explain the equivalent systems which are used for corporation tax, inheritance tax and VAT.

For tax years up to and including 1995/96, the assessment of an individual's tax liability was entirely the responsibility of the Inland Revenue and it was possible for taxpayers to delay the assessment and payment of tax by withholding information from the Inland Revenue for as long as possible. The introduction of Self Assessment in 1996/97 shifted responsibility from the Inland Revenue to the taxpayer and made it much more likely that tax is assessed and paid on time.

Self Assessment

If an individual's tax liability for a tax year cannot be collected entirely by deduction at source (see Chapter 2) or via the PAYE system (see Chapter 7), then the tax liability must be the subject of a formal tax assessment. The amount of tax which is due for the year may be calculated by the taxpayer (or by the taxpayer's accountant) and then checked by the Inland Revenue. Alternatively, if the taxpayer prefers not to perform the calculation, the amount due is calculated by the Inland Revenue. In either case, the first step is the completion of a *tax return*. The annual procedure is as follows :

(a) In early April each year, the Inland Revenue issues tax returns to those taxpayers who are likely to need them. The tax return consists of a basic 8-page form plus a number of "supplementary pages", each dealing with a different type of income or gains (e.g. income from employment, income from property etc.). Taxpayers are sent only those supplementary pages which are thought to be relevant to their circumstances, but can request further supplementary pages if necessary.

(b) A disk version of the return is available for tax practitioners who wish to complete their clients' tax returns with the aid of a computer system and then submit the completed returns electronically (the "Electronic Lodgement Service"). As from tax year 2000/01, individual taxpayers can also file their tax returns electronically, via the Internet. A taxpayer who files his or her return in this way in 2000/01 (and pays any tax due electronically) qualifies for a one-off discount of £10.

(c) The information requested in a tax return relates to the tax year just ended. For example, the tax returns which were issued in April 2000 required taxpayers to declare their income and gains for tax year 1999/00 and to claim allowances and reliefs (see Chapters 3 and 4) for the same year.

(d) The tax return must be completed in full. It is not permissible to omit figures or to make entries such as "see accounts" or "as submitted by employer". Unless asked to submit accounts or other supporting documentation with the return, a taxpayer is under no obligation to do so. However, it is necessary to retain all supporting documentation in case the Inland Revenue enquires into the accuracy of a return.

(e) The tax return includes an optional tax calculation section in which the taxpayer may calculate his or her own tax liability. If this section is left blank, the Inland Revenue will calculate the tax liability on the taxpayer's behalf and send a copy of this calculation to the taxpayer. In either case, the resulting assessment is referred to as a "self-assessment".

(f) The tax return must be "filed" (i.e. sent back to the Inland Revenue) on or before the following dates :

(i) 31 January following the end of the tax year to which the return relates (or within 3 months of the date of issue of the return, if later) for taxpayers who have calculated their own tax liability

(ii) 30 September following the end of the tax year to which the return relates (or within 2 months of the date of issue of the return, if later) for taxpayers who wish the Inland Revenue to calculate their tax liability.

The 31 January following the end of a tax year is known as the "annual filing date" for that year. For example, the annual filing date for tax year 2000/01 is 31 January 2002. A regime of automatic penalties (see Chapter 14) applies if a return is filed late.

(g) Taxpayers who fail to submit a tax return by the 30 September deadline have lost the right to ignore the optional tax calculation section of the return and the Inland Revenue is entitled to reject (as incomplete) any return which is received after 30 September unless this section has been filled in. If a return is rejected in these circumstances and the taxpayer then completes the tax calculation section, it is possible that eventual submission of the completed return will be delayed beyond the annual filing date and an automatic penalty will be incurred (see Chapter 14). Surcharges and interest might also be charged if tax is paid late as a consequence of the late submission of the return (see Chapter 14).

(h) The Inland Revenue has the right to "repair" a taxpayer's self-assessment (i.e. to correct any obvious mistakes) within 9 months of the date on which the return is filed by the taxpayer.

(i) The taxpayer has the right to amend his or her tax return and self-assessment within 12 months of the annual filing date for that return. Taxpayers who believe that an error or mistake in their tax return has resulted in an excessive self-assessment may make an "error or mistake" claim within five years of the annual filing date for the year to which the claim relates.

(j) The tax due in relation to a self-assessment is normally payable as follows :

(i) A first payment on account (POA) is due on 31 January in the tax year to which the self-assessment relates.

(ii) A second POA is due on the following 31 July.

(iii) A final balancing payment is due on the annual filing date (i.e. 31 January following the end of the tax year).

For example, the tax due in relation to a 2000/01 self-assessment would normally be payable on 31 January 2001 (first POA), 31 July 2001 (second POA) and 31 January 2002 (balancing payment). Further information regarding the payment of tax is given in Chapter 14.

Notification of chargeability to tax

Individuals who have not received a tax return, but have taxable income or gains of which the Inland Revenue is not aware, must notify the Revenue of their chargeability to tax within 6 months of the end of the tax year in which the income arises. Penalties are imposed for non-compliance with this requirement (see Chapter 14). Notification of chargeability to tax is *not* required if :

(a) the taxpayer has no capital gains, and

(b) the taxpayer is not a higher rate taxpayer (see Chapter 2), and

(c) all of the taxpayer's income has been subject to deduction of tax at source (see Chapter 2) or has been dealt with via the PAYE system (see Chapter 7).

Enquiries

The Inland Revenue adopts a "process now - check later" approach to tax returns filed under the Self Assessment system. The information supplied in tax returns is processed when the returns are filed and any obvious errors in taxpayers' self-assessments are repaired (see above) but no attempt is made at that time to check that the correct amount of income and gains has been declared. However, all returns are eventually checked and some are selected for detailed enquiry. Note that :

(a) Most enquiries arise because the Inland Revenue wishes to ask questions about the information given in a tax return, but it is not necessary for the Revenue to justify an enquiry and some enquiry cases are chosen entirely at random.

(b) In general, enquiries must begin within 12 months of the annual filing date for the year to which the enquiry relates. This means that a taxpayer who has made full disclosure of all relevant facts in a tax return can be sure that the corresponding self-assessment is final if no enquiry has begun within 12 months of the annual filing date. However, the Inland Revenue may raise a "discovery assessment" after these 12 months have elapsed if it is discovered that full disclosure has not been made. The time limits for discovery assessments under the Self Assessment system are as follows :

(i) 31 January in the sixth tax year following the year to which the assessment relates, in the case of incomplete disclosure of facts without negligence or fraud

(ii) 31 January in the twenty-first tax year following the year to which the assessment relates, in the case of negligence or fraud.

Determinations

If a taxpayer fails to file a tax return by the required date, an Officer of the Board may make a "determination" of the amount of tax due, calculated according to "the best of his information and belief". The taxpayer cannot appeal against this determination and cannot apply for the tax due to be postponed (see below). A determination can be displaced only if the taxpayer files the required return.

Appeals

Under Self Assessment, taxpayers have the right of appeal in relation to certain Inland Revenue decisions. The main classes of appeal are :

(a) an appeal against the imposition of a penalty (see Chapter 14)

(b) an appeal against the imposition of a surcharge (see Chapter 14)

(c) an appeal against a request by the Inland Revenue that the taxpayer should submit documents, records etc. in the course of an enquiry

(d) an appeal against amendments made to a self-assessment as a consequence of an enquiry

(e) an appeal to the effect that the relevant conditions for the making of a discovery assessment do not exist

(f) an appeal against a discovery assessment.

The appeals procedure

In general, appeals must be made in writing to the Inland Revenue and must be made within 30 days of the relevant Inland Revenue decision. In the case of disputed amendments to self-assessments and disputed discovery assessments, the taxpayer may also apply to postpone payment of all or part of the tax assessed, pending settlement of the appeal. Note that :

(a) Applications to postpone payment are subject to the agreement of the Inland Revenue. Applications which cannot be accepted by the Inland Revenue may be referred to the appeal Commissioners (see below).

(b) Any non-postponed part of the tax due on a disputed assessment is payable on the due date in the usual way. If the appeal is subsequently determined in the taxpayer's favour, any overpaid tax is refunded.

(c) Most appeals are settled by means of an informal discussion between the Inland Revenue and the taxpayer (or the taxpayer's accountant), culminating in an agreement of the amount of tax due. Appeals which cannot be resolved amicably in this way are referred to the appeal Commissioners (who should not be confused with the Commissioners of Inland Revenue mentioned earlier in this chapter). Appeal Commissioners fall into two categories, the *General Commissioners* and the *Special Commissioners.*

(d) The General Commissioners are appointed by the Lord Chancellor to hear appeals locally. They do not usually possess any formal tax qualifications and are similar in many ways to magistrates, being part-time and unpaid. They are assisted by a paid clerk who is normally a local solicitor or accountant. The appeals brought before the General Commissioners are usually of a fairly straightforward nature.

(e) The Special Commissioners, who are also appointed by the Lord Chancellor, are similar to circuit judges and travel the country hearing appeals which involve complex matters of tax law. They are full-time tax professionals and they are paid for their services.

(f) The appeal Commissioners may confirm, reduce or increase a disputed assessment and their decision on a matter of fact is final. But either the Inland Revenue or the taxpayer may express dissatisfaction with the Commissioners' decision on a point of law and take the appeal further, first to the High Court, then to the Court of Appeal and ultimately to the House of Lords.

(g) The costs of bringing an appeal before the appeal Commissioners are usually fairly modest. Each party bears their own costs and the Commissioners cannot normally require the losing party to pay the costs of the victor (though the Special Commissioners may do so if they believe that a taxpayer has acted wholly unreasonably). The costs of taking an appeal to the High Court and beyond can be extremely high and an unsuccessful taxpayer may be required to pay the costs of the Inland Revenue in defending the appeal as well as his or her own costs.

Record keeping

It is compulsory for taxpayers to keep proper records so that they can make a correct tax return. Business records relating to a given tax year must be retained for 5 years after the annual filing date for that year. Personal records must be retained for 12 months after the annual filing date.

The Adjudicator

An independent and impartial Adjudicator (who is not part of the Inland Revenue management structure) considers complaints made by taxpayers who are not satisfied with the quality of the service which they have received from the Inland Revenue. The Adjudicator produces an annual report and makes recommendations for improvements to Inland Revenue procedures and practices. The Adjudicator is not empowered to hear tax appeals.

The Adjudicator for the Inland Revenue is also the Adjudicator for the Customs and Excise. As a result, complainants have a single point of contact for complaints about any tax matter.

Taxpayer's Charter

The Taxpayer's Charter (which was produced jointly by the Inland Revenue and the Customs and Excise) sets out the standards of service which a taxpayer has the right to expect from the tax authorities. The Charter also describes the tax authorities' expectations of the taxpayer. In summary, a taxpayer has the right to expect that the tax authorities will be fair, helpful and efficient, whilst the authorities expect the taxpayer to be honest, to provide accurate information and to pay tax on the due date. A series of codes of practice is being published by the Inland Revenue in support of the Taxpayer's Charter, each relating to a specific aspect of the Revenue's work.

Tax evasion and tax avoidance

As stated above, the Inland Revenue expects a taxpayer to be honest. Dishonest behaviour (such as concealing a source of income) is known as *tax evasion* and is punishable by law. On the other hand, taxpayers are entitled to organise their financial affairs in any way that they please and may choose to do so in such a way that their tax burden is minimised. This perfectly legal activity is known as *tax avoidance*.

Over the years, taxpayers (or their advisors) have shown great ingenuity in exploiting "loopholes" in the tax system and it has been necessary to "plug" each of the most important loopholes with specific anti-avoidance legislation. A permanent solution to this problem would be to establish a *general anti-avoidance rule* (GAAR). If such a rule existed, an entirely lawful transaction which a taxpayer had performed solely for tax avoidance purposes could be set aside when computing his or her tax liability. The Government has in fact considered the introduction of a GAAR in relation to corporate taxation but has decided not to proceed, at least for the immediate future.

Summary

► Direct taxes are charged on income, profits and other gains and are often paid directly to the tax authorities. The main direct taxes are income tax, capital gains tax, inheritance tax and corporation tax. National Insurance contributions are also a form of direct taxation. Indirect taxes are taxes on spending and are paid as part of the price of a bought item. The main indirect taxes are VAT, customs duties and excise duties.

► Taxation law is a combination of statute law and case law. Statements made by the tax authorities have no legal force but provide information on the authorities' interpretation of the law.

► The fiscal year runs from 6 April to the following 5 April. The corporation tax financial year runs from 1 April to the following 31 March.

► The Inland Revenue calculates a taxpayer's tax liability (or checks the taxpayer's own calculation of the liability) on the basis of the information provided in an annual tax return.

► Under the Self Assessment system, taxpayers have the option of calculating their own tax liabilities. A tax return must normally be filed by 30 September following the end of the tax year if the taxpayer wishes the Inland Revenue to calculate the liability. Otherwise, the return must be filed by 31 January following the end of the tax year.

► A taxpayer who has not received a tax return, but has taxable income or gains of which the Inland Revenue is not aware, must notify the Revenue of his or her chargeability to tax within 6 months of the end of the tax year in which the income arises.

▶ The Inland Revenue may initiate an enquiry within 12 months of the annual filing date for the year to which the enquiry relates. Discovery assessments may be made after these 12 months have elapsed if it is discovered that the taxpayer has not made full disclosure of all relevant facts.

▶ In certain circumstances, taxpayers have the right of appeal against Inland Revenue decisions. Appeals are heard initially by the General Commissioners or the Special Commissioners but may progress to the Courts.

▶ Tax evasion should be distinguished from tax avoidance. The former involves dishonest conduct by the taxpayer and is illegal. The latter involves the sensible arrangement of the taxpayer's affairs so as to minimise the liability to tax and is perfectly legal.

Chapter 2

Introduction to income tax

Introduction

Income tax assessments are computed for a tax year (or "year of assessment") and are based on the taxpayer's aggregate income for that year from all sources, ignoring any income which is exempt from income tax. The computation takes into account any tax-deductible payments made by the taxpayer during the year and the taxpayer's entitlement to personal allowances and reliefs. This chapter explains the main features of an income tax computation, in preparation for the much more detailed information which is provided in subsequent chapters.

As stated in Chapter 1, current income tax legislation is to be found in the Income and Corporation Taxes Act 1988, as amended by subsequent Finance Acts.

Taxable persons

In general, an individual who is resident in the UK for a tax year is liable to pay income tax on all of his or her income for that year, including both income arising in the UK and income which is derived from an overseas source. However, there are two main exceptions to this general rule :

(a) Certain forms of income are exempt from income tax altogether (see later in this chapter).

(b) Income derived from an overseas source by a UK resident who is not domiciled in the UK (i.e. whose natural home is not the UK) is only subject to income tax to the extent that the income is remitted to the UK.

Individuals who are not UK residents are liable to pay income tax on their UK income only. (Chapter 32 provides a detailed explanation of "residence" and its application to income tax). Income tax is payable by :

(a) adults, on their own income and on their share of the income of a partnership

(b) children, if they have sufficient income to pay tax

(c)   trustees, on the income of a trust or settlement

(d)   personal representatives, on income arising from the estate of a deceased person.

The following persons and organisations are *not* liable to pay income tax, whether or not they are resident in the UK :

(a)   companies (which pay corporation tax on their income instead of income tax)

(b)   registered charities and scientific research associations (except on trading income other than the income derived from certain small trading activities)

(c)   approved pension funds

(d)   representatives of foreign countries (e.g. ambassadors) and visiting members of foreign armed forces (on their service pay only)

(e)   local authorities

(f)   trade unions (on certain types of income).

The schedular system

Some types of income are *taxed at source* (i.e. tax is deducted from the income before the taxpayer receives it). Typical examples are building society interest and most forms of bank interest. Other types of income are received *gross* (i.e. without deduction of any tax at source). Typical examples are the profits of a self-employed person and the rents received by a landlord. The tax due on these types of income has to be assessed by the Inland Revenue (or self-assessed by the taxpayer) and therefore such income is often referred to as income which is *taxed by direct assessment*.

Income taxed by direct assessment is classified into a number of "Schedules", each identified by a letter of the alphabet. Two of the Schedules are further subdivided into "Cases". The main types of income which are assessed under each Schedule and Case are as follows :

Schedule A		- Income from property (e.g. rents)
Schedule D	Case I	- Profits of a trade
	Case II	- Profits of a profession or vocation
	Case III	- Interest received without deduction of tax at source
	Case IV	- Interest on overseas securities
	Case V	- Income from overseas possessions
	Case VI	- Income not assessed under any other Schedule or Case
Schedule E	Case I	- } Emoluments of an office or employment (the applicable
	Case II	- } Case depends upon the employee's residence status and
	Case III	- } whether the work is performed in the UK or abroad)
Schedule F		- Dividends received from UK companies.

The missing Schedules B and C have been abolished.

Each Schedule and Case has its own rules for determining the amount of income arising in a given tax year. Since the rules differ from one Schedule and Case to another it is vitally important to allocate income to the correct category.

Note that the tax due under Schedule E is usually deducted from employees' wages and salaries by their employers and then paid over to the Inland Revenue. In general, therefore, employees receive their emoluments net of tax. However, the amount of tax which is deducted from an employee depends upon the employee's "tax code" (see Chapter 7) and this code has to be determined for each employee individually by the Inland Revenue. Consequently, this type of income is regarded as assessed income rather than as income which is taxed at source.

Non-taxable income

Schedule D Case VI seems to catch any income not already caught by any of the other Schedules and Cases. However, certain types of income are specifically exempt from income tax. Some of the most important sources of non-taxable income are :

(a) the first £70 per annum of interest received on a National Savings Bank Ordinary account (see Chapter 6)

(b) interest on National Savings Certificates

(c) interest on Tax Exempt Special Savings Accounts (see Chapter 6)

(d) income from Personal Equity Plans (see Chapter 6)

(e) income from Individual Savings Accounts (see Chapter 6)

(f) dividends received on shares held in a Venture Capital Trust, so long as certain conditions are satisfied (see Chapter 6)

(g) winnings from betting, competition prizes and premium bond prizes

(h) certain social security benefits (e.g. housing benefit, child benefit) though others are taxable (e.g. the state retirement pension)

(i) wound and disability pensions.

(j) statutory redundancy pay and the first £30,000 of compensation received for loss of employment (see Chapter 7)

(k) income of up to £4,250 per annum received under the "rent-a-room" scheme (see Chapter 5)

(l) income from scholarships

(m) most commissions, discounts and cashbacks received by ordinary retail customers when purchasing goods, investments or services

(n) compensation for mis-sold personal pensions or (by concession) mis-sold free-standing additional voluntary contribution schemes taken out between certain dates.

Structure of an income tax computation

In order to calculate a taxpayer's income tax liability for a tax year it is necessary to bring together *all* of the taxpayer's income into a single tax computation. For reasons which are explained below, income which has already been taxed at source must also be included in this computation. A typical income tax computation for the year 2000/01 might appear as follows :

		£
Schedule A (Income from property)		4,000
Schedule D Case I (Income from self-employment)	39,760	
<u>Less</u> : Personal pension premiums	5,300	34,460
Schedule D Case III (Interest received gross)		2,289
Building society interest taxed at source (pre-tax equivalent)		700
Total income		41,449
<u>Less</u> : Charges on income		1,000
Statutory total income		40,449
<u>Less</u> : Personal allowance		4,385
Taxable Income		36,064

Income tax		
1,520	@ 10%	152.00
26,880	@ 22%	5,913.60
7,664	@ 40%	3,065.60
36,064		9,131.20
<u>Less</u> : Tax reducers		0.00
Tax borne		9,131.20
<u>Add</u> : Tax withheld on charges		220.00
Tax liability for the year		9,351.20
<u>Less</u> : Tax paid by deduction at source		140.00
Tax payable		9,211.20

All of the terms used in this computation are explained in great detail in this chapter and in later chapters. For the time being it is sufficient to understand the main features of the computation, which are as follows :

(a) The taxpayer's total income for the year is calculated by adding together income from all sources, including the pre-tax equivalent of any income which has already been taxed but excluding any income which is exempt from income tax.

(b) Certain payments made by the taxpayer known as "charges on income" are deducted from total income, giving statutory total income (STI).

(c) The taxpayer's personal allowance is deducted from STI, giving taxable income. The personal allowance (£4,385 in 2000/01) acts as a tax threshold, ensuring that those on very low incomes do not have to pay income tax.

(d) Income tax is charged on the taxable income, using the rates of tax in force for the year in question. The amount of tax calculated in this way is then subject to a number of adjustments and the result is the tax payable to the Inland Revenue.

(e) The *tax borne* by the taxpayer is the amount of tax suffered for the year. This may be different from the *tax liability*, which is the amount of tax which the taxpayer must account for to the Inland Revenue and the *tax payable* which is the tax remaining to be paid after deducting any tax already paid for the year. These distinctions will become clearer in the course of the next two chapters.

A tax computation is not required for every taxpayer. For example, a computation is not usually required for an individual whose income is derived entirely from employment, since the correct amount of tax is deducted automatically by the PAYE system (see Chapter 7). However, the only way to calculate the tax liability in more complex cases is to prepare a computation and this approach should always be adopted when answering examination questions.

Married couples

At one time, a wife's income was aggregated with that of her husband into a single joint assessment but this arrangement ceased in tax year 1989/90. Married couples are now taxed independently, which means that the husband's income and the wife's income are taxed completely separately. If a married couple receive joint income (e.g. interest received on a joint bank account) then the income is normally divided between them equally for tax purposes. However, if the source of the income is genuinely held between them in some other proportion, the couple may make a declaration to that effect and the income will then be divided between them as appropriate.

The rates of income tax

An individual's taxable income is taxed according to the rates of income tax in force for the year in question. For 2000/01, the rates of income tax are as follows :

First £1,520 of taxable income	10% (the "starting rate")
Next £26,880 of taxable income	22% (the "basic rate")
Remainder of taxable income after first £28,400	40% (the "higher rate")

Note that :

(a) The first £1,520 of taxable income is referred to as the "starting rate band" and the next £26,880 of taxable income is referred to as the "basic rate band".

(b) Calculations are normally made to the nearest pound when calculating taxable income but the tax due should be calculated to the nearest penny.

(c) Savings income and dividend income are treated specially, as explained below.

(d) The Scottish Parliament has the power to increase or decrease (by up to 3%) the basic rate of income tax which is set by the UK Parliament. The resulting "Scottish variable rate" applies to the income of Scottish taxpayers only. The examples and exercises in this book all assume that the taxpayers referred to are liable to income tax at unvaried UK rates.

EXAMPLE 1

Calculate the income tax payable in 2000/01 on a taxable income (i.e. income after deducting charges and the personal allowance) of :

(a) £1,250

(b) £19,820

(c) £39,103

(Assume that none of the income is derived from savings or dividends).

SOLUTION

(a) 1,250 @ 10% = £125.00.

(b) 1,520 @ 10% + 18,300 @ 22% = £4,178.00.

(c) 1,520 @ 10% + 26,880 @ 22% + 10,703 @ 40% = £10,346.80.

Income taxed at source

If tax is deducted from a source of income before the taxpayer receives it (e.g. wages received after deduction of tax, bank interest received net of tax) such income must still be included in the taxpayer's tax computation. This may seem to be unnecessary since tax has already been paid but there are two good reasons for including the income in the computation :

(a) It is important to derive the correct figures for total income and statutory total income, as will become clearer in later chapters.

(b) The amount of tax which has already been deducted might not be the correct amount. The only way to check this is to aggregate the income concerned with all of the taxpayer's other income in a single tax computation.

In a tax computation, all income must be shown "gross" (i.e. the amount shown must be the amount of the income *before* any income tax was deducted at source). When the tax liability has been calculated, tax paid by deduction at source is subtracted and the taxpayer is then required to pay only the balance of the liability. A tax refund is given if tax deducted at source exceeds the tax liability for the year.

Grossing up

If wages and salaries are received net of income tax, the gross pay and the amount of tax deducted can easily be found by examining the end-of-year certificate supplied by the taxpayer's employer. But for other types of income which are received net of tax it is often necessary to deduce the gross figure from the net figure. For reasons which will become clear later in this chapter, some types of income are received net of 20% tax. Some other types of income are received net of basic rate (22%) tax. In each case, the gross income can be calculated by "grossing up" the net income, as follows :

(a) If income is received net of 20% tax, the gross income is equal to the net income multiplied by 100/80. The amount of tax deducted at source is equal to the net income multiplied by 20/80 (or 20% of gross income). The main types of income which are received net of 20% tax are :

(i) building society interest and most forms of bank interest

(ii) debenture and other loan interest paid by UK companies

(iii) the income element of purchased life annuities.

Interest on most UK Government securities ("gilt-edged" securities or "gilts") used to be received net of 20% tax. But, as from 6 April 1998, anyone receiving such interest may choose whether to receive the interest gross or net. As from that date, new holders of gilts automatically receive their interest gross unless they ask for it to be paid net. Those who held gilts on 6 April 1998 continue to receive their interest net of 20% tax unless they ask for it to be paid gross. Interest received gross is assessed under Schedule D Case III.

(b) If income is received net of basic rate (22%) tax, the gross income is equal to the net income multiplied by 100/78. The amount of tax deducted at source is equal to the net income multiplied by 22/78 (or 22% of gross income). Patent royalties are an example of income which is received net of basic rate tax.

EXAMPLE 2

In 2000/01, an individual receives net income of £1,248. Compute the equivalent gross income and the amount of tax deducted at source if the income consists entirely of :

(a)   building society interest

(b)   patent royalties.

SOLUTION

(a)   If the income consists of building society interest then the equivalent gross income is £1,248 x 100/80 = £1,560 and the tax deducted at source is £1,248 x 20/80 = £312.

(b)   If the income consists of patent royalties then the equivalent gross income is £1,248 x 100/78 = £1,600 and the tax deducted at source is £1,248 x 22/78 = £352.

Savings income

The tax liability on a taxpayer's "savings income" is calculated differently from the tax liability on non-savings income. The main categories of savings income are :

(a)   interest from banks and building societies

(b)   interest from gilt-edged securities and corporate bonds (i.e. debentures)

(c)   the income element of purchased life annuities

(d)   certain "equivalent foreign income" (see Chapter 32).

The crucial difference between savings income and non-savings income is that savings income falling into the basic rate band is taxed at the *lower rate* of 20% (*not* the 22% basic rate). Therefore, if a taxpayer has both savings income and non-savings income, it is necessary to split taxable income between the two categories before calculating the tax liability. Note that :

(a)   Non-savings income is regarded as the bottom layer or "slice" of taxable income and savings income is regarded as a higher layer. This means that the starting rate and basic rate bands are made available to non-savings income in priority to savings income.

(b)   Charges on income and the personal allowance are set against income in the order which will result in the lowest tax liability. The best approach is to make these deductions from non-savings income in priority to savings income (so that as little income as possible is taxed at 22%).

(c)   The effect of these rules is that the tax liability on savings income is generally calculated at the lower rate (20%), sometimes at the starting rate (10%) or higher rate (40%), but *never* at the basic rate (22%). This is why the tax deducted at source (if any) from savings income is calculated at 20%.

2 INTRODUCTION TO INCOME TAX

(d) Dividends from UK companies used to be regarded as savings income but this ceased to be the case as from 6 April 1999. The special tax regime which now applies to UK dividends is explained later in this chapter.

EXAMPLE 3

In 2000/01, Robert has business profits of £14,280, net bank interest of £360 and no charges on income. He claims the personal allowance of £4,385. Calculate the income tax payable for the year.

SOLUTION

	Total £	Non-savings £	Savings £
Schedule D Case I/II	14,280	14,280	
Bank interest £360 x 100/80	450		450
Statutory total income	14,730	14,280	450
Less : Personal allowance	4,385	4,385	
Taxable income	10,345	9,895	450

Income tax due

Starting rate band	: Non-savings	1,520	@ 10%	152.00
Basic rate band	: Non-savings	8,375	@ 22%	1,842.50
	: Savings	450	@ 20%	90.00
		10,345		

Tax borne	2,084.50
Less : Tax deducted at source	90.00
Tax payable	1,994.50

Non-savings income occupies the whole of the starting rate band and the first £8,375 (£9,895 - £1,520) of the basic rate band. Savings income falls entirely into the basic rate band and is taxed at 20%.

EXAMPLE 4

In 2000/01, Roberta has rents of £20,685, net bank interest of £6,080 and net building society interest of £4,000. She has no charges on income and she claims the personal allowance of £4,385. Calculate the income tax payable for the year.

SOLUTION

	Total £	Non-savings £	Savings £
Schedule A	20,685	20,685	
Bank interest £6,080 x 100/80	7,600		7,600
BSI £4,000 x 100/80	5,000		5,000
Statutory total income	33,285	20,685	12,600
Less : Personal allowance	4,385	4,385	
Taxable income	28,900	16,300	12,600

Income tax due

Starting rate band	: Non-savings	1,520	@ 10%	152.00	
Basic rate band	: Non-savings	14,780	@ 22%	3,251.60	
	: Savings	12,100	@ 20%	2,420.00	
Higher rate	: Savings	500	@ 40%	200.00	
		28,900			

Tax borne	6,023.60
Less : Tax deducted at source	2,520.00
Tax payable	3,503.60

Non-savings income occupies the whole of the starting rate band and the first £14,780 (£16,300 - £1,520) of the basic rate band. This leaves £12,100 (£26,880 - £14,780) of the basic rate band for savings income. The remaining £500 is taxed at the higher rate.

EXAMPLE 5

In 2000/01, Philip has business profits of £35,620 and net bank interest of £4,000. He has no charges on income and he claims the personal allowance of £4,385. Calculate the income tax payable for the year.

SOLUTION

	Total £	Non-savings £	Savings £
Schedule D Case I/II	35,620	35,620	
Bank interest £4,000 x 100/80	5,000		5,000
Statutory total income	40,620	35,620	5,000
Less : Personal allowance	4,385	4,385	
Taxable income	36,235	31,235	5,000

Income tax due

Starting rate band	: Non-savings	1,520	@ 10%	152.00
Basic rate band	: Non-savings	26,880	@ 22%	5,913.60
Higher rate	: Non-savings	2,835	@ 40%	1,134.00
	: Savings	5,000	@ 40%	2,000.00
		36,235		

Tax borne	9,199.60
Less : Tax deducted at source	1,000.00
Tax payable	8,199.60

Non-savings income occupies the whole of the starting and basic rate bands so savings income (and the balance of non-savings income) is taxed entirely at the higher rate.

EXAMPLE 6

In 2000/01, Philippa has business profits of £1,060, National Savings Bank investment account interest (received gross) of £2,080, net debenture interest of £35,504 and no charges on income. She claims the personal allowance of £4,385. Calculate the income tax payable for the year.

SOLUTION

	Total £	Non-savings £	Savings £
Schedule D Case I/II	1,060	1,060	
Schedule D Case III	2,080		2,080
Debenture interest £35,504 x 100/80	44,380		44,380
Statutory total income	47,520	1,060	46,460
Less : Personal allowance	4,385	1,060	3,325
Taxable income	43,135	nil	43,135

Income tax due

Starting rate band	: Savings	1,520	@ 10%	152.00
Basic rate band	: Savings	26,880	@ 20%	5,376.00
Higher rate	: Savings	14,735	@ 40%	5,894.00
		43,135		

Tax borne	11,422.00
Less : Tax deducted at source	8,876.00
Tax payable	2,546.00

Dividends from UK companies

Until 6 April 1999, dividends received from UK companies were regarded as savings income and were treated in a similar way to income received net of tax. However, a new tax regime applies to UK dividends as from tax year 1999/00. The main points of this regime are as follows :

(a) UK dividends have an attached "tax credit" which is equal to *one-ninth* of the amount of the dividend. A taxpayer's Schedule F income for a tax year is equal to the amount of UK dividends received in that year plus the attached tax credits. For example, a taxpayer who receives UK dividends of £720 has Schedule F income of £800 (£720 plus the tax credits of £80).

(b) The tax credits attached to UK dividends are deducted from the taxpayer's tax liability on those dividends. It is *not* possible to claim payment of any tax credits which exceed this liability. Tax credits can be deducted only from the tax due on dividends, *not* from the tax due on other forms of income.

(c) UK dividends are not classed as savings income or non-savings income. Dividends constitute a third layer which is treated as the top slice of taxable income, ranking above both non-savings and savings income.

(d) Dividends which fall into the starting rate band or basic rate band are taxed at the "Schedule F ordinary rate" of 10%. Dividends which lie above these bands are taxed at the "Schedule F upper rate" of 32.5%.

Before 1999/00, the tax credit attached to a UK dividend was equal to *one-quarter* of the amount of the dividend and taxpayers with tax credits which exceeded their tax liability *could* claim payment of the excess amount. Exempt persons and organisations (apart from companies and pension funds) could claim payment of the tax credits on *all* of their dividend income. The general abolition of the payment of tax credits as from 6 April 1999 has had an adverse effect on all such persons and organisations, but charities have been especially hard-hit. In recognition of this, charities are receiving special compensation payments (funded from public expenditure) for years 1999/00 to 2003/04. These special payments are calculated as a diminishing percentage of the dividends received by a charity, beginning with 21% in 1999/00 and ending with 4% in 2003/04.

Note that the tax treatment of dividends received from overseas companies is described in Chapter 32.

EXAMPLE 7

In 2000/01, Ewan has rents of £25,735, net bank interest of £3,240, UK dividends of £3,690 and no charges on income. He claims the personal allowance of £4,385. Calculate the income tax payable for the year.

SOLUTION

	Total £	Non-savings £	Savings £	Dividends £
Schedule A	25,735	25,735		
Bank interest £3,240 x 100/80	4,050		4,050	
Schedule F £3,690 + £410	4,100			4,100
Statutory total income	33,885	25,735	4,050	4,100
Less : Personal allowance	4,385	4,385		
Taxable income	29,500	21,350	4,050	4,100

Income tax due

Starting rate band	: Non-savings	1,520	@ 10%	152.00
Basic rate band	: Non-savings	19,830	@ 22%	4,362.60
	: Savings	4,050	@ 20%	810.00
	: Dividends	3,000	@ 10%	300.00
Higher rate	: Dividends	1,100	@ 32.5%	357.50
		29,500		

Tax borne	5,982.10
Less : Tax credits on dividends	410.00
Tax payable	5,572.10
Less : Tax deducted at source	810.00
Tax payable	4,762.10

The dividends are treated as the top slice of income and are taxed at 10% to the extent that they occupy the basic rate band and at 32.5% in the higher rate band. The total tax due on dividends is £657.50, so the tax credits of £410 may be deducted in full.

EXAMPLE 8

Imagine now that Ewan (in the previous example) has no rental income but that all of the other figures remain unchanged. Calculate the income tax payable for the year.

SOLUTION

	Total £	Non-savings £	Savings £	Dividends £
Bank interest £3,240 x 100/80	4,050		4,050	
Schedule F £3,690 + £410	4,100			4,100
Statutory total income	8,150		4,050	4,100
Less : Personal allowance	4,385		4,050	335
Taxable income	3,765		-	3,765

Income tax due

		Total			
Starting rate band	: Dividends	1,520	@ 10%	152.00	
Basic rate band	: Dividends	2,245	@ 10%	224.50	
		3,765			

Tax borne	376.50
Less : Tax credits on dividends (restricted)	376.50
Tax payable	0.00
Less : Tax deducted at source	810.00
Tax repayable	(810.00)

The dividends all fall into the starting rate and basic rate bands and are taxed at 10%. The total tax due on the dividends is only £376.50, so the tax credits which may be deducted are restricted to this amount. Ewan cannot claim payment of the remaining £33.50 of tax credits.

Summary

▶ In general, income tax is chargeable on all of the income of UK residents and on the UK income of non-residents.

▶ Income is classified into a number of Schedules and Cases, each of which has its own rules for determining the amount of assessable income in a tax year.

▶ Certain types of income are specifically exempt from income tax.

▶ To calculate a taxpayer's income tax liability it is necessary to bring together all of the taxpayer's income into a single computation. The gross equivalent of income received net of income tax must be included in the computation.

▶ Husband and wife are assessed to income tax independently.

▶ In 2000/01 the rates of income tax are 10% (the starting rate), 22% (the basic rate) and 40% (the higher rate).

▶ Savings income falling into the basic rate band is taxed at the lower rate of 20%.

▶ UK dividends are accompanied by tax credits which may be set against the tax liability on those dividends. This liability is calculated at 10% (the Schedule F ordinary rate) and 32.5% (the Schedule F upper rate).

▶ If the tax credit attached to a UK dividend exceeds the recipient's tax liability with regard to that dividend, the excess tax credit cannot be paid to the recipient under any circumstances.

Exercises

2.1 Calculate the income tax payable in 2000/01 on a taxable income (i.e. income after deducting charges and the personal allowance) of :

(a) £12,120 (b) £36,100 (c) £62,103.

(Assume in each case that none of the income is derived from savings or dividends).

2.2 Calculate the income tax payable in 2000/01 on the following incomes, assuming no charges on income and a personal allowance of £4,385 :

(a) Business profits of £19,280 and net bank interest of £720.

(b) Business profits of £20,520, net building society interest of £8,000 and net bank interest of £2,300.

(c) Net building society interest of £26,912.

2.3 Stephanie has the following income in 2000/01 :

	£
Income from employment	19,395
Rents received	13,000
Bank interest (net)	160
NSB ordinary account interest, received gross	63
UK dividends	225

(a) Identify the Schedules or Cases under which each of the above sources of income is assessed, assuming that the rents received are not within the "rent-a-room" scheme.

(b) Compute the income tax payable by Stephanie for the year, assuming that there are no charges on income and that Stephanie is entitled to the personal allowance of £4,385.

2.4   Ernest has a retirement pension in 2000/01 of £3,375. He also receives net bank interest of £416. Compute the income tax payable by Ernest for the year, assuming a personal allowance of £4,385 and no charges on income.

What difference would it make if Ernest had received UK dividends of £468 instead of the bank interest ?

*2.5   Ivan's income for the tax year 2000/01 is as follows :

	£
Salary	16,040
Building society interest (net)	560
Premium bond prize	50
NSB investment account interest, received gross	60

Compute the income tax payable by Ivan for the year, assuming a personal allowance of £4,385 and no charges on income.

*2.6   Mary's income for the tax year 2000/01 is as follows :

	£
Business profits	28,215
Rents received	2,600
UK dividends	1,890

Compute the income tax payable by Mary for the year, assuming that the rents received are not within the "rent-a-room" scheme. Mary is entitled to a personal allowance of £4,385 and has no charges on income.

Chapter 3
Personal allowances

Introduction

One of the factors which must be taken into account when preparing an income tax computation is the taxpayer's entitlement to *personal allowances*. Personal allowances are intended to adjust the income tax liability of a taxpayer so as to reflect his or her personal circumstances. Some allowances are deducted from the taxpayer's statutory total income. Others are ignored until taxable income has been calculated but then take effect by reducing the amount of tax due on the taxpayer's taxable income. The main purpose of this chapter is to describe the allowances available in tax year 2000/01 and to explain the way in which relief is given for each allowance. A new allowance which will be available as from tax year 2001/02 is introduced at the end of the chapter.

It is important to appreciate that personal allowances are indeed "personal". If all or part of an allowance cannot be used by the person to whom it is available, then any unused part of the allowance is generally lost. Excess allowances cannot normally be transferred to anyone else and cannot be carried back to previous years or forward to future years. However, some limited provisions exist for transferring excess allowances between husband and wife (see later in this chapter).

Personal allowances for 2000/01

Personal allowances may be claimed by UK residents and by some non-residents. The main classes of non-resident who may claim personal allowances are :

(a) citizens of the Commonwealth or of the European Economic Area (EEA), which comprises all EU states plus Norway, Iceland and Liechtenstein

(b) residents in the Isle of Man or the Channel Islands and persons who used to reside in the UK but now reside abroad for health reasons

(c) Crown servants, ex-Crown servants, their widows/widowers and missionaries.

The personal allowances for 2000/01 are as follows :

Allowances which are deducted from STI : £

Personal allowance	
Age 0-64	4,385
Age 65-74	5,790
Age 75 and over	6,050
Blind person's allowance	1,400
Income limit for age-related allowances	17,000

Allowances which are "tax reducers" : £

Married couple's allowance	
Age 65-74	5,185
Age 75 and over	5,255
Minimum amount	2,000
Widow's bereavement allowance	2,000
Income limit for age-related allowances	17,000

The personal allowance (PA)

Anyone who is entitled to claim personal allowances is entitled to at least the basic personal allowance (£4,385 in 2000/01). The allowance is given in full in the tax year in which a taxpayer is born or dies.

The personal allowance is available to adults and children alike, though the income of most children is insufficient to enable them to make full use of the allowance. If an unmarried minor child receives investment income which is derived from a parent then this income is treated for tax purposes as the income of the parent, not the child, unless the amount involved does not exceed £100. This prevents parents (but not other relatives e.g. grandparents) from transferring income-bearing assets to a child so as to utilise the child's personal allowance.

Older taxpayers

As can be seen from the list of allowances given above, the amount of the personal allowance depends upon the taxpayer's age :

(a) A taxpayer who is over 65 years old, or who reaches the age of 65 during the tax year, is entitled to an increased personal allowance (£5,790 in 2000/01), and

(b) the allowance is higher still (£6,050 in 2000/01) for taxpayers who are over 75 years old or who reach the age of 75 during the tax year.

These higher age-related personal allowances are granted *instead* of the usual personal allowance, not in addition to it. A taxpayer who dies in the tax year in which he or she would have reached the age of 65 or 75 is granted the higher allowance for the year of death.

The age-related personal allowances are reduced if the taxpayer's statutory total income exceeds a specified limit (£17,000 in 2000/01). If STI exceeds this limit, then the personal allowance is reduced by one-half of the excess. However, the allowance is never reduced to less than the personal allowance for those aged 0-64.

EXAMPLE 1

Calculate the personal allowance due in 2000/01 to each of the following taxpayers :

(a)   Born 31 July 1935, STI £9,300

(b)   Born 31 July 1925, STI £8,650

(c)   Born 22 November 1932, STI £17,600

(d)   Born 2 May 1931, STI £20,000

(e)   Born 22 November 1922, STI £17,200

(f)   Born 2 May 1921, STI £20,350.

SOLUTION

(a)   This taxpayer reaches the age of 65 during 2000/01 and is therefore entitled to a PA of £5,790 for the year.

(b)   This taxpayer reaches the age of 75 during 2000/01 and is therefore entitled to a PA of £6,050 for the year.

(c)   This taxpayer is in the 65-74 age group and has an STI which exceeds the limit by £600, giving a PA of £5,490 (£5,790 - 1/2 x £600).

(d)   This taxpayer is in the 65-74 age group and has an STI which exceeds the income limit by £3,000. This would give a PA of £4,290 (£5,790 - 1/2 x £3,000) but the allowance is never reduced to less than the PA for those aged 0-64 so the taxpayer will claim £4,385.

(e)   This taxpayer is over 75 and has an STI which exceeds the limit by £200, giving a PA of £5,950 (£6,050 - 1/2 x £200).

(f)   This taxpayer is over 75 and has an STI which exceeds the limit by £3,350. This would give a PA of £4,375 (£6,050 - 1/2 x £3,350) so the taxpayer will claim £4,385.

Blind person's allowance (BPA)

This allowance (£1,400 in 2000/01) is granted to registered blind persons. If both a husband and wife are registered blind persons they can each claim the allowance. The allowance is given in full in the tax year in which the taxpayer is first registered as a blind person.

If a husband or a wife who is granted the blind person's allowance cannot make full use of it, then the unused part can be transferred to the other spouse, even if that spouse is not a registered blind person.

Tax reducers

The personal allowance and the blind person's allowance are the only allowances which are deducted from STI when calculating taxable income. The remaining allowances are relieved by reducing the amount of tax due on the taxpayer's taxable income. For this reason, these allowances are often referred to as "tax reducers". Note the following points :

(a) In 2000/01, the amount of the tax reduction is calculated as 10% of the amount of the allowance.

(b) Tax reductions for 2000/01 are made in the following order :

   (i)   the tax reduction relating to the widow's bereavement allowance

   (ii) the tax reduction relating to the married couple's allowance.

(c) The amount of tax borne can never be reduced to less than zero as a result of this tax reduction process. If the available tax reductions exceed the tax due on taxable income, there is no repayment of the excess. Any unused part of a tax reduction is simply lost (though the tax reduction relating to the married couple's allowance can sometimes be transferred between spouses, as explained below).

EXAMPLE 2

In 2000/01, a taxpayer aged 45 claims the personal allowance and the widow's bereavement allowance. Calculate the tax borne if the taxpayer's STI (none of which is derived from savings or dividends) is equal to :

(a) £34,640

(b) £10,560

(c) £4,620.

SOLUTION

	(a) £	(b) £	(c) £
Statutory total income	34,640	10,560	4,620
Less : Personal allowance	4,385	4,385	4,385
Taxable income	30,255	6,175	235

				£	£	£
Income tax						
(a)	(b)	(c)				
1,520	1,520	235	@ 10%	152.00	152.00	23.50
26,880	4,655		@ 22%	5,913.60	1,024.10	
1,855			@ 40%	742.00		
30,255	6,175	235		6,807.60	1,176.10	23.50
<u>Less</u> : WBA £2,000 @ 10%				200.00	200.00	23.50
Tax borne				6,607.60	976.10	0.00

Note :

In case (c), £176.50 (£200.00 - £23.50) of the tax reduction relating to the WBA cannot be used. This is lost and cannot be paid to the taxpayer.

Married couple's allowance (MCA)

For 2000/01 and subsequent tax years, the married couple's allowance is available to a legally married couple who live together for at least part of the tax year, *so long as at least one of the spouses was born before 6 April 1935*. For 1999/00 and previous years, the MCA was also available to younger couples but the allowance is now available only to those who were at least 65 years old on 5 April 2000. Note the following points :

(a) The allowance is not available to a married couple who are separated for the whole of the tax year. A couple are regarded as "separated" for tax purposes if they are legally separated or if they are separated in circumstances which make it likely that separation will be permanent.

(b) There is no requirement that the couple were already married by the start of tax year 2000/01. Couples who marry during 2000/01 or in subsequent years will be eligible for MCA so long as at least one of them was born before 6 April 1935.

(c) The amount of the MCA depends upon the age of the older spouse. For 2000/01, the allowance is £5,185 unless the older spouse is aged 75 (or older) at any time during the tax year, in which case the allowance rises to £5,255. If the older spouse dies in the tax year in which he or she would have reached the age of 75, the higher MCA is available for that year.

(d) In the same way as the age-related personal allowance is reduced for taxpayers whose STI exceeds a specified limit, the MCA is reduced if the *husband's* STI exceeds the same limit (£17,000 in 2000/01). However, the allowance is never reduced to less than a specified minimum amount (£2,000 in 2000/01). It is noteworthy that the *wife's* STI is not taken into account for this purpose, even if the MCA is being given because of her age rather than her husband's age.

(e) If a husband is over 65, his STI will be taken into account when calculating both his own PA and the MCA. The method of calculation is as follows :

    (i) The excess of the husband's STI over the income limit is divided by two, giving the required reduction in allowances.

    (ii) The husband's own personal allowance is reduced first, but never to an amount which is less than the personal allowance for those aged 0-64.

    (iii) If the reduction made in the husband's own personal allowance has not fully achieved the required reduction in allowances, the MCA is reduced next, but never to less than the specified minimum amount.

EXAMPLE 3

Calculate the allowances available to a husband and wife in 2000/01, given the following information :

(a) Husband born 1 March 1933 STI £12,700, wife born 5 July 1928 STI £7,700.

(b) Husband born 2 April 1937 STI £nil, wife born 6 August 1933 STI £22,800.

(c) Husband born 3 May 1923 STI £17,150, wife born 7 September 1932 STI £nil.

(d) Husband born 4 June 1927 STI £21,000, wife born 8 October 1922 STI £8,200.

SOLUTION

(a) Husband and wife are both over 65 and are each entitled to a PA of £5,790. An MCA of £5,185 is also available.

(b) The husband is under 65 and is therefore entitled to a PA of £4,385, all of which is unused. His wife is over 65 but her STI exceeds the income limit by £5,800. This would give her a PA of only £2,890 (£5,790 - 1/2 x £5,800) but the allowance is never reduced to less than the PA for those aged 0-64 so she will claim a PA of £4,385.

An MCA of £5,185 is available by virtue of the wife's age. The MCA is not reduced at all since the husband's STI does not exceed the income limit.

(c) The husband is over 75 but his STI exceeds the limit by £150. This gives him a PA of £5,975 (£6,050 - 1/2 x £150). His wife is over 65 and she is entitled to a PA of £5,790, all of which is unused.

An MCA of £5,255 is available by virtue of the husband's age. This is not reduced at all since the reduction required because of the size of his STI has already been made in full against his own PA.

(d) The husband is over 65 but his STI exceeds the limit by £4,000. Therefore he must lose a total of £2,000 in allowances. His own PA is first reduced from £5,790 to the minimum of £4,385 (a reduction of £1,405). The remaining £595 is deducted from the MCA of £5,255 (available by virtue of the wife's age) giving an MCA of £4,660.

His wife is over 75 and she is entitled to a PA of £6,050.

Allocation of the MCA

The tax reduction relating to the MCA is normally set against the husband's tax, but there are three exceptions to this general rule :

(a) The husband and wife may elect jointly that the tax reduction relating to the MCA minimum amount (£2,000 for 2000/01) should be set against the wife's tax.

(b) The wife may elect unilaterally that 50% of the tax reduction relating to the MCA minimum amount should be set against her tax.

(c) If either spouse is unable to use their MCA-related tax reduction in full or in part, the unused part may be transferred to the other spouse (assuming that the other spouse can use it).

The elections described in (a) and (b) must normally be made before the start of the tax year to which they relate, but the elections can be made during the tax year if this is the year of marriage. If either of these elections is made, any remaining part of the MCA (above the minimum amount) is dealt with in the husband's tax computation.

The transfer described in (c) may be claimed at any time up to 31 January in the sixth tax year following the year to which it relates. This transfer applies to the whole of the unused MCA, not just to the unused part (if any) of the minimum amount.

Year of marriage

In the tax year in which a marriage takes place the MCA is calculated in the usual way but is then reduced by one-twelfth for each full tax month which has elapsed between the start of the year and the date of the marriage. (A tax month runs from the 6th of one month to the 5th of the next month, inclusive).

If an election is made to transfer all or 50% of the MCA minimum amount to the wife in the year of marriage, it applies only to that amount reduced by 1/12th for each full tax month between the start of the year and the date of the marriage.

EXAMPLE 4

Calculate the MCA available in 2000/01 to a husband and wife (both born in 1930) who marry on each of the following dates :

(a) 5 April 2000   (b) 9 April 2000   (c) 23 June 2000   (d) 4 April 2001

Assume in each case that the husband's STI does not exceed £17,000.

SOLUTION

(a) A couple who marry on 5 April 2000 are already married by the start of tax year 2000/01. Therefore the MCA of £5,185 is available in full.

(b) A couple who marry on 9 April 2000 are not married for the whole of 2000/01 but no full tax months have passed between the start of the tax year and the date of the marriage. Therefore the full MCA of £5,185 is available.

(c) If the marriage takes place on 23 June 2000, two full tax months have passed since the start of the tax year (6 April 2000 to 5 May 2000 and 6 May 2000 to 5 June 2000). The MCA is reduced by two twelfths, giving an MCA of £5,185 x 10/12 = £4,321.

(d) If the marriage takes place on 4 April 2001, eleven full tax months have passed since the start of the tax year. Therefore the MCA is reduced by eleven twelfths, giving an MCA of £5,185 x 1/12 = £432.

Year of divorce, separation or death

The MCA is available in full in the tax year in which a couple divorce or separate or in which one of them dies.

EXAMPLE 5

Calculate the tax borne in 2000/01 by a husband and wife (both born in 1932), given the information shown below. In each case, an election has been made for 50% of the tax reduction relating to the MCA minimum amount to be set against the wife's tax and none of the income shown is derived from savings or dividends.

(a) Married all year, husband's STI £18,480, wife's STI £16,170.

(b) Married 1 March 2001, husband's STI £6,765, wife's STI £20,430.

(c) Husband dies on 12 October 2000, husband's STI to date of death £8,085, wife's STI for the year £16,835.

SOLUTION

	(a) £	(b) £	(c) £
HUSBAND			
Statutory total income	18,480	6,765	8,085
Less : Personal allowance	5,050	5,790	5,790
Taxable income	13,430	975	2,295

				£	£	£
Income tax						
(a)	(b)	(c)				
1,520	975	1,520	@ 10%	152.00	97.50	152.00
11,910		775	@ 22%	2,620.20		170.50
13,430	975	2,295		2,772.20	97.50	322.50
Less : MCA £4,185 @ 10%				418.50		
MCA £697 @ 10%					69.70	
MCA £4,185 @ 10% = £418.50						322.50
Tax borne				2,353.70	27.80	nil
WIFE						
Statutory total income				16,170	20,430	16,835
Less : Personal allowance				5,790	4,385	5,790
Taxable income				10,380	16,045	11,045
Income tax						
(a)	(b)	(c)				
1,520	1,520	1,520	@ 10%	152.00	152.00	152.00
8,860	14,525	9,525	@ 22%	1,949.20	3,195.50	2,095.50
10,380	16,045	11,045		2,101.20	3,347.50	2,247.50
Less : MCA £1,000 @ 10%				100.00		
MCA £167 @ 10%					16.70	
MCA £1,000 @ 10% + £96						196.00
Tax borne				2,001.20	3,330.80	2,051.50

Notes :

(i) In case (a), the husband's income is £1,480 over the income limit, therefore his PA is reduced to £5,050 (£5,790 - 1/2 x £1,480). The MCA is available in full. £1,000 (half of the minimum amount) is claimed by the wife, leaving £4,185 for the husband.

(ii) In case (b), the available MCA is 2/12 x £5,185 = £864. The wife claims 2/12 x £1,000 = £167, leaving £697 for the husband. The wife's income exceeds the income limit by £3,430. The reduced age-related PA would be £4,075 (£5,790 - 1/2 x £3,430) so she claims £4,385.

(iii) In case (c), the MCA is available in full in the year of the husband's death. £1,000 is claimed by the wife, leaving £4,185 for the husband. The tax reduction that he cannot use (£96) is transferred to his wife.

Widow's bereavement allowance (WBA)

In 2000/01, the only taxpayers who may claim the widow's bereavement allowance are widows whose husbands died during 1999/00 and who did not remarry before 6 April 2000. There is no equivalent allowance for widowers. The WBA is £2,000 in 2000/01 but is abolished for tax year 2001/02 and for subsequent years.

Children's tax credit (CTC)

The Finance Act 1999 abolished a number of personal allowances (including the MCA for younger couples and the WBA) but made provision for the introduction of a new allowance known as the *children's tax credit*. The main features of this new allowance, which will be available as from 6 April 2001, are as follows :

(a) The children's tax credit will be available to taxpayers who have one or more children living with them who are under the age of 16. The credit will take the form of a tax reducer relieved at 10%. For 2001/02, the amount of the credit has been set at £4,420, giving a maximum tax reduction of £442.

(b) If a child is living with a couple (whether married or unmarried) the children's tax credit will usually go to the partner with the higher income. But so long as neither partner is a higher-rate taxpayer, the couple will be able to choose whether to allocate the whole credit to either one of them or to share it equally.

(c) Higher-rate taxpayers who claim the children's tax credit will lose £2 of the credit for every £3 of income which is charged at the higher rate, until their entitlement to the credit is exhausted. This will occur when income of £6,630 or more (£4,420 x 3/2) is taxed at the higher rate.

(d) It will not be possible to claim the children's tax credit whilst simultaneously claiming the MCA (for older taxpayers). A taxpayer who is entitled to claim MCA may elect to give up that entitlement and claim children's tax credit instead, if that would be beneficial.

Summary

▶ Everyone is entitled to at least the basic personal allowance. Older taxpayers are entitled to a higher personal allowance but this allowance is reduced if income exceeds a specified limit.

▶ The blind person's allowance is granted to registered blind persons.

▶ The married couple's allowance is available to a legally married couple who live together for at least part of the tax year, so long as at least one of the spouses was born before 6 April 1935. The MCA is reduced if the husband's income exceeds a specified limit.

▶ The widow's bereavement allowance is available in 2000/01 to widows whose husbands died during 1999/00 and who did not remarry before 6 April 2000.

▶ Tax relief for the personal allowance and the blind person's allowance is given by deducting these allowances from the taxpayer's STI. All of the other allowances reduce tax borne by 10% of the amount of the allowance.

▶ Any part of an allowance that cannot be used by the person to whom it is available is lost (except that the married couple's allowance and the blind person's allowance can sometimes be transferred between husband and wife).

▶ The new children's tax credit will be available as from 6 April 2001.

Exercises

3.1 Calculate the personal allowance due in 2000/01 to each of the following taxpayers :

(a) Born on 28 August 1933, STI £12,300

(b) Born on 25 May 1924, STI £18,000

(c) Born on 2 February 1936, STI £20,600.

3.2 Calculate the allowances available to a husband and wife in 2000/01, given the following information :

(a) Husband born 1922 STI £14,500 , wife born 1928 STI £17,300

(b) Husband born 1930 STI £17,700, wife born 1930 STI £5,200

(c) Husband born 1933 STI £21,560, wife born 1939 STI £17,200.

3.3 Calculate the tax borne in 2000/01 by a husband and wife (both born in 1924), given the information shown below. No elections have been made in relation to the married couple's allowance and none of the income is derived from savings or dividends.

(a) Married all year, husband's STI £11,980, wife's STI £13,280

(b) Married 17 August 2000, husband's STI £5,000, wife's STI £10,705

(c) Husband dies on 16 September 2000, husband's STI to date of death £6,385, wife's STI for the year £13,145.

3.4 Calculate the married couple's allowance available in 2000/01 to a married couple who marry on each of the following dates :

(a) 4 May 2000 (both aged 21)

(b) 14 February 2001 (husband aged 62 STI £12,500, wife aged 68 STI £7,500)

(c) 25 December 2000 (husband aged 58 STI £18,100, wife aged 67 STI £100,000).

3.5   Toby is a widower. He was born in August 1924 and his income for 2000/01 is as follows :

	£
Retirement pension	5,030
Bank interest (net)	912

Calculate the amount of income tax repayable to Toby for 2000/01.

3.6   What personal allowances may be claimed by each of the following taxpayers in 2000/01 ?

(a)   John is single, 45 years old and registered blind.

(b)   June is 28 years old. Her husband died in September 1999, leaving her with two young children.

(c)   James is 14 years old. He earns about £15 per week from his paper round.

(d)   Jeremy is 68 years old and has a total income of £25,800. His wife died in May 1999.

3.7   Richard was born on 5 February 1938. His wife, Patricia, was born on 5 April 1935. They were married in 1965. Their income for 2000/01 is as follows :

	£
Richard :	
Business profits	18,040
Patricia :	
UK dividends	1,800

Calculate their tax borne and tax payable in 2000/01.

*3.8   A married man (born 3 November 1925) died on 8 July 2000. He received a retirement pension of £7,280 between 6 April 2000 and the date of his death. His wife (born 12 August 1935) had no income whilst her husband was alive but received a pension of £12,265 between 8 July 2000 and 5 April 2001.

Calculate their tax borne in 2000/01.

*3.9   Bill was born in 1933. He is married to Hilary who was born in 1937. They have elected that Hilary should receive the whole of the MCA minimum amount.

In 2000/01, Bill received business profits of £37,010 and dividends of £4,680. Hilary received a salary of £17,770 and net bank interest of £2,432. Calculate their tax payable for the year.

Chapter 4

Charges on income and other payments

Introduction

Certain types of payment made by a taxpayer are eligible for tax relief. Some of these payments, known as *charges on income*, are relieved by deducting them from the taxpayer's total income when calculating STI. Other payments act as tax reducers and are relieved by reducing the tax due on the taxpayer's taxable income. As from 6 April 2000, a special tax regime applies to certain charitable donations.

The purpose of this chapter is to describe the main types of payment which attract tax relief and to explain how relief is given for each type of payment.

Charges on income

As from 6 April 2000, the following items are treated as charges on income and are deducted when calculating the taxpayer's statutory total income for the year in which the items occur :

(a) eligible interest payments

(b) patent royalties paid and copyright royalties paid

(c) gifts of listed shares or securities to a charity.

Each of these items is explained in more detail later in this chapter. Before 6 April 2000, certain charitable donations were also treated as charges on income but this is no longer the case. The tax regime which now applies to charitable donations is explained at the end of this chapter.

Tax relief for charges on income is given at the highest rates of tax to which the taxpayer is liable. Deducting charges from total income automatically gives the right amount of relief, since the effect of the deduction is to reduce the amount of taxable income falling into the upper tax bands.

Charges paid gross or net

Some charges are paid gross (without deduction of tax) whilst others are paid net (after deduction of *basic rate* tax). Charges paid gross are deducted from the taxpayer's total income when computing STI, but it is tempting to ignore any charges paid net since the taxpayer has already taken tax relief at source. However, the tax deducted at source is always calculated at the basic rate and this will not give the right amount of relief to a taxpayer whose highest rate of tax is not the basic rate. The only way to be sure that the right amount of tax relief is given for a charge paid net is to :

(a) calculate the gross amount of the charge (net payment x 100/78)

(b) subtract the gross figure from total income when calculating STI (thus giving the correct amount of tax relief)

(c) increase the taxpayer's income tax liability by the amount of basic rate tax which was deducted from the payment when it was made. (In effect, the person making the payment is regarded as having collected basic rate income tax from the recipient on behalf of the Inland Revenue and must therefore account to the Inland Revenue for this tax as part of his or her income tax liability).

It is worth noting that this treatment of charges paid net is entirely consistent with the treatment of income received net (see Chapter 2). Income received net of tax is shown gross in the taxpayer's computation and the tax deducted at source is subtracted when calculating tax payable. Similarly, charges paid net are shown gross in the taxpayer's computation and the tax deducted at source is added when calculating tax payable.

EXAMPLE 1

Bob has income of £13,620 in 2000/01. None of the income is derived from savings or dividends. He is subject to an annual charge of £200, which he pays gross. Cathy's circumstances are precisely the same as Bob's in all respects except that she pays her charge net (i.e. she pays a net £156 in the year).

Compute Bob and Cathy's tax liabilities for 2000/01. Does it seem to be better to pay charges gross or net ?

SOLUTION

	Bob £	Cathy £
Total income	13,620	13,620
Less : Charge on income	200	
Charge on income £156 x 100/78		200
Statutory total income	13,420	13,420
Less : Personal allowance	4,385	4,385
Taxable income	9,035	9,035

				£	£
Income tax					
Bob	*Cathy*				
1,520	1,520	@ 10%		152.00	152.00
7,515	7,515	@ 22%		1,653.30	1,653.30
9,035	9,035				
Tax borne				1,805.30	1,805.30
Add : Tax deducted from charge				0.00	44.00
Tax liability				1,805.30	1,849.30

Note :

Bob has paid a charge of £200 and has a tax liability of £1,805.30, a total of £2,005.30. Cathy has paid a charge of £156 and has a tax liability of £1,849.30, again a total of £2,005.30. It makes no difference whether the charge is paid gross or net and this is evidenced by the fact that tax borne is the same for both taxpayers.

Higher rate taxpayers

A charge on income costs a higher rate (or Schedule F upper rate) taxpayer less than it costs a basic rate taxpayer, since relief is given at the highest rate of tax to which the taxpayer is liable. However, there is no need to adjust the method of computation to deal specially with such taxpayers. The method described above will give the correct result for all taxpayers.

EXAMPLE 2

Derek has income in 2000/01 of £23,100 (none of which is derived from savings or dividends). He pays a net annual charge of £234. Show his income tax computation :

(a)   with the annual charge

(b)   as it would have been without the annual charge.

How much has the annual charge effectively cost him ? How much would it have cost him if his income for the year had been £10,000 higher ?

SOLUTION

	Income £23,100		Income £33,100	
	(a)	(b)	(a)	(b)
	£	£	£	£
Total income	23,100	23,100	33,100	33,100
Less : Charge £234 x 100/78	300		300	
Statutory total income	22,800	23,100	32,800	33,100
Less : Personal allowance	4,385	4,385	4,385	4,385
Taxable income	18,415	18,715	28,415	28,715

Income tax

(a)	(b)					
1,520	1,520	@ 10%	152.00	152.00		
16,895	17,195	@ 22%	3,716.90	3,782.90		
18,415	18,715					

(a)	(b)					
1,520	1,520	@ 10%			152.00	152.00
26,880	26,880	@ 22%			5,913.60	5,913.60
15	315	@ 40%			6.00	126.00
28,415	28,715					

Tax borne	3,868.90	3,934.90	6,071.60	6,191.60
Add : Tax deducted from charge	66.00		66.00	
Tax liability	3,934.90	3,934.90	6,137.60	6,191.60

Notes :

(i) With income of £23,100, Derek's tax liability is the same whether or not he pays the annual charge. This is to be expected since he is a basic rate taxpayer and he has paid the charge net of basic rate tax (giving him the right amount of tax relief at source). The cost of the charge to him is therefore just £234.

(ii) With income of £33,100, Derek becomes a higher rate taxpayer and his tax liability is reduced by £54 if he pays the annual charge. The cost of the charge to him is only £180 (payment £234 less reduction in tax liability £54). In effect, the gross charge of £300 is reduced by tax relief at 40% (£120), leaving £180 as the cost to Derek. An alternative way of looking at the situation is to say that Derek takes 22% tax relief when making the payment but is entitled to 40% tax relief. Therefore the extra 18% is given via Derek's tax computation (18% of £300 = £54).

Starting rate and lower rate taxpayers

A taxpayer whose highest rate of tax is the starting rate or the Schedule F ordinary rate is entitled to tax relief on charges at that rate only. Similarly, a taxpayer whose highest rate of tax is the lower rate which applies to savings income is entitled to tax relief on charges at that rate only. But there is no need to adjust the method of computation to deal specially with such taxpayers. The method described above will automatically ensure that relief is given at the correct rate.

EXAMPLE 3

Esmé has income of £4,940 in 2000/01 and she is subject to a net annual charge of £124.80. Show her income tax computation :

(a)   with the annual charge

(b)   as it would have been without the annual charge.

How much has the annual charge effectively cost her ?

SOLUTION

	(a) £	(b) £
Total income	4,940	4,940
Less : Charge £124.80 x 100/78	160	
Statutory total income	4,780	4,940
Less : Personal allowance	4,385	4,385
Taxable income	395	555
Income tax		
Tax borne @ 10%	39.50	55.50
Add : Tax deducted from charge	35.20	
Tax liability	74.70	55.50

Notes :

(i)   As a starting rate taxpayer, Esmé's tax liability is increased by £19.20 if she pays the annual charge. This is logical since she takes 22% tax relief when making the payment but is entitled to only 10% tax relief. Therefore the difference of 12% is "clawed back" by the tax system (12% of £160 = £19.20). The £19.20 assessment would be raised under Section 350 of ICTA 1988 and assessments of this type are often referred to as "Section 350 assessments".

(ii)   The cost of the charge to her is therefore £144 (payment £124.80 plus increase in tax liability £19.20). In effect, the gross charge of £160 is reduced by tax relief at 10% (£16), leaving £144 as the cost to Esmé.

45

Non-taxpayers

Non-taxpayers (whose taxable income is zero) are not entitled to any tax relief at all on the charges that they pay. Once again, there is no need to adjust the method of computation to deal specially with non-taxpayers. The method described above will automatically ensure that no relief is given.

If charges cannot be relieved in the year in which they are paid, the opportunity for tax relief on those charges is permanently lost. In general, it is not possible to carry the unrelieved charges back to previous years or forward to future years. However, a special rule applies to unrelieved trade charges (see Chapter 11).

EXAMPLE 4

Glenda has income of £4,250 in 2000/01. She is subject to a net annual charge of £39. Show her income tax computation :

(a) with the annual charge

(b) as it would have been without the annual charge.

How much has the annual charge effectively cost her ?

SOLUTION

	(a) £	(b) £
Total income	4,250	4,250
Less : Charge £39 x 100/78	50	
Statutory total income	4,200	4,250
Less : Personal allowance (restricted)	4,200	4,250
Taxable income	0	0
Income tax		
Tax borne	0.00	0.00
Add : Tax deducted from charge	11.00	
Tax liability	11.00	0.00

Notes :

(i)   As a non-taxpayer, Glenda's tax liability is increased by £11.00 if she pays the annual charge. This is logical since she takes 22% tax relief when making the payment but is entitled to no tax relief. Therefore the tax relief which she deducts at source is clawed back by means of a Section 350 assessment.

(ii) The cost of the charge to her is £50 (payment £39 plus increase in tax liability £11). In effect, she pays the full gross amount of the charge, with no reduction for tax relief.

Eligible interest payments

The interest paid on certain loans is treated as a charge on income. This interest is paid gross. The main types of eligible loan are :

(a) A loan to purchase plant or machinery for use in the taxpayer's employment or for use in the business of a partnership in which the taxpayer is a partner. The interest paid on such a loan is eligible for relief in the tax year in which the loan is taken out and for the next three years.

(b) A loan to purchase shares in an employee-controlled company or to purchase an interest in a partnership.

(c) A loan to purchase ordinary shares in a close company (see Chapter 27), so long as the taxpayer has a material interest in the company or works for the greater part of his or her time in the management of the company.

(d) A loan to pay inheritance tax. The interest paid on such a loan is eligible for tax relief for 12 months only.

Interest paid wholly and exclusively for business purposes is generally treated as an allowable business expense and is deducted from the business profits assessed under Schedule D Case I or II (see Chapter 8). In this case, the interest is not regarded as a charge on income and it is not necessary for the loan to fall into one of the above categories for relief to be given.

Royalties

Patent royalties are paid net but copyright royalties are paid gross. These types of payment are most likely to be made in the course of business and are considered more fully in Chapter 8.

Gifts of listed shares and securities

As from 6 April 2000, a gift of listed shares and securities to a charity attracts tax relief as a charge on income. The amount of the charge is taken as the market value of the shares on the date of the gift. This new tax relief is in addition to the relief from capital gains tax which arises when assets are given to charities (see Chapter 16).

EXAMPLE 5

In 2000/01, a taxpayer who pays both income tax and capital gains tax at 40% gives listed shares with a market value of £20,000 to a charity. A capital gain of £17,000 would have arisen if the shares had been sold. In effect, how much has this gift cost the taxpayer ?

SOLUTION

The taxpayer will save income tax of £8,000 (40% x £20,000) and capital gains tax of £6,800 (40% x £17,000). The total tax saving is £14,800. This amounts to tax relief at 74% and the gift has cost the taxpayer only £5,200.

Payments which are tax reducers

The following payments are granted tax relief by means of a reduction in the tax due on the taxpayer's taxable income :

(a) certain maintenance payments made to an ex-spouse (so long as either the payer or the recipient was born before 6 April 1935)

(b) interest on a loan secured on the taxpayer's main residence and used to purchase an annuity (so long as the loan was taken out before 9 March 1999).

If such a payment is made gross, the appropriate tax reduction (see below) is given in the payer's tax computation. This tax reduction takes priority over the tax reductions which relate to personal allowances (see Chapter 3) and no tax refund is available if the available tax reductions exceed the tax due on the payer's taxable income. If the payment is made net, it should be *entirely omitted* from the payer's tax computation. This is because precisely the right amount of tax relief has been given at source and the tax system does *not* claw back excess relief from those whose tax liability is less than the tax deducted at source.

Before tax year 2000/01, maintenance payments were eligible for tax relief regardless of the age of the payer or recipient and tax relief was also available in relation to mortgage interest and payments made for vocational training. All of these reliefs have now been abolished.

Maintenance payments

Maintenance payments consist of payments to support a spouse or child, made by one spouse to the other after they have separated or divorced. The tax regime which applies to payments made under maintenance agreements is as follows :

(a) Maintenance payments are made gross, without any deduction of tax at source.

(b) Tax relief is available to the person making the payments only if one or both of the spouses was born before 6 April 1935 and the payments are made under a court order or legally binding agreement (or have been assessed by the Child Support Agency). Relief ceases when the *recipient* re-marries.

(c) Maintenance payments made directly to children do not attract tax relief.

(d) In 2000/01, a taxpayer making qualifying maintenance payments is entitled to a tax reduction equal to 10% of the *lower* of :

    (i)   the payments falling due and made in the tax year, and

    (ii) the minimum married couple's allowance (£2,000).

(e) The recipient of maintenance payments is not liable to pay income tax on them.

Loans used to purchase an annuity

Tax relief is available in relation to the interest paid on the first £30,000 of a loan taken out *before 9 March 1999* and which is :

(a) made to a taxpayer aged 65 or over, and

(b) used to purchase a life annuity, and

(c) secured on the taxpayer's main residence.

Such arrangements are often referred to as *home income plans*. Relief takes the form of a tax reduction equal to 23% of the qualifying interest. This rate remains at 23% even though the basic rate of income tax has now fallen to 22%. If the interest is paid gross, relief is given in the payer's tax computation. If the interest is paid net it should be entirely omitted from the payer's tax computation (as explained above).

Gift Aid

The Gift Aid scheme was established several years ago as a means of providing a tax incentive for individuals (and companies) to make charitable donations. Until recently, the scheme applied only to one-off charitable gifts of at least £250. Regular gifts made under the terms of a deed of covenant (a legally binding agreement) were covered by separate legislation. However, the Gift Aid scheme has undergone radical reform for tax year 2000/01 and subsequent tax years. The revised scheme as it now applies to individuals is explained below. The way in which the scheme now works for companies is explained in Chapter 23.

Gift Aid as from 6 April 2000

As from 6 April 2000, the Gift Aid scheme applies to any charitable donation, however large or small, whether one-off or made regularly according to the terms of a deed of covenant, provided that :

(a) the donor is either :

    (i)   a UK resident, or

    (ii) a Crown servant or member of the UK armed forces working overseas, or

    (iii) a non-resident with income or gains charged to UK tax (see Chapter 32)

(b) the gift is not covered by the payroll giving scheme (see Chapter 7) and is not repayable to the donor

(c) the donor receives no benefit from making the gift, or receives a benefit which does not exceed the following limits :

    (i)   25% of the amount of the gift, if the gift does not exceed £100

    (ii) £25, if the gift exceeds £100 but does not exceed £1,000

    (iii) 2.5% of the amount of the gift, if the gift exceeds £1,000

(d) the donor gives an appropriate declaration to the charity concerned (either orally, in writing, by telephone or via the Internet).

If all of these conditions are satisfied, the gift is treated as if it were made net of basic rate income tax and the charity can then recover the amount of tax which is deemed to have been deducted at source. For instance, a £20 gift would be treated as a gross gift of £25.64 (£20 x 100/78) less tax deducted of £5.64. In this case, the charity would receive £20 from the donor and a further £5.64 from the Inland Revenue. The gift is *not* shown in the donor's tax computation, but the following provisions apply :

(a) The donor must pay income tax and capital gains tax equal to at least the amount of tax deemed to have been deducted from the gift. If this is not the case, then the donor's entitlement to personal allowances is restricted to ensure that this amount of tax is in fact paid. If the restriction of personal allowances does not give the required result, the donor is charged to income tax at the basic rate on as much of the gift as is necessary to ensure that the required amount of tax is paid.

(b) The donor's basic rate band is extended by the gross amount of the gift. This extension ensures that relief at the higher rate is automatically given to higher-rate taxpayers. If the taxpayer has capital gains, some or all of the relief might be given against capital gains tax (see Chapter 16) rather than income tax.

(c) When determining the donor's entitlement to age-related personal allowances (see Chapter 3) the donor's STI is deemed *for this purpose only* to be reduced by the gross amount of the gift.

EXAMPLE 6

In 2000/01, Owen makes qualifying Gift Aid donations totalling £351. He is under 65 and he has no capital gains tax liability for the year. Show his income tax computation if his only income for the year consists of business profits of :

(a) £20,000

(b) £4,500

(c) £35,000.

SOLUTION

	(a) £	(b) £	(c) £
Schedule D Case I/II	20,000	4,500	35,000
<u>Less</u> : Personal allowance	4,385	4,385	4,385
Taxable income	15,615	115	30,615

Income tax

(a)	(b)	(c)				
1,520	115	1,520	@ 10%	152.00	11.50	152.00
14,095		27,330	@ 22%	3,100.90		6,012.60
		1,765	@ 40%			706.00
15,615	115	30,615				
Tax borne				3,252.90	11.50	6,870.60

Notes :

(i) The donations of £351 are grossed-up to £450 (£351 x 100/78) and are treated as if paid net of 22% tax. Deemed tax deducted is £99.

(ii) In case (a), Owen's income tax liability far exceeds £99 so there is no more to be done.

(iii) In case (b), Owen's income tax liability falls short of £99 by £87.50. Therefore he must pay a further £87.50 of income tax. This is achieved by reducing his personal allowance by £875, so increasing his tax liability by £875 x 10% = £87.50.

(iv) In case (c), Owen's basic rate band is extended by £450 from the normal figure of £26,880 to £27,330. This moves £450 of taxable income from the higher rate to the basic rate and saves tax of £81 (£450 x 18%). Together with the £99 deemed to have been deducted at source, total tax relief is now £180 (i.e. £450 x 40%).

Millennium Gift Aid

Millennium Gift Aid is an extension to the Gift Aid scheme which provides tax relief on gifts made to support educational and anti-poverty projects in countries designated as "low income countries" by the World Bank. Millennium Gift Aid will cease on 31 December 2000.

Summary

- ▶ Certain payments made by a taxpayer attract tax relief either as a charge on income or as a tax reducer.

- ▶ Charges must always be shown gross in the tax computation. Any tax deducted when the payment was made is added to the tax liability of the payer.

- ▶ If a payment which ranks as a tax reducer is made gross, the appropriate tax reduction is given in the payer's income tax computation. But payments made net should be omitted from the computation entirely.

- ▶ Charges on income comprise eligible interest payments, patent royalties paid and copyright royalties paid. As from 6 April 2000, a gift of listed shares or securities to a charity also ranks as a charge on income.

- ▶ Qualifying maintenance payments of up to the amount of the minimum married couple's allowance are relieved at 10% in 2000/01. This relief is available only if either the payer or the recipient was born before 6 April 1935.

- ▶ Subject to certain conditions, the interest paid on a home loan which is used to buy a life annuity is relieved at 23%. This relief is available only if the loan was taken out before 9 March 1999.

- ▶ The revised Gift Aid scheme covers both one-off donations to charity and regular donations made under the terms of a deed of covenant. Qualifying donations are deemed to have been made net of basic rate tax.

- ▶ A taxpayer making a Gift Aid donation must pay income tax and capital gains tax equal to at least the amount of tax deemed to have been deducted from the donation. Higher-rate taxpayers obtain higher-rate relief on such donations.

Exercises

4.1 Mabel has income of £18,380 in 2000/01, none of which is derived from savings or dividends. During the year she pays a net charge of £195. Show her income tax computation for the year.

4.2 Paul has income of £36,890 in 2000/01, none of which is derived from savings or dividends. During the year he pays a net charge of £1,248. Show his income tax computation :

(a) with the charge

(b) as it would have been without the charge.

How much has the charge effectively cost him ?

4.3 Rose has income of £4,375 in 2000/01. During the year she pays a net charge of £19.50. Show her income tax computation for the year.

4.4 At what rate of income tax is each of the following types of payment relieved in 2000/01 ?

(a) interest on a qualifying home loan used to buy an annuity

(b) interest on a loan used to buy an interest in a partnership

(c) qualifying maintenance payments

(d) patent royalties.

4.5 A taxpayer with no capital gains tax liability makes a qualifying Gift Aid donation of £936 in tax year 2000/01. Explain :

(a) why this donation is worth more than £936 to the charity which receives it

(b) why this donation might cost the taxpayer more than £936

(c) why this donation might cost the taxpayer less than £936.

4.6 Raj is was born in 1933 and is single. In 2000/01, he has business profits of £18,000 and no other income. He makes a qualifying Gift Aid donation of £273 during the year. Show his 2000/01 income tax computation.

4.7 Geoffrey is married, aged 48 and has two children under the age of 16. His wife is 47 years old. Geoffrey's only income for 2000/01 consists of a salary of £31,365 and UK dividends of £2,700. He pays £312 per annum to a charity under the terms of a deed of covenant. Show his 2000/01 income tax computation.

*4.8   Pauline (born August 1934) marries Adrian (born June 1938) on 17 October 2000. Their income for 2000/01 is as follows :

	£
Pauline :	
Retirement pension	9,370
Net building society interest	20
Adrian :	
Business profits	20,010
UK dividends	1,575

Adrian pays maintenance of £3,000 per annum to his former wife (born March 1935) as required by a court order.

Show Pauline and Adrian's income tax computations for 2000/01.

*4.9   Matthew dies on 23 December 2000 at the age of 67, leaving a widow aged 59. His only income in 2000/01 is a retirement pension of £18,110. His wife has income from property of £13,470 and no other income. She pays a net charge of £390 during the year and also makes a Gift Aid donation of £100.

Calculate their tax liabilities for 2000/01.

Chapter 5

Income from property

Introduction

Income from UK property is assessed under Schedule A. The purpose of this chapter is to list the types of income which fall within Schedule A and to explain how a taxpayer's Schedule A assessment for a tax year is calculated. Income from overseas property (which is assessed under Schedule D Case V) is considered separately in Chapter 32.

Schedule A income and expenditure

Section 15 of ICTA 1988 states that tax is charged under Schedule A on the profits arising from "*a business carried on for the exploitation, as a source of rents or other receipts, of any estate, interest or rights in or over land in the United Kingdom*". This is a very broad definition but, in practice, the main types of income assessed under Schedule A are :

(a) rents (including amounts receivable for the use of furniture if the property is let furnished)

(b) lease premiums, if the length of the lease does not exceed 50 years

(c) amounts receivable in respect of rights of way, sporting rights etc.

(d) income from the letting of fixed caravans or permanently moored houseboats.

Despite the use of the word "business" above, it is important to realise that income from property is almost always *unearned* income. The only occasion on which income from property is treated as earned income is when the income derives from the commercial letting of furnished holiday accommodation (see later in this chapter). The distinction between earned and unearned income is especially important if the owner of the property is hoping to obtain tax relief on premiums paid into a personal pension scheme (see Chapter 13).

Basis of assessment and allowable expenditure

The income assessable under Schedule A for a tax year is calculated on the accruals basis, using ordinary accounting principles. An exception to this rule occurs in the case of short lease premiums, which are dealt with in a special way (see later in this chapter). Expenditure which is incurred wholly and exclusively for the purposes of the property letting business is deducted from the assessable income, giving the Schedule A assessment for the year. This "wholly and exclusively" rule is copied directly from Schedule D Case I and is considered fully in Chapter 8, but the types of expenditure which are likely to be deductible in a Schedule A assessment include the following :

(a) repairs and maintenance to the property (excluding improvements)

(b) insurance of the property and/or its contents

(c) the cost of providing services to tenants

(d) administrative and management costs, including bad debts incurred

(e) rent paid to a superior landlord (if the property is sub-let)

(f) business rates, water rates or council tax (these are the responsibility of the occupier of premises, not the owner, but may be paid by a landlord on behalf of a tenant and then recouped via an increased rent)

(g) interest paid on a loan to buy or improve the property concerned.

If a property is partly let and partly owner-occupied, it is necessary to apportion the expenditure accordingly.

When a taxpayer derives income from two or more properties it is *not* necessary to calculate the amount of profit (or loss) arising on each property individually. In each tax year, total property expenditure is deducted from total property income, giving a single profit (or loss) figure for the year.

EXAMPLE 1

Ryan owns a house which he lets to a tenant. Rent is payable monthly in advance on the 6th day of each month. For some years the rent has been fixed at £2,400 per annum but this was increased to £3,000 per annum with effect from 6 December 2000. The rent due on 6 March 2001 was not paid until 7 April 2001.

Compute Ryan's 2000/01 Schedule A assessment, given that his allowable expenditure for the year is £800.

SOLUTION

The rent relating to 2000/01 is £2,600 (£2,400 x 8/12 + £3,000 x 4/12), so the Schedule A assessment for the year is £1,800 (£2,600 - £800). The fact that some of the rent was not received until early 2001/02 is irrelevant, since the accruals basis takes into account accrued rent as well as rent actually received.

Capital expenditure

Capital expenditure is never deductible in a Schedule A assessment but tax relief may be obtained on certain types of capital expenditure as follows :

(a) Capital allowances (see Chapter 10) are available in relation to expenditure on :

   (i) plant and machinery used in the repair, maintenance or management of let property, and

   (ii) qualifying industrial buildings let for industrial use.

   Capital allowances are standardised depreciation allowances which are deductible when computing the Schedule A assessment.

(b) A "wear and tear allowance" may be available in relation to expenditure on furniture and other equipment let to a tenant (which does not qualify for capital allowances). The wear and tear allowance is commonly calculated as 10% of the rent for the year, net of any council tax or rates borne by the landlord on behalf of the tenant.

(c) An alternative to the wear and tear allowance is the "renewals basis". If this basis applies, no tax relief is available in relation to the initial cost of providing furniture etc., but subsequent expenditure on replacements (not improvements) is allowed as a deduction in the Schedule A assessment for the year in which the expenditure is incurred.

EXAMPLE 2

Ursula owns a flat which she lets furnished. In 2000/01 the flat was let for 46 weeks at £40 per week. For the remaining 6 weeks of the year, Ursula occupied the flat herself. Her expenditure during the year was as follows :

	£
Council tax	380
Water rates	240
Minor repairs	135
Advertising for tenants	38
Cleaning (only when the property was let)	296
Painting and decorating	250
Insurance	120

Compute Ursula's Schedule A assessment for 2000/01, assuming that the wear and tear allowance is claimed.

SOLUTION

	£	£	£
Rents for the year £40 x 46			1,840
Less : Expenses allowed in full :			
Advertising for tenants		38	
Cleaning		296	
Apportioned expenses :			
Council tax	380		
Water rates	240		
Minor repairs	135		
Painting and decorating	250		
Insurance	120		
$\frac{46}{52}$ x 1,125		995	
Wear and tear allowance (see note)		129	1,458
Schedule A assessment			382

Note :

The wear and tear allowance is calculated at 10% of the rents, less any part of those rents which are deemed to reimburse Ursula for expenses incurred by her which are legally the tenants' responsibility (i.e. council tax and water rates). The tenants were in occupation for 46 weeks, so 46/52th of the council tax and water rates were their responsibility. The wear and tear allowance is therefore 10% of (£1,840 - 46/52th of (£380 + £240)) = £129.

Schedule A losses

If a taxpayer's total property income for a tax year is exceeded by the total allowable expenditure, the taxpayer has incurred a loss and the Schedule A assessment for the year is £nil. The loss is carried forward and relieved against the first available Schedule A income in subsequent tax years.

Note that any loss incurred on an individual property in a tax year will automatically be set against the profits arising on other properties in the same year, since all property income and all property expenses are pooled to give an overall Schedule A profit or loss for the year.

EXAMPLE 3

Sandra's entire income is derived from the letting of property. She has the following income and expenditure in tax years 1998/99 through to 2000/01 :

	1998/99	1999/00	2000/01
	£	£	£
Total income from property	19,320	19,650	21,100
Total allowable expenditure	27,410	15,430	7,540

Compute her Schedule A assessment for each year.

SOLUTION

	1998/99	1999/00	2000/01
	£	£	£
Total income from property	19,320	19,650	21,100
Total allowable expenditure	27,410	15,430	7,540
Profit/(loss)	(8,090)	4,220	13,560
Assessment before loss relief	0	4,220	13,560
Less : Losses b/f	-	(4,220)	(3,870)
Schedule A assessment	0	0	9,690

Note :

The 1998/99 loss must be set against the first available Schedule A income in subsequent years. This means that Sandra's Schedule A income for 1999/00 is reduced to £nil and (since this is her only source of income) her personal allowance for that year is wasted. However, it is not possible to conserve personal allowances by restricting the amount of loss relief claimed in 1999/00.

Lease premiums

A premium is a lump sum payable to a landlord by a tenant on the grant of a lease. The way in which such premiums are taxed depends upon the length of the lease :

(a) If the lease is for more than 50 years, any premium payable to the landlord is not subject to income tax but to capital gains tax (see Chapter 18).

(b) If the lease is for 50 years or less, any premium payable to the landlord on the grant of the lease is assessed to income tax under Schedule A in the tax year in which the lease is granted. The amount assessed is equal to the amount of the premium, reduced by 2% for each year of the lease except for the first year.

It should be noted that the above provisions relate only to the *grant* of a lease not to the *assignment* of a lease. The grant of a lease occurs when a new lease is created, under the terms of which the property will eventually revert to the landlord. The assignment of a lease occurs when an existing lease is sold to a new owner. This distinction is discussed further in Chapter 18.

EXAMPLE 4

In 2000/01, a landlord receives a premium of £36,000 when granting a 25 year lease to a tenant. What is the Schedule A assessment on this premium ?

SOLUTION

The assessable premium is reduced by 2% for each year of the lease except for the first year. Therefore 48% (24 x 2%) of the premium is not taxable and the remaining 52% is taxable. The Schedule A assessment on the premium is therefore £18,720 (52% of £36,000).

Relief for premiums paid

A tenant who pays a premium on being granted a short lease may obtain tax relief on the premium paid in one of two ways :

(a) If the tenant uses the property for business purposes then, throughout the duration of the lease, the tenant may claim an annual deduction from his or her trading profits assessed under Schedule D Case I or II (see Chapter 8). This annual deduction is equal to the amount of the landlord's Schedule A assessment on the premium, divided by the number of years of the lease.

(b) If the tenant sublets the property to someone else and receives a premium from the sub-lessee, then the assessable amount of the premium received is reduced by virtue of the premium paid. The reduction is equal to :

$$\text{Landlord's Sch. A assessment on premium paid} \times \frac{\text{Duration of sub-lease}}{\text{Duration of head-lease}}$$

If full relief cannot be given in this way for the premium paid (either because the premium received is too small or because no premium was received at all) the excess is spread evenly over the period of the sub-lease and set against the rents due from the sub-lessee.

EXAMPLE 5

Susan is granted a 20-year lease on a property, paying a premium of £76,000. To what extent will she be allowed tax relief in relation to this premium if :

(a) she uses the property for trading purposes, or

(b) she grants a sub-lease to Timothy for 5 years, receiving a premium of :

    (i)   £25,000

    (ii) £10,000.

SOLUTION

(a) The amount assessable on Susan's landlord is £47,120 (£76,000 less 38% of £76,000). If Susan uses the premises for trading purposes she will be able to claim an annual deduction of £2,356 from her trading profits for each of the next 20 years. (£47,120 divided by 20 = £2,356).

(b)

	(i)	(ii)
	£	£
Premium received	25,000	10,000
Less : 2% x 4 x £25,000	2,000	
2% x 4 x £10,000		800
	23,000	9,200
Less : Premium paid £47,120 x $\frac{5}{20}$	11,780	11,780
Assessable premium	11,220	nil

In case (ii) it is not possible to relieve the whole of the part of the premium paid which relates to the sub-letting period against the premium received for the sub-let. The amount unrelieved is £2,580 (£11,780 - £9,200). No assessment will be raised on the premium received and an annual deduction of £516 will be made from Susan's Schedule A assessment on the rents falling due from the sub-lessee. (£2,580 divided by 5 = £516).

Reverse premiums

It is not uncommon for a landlord to pay a so-called "reverse premium" to a potential tenant so as to induce that tenant to take out a lease. This arises most frequently when commercial premises are let to business tenants. The amount of any reverse premium paid by a landlord will usually be treated as enhancement expenditure for capital gains tax purposes when the landlord disposes of the property (see Chapter 17). But if the landlord is a property developer or dealer, the premium may be an allowable expense under Schedule D Case I (see Chapter 8).

From the point of view of a tenant who receives a reverse premium, this premium is chargeable to income tax (or corporation tax for a corporate tenant). If the premises are used for business purposes, the amount received is treated as trading income and is assessable under Schedule D Case I (see Chapter 8). Otherwise the amount received is assessable under Schedule A. In both cases, the timing of the tax charge will usually follow accepted accountancy practice, so that the tax liability arising on the receipt of a reverse premium will probably be spread over the period of the lease.

"Rent-a-room" relief

If an individual lets furnished accommodation which is part of his or her only or main residence, gross annual rents of up to a specified limit (£4,250 for 2000/01) are exempt from income tax. However, the taxpayer concerned may elect to ignore this exemption and to be assessed according to the usual Schedule A rules. This might be beneficial if the rents were exceeded by expenses, so that a loss could be claimed.

If gross rents exceed the limit, the exemption does not apply and rents less expenses will be assessed under Schedule A in the normal way. However, the taxpayer may elect to be assessed instead on the excess of the gross rents over the limit, without deducting expenses of any kind.

Both of the elections referred to above must be made by 31 January in the second tax year following the tax year to which the election relates. The election to ignore the exemption applies only to the year for which it is made. The election to be assessed on the excess of gross rents over the limit applies to all subsequent tax years until a year arises in which gross rents do not exceed the limit (or until the taxpayer withdraws the election).

EXAMPLE 6

In 2000/01, Victor rents out two rooms in his house and receives rents totalling £4,900. He incurs allowable expenses of £820. No elections are currently in force. What elections (if any) should he make ?

SOLUTION

The rent-a-room exemption does not apply since gross rents exceed £4,250. If Victor does nothing, he will be assessed on £4,080 (£4,900 - £820). If he elects to be assessed on the excess of gross rents over the rent-a-room relief limit, his assessment will be only £650 (£4,900 - £4,250). He should make this election and he has until 31 January 2003 to do so.

Furnished holiday lettings

If the letting of furnished property satisfies certain conditions, it qualifies as income from the "commercial letting of furnished holiday accommodation". Such income is still assessed under Schedule A but is regarded as trading income. The main beneficial effects of this are as follows :

(a) The income is regarded as earned income and personal pension premiums may therefore be relieved against it (see Chapter 13).

(b) Losses are treated as trading losses and may be relieved as such under the rules of Schedule D Case I (see Chapter 11).

(c) Capital allowances are available in respect of the furniture (see Chapter 10). The wear and tear allowance and the renewals basis do not apply.

(d) Business-related capital gains tax reliefs may be available (see Chapter 22).

The conditions which must be satisfied in order that the letting of property should qualify as the commercial letting of furnished holiday accommodation are :

(a) The property must be let furnished and it must be let with a view to profit.

(b) The property must be :

(i) available for letting to the general public as holiday accommodation for at least 140 days in the tax year, and

(ii) actually let to the general public as holiday accommodation for at least 70 days in the tax year, and

(iii) not normally in the same occupation for more than 31 consecutive days (for at least 7 months of the tax year).

If a taxpayer owns two or more properties each of which satisfies the 140-day rule but which do not all satisfy the 70-day rule, these properties will all be regarded as satisfying the 70-day rule so long as their average number of days let is at least 70.

EXAMPLE 7

Yvonne owns four cottages, all of which she lets furnished with a view to profit. None of the cottages is normally in the same occupation for more than 31 consecutive days. In 2000/01 the number of days for which each cottage was available for letting and the number of days actually let were :

	Days available	Days actually let
Cottage A	150	80
Cottage B	170	56
Cottage C	120	113
Cottage D	180	68

Show Yvonne's potential averaging claims.

SOLUTION

Cottage C cannot be regarded as furnished holiday accommodation since it does not pass the 140-day test. Cottages A, B and D all pass this test but only Cottage A also passes the 70-day test. Without any averaging claims, therefore, only Cottage A will be regarded as furnished holiday accommodation. Possible averaging claims are :

(a) Average Cottage A with Cottage B. This is no use since the average number of days let is only 68.

(b) Average Cottage B with Cottage D. This is no use since the average number of days let is only 62.

(c) Average Cottage A with Cottage D. This would be beneficial since the average number of days let is 74.

(d) Average Cottage A with Cottage B and Cottage D. This is no use since the average number of days let is only 68.

Therefore, Yvonne should claim that Cottage A should be averaged with Cottage D, in which case both cottages would qualify as furnished holiday accommodation.

Summary

▶ Income tax is charged under Schedule A on the profits of a business of letting property situated in the UK.

▶ Schedule A income is treated as unearned income unless it arises from the commercial letting of furnished holiday accommodation.

▶ The Schedule A assessment for a tax year is equal to the income for that year, calculated according to ordinary accounting principles, less any expenditure incurred wholly and exclusively for the purposes of the property letting business.

▶ Capital allowances are available in relation to certain types of capital expenditure incurred in relation to a property letting business.

▶ Schedule A losses are carried forward and set against the first available Schedule A income in subsequent years.

▶ A premium received on the grant of a lease is assessable if the lease does not exceed 50 years. The amount assessed is the amount of the premium less 2% for each year of the lease except the first.

▶ A tenant paying a lease premium will receive tax relief on the premium if the property is sublet or is used for the purposes of a trade.

▶ Rent-a-room relief is available if a taxpayer receives rents of up to £4,250 p.a. from the letting of furnished rooms in his or her main residence.

▶ Under certain conditions, the letting of furnished property qualifies as the commercial letting of furnished holiday accommodation. This offers a number of benefits to the taxpayer.

Exercises

5.1 Andrew owns a house which he lets to tenants. Rent is payable quarterly in advance on 1 January, 1 April, 1 July and 1 October. The rent was £4,000 per annum until it was increased to £4,400 per annum with effect from 1 January 2001. Rent received by Andrew during 2000/01 was as follows :

	£
2 July 2000	1,000
30 September 2000	1,000
3 January 2001	1,100
	3,100

Andrew did not receive the payment due on 1 April 2001 until 7 April 2001. Compute the income assessable under Schedule A in 2000/01.

5.2 Simon owns a country cottage which he uses as a holiday home for 4 weeks per year and lets furnished at £120 per week for the remaining 48 weeks of the year. Simon's expenses in relation to the cottage in 2000/01 were as follows :

	£
Council tax	400
Accountant's fee	35
Repairs to furniture (damaged by tenant)	50
Gardener's wages (£10 per week)	520
Insurance	230

Compute Simon's Schedule A assessment for 2000/01.

5.3 In 2000/01, a landlord receives a premium of £12,000 when granting a lease to a tenant. What is the Schedule A assessment on this premium if the length of the lease is :

(a) 60 years

(b) 50 years

(c) 20 years.

5.4 In 2000/01, Jasper is granted a 10-year lease on a property, paying a premium of £15,000. He uses the property for trading purposes. Compute the tax relief which he will be allowed in respect of the lease premium.

5.5   Georgina owns three holiday flats, all of which she lets furnished with a view to profit. None of the flats is normally in the same occupation for more than 31 consecutive days. In 2000/01 the number of days for which each flat was available for letting, and the number of days actually let, were :

	Days available	Days actually let
Flat 1	140	64
Flat 2	150	72
Flat 3	182	74

Show Georgina 's potential averaging claims.

*5.6   In 2000/01, Peter is granted a 12-year lease on a property, paying a premium of £40,000. He immediately grants a 4-year sub-lease to Paula, receiving a premium of £14,000. Calculate the Schedule A assessment on the premium received by Peter.

*5.7   Melissa is single and was born in 1931. She owns a house which she lets unfurnished at a rent of £100 per week. Her allowable expenditure in 2000/01 was £4,100 and she had Schedule A losses brought forward from 1999/00 of £1,350. Her other income in 2000/01 was as follows :

	£
Retirement pension	6,584
Net building society interest	9,200

Compute the income tax payable by Melissa for the year.

Chapter 6

Investment income and miscellaneous income

Introduction

This chapter deals with the tax treatment of income arising from investments other than property. The main options available to a taxpayer who wishes to make an investment are to invest in stocks and shares or to save money in bank and building society accounts. Each of these types of investment has its taxation implications and the purpose of this chapter is to explain those implications.

The chapter also briefly considers the taxation of income from trusts and settlements and the tax treatment of some miscellaneous sources of income.

Dividends received

As explained in Chapter 2, UK dividends have an attached tax credit which is equal to one-ninth of the amount of the dividend. A taxpayer's Schedule F income for a tax year is equal to the amount of UK dividends received in that year plus the attached tax credits. Dividends are treated as the top slice of taxable income and are taxed at 10% in the starting rate and basic rate bands. Dividends which lie above these bands are taxed at 32.5%. Tax credits are set against the tax liability on dividends but tax credits which exceed this liability cannot be paid to the taxpayer or set against the tax liability on any other form of income. Note that :

(a) No expenses are allowed against this form of income.

(b) Overseas dividends are assessed under Schedule D Case V (see Chapter 32).

Personal Equity Plans

If a taxpayer buys shares directly in a UK company, any dividends received are subject to income tax and any capital gain arising on the disposal of the shares is subject to capital gains tax (see Chapter 19). An alternative, tax-efficient means of investing in stocks and shares used to be provided by Personal Equity Plans (PEP's) but with the introduction of Individual Savings Accounts (ISA's) on 6 April 1999 (see later in this chapter) it is no longer possible to set up a new PEP. Investors who held PEP's on 5 April 1999 may continue to hold them if they so wish *and retain the tax exemptions described below*. However, no further investment may now be made in a PEP. The main features of PEP's which are still relevant in tax year 2000/01 are as follows :

(a) The funds invested in a PEP are managed by a plan manager who uses these funds to make qualifying investments. The main qualifying investments are listed ordinary or preference shares in companies incorporated in the UK or elsewhere in the EU.

(b) Dividends and interest paid on PEP investments are exempt from income tax. Tax deducted at source may be reclaimed by the plan manager. Although payment of the tax credits on dividends was generally abolished as from 6 April 1999, plan managers are able to claim payment of tax credits until 5 April 2004.

(c) Disposals of investments in a PEP are exempt from capital gains tax. This means that investors do not have to pay any CGT when disposing of PEP investments which have increased in value but also means that no loss relief is available if investments are sold which have declined in value (see Chapter 16).

Enterprise Investment Scheme

The Enterprise Investment Scheme (EIS) was established in 1994 to provide a means of encouraging investment in industry. It replaced a previous scheme known as the Business Expansion Scheme (BES). The main features of the EIS are as follows :

(a) Income tax relief is available to taxpayers who *subscribe* for newly-issued shares in certain "qualifying" companies. Essentially, these are unlisted UK trading companies whose gross assets are no more than £15 million immediately before the investment is made and no more than £16 million immediately afterwards.

(b) Relief takes the form of a reduction in the amount of tax due on the taxpayer's taxable income, equal to 20% of the amount invested in qualifying companies during the tax year. This reduction takes priority over the tax reductions relating to certain payments made by the taxpayer (see Chapter 4) and the tax reductions relating to certain personal allowances (see Chapter 3).

(c) A minimum of £500 and a maximum of £150,000 may be invested in each tax year. A taxpayer may claim that up to one-half of the EIS investments made in the first half of a tax year (subject to a limit of £25,000) should be treated as if paid in the previous tax year.

(d) The taxpayer must not be connected with the company at any time during the two years prior to the date of the investment and the five years after that date. Broadly speaking, an individual is connected with a company for this purpose if he or she is an employee of the company or, together with associates, owns more than 30% of the company's ordinary shares.

(e) Dividends received on the shares are subject to income tax in the usual way.

(f) Any capital gain arising on the eventual disposal of the shares is exempt from capital gains tax but any loss arising on the disposal is eligible for relief. A loss may be relieved either :

    (i) as a capital loss, in the usual way (see Chapter 16), or

    (ii) under Section 574 of ICTA 1988, against the taxpayer's income of the year in which the loss is incurred or the previous year (see Chapter 11).

When calculating the gain or loss arising on disposal, the shares are deemed to have been acquired for their issue price, less the tax reduction obtained by the taxpayer when the shares were purchased.

(g) The taxpayer must retain the shares for a minimum holding period of at least 3 years or both the income tax and capital gains tax reliefs are lost. For shares acquired before 6 April 2000, the minimum holding period is 5 years.

Venture Capital Trusts

A Venture Capital Trust (VCT) is a company approved as such by the Board of Inland Revenue. The main conditions which must be satisfied before Board approval can be obtained are :

(a) The company's ordinary shares must be listed on the Stock Exchange.

(b) Its income must be derived wholly or mainly from shares or securities and no more than 15% of this income may be retained by the company.

(c) At least 70% of its total investments must consist of "qualifying holdings" and at least 30% must consist of ordinary shares. Broadly, shares or securities owned by a VCT rank as qualifying holdings if they were newly issued to the VCT and if they consist of shares or securities in unlisted companies carrying on a qualifying trade in the UK.

(d) No holding in any one company (other than in another VCT) can represent more than 15% of a VCT's investments. At least 10% of a VCT's investment in any one company must be held in the form of ordinary shares.

(e) An investment does not count as a qualifying holding unless the company which is issuing shares to the VCT satisfies the same gross assets test as a qualifying company for EIS purposes (see above). If a VCT invests more than £1 million in any one company in the *longer* of the period of six months leading up to a share issue and the period from the start of the tax year up to the date of the issue, the excess over £1 million does not count as a qualifying holding.

An individual who is at least 18 years old can obtain income tax relief in respect of an investment in newly-issued shares of a VCT. The relief is equal to 20% of the amount invested (subject to a limit of £100,000 per tax year) providing that the shares are held for a minimum holding period of at least 3 years. For shares acquired before 6 April 2000, the minimum holding period is 5 years.

Dividends received on the first £100,000 of VCT shares acquired in each tax year are exempt from income tax and any capital gain (or loss) arising on the disposal of these shares is exempt from capital gains tax, regardless of whether or not the shares have been held for the minimum holding period.

Interest taxed at source

A taxpayer who receives interest on an investment is likely to receive the interest net of 20% income tax. Some investments do pay gross interest but these are comparatively few (see later in this chapter). The main categories of interest taxed at source are :

(a) building society interest

(b) bank interest (other than interest from the National Savings Bank)

(c) debenture and other loan interest from UK companies.

Interest from most Government securities or "gilts" used to be taxed at source (with the notable exception of 3.5% War Loan which has always paid gross interest). However, as from 6 April 1998, anyone receiving interest on gilts may choose whether to receive the interest gross or net (see Chapter 2).

The gross equivalent of any interest received net by a taxpayer during a tax year is included in the taxpayer's total income. The tax suffered by deduction at source is then subtracted when calculating tax payable. All of the above types of interest rank as savings income so that any amount falling into the basic rate band is taxed at the lower rate of 20%. No expenses are allowed against this form of income.

Self-certification

Individuals resident in the UK who are unlikely to be liable to income tax for a given tax year may supply a certificate to this effect to their bank or building society. Interest is then paid to such individuals without deduction of tax at source, so avoiding the need for repayment claims at the end of the year. As might be expected, there are penalties for supplying such certificates fraudulently or negligently.

EXAMPLE 1

Alfred is single and 66 years old. He receives the following income in 2000/01 :

	£
Retirement pension	4,820
Building society interest (net)	352

(a) Calculate the amount of income tax reclaimed by Alfred at the end of 2000/01.

(b) Could the need to make a repayment claim have been avoided ?

SOLUTION

(a) Alfred's total income for the year is £5,260 (£4,820 + £352 x 100/80). This is less than his personal allowance of £5,790 (over 65), resulting in a zero income tax liability for the year. He may reclaim the £88 tax deducted at source from the interest.

(b) Since it was probably evident at the beginning of the year that Alfred was going to be a non-taxpayer in 2000/01, he could have supplied his building society with a certificate to that effect. He would then have received his interest without deduction of tax (i.e. he would have received £440).

Interest not taxed at source

Interest not taxed at source is assessed under Schedule D Case III and ranks as savings income (see Chapter 2). No expenses are allowed against this form of income. The main sources of Schedule D Case III income are :

(a) National Savings Bank (NSB) ordinary account interest (apart from the first £70 per annum which is exempt from income tax)

(b) National Savings Bank investment account interest

(c) Interest on gilt-edged securities if the recipient has chosen to receive the interest gross (see Chapter 2).

(d) Interest which would normally be taxed at source but which has been received gross by an individual who is self-certificated as a non-taxpayer. Such interest will only be taxable if it transpires that the individual is a taxpayer after all.

Schedule D Case III income is assessed on the "current year" basis (also known as the "actual basis"). On this basis, the income assessed in a tax year is simply the income arising in that year. Interest arises when it is paid to the taxpayer or credited to the taxpayer's account. Any interest accrued at the end of a tax year but not yet paid or credited to the taxpayer is ignored when computing the Schedule D Case III assessment for that year.

Tax Exempt Special Savings Accounts

Until 6 April 1999, banks and building societies were able to offer Tax Exempt Special Savings Accounts (TESSA's) to their investors. These accounts offered tax advantages and were designed to encourage saving. With the introduction of Individual Savings Accounts (ISA's) as from 6 April 1999, no new TESSA's may be opened on or after that date. However, savers who held TESSA's on 5 April 1999 may continue to pay money into their TESSA's if they so wish and *these accounts will retain their tax-exempt status* for the remainder of their 5-year lives (see below). The main features of TESSA's which are still relevant in tax year 2000/01 are as follows :

(a) Interest received on a TESSA is exempt from income tax, whether or not the interest is withdrawn from the account.

(b) A TESSA retains its tax exempt status for five years after the account is opened, so long as no capital is withdrawn. If any capital is withdrawn during the five-year period the account loses its tax exempt status and all interest credited to the account since it was opened becomes taxable.

(c) At the end of five years the account ceases to be a TESSA and any interest subsequently received on the account is taxed as usual. Capital from a maturing TESSA can be transferred into the cash component of an ISA (see below).

(d) Up to £9,000 in total may be invested in a TESSA, but no more than £3,000 may be invested in the first year and no more than £1,800 per annum may be invested in each of the remaining four years.

Individual Savings Accounts

The tax-free Individual Savings Account (ISA) was introduced on 6 April 1999 as a replacement for both PEP's and TESSA's. The main features of this account are as follows :

(a) Individuals who are both resident and ordinarily resident in the UK (see Chapter 32) and are aged 18 or over are eligible to hold an ISA.

(b) An ISA may include three components. These are cash deposits, stocks and shares and life insurance products. A "maxi-ISA" is an ISA which includes a stocks and shares component plus either or both of the other two components. A "mini-ISA" is an ISA which includes only one of the components.

(c) The cash component of an ISA is likely to consist of a bank or building society account or a specially-designed National Savings product. The stocks and shares component can include qualifying shares and securities listed on a stock exchange anywhere in the world. The life insurance component can only include policies on the saver's own life which have been specially designed for ISA's.

(d) Each tax year, a saver may put money into *either* a single maxi-ISA *or* up to three mini-ISA's, one for each component. In the first two years of the scheme (1999/00 and 2000/01) no more than £7,000 may be invested in each year. In subsequent years, this limit reduces to £5,000. These limits are unaffected by the value of any PEP and/or TESSA also held by a saver.

(e) Within the overall annual limits, there are limits on the amount which can be invested in each component, as follows :

	1999/00 and 2000/01	*Later years*
Maxi-ISA	no more than £3,000 in cash and £1,000 in life insurance	no more than £1,000 in cash and £1,000 in life insurance
Mini-ISA's	no more than £3,000 in a stocks and shares ISA no more than £3,000 in a cash ISA no more than £1,000 in a life insurance ISA	no more than £3,000 in a stocks and shares ISA no more than £1,000 in a cash ISA no more than £1,000 in a life insurance ISA

(f) Savers may transfer capital from a maturing TESSA into the cash component of an ISA without regard to the above limits. Capital transferred from a TESSA during a tax year does not count towards the overall limit for that year.

(g) There is no cumulative limit on the total amount which an individual can save in ISA's during his or her lifetime. Nor is there a specified minimum level of saving. Savers are able to save as little as they wish in an ISA.

(h) In each tax year, savers may start fresh ISA's (maxi or mini) or may continue to put money into ISA's started in previous years. However, it is not possible to put money into more than one maxi-ISA, or one mini-ISA of each type, in any year.

(i) ISA's are run by ISA managers, typically banks, building societies, insurance companies and some high street stores and supermarkets.

(j) Interest, dividends and bonuses from ISA investments are exempt from income tax. In addition, ISA managers are able to claim payment of the tax credits on dividends until 5 April 2004. Capital gains (and losses) arising on ISA investments are exempt from capital gains tax.

(k) Withdrawals may be made from an ISA at any time without loss of tax relief. But once the maximum amount has been subscribed to an ISA for a tax year, no further subscriptions will be allowed in that year, regardless of how much is withdrawn from the account.

The ISA scheme is guaranteed to run for at least ten years and will be reviewed after seven years to decide on any changes required at the end of the ten-year period.

Income from trusts and settlements

A trust or settlement is an arrangement whereby property is held by persons known as *trustees*, for the benefit of other persons known as *beneficiaries*. Trusts fall into two main categories, as follows :

(a) If one or more persons are entitled to receive all of the income generated by the trust property, those persons are "life tenants" and the trust is a "trust with an interest in possession".

(b) If there is no life tenant and the trustees have the discretion to distribute as much or as little of the trust income to the beneficiaries as they see fit, the trust is a "discretionary trust".

Trusts with an interest in possession

The trustees of a trust with an interest in possession are liable to tax at the Schedule F ordinary rate (10%) on the trust's dividend income, the lower rate (20%) on its savings income and the basic rate (22%) on all of its other income. Note that :

(a) The tax liability of the trustees is never calculated at the starting rate, the higher rate or the Schedule F upper rate.

(b) The expenses of administering the trust are *not* allowed when computing the trustees' liability but expenses which relate to specific items of trust income (e.g. expenses normally deductible from property income) are set against that income.

(c) The trustees' tax liability is calculated without deduction of personal allowances.

(d) Relief is given in the usual way for income tax deducted at source and non-payable tax credits on dividends.

The income which remains after tax and all expenses have been deducted (including administration expenses) is paid to the life tenants and is dealt with in their personal tax computations. In those computations :

(a) trust non-savings income is treated as income received net of basic rate tax

(b) trust savings income is treated as income received net of lower rate tax

(c) trust dividend income is treated as dividend income received with an attached one-ninth tax credit.

The administration expenses of the trust are deemed to have been paid out of dividends in priority to savings income and out of savings income in priority to non-savings income.

EXAMPLE 2

An interest in possession trust with a single life tenant has the following income in 2000/01 :

	£
Rents receivable	30,200
Bank interest (net)	7,200
UK dividends	1,350

Expenses were incurred in the year as follows :

	£
Property expenses	6,900
Administration expenses	1,990

(a) Compute the trustees' income tax liability for 2000/01.

(b) How much income does the life tenant receive from the trust in 2000/01 and how will this be treated in his or her personal tax computation ?

SOLUTION

	Total £	Non-Savings £	Savings £	Dividends £
Schedule A £30,200 - £6,900	23,300	23,300		
Bank interest £7,200 x 100/80	9,000		9,000	
Sch. F £1,350 + tax credit £150	1,500			1,500
	33,800	23,300	9,000	1,500
Income tax @ 22%	(5,126)	(5,126)		
Income tax @ 20%	(1,800)		(1,800)	
Income tax @ 10%	(150)			(150)
Income after tax	26,724	18,174	7,200	1,350
Administration expenses	(1,990)		(640)	(1,350)
Income after tax and expenses	24,734	18,174	6,560	0

(a) The trustees' tax liability for the year is £7,076 (£5,126 + £1,800 + £150). The £1,800 of tax deducted at source and the £150 of tax credits are deducted, leaving tax payable by the trustees of £5,126.

(b) The income of the life tenant is :

	Gross £	Tax deducted £
Non-savings £18,174 x 100/78	23,300	5,126
Savings £6,560 x 100/80	8,200	1,640
Total	31,500	6,766

This income will be included in the life tenant's tax computation for 2000/01 and the tax deducted at source of £6,766 will be subtracted when computing tax payable for the year.

Discretionary trusts

The tax liability of the trustees of a discretionary trust is calculated at the "Schedule F trust rate" (25%) on the trust's dividend income and at the "rate applicable to trusts" (34%) on all of its other income. However, these special rates do not apply to income which has been used to fund the expenses of administering the trust. Such income is taxed at the Schedule F ordinary rate (dividends), the lower rate (savings income) or the basic rate (non-savings income).

Any payments made to beneficiaries are deemed to have been made net of tax at the rate applicable to trusts and must therefore be grossed-up at 100/66 in their personal income tax computations.

EXAMPLE 3

Assume that a discretionary trust has the same income and expenses in 2000/01 as the trust described in the above example. Assume also that a payment of £4,950 was made to a beneficiary during the year.

(a)   Compute the trustees' income tax liability for 2000/01.

(b)   Show how the £4,950 received by the beneficiary will be treated in his or her personal tax computation.

SOLUTION

	Total £	Non-Savings £	Savings £	Dividends £
Schedule A £30,200 - £6,900	23,300	23,300		
Bank interest £7,200 x 100/80	9,000		9,000	
Sch. F £1,350 + tax credit £150	1,500			1,500
	33,800	23,300	9,000	1,500
Income tax @ 10%	(150)			(150)
Income tax @ 20%	(160)		(160)	
Income tax @ 34%	(10,710)	(7,922)	(2,788)	
Income after tax	22,780	15,378	6,052	1,350
Administration expenses	(1,990)		(640)	(1,350)
Income after tax and expenses	20,790	15,378	5,412	0

Note :

The administration expenses of £1,990 are deemed to have been paid out of the trust's after-tax income, first out of dividends (£1,350) and then out of savings income (£640). As £640 of net savings income has been used for this purpose, gross savings income of £800 is taxed at only 20% and not at the special rate of 34%.

(a)   The trustees' tax liability for the year is £11,020 (£150 + £160 + £10,710). The tax deducted at source of £1,800 and tax credits of £150 are deducted, leaving tax payable by the trustees of £9,070. This consists of the £7,922 payable on the non-savings income and an extra 14% (34% - 20%) on the £8,200 of savings income which is taxed at the trust rate.

(b) The payment of £4,950 is grossed-up at 100/66, giving gross income of £7,500. This income is included in the beneficiary's tax computation for 2000/01 and the £2,550 of tax deducted at source is subtracted when computing tax payable for the year.

Miscellaneous income

Miscellaneous income (i.e. income which does not fall within any of the other Schedules and Cases) is assessed under Schedule D Case VI. Some examples of income assessed under Schedule D Case VI are :

(a) receipts from casual authorship

(b) casual commissions

(c) post-cessation receipts (i.e. income received after a business has ceased trading)

(d) receipts from the sale of patent rights

(e) income assessable under the accrued income scheme (see below).

The basis of assessment is the income actually arising in the tax year, less any allowable expenses.

Accrued income scheme

The accrued income scheme exists in order to prevent a form of tax avoidance known as "bond washing". Bond washing involves selling a security cum interest (so that the buyer of the security will receive the next interest payment) just before an interest payment is due. The price paid by the buyer reflects the fact that the sale is cum interest, so the seller is not disadvantaged. However, the effect of the transaction from the tax point of view is that the seller has converted what would have been income into a capital gain. Since capital gains on certain securities are exempt from capital gains tax (see Chapter 19) the seller appears to have avoided tax.

The accrued income scheme overcomes this potential loss of tax by charging the seller income tax under Schedule D Case VI on the interest which has accrued up to the date of the sale. The buyer of the securities is entitled to tax relief on the same amount and this is given by deduction from the next interest payment which the buyer receives.

Similar arrangements apply if securities are transferred ex interest (so that the seller will receive the next interest payment). In this case, the buyer is taxed on the interest accruing from the date of the sale to the date of the next interest payment and the seller is entitled to tax relief on the same amount.

The accrued income scheme applies to securities such as gilt-edged stocks, local authority bonds and company debentures. It does not apply to ordinary or preference shares in a company. Transfers made by individuals who have not held securities with a total nominal value exceeding £5,000 in the current tax year or in the preceding tax year are excluded from the accrued income scheme.

Summary

► Personal Equity Plans used to provide a tax-efficient means of investing in stocks and shares. Because of the introduction of the Individual Savings Account, no further investment may be made in a PEP after 5 April 1999.

► The Enterprise Investment Scheme provides tax incentives for those subscribing for the newly-issued shares of unlisted UK trading companies.

► Subject to certain conditions, tax relief is available in relation to an investment in a Venture Capital Trust.

► Most interest received is taxed at source. Non-taxpayers may receive interest gross if they certify that they are non-taxpayers.

► Interest not taxed at source is taxed under Schedule D Case III on the actual basis.

► A Tax Exempt Special Savings Account provides a tax-efficient means of saving money with a bank or building society. Because of the introduction of the Individual Savings Account, no new TESSA's may be opened after 5 April 1999.

► The Individual Savings Account (ISA) provides a tax-free means of saving cash or investing in life insurance products or stocks and shares.

► Trustees must account to the Inland Revenue for income tax on the income of a trust. The administration expenses of the trust are not allowed when computing the trustees' tax liability.

► Special tax rates apply to the income of a discretionary trust.

► Miscellaneous income is taxed under Schedule D Case VI.

Exercises

6.1   Edward has the following income in 2000/01 :

	£
Building society interest (net)	6,900
UK dividends	27,468

Compute the income tax payable by Edward for the year, assuming that there are no charges on income and that he claims only the personal allowance.

6.2   Anne is single and aged 76. She has the following income in 2000/01 :

	£
Bank interest :	
Interest on deposit account (net)	384
Interest credited to TESSA	210
Interest credited to cash mini-ISA	83
UK dividends	585
Retirement pension	5,436

Compute the income tax payable by (or repayable to) Anne for the year, assuming that she has no charges on income and that no capital has been withdrawn from the TESSA.

6.3   Outline the income tax advantages of investing in :

(a)   the Enterprise Investment Scheme

(b)   a Venture Capital Trust.

6.4   Outline the main features of the Individual Savings Account and explain how the introduction of this account affects a taxpayer who had a PEP or a TESSA as at 5 April 1999.

6.5   Bernice was born on 1 March 1936 and is a widow (her husband died in February 2000). Her income for 2000/01 is as follows :

	£
Pension	12,470
NSB ordinary account interest	78
NSB investment account interest	52
Building society interest (net)	3,784

Compute the income tax payable by Bernice for 2000/01.

*6.6   An interest in possession trust with two life tenants has the following income in 2000/01 :

	£
Rents received	12,620
Bank deposit interest (net)	992
Interest received gross	1,800
UK dividends	12,600

Property expenses incurred in the year were £2,220 and general administration expenses amounted to £2,700.

(a)   Compute the trustees' income tax liability for 2000/01.

(b)   Assuming that the trust income is divided equally between the two life tenants, calculate each life tenant's income from the trust in 2000/01.

Chapter 7
Income from employment

Introduction

Income from employment is taxed under Schedule E. This chapter explains the way in which employment income is assessed and considers the expenses which may be deducted when computing a Schedule E assessment. There is also a brief description of the Pay As You Earn system, through which most employees pay their income tax.

This chapter is concerned only with those employees whose duties are performed within the UK. The taxation of overseas earnings is considered in Chapter 32.

Employment and self-employment

As will become clear in the next few chapters, self-employed people, who are assessed under Schedule D Case I or II, enjoy considerable tax advantages when compared with employees, who are assessed under Schedule E. Two of the main advantages of being self-employed are :

(a) A much wider range of expenses is allowed against the income of self-employed people than against the income of employees (see this chapter and Chapter 8).

(b) Self-employed people pay their income tax by instalments (see Chapter 14) and effectively pay their tax much later than employees, who normally pay income tax under the PAYE system (see later in this chapter).

It is usually quite obvious whether someone is employed or self-employed but sometimes there are borderline cases. For example, it may be difficult to distinguish between an employee with a number of part-time jobs and a self-employed person with several clients. In such cases, the taxpayer (mindful of the tax advantages of being self-employed) will usually wish to claim self-employed status whilst the Inland Revenue will often feel that the taxpayer should be treated as an employee. The key test to be applied when trying to establish a taxpayer's status in cases like these is concerned with the nature of the contract between the taxpayer and the person who is paying for the work done by that taxpayer. There are two possibilities :

(a) If it can be shown that a *contract of service* exists, then the taxpayer is regarded as an employee who is in service to an employer.

(b) If it can be shown that a *contract for services* exists, then the taxpayer is regarded as a self-employed person who is rendering services to a client.

A great deal of case law has accumulated on this subject over the years and several criteria have been established which may be used to distinguish between the two types of contract (and, therefore, between employment and self-employment). The main criteria are as follows :

(a) **Control**. The more control that the person who is paying for the work has over the person who is doing the work, the more likely it is that a contract of service exists. Employees are usually unable to choose whether or not to do certain work, how to do the work, when to do the work or where to do the work. Self-employed people are usually able to decide these matters for themselves.

(b) **Financial risk**. Employees do not usually risk their own capital in the business for which they work and they receive their remuneration regularly, whether or not their employer is making a profit. Self-employed people may make losses as well as profits and may lose their capital if the business fails.

(c) **Equipment**. In general, employees do not provide their own equipment but self-employed people do.

(d) **Work performance and correction**. Employees are usually expected to do their work themselves. If they make mistakes they usually correct the work during working hours and so get paid both for the original work and for the corrections. Self-employed people often delegate their work to staff or to subcontractors. If the work done is unsatisfactory, the client will not expect to have to pay again for it to be corrected.

(e) **Holidays and sickness**. Employees are likely to receive holiday pay and sick pay from their employers. Self-employed people are paid by their clients only for the work that they do and do not get paid when on holiday or when ill.

(f) **Exclusivity**. Employees (on the whole) work for a single employer. Self-employed people normally have a number of clients.

There are exceptions to all of the general statements given above and therefore these criteria should be applied with caution. It is vitally important to consider the facts of each case as a whole and not to rely upon just one criterion when trying to decide whether a taxpayer should be regarded as employed or self-employed.

Personal services provided through intermediaries

A specific situation about which the Government has been concerned for some time is the hiring of individuals through their own personal service companies, thus enabling those individuals to exploit the tax (and National Insurance) advantages offered by corporate status. Anti-avoidance legislation designed to thwart this kind of disguised employment took effect as from 6 April 2000. The main points are as follows :

(a) The legislation applies to "relevant engagements" where a worker provides services to a client through an intermediary (usually a company) in circumstances such that the income arising from the engagement would have been treated as income from employment if it had not been for the presence of the intermediary.

(b) The legislation does *not* apply if the worker receives income from the intermediary only in a form which is taxable under Schedule E and has no other rights to income or capital from the intermediary.

(c) If a intermediary company receives income from relevant engagements and this income (less allowable expenses) is greater than the worker's Schedule E income from the company, then the excess is subject to both Schedule E income tax and National Insurance contributions.

(d) The allowable expenses referred to above include all expenses generally allowable under Schedule E, plus employer's pension and National Insurance contributions made by the intermediary company, plus a further flat-rate 5% of the income arising from relevant engagements (to cover running costs of the intermediary).

Basis of assessment

The income taxed under Schedule E for a tax year is the income actually received in that year (the "receipts basis"). Income is deemed to be received on the *earliest* of the following dates :

(a) the date that the income is actually received by the employee

(b) the date that the employee becomes entitled to receive the income

and, for a company director only :

(c) the date that the income is credited to the director in the company's records

(d) the end of an accounting period, if the amount of the director's income for that period is determined before it ends

(e) the date that the amount of the director's income for an accounting period is determined, if this falls after the end of that accounting period.

Note that the income received in a tax year is not necessarily the same as the income earned during that year.

EXAMPLE 1

Barry is a sales manager. He receives a basic salary plus an annual bonus (received in February), based on the sales achieved in the previous calendar year. Compute his total Schedule E income in 2000/01, given that his basic salary for the year was £35,000 and that bonuses for calendar years 1999, 2000 and 2001 are as follows :

	£
year ended 31 December 1999 (received February 2000)	6,250
year ended 31 December 2000 (received February 2001)	7,350
year ended 31 December 2001 (received February 2002)	7,900

SOLUTION

Barry's Schedule E income for 2000/01 is £42,350 (£35,000 + £7,350). The bonus he received in February 2001 is assessed in 2000/01, regardless of the fact that some of it relates to sales achieved in 1999/00.

Income assessable under Schedule E

Income tax under Schedule E is charged on the emoluments of an office or employment. The term "emoluments" includes practically anything that could conceivably be received by an employee in respect of an employment e.g. wages, salaries, bonuses, commissions, fees, expense allowances, payments on the termination of employment, pensions arising from an employment and benefits in kind. Also, certain social security benefits are taxable under Schedule E, including :

(a) the retirement pension and the widow's pension

(b) the job seeker's allowance

(c) statutory sick pay and maternity pay

(d) incapacity benefit (except for short-term benefit paid in the first 28 weeks)

(e) the invalid care allowance and industrial death benefit.

Note that it is not necessary for the employee to receive the emoluments directly from the employer. So long as the emoluments are received as a result of the office or employment they are taxable under Schedule E, no matter who has paid them. For example, a waiter's tips are taxable under Schedule E, even though these are paid by customers rather than by the waiter's employer.

Non-taxable emoluments

Although the above definition of emoluments seems to be all-embracing, certain forms of income from employment are in fact exempt from income tax. The main types of exempt income are as follows :

(a) luncheon vouchers provided by an employer of up to 15p per day in value

(b) free or subsidised meals in a staff canteen, if available to all employees

(c) an annual Christmas party or similar function paid for by the employer, so long as the function is open to staff generally and the cost does not exceed £75 per head, but note that :

   (i) if a function costs over £75 per head, the whole cost of the function is taxable

   (ii) if there is more than one function during the year and their total cost exceeds £75 per head, functions totalling £75 per head or less are exempt from tax but any other functions are taxed in full

(d) the provision of a parking space at or near the employee's place of work

(e) the provision of private transport (e.g. a taxi) for the journey home of employees who are occasionally required to work until 9pm or later

(f) the payment by an employer of the costs of an employee's journey home if the employee travels to work in a shared car (in accordance with a regular car-sharing arrangement) and is prevented from travelling home in the shared car because of unforeseen and exceptional circumstances

(g) "green commuting" benefits paid for by an employer and used by employees for travel between home and work, including the provision of bicycles, cycling safety equipment, works buses and subsidies to public bus services

(h) reasonable mileage allowances (see "fixed profit car scheme" below)

(i) the payment by an employer of an employee's personal incidental expenses (e.g. the cost of telephone calls home) when the employee is staying away from home overnight on business, of up to £5 per night for stays within the UK or £10 per night for stays outside the UK

(j) reasonable removal expenses (up to a maximum of £8,000) paid for by an employer when an employee first takes up an employment or transfers to a new location within the organisation

(k) reasonable gifts made by an employer to an employee on special occasions (e.g. marriage, exam success)

(l) non-cash long service awards so long as the award is in respect of at least 20 years of service and does not cost the employer more than £20 per year of service

(m) non-cash gifts received by virtue of the employment from someone other than the employer (so long as the value of the gifts from any one source amounts to no more than £150 in the tax year and the gifts are not made in recognition of the performance of particular services in the course of the employment)

(n) awards of up to £5,000 made under a staff suggestion scheme

(o) the cost of work-related training courses for an employee and contributions made by an employer to an employee's Individual Learning Account

(p) the loan of computer equipment to an employee, so long as the benefit arising under the usual rules (see later in this chapter) would not exceed £500 p.a.

(q) the provision of a mobile telephone for an employee's use

(r) the provision of workplace child care, sports or recreation facilities

(s) the provision of a low-interest or interest-free loan to an employee if the loan is of the type that qualifies for tax relief (see Chapter 4).

Fixed profit car scheme (FPCS)

Employees who use their own cars on business may receive mileage allowances from their employers, calculated at some number of pence per mile. Strictly speaking, these allowances should be regarded as part of an employee's income for tax purposes and the employee should then claim tax relief for the motor expenses actually incurred by him or her on business trips. This would require the employee to keep fairly extensive records of business and private mileage, fuel costs, car maintenance costs etc.

An alternative (but optional) approach is the "fixed profit car scheme", which works by reference to a table of tax-free mileage rates fixed by the Inland Revenue. For 2000/01, these rates (in pence per mile) are as follows :

Engine size	first 4,000 miles in the year	miles in excess of 4,000
up to 1,000 cc	28p	17p
1,001 - 1,500 cc	35p	20p
1,501 - 2,000 cc	45p	25p
over 2,000 cc	63p	36p

If the mileage allowances paid to an employee exceed the sum calculated using these rates, then the excess is taxable. On the other hand, if the mileage allowances paid to an employee are less than the sum calculated using these rates, the deficit is an allowable expense. Note that :

(a) If an employer pays a mileage allowance to employees who use their own motor-cycles or bicycles for business travel, tax-free mileage rates apply of 24p and 12p per mile respectively.

(b) Employees who use their own car, motor cycle or cycle for business travel may claim capital allowances (see Chapter 10) on a proportion of the vehicle's cost.

EXAMPLE 2

Julie uses her own 1,800 cc car when travelling on her employer's business. In 2000/01 she drives 5,000 business miles. Explain the taxation implications if her employer pays her a mileage allowance of :

(a)   42p per mile   (b)   32p per mile   (c)   None.

SOLUTION

(a)   Having driven 5,000 business miles in an 1,800 cc car, Julie may receive a tax-free mileage allowance of up to £2,050 (4,000 @ 45p + 1,000 @ 25p) for the year. She actually receives £2,100 (5,000 @ 42p) so her taxable mileage allowance is £50.

(b)   If the mileage allowance is only 32p per mile, Julie receives only £1,600 from her employer. Therefore she has incurred an allowable Schedule E expense of £450 (£2,050 - £1,600) which may be set against her income from employment.

(c)   If Julie receives nothing, she has an allowable Schedule E expense of £2,050.

Allowable expenses

If an employee incurs expenses by virtue of his or her employment, then one of two situations may arise :

(a)   The employer does not reimburse the employee for the expenses. In this case the expenses (if allowable) will be deducted from the employee's Schedule E income.

(b)   The employer reimburses the employee. In this case the amount reimbursed by the employer will be treated as part of the employee's emoluments and the expenses (if allowable) will be deducted from the employee's Schedule E income.

Expenses incurred by an employee are allowable for tax purposes only if they fall into one of the following categories :

(a)   contributions to an approved occupational pension scheme or premiums paid to secure a personal pension or retirement annuity (see Chapter 13)

(b)   subscriptions to relevant professional bodies

(c)   donations made under a payroll giving scheme (see later in this chapter)

(d)   travel and subsistence expenses necessarily incurred in the performance of the duties of the employment (see below)

(e)   other expenses incurred "wholly, exclusively and necessarily in the performance of the duties of the employment".

The "wholly, exclusively and necessarily" rule is applied stringently. In particular, the "necessarily" part of the rule means that an expense will not be allowed unless it can be shown that the duties of the employment could not be performed (by anyone) if the expense were not incurred.

Travel and subsistence expenses

As stated above, travel and subsistence expenses are allowable for tax purposes only if they are necessarily incurred in the performance of the duties of the employment. This means that the cost of travel between home and work is normally disallowed on the grounds that the duties of the employment do not begin until the employee arrives at work. However, the following costs of travel between home and work are allowable :

(a) travel and subsistence costs incurred by a "site based" employee (i.e. an employee who has no normal place of work) when travelling between home and the site

(b) travel and subsistence costs incurred by an employee who has a normal place of work, when undertaking business journeys which start from home

(c) travel and subsistence costs incurred by an employee who is seconded to a temporary place of work, so long as it is expected that he or she will return to the normal place of work within 24 months.

EXAMPLE 3

In which of the following cases will the expenses described be allowable against the employee's income for tax purposes ?

(a) A bank manager voluntarily pays an annual subscription to a London club (he uses the club only for the purpose of meeting the bank's clients).

(b) A workman is required to provide his own tools and protective clothing.

(c) A clerk pays to attend a college course in the evenings, so as to gain qualifications and improve her career prospects.

(d) The finance director of a company pays an annual subscription to the Institute of Chartered Accountants.

(e) A college lecturer teaches at the main college building and then drives to one of the college's annexes to take his next class. He pays his own travel costs.

(f) A barrister living and practising in London is appointed Recorder of Portsmouth. He pays his own travel costs between London and Portsmouth.

SOLUTION

(a) The bank manager uses the club wholly and exclusively for business purposes, but it is not necessary for him to be a member of the club in order to perform his duties. Therefore the cost of the subscription will be disallowed. The facts of this case are similar to those of *Brown* v *Bullock* (1961).

(b) The cost of necessary tools and protective clothing will be allowed. In some cases, the Inland Revenue has agreed flat-rate tax allowances with the relevant trade union for such expenses as tools, protective clothing, uniforms and laundry costs.

(c) Whilst attending college, the clerk is not performing the duties of her employment. Therefore the cost of the college course will be disallowed. The facts of this case are similar to those of *Blackwell* v *Mills* (1945).

(d) Relevant professional subscriptions of this nature are specifically allowed by statute. Therefore the cost of the subscription will be allowed.

(e) Travel between the two buildings will be allowed, since the travel is necessary and is incurred in the performance of the duties of the employment.

(f) The duties of the employment are carried out entirely in Portsmouth. Whilst travelling from London, the barrister is not performing those duties so the expense will be disallowed. The facts of this case are similar to those of *Ricketts* v *Colquhoun* (1935).

Entertaining expenses

In general, entertaining expenses (e.g. expenses incurred when entertaining clients) are not allowable under Schedule E and an employee who is obliged to defray such expenses personally cannot claim them as a deduction from income. However, if an employer either :

(a) reimburses an employee for entertaining expenses incurred, or

(b) pays an employee an allowance which is specifically intended for entertaining purposes

then the entertaining expenses incurred by the employee may be set against the sums received from the employer. This rule is subject to the overriding rule that the entertaining expenses must be incurred wholly, exclusively and necessarily in the performance of the duties of the employment.

Payroll giving scheme

Employees whose employers operate a "payroll giving scheme" may make charitable donations by asking that the donations should be deducted from their gross earnings. Income tax is payable on the earnings remaining *after* the charitable donations have been deducted, thus providing tax relief. The employer, who must gain Inland Revenue approval to operate the scheme, passes the donations on to an approved charity or charity agency. The Government will add a 10% supplement to all donations made under the scheme between 6 April 2000 and 5 April 2003 inclusive.

Benefits in kind

The definition of "emoluments" given above includes benefits in kind. Benefits in kind consist of goods or services received by an employee, rather than money. For the purpose of assessing benefits in kind, employees are divided into "P11D employees" and "non-P11D employees" :

(a) P11D employees comprise those employees who earn at least £8,500 per annum and most company directors. The only exceptions are full-time working directors who earn less than £8,500 per annum and who do not control more than 5% of their company's ordinary share capital. Employers are required to submit a form P11D to the Inland Revenue for each such employee each year, listing the employee's benefits in kind.

(b) All other employees are non-P11D employees or "lower-paid employees".

As a general rule, lower-paid employees are taxed only on benefits in kind that are convertible into money, and then only on the amount of money that the employee could obtain in this way. In other words, lower-paid employees are taxed on the *second-hand value* of their benefits in kind. P11D employees are generally taxed on the *cost to the employer* of providing the benefits in kind, whether or not these benefits are convertible into money.

The cost of providing a benefit is to be taken as the marginal cost incurred by the employer i.e. the additional cost borne by the employer as a consequence of providing the benefit. This rule was established in the case of *Pepper* v *Hart* (1992), which concerned the provision of school places for the children of masters at the school. It was held that the cost of this provision for Schedule E purposes should consist only of the additional costs borne by the school (e.g. extra food and laundry costs) rather than the average cost per pupil which would be obtained by dividing the total running costs of the school by the total number of pupils.

When comparing an employee's emoluments with the watershed figure of £8,500, it is necessary to take into account all of the employee's emoluments including benefits in kind *valued as if the employee were a P11D employee*. No expenses may be deducted from the employee's emoluments for this purpose, apart from contributions made to an approved superannuation scheme and contributions to a payroll giving scheme.

If an employee works for more than one employer and the employers are connected in some way (e.g. they are both subsidiaries of the same parent company) the employee's emoluments from all connected employers must be aggregated for the purpose of deciding the employee's classification for benefits in kind purposes.

EXAMPLE 4

Classify each of the following employees for benefits in kind purposes :

(a) Joan has a salary of £7,300 p.a. She also receives benefits in kind which cost her employer £900 but which have a second-hand value of £500.

(b) Kate has a salary of £8,320 p.a. She also receives benefits in kind which cost her employer £600 with a second-hand value of £300. She has allowable expenses of £535, including contributions of £416 to an approved superannuation scheme.

(c) Lawrence is a company director. He has 10% of the company's share capital, works one day per week on company business and receives an annual director's fee of £8,000. Benefits in kind cost his company £250 with a second-hand value of £150.

SOLUTION

(a) Joan's salary, plus the cost of her benefits in kind, total £8,200. This is less than £8,500 and therefore she is a lower-paid employee. She will be taxed on her salary and on the second-hand value of her benefits, a total of £7,800.

(b) Kate's salary, plus the cost of her benefits, total £8,920. Her superannuation contributions of £416 reduce this total to £8,504 but this is not less than £8,500 so she is a P11D employee. She will be taxed on her salary, plus the full cost of her benefits, less her allowable expenses i.e. £8,385 (£8,320 + £600 - £535).

(c) Lawrence is a P11D employee by virtue of being a company director who does not work full-time and who owns more than 5% of his company's share capital. He will be taxed on his fees, plus the full cost of his benefits i.e. £8,250.

Benefits assessable on all employees

The tax treatment of an employee's benefits in kind usually depends upon the employee's classification, as explained above. But certain benefits are assessable in the same way on all employees, regardless of their classification. The two main benefits concerned are :

(a) vouchers which may be exchanged for goods or services

(b) living accommodation.

Vouchers for goods or services

All employees are taxed on the cost to their employer of providing vouchers which may be exchanged for goods or services (e.g. gift vouchers, season tickets). However, the first 15p per day of luncheon vouchers is exempt from income tax and vouchers for a car parking space at or near the employee's workplace are also exempt. Note the following points :

(a) Entertainment and hospitality vouchers provided by a person other than the employer or someone connected with the employer are exempt from income tax unless provided as a reward for specific services rendered by the employee.

(b) The provision of a cash voucher (i.e. a voucher which may be converted directly into cash) results in an assessable benefit equal to the amount of cash into which the voucher can be converted.

Living accommodation

All employees are taxed in the same way on the value of any living accommodation provided for them by their employer. The employee is assessed on either :

(a) the rateable value of the accommodation (if the employer owns the accommodation), or

(b) the rent that the employer pays for the accommodation (if the employer rents the accommodation and the rent paid exceeds its rateable value).

The abolition of domestic rates in 1990 means that the rateable value of newer properties has to be estimated. In either case, the assessable benefit is reduced by any contribution made by the employee.

Accommodation costing the employer more than £75,000 is regarded as "expensive" and gives rise to an increase in the assessable benefit. This increase is calculated by applying an appropriate percentage to the amount by which the cost of the accommodation exceeds £75,000. Note the following points :

(a) The "appropriate percentage" used for this purpose is the same as the official rate of interest used in beneficial loan calculations (see below), as it stood at the beginning of the tax year.

(b) The cost of providing accommodation is equal to the purchase price of the property, plus the cost of any improvements made to the property before the start of the tax year, less any capital contribution made by the employee.

(c) If the property was acquired by the employer more than 6 years before it was made available to the employee, then the purchase price of the property may be replaced for benefits in kind purposes by its market value on the date that it was first occupied by the employee.

EXAMPLE 5

As from 1 January 2000, an employee is provided with the use of a house which has a rateable value of £2,300. The employer bought the house in 1997 for £70,000 and spent £35,000 on improvements in 1999. A further £10,000 is spent on improvements in July 2000. The employee pays £1,000 per annum to his employer in relation to this benefit. Calculate the taxable benefit in 2000/01 (assuming an official rate of interest of 6.25% per annum).

SOLUTION

	£
Rateable value	2,300
<u>Add</u> : 6.25% x (£70,000 + £35,000 - £75,000)	1,875
	4,175
<u>Less</u> : Employee contribution	1,000
Assessable benefit	3,175

Job-related accommodation

If accommodation provided by an employer is "job-related" then no taxable benefit arises. Accommodation is job-related if :

(a) it is necessary for the employee to reside in the accommodation for the proper performance of his or her duties (e.g. a caretaker who is required to live in a caretaker's flat on an employer's premises)

(b) the accommodation is provided for the better performance of the employee's duties and it is customary for such accommodation to be provided (e.g. a clergyman living in a vicarage provided by an employer)

(c) the accommodation is provided as part of security arrangements (if there is a special threat to the employee's security).

Special rules for P11D employees

Certain types of benefits in kind are assessed on P11D employees according to special rules. The main benefits for which special rules exist are :

(a) assets loaned to the employee for private use

(b) ancillary services connected with living accommodation

(c) cars provided for private use

(d) fuel provided for private use

(e) vans provided for private use

(f) beneficial loans.

Lower-paid employees would be taxed on these benefits only if they were capable of being converted into cash in some way, and then only on the amount of cash obtainable.

Assets loaned to the employee for private use

If an employer lends an asset to a P11D employee for his or her own private use, the employee is assessed annually on 20% of the asset's market value on the date of the loan. If the period of the loan exceeds five years, the total of the annual assessments will exceed the total value of the asset. If the asset is subsequently sold or given to the employee, he or she is additionally assessed on the *greater* of :

(a) the market value of the asset when sold or given to the employee, less any amount paid for the asset by the employee, and

(b) the market value of the asset when first loaned to the employee, less the amounts already assessed during the period of the loan, less any amount paid for the asset by the employee.

As mentioned earlier, the loan of computer equipment is exempt from tax so long as the amount of the assessable benefit under the above rules would not exceed £500 p.a.

EXAMPLE 6

On 6 April 1998, an employer purchases a hi-fi system for £400 and immediately lends the system to a P11D employee for his private use. The system remains in the employee's possession until 6 October 2000 when the employee buys it from his employer for £50, its market value on that day being £120. Calculate the assessable benefit for the years 1998/99 to 2000/01 inclusive.

SOLUTION

			£
1998/99	20% of £400		80
1999/00	20% of £400		80
2000/01	20% of £400 x 6/12	40	
	plus, the greater of :		
	(i) £120 - £50 = £70		
	(ii) £400 - £80 - £80 - £40 - £50 = £150	150	190
Total benefit in kind assessed over period of the loan			350

Ancillary services connected with living accommodation

If an employer provides living accommodation for a P11D employee, the employee is taxed not only on the accommodation itself but also on the cost to the employer of providing ancillary services in connection with the accommodation. Such services include cleaning, heating and lighting, repairs and maintenance etc. The provision of furniture for the employee's use is also included under the heading of ancillary services and is assessed as an asset loaned for private use (see above). The assessable benefit is reduced by any contribution made by the employee.

However, if the accommodation is job-related, the assessment with regard to these ancillary services is limited to no more than 10% of the employee's net emoluments for the year (i.e. total emoluments, excluding the ancillary services, less all allowable expenses), less any contribution made by the employee.

EXAMPLE 7

In 2000/01, an employer provides living accommodation for a P11D employee and also provides the following services in connection with this accommodation :

	£
Cleaning	520
Heating and lighting	850
Repairs and maintenance	235
Loan of furniture, cost to the employer	12,000

The employee contributes £100 per month towards the cost of these services. Compute the assessable benefit in kind, given that the employee has net emoluments for the year of £37,500 (excluding the ancillary services).

SOLUTION

If the accommodation is not job-related, the assessable benefit is £2,805 (£520 + £850 + £235 + 20% of £12,000, less £1,200). If the accommodation is job-related, the assessment is limited to 10% of £37,500, less £1,200 = £2,550.

Cars provided for private use

A P11D employee is assessed on the provision of a car unless the car is totally unavailable for the employee's private use. The assessable benefit for a given tax year is based upon the price of the car when new (even if the employer bought it second-hand) but is adjusted to reflect the car's age and the number of business miles driven in the year. The method of computation is as follows :

(a) The price of a car for benefits in kind purposes is found by taking the lower of £80,000 and :

    (i) the list price of the car when new, including standard accessories and delivery charges, plus

    (ii) the cost of all optional accessories (other than mobile telephones), fitted to the car before it is made available to the employee, plus

    (iii) the cost of any optional accessories (other than mobile telephones) costing £100 or more and fitted to the car after it is made available to the employee.

(b) Accessories which are designed for use by a disabled person only are ignored when calculating the price of the car. If the employee holds a disabled person's orange badge, this exemption extends to any accessories required because of the employee's disability (e.g. power steering) and is not limited to accessories designed for use solely by the disabled.

(c) If the car is a "classic car", defined as a car which :

(i)   is over 15 years old at the end of the tax year, and

(ii) has a market value at the end of the year exceeding £15,000 and exceeding the price calculated at (a) above

then the car's market value (or £80,000 if lower) is substituted for the car's price when calculating the assessable benefit.

(d) The price calculated at (a) or (c) above is reduced by any capital contribution made by the employee towards the cost of the car or its accessories, up to a maximum of £5,000. If the employee makes a capital contribution exceeding £5,000, the excess over £5,000 is ignored.

(e) The assessable benefit in kind for a tax year is calculated as a percentage of the price of the car (less capital contributions) which was calculated at (d) above. The percentage to be applied depends upon the number of business miles driven in that year, as follows :

Number of business miles	Applicable percentage
under 2,500	35%
2,500 - 17,999	25%
18,000 or more	15%

(f) If the employee simultaneously has a second (or subsequent) car, the assessable benefit in kind on this car is generally calculated at 35%. However, the charge is reduced to 25% if such a car is used for at least 18,000 business miles per year.

(g) The assessable benefit on a car is reduced by one-quarter if the car is 4 years old (or more) at the end of the tax year.

(h) If a car is available to the employee for only part of the year, the assessed benefit in that year is reduced proportionately, depending upon the number of days for which the car is available. This applies if the car is not made available to the employee for the whole of the year or if the car is unusable for a continuous period of at least 30 days during the year. The mileage thresholds of 2,500 and 18,000 miles are also reduced proportionately in these circumstances.

(i) Finally, the assessable benefit is reduced by any contribution which the employee pays to the employer for private use of the car.

It has been announced that, with effect from 6 April 2002, the above system will be replaced by one in which the assessable benefit in kind will be based upon a car's price, but graduated according to the level of the car's carbon dioxide emissions. There will be no discount to reflect either business mileage or the age of the car.

EXAMPLE 8

(a) Throughout the whole of 2000/01, Lucy (a P11D employee) is provided by her employer with the use of a car first registered on 1 February 1999, costing £12,400 new. She contributed £1,000 towards the cost of the car. Her mileage for the year is 26,100 miles, of which 70% is business mileage. She contributes £300 per annum to her employer for private use of the car. Calculate the benefit assessable in 2000/01.

(b) During 2000/01, Luke (a P11D employee) is provided by his employer with the use of a car first registered in 1996, with a list price at that time of £20,000. His employer bought the car for £15,700 in 1998. Luke's mileage in the car is 40% business and 60% private. Calculate the benefit assessable in 2000/01 if :

   (i) the car is available to Luke throughout the entire year and he drives a total of 6,000 miles during the year

   (ii) the car is made available to Luke only from 6 October 2000 and he drives 6,000 miles between that date and 5 April 2001.

SOLUTION

(a) Lucy has driven 18,270 business miles (70% of 26,100) and therefore the benefit in kind is calculated at 15% of the car's price. The calculation is as follows :

	£
15% of (£12,400 - £1,000)	1,710
Less : contribution for private use	300
Assessable benefit	1,410

(b) The fact that Luke's employer bought the car for £15,700 is irrelevant. The benefit is based on the original list price of the car. The calculation is :

   (i) *Car available all year*

   Luke's business mileage of 2,400 during the year (40% of 6,000) is less than 2,500 so the calculation is :

	£
35% of £20,000	7,000
Less : one-quarter reduction (age of car)	1,750
Assessable benefit	5,250

   (ii) *Car available from 6 October 2000*

   Luke has the car for only 6 months during the tax year and is therefore assessed on only 6/12ths of the usual benefit. The mileage thresholds are reduced proportionately to 1,250 and 9,000 miles respectively, so his 2,400 business miles mean that the benefit is calculated at 25% . The assessable benefit is :

	£
25% of £20,000 x 6/12	2,500
Less : one-quarter reduction (age of car)	625
Assessable benefit	1,875

Pool cars

The above provisions do not apply to "pool cars". A pool car is one which satisfies all of the following criteria :

(a) It is available for use by more than one employee and is not ordinarily used by one employee exclusively.

(b) It is not normally kept at an employee's residence overnight.

(c) It is used for private purposes only incidentally to its use for business purposes.

If all these criteria are satisfied, no assessable benefit will arise.

Fuel provided for private use

The assessable benefit described above is intended to cover the cost of providing the car itself, together with the costs of road fund licence, insurance and maintenance. But a separate assessable benefit arises if any fuel at all is supplied by the employer to the employee for private purposes during the year. The assessable benefit in 2000/01 is calculated by reference to the following table.

	Petrol engines £	Diesel engines £
up to 1,400 cc	1,700	2,170
up to 2,000 cc	2,170	2,170
2,001 cc or more	3,200	3,200

It is important to note that the assessed benefit is *not* reduced by any contribution which the employee makes towards the cost of private fuel. Employees either pay the full cost of all private fuel (in which case there is no assessable benefit) or pay less than the full cost of all private fuel (in which case they are assessed according to the above table). However, the assessed benefit *is* reduced proportionately if the car is not made available to the employee for the entire tax year.

EXAMPLE 9

Miranda (a P11D employee) is supplied with a 1,600cc petrol-engined company car for both business and private use and her employer pays all running costs. Calculate her assessable fuel benefit in 2000/01 if :

(a) she contributes nothing towards private fuel

(b) she reimburses her employer for the cost of all private fuel

(c) she reimburses her employer £1,500 per year towards the cost of private fuel but this does not cover the entire cost of the private fuel provided.

SOLUTION

(a) £2,170, taken from the standard table.

(b) £nil (since the employer pays for no private fuel at all).

(c) £2,170, taken from the standard table. Miranda's contribution is less than 100% and so has no effect on the assessed benefit.

Vans provided for private use

If an employee is provided with a van (weighing 3.5 tonnes or less) for private use then the assessable benefit in 2000/01 is as follows :

	£
Under 4 years old at end of the tax year	500
Over 4 years old at end of the tax year	350

There is no separate assessable benefit in respect of van fuel provided for private use. If the van weighs more than 3.5 tonnes no assessable benefit will arise unless the van is used wholly or mainly for private purposes.

Beneficial loans

A beneficial loan is one that is granted by an employer to an employee (or to a member of the employee's family) either interest-free or at a low rate of interest. A loan is deemed to be at a low rate of interest if the rate charged is less than the "official rate" which is set by the Treasury and which is changed from time to time. P11D employees are taxed on the difference between the interest actually payable to the employer and the interest that would have been payable at the official rate. Note that :

(a) Loans made in the ordinary course of the employer's money-lending business and made on the same terms and conditions as loans made to the general public are ignored when calculating the assessable benefit arising in connection with low-interest loans.

(b) As from 6 April 2000, "qualifying loans" are also ignored. Qualifying loans are loans which are eligible for tax relief (see Chapter 4).

(c) No assessable benefit arises in relation to a low-interest loan if the total amount outstanding on all loans made by the employer to the employee does not exceed £5,000 at any time during the tax year.

If a loan is wholly or partly written off by the employer, the amount written off is assessed on the employee in the tax year in which the write-off takes place. This provision applies to all loans, including those made in the ordinary course of a money-lending business. However, no assessable benefit will arise if the loan is written off on the death of the employee or if the loan is to a relative of the employee and it can be shown that the employee has derived no benefit from the write-off.

EXAMPLE 10

Adam (a P11D employee) has the following four loans from his employer :

(a) A £36,000 loan at 3% p.a. interest to enable Adam to buy his own home.
(b) An interest-free season ticket loan of £2,000.
(c) A £2,400 personal loan at 4% p.a. interest.
(d) A £6,000 loan to buy equipment for use in his employment.

The full amount of each loan was outstanding at 6 April 2000 and no repayments were made during 2000/01.

Calculate Adam's assessable benefit in 2000/01 (assuming an official rate of interest of 6.25% per annum).

SOLUTION

The £6,000 loan is a qualifying loan and is ignored. The remaining loans total more than £5,000 and so give rise to assessable benefits in kind. The amount assessed is :

	£
£36,000 x (6.25% - 3%)	1,170
£2,000 x 6.25%	125
£2,400 x (6.25% - 4%)	54
	1,349

In the above example, it was assumed that the amount of the loans did not vary during the tax year. However, if the amount of a beneficial loan does vary during the year, the assessable benefit can be calculated in one of two ways :

(a) The amount of the loan outstanding at the start of the tax year and at the end of the tax year are averaged and then multiplied by the average official rate in force during the year. Interest actually paid to the employer is then subtracted, giving the assessable benefit.

(b) Interest at the official rate is calculated precisely on the day-to-day outstanding balance. Interest actually paid is then subtracted, giving the assessable benefit.

Clearly, the first method will be quicker and easier and is generally used. However, either the employee or the Inland Revenue may insist that the precise method should be used. The employee will presumably do so if this results in a lower assessment and the Inland Revenue may do so if it appears that the "average" method is being deliberately exploited for tax avoidance purposes.

Payments made on termination of employment

Payments received by an employee on the termination of employment fall into three distinct categories :

(a) **Fully exempt**. The following types of termination payment are fully exempt from income tax :

    (i)   payments made on the death of the employee

    (ii) payments made to the employee because of injury or disability

    (iii) lump sum payments under approved superannuation schemes

    (iv) statutory redundancy pay.

(b) **Fully taxable**. If an employee receives a termination payment which does not fall into any of the categories listed above (and which is made by way of reward for the employee's services) then the payment is fully taxable in the year in which it is received. This applies if the employee was contractually entitled to the payment or if there was a reasonable expectation that the payment would be made.

(c) **Partially exempt**. Payments made at the employer's discretion so to compensate an employee for loss of employment are exempt up to £30,000. Any excess over £30,000 is taxable in the year in which it is received. If the employee also receives statutory redundancy pay then the amount of statutory redundancy pay received reduces the £30,000 exemption.

The taxable part of a partially exempt termination payment is treated as the top slice of income, ranking above even savings income and dividends. This provision ensures that savings and dividend income are not moved out of the basic rate band (where they are taxed at only 20% and 10% respectively) as a consequence of the taxpayer receiving a partially exempt termination payment.

EXAMPLE 11

Henrietta is made redundant in March 2001. She receives statutory redundancy pay of £2,500 and an ex gratia payment of £40,000 from her employer as compensation for loss of office. Her only other income in 2000/01 consists of her salary of £26,960 and net building society interest of £4,000. Calculate her tax payable for 2000/01, assuming that she claims only the personal allowance.

SOLUTION

	Total £	Non-savings £	Savings £	Compensation £
Salary	26,960	26,960		
BSI £4,000 x 100/80	5,000		5,000	
Compensation £40,000 - £27,500	12,500			12,500
Statutory total income	44,460	26,960	5,000	12,500
Less : Personal allowance	4,385	4,385		
Taxable income	40,075	22,575	5,000	12,500

Non-savings income occupies the whole of the starting rate band and the first £21,055 of the basic rate band. Savings income falls entirely into the basic rate band, leaving £825 of this band for the compensation. The remaining compensation is taxed at the higher rate.

Income tax due

Starting rate band	: Non-savings	1,520	@ 10%	152.00
Basic rate band	: Non-savings	21,055	@ 22%	4,632.10
	: Savings	5,000	@ 20%	1,000.00
	: Compensation	825	@ 22%	181.50
Higher rate	: Compensation	11,675	@ 40%	4,670.00
		40,075		

Tax borne	10,635.60
Less : Tax deducted at source	1,000.00
Tax payable	9,635.60

Notes :

(i) The statutory redundancy pay of £2,500 is exempt from income tax but reduces the £30,000 exemption to £27,500.

(ii) Any tax paid by means of the PAYE system would also be deducted.

The PAYE system

Under the "Pay As You Earn" (PAYE) system, employers deduct both income tax and National Insurance contributions from their employees when paying them their wages and salaries. The amounts deducted, together with the employer's secondary National Insurance contributions (see Chapter 15), must be accounted for to the Inland Revenue within 14 days of the end of the tax month in which the employees are paid. A tax month runs from the 6th of one month to the 5th of the next month, so employers generally make a payment to the Inland Revenue on or before the 19th of each month. But employers whose payments do not exceed an average of £1,500 per month are allowed to make quarterly payments instead of monthly payments. The PAYE system applies to all payments assessable under Schedule E. The system obviously applies to wages, salaries, bonuses, commissions etc. but it also covers :

(a) payments taking the form of assets which are readily convertible into cash, such as shares, gold bars, coffee beans or other similar commodities, but excluding "own company" shares provided under an approved share scheme (see later in this chapter)

(b) vouchers exchangeable either for cash or for readily convertible assets

(c) remuneration schemes involving trade debts, whereby employers assign trade debts (i.e. amounts owed to them by their customers) to employees, who then receive cash when the debts are settled.

Tax codes

The PAYE system is based upon the concept of "tax codes". It is the responsibility of the Inland Revenue to issue a tax code for each employee each tax year, representing the amount which the employee may earn in that year before becoming liable to tax. The tax code takes into account a number of factors affecting the employee's income tax liability, including :

(a) the personal allowances to which the employee is entitled

(b) the employee's charges on income

(c) the employee's allowable expenses

(d) adjustments made in order to collect tax on benefits in kind

(e) adjustments for tax overpaid or underpaid in previous years.

The tax code allocated to an employee is equal to one-tenth of the aggregate of the above items, rounded down to a whole number.

EXAMPLE 12

Henry is single and claims only the personal allowance. He pays a gross charge of £100 per annum and a professional subscription (allowable under Schedule E) of £80 per annum. In 2000/01 he has assessable benefits in kind of £500. Calculate his 2000/01 tax code.

SOLUTION

By virtue of his personal allowance, his charges on income and his allowable expenses, Henry is entitled to earn £4,565 (£4,385 + £100 + £80) in the year before paying tax. But some of this must be set against his benefits in kind of £500, leaving only £4,065 to set against his salary. Therefore Henry's tax code for the year would be 406, which is one-tenth of £4,065, rounded down to a whole number.

Note that the same result would be obtained if the aggregate figure of £4,065 were anywhere in the range £4,060 - £4,069, so tax codes are not absolutely precise. But dividing the aggregate figure by ten results in only one-tenth as many different tax codes as would be obtained otherwise and cuts down the size of the tax tables used by employers (see below).

Tax code suffixes

A tax code also has a suffix, which is generally a letter of the alphabet. The most common suffix is L which stands for "low" and indicates that the employee is entitled to the basic personal allowance only. So Henry's full tax code in the above example would be 406L. Other suffixes in general use include :

P - the employee is entitled to the personal allowance for those aged 65-74

V - the employee is entitled to the personal allowance and the MCA for those aged 65-74

BR - which instructs the employer to deduct tax at the basic rate from all payments made to the employee

NT - which instructs the employer not to deduct tax from the employee at all.

Codes prefixed with the letter K are negative codes, used mainly for employees whose benefits in kind exceed their allowances. Tax on the excess benefits is collected by increasing the amount of tax charged on the employee's wage or salary.

The purpose of tax code suffixes is to facilitate the recoding exercise which is needed whenever personal allowances are increased. When this happens, the Inland Revenue instructs employers to increase all L codes by the amount required to reflect the increase in the basic personal allowance, to increase all P codes by the amount required to reflect the increase in the 65-74 personal allowance, and so on. This avoids the need to individually recode every employee in the country.

Operation of the PAYE system

Employers who operate manual payroll systems are issued with sets of tax tables which enable them to calculate the amount of income tax that should be deducted from an employee in a given week or month. The main tables used are :

Table A   This table (also known as the Pay Adjustment Table) contains pages for each week or month of the year and shows, for each tax code, the amount of tax-free pay to which the employee is entitled for the year to date. In effect, the table spreads an employee's allowances evenly over the year, giving 1/12th of the allowances per month or 1/52th of the allowances per week.

Table B   This table (also known as the Taxable Pay Table) is used to look up an employee's income tax liability for the year to date, after the entitlement to tax-free pay has been taken into account.

In outline, the procedure followed for each employee in each week or month is :

(a)   The employee's tax code is looked up in Table A, which shows the amount of tax-free pay to which the employee is entitled for the year to date.

(b)   This is then subtracted from the employee's gross pay for the year to date giving the employee's taxable pay for the year to date.

(c)   The employee's taxable pay for the year to date is then looked up in Table B, which shows the tax due for the year to date. Tables C and D are used if the employee is a higher rate taxpayer.

(d)   Finally, the tax paid to date by the employee in previous weeks or months is subtracted from the tax due for the year to date, giving the employee's income tax liability for the current week or month.

The entire system is cumulative and requires the employer to keep track of an employee's gross pay and tax paid "to date" (i.e. since the beginning of the tax year on 6 April). Employers are provided with deductions working sheets (form P11) which facilitate the accumulation of the necessary "to date" figures.

PAYE forms

P6   An employee's notice of coding, sent to the employer by the Inland Revenue.

P9D   An end of year return showing the benefits in kind and expenses of a lower-paid employee. P9D's must be submitted to the Inland Revenue by 6 July following the end of the tax year and the employees concerned must be provided with copies by the same date.

P11D An end of year return showing the benefits in kind and expenses of a director or employee earning at least £8,500. P11D's must be submitted to the Inland Revenue by 6 July following the end of the tax year and the employees concerned must be provided with copies by the same date.

P11   Deductions working sheet (see above).

P14   An end of year return, sent to the Inland Revenue by the employer, showing an individual employee's gross pay, tax paid and National Insurance paid for the year.

P35   An end of year return, sent to the Inland Revenue by the employer, showing and summarising all employees' gross pay, tax paid and National Insurance paid for the year. The P35, together with the P14's, must be submitted to the Inland Revenue by 19 May following the end of the tax year.

P45   A 4-part form used when an employee leaves an employment, showing the employee's tax code, gross pay to date and tax paid to date. Part 1 is sent to the Inland Revenue by the employer and Parts 2, 3 & 4 are given to the leaving employee. The employee gives Parts 2 & 3 of the form to his or her new employer who retains Part 2 (using it to fill in a P11 for the employee) and sends Part 3 to the Inland Revenue. The employee retains Part 4.

P60   Certificate of gross pay and tax deducted, given to employees by employers at the end of the tax year. P60's must be provided to employees by 31 May following the end of the tax year.

There is an increasing use of electronic means of communication between employers and the Inland Revenue. Employers may now submit employee expenses and benefits information electronically and services are being developed which will enable employers to submit PAYE returns to the Inland Revenue via the Internet by April 2001. Employers who submit their PAYE end-of-year returns for 2000/01 in this way (and pay any tax due electronically) will receive a one-off discount of £50.

Working Families and Disabled Person's Tax Credits

Working families on low or middle incomes may be able to claim a benefit known as the Working Families Tax Credit (WFTC). Similarly, disabled working people may be able to claim the Disabled Person's Tax Credit (DPTC). These tax credits *which should not be confused with the tax credit on dividends* are administered by the Inland Revenue and, as from 6 April 2000, are paid by employers to those of their employees who qualify. The system works as follows :

(a) The Inland Revenue calculates the amount to be paid to a claimant and notifies the claimant's employer of the required daily rate of payment.

(b) In each pay period, the employer calculates the amount of tax credit due to be paid to the employee (according to the number of days in the period) and adds this onto the employee's net pay. The tax credit is shown separately on the employee's payslip.

(c) The amount of PAYE and National Insurance contributions which the employer is due to pay over to the Inland Revenue each month or quarter is reduced by the tax credits paid to employees in that month or quarter.

(d) Forms P14, P35 and P60 show the tax credits separately. Employees receiving tax credits who leave their employment are given a Certificate of Payments to show the amount of tax credits paid by their employer up to the date of leaving and the period covered.

Employers who pay tax credits to one or more employees in 2000/01 and then qualify for the £50 discount for filing the end-of-year PAYE return via the Internet (see above) will receive a further discount of £50.

Construction industry tax deduction scheme

The construction industry tax deduction scheme applies when payments are made by a contractor to a subcontractor under a contract relating to construction operations. As from 1 August 1999, the main features of this scheme are as follows :

(a) Payments made by a contractor to a subcontractor must be made net of tax unless the subcontractor holds a gross payment certificate. Any part of a payment which represents a reimbursement of the cost of materials supplied by the subcontractor may be excluded from the amount which is subject to deduction of tax.

(b) Gross payment certificates are issued only to subcontractors who are carrying on a genuine construction business in the UK with proper premises, equipment etc. The business must have its own bank account and proper accounting records must be maintained. Furthermore, the subcontractor must have complied with all tax and National Insurance obligations throughout the three years prior to the application for a certificate.

(c) A gross payment certificate is not issued unless the subcontractor meets certain minimum turnover requirements. The annual threshold is £30,000 for individuals and £30,000 multiplied by the number of partners or directors for a partnership or company (subject to a maximum requirement of £200,000).

(d) Subcontractors who are ineligible for a gross payment certificate are issued with a registration card. Contractors must deduct tax from such subcontractors and make accurate returns of registration card payments to the Inland Revenue.

(e) The amount of tax deducted from subcontractors who do not have gross payment certificates is calculated at a percentage rate which is determined by order of the Treasury (but cannot exceed basic rate). As from 6 April 2000, this rate is 18%.

Employee incentive schemes

An employee incentive scheme provides financial incentives for employees to improve their work performance. The main types of scheme which currently have income tax implications are :

(a) older schemes which are being phased out :

    (i) approved profit-related pay (PRP) schemes

    (ii) approved profit-sharing (APS) schemes

(b) schemes which are set to continue for the foreseeable future :

    (i) all-employee share ownership plans (AESOP's)

    (ii) approved share option schemes

    (iii) enterprise management incentives (EMI's).

A brief description of each of these types of scheme is given below.

Approved profit-related pay schemes

Subject to certain conditions, that part of an employee's pay which derives from an approved profit-related pay (PRP) scheme is exempt from income tax, but not from National Insurance contributions. The main conditions that must be satisfied by a PRP scheme in order to gain approval are as follows :

(a) There must be a clear relationship between the employer's profits and the amount of PRP paid to employees.

(b) At least 80% of employees must be included in the scheme.

(c) The scheme must treat all eligible employees in a similar way, though it is permitted for the amount of PRP paid to an employee to depend upon his or her remuneration or length of service.

As mentioned above, tax relief for PRP is being phased out. This is being achieved by reducing the maximum amount of tax-free PRP which can be paid to any employee for a profit period. The maximum tax-free PRP used to be the *lower* of £4,000 p.a. and 20% of the employee's pay for the period (including PRP but excluding benefits in kind). However, the £4,000 ceiling was reduced to £2,000 for profit periods beginning during 1998 and is reduced to £1,000 for profit periods beginning during 1999. No relief at all is available for profit periods beginning on or after 1 January 2000.

Approved profit-sharing schemes

An employee who works for a company and is given shares in that company as part of his or her emoluments will normally be charged income tax on the market value of the shares on the date of the gift. An approved profit-sharing (APS) scheme is a means by which employees can be given shares in the company for which they work without incurring this income tax liability. The main features of an APS scheme are :

(a) The company sets up a trust and gives it money which is used to purchase shares in the company. These shares are immediately appropriated to employees but are held on their behalf by the trustees. All employees who have been employed for a stated qualifying period (not to exceed 5 years) must be eligible to receive shares.

(b) The maximum annual value of the shares which may be appropriated to an employee under a profit-sharing scheme is the *greater* of £3,000 and 10% of the employee's salary. If the employee's salary exceeds £80,000, it is deemed to be £80,000 for the purpose of calculating this maximum.

(c) The shares appropriated to an employee are held by the trustees during the "period of retention". This begins when the shares are appropriated and ends two years later or (if earlier) when the employee reaches retirement age or employment ceases because of death, injury, disability or redundancy.

(d) No income tax is charged if the shares are held by the trustees for at least three years. But if an employee directs the trustees to sell the shares on his or her behalf within three years, income tax is charged on the *lower* of the sale proceeds and the market value of the shares when they were appropriated to the employee. Only 50% of this is charged to tax if the disposal occurs after the employee has left the company through injury, disability, redundancy or reaching retirement age.

(e) When an employee disposes of shares acquired under a profit-sharing scheme, the allowable cost of the shares for capital gains tax purposes (see Chapter 17) is deemed to be their market value on the day that they were appropriated to the employee.

With the introduction of the new all-employee share ownership plan (see below), no further awards of shares under APS schemes will be allowed after 5 April 2002.

All-employee share ownership plans

All-employee share ownership plans (AESOP's) are to be introduced during tax year 2000/01. The main features of these new plans are as follows :

(a) Companies which set up an AESOP may offer their employees :

    (i) *free shares* in the company worth up to £3,000 per annum per employee

    (ii) the opportunity to use salary of up to £125 per month to buy *partnership shares* in the company (without having to pay income tax or National Insurance contributions on the salary used for this purpose)

    (iii) up to two free *matching shares* for each partnership share bought by an employee.

(b) The company may offer free shares only, partnership shares only, free shares and partnership shares only, partnership shares and matching shares only, or all three types of shares.

(c) Subject to certain conditions, the plan may link the provision of free shares to the achievement of employee performance targets.

(d) In general, all employees must be eligible to participate in the plan. However, the plan may specify that employees do not become eligible until they have been employed by the company for a qualifying period of not more than 18 months.

(e) Employees who hold over 25% of the company's ordinary shares (a "material interest") are not eligible to participate in the plan.

(f) The plan must specify a holding period of between 3 and 5 years for free shares and matching shares. Employees are contractually bound to keep their shares in the plan during this period but this obligation ceases when an employee leaves the company. The plan may specify that employees who leave within 3 years should forfeit their free and matching shares.

(g) The plan may allow (or compel) dividends of up to £1,500 per annum arising on an employee's shares to be re-invested in the plan tax-free. The holding period for such *dividend shares* must be exactly 3 years.

(h) Employees who keep their shares in the plan for 5 years will pay no income tax or National Insurance in respect of those shares. Employees who keep their shares in the plan for at least 3 years but less than 5 years will be charged to income tax and NI on the *lower* of the market value of the shares when originally awarded and the market value of the shares when leaving the plan.

(i) Employees who keep their shares in the plan until they sell them will incur no liability to capital gains tax. Employees who take their shares out of the plan and sell them later will pay capital gains tax on any increase in value since the shares were taken out of the plan.

Approved share option schemes

In general, an income tax liability will arise if an employee who works for a company is granted an option to buy shares in that company. The liability will usually arise only when the option is exercised but if the option can be exercised more than 10 years after it is granted, a liability also arises at the time of the grant. The total Schedule E assessment is equal to the market value of the shares obtained when the option is exercised, less the amount paid for the shares, less the amount (if any) paid to acquire the option. A tax liability can be avoided if the option falls within an approved share option scheme. Approved schemes are of two main types :

(a) **Savings-related share option schemes**. Under such a scheme, employees are granted an option to buy shares and then save through a tax-free savings scheme in order to raise funds to exercise the option. The amount saved must be between £5 and £250 per month and the savings contract may last for 3 or 5 years. The scheme must be open to all employees who have worked for the company for a specified qualifying period (which cannot exceed 5 years). The price at which employees are given the option to buy shares must be at least 80% of the shares' market value at the time that the option is granted.

(b) **Company share option plans**. These schemes are less restrictive than savings-related schemes. The company can select the employees to which it would like to offer share options and can set these employees performance targets which must be achieved before the options are made available. The price at which an option may be exercised must not be manifestly less than the market value of the shares at the time that the option is granted and options must be exercised no earlier than 3 years and no later than 10 years after they are granted. There is an upper limit of £30,000 on the value of the shares for which an employee may hold options at any one time.

If a share option is granted under an approved scheme of either type and all necessary conditions are satisfied, then no income tax is payable on either the grant or the exercise of the option. For capital gains tax purposes (see Chapter 17) the allowable cost of shares acquired under an approved share option scheme is the price actually paid for the shares by the employee.

Enterprise Management Incentives

Enterprise Management Incentives (EMI's) are to be introduced in 2000/01 and offer independent trading companies with gross assets not exceeding £15 million the chance to reward up to 15 key employees with tax-free share options. An employee may be granted options in respect of shares with a total value of up to £100,000 and (subject to certain conditions) there will be no liability to income tax or National Insurance contributions on either the grant or the exercise of such options.

Summary

▶ Several criteria have been established which may be used to distinguish employment from self-employment.

▶ The basis of assessment for income taxed under Schedule E is the income actually received in the year.

▶ Income tax is payable on all the income received in respect of an employment, including benefits in kind. Certain social security benefits are also taxable.

▶ In general, an employee's expenses are allowed only if they are incurred wholly, exclusively and necessarily in the performance of the duties of the employment.

▶ The way in which an employee's benefits in kind are taxed depends upon whether or not the employee is a P11D employee, though some benefits are taxable in the same way on all employees.

▶ Any amount to which an employee is contractually entitled on the termination of employment is fully taxable. Certain termination payments (e.g. on death or injury) are fully exempt and ex gratia termination payments are partially exempt.

▶ The PAYE system is used to deduct income tax and National Insurance contributions from employees' wages and salaries.

▶ Certain employee incentive schemes offer tax advantages. Profit-related pay and approved profit-sharing schemes are being phased out in favour of all-employee share ownership plans, approved share option schemes and enterprise management incentives.

Exercises

7.1 List the criteria which might be used to distinguish employment from self-employment.

7.2 Malcolm earns a basic salary of £17,500 in 2000/01. He also receives an annual bonus based on his employer's profits for the accounting year, which ends on 31 March. The bonus for the year ended 31 March 2000 (received 1 June 2000) was £2,350 and the bonus for the year ended 31 March 2001 (received 1 June 2001) was £2,570. Compute Malcolm's 2000/01 Schedule E assessment.

7.3 Which of the following forms of income from employment would be exempt from income tax ?

    (a) Luncheon vouchers of £2 per working day.

    (b) Free meals in the company canteen.

    (c) Removal expenses of £4,500.

111

(d) A cheque for £1,000 given to an employee on reaching 25 years of service with his employer.

(e) A canteen of cutlery given to an employee on her marriage.

(f) A mileage allowance of 25p per mile given to an employee who drives his own 1,300 cc car on 2,500 business miles per year.

7.4 Which of the following expenses incurred by an employee would be allowable under Schedule E ?

(a) Travel costs between work and home.

(b) Travel costs between employment sites.

(c) Subscriptions to professional bodies.

(d) The cost of protective clothing.

(e) The cost of a suit to wear at the office.

(f) Entertaining expenses.

7.5 Kim is an employee earning a salary of £7,000 per annum, out of which she pays 5% to her employer's superannuation scheme. She has allowable expenses of £1,000, all of which are reimbursed by her employer and is provided with a company car on which the assessable benefit if she were a P11D employee would be £1,800. Is she a P11D employee or a lower-paid employee ?

7.6 Niall (a P11D employee) is provided with a diesel-engined 2,800 cc company car which had a list price of £18,800 when it was new on 1 April 1997. His employer pays for all running expenses including fuel for private use. In 2000/01 Niall drove 27,000 miles of which 25% was private mileage. Compute the assessable benefit in 2000/01.

7.7 On being made redundant by her employer, Penny received statutory redundancy pay of £1,750 and an ex gratia payment from her employer as compensation for the loss of employment. Compute the amount assessable if the ex gratia payment was :

(a) £12,000

(b) £29,000.

*7.8 Emma is the sales director of a company. She earns an annual salary of £40,000 together with a bonus (received in September each year) based on the company's profits for the accounting year ending on the previous 30 June. She also receives a general expenses allowance of £5,000 per annum, which she uses for business travel and entertaining. The company provides her with a new BMW motor car every two years and pays all running costs. She has an interest-free loan from the company of £20,000 and the company pays her annual subscription to a private medical insurance scheme, costing £300. Explain the taxation implications of each of the elements of Emma's remuneration package.

*7.9   Jim is the managing director of a company and earns a basic salary in 2000/01 of £100,000. He receives benefits in kind from the company during the year as follows :

(a)   He is provided with the use of a company house which has a rateable value of £4,750 and which cost his employer £250,000. Jim makes no contribution towards the cost of the house or towards its running costs which cost the company £2,300 in 2000/01. The company has also furnished the house at a cost of £8,500. Jim's occupation of the house is not job-related.

(b)   He is provided with a 3,000 cc petrol-engined company car which is one year old and had a list price when purchased of £45,000. The company pays all running costs and Jim drove 20,000 miles in 2000/01, of which one-quarter was business mileage.

(c)   He is provided with a company loan of £50,000 on which he pays interest at 2% per annum.

Calculate Jim's assessable benefits in 2000/01 (assuming an official rate of interest of 6.25%).

Chapter 8

Income from self-employment : Computation of income

Introduction

This is the first of five chapters concerned with the assessment of self-employed people under the rules of Schedule D Cases I and II.

The profits of a trade are assessed under Schedule D Case I whilst the profits of a profession or a vocation are assessed under Schedule D Case II. As there are no significant differences between the two Cases, references in this chapter and subsequent chapters to Case I should be taken to include Case II unless the context indicates otherwise. Similarly, the terms "trader" and "sole trader" will be used to refer to any self-employed person, regardless of whether the person in question is actually conducting a trade, a profession or a vocation.

The badges of trade

When deciding whether or not a person's activities make that person liable to income tax under Schedule D Case I or II, two important distinctions must be drawn :

(a) the distinction between employment and self-employment (see Chapter 7)

(b) for a taxpayer who sells goods or other assets, the distinction between :

    (i) trading activities, giving rise to trading profits which are charged to income tax under Schedule D Case I, and

    (ii) non-trading activities, giving rise either to profits which are assessed under Schedule D Case VI or to capital gains which may be chargeable to capital gains tax (see Chapter 16).

ICTA 1988 states that the term "trade" includes "*every trade, manufacture, adventure or concern in the nature of trade*". This circular definition is of little real help and it has been left largely to the courts to decide whether or not a given activity constitutes trading.

In 1955, a Royal Commission summarised the guidance provided by case law up to that time and produced a list of the main criteria which may be used to distinguish between trading and non-trading activities. These criteria (which are known as the "badges of trade") are as follows :

(a) **Subject matter of the transaction**

If the assets which the taxpayer has sold are of a type which might normally be acquired for personal enjoyment or as an investment (e.g. works of art, stocks and shares), this may suggest that any profit arising on their sale should be treated as a capital gain rather than a trading profit.

But if the assets concerned do not provide personal enjoyment and would not normally be held as an investment, any profit arising on their sale is more likely to be treated as a trading profit assessable to income tax. In *Martin* v *Lowry* (1926) the taxpayer bought and sold 44 million yards of war surplus linen and in *Rutledge* v *CIR* (1929) the taxpayer bought and sold 1 million toilet rolls. In both of these cases, it was held that the subject matter of the transaction was such that the activity must be construed as trading.

(b) **Length of the period of ownership**

Trading stocks are normally retained for only a short period before being sold, whereas assets acquired for personal use or as an investment are generally retained for much longer. Therefore, if assets are bought and sold within a short space of time it is more likely that any profit made will be treated as a trading profit.

(c) **Frequency of transactions**

The more often that a taxpayer repeats a certain type of transaction, the more likely it is that the activity will be construed as trading. In *Pickford* v *Quirke* (1927) the taxpayer bought a cotton mill and sold off its assets at a profit. This was the fourth time that the taxpayer had carried out this particular type of transaction and therefore he was held to be trading.

(d) **Supplementary work**

A taxpayer who buys an asset, performs work on it so as to make it more saleable and then sells it, is more likely to be regarded as trading than someone who simply buys and sells an asset without performing any supplementary work. In *Cape Brandy Syndicate* v *CIR* (1921) a group of individuals bought a large quantity of brandy which they first blended and then sold. They were held to be trading.

(e) **Reason for the sale**

The circumstances which have prompted the sale of an asset might be taken into account when deciding whether trading has occurred. A sale necessitated by a sudden urgent need for cash is less likely to be regarded as a trading activity than a sale made in the normal course of events.

(f) **Motive**

The presence of a profit motive in the mind of the taxpayer when acquiring the asset provides strong evidence of trading. In *Wisdom* v *Chamberlain* (1969) the taxpayer acquired silver bullion with the intention of selling it at a profit and eventually did so. He was held to be trading.

However, this test is not always conclusive. After all, many investments are bought at least partially with a view to their long-term sale at a profit and yet such profits are generally treated as capital gains. This point emphasises the need to consider the evidence provided by *all* of the badges of trade (not just one) when trying to decide whether or not trading has occurred.

Since trading requires the presence of a profit motive when the asset was acquired, the sale of an asset originally acquired by inheritance or by gift (or in any way otherwise than by purchase) is very unlikely to be construed as trading.

The calculation of adjusted profits

The computation of a self-employed person's taxable profit begins with the net profit shown by that person's accounts. Business accounts are normally drawn up in accordance with UK GAAP (generally accepted accounting practice) which measures income and expenditure on the accruals basis. This is also the basis used for the purposes of Schedule D Case I. Self-employed professionals were allowed at one time to calculate their profits on a cash basis but this concession has now been withdrawn (except for new barristers in their first 7 years of practice).

It is usually necessary to make a number of adjustments to the net profit shown by the accounts in order to arrive at the taxable profit. These adjustments can be summarised as follows :

		£	£
Net profit shown by the accounts			x
Add :	Expenditure shown in the accounts but not deductible under Schedule D Case I	x	
	Income assessable under Schedule D Case I but not shown in the accounts	x	x
			x
Less :	Income shown in the accounts but not assessable under Schedule D Case I	x	
	Expenditure deductible under Schedule D Case I but not shown in the accounts	x	x
Profit adjusted for tax purposes			x

Each of these adjustments is explained below.

Deductibility of expenditure

In general, expenditure is deductible (allowable) under Schedule D Case I only if it is incurred *wholly and exclusively for the purposes of the trade*. This rule is not as restrictive as the "wholly, exclusively and necessarily" rule applied under Schedule E but it does have the following implications :

(a) Expenditure which has no connection with the trade will be disallowed (the "remoteness test"). In *Strong & Co of Romsey Ltd* v *Woodifield* (1906), damages paid by a brewery to a hotel guest injured by a falling chimney were disallowed. The damages were incurred by the brewery in its capacity as a property owner, not in its capacity as a trader, and therefore failed the remoteness test.

(b) Expenditure which serves both a business purpose and a private purpose should, in principle, be entirely disallowed (the "duality test"). In practice, however, it is usual to disallow only the private element so long as the expenditure can be apportioned with reasonable accuracy. In *Mallalieu* v *Drummond* (1983) the cost of black clothing worn in court by a lady barrister was disallowed. The clothing provided warmth and decency as well as satisfying professional standards of dress and therefore failed the duality test.

Even if expenditure passes both the remoteness test and the duality test it may still be disallowed by statute.

Disallowed expenditure

The main categories of expenditure which are disallowed in a Schedule D Case I computation (either by statute or as a consequence of case law decisions) are as follows :

Capital expenditure

Capital expenditure is specifically disallowed by ICTA 1988 but the Act does not provide a definition of the term "capital". Consequently, there is a great deal of case law on this subject, much of which is concerned with distinguishing between repairs (allowable) and improvements (disallowed as capital expenditure). In *Atherton* v *British Insulated & Helsby Cables Ltd* (1926), it was stated that capital expenditure is such that it brings an "enduring benefit" to the business, and this test is still widely used. The following capital-related expenses are also disallowed :

(a) legal or professional fees incurred in relation to an item of capital expenditure

(b) depreciation and amortisation charges, though capital allowances may be available instead (see Chapter 10)

(c) losses on the disposal of fixed assets.

Even repairs may be disallowed if they relate to a newly acquired asset and are required in order to put the asset into usable condition. In *Law Shipping Co Ltd v CIR* (1923) the cost of putting a newly acquired ship into seaworthy condition was disallowed for this reason. However, repairs to a newly acquired asset which was usable before the repairs were carried out are generally allowed. In *Odeon Associated Theatres Ltd v Jones* (1971) repairs to cinemas which had been bought in a state of disrepair (but were nonetheless usable) were allowed.

Appropriations of profit

Any appropriations of profit made by the owner of a business (whether described as drawings, proprietor's salary, interest on capital or anything else) are disallowed, as are the owner's personal income tax payments and National Insurance contributions.

Provisions

Provisions are generally allowed so long as they are in respect of revenue expenditure and are required by UK GAAP. However, a provision will be disallowed if it cannot be estimated with sufficient accuracy. For this reason, transfers to general provisions (e.g. a general provision for bad and doubtful debts) are generally disallowed.

Charges on income

Payments which are treated as a charge on income (e.g. patent royalties) are relieved against the taxpayer's total income (see Chapter 4) and must therefore be disallowed in the Schedule D Case I computation. It should be noted that :

(a) the amount disallowed is the amount shown in the accounts (usually the amount *accrued* in the accounting period), but

(b) the amount relieved as a charge on income for a given tax year is the amount actually *paid* in that year.

Entertainment and gifts

Entertaining expenses are disallowed unless they relate to staff entertaining (in which case the employees concerned may incur a Schedule E liability if the amount involved is excessive, as explained in Chapter 7). The cost of gifts is also disallowed, other than :

(a) gifts to employees (but again, the employees may incur a Schedule E liability)

(b) gifts to customers costing no more than £10 per head, displaying a prominent advertisement for the business and not consisting of food, drink or tobacco

(c) gifts to charities or designated UK educational establishments of trading stock or used plant and machinery (and, until 31 December 2000, similar gifts made for educational or medical purposes in designated low-income countries)

(d) reasonably small gifts to local charities, so long as the "wholly and exclusively" test is satisfied (e.g. if the gift attracts favourable publicity and enhances the firm's public image).

Note that charitable donations made within the Gift Aid scheme (including charitable covenants) are given tax relief in the taxpayer's overall computation and are therefore disallowed in the Schedule D Case I computation (see Chapter 4).

Political donations and subscriptions are usually not allowed. But political donations which result in a definite benefit to the trade may be allowed. In *Morgan* v *Tate & Lyle Ltd* (1954) the costs of a political campaign against nationalisation were allowed on the grounds that the campaign was waged for the survival of the trade.

Non-trade bad debts

Bad debts incurred in the course of trade are allowable. But employee loans written off are not allowable unless :

(a) the loan was made in the course of trade (i.e. the firm is in the business of lending money), or

(b) the written-off loan forms part of the employee's remuneration and is therefore taxable under Schedule E.

Transfers to a *specific* bad debts provision are allowable but transfers to a general provision are disallowed, as stated earlier. Bad debts recovered and reductions in a specific bad debts provision are both treated as trading income.

EXAMPLE 1

A sole trader's nominal ledger contains the following bad and doubtful debts account for the year ended 30 June :

	£	£		£	£
Trade debts w/o		812	Provisions b/f at 1 July :		
Staff loan w/o		50	General	432	
			Specific	312	744
Provisions c/f at 30 June :					
General	459		Trade debt recovered		42
Specific	288	747	P & L Account		823
		1,609			1,609

How much of the £823 charged to the profit and loss account for the year should be added back when calculating the Schedule D Case I adjusted profit ?

SOLUTION

The figure of £823 charged to the profit and loss account can be analysed as follows :

	£
Trade debts written off, less trade debts recovered (£812 - £42)	770
Staff loan written off	50
Increase in general provision for bad debts (£459 - £432)	27
Decrease in specific provision for bad debts (£312 - £288)	(24)
	823

The £50 staff loan written off and the £27 increase in the general provision are disallowed, so a total of £77 should be added back when calculating the adjusted profit.

Criminal payments

A payment will be disallowed if the making of the payment in itself constitutes a criminal offence (e.g. the payment of a bribe). Payments to a blackmailer or extortionist are also disallowed.

Fines and penalties

Fines or penalties incurred because of infringements of the law are not regarded as trading expenses and are disallowed. An exception occurs if an employer pays parking fines incurred by employees whilst on their employer's business. Such payments are usually allowed under Schedule D Case I but may then be assessed under Schedule E as emoluments of the employee.

Allowable expenditure

As explained earlier, expenditure is allowable under Schedule D Case I if it has been incurred wholly and exclusively for the purposes of the trade and is not specifically disallowed by statute. Other than the disallowed items listed above, most of the expenditure shown in a typical profit and loss account will probably be allowable but the following points should be noted :

(a) **Interest**. Interest of all types, including credit card and overdraft interest, is allowable if incurred for the purposes of the trade. But interest which constitutes a charge on income is disallowed (see above) and interest paid on overdue tax is also disallowed.

(b) **Legal and professional fees**. Legal and professional fees relating to capital expenditure are specifically disallowed (see above) but fees incurred for other trade purposes are normally allowable. For example, fees are allowed if incurred in connection with such matters as the collection of trade debts, the raising of long-term loan finance, the renewal of a short lease (i.e. a lease of up to 50 years), an action for breach of contract or the preservation of trading rights.

Audit and accountancy fees incurred in relation to the preparation of accounts and the agreement of tax liabilities are normally allowed. Fees incurred in relation to tax appeals and investigations are incurred in the role of taxpayer rather than trader and should be disallowed.

(c) **Short lease premiums**. A premium paid for the grant of a short lease of business premises is discounted according to the length of the lease and is then allowed in equal annual instalments over the period of the lease (see Chapter 5). A "reverse premium" received by a tenant using premises for business purposes is taxable as trading income.

(d) **Damages**. Damages and compensation payments are allowed if incurred for the purposes of the trade.

(e) **Value Added Tax**. If a trader pays VAT in relation to an item of expenditure and is unable to reclaim that VAT (see Chapter 30), the amount of VAT suffered will be allowable so long as the item of expenditure is itself allowable.

(f) **Trade subscriptions**. Subscriptions payable to professional and trade associations are generally regarded as having been incurred for the purposes of the trade and are allowable. Political subscriptions are generally disallowed (see above).

(g) **Employees' remuneration**. Remuneration paid to employees is allowable so long as it is genuinely expended for business purposes. In *Copeman* v *Flood (William) & Sons Ltd* (1941) it was held that large salaries paid to family members could be allowed only to the extent that they were expended for trading purposes.

Remuneration which is not actually paid to employees within 9 months of the end of the accounting period in which it is accrued is disallowed in that period but allowed in the period of payment.

Employers' contributions to approved occupational pension schemes (see Chapter 13) are allowed in the *accounting period in which they are paid*.

Redundancy payments and compensation payments for loss of office are normally allowable, as are lump sum payments made to employees on retirement. When a firm ceases trading, statutory redundancy payments made to staff are allowed, together with further compensation payments of up to three times the statutory payments.

The cost of educational courses provided for employees is allowable if incurred for trade purposes. Employer contributions to an employee's Individual Learning Account are also allowable. The cost of retraining employees who are about to leave (or have recently left) is allowable subject to certain conditions. The cost of temporarily seconding an employee to a charity or an educational establishment is allowable.

(h) **Staff defalcations**. Losses caused by the dishonesty of an employee are normally allowable. But, following the decision in *Curtis* v *J & G Oldfield Ltd* (1925), the defalcations of a person having control over the business (e.g. the proprietor or a senior employee) are disallowed.

(i) **Travel expenses**. The cost of business travel is allowable but the cost of travelling between home and work is not. In *Newsom* v *Robertson* (1952) the travelling expenses of a barrister between his home and his chambers were disallowed. But in *Horton* v *Young* (1971) the travelling expenses of a self-employed bricklayer between his home and the building sites at which he worked was allowed, on the grounds that his business was conducted from his home.

(j) **Car leasing and rental costs**. The costs of hiring, leasing or renting plant and equipment are normally allowable. But in the case of "expensive" cars (defined as those costing more than £12,000) the allowable amount is restricted to :

$$\text{Hire charge} \times \frac{£12,000 + 1/2(\text{Cost of car} - £12,000)}{\text{Cost of car}}$$

For example, if a car costing £18,000 is rented at a cost of £3,600 per annum, then the amount allowed is restricted to :

$$£3,600 \times \frac{£12,000 + 1/2(£18,000 - £12,000)}{£18,000} = £3,000.$$

(k) **Pre-trading expenditure**. Expenditure incurred during the seven years before starting to trade is treated as if it had been incurred on the first day of trading and is allowable so long as the expenditure is of a type which would normally be allowable under the rules of Schedule D Case I.

(l) **Registration of patents and trademarks**. The cost of registering a patent or trademark is allowable.

Trading income not shown in the accounts

The most common example of trading income not being shown in the accounts of a business occurs when the owner takes goods from the business for personal use, either without paying for them or paying less than their full value. This is often known as "own consumption".

If own consumption occurs, then an amount equal to the normal *selling price* of the goods (less any amount paid for the goods by the owner) must be added to the net profit shown by the accounts when computing the adjusted profit. This rule stems from the case of *Sharkey* v *Wernher* (1955) in which horses were transferred from a stud farm to the owner's private stables. It was held that the profits of the stud farm should be increased, for tax purposes, by the full market value of the horses.

Non-trading income shown in the accounts

Any non-trading income shown in the accounts of a business must be deducted when computing the adjusted profit for Schedule D Case I purposes. The main categories of non-trading income which might be found in the accounts of a business are :

(a) income which is taxed under other Schedules and Cases of income tax or which has been taxed at source (e.g. income from property, interest received)

(b) profits on the disposal of fixed assets (these are usually depreciation adjustments but a genuine gain may be chargeable to capital gains tax)

(c) interest received from the Inland Revenue in connection with a repayment of income tax (see Chapter 14)

(d) decreases in general provisions.

Expenditure not shown in the accounts

The most common example of allowable expenditure not shown in the accounts of a business is the trader's claim (if any) to capital allowances. The types of expenditure which attract capital allowances and the way in which capital allowances are calculated are considered in Chapter 10.

Another instance of allowable expenditure not shown in the accounts is a premium paid for the grant of a short lease of business premises. As explained earlier, part of such a premium is deductible from trading income in equal annual instalments over the period of the lease. If a premium is being amortised in the business accounts, the amortisation charges shown in the accounts are added back and the allowable amount of the premium (according to the rules given in Chapter 5) is deducted instead.

Summary

► A set of criteria known as the "badges of trade" may be used to distinguish between trading activities and non-trading activities.

► The net profit shown in the accounts of a self-employed person needs adjusting for tax purposes.

► Expenditure is allowable under Schedule D Case I if it is wholly and exclusively incurred for the purposes of the trade. Expenditure which is not so incurred will be disallowed. Certain categories of expenditure are disallowed by statute.

► If the owner of a business takes goods for personal use, the full market value of the goods (less any amount paid by the owner) must be added to the net profit shown by the accounts when computing the adjusted profit.

▶ Non-trading income included in the accounts of a business must be deducted from the net profit shown by those accounts when computing the adjusted profit.

▶ Any allowable expenditure not shown in the accounts (e.g. the deductible part of a premium paid for the grant of a short lease) must be deducted from the net profit shown by the accounts when computing the adjusted profit.

Exercises

8.1 List the six badges of trade.

8.2 State the general rule which governs whether or not expenditure is deductible under the rules of Schedule D Case I.

8.3 Which of the following items of expenditure would be allowed under the rules of Schedule D Case I ?

    (a) the salary paid to a sole trader's wife

    (b) a deed of covenant to charity

    (c) a new lathe bought by an engineering business

    (d) diaries costing £3 each given to customers

    (e) the cost of the annual staff outing to Blackpool

    (f) the black suit worn at work by a self-employed undertaker

    (g) the legal costs of acquiring new freehold premises

    (h) a subscription to the local chamber of commerce

    (i) bottles of whisky costing £9.99 each given to customers at Christmas

    (j) the legal costs of suing a trade debtor for non-payment.

8.4 Julian, a self-employed shopkeeper, takes goods costing £30 from his business stock for his own personal use. If he had sold the stock to a customer he would have charged £45. What adjustment would need to be made for tax purposes to his net profit if :

    (a) he pays nothing for the goods

    (b) he puts £30 of his own money into the till so as to pay for the goods

    (c) he puts £45 of his own money into the till.

8.5 (a) A motor car with an original cost of £21,000 is leased for an annual rental of £5,670. How much of the £5,670 should be added back each year when calculating the Schedule D Case I adjusted profit ?

    (b) A sole trader is granted a 15 year lease on premises which he uses for business purposes. He pays a premium of £15,000 and writes off £1,000 per year in his business accounts. How much of the £1,000 should be added back each year when calculating the Schedule D Case I adjusted profit ?

8.6   Linda's profit and loss account for the year ended 31 March 2001 is as follows :

	£	£
Sales		82,500
Less : Cost of sales		37,200
Gross profit		45,300
Add : Rents receivable	1,200	
Bank interest receivable	80	
Profit on sale of fixed assets	310	1,590
		46,890
Less : Wages and salaries	22,620	
Business rates and insurance	1,750	
Heating and lighting	2,170	
Repairs and renewals	4,280	
Telephone	880	
Motor expenses	3,250	
Sundry expenses	1,650	
Bad and doubtful debts	640	
Credit card interest	120	
Loss on sale of fixed asset	70	
Depreciation	2,500	39,930
Net profit for the year		6,960

Notes :

(a)   Linda draws a salary of £200 per week from the business. This is included in the wages and salaries figure.

(b)   Repairs and renewals are as follows :

	£
Decoration of business premises	400
Installation of new improved heating system	3,800
Minor repair	80
	4,280

(c)   It has been agreed with the Inland Revenue that one-quarter of telephone costs and one-fifth of motor expenses relate to private use.

(d)   Sundry expenses include business entertaining of £520.

(e)   Trade debts written off in the year amount to £440 and £200 has been set aside as a general provision for bad and doubtful debts.

Compute the Schedule D Case I adjusted profit (before deduction of capital allowances) for the year ended 31 March 2001.

*8.7   A sole trader's bad and doubtful debts account for the year ended 31 March 2001 is as follows :

	£	£		£	£
Trade debts written off		638	Provisions b/f		
Provisions c/f			General	200	
General	150		Specific	231	431
Specific	317	467			
			Staff loan recovered		500
			P & L Account		174
		1,105			1,105

How much of the £174 charged to the profit and loss account for the year should be added back when calculating the Schedule D Case I adjusted profit ?

*8.8   Imran owns a wholesaling business which operates from rented premises. He has a 10-year lease on the premises and paid a premium of £7,000 in order to obtain the lease. His profit and loss account for the year ended 31 December 2000 is as follows :

		£	£
Gross profit for the year			52,618
Add :	Interest receivable	212	
	Surplus on sale of office equipment	300	512
			53,130
Less :	Wages (see Note 1)	19,280	
	Rent, rates and insurance (see Note 2)	6,915	
	Electricity	4,328	
	Telephone (see Note 3)	1,650	
	Repairs (see Note 4)	2,286	
	Printing and advertising	1,250	
	Motor expenses (see Note 5)	5,712	
	Legal and professional expenses (see Note 6)	3,000	
	Sundry expenses (see Note 7)	4,777	
	Bad and doubtful debts (see Note 8)	860	
	Bank charges and interest	2,765	
	Lease premium amortisation	700	
	Depreciation	8,749	62,272
Net loss for the year			(9,142)

Notes :

1.   Wages include £5,800 for Imran's wife (who works full-time for the business) and £1,000 for his son (a student who does not work for the business at all). Also included is Imran's personal Schedule D Case I income tax of £3,187 and personal National Insurance contributions of £328.

2.   Rent, rates and insurance includes Imran's private medical insurance premium of £414.

3. It has been agreed that one-sixth of telephone costs relate to private use.

4. Repairs include £750 for the cost of essential repairs to a newly-acquired second-hand forklift truck which could not be used until the repairs had been carried out.

5. Motor expenses are as follows :

	£
Vehicle servicing and repairs	1,165
Fuel and oil	2,815
Loss on disposal of motor vehicle	422
Road fund licences and insurance	610
Fine for speeding by Imran	700
	5,712

It has been agreed that one-tenth of motor expenses relate to private use.

6. Legal and professional expenses consist of :

	£
Fees relating to renewal of lease	500
Debt collection	1,500
Accountancy fees	1,000
	3,000

7. Sundry expenses are :

	£
Entertaining UK customers	630
Entertaining overseas customer	150
Staff Christmas dinner	312
Gift to employee on examination success	100
Patent royalties	2,540
Subscription to trade association	250
Donation to political party	200
Miscellaneous small items (all allowable)	595
	4,777

8. Trade debts of £500 were written off during the year. The general provision for bad debts was reduced by £100 and the specific provision for bad debts was increased by £460.

9. During the year, Imran took goods costing £220 from stock for personal use, paying £220 of his own money into the business bank account. His gross profit percentage on turnover is 20%.

Compute the Schedule D Case I adjusted profit (before deduction of capital allowances) for the year ended 31 December 2000.

Chapter 9

Income from self-employment : Basis periods

Introduction

Income tax assessments are raised for tax years or "years of assessment", which run from 6 April to the following 5 April. It would be convenient, therefore, if all traders were required to choose 5 April as their annual accounting date, so that the profits for a given tax year could be readily identified. However, traders are free to choose any accounting date they wish and so it is necessary to devise some means of establishing a link between the accounting periods for which profits are calculated and the tax years in which those profits are charged to tax.

The profits charged to tax in a tax year are the profits earned during the *basis period* for that year and the purpose of this chapter is to explain the rules which are used to determine the basis period for any given tax year. The basis period rules which are now in use were introduced by Finance Act 1994 and the old rules which these rules replaced are no longer of interest. However, one aspect of the transition from the old rules to the FA1994 rules which remains relevant today is considered briefly at the end of this chapter.

The current year basis

The main principle of the basis period rules is that the basis period for a year of assessment is *the accounting year ending in that year of assessment*. This is known as the "current year basis" (CYB). However, special rules apply when a business starts trading, ceases trading or changes its accounting date (see below).

EXAMPLE 1

(a) A trader prepares accounts annually to 31 December. Identify the basis period for the 2000/01 Schedule D Case I assessment.

(b) A trader prepares accounts annually to 30 April. For which tax year will the accounting year to 30 April 2001 form the basis period ?

Assume in both cases that the special rules which are used on commencement, cessation or change of accounting date do not apply in any of the years concerned.

SOLUTION

(a) The accounting year to 31 December 2000 ends during 2000/01 and therefore forms the basis period for the 2000/01 assessment.

(b) The accounting year to 30 April 2001 ends during 2001/02 and therefore forms the basis period for the 2001/02 assessment.

Commencement of trade

Special rules are used to determine basis periods when a business starts trading. The basis periods for the opening years of assessment for a new business are as follows :

Year of assessment		Basis period
1		Date of commencement to the following 5 April (the "actual basis")
2	*either* (a)	12 months to the accounting date in year 2 (if possible)
	or (b)	First 12 months of trading (if the accounting date in year 2 is less than 12 months after commencement)
	or (c)	Actual i.e. 6 April to 5 April (if there is no accounting date in year 2)
3	*either* (a)	Current year basis (if possible)
	or (b)	12 months to the accounting date in year 3
4 etc.		Current year basis.

Note the following points :

(a) Basis periods for the opening tax years may overlap to some extent and therefore some of the profits made in the early years of trading may be the subject of more than one tax assessment (see below).

(b) If necessary, the adjusted profits for early accounting periods are apportioned on a time basis in order to compute the assessments in the opening years.

(c) Strictly speaking, all apportionments required for the purposes of Schedule D Case I or II should be made exactly, according to the number of days in the relevant basis period. However, the Inland Revenue will accept any other reasonable time-based apportionment so long as it is applied consistently. In practice, calculations are usually made to the nearest month and this is the approach adopted in this book. However, *some examining bodies may require exact apportionments*. Therefore the reader is advised to find out whether his or her examining body requires apportionments to be made in days or months and to proceed accordingly when answering examination questions.

EXAMPLE 2

(a)   Vera commences trading on 1 January 2000, preparing accounts annually to 31 December. Identify the basis periods for the first four tax years.

(b)   Wilbur commences trading on 1 October 1999. He chooses 30 June as his annual accounting date and prepares his first accounts for the 9 months to 30 June 2000. Identify the basis periods for the first four tax years.

(c)   Yasmin commences trading on 1 February 1999 and chooses 30 April as her annual accounting date. She prepares her first accounts for the 15 months to 30 April 2000. Identify the basis periods for the first four tax years.

SOLUTION

(a)

	1999/00	Actual	1 January 2000 to 5 April 2000
	2000/01	12 months to a/c date in year 2	1 January 2000 to 31 December 2000
	2001/02	CYB	year to 31 December 2001
	2002/03	CYB	year to 31 December 2002

(b)

	1999/00	Actual	1 October 1999 to 5 April 2000
	2000/01	First 12 months	1 October 1999 to 30 September 2000
	2001/02	CYB	year to 30 June 2001
	2002/03	CYB	year to 30 June 2002

(c)

	1998/99	Actual	1 February 1999 to 5 April 1999
	1999/00	Actual	6 April 1999 to 5 April 2000
	2000/01	12 months to a/c date in year 3	1 May 1999 to 30 April 2000
	2001/02	CYB	year to 30 April 2001

Overlap profits

If a business chooses 5 April as its annual accounting date, the basis periods used in the opening tax years will not overlap at all. In most cases, however, the opening basis periods will overlap and some profits will form the basis of more than one assessment. Such profits are known as "overlap profits".

EXAMPLE 3

Albert begins trading on 1 May 1999 and has the following results :

	Adjusted profit
	£
15 months to 31 July 2000	16,800
year to 31 July 2001	21,600

Compute Albert's Schedule D Case I assessments for the first three tax years and calculate the amount of any overlap profits.

SOLUTION

Albert's first accounting period contains 15 months and his first assessment is based on the profits of the 11 months from 1 May 1999 to 5 April 2000. The assessments for the first three tax years are as follows :

Year	Basis	Basis period	Workings	Assessment
				£
1999/00	Actual	1/5/99 to 5/4/00	£16,800 x 11/15	12,320
2000/01	12 months to a/c date in year 2	1/8/99 to 31/7/00	£16,800 x 12/15	13,440
2001/02	CYB	y/e 31/7/01		21,600

The overlap period consists of the 8 months from 1 August 1999 to 5 April 2000, which are common to the basis periods for 1999/00 and 2000/01. The overlap profits are therefore £8,960 (£16,800 x 8/15).

Overlap relief

In general, any overlap profits arising in the opening tax years of a business are deducted from the assessment raised for the final tax year when the business ceases trading. Note the following points regarding "overlap relief" :

(a) Overlap relief ensures that, over the entire lifetime of a business, the total of all the assessments raised is equal to the total adjusted profits.

(b) Overlap profits are not index-linked. The real value of overlap relief will therefore be eroded by inflation, especially in the case of businesses which trade for many years.

(c) If overlap profits exceed the final year's assessment, the resulting loss is dealt with in the usual way (see Chapter 11).

However, if a business changes its accounting date at some point during its lifetime, it is possible that some of the overlap profits arising in the opening years may be relieved by deduction from the assessment raised for the year of the change. It is also possible that further overlap profits might arise on a change of accounting date (see later in this chapter).

Cessation of trade

A cessation of trade occurs when the owner of a business retires, sells the business or dies and the final tax year in which the trader is assessed under Schedule D Case I is the tax year in which the cessation occurs. The basis period for this final tax year is determined as follows :

(a) If a business commences trading and ceases trading in the same tax year, the basis period for that year consists of the entire lifespan of the business.

(b) If a business ceases trading in its second tax year, the basis period for that year runs from 6 April at the start of the year up to the date of cessation. (This rule overrides the usual commencement rules for the second year of assessment).

(c) Otherwise, the basis period for the final tax year runs from the end of the basis period for the previous tax year up to the date of the cessation. This basis period may be less than, equal to or more than 12 months in length. (The usual commencement rules for the third year are overridden if a business ceases trading in its third tax year).

If the final set of accounts prepared for a business covers a period of more than 12 months, it is possible that no accounting date at all falls into the penultimate tax year (i.e. the last year but one). This makes it impossible to apply the usual current year basis in that year. In these circumstances, the basis period for the penultimate tax year is the 12 months up to the normal accounting date falling in that year.

It is important to appreciate that Schedule D Case I assessments are raised on the owner of a business and not on the business itself, so that a change in the ownership of a business is treated for tax purposes as a cessation of one business followed by the commencement of another.

EXAMPLE 4

Carmen starts trading on 1 July 1999 and chooses 30 June as her annual accounting date. Identify the basis periods for her last two tax years if she ceases trading as follows :

	Date of cessation	Final set of accounts
(a)	31 March 2000	9 months to 31 March 2000
(b)	30 June 2000	year to 30 June 2000
(c)	30 June 2007	year to 30 June 2007
(d)	31 May 2007	11 months to 31 May 2007
(e)	30 April 2007	22 months to 30 April 2007

SOLUTION

(a) Trade both commences and ceases in 1999/00. The basis period for this single tax year is the entire lifespan of the business i.e. 1 July 1999 to 31 March 2000.

(b) The cessation occurs in 2000/01, which is the second year of assessment. The basis periods are :

1999/00	Actual	1 July 1999 to 5 April 2000
2000/01	6 April to date of cessation	6 April 2000 to 30 June 2000

(c)
2006/07	CYB	y/e 30 June 2006
2007/08	End of previous basis period up to date of cessation	1 July 2006 to 30 June 2007

(d)
2006/07	CYB	y/e 30 June 2006
2007/08	End of previous basis period up to date of cessation	1 July 2006 to 31 May 2007

(e)
2006/07	12 months to normal a/c date	1 July 2005 to 30 June 2006
2007/08	End of previous basis period up to date of cessation	1 July 2006 to 30 April 2007

EXAMPLE 5

Damien starts trading on 1 July 1995 and chooses 31 December as his annual accounting date. He ceases trading on 30 September 2000 and has the following results :

	Adjusted profit £
6 months to 31 December 1995	8,400
year to 31 December 1996	9,200
year to 31 December 1997	10,500
year to 31 December 1998	7,500
year to 31 December 1999	6,400
9 months to 30 September 2000	5,800

Compute the Schedule D Case I assessments for all years. Show that the total of these assessments is equal to the total of the adjusted profits.

SOLUTION

Year	Basis period	Workings	Assessment £
1995/96	1/7/95 to 5/4/96	£8,400 + £9,200 x 3/12	10,700
1996/97	y/e 31/12/96		9,200
1997/98	y/e 31/12/97		10,500
1998/99	y/e 31/12/98		7,500
1999/00	y/e 31/12/99		6,400
2000/01	1/1/00 to 30/9/00	£5,800 - overlap relief £2,300	3,500
			47,800

Notes :

(a) The overlap period is from 1 January 1996 to 5 April 1996 (3 months) and the overlap profits are £2,300 (£9,200 x 3/12).

(b) The total of the assessments is £47,800, the same as the total of the adjusted profits.

Change of accounting date

If a business changes its accounting date from one date (the "old date") to another (the "new date") special rules are used to determine the basis period for the year of the change. The year of change is defined as the first year of assessment in which accounts are *not* made up to the old date or *are* made up to the new date (or both). There will be a change of basis period for a year of change so long as all of the following conditions are satisfied :

(a) The first set of accounts made up to the new date does not cover a period of more than 18 months.

(b) Notice of the change of accounting date is given to the Inland Revenue in a tax return on or before the due filing date for that return.

(c) Either :

 (i) None of the previous five years of assessment has been a year of change resulting in a change of basis period, or

 (ii) The Inland Revenue is satisfied that the change of date has been made for genuine commercial reasons and not for tax avoidance purposes.

If all of these conditions are satisfied, the basis period for the year of change is determined as follows :

(a) The "relevant period" is identified as the period beginning immediately after the end of the basis period for the previous year of assessment and ending with the new date in the year of change.

(b) If the length of the relevant period is less than 12 months, the basis period for the year of change is the 12 months to the new date in the year of change.

(c) If the length of the relevant period is not less than 12 months, the basis period for the year of change is the relevant period itself.

(d) In consequence, the basis period for a year of change will always be of at least 12 months' duration.

If all of the required conditions are *not* satisfied, the basis period for the year of change is the 12 months to the old date in that year. However, the following year of assessment is then regarded as a year of change (the taxpayer being treated as though this were the first year in which the new date had been used) and a change of basis period will occur in that year if all of the conditions are satisfied in relation to that year. A change of accounting date can be carried forward indefinitely in this way until such time as the necessary conditions for a change of basis period are satisfied.

EXAMPLE 6

(a) Gary began trading many years ago, preparing accounts to 30 September each year. He decided to change his accounting date to 30 June and the first accounts made up to the new date were for the period from 1 October 1999 to 30 June 2000. The conditions necessary for a change of basis period were all satisfied. Identify the basis periods for years 1998/99 to 2001/02 inclusive.

(b) Audrey began trading on 1 January 1997, preparing accounts to 31 December each year. She decided to change her accounting date to 31 March and the first accounts made up to the new date were for the period from 1 January 1999 to 31 March 2000. The conditions necessary for a change of basis period were all satisfied. Identify the basis periods for years 1996/97 to 2001/02 inclusive.

(c) Grant began trading many years ago, preparing accounts to 30 June each year. He decided to change his accounting date to 31 December and the first accounts made up to the new date were for the period from 1 July 2000 to 31 December 2000. The conditions necessary for a change of basis period were all satisfied. Identify the basis periods for years 1999/00 to 2002/03 inclusive.

(d) Clare began trading on 1 March 1996, preparing accounts to 31 January each year. Her first accounts were for the period to 31 January 1997. She decided to change her accounting date to 30 April and the first accounts made up to the new date were for the period from 1 February 1999 to 30 April 2000. The conditions necessary for a change of basis period were all satisfied. Identify the basis periods for years 1995/96 to 2001/02 inclusive.

SOLUTION

(a) The year of change is 2000/01 (the first year in which the old date was not used and the new date was used). The basis period for 1999/00 ended on 30 September 1999, so the relevant period is from 1 October 1999 to 30 June 2000. This is less than 12 months in length so the basis period for 2000/01 is the 12 months to 30 June 2000. Basis periods for 1998/99 to 2001/02 are :

1998/99   year to 30 September 1998
1999/00   year to 30 September 1999
2000/01   year to 30 June 2000
2001/02   year to 30 June 2001

Note that there is an overlap between the basis periods for 1999/00 and 2000/01. The treatment of overlap profits on a change of accounting date is explained below.

(b)   The year of change is 1999/00 (the first year in which the old date was not used and the new date was used). The basis period for 1998/99 ended on 31 December 1998, so the relevant period is from 1 January 1999 to 31 March 2000. This is not less than 12 months in length so the basis period for 1999/00 is the same as the relevant period. Basis periods for 1996/97 to 2001/02 are :

1996/97   1 January 1997 to 5 April 1997
1997/98   year to 31 December 1997
1998/99   year to 31 December 1998
1999/00   1 January 1999 to 31 March 2000
2000/01   year to 31 March 2001
2001/02   year to 31 March 2002

(c)   The year of change is 2000/01 (the first year in which the new date was used). The basis period for 1999/00 ended on 30 June 1999, so the relevant period is from 1 July 1999 to 31 December 2000. This is not less than 12 months in length so the basis period for 2000/01 is the same as the relevant period. Basis periods are :

1999/00   year to 30 June 1999
2000/01   1 July 1999 to 31 December 2000
2001/02   year to 31 December 2001
2002/03   year to 31 December 2002

(d)   The year of change is 1999/00 (the first year in which the old date was not used). The basis period for 1998/99 ended on 31 January 1999, so the relevant period is from 1 February 1999 to 30 April 1999. This is less than 12 months in length so the basis period for 1999/00 is the 12 months to 30 April 1999 (even though this accounting date was not used in 1999/00). Basis periods for 1995/96 to 2001/02 are :

1995/96   1 March 1996 to 5 April 1996
1996/97   1 March 1996 to 28 February 1997
1997/98   year to 31 January 1998
1998/99   year to 31 January 1999
1999/00   year to 30 April 1999
2000/01   year to 30 April 2000
2001/02   year to 30 April 2001

There is an overlap between the basis periods for 1998/99 and 1999/00 (as well as the usual overlap arising on the commencement of trade).

Overlap profits on a change of accounting date

If a change of accounting date results in profits being assessed more than once, these overlap profits are added to any earlier overlap profits (which arose in the opening years or on a previous change of accounting date) and the total is carried forward for relief on cessation or on a subsequent change of accounting date.

Alternatively, if the basis period for a year of change exceeds 12 months, a part of the overlap profits brought forward from previous years may be relieved in the year of change. The amount to be relieved is calculated according to the following formula :

$$\text{Amount relieved} = A \times \frac{(B - C)}{D}$$

where : A = Total overlap profits brought forward and not yet relieved

B = Length of the relevant period

C = 12 (or 365 if strict daily apportionments are being used)

D = Total length of the overlap period(s) to which the total overlap profits brought forward relate.

EXAMPLE 7

(a) Byron began trading on 1 November 1997, preparing accounts to 31 October each year. He decided to change his accounting date to 31 August and the first accounts made up to the new date were for the period from 1 November 1999 to 31 August 2000. The conditions necessary for a change of basis period were all satisfied. The adjusted profits for Byron's first five accounting periods were as follows :

	£
Year to 31 October 1998	12,000
Year to 31 October 1999	18,000
Period to 31 August 2000	16,000
Year to 31 August 2001	21,000
Year to 31 August 2002	24,000

Compute Byron's Schedule D Case I assessments for years 1997/98 to 2002/03.

(b) Michelle began trading on 1 January 1997, preparing accounts to 31 December each year. She decided to change her accounting date to 28 February and the first accounts made up to the new date were for the period from 1 January 2000 to 28 February 2001. The conditions necessary for a change of basis period were all satisfied. The adjusted profits for Michelle's first five accounting periods were :

	£
Year to 31 December 1997	4,560
Year to 31 December 1998	5,250
Year to 31 December 1999	11,680
Period to 28 February 2001	14,390
Year to 28 February 2002	16,270

Compute Michelle's Schedule D Case I assessments for years 1996/97 to 2001/02.

SOLUTION

(a) The year of change is 2000/01 (the first year in which the old date was not used and the new date was used). The basis period for 1999/00 ended on 31 October 1999, so the relevant period is from 1 November 1999 to 31 August 2000. This is less than 12 months in length so the basis period for 2000/01 is the 12 months to 31 August 2000. The assessments for 1997/98 to 2002/03 are :

Year	Basis period	Workings	Assessment £
1997/98	1/11/97 to 5/4/98	£12,000 x 5/12	5,000
1998/99	y/e 31/10/98		12,000
1999/00	y/e 31/10/99		18,000
2000/01	y/e 31/8/00	£18,000 x 2/12 + £16,000	19,000
2001/02	y/e 31/8/01		21,000
2002/03	y/e 31/8/02		24,000

There are overlap profits of £5,000 (5 months) on the commencement of trade and a further £3,000 (2 months) on the change of accounting date. Total overlap profits carried forward are £8,000 (7 months).

(b) The year of change is 2000/01 (the first year in which the old date was not used and the new date was used). The basis period for 1999/00 ended on 31 December 1999, so the relevant period is from 1 January 2000 to 28 February 2001. This is not less than 12 months in length so the basis period for 2000/01 is the relevant period itself. The assessments for 1996/97 to 2001/02 are :

Year	Basis period	Workings	Assessment £
1996/97	1/1/97 to 5/4/97	£4,560 x 3/12	1,140
1997/98	y/e 31/12/97		4,560
1998/99	y/e 31/12/98		5,250
1999/00	y/e 31/12/99		11,680
2000/01	1/1/00 to 28/2/01	£14,390 - overlap relief £760	13,630
2001/02	y/e 28/2/02		16,270

There are overlap profits of £1,140 (3 months) on the commencement of trade. The relevant period is 14 months long, which exceeds 12 months by 2 months. Overlap relief in the year of change is calculated as £1,140 x 2/3 = £760. Overlap profits carried forward are £380 (1 month).

Transitional overlap relief

As explained earlier, the basis period rules now in use were introduced by Finance Act 1994. Businesses which were in existence before 6 April 1994 used to be assessed on the *preceding year basis*, which meant that the basis period for a tax year was the accounting year ending in the previous tax year. The switch to the current year basis for these older businesses occurred as from 1997/98 with a special transitional rule for 1996/97. Broadly, the basis period for tax year 1996/97 was the 24 months to the accounting date in that year and the assessment for the year was computed as 50% of the profits occurring during this 24-month period.

An aspect of this transition which will remain relevant for many years to come is that the period between the end of the basis period for 1996/97 and 5 April 1997 is treated as an overlap period. Ordinary overlap relief (arising on commencement of trade) is not available to these older businesses but the profits of this special overlap period are eligible for *transitional overlap relief* on a subsequent change of accounting date or on the cessation of trade.

EXAMPLE 8

Norman began trading in 1975. He ceases trading on 31 October 2000. Recent adjusted profits have been as follows :

	£
year to 31 October 1995	25,460
year to 31 October 1996	26,820
year to 31 October 1997	28,560
year to 31 October 1998	31,370
year to 31 October 1999	27,430
year to 31 October 2000	28,100

Compute Norman's Schedule D Case I assessment for 2000/01.

SOLUTION

Norman's 1996/97 assessment would have been 50% of the profits for the 24 months to 31 October 1996. Transitional overlap relief is available in relation to the profits of the period from 1 November 1996 to 5 April 1997 (£28,560 x 5/12 = £11,900).

The business ceases in 2000/01 so the basis period for 2000/01 runs from the end of the basis period for 1999/00 up to the date of cessation (from 1 November 1999 to 31 October 2000). The 2000/01 assessment is therefore £16,200 (£28,100 less transitional overlap relief of £11,900).

Averaging of agricultural profits

More than any other trade, the trade of farming and market gardening is at the mercy of the weather. As a consequence, farming profits may fluctuate considerably from one year to the next, leading to corresponding fluctuations in Schedule D Case I assessments. Such fluctuations may be smoothed out by a claim for *averaging*.

The Schedule D Case I assessments of two consecutive tax years may be averaged if the difference between them is at least 30% of the higher assessment. The effect of an averaging claim is to replace the normal assessment in each of the two years concerned by the average of the two assessments which would otherwise be raised.

EXAMPLE 9

The recent tax-adjusted profits of a self-employed farmer who began trading many years ago are as follows :

	£
year to 30 November 1999	36,200
year to 30 November 2000	10,640

He has no other income.

(a) May an averaging claim be made ?

(b) Would the farmer benefit from an averaging claim ?

SOLUTION

(a) The tax years in question are 1999/00 and 2000/01. The difference between the two profit figures is £25,560, which is far more than 30% of £36,200 so an averaging claim may be made.

(b) If an averaging claim is made, the 1999/00 and 2000/01 assessments are each revised to £23,420 (the average of £36,200 and £10,640). The farmer benefits from this claim in two ways :

(i)   the likelihood of paying 40% tax for 1999/00 is removed, so reducing the total tax liability for the two years, and

(ii) the farmer's cash flow situation is improved, since the 1999/00 tax liability is reduced and the 2000/01 tax liability is increased.

Note the following points in relation to the averaging of agricultural profits :

(a) If a loss has been incurred in either of the two years involved in an averaging claim, the loss counts as zero in the averaging calculation. (The loss is then relieved in the usual way, as described in Chapter 11).

(b) An averaging claim may not be made for the tax year in which trade commences or for the tax year in which trade ceases.

(c) If an averaging claim has been made for two tax years, then the revised assessment for the second year may subsequently be used in another averaging claim. For example, if a claim has already been made for 1998/99 and 1999/00, then another claim may be made for 1999/00 and 2000/01. Overlapping claims of this nature must be made in chronological order.

(d) An averaging claim must be made by the first anniversary of the 31 January which follows the end of the second tax year to which the claim relates. For example, an averaging claim which relates to 1999/00 and 2000/01 must be made by 31 January 2003.

EXAMPLE 10

A market gardener who began trading many years ago has the following recent results :

	Adjusted profit (loss)
	£
year to 31 December 1997	21,500
year to 31 December 1998	14,200
year to 31 December 1999	(5,400)
year to 31 December 2000	6,900
year to 31 December 2001	10,800

Compute the assessments for 1997/98 to 2001/02 inclusive, assuming that all possible averaging claims are made.

SOLUTION

1997/98 and 1998/99

	£	
Original assessment for 1997/98 (y/e 31/12/97)	21,500	
Original assessment for 1998/99 (y/e 31/12/98)	14,200	
Difference	7,300	(more than 30% of £21,500)

Averaging gives revised assessments of £17,850 in 1997/98 & 1998/99.

1998/99 and 1999/00

	£	
Revised assessment for 1998/99	17,850	
Original assessment for 1999/00 (y/e 31/12/99)	0	
Difference	17,850	(more than 30% of £17,850)

Averaging gives revised assessments of £8,925 in 1998/99 & 1999/00.

1999/00 and 2000/01

	£	
Revised assessment for 1999/00	8,925	
Original assessment for 2000/01 (y/e 31/12/00)	6,900	
Difference	2,025	(less than 30% of £8,925)

No averaging is possible so assessments are unaltered.

2000/01 and 2001/02

	£	
Original assessment for 2000/01 (y/e 31/12/00)	6,900	
Original assessment for 2001/02 (y/e 31/12/01)	10,800	
Difference	3,900	(more than 30% of £10,800)

Averaging gives revised assessments of £8,850 in 2000/01 & 2001/02. The final assessments for all years concerned are as follows :

	£	
1997/98	17,850	
1998/99	8,925	
1999/00	8,925	
2000/01	8,850	
2001/02	8,850	(which may perhaps be averaged with 2002/03).

Marginal relief

As explained above, an averaging claim may not be made if the difference between the assessments for the two years concerned is less than 30% of the higher assessment. If, however, this difference is at least 25% of the higher assessment, a form of averaging known as "marginal relief" may be claimed. The effect of marginal relief is to reduce the higher assessment (H) and to increase the lower assessment (L) by an amount given by the following formula :

$$3 \times (H - L) - 0.75 \times H$$

If the difference between H and L is exactly 30% of H, this formula has the same effect as an ordinary averaging claim. If the difference between H and L is exactly 25% of H, this formula has no effect at all.

EXAMPLE 11

A farmer's Schedule D Case I assessment for 1999/00 is £12,000. What averaging claims (if any) can he make if his Schedule D Case I assessment for 2000/01 is :

(a) £7,600

(b) £8,600

(c) £9,600.

SOLUTION

(a) The difference between the two assessments is £4,400, which is more than 30% of £12,000 so a normal averaging claim can be made, revising both assessments to £9,800 (the average of £12,000 and £7,600).

(b) The difference between the two assessments is £3,400, which is between 25% and 30% of £12,000 so a marginal relief claim can be made. The adjustment to each assessment is :

$$3 \times (£12,000 - £8,600) - 0.75 \times £12,000 = £1,200.$$

The assessment for 1999/00 is reduced to £10,800 and the assessment for 2000/01 is increased to £9,800.

(c) The difference between the two assessments is £2,400, which is less than 25% of £12,000 so no averaging is possible at all.

Summary

▶ Schedule D Case I assessments are made on the current year basis. Special rules apply in the opening and closing years of a business and on a change of accounting date.

▶ Overlap profits arising in the opening years of a new business are relieved either on the cessation of trade or on a change of accounting date.

▶ Further overlap profits may arise on a change of accounting date.

▶ Transitional overlap relief may be available when a business which commenced before 6 April 1994 ceases trading.

▶ In certain circumstances, farmers and market gardeners may claim that the profits of two consecutive tax years should be averaged.

Exercises

9.1 Under the *current year basis*, for which tax years would the following accounting years form the basis period ?

(a) year to 31 October 2000   (b) year to 31 March 2001

(c) year to 30 April 2002   (d) year to 5 April 2002.

9.2 Frank began trading on 1 July 1999. Identify the basis periods for his first 4 years of assessment if he :

(a) chooses 30 June as his annual accounting date and prepares his first accounts for the year to 30 June 2000

(b) chooses 30 April as his annual accounting date and prepares his first accounts for the 22 months to 30 April 2001

(c) chooses 30 April as his annual accounting date and prepares his first accounts for the 10 months to 30 April 2000.

Also identify any overlap periods which arise in each case.

9.3 Greta commences trading on 1 January 2000 and chooses 30 June as her annual accounting date. Her first accounts are made up for the 18 months to 30 June 2001 and show an adjusted profit of £27,300. Compute Greta's assessments for the first three tax years and calculate the amount of any overlap profits.

9.4   Hitesh has been trading for many years, preparing accounts to 31 January each year. His last full year of trading is the year to 31 January 2001. Identify the basis periods for the last three tax years in each of the following cases :

	Date of cessation	*Final set of accounts*
(a)	31 May 2001	4 months to 31 May 2001
(b)	31 March 2002	14 months to 31 March 2002
(c)	30 April 2002	15 months to 30 April 2002

9.5   Larry began trading in 1981, preparing accounts to 31 July each year. He ceases trading on 31 July 2000 and his adjusted profits in the closing years are as follows :

	£
year to 31 July 1997	15,900
year to 31 July 1998	12,800
year to 31 July 1999	13,400
year to 31 July 2000	11,200

Compute the Schedule D Case I assessment for 2000/01.

*9.6   Ivy begins trading as a market gardener on 1 January 1999, making up annual accounts to 31 December. Her adjusted profits in the opening years are as follows :

	£
year to 31 December 1999	7,200
year to 31 December 2000	5,010
year to 31 December 2001	4,570

(a)   Compute the Schedule D Case I assessments for the first four tax years, assuming that no averaging claims are made.

(b)   Compute the revised Schedule D Case I assessments for the first four tax years, assuming that all possible averaging claims are made.

*9.7   Ken starts trading on 1 October 1995 and chooses 30 April as his annual accounting date. He ceases trading on 31 January 2001 and has the following results :

	Adjusted profit
	£
7 months to 30 April 1996	3,500
year to 30 April 1997	6,480
year to 30 April 1998	7,700
year to 30 April 1999	7,900
year to 30 April 2000	8,200
9 months to 31 January 2001	7,300

Compute the Schedule D Case I assessments for all years.

*9.8   Belinda began trading on 1 March 1997 and chose 31 December as her accounting date. Her first accounts were for the period to 31 December 1997. She eventually decided to change her accounting date to 31 May and the first accounts made up to the new date were for the 17 months to 31 May 2001. The conditions necessary for a change of basis period were all satisfied. The adjusted profits for her first five accounting periods were as follows :

	Adjusted profit
	£
1 March 1997 to 31 December 1997	43,700
year to 31 December 1998	52,590
year to 31 December 1999	54,300
1 January 2000 to 31 May 2001	71,060
year to 31 May 2002	68,200

Compute the Schedule D Case I assessments for 1996/97 to 2002/03 inclusive, showing the amounts of any overlap profits or overlap relief.

*9.9   Roger began trading on 1 January 1996, preparing accounts to 30 April each year. His first accounts were for the 16 months to 30 April 1997. In 1999 he decided to change his accounting date to 30 June. The first accounts made up to the new date were for the 14 months to 30 June 1999 and the conditions necessary for a change of basis period were all satisfied. Roger ceased trading on 31 May 2002. His adjusted profits were as follows :

	Adjusted profit
	£
1 January 1996 to 30 April 1997	33,920
year to 30 April 1998	29,700
1 May 1998 to 30 June 1999	33,300
year to 30 June 2000	41,600
year to 30 June 2001	37,900
1 July 2001 to 31 May 2002	23,500

Compute the Schedule D Case I assessments for all years.

Chapter 10

Income from self-employment : Capital allowances

Introduction

Capital expenditure is not in itself deductible under the rules of Schedule D Case I, but certain types of capital expenditure do attract tax relief in the form of standardised depreciation allowances known as *capital allowances*. The purpose of this chapter is to define the categories of capital expenditure which are eligible for capital allowances and to explain how capital allowances are calculated.

Eligible expenditure

In order to be eligible for capital allowances, expenditure must fall into one of the following categories :

(a) plant and machinery

(b) industrial buildings

(c) agricultural buildings

(d) patents, know-how and scientific research

(e) mineral extraction, dredging and crematoria.

Each of these categories (other than the last) is considered in this chapter.

Chargeable periods

Capital allowances are granted in respect of *chargeable periods*. In most cases, each accounting period ranks as a chargeable period and so there is one capital allowances computation per accounting period, taking into account the acquisitions and disposals of qualifying assets made during that period. The only exception occurs if an accounting period lasts for more than 18 months, in which case it is divided into one or more 12-month chargeable periods with (possibly) a short chargeable period at the end.

When the capital allowances due for an accounting period have been calculated, they are treated as a trading expense of that period and are deducted when calculating the adjusted profit assessable under Schedule D Case I. The basis period rules described in Chapter 9 are then applied to the profit *after* deduction of capital allowances.

EXAMPLE 1

A trade commences on 1 January 2000 and accounts are made up annually to 31 December. The adjusted profits for the year to 31 December 2000 (before deduction of capital allowances) are £9,000 and capital allowances of £1,200 are claimed for that year. Compute the first two Schedule D Case I assessments.

SOLUTION

The adjusted profits (after deduction of capital allowances) are £7,800. Therefore the assessments for the first two tax years are :

Year	Basis	Basis period	Workings	Assessment £
1999/00	Actual	1/1/00 to 5/4/00	£7,800 x 3/12	1,950
2000/01	12 months to a/c date in year 2	1/1/00 to 31/12/00		7,800

Plant and machinery

Capital Allowances Act 1990 (the main statute concerned with capital allowances) does not provide a definition of the term "plant and machinery". Therefore it has been left mainly to case law to decide whether or not any given item should qualify as plant and machinery and so attract capital allowances. In *Yarmouth* v *France* (1887) it was stated that plant and machinery includes :

"whatever apparatus is used by a businessman for carrying on his business, not his stock in trade which he buys or makes for sale, but all goods and chattels, fixed or moveable, live or dead, which he keeps for permanent employment in his business".

It is clear that machinery of all types, motor vehicles and items such as office furniture and equipment all qualify as plant and machinery but difficulties arise in connection with expenditure on buildings and fixtures to buildings. Much case law has been concerned with the distinction between :

(a) assets which perform an *active function* in the carrying on of the business i.e. the apparatus *with which* the business is carried on, and

(b) assets which perform a *passive function* in the carrying on of the business i.e. the setting *in which* the business is carried on.

Assets in the first of these categories qualify as plant and machinery whilst assets in the second category do not, but the distinction between the categories can be a very fine one. Some of the more important case law decisions have been as follows :

Held to be plant and machinery :

(a) a dry dock built for the repair and maintenance of ships, in *CIR v Barclay Curle & Co Ltd* (1969)

(b) a swimming and paddling pool, in *Cooke v Beach Station Caravans Ltd* (1974)

(c) a concrete grain silo, in *Schofield v R & H Hall Ltd* (1975)

(d) decorative screens placed in the window of a building society's offices and incorporating the name of the building society, in *Leeds Permanent Building Society v Proctor* (1982)

(e) moveable office partitions, in *Jarrold v John Good & Sons Ltd* (1962)

(f) display lighting in a store window, in *Cole Brothers Ltd v Phillips* (1982)

(g) light fittings, plaques and pictures on the walls of an hotel, in *IRC v Scottish and Newcastle Breweries Ltd* (1982)

(h) storage platforms built in a warehouse, in *Hunt v Henry Quick Ltd* (1992)

(i) a barrister's law books, in *Munby v Furlong* (1977).

Held *not* to be plant and machinery :

(a) prefabricated school buildings, in *St John's School v Ward* (1974)

(b) a moored ship used as a restaurant, in *Benson v The Yard Arm Club Ltd* (1979)

(c) a petrol station forecourt canopy, in *Dixon v Fitch's Garage Ltd* (1975)

(d) a football stand, in *Brown v Burnley Football and Athletic Co Ltd* (1980)

(e) a false ceiling built to hide electrical conduits, in *Hampton v Fortes Autogrill Ltd* (1979)

(f) a false ceiling, mezzanine floors, staircases, decorative floor and wall tiles all used to create ambience in a restaurant, in *Wimpey International Ltd v Warland* (1988).

In an attempt to clarify the distinction between buildings and plant, Finance Act 1994 provides a detailed list of types of expenditure on buildings (or structures) which are statutorily excluded from qualifying as plant. The Act also provides a detailed list of types of expenditure on buildings (or structures) which are not statutorily excluded from qualifying as plant, and may therefore qualify if permitted by case law.

Expenditure statutorily deemed to be plant and machinery

By statute, expenditure of the following types always qualifies as plant and machinery :

(a) expenditure incurred so as to comply with fire regulations

(b) expenditure on the thermal insulation of industrial buildings

(c) expenditure incurred so as to comply with safety regulations at sports grounds

(d) expenditure on assets necessary to safeguard personal security

(e) expenditure on computer software

(f) expenditure incurred on building alterations, incidental to the installation of plant and machinery.

Capital allowances on plant and machinery

Capital allowances are available to a person who incurs capital expenditure on plant and machinery which is provided :

(a) for the purposes of a trade, profession or vocation carried on by that person, or

(b) for the purposes of a Schedule A business carried on by that person (excluding plant which is let for use in a dwelling house e.g. furniture let to a tenant).

An item of plant and machinery acquired by hire purchase is treated as if bought for its cash price on the date of the HP agreement. HP interest is an allowable expense under Schedule D Case I and may be written off over the life of the HP contract.

Writing down allowance (WDA)

With some exceptions (see later in this chapter) capital allowances are not calculated individually for each item of plant and machinery acquired by a business. Instead, expenditure on plant and machinery is pooled and capital allowances are calculated with reference to the value of the pool. The basic procedure for each chargeable period is as follows :

(a) The written down value (WDV) of the pool at the end of the previous chargeable period is brought forward.

(b) The cost of any plant and machinery acquired during the chargeable period is added into the pool. Items of plant and machinery originally owned personally by the trader, and then brought into the business at a later date, are treated as if purchased at their market value on the date when brought into the business.

(c) If any items have been disposed of during the chargeable period a disposal value is subtracted from the pool, equal to :

   (i)   the sale proceeds, if the asset is sold in the open market

    (ii) the market value on the date of disposal, if the asset is given away or sold for less than market value (unless the new owner will be claiming capital allowances, in which case the sale proceeds are used)

    (iii) the scrap value or any compensation received, if the asset is scrapped or destroyed.

But if the disposal value exceeds the original cost of the item, only the original cost is subtracted from the pool. The profit on the disposal may give rise to a capital gains tax liability (see Chapter 18).

(d)   A *writing down allowance* (WDA) is then given, calculated at 25% per annum on the pool balance.

(e)   The WDA given for the chargeable period is subtracted from the pool, leaving a WDV which is carried forward to the next chargeable period. This WDV will then attract WDA's in future chargeable periods (even if all the plant and machinery has now been sold).

(f)   It is not mandatory to claim the maximum allowances available for a chargeable period and a trader with low profits (or a loss) may wish to claim less than the maximum amount, usually to avoid wasting personal allowances. This applies to both WDA and FYA (see below) and is discussed further in Chapter 11. The effect of claiming less than the maximum permitted capital allowances for a chargeable period is to increase the WDV carried forward, thus increasing the allowances available in future chargeable periods.

Note that WDA is calculated at a rate of 25% *per annum*. The "per annum" refers to the length of the chargeable period for which capital allowances are being claimed and WDA is scaled up or down accordingly if the length of this period is not 12 months.

First year allowance (FYA)

Expenditure on plant and machinery incurred *by small and medium-sized businesses* on or after 2 July 1998 qualifies for a first year allowance (FYA) of 40%. A 50% FYA is available if the expenditure was incurred between 2 July 1997 and 1 July 1998. Note that :

(a)   FYA is not available in relation to plant and machinery for leasing, cars, sea-going ships and railway assets.

(b)   Unlike WDA, FYA is not scaled up or down in accordance with the length of the chargeable period in which it is being given.

(c)   Expenditure on information and communications technology incurred *by small businesses* between 1 April 2000 and 31 March 2003 qualifies for a 100% FYA. Qualifying expenditure includes computer equipment, high-tech communications equipment (e.g. WAP telephones) and software.

(d) Expenditure on plant and machinery *for use primarily in Northern Ireland* which is incurred by small and medium-sized businesses between 12 May 1998 and 11 May 2002 qualifies in most cases for a first year allowance of 100%.

(e) A business (whether sole trader, partnership or company) is a small or medium-sized business for this purpose if it meets the criteria for small and medium-sized companies laid down in company law. Any two of the following three conditions must be satisfied :

	Small	*Medium*
Total assets	£1.4 million or less	£5.6 million or less
Turnover	£2.8 million or less	£11.2 million or less
Average number of employees	50 or less	250 or less

In fact, more than 99% of all businesses qualify as small or medium-sized. (It is assumed for the remainder of this chapter that all of the businesses referred to in examples and exercises are small or medium-sized).

(f) A company which is a member of a group (see Chapter 28) cannot claim FYA unless the group is small or medium-sized.

If FYA is available in relation to an item of plant and machinery, it is nearly always given *instead* of WDA in the chargeable period in which the item first attracts capital allowances. The remainder of the cost of the asset (after deducting FYA) then enters the pool and is eligible for WDA in subsequent chargeable periods. An exception to this rule occurs if an item which is eligible for FYA is acquired and disposed of in the same chargeable period. In these circumstances, FYA and WDA are both available in relation to the item for the period in question.

EXAMPLE 2

(a) Sharon began trading on 1 February 1999 and chose 30 April as her annual accounting date. Her first accounts covered the period from 1 February 1999 to 30 April 2000 and showed an adjusted profit (before capital allowances) of £28,450. During this period she bought and sold plant and machinery as follows :

		£
1 February 1999	Bought car	7,840
1 April 1999	Bought plant	8,000

Compute the first three Schedule D Case I assessments.

(b) Sharon's adjusted profit (before capital allowances) for the year to 30 April 2001 was £31,720. Her purchases and sales of plant and machinery during this year were :

		£
1 June 2000	Bought plant	4,750
30 June 2000	Sold plant (original cost £3,500 on 1/4/99)	2,610
28 February 2001	Bought plant	1,240

Compute Sharon's Schedule D Case I assessment for 2001/02.

SOLUTION

(a) The computation for the 15-month period from 1 February 1999 to 30 April 2000 is :

		Pool £	Allowances £
1/2/99 - 30/4/00			
Additions not qualifying for FYA		7,840	
WDA @ 25% x 15/12		2,450	2,450
		5,390	
Additions qualifying for 40% FYA	8,000		
FYA @ 40%	3,200	4,800	3,200
WDV c/f		10,190	
Total allowances			5,650

Capital allowances due for the period are £5,650, reducing the adjusted profit to £22,800. The first three Schedule D Case I assessments are therefore :

Year	Basis period	Workings	Assessment £
1998/99	1/2/99 to 5/4/99	£22,800 x 2/15	3,040
1999/00	6/4/99 to 5/4/00	£22,800 x 12/15	18,240
2000/01	1/5/99 to 30/4/00	£22,800 x 12/15	18,240

There is an overlap period from 1 May 1999 to 5 April 2000 (11 months) and overlap profits are £22,800 x 11/15 = £16,720.

(b) The capital allowances computation for the year to 30 April 2001 is as follows :

		Pool £	Allowances £
y/e 30/4/01			
WDV b/f		10,190	
Disposals		(2,610)	
		7,580	
WDA @ 25%		1,895	1,895
		5,685	
Additions qualifying for 40% FYA	5,990		
FYA @ 40%	2,396	3,594	2,396
WDV c/f		9,279	
Total allowances			4,291

Capital allowances available in the year to 30 April 2001 are £4,291, reducing the adjusted profit for the year to £27,429 (£31,720 - £4,291). Therefore the 2001/02 Schedule D Case I assessment is £27,429.

EXAMPLE 3

Ian began trading on 1 September 1999, preparing accounts to 31 March each year. His first accounts covered the period from 1 September 1999 to 31 March 2001 and showed an adjusted profit (before deduction of capital allowances) of £72,598. Ian bought and sold plant and machinery as follows :

		£
1 September 1999	Bought plant and machinery	16,000
21 August 2000	Bought plant and machinery	12,000
5 September 2000	Bought plant and machinery	8,000
1 January 2001	Sold plant (original cost £3,700 on 1/9/99)	3,000
31 March 2001	Bought plant and machinery	2,000

Compute Ian's Schedule D Case I assessments for the first two years of assessment.

SOLUTION

Ian's first accounting period covers 19 months. Since this exceeds 18 months it must be divided into two chargeable periods for capital allowances purposes. The first chargeable period is the year to 31 August 2000. The second chargeable period runs from 1 September 2000 to 31 March 2001. The capital allowances computation is as follows :

		Pool	Allowances
		£	£
y/e 31/8/00			
Additions qualifying for 40% FYA		28,000	
FYA @ 40%		11,200	11,200
		———	
		16,800	
1/9/00 - 31/3/01			
Disposals		(3,000)	
		———	
		13,800	
WDA @ 25% x 7/12		2,013	2,013
		———	
		11,787	
Additions qualifying for 40% FYA	10,000		
FYA @ 40%	4,000	6,000	4,000
	———		
WDV c/f		17,787	
		———	
Total allowances			17,213

Ian's profit after deduction of capital allowances is £55,385 (£72,598 - £17,213). His first two Schedule D Case I assessments are :

Year	Basis	Basis period	Workings	Assessment
				£
1999/00	Actual	1/9/99 to 5/4/00	£55,385 x 7/19	20,405
2000/01	12 months to a/c date in year 2	1/4/00 to 31/3/01	£55,385 x 12/19	34,980

Strictly speaking, there is an overlap period from 1 April 2000 to 5 April 2000 but since we are working to the nearest month, the length of this period is zero months and overlap profits are zero.

Balancing allowances and charges

If the total disposal value of the disposals for a chargeable period exceeds the balance of expenditure in the pool (before disposals are deducted) then this is evidence that the capital allowances given to date are greater than the depreciation which has actually occurred. In these circumstances the written down value of the pool is set to zero and a *balancing charge* (a negative capital allowance) is made, equal to the amount of the excess. Balancing adjustments may also be required in the following circumstances:

(a) when a business ceases trading (see later in this chapter)

(b) when a non-pooled asset is disposed of.

Non-pooled assets are those assets which are treated individually for capital allowances purposes and not brought into the pool (see below). When a non-pooled asset is sold, a balancing adjustment is required to ensure that the total capital allowances granted in relation to the asset are exactly equal to the depreciation of the asset whilst owned by the business. The balancing adjustment is calculated as follows:

(a) if the disposal value of the asset exceeds its written down value, a *balancing charge* is made, equal to the excess

(b) if the written down value of the asset exceeds its disposal value, a *balancing allowance* is given, equal to the excess.

Non-pooled assets

The following types of plant and machinery are not brought into the pool:

(a) expensive motor cars

(b) assets with some private use

(c) short-life assets

(d) long-life assets (for certain businesses).

The treatment of each of these types of asset is explained below.

Motor cars

Motor cars costing more than £12,000 do not join the pool but are dealt with on an individual basis and attract a maximum WDA of £3,000 p.a. This rule does not apply to vans and lorries, which join the pool regardless of their cost.

For chargeable periods ending before 6 April 2000, cheaper motors cars were pooled together but were held in a separate pool from the main pool. This separate pool has now been abolished. The balance brought forward on the cars pool is added into the main pool in the first chargeable period ending on or after 6 April 2000.

EXAMPLE 4

Bianca began trading on 1 September 1997 and chose 31 December as her annual accounting date. Her first accounts covered the 16 months to 31 December 1998. On 21 October 1997 she bought a motor car costing £17,600. Compute the capital allowances available on this car for the first three chargeable periods.

SOLUTION

Bianca's first accounts cover a 16-month period. The capital allowances computation is as follows :

	Expensive Car £	Allowances £
1/9/97 - 31/12/98		
Addition	17,600	
WDA restricted to £3,000 x 16/12	4,000	4,000
WDV c/f	13,600	
y/e 31/12/99		
WDA restricted to £3,000	3,000	3,000
WDV c/f	10,600	
y/e 31/12/00		
WDA @ 25% (no restriction necessary)	2,650	2,650
WDV c/f	7,950	

Assets with some private use

An asset which is used partly for private purposes by the *owner* of a business is not pooled but is treated on an individual basis. The capital allowances calculation is carried out in the usual way but the owner of the business may then claim only the business proportion of the allowances which have been calculated.

Note that capital allowances are available in full on assets used partly for private purposes by an *employee* of the business (but the employee may then be assessed on a benefit in kind under Schedule E).

EXAMPLE 5

Allan prepares annual accounts to 31 May. On 1 July 1999 he bought a motor car costing £14,000. Compute the capital allowances available on this car for the first two chargeable periods, assuming 30% private use of the car by Allan.

SOLUTION

	Expensive car (30% private) £	Allowances £
y/e 31/5/00		
Addition	14,000	
WDA restricted to £3,000	3,000 x 70% =	2,100
WDV c/f	11,000	
y/e 31/5/01		
WDA @ 25%	2,750 x 70% =	1,925
WDV c/f	8,250	

Short-life assets

A trader may elect that an asset (other than a motor car) should be treated as a "short-life asset". Such an election has the following consequences :

(a) The asset does not join the pool but is treated on an individual basis (for this reason, the election is known as a "de-pooling" election).

(b) If the asset is not disposed of within four years of the end of the chargeable period in which it is acquired, it joins the pool at its written down value and the de-pooling election will have had no effect.

(c) If the asset is disposed of within the four-year period, a balancing allowance will be given (or a balancing charge will be made).

The election is usually made for assets which are likely to be sold or scrapped within the stated four-year period for less than their WDV's. De-pooling such assets generates balancing allowances on their disposal, so ensuring that capital allowances are given as quickly as possible. A de-pooling election in relation to expenditure incurred during a chargeable period must be made by 31 January in the second tax year following the tax year in which the chargeable period ends.

EXAMPLE 6

Anita begins trading on 1 January 1998, preparing annual accounts to 31 December. On 1 August 1998 she buys general plant and machinery costing £20,000 and a computer system costing £4,000. She sells the computer on 31 October 2000 for £800. Compute her capital allowances for the first three accounting periods if :

(a)   she makes a de-pooling election with regard to the computer

(b)   she does not make the de-pooling election.

SOLUTION

(a)	Pool	Short-life asset	Allowances
	£	£	£
y/e 31/12/98			
Additions	20,000	4,000	
FYA @ 40%	8,000	1,600	9,600
WDV c/f	12,000	2,400	
y/e 31/12/99			
WDA @ 25%	3,000	600	3,600
WDV c/f	9,000	1,800	
y/e 31/12/00			
Disposal		(800)	
Balancing allowance		1,000	1,000
WDA @ 25%	2,250		2,250
WDV c/f	6,750		
Total allowances			3,250

(b)	Pool		Allowances
	£		£
y/e 31/12/98			
Additions	24,000		
FYA @ 40%	9,600		9,600
WDV c/f	14,400		
y/e 31/12/99			
WDA @ 25%	3,600		3,600
WDV c/f	10,800		
y/e 31/12/00			
Disposal	(800)		
	10,000		
WDA @ 25%	2,500		2,500
WDV c/f	7,500		

The de-pooling election increases the capital allowances in the year to 31 December 2000 by £750, at the expense of reducing the WDV c/f (and therefore future capital allowances) by the same amount.

If the computer had been acquired between 1 April 2000 and 31 March 2003 (and if Anita's business is small) the expenditure would have qualified for an FYA of 100% and the short-life asset treatment would have been unnecessary.

Long-life assets

A long-life asset is one with a working life of 25 years or more. As from 26 November 1996, the rate of WDA available in relation to long-life assets acquired by businesses *spending more than £100,000 a year on such assets* is reduced from 25% per annum to 6% per annum. Businesses affected by this rule maintain a separate pool of long-life assets and calculate WDA at 6% per annum on the balance of expenditure in this pool.

In the unlikely event that a small or medium-sized business is affected by the rule on long-life assets, an FYA of 12% is available in relation to long-life assets acquired between 2 July 1997 and 1 July 1998. The types of asset which do not normally qualify for FYA (see above) are also ineligible for this 12% FYA. No FYA is available on long-life assets acquired after 1 July 1998.

Allowances on cessation of trade

When a business ceases trading and all the plant and machinery is disposed of, capital allowances for the final chargeable period are computed as follows :

(a) Items acquired in the final period are added onto the WDV brought forward.

(b) No WDA's or FYA's are given for the final chargeable period.

(c) The disposal value of the pool (and each non-pooled asset) is subtracted from the balance of unrelieved expenditure, giving rise to balancing allowances or balancing charges. Assets taken over personally by the trader are treated as if sold for their market value on the date taken over.

The balancing adjustments normally made on a cessation of trade can be avoided if the business is being taken over by a "connected person" (e.g. the trader's spouse or other relative or a company which the trader controls) so long as an election to this effect is made by both parties. In this case, the final chargeable period is treated in exactly the same way as any other chargeable period (with WDA's and FYA's as appropriate) and the assets are then transferred to the new owner at their WDV's.

EXAMPLE 7

Jake has been trading for many years, preparing accounts to 30 September each year. The written down value of his plant and machinery at 30 September 1999 was :

	£
Pool	11,350
Expensive motor car (20% private use by Jake)	13,200

Jake ceases trading on 30 June 2000. His purchases and sales of plant and machinery in the 9 months to 30 June 2000 are :

		£
15 October 1999	Bought plant	1,150
30 June 2000	Sold all pool items (all for less than original cost)	12,850
30 June 2000	Sold car	12,000

Prepare the capital allowances computation for the 9 months to 30 June 2000.

SOLUTION

	Pool	Expensive car (20% private)	Allowances
	£	£	£
1/10/99 - 30/6/00			
WDV b/f	11,350	13,200	
Additions	1,150		
	12,500		
Disposals	(12,850)	(12,000)	
Balancing allowance/(charge)	(350)	1,200 x 80% = 960	610

Industrial buildings allowances

Capital allowances known as *industrial buildings allowances* (IBA's) are available in relation to "qualifying buildings", which consist of :

(a) industrial buildings

(b) certain hotels.

Industrial buildings

The term "industrial buildings" includes such buildings as :

(a) factories used for manufacturing purposes, or for processing goods and materials in some way

(b) ancillary buildings associated with such factories e.g. warehouses for the storage of raw materials or finished goods

(c) staff welfare buildings (e.g. canteens) provided for the welfare of those working in factories and ancillary buildings

(d) sports pavilions provided for the welfare of employees in *any* trade.

The term does *not* include buildings such as dwelling houses, shops, showrooms and offices (other than drawing offices attached to an industrial building). If a building is used partly as a qualifying industrial building and partly for a non-qualifying purpose, the whole building will qualify for IBA's if the cost of the non-qualifying part does not exceed 25% of the cost of the entire building. If the 25% limit is exceeded only the qualifying part of the building attracts IBA's.

Hotels

IBA's may be claimed in relation to an hotel which satisfies the following conditions :

(a) It offers sleeping accommodation consisting wholly or mainly of "letting bed-rooms" available to the general public and not normally occupied by the same person for more than one month.

(b) It has at least 10 letting bedrooms.

(c) It offers ancillary services including (at least) breakfast, evening meals, cleaning of rooms and bed-making.

(d) It is open for at least four months between April and October.

Accommodation for hotel staff (either in a separate building or forming part of the hotel itself) is regarded as part of the hotel but accommodation for the proprietor's own use is not. For the remainder of this chapter, references to industrial buildings should be taken to include qualifying hotels.

Qualifying expenditure

The IBA's available in relation to an industrial building are based on the "qualifying expenditure" of the person who first uses the building. This is either :

(a) the cost of constructing the building, if constructed by the user

(b) the price paid for the building, if bought unused from a builder

(c) the lower of the price paid for the building and the building's construction cost, if bought unused from someone other than a builder.

In all cases, the cost of land is excluded but the costs of land preparation are allowed, as are professional fees such as those paid to an architect.

EXAMPLE 8

(a) Smith (who does not trade as a builder) buys a building site for £100,000 and then incurs the following costs on the erection of an industrial building on that site :

	£
Levelling the site and preparing foundations	95,000
Architect's fees	50,000
Building costs	650,000

What is Smith's qualifying expenditure for IBA's purposes ?

(b) If the building is sold unused to Brown for £1,000,000 (including £120,000 for the land), what is Brown's qualifying expenditure ?

(c) If instead of buying Smith's building, Brown buys a similar unused building for the same price from a firm of builders, what is Brown's qualifying expenditure ?

SOLUTION

(a) The costs of construction (excluding land) amount to £795,000. This is Smith's qualifying expenditure.

(b) Brown's qualifying expenditure is also £795,000 (i.e. the lower of Smith's original construction cost and £880,000, the price paid by Brown).

(c) If Brown purchases an industrial building from a firm of builders, then the price paid to that builder (which will, of course, include the builder's profit) is fully eligible for IBA's. Therefore Brown's qualifying expenditure is £1,000,000 less the part of that price which is allocated to the land.

Initial allowance

At various times in the past, expenditure on industrial buildings has qualified for an *initial allowance* (IA). IA was most recently available (at a rate of 20%) in relation to expenditure incurred between 1 November 1992 and 31 October 1993, so long as the building concerned was brought into industrial use by the end of 1994.

In general, the chargeable period in which IA is available depends upon the date of the expenditure rather than the date that the building is first brought into industrial use. IA may be disclaimed (wholly or in part) by a trader with low profits (or a loss) so as to avoid wasting personal allowances.

Writing down allowance

A *writing down allowance* (WDA) is available in relation to an industrial building so long as the building is in industrial use at the end of the chargeable period in which IBA's are claimed. The annual WDA is calculated as 4% of qualifying expenditure (2% if the expenditure was incurred before 6 November 1962). Note that :

(a) WDA is available to the holder of the "relevant interest" in a building. This is the interest of the person who first acquired the building (usually the freehold) and is transferred to the new owner when the building is sold.

(b) The relevant interest is *not* transferred when a building is leased, so that WDA is normally given to the landlord of a leased building, not to the tenant. However, the landlord and tenant may jointly elect that the grant of a long lease (i.e. a lease of more than 50 years) should be treated as a sale for capital allowances purposes, in which case WDA will be given to the tenant.

(c) Industrial buildings are treated on an individual basis and are not pooled.

(d) WDA is calculated on the straight line basis (as opposed to the reducing balance basis used for plant and machinery) and is given in proportion to the length of the chargeable period for which allowances are claimed.

(e) Although the Capital Allowances Act 1990 does not provide for partial WDA claims on industrial buildings, the Inland Revenue seems to allow taxpayers to disclaim the WDA wholly or in part.

(f) IA (if available) and WDA can both be claimed in the same chargeable period.

(g) The total allowances given in relation to an industrial building can never exceed the qualifying expenditure. In general, WDA will be given at 4% p.a. for 25 years (or 2% p.a. for 50 years). However, WDA will cease earlier than this if IA has been claimed and may continue beyond the 25 (or 50) years if IBA's are disclaimed in some years.

(h) A building has a "tax life" of 25 (or 50) years, as from the date on which it is first used for any purpose. If a building is used for non-industrial purposes and then later put to industrial use, WDA's may be claimed for the remainder of the building's tax life. In this case, the total WDA's available will be less than 100% of qualifying expenditure. The period between the date on which the building was first used and the date on which it is first used for industrial purposes is covered by "notional allowances" (see below).

EXAMPLE 9

Brian began trading on 1 April 1998, preparing accounts annually to 31 December. His first accounts were for the 9 months to 31 December 1998. On 12 May 1998, he bought a new factory building for £250,000 (excluding the cost of land) and immediately put the building to industrial use. Calculate the IBA's available for Brian's first three chargeable periods.

SOLUTION

	Factory £	Allowances £
1/4/98 - 31/12/98		
Cost	250,000	
WDA @ 4% of £250,000 x 9/12	7,500	7,500
WDV c/f	242,500	
y/e 31/12/99		
WDA @ 4% of £250,000	10,000	10,000
WDV c/f	232,500	
y/e 31/12/00		
WDA @ 4% of £250,000	10,000	10,000
WDV c/f	222,500	

If Brian keeps the building and uses it for industrial purposes throughout its entire tax life, a WDA of £10,000 per annum will be available up to and including the year to 31 December 2022, with a final WDA of £2,500 in the year to 31 December 2023.

Non-industrial use

A building which is not in industrial use at the end of a chargeable period will either be disused or will be in use for a non-industrial purpose. IBA's may be claimed during a period of temporary disuse following a period of industrial use but IBA's may *not* be claimed if a building is being used for a non-industrial purpose.

A "notional WDA" is calculated for a building which is in non-industrial use at the end of a chargeable period and this notional WDA is deducted from the WDV of the building in the usual way. However, the notional WDA is *not* available to the trader.

EXAMPLE 10

Carole prepares annual accounts to 31 March. On 1 July 1998, she buys a new building for £200,000 (excluding the cost of land) and immediately puts it to industrial use. This use continues until 1 October 2001, when she starts using the building for a non-industrial purpose. The building reverts to industrial use on 1 May 2003. Show the capital allowances computation for all years up to and including the year ending 31 March 2004.

SOLUTION

	Building £	Allowances £
y/e 31/3/99, 00 & 01		
Cost	200,000	
WDA @ 4% of £200,000 for 3 years	24,000	24,000
WDV c/f	176,000	
y/e 31/3/02 & y/e 31/3/03		
Notional WDA @ 4% of £200,000 for 2 years	16,000	
WDV c/f	160,000	
y/e 31/3/04		
WDA @ 4% of £200,000	8,000	8,000
WDV c/f	152,000	

Note :

The notional WDA's of £16,000 given in the years to 31 March 2002 and 31 March 2003 serve to reduce the building's WDV but are not available to Carole.

Sale of a building after continual industrial use

If an industrial building which has been in continual industrial use is sold during its tax life of 25 (or 50) years, then :

(a) No WDA is given in the final chargeable period and a balancing adjustment is made in the usual way, calculated by comparing the building's WDV with the disposal proceeds (or original cost, if lower).

(b) The second-hand buyer of the building takes over the right to claim a WDA for the remainder of the building's tax life, calculated by dividing the "residue of expenditure" by the number of years remaining of the tax life. The residue of expenditure is equal to the WDV of the building before the sale, plus any balancing charge and less any balancing allowance made on the sale. In effect, the second-hand buyer's WDA's are calculated on the lower of the original cost of the building and the price for which it was sold.

If a building is sold after the expiry of its tax life then no balancing adjustments are made and the second-hand buyer is unable to claim any WDA.

EXAMPLE 11

Christopher prepares annual accounts to 31 December. On 1 January 1998 he bought a new building for £150,000 (excluding land) and started using it immediately for an industrial purpose. Show the capital allowances computation for all affected years if he sells the building to Dean on 1 July 2001 for :

(a)   £110,000 (excluding land)   (b)   £175,000 (excluding land)

Also calculate the WDA's available to Dean, assuming that he prepares accounts to 31 March each year.

SOLUTION

(a)	Building £	Allowances £
y/e 31/12/98, 99 & 00		
Cost	150,000	
WDA @ 4% of £150,000 for 3 years	18,000	18,000
WDV c/f	132,000	
y/e 31/12/01		
Disposal value	110,000	
Balancing allowance	22,000	22,000

The residue of expenditure is £110,000 (£132,000 - £22,000). The tax life of the building ends on 31 December 2022, giving an unexpired life of 21 years 6 months (21.5 years) on the date of the second-hand purchase by Dean. Dean may therefore claim an annual WDA of £110,000/21.5 = £5,116 for each of the 21 years to 31 March 2022 and a final WDA of £2,564 (to bring the total to £110,000) in the year to 31 March 2023.

(b)	Building	Allowances
	£	£
y/e 31/12/01		
WDV b/f	132,000	
Disposal value (limited to original cost)	150,000	
Balancing charge	(18,000)	(18,000)

The residue of expenditure is £150,000 (£132,000 + £18,000). Therefore Dean may claim an annual WDA of £150,000/21.5 = £6,977 for each of the 21 years to 31 March 2022 and a final WDA of £3,483 in the year to 31 March 2023.

Sale of a building after non-industrial use

As explained above, an industrial building is written down by notional WDA's during a period of non-industrial use. If the building is then sold (within its tax life) the balancing adjustments made on the sale depend upon whether the building is sold for more or less than its original cost.

(a) If the building is sold for *more* than original cost, the balancing charge made on the sale is restricted to the actual allowances given to date (i.e. excluding the notional WDA's).

(b) If the building is sold for *less* than original cost, the required balancing adjustment is calculated as follows :

   (i) "Net cost" $\quad$ = original cost - sale proceeds

   (ii) "Adjusted net cost" $\quad = $ net cost $\times \dfrac{\text{period of industrial use}}{\text{period of total use}}$

   (iii) Balancing adjustment $\quad$ = adjusted net cost - actual allowances given.

(c) The second-hand buyer's WDA's are based on the lower of the residue of expenditure (calculated as before) and the second-hand price paid.

EXAMPLE 12

Rework the above example, assuming that Christopher uses the building for non-industrial purposes between 1 July 1999 and 30 June 2000.

SOLUTION

(a) The period of total use by Christopher is 3 years 6 months (3.5 years), of which 1 year comprises non-industrial use and the remainder comprises industrial use. The building was not in industrial use on 31 December 1999, so only notional WDA's would be calculated for the year to 31 December 1999. The actual allowances given (in the other 2 chargeable periods) are 4% of £150,000 for 2 years = £12,000.

Net cost is £40,000 (£150,000 - £110,000) and adjusted net cost is £28,571 (£40,000 x 2.5/3.5). A balancing allowance of £16,571 (£28,571 - £12,000) would be made.

The residue of expenditure is now £115,429 (£132,000 - £16,571). This exceeds the price paid by Dean so Dean's annual WDA's are equal to £110,000 divided by 21.5.

(b)   The balancing charge is limited to the actual allowances given i.e. £12,000. The residue of expenditure is £144,000 (£132,000 + £12,000) and Dean's annual WDA's are equal to this figure divided by 21.5.

Commercial buildings in enterprise zones

Certain areas of the country are designated as "enterprise zones". IBA's are available in relation to *any* commercial building constructed in an enterprise zone (including shops, showrooms and offices, but not dwellings) so long as the construction expenditure :

(a)   is contracted for within 10 years of the zone's designation, and

(b)   is actually incurred within 20 years of the zone's designation.

An initial allowance of 100% is available for the chargeable period in which the expenditure is incurred. If the full allowance is not claimed, the remaining expenditure is eligible for an annual WDA of 25%, calculated straight-line on the cost of the building and beginning when the building is first brought into use. For example, if an initial allowance of only 30% is claimed, the remaining 70% of the expenditure is eligible for WDA's equal to 25% of the cost of the building in each of the first two years of use and 20% of the cost in the third year.

Agricultural buildings

Agricultural buildings allowances (ABA's) are available in relation to capital expenditure on the construction of farmhouses, farm cottages, farm buildings, fences, drainage works etc. However, no more than one-third of the expenditure on a farmhouse is eligible for ABA's. The cost of land is always excluded. The system of granting allowances is similar (but not identical) to that used for industrial buildings :

(a)   An annual WDA, calculated at 4% per annum on the straight line basis, is given in relation to qualifying expenditure. WDA begins in the chargeable period in which the expenditure is incurred.

(b) Qualifying expenditure incurred between 1 November 1992 and 31 October 1993 attracted an initial allowance of 20%, so long as the building was brought into use by the end of 1994.

(c) The 25-year tax life of an agricultural building begins on the first day of the chargeable period in which ABA's are first given.

Sale of an agricultural building

If an agricultural building is sold during its tax life, and the vendor and buyer do not elect for a balancing adjustment to be made (see below), the buyer simply takes over the right to receive the WDA's that the vendor would have received if the sale had not occurred. The procedure is as follows :

(a) No balancing adjustments are made on the sale and the price paid by the second-hand buyer is totally ignored.

(b) For the chargeable period in which the sale is dealt with, the vendor receives WDA on the building for the last time, calculated at 4% per annum from the start of the chargeable period to the date of the sale.

(c) For the chargeable period in which the purchase is dealt with, the buyer receives WDA for the first time, calculated (on the original cost of the building) at 4% per annum from the date of purchase to the end of the chargeable period.

(d) The buyer then receives WDA of 4% p.a. until the building is fully written off.

If vendor and buyer both elect for the sale of an agricultural building to be treated as a balancing event, then the capital allowances computation is exactly the same as that performed on the sale of an industrial building (see above).

EXAMPLE 13

Bill trades as a farmer, preparing accounts to 31 December each year. On 1 December 1998 he constructed a barn at a cost of £50,000 (excluding land). On 1 August 2000 he sells the barn to Ben for £47,000 (excluding land). Ben also trades as a farmer, preparing accounts to 30 June each year. No election is made for the sale to be treated as a balancing event. Calculate the ABA's available to Bill and Ben.

SOLUTION

Bill's allowances are :

		£
y/e 31/12/98	£50,000 x 4%	2,000
y/e 31/12/99	£50,000 x 4%	2,000
y/e 31/12/00	£50,000 x 4% x 7/12	1,167

Ben's allowances are :

		£
y/e 30/6/01	£50,000 x 4% x 11/12	1,833
y/e 30/6/02 etc.	£50,000 x 4%	2,000

Notes :

(a) Bill's sale is made after 7 months of the accounting period have elapsed, so his final WDA is calculated at 7/12th of 4%.

(b) Ben's purchase is made with 11 months of the accounting period remaining, so his first WDA is calculated at 11/12th of 4%.

(c) Ben will continue to receive WDA's of £2,000 per annum until the barn's WDV reaches zero.

EXAMPLE 14

Rework the Bill and Ben example above, given that an election is made for the sale to be treated as a balancing event.

SOLUTION

Bill's allowances in the years to 31 December 1998 and 1999 total £4,000, reducing the WDV of the barn to £46,000. The barn is sold for £47,000, so a balancing charge of £1,000 is made in the year to 31 December 2000.

The tax life of the building began on 1 January 1998 (the first day of the chargeable period in which ABA's were first given) and ends on 31 December 2022, giving an unexpired life of 22 years and 5 months (22.417 years) on the date of the second-hand purchase by Ben. The residue of expenditure is £47,000 (£46,000 + £1,000). Therefore Ben's annual WDA is £2,097 (£47,000/22.417).

Miscellaneous capital allowances

Capital allowances are available in relation to some miscellaneous categories of capital expenditure, including expenditure on patent rights, know-how and scientific research.

Patent rights

Purchased patent rights are treated in a similar way to plant and machinery for capital allowances purposes.

(a) All patent rights are pooled together.

(b) The pool is adjusted in each chargeable period for acquisitions and disposals and a WDA is then given calculated at 25% per annum on the reducing balance.

(c) As with plant and machinery, disposal value is limited to original cost. But whereas a sale of plant and machinery for more than original cost may give rise to a capital gains tax liability (see Chapter 18), a sale of patent rights for more than original cost gives rise to a Schedule D Case VI income tax liability (see Chapter 6).

(d) If the disposal value of a patent exceeds the balance of unrelieved expenditure in the pool, a balancing charge is made and the pool value is set to zero.

(e) A balancing allowance will arise if :

   (i) there is a cessation of trade and the patents are sold for less than the balance of unrelieved expenditure in the pool, or

   (ii) there is no cessation of trade but the last patent in the pool is sold (or comes to the end of its term) and the disposal value is less than the balance of unrelieved expenditure in the pool. (This treatment is different from that used for plant and machinery).

EXAMPLE 15

Gemma prepares accounts to 31 July each year. At the end of the capital allowances computation for the year to 31 July 1999, the WDV of her patents pool was £3,800.

(a) Calculate the capital allowances due for the year to 31 July 2000 if she acquires no further patents during the year but sells for £1,500 a patent which had cost her £2,000.

(b) Rework the computation given that the sold patent is Gemma's last remaining patent.

SOLUTION

(a)

	Patents pool £	Allowances £
y/e 31/7/00		
WDV b/f	3,800	
Disposals	(1,500)	
	2,300	
WDA @ 25%	575	575
WDV c/f	1,725	

(b) If the last patent has been sold, then a balancing allowance of £2,300 will be given instead of the £575 WDA and the pool will be closed.

Know-how

"Know-how" is defined as industrial information and techniques, of use in either :

(a) manufacturing, or

(b) the processing of goods or materials, or

(c) the working of mineral deposits, or

(d) agricultural, fishing or forestry operations.

All expenditure on know-how is pooled and, in general, capital allowances are calculated as for patent rights. However, if know-how is sold for more than original cost, the disposal value used in the capital allowances computation is the *full sale proceeds*. Depending upon the balance of unrelieved expenditure in the pool prior to the disposal, this will either create a balancing charge or restrict the value of subsequent WDA's. In either case, the profit made on the disposal is, in effect, taxed under Schedule D Case I, thus avoiding the need for a Schedule D Case VI assessment (which would be required if the sale had been of patent rights).

Scientific research

Capital expenditure on scientific research related to the claimant's trade attracts a first year allowance of 100%. Any proceeds subsequently received on the disposal of a scientific research asset are treated as a trading receipt.

Summary

▶ Capital allowances are granted for chargeable periods. Each accounting period ranks as a chargeable period, except that accounting periods exceeding 18 months in length are divided into two or more chargeable periods.

▶ In order to qualify as plant and machinery, an asset must perform an active function in the trade, not merely provide a setting in which the trade is carried on.

▶ Writing down allowances on plant and machinery are granted at 25% per annum, calculated on the reducing balance basis.

▶ A 50% FYA is available on qualifying plant and machinery bought by a small or medium-sized business between 2 July 1997 and 1 July 1998. The FYA is 40% if the expenditure is incurred on or after 2 July 1998. An FYA of 100% is available to small businesses which incur expenditure on information and communications technology between 1 April 2000 and 31 March 2003.

▶ In general, expenditure on plant and machinery is pooled and capital allowances are calculated by reference to the value of the pool. Expensive motor cars are treated individually, as are assets with private use and short-life assets. Long-life assets acquired by certain businesses are pooled separately and attract an annual WDA of 6%, calculated on the reducing balance basis.

► On the cessation of a business, the disposal value of the pool (and of each non-pooled asset) is subtracted from the balance of unrelieved expenditure, giving rise to balancing adjustments.

► Writing down allowances are available on qualifying industrial buildings, hotels and agricultural buildings at a rate of 4% per annum, calculated on the straight line basis. Notional WDA's are deducted if an industrial building is put to non-industrial use. Commercial buildings constructed in enterprise zones are granted an initial allowance of 100%.

► Capital allowances are also available in relation to patent rights, know-how and scientific research expenditure.

Exercises

10.1   Laura began trading on 1 June 1999 and chose 30 June as her annual accounting date. Her first accounts covered the period from 1 June 1999 to 30 June 2000 and showed an adjusted profit (before capital allowances) of £41,780. During this period she bought plant and machinery as follows :

		£
1 June 1999	Bought machinery	8,000
1 June 1999	Bought motor car	15,000
1 July 1999	Bought machinery	4,000
31 March 2000	Bought machinery	6,000

Compute the first two Schedule D Case I assessments, assuming 40% private use of the car by Laura. Also compute the amount of any overlap profits.

10.2   Maurice prepares annual accounts to 31 March. The tax written down values of his plant and machinery at 31 March 2000 were :

	£
Main pool	2,700
Motor cars pool	7,600

He had the following transactions during the year to 31 March 2001 :

		£
1 May 2000	Bought plant	600
11 July 2000	Sold motor car (original cost £7,000)	3,000
11 July 2000	Bought motor car	8,000
1 November 2000	Bought machinery	400
12 January 2001	Sold machinery (original cost £4,000 in 1999)	4,200

Compute the capital allowances claimable for the year to 31 March 2001, assuming no private use of any of the assets.

10.3 Norma began trading on 1 November 1997 and chose 30 June as her annual accounting date. Her first accounts covered the period to 30 June 1999 and showed an adjusted profit (before deduction of capital allowances) of £56,200. Her accounts for the year to 30 June 2000 showed an adjusted profit (before deduction of capital allowances) of £59,900. Plant and machinery was bought and sold as follows :

		£
1 November 1997	Bought plant	10,000
17 May 1998	Bought plant	17,400
12 October 1998	Bought car (40% private use by Norma)	8,800
3 November 1998	Sold plant (original cost £2,000 in November 1997)	1,750
3 November 1998	Bought plant	4,600
1 February 1999	Bought car	7,200
7 August 1999	Sold plant (original cost £1,500 in November 1998)	1,600
8 August 1999	Bought plant	11,500
31 March 2000	Sold car bought on 12 October 1998	6,300
31 March 2000	Bought car (40% private use by Norma)	14,100

Compute Norma's Schedule D Case I assessments for her first four years of assessment. and calculate the amount of any overlap profits.

10.4 Oliver prepares accounts to 30 June each year. On 1 May 1999 he acquired a brand new factory for £100,000 and put the factory to immediate industrial use. The cost of £100,000 included land of £20,000 and offices of £22,500. Calculate the IBA's available for the years to 30 June 1999 and 2000.

10.5 Francesco begins trading on 1 January 1996, producing annual accounts to 31 December. On 1 December 1996 he buys a new workshop for £56,000 (including land £11,000). He begins using the workshop on 1 January 1997 and it is in continual industrial use until 1 July 2004, when he sells it to Maria for £45,000 (including land £15,000). Maria immediately begins to use the workshop for an industrial purpose.

(a) Compute the IBA's available to Francesco for all affected years.

(b) Compute the IBA's available to Maria, who starts trading on 1 May 2004, making her first accounts up to 30 November 2004, and then producing accounts annually to 30 November thereafter.

10.6 Giles has traded as a farmer for many years, preparing annual accounts to 31 March. On 1 July 1999 he constructed a barn at a cost (excluding land) of £30,000. On 1 October 2000, he sold the barn to Pam for £35,000 (excluding land). Pam also trades as a farmer and began trading on 1 May 2000. She made up her first accounts for the period from 1 May 2000 to 31 December 2000 and intends to produce accounts for calendar years thereafter. Calculate the ABA's available to Giles and to Pam :

(a) if no election is made for the sale to be treated as a balancing event

(b) if such an election is made.

*10.7   David has traded for many years, preparing accounts to 31 March annually. On 1 July 1998 he buys a new industrial building for £80,000 (excluding land) and puts the building to immediate industrial use. Throughout David's ownership, the building is always in industrial use apart from the period between 1 January 2001 and 31 December 2003 when it is used for a non-industrial purpose. On 1 February 2006, he sells the building to Diana, who started business on 1 July 2005 and makes up accounts to 30 June each year. Calculate the IBA's available to David and to Diana, if the building was sold for :

(a)   £60,000 (excluding land)   (b)   £120,000 (excluding land).

*10.8   Talat prepares accounts to 31 October each year. The written down value of his plant and machinery after deducting capital allowances for the year to 31 October 1997 was as follows :

	£
Main pool	8,290
Motor cars pool	4,900
Motor car (30% private use by Talat)	14,500

He had the following transactions during the next three years :

		£
y/e 31/10/98		
10 November 1997	Bought plant	2,000
1 January 1998	Sold plant (original cost £4,200 in 1992)	1,310
y/e 31/10/99		
5 May 1999	Sold pool car (original cost £7,500)	3,000
5 May 1999	Bought pool car	8,200
12 June 1999	Bought plant	600
y/e 31/10/00		
5 April 2000	Sold plant (original cost £1,000 in November 1997)	1,150
6 August 2000	Bought plant	900

There were no capital transactions between 1 November 2000 and 31 March 2001, when Talat ceased trading. On 31 March 2001, the plant and machinery was disposed of as follows :

(i)   All of the plant and machinery other than cars was sold for £4,000.

(ii)   Talat took over his own car. Its market value on 31 March 2001 was £8,000.

(iii) There was only one other car remaining and Talat gave this to his brother, who will be using it for private purposes. The market value of the car on 31 March 2001 was £5,900.

Prepare the capital allowances computations for the years to 31 October 1998, 1999 and 2000 and for the period from 1 November 2000 to 31 March 2001.

Chapter 11

Income from self-employment : Trading losses

Introduction

If the computation of a trader's adjusted profit for an accounting period produces a negative result, then a trading loss has been incurred. Such a loss has two main consequences :

(a) the Schedule D Case I assessment for the relevant tax year is set to £nil, and

(b) the trader may be able to claim tax relief in respect of the loss.

Several forms of relief are available and each involves offsetting the trading loss against other income or gains of the trader, so reducing the tax payable on that income or on those gains. The purpose of this chapter is to explain the main features of each form of relief.

Relief for trading losses

In general, trading losses may be relieved in one of two ways :

(a) Under Section 385 of ICTA 1988, a trading loss may be carried forward and relieved against future profits of the same trade.

(b) Under Section 380 of ICTA 1988, trading losses may be relieved against the statutory total income of the trader. A claim under Section 380 may also be extended by a further claim, under Section 72 of the Finance Act 1991, that unrelieved trading losses should be relieved against the trader's capital gains.

Each of these forms of loss relief is described below. The loss reliefs are usually referred to by their section numbers in ICTA 1988 or Finance Act 1991 and this practice is followed for the remainder of this chapter.

Section 385 relief

Unless a trader claims any other form of loss relief, a trading loss is automatically carried forward under Section 385 and relieved against future trading profits. It is important to note the following points :

(a) Relief under Section 385 is given only against future *trading* profits, not against any other form of income.

(b) Furthermore, relief is given only against future trading profits arising from *the same trade* as that in which the loss was incurred. Therefore, if a trader ceases one trade and commences another, the losses of the old trade cannot be carried forward and relieved against the future profits of the new trade. Similarly, if a trader carries on two trades simultaneously, a loss incurred in one of the trades cannot be carried forward and relieved against the future profits of the other trade.

(c) Relief must be given against the *first available* trading profits arising in the future. The maximum possible amount of relief must be taken in each future year until the loss is fully relieved, even if this leaves insufficient income to absorb personal allowances.

EXAMPLE 1

Carla incurred a trading loss of £8,700 in the year to 30 June 1999. Her projected trading profits for the next three years (adjusted for tax purposes) are as follows :

	£
year to 30 June 2000	3,800
year to 30 June 2001	4,200
year to 30 June 2002	18,500

Carla's only other income consists of rents receivable of £500 per annum. Assuming that the trading loss is carried forward under Section 385, calculate her total income for 1999/00 to 2002/03 inclusive.

SOLUTION

	1999/00 £	2000/01 £	2001/02 £	2002/03 £
Schedule D Case I	nil	3,800	4,200	18,500
Less : S385 relief	-	(3,800)	(4,200)	(700)
	-	-	-	17,800
Schedule A	500	500	500	500
Total income	500	500	500	18,300

Notes :

(a)   The Schedule D Case I assessment in 1999/00 is £nil since there is a loss in the basis period for that year.

(b)   The trading loss carried forward is relieved only against future trading profits (not against the rents) and the maximum relief must be given in each year. This results in a waste of personal allowances in 2000/01 and 2001/02. Carla would probably prefer to carry forward the loss in its entirety to 2002/03, where it can be put to good use, but this is not possible.

Capital allowances

As explained in Chapter 8, any capital allowances claimed for an accounting period are treated as a trading expense of that period. Therefore capital allowances are included automatically in the calculation of a trading loss.

It is important to remember that it is not mandatory to claim the maximum capital allowances available for a chargeable period. If a trading loss has been incurred it may be advisable to claim less than the maximum capital allowances (or even none at all) so as to avoid wasting personal allowances. Disclaimed capital allowances are not lost permanently, since higher WDV's are carried forward than would otherwise have been the case and this results in higher capital allowances in future years (see Chapter 10).

EXAMPLE 2

Colin's adjusted trading profits/(losses) for the years to 31 August 1999 and 2000 are :

	Before capital allowances	*Capital allowances available*	*After capital allowances*
	£	£	£
year to 31 August 1999	(8,300)	1,900	(10,200)
year to 31 August 2000	12,400	2,000	10,400

He has no other income. If the trading loss is carried forward under Section 385, should Colin claim maximum capital allowances in these two years ?

SOLUTION

If Colin claims maximum capital allowances in both years, S385 relief in 2000/01 will be £10,200. This will almost entirely absorb the trading profit of £10,400 assessed in that year, leaving only £200 against which to set personal allowances, most of which will therefore be wasted.

It would be better to claim no capital allowances at all for the two years concerned. The loss carried forward under S385 would then be only £8,300 and this would be relieved in 2000/01 against the trading profit of £12,400, leaving income of £4,100 against which to set personal allowances. There would be minimal waste of personal allowances and the capital allowances available to Colin in future years would be increased.

Relief for trade ch[arges]

If a trading loss is incurred in [t]... s is brought forward under Section 385 and ... uite possible that the trader's total income fo... even zero. In consequence, the trader may b... only 10% or 20% and the Inland Revenue r... to claw back all or part of the basic rate tax... Chapter 4).

In these circumstances, Sect... t of any *trade* charges which have been the ... carried forward and set against future trading ... g losses carried forward under Section 385. ... red wholly and exclusively for trade purpose...

Non-trade charges which ... sessment *cannot* be carried forward. If a tr... s in a year, any Section 350 assessment can ... ch can be carried forward) in priority to non...

EXAMPLE 3

Joyce has been self-empl... 31 December each year. Her recent adjusted ...

year to 31 Decembe...
year to 31 Decembe...

She has no other incom... me tax was 23%) she paid trade charges (net) ... 770. In 2000/01, these payments are £1,560 a... 1999/00 and 2000/01, assuming that the tradi...

SOLUTION

		2000/01
		£
Schedule D Case I		18,000
Less : Section 385	1,700	
Section 387 relief	2,000	3,700
	—	14,300
Less : Charges (£2,310 x 100/77)	—	
Charges (£2,340 x 100/78)		3,000
Statutory total income	—	11,300

A Section 350 assessment would be raised for 1999/00 to recover the basic rate tax deducted from the charges of £3,000 (gross). To the extent that this assessment relates to trade charges (£1,540 x 100/77 = £2,000) it is carried forward along with the trading loss.

Section 380 relief

As illustrated earlier, carrying losses forward under Section 385 does not always provide the most satisfactory form of loss relief. Problems associated with Section 385 relief include :

(a) Relief is delayed until sufficient profits arise from the same trade in future years (if, indeed, they ever do).

(b) The trader has no control over the amount of relief given in each year and therefore personal allowances may be wasted.

(c) If tax rates are falling, relief may be given at a lower rate than the rates which were in force when the loss was incurred.

An alternative form of loss relief, which overcomes some of these problems, is provided by Section 380, under which trading losses may be set against the trader's *statutory total income* (i.e. the total income from all sources, less charges on income) for a period of up to two years. It is important to note that :

(a) The trader is under no obligation to make a Section 380 claim. If no such claim is made, trading losses are automatically carried forward under Section 385.

(b) Any unrelieved losses remaining after a Section 380 claim has been made are automatically carried forward under Section 385.

(c) Section 380 relief is available only if the business is being carried on on a commercial basis with a view to making profits. If this is not the case then only Section 385 relief is available.

(d) In the case of farmers and market gardeners (see Chapter 9), a loss is not eligible for Section 380 relief if losses have also been incurred in each of the previous 5 tax years. In these circumstances only Section 385 relief is available.

(e) Section 380 relief is set against income in the order which will result in the lowest tax liability. The best approach is to deduct the relief first from non-savings income, then from savings income and finally from dividends.

Relieving a trading loss under Section 380

Section 380 relief is available in respect of the trading loss "incurred in a year of assessment". In most cases, the loss incurred in a year of assessment is simply the loss incurred in the basis period for that year. The only exception to this rule occurs if a trading loss occurs in an overlap period (see later in this chapter). A trading loss incurred in a tax year may be set against the statutory total income of either :

(a) the tax year in which the loss is incurred, or

(b) the previous tax year, or

(c) both of these years.

A claim for Section 380 relief must be made by 31 January in the second tax year following the tax year in which the loss was incurred. For example, a Section 380 claim in relation to a loss incurred in 2000/01 must be made by 31 January 2003.

The trader can decide whether to make a Section 380 claim for one of the available years, for both years, or for neither of them. But partial claims are not allowed. A Section 380 claim must be for the whole of the trading loss, even if this leaves insufficient income to absorb personal allowances. However, if a claim is made for both available years, and the combined STI of the two years exceeds the amount of the loss, then the trader can decide whether to claim maximum relief in the year of the loss, relieving the remainder of the loss in the previous year, or vice versa. A trading loss may be set against the STI of the previous tax year whether or not the loss-making trade was being carried on in that year.

If two Section 380 claims are made for the same year (one for a trading loss incurred in the current year and one for a trading loss incurred in the subsequent year) the claim in respect of the current year's loss takes priority.

EXAMPLE 4

Ashok has been trading for many years, preparing annual accounts to 30 June. Recent trading profits/(losses), adjusted for tax purposes, are as follows :

	£
year to 30 June 1998	12,400
year to 30 June 1999	9,300
year to 30 June 2000	(9,500)

He has other income amounting to £4,000 per annum and claims only the personal allowance. Show his possible Section 380 claims. Which of these claims (if any) should be recommended ?

SOLUTION

The Schedule D Case I assessments are :

Year	Basis period	Assessment
		£
1998/99	y/e 30/6/98	12,400
1999/00	y/e 30/6/99	9,300
2000/01	y/e 30/6/00	nil

Ashok could make a Section 380 claim for 2000/01, or for 1999/00, or for both years, or for neither year :

(a)   A claim for 2000/01 only would relieve £4,000 of the loss against his other income, leaving no tax liability for the year and losses of £5,500 to carry forward under Section 385. This would be a waste, since the other income of £4,000 would have been covered by personal allowances anyway.

(b)   A claim for 1999/00 only would relieve the entire loss against that year's STI of £13,300 (£9,300 + £4,000), leaving income of £3,800 (£13,300 - £9,500) against which to set personal allowances. There would be some wastage of personal allowances but the tax liability for 1999/00 would become zero. This seems to be a fairly efficient way of relieving the loss.

(c)   A claim for both years is pointless, since :

   (i)   a claim giving maximum relief in 1999/00 would leave no losses to relieve in 2000/01, and

   (ii)   a claim giving maximum relief in 2000/01 leads to a waste of personal allowances in that year (see above).

(d)   A claim for neither year would result in the entire loss being carried forward under Section 385. This would mean that loss relief would be delayed until such time as sufficient profits of the same trade arose in future years.

On balance, a Section 380 claim for 1999/00 might be recommended. This claim combines early relief of the loss with a fairly small wastage of personal allowances. The claim would have to be made by 31 January 2003.

Section 72 relief

If a Section 380 claim is made for a tax year and the effect of that claim is to reduce the trader's total income for the year to nil, a claim may also be made under Section 72 of the Finance Act 1991 for any unrelieved part of the loss to be set against the trader's capital gains for the year. The time limit for making such a claim is the same as for Section 380 relief. Section 72 relief is considered further in Chapter 16.

Losses on commencement of trade

Losses incurred in the opening years of trading may, just like any other trading losses, be carried forward under Section 385 or set against statutory total income under Section 380. But, in addition to these forms of relief, Section 381 of ICTA 1988 allows trading losses incurred in any of the first 4 tax years to be set against the statutory total income of the three previous years. Note that :

(a) Section 381 relieves the trading loss incurred in a tax year against the STI of the three previous tax years, beginning with the earliest year. For example, a trading loss incurred in 2000/01 could be set against the STI of 1997/98, 1998/99 and 1999/00, in that order.

(b) A Section 381 claim, if made, applies to *all* of the three years previous to the loss-making year. The trader cannot specify the years in which relief is to be given or the amount of relief to be given in each year. The maximum possible relief is given in each year and this may result in a wastage of personal allowances.

(c) Relief is given against income in the order which results in the lowest tax liability.

(d) Claims under Section 381 must be made by 31 January in the second tax year following the loss-making tax year.

(e) Unlike a Section 380 claim, a claim under Section 381 cannot be extended so as to set unrelieved trading losses against capital gains.

(f) A loss incurred in an overlap period is treated as *a loss of the earlier tax year only*. This rule ensures that a loss is relieved only once.

EXAMPLE 5

Carl begins trading on 1 July 1998 and chooses 30 June as his accounting date. His adjusted profits/(losses) for the first two accounting years are as follows :

	£
year to 30 June 1999	(31,200)
year to 30 June 2000	(12,400)

Now that he is self-employed, Carl has no other income. Prior to becoming self-employed his only income was from employment, as follows :

	£
1995/96	14,900
1996/97	15,760
1997/98	16,120
1998/99 (to 30 June 1998)	4,180

Assuming that Carl makes all possible Section 381 claims, calculate his total income for years 1995/96 to 1998/99 inclusive.

SOLUTION

The losses which are eligible for Section 381 relief are :

Year	Basis period	Workings	Loss	Years for S381 claim
			£	
1998/99	1/7/98 to 5/4/99	£(31,200) x 9/12	(23,400)	95/96-97/98
1999/00	1/7/98 to 30/6/99	£(31,200) - overlap £(23,400)	(7,800)	96/97-98/99
2000/01	y/e 30/6/00		(12,400)	97/98-99/00

The Schedule D Case I assessments for 1998/99 through to 2000/01 will of course be £nil. If all possible Section 381 claims are made, total income for years 1995/96 to 1998/99 is :

	1995/96 £	1996/97 £	1997/98 £	1998/99 £
Schedule E	14,900	15,760	16,120	4,180
Less : Section 381 relief :				
1998/99 loss	(14,900)	(8,500)		
1999/00 loss		(7,260)	(540)	
2000/01 loss			(12,400)	
Total income (after loss reliefs)	-	-	3,180	4,180

Losses on cessation of trade

In normal circumstances, a trader has a choice between carrying forward trading losses under Section 385 or relieving such losses against total income under Section 380. But if a loss is incurred in the final year of trading the first of these alternatives is not available since there can be no future profits against which to set the loss. In order to remedy this situation, Section 388 of ICTA 1988 provides a relief known as "terminal loss relief" which allows a trading loss incurred in the last 12 months of trading to be set against the trading profits of the tax year in which the cessation occurs and the previous three tax years.

In effect, terminal loss relief is a form of Section 385 relief which works backwards rather than forwards.

Calculating the terminal loss

The "terminal loss" eligible for relief is the trading loss incurred in the final 12 months of trading, excluding any part of the loss which is relieved under Section 380. The terminal loss is calculated by adding together the following components :

(a) *Losses* :

    (i)   the actual trading loss incurred from 6 April to the date of the cessation

    (ii) the actual trading loss incurred from a date 12 months before the cessation to the following 5 April

(b) *Trade charges* :

    (i)   any trade charges of the final tax year on which a Section 350 assessment has been raised

    (ii) any trade charges of the previous tax year on which a Section 350 assessment has been raised (restricted so that only trade charges of the final 12 months are included in the calculation altogether).

If either (a)(i) or (a)(ii) yields a profit, this profit counts as zero in the calculation of the terminal loss. Any available overlap relief is added to the terminal loss.

EXAMPLE 6

Andrea ceases trading on 31 October 2001. Her adjusted profits/(losses) for the closing accounting periods are as follows :

	£
year to 31 December 1999	6,600
year to 31 December 2000	2,400
10 months to 31 October 2001	(22,500)

Her trade charges and her other income are as follows :

	2000/01	2001/02
	£	£
Trade charges paid net (gross amounts)	6,000	3,000
Other income	nil	nil

Overlap profits of £3,200 arose when Andrea began trading. Calculate the amount of the terminal loss, assuming that no Section 380 claims are made.

SOLUTION

			£
(a)	*Losses* :		
	(i) 6/4/01 to 31/10/01	£(22,500) x 7/10	(15,750)
	Overlap relief		(3,200)
	(ii) 1/11/00 to 5/4/01	£2,400 x 2/12 + £(22,500) x 3/10	(6,350)
(b)	*Trade charges* :		
	(i) S350 assessment in 2001/02		(3,000)
	(ii) S350 assessment in 2000/01 £6,000, restricted to £6,000 x 5/12		(2,500)
Terminal loss			(30,800)

Notes :

1. Taxable income for 2000/01 is £nil (profits of £2,400 are covered by the personal allowance). Taxable income for 2001/02 is also £nil. Section 350 assessments would be raised in both years to recover the basic rate tax deducted from charges.
2. Trade charges for 2001/02 cover 7 months (6 April 2001 to 31 October 2001) so no more than 5 months' worth of the trade charges for 2000/01 can be taken into account when calculating the terminal loss.

Relieving the terminal loss

As stated above, the terminal loss may be relieved against the trading profits of the year of cessation and the three tax years preceding the year of cessation. Note that :

(a) Relief is given in later years first. For example, a terminal loss arising as a consequence of a business ceasing to trade during 2000/01 would be set against the trading profits of 2000/01, 1999/00, 1998/99 and 1997/98, in that order.

(b) The trader cannot specify how much relief is given in each year. The maximum possible relief must be given in each year even if this results in a wastage of personal allowances.

(c) Relief is given after the deduction from trading profits of any charges paid net which are not covered by other income.

EXAMPLE 7

Brendan ceases trading on 30 June 2000. His recent profits/(losses) are as follows :

	£
year to 31 January 1998	24,700
year to 31 January 1999	12,500
year to 31 January 2000	10,560
5 months to 30 June 2000	(27,300)

He pays charges (net of income tax) and receives other income as follows :

	1997/98	1998/99	1999/00	2000/01
	£	£	£	£
Trade charges (gross amounts)	2,000	2,000	2,000	2,000
Non-trade charges (gross amounts)	500	500	500	500
Other income	nil	nil	nil	nil

Overlap profits of £2,700 arose when Brendan began trading. Calculate the amount of the terminal loss (assuming that no Section 380 claims are made) and show how this may be relieved.

SOLUTION

The calculation of the terminal loss is as follows :

			£
(a)	*Losses* :		
	(i) 6/4/00 to 30/6/00	£(27,300) x 3/5	(16,380)
	Overlap relief		(2,700)
	(ii) 1/7/99 to 5/4/00	£10,560 x 7/12 + £(27,300) x 2/5	(4,760)
(b)	*Trade charges* :		
	(i) Section 350 assessment in 2000/01		(2,000)
	(ii) Section 350 assessment in 1999/00		nil
Terminal loss			(25,840)

The loss may be relieved as follows :

	1997/98	1998/99	1999/00	2000/01
	£	£	£	£
Adjusted profit	24,700	12,500	10,600	nil
<u>Less</u> : Charges	2,500	2,500	2,500	-
	22,200	10,000	8,100	-
<u>Less</u> : Terminal loss relief :				
(i) 1999/00			(8,100)	
(ii) 1998/99		(10,000)		
(iii) 1997/98	(7,740)			
Total income	14,460	-	-	-

Post-cessation expenditure

As a general rule, post-cessation expenditure which was not provided for in the final accounts of a business is relieved against any post-cessation receipts assessed under Schedule D Case VI. If post-cessation receipts are insufficient to absorb post-cessation expenditure, the excess expenditure is normally unrelieved.

However, certain categories of unrelieved post-cessation expenditure may be set against the taxpayer's income and capital gains for the year of assessment in which the expenditure is incurred. The main categories of post-cessation expenditure which may be relieved in this way are :

(a) the costs of remedying defective work done whilst the business was operating, together with associated legal costs and insurance premiums

(b) bad debts which were not provided for in the accounts of the business, together with associated debt collection costs.

Transfer of a business to a company

If the owner of a business transfers that business to a limited company, there is a change in the legal ownership of the business and the vendor is deemed to have ceased trading. As a consequence, any trading losses sustained by the vendor before the date of the transfer cannot be carried forward and set against the company's trading profits.

Relief for these losses might be sought under Section 380 or (if the losses were incurred in the final 12 months of trading) in the form of terminal loss relief, but an alternative is provided by Section 386 of ICTA 1988. Section 386 provides that :

(a) if a business is transferred wholly or mainly in exchange for shares in a company, and

(b) the vendor of the business continues to hold those shares, and

(c) the company continues to carry on the transferred business, then

(d) the vendor may set his or her unrelieved trading losses against the first available income that he or she receives from the company.

The offset is against earned income (e.g. salaries and directors' fees) in priority to dividends.

Losses on shares in unlisted trading companies

An individual who *subscribes* for shares in an unlisted UK trading company and then incurs a capital loss on the disposal of those shares may claim that this loss should be set against his or her total income as if it were a trading loss being relieved under Section 380. This relief is provided by Section 574 of ICTA 1988 and a Section 574 claim in a year of assessment takes priority over any Section 380 or Section 381 claims made for the same year.

Tax relief under Section 574 is available only if the trading company concerned is of a type which would qualify for the purposes of the Enterprise Investment Scheme (see Chapter 6).

Summary

► Under Section 385 of ICTA 1988, a trading loss may be carried forward and relieved against future profits of the same trade.

► Under Section 380 of ICTA 1988, trading losses may be relieved against the statutory total income of the trader for a specified two-year period.

► Under Section 72 of the Finance Act 1991, any losses remaining unrelieved after a Section 380 claim has been made for a tax year may be set against the trader's capital gains for that year.

► Trade charges which have been the subject of a Section 350 assessment may be carried forward as if they were trading losses.

► On a commencement of trade, a loss incurred in any of the first four tax years may be set against the STI of the previous three tax years.

► On a cessation of trade, a trading loss incurred during the final 12 months of trading may be set against the trading profits of the year in which trade ceases and the previous 3 years.

► If a business is transferred to a company, the unrelieved trading losses of the vendor may (subject to certain conditions) be set against the first available income which the vendor receives from the company.

Exercises

11.1   Sally, who has been trading for many years, incurs an adjusted trading loss of £10,000 in the year to 31 December 2000.

(a)   What is her Schedule D Case I assessment for 2000/01 ?

(b)   If she makes no claim under Section 380, how will the loss be relieved ?

(c)   How will the loss be relieved if she does make a Section 380 claim ?

11.2   Jane is self-employed. Her recent adjusted trading profits/(losses) are :

	£
year to 31 May 1998	(18,860)
year to 31 May 1999	4,710
year to 31 May 2000	6,210
year to 31 May 2001	14,810

Jane has other income of £5,000 per annum. Assuming that the trading loss is carried forward under Section 385, calculate her total income for tax years 1998/99 through to 2001/02.

11.3   Marcus begins trading on 1 January 1999 and has the following results :

	Adjusted profits/(losses) before capital allces £	Capital allowances claimed £
year to 31 December 1999	12,720	2,460
year to 31 December 2000	(8,480)	1,320

(a)   Compute the Schedule D Case I assessments (before any loss relief) for 1998/99 to 2000/01.

(b)   Assuming that Marcus has no other income, show his possible Section 380 claims. Which (if any) of these claims should be recommended ?

11.4   Nathan begins trading on 1 October 1998, making up accounts to 31 December each year. His first two sets of accounts show the following adjusted losses :

	£
15 months to 31 December 1999	(11,850)
year to 31 December 2000	(9,660)

He has had no other income since becoming self-employed but his income before he started trading was as follows :

	£
1995/96	6,100
1996/97	6,250
1997/98	6,400
1998/99 (to 30 September 1998)	3,450

Assuming that all possible Section 381 claims are made, calculate Nathan's total income for years 1995/96 to 1998/99.

***11.5**   Olive ceases trading on 31 May 2001. Her recent adjusted profits/(losses) are :

	£
year to 30 June 1997	37,450
year to 30 June 1998	39,190
year to 30 June 1999	22,870
year to 30 June 2000	(6,840)
11 months to 31 May 2001	(36,300)

Her charges (paid net) are as follows :

	1998/99 £	1999/00 £	2000/01 £	2001/02 £
Trade charges (gross amounts)	1,500	1,500	1,500	1,500
Non-trade charges (gross amounts)	6,750	6,750	6,750	6,750

She had no other income in any of these years. Overlap relief of £4,390 is available. Calculate the terminal loss and show how this would be relieved (assuming that no Section 380 claims are made).

*11.6   Craig began trading on 1 August 1998 and has the following results :

	Adjusted profits/(losses) before capital allces £	Capital allowances claimed £
year to 31 July 1999	5,460	1,140
year to 31 July 2000	(17,400)	1,920

Before commencing to trade, Craig had only investment income. He sold all of his investments in July 1999 (realising a large capital gain) so as to raise extra working capital for his own business. His income from investments in recent years has been :

	£
1996/97	3,150
1997/98	3,040
1998/99	1,390
1999/00 (to July 1999)	110

(a)   Compute the Schedule D Case I assessments for 1998/99 to 2000/01.

(b)   Explain the loss reliefs available to Craig. Which would you recommend ?

Chapter 12

Income from self-employment : Partnerships

Introduction

The purpose of this chapter is to explain the taxation treatment of partnerships. In many ways, a partnership is treated for tax purposes in much the same way as a sole trader, and the rules given in Chapters 8 to 11 as regards computation of the adjusted profit, basis periods, capital allowances and losses apply to partnerships as well as to sole traders. The important new problem which arises when considering partnership taxation is that of calculating each partner's individual tax liability and much of this chapter is devoted to that problem.

Principles of partnership taxation

Under the partnership tax rules, a partnership is not regarded as a separate entity for taxation purposes and assessments are not raised on the partnership itself. Instead, the profits of the partnership are allocated between the partners and assessments are then raised on the partners as individuals. In detail, the procedure for each tax year is as follows :

(a) The partnership submits a tax return to the Inland Revenue. This return provides information on the profit or loss for the accounting period ending in the tax year and gives details of the profit-sharing agreement in force during that period. The return is also used to :

   (i) claim capital allowances for the accounting period (both on partnership assets and on individual partners' assets)

   (ii) claim relief for any business expenses which have been incurred by partners personally.

(b) The adjusted trading profit or loss of the partnership is calculated in the usual way. Any drawings or other appropriations of profit made by the partners are disallowed. Capital allowances on partnership assets are treated as a trading expense.

(c) The adjusted trading profit or loss is then allocated between the partners according to the profit-sharing agreement in force during the accounting period. If the agreement changes during the period, it is necessary to time-apportion the profit or loss, applying the old agreement to the pre-change profit or loss and the new agreement to the post-change profit or loss.

(d) Any capital allowances claimed on an individual partner's assets and any expenses incurred personally by a partner are deducted from the relevant partner's share of the adjusted profit or added to that partner's share of the adjusted loss.

(e) Partners are then assessed to tax individually, as if each partner's share of the partnership profit or loss had arisen from a trade carried on by that partner alone. In effect, each partner is treated as a sole trader who :

   (i)   begins trading when joining the partnership

   (ii) has the same accounting periods as the partnership (except that a partner who joins or leaves the partnership part-way through an accounting period will have an individual accounting period which begins or ends part-way through a partnership accounting period)

   (iii) ceases trading when leaving the partnership.

(f) Each partner is solely responsible for the tax due on his or her share of the partnership profit. Partners must include their share of the partnership profit or loss in their own tax returns and in their self-assessment calculations.

EXAMPLE 1

Tom, Dick and Harry begin trading as a partnership on 1 January 1999, sharing profits in the ratio 3:2:1. With effect from 1 January 2000, they agree that Harry should receive a salary of £4,000 p.a., that partners should be entitled to 4% p.a. interest on capital and that remaining profits should be shared in the ratio 5:3:2. The adjusted profits of the partnership are :

	£
y/e 31/12/99	18,000
y/e 31/12/00	22,000

Fixed capitals are Tom £10,000, Dick £12,000, Harry £16,000. Compute each partner's Schedule D Case I assessment for 1998/99, 1999/00 and 2000/01.

SOLUTION

The allocation of profit for each accounting period is :

	Tom £	Dick £	Harry £	Total £
y/e 31/12/99				
Profit (shared 3:2:1)	9,000	6,000	3,000	18,000
y/e 31/12/00				
Salary	-	-	4,000	4,000
Interest on capital	400	480	640	1,520
Remainder of profit (shared 5:3:2)	8,240	4,944	3,296	16,480
	8,640	5,424	7,936	22,000

Each partner is treated as a sole trader, commencing trade on 1 January 1999, making up accounts to 31 December and with profits for the first two accounting years as shown above. The assessments on each partner are :

Tom

Year	Basis period	Workings	Assessment £
1998/99	1/1/99 to 5/4/99	£9,000 x 3/12	2,250
1999/00	y/e 31/12/99		9,000
2000/01	y/e 31/12/00		8,640

Dick

Year	Basis period	Workings	Assessment £
1998/99	1/1/99 to 5/4/99	£6,000 x 3/12	1,500
1999/00	y/e 31/12/99		6,000
2000/01	y/e 31/12/00		5,424

Harry

Year	Basis period	Workings	Assessment £
1998/99	1/1/99 to 5/4/99	£3,000 x 3/12	750
1999/00	y/e 31/12/99		3,000
2000/01	y/e 31/12/00		7,936

Note :

In each case, the overlap period is from 1 January 1999 to 5 April 1999. Overlap profits are Tom £2,250, Dick £1,500 and Harry £750. These overlap profits will be relieved when the relevant partner leaves the partnership (or on a change of accounting date).

Notional profits and losses

Occasionally, the effect of taking into account partners' salaries and/or interest on capital is to allocate a loss to an individual partner, even though the partnership as a whole has made a profit. In these circumstances, that partner's share of the partnership assessment is set to £nil and then his or her "notional loss" is allocated between the remaining partners in proportion to their original profit allocations. A similar procedure is followed if a partner is allocated a "notional profit" in a year in which the partnership as a whole has sustained a loss.

EXAMPLE 2

(a) Lock, Stock and Barrel are in partnership, making up accounts to 30 June each year. Their profit-sharing agreement specifies that Lock and Barrel should receive annual salaries of £20,000 and £24,000 respectively and that remaining profits or losses should be divided equally. The partnership has an adjusted profit of £26,000 in the year to 30 June 2000. Show how this profit will be allocated between the partners.

(b) Rod, Pole and Perch are in partnership, also making up accounts to 30 June each year. Their profit-sharing agreement specifies that Perch should receive an annual salary of £25,000 and that remaining profits or losses should be shared in the ratio 3:2:1. The partnership has an adjusted loss of £5,000 in the year to 30 June 2000. Show how this loss will be allocated between the partners.

SOLUTION

(a)

	Lock £	Stock £	Barrel £	Total £
Salaries	20,000	-	24,000	44,000
Remainder (£26,000 - £44,000)	(6,000)	(6,000)	(6,000)	(18,000)
	14,000	(6,000)	18,000	26,000
Stock's notional loss divided in the ratio 14,000 : 18,000	(2,625)	6,000	(3,375)	-
Allocation of profit for the year	11,375	-	14,625	26,000

(b)

	Rod £	Pole £	Perch £	Total £
Salaries	-	-	25,000	25,000
Remainder (£5,000 + £25,000)	(15,000)	(10,000)	(5,000)	(30,000)
	(15,000)	(10,000)	20,000	(5,000)
Perch's notional profit divided 15,000 : 10,000	12,000	8,000	(20,000)	-
Allocation of loss for the year	(3,000)	(2,000)	-	(5,000)

Change in partnership composition

A change in partnership composition occurs if a new partner joins the partnership or if an existing partner dies or leaves the partnership. Such a change has no effect on those persons who were carrying on the trade before the change (either alone or in partnership) and who continue to carry on the trade after the change (either alone or in partnership). Such persons are taxed on the current year basis as if the change had not taken place. But new partners have commenced trading and are subject to the commencement rules, whilst leaving partners have ceased trading and are subject to the cessation rules.

EXAMPLE 3

Red and White begin trading as a partnership on 1 October 1997, sharing profits equally. On 1 January 1999, they agree to admit Blue as a partner and to share profits in the ratio 3:2:1. The adjusted profits of the partnership are :

	£
y/e 30/9/98	21,000
y/e 30/9/99	24,000
y/e 30/9/00	27,000

Compute each partner's Schedule D Case I assessment for the years 1997/98 through to 2000/01.

SOLUTION

The allocation of profit for each accounting period is :

	Red £	White £	Blue £	Total £
y/e 30/9/98 (shared equally)	10,500	10,500	-	21,000
y/e 30/9/99				
1/10/98 - 31/12/98				
£24,000 x 3/12 (shared equally)	3,000	3,000	-	6,000
1/1/99 - 30/9/99				
£24,000 x 9/12 (shared 3:2:1)	9,000	6,000	3,000	18,000
	12,000	9,000	3,000	24,000
y/e 30/9/00 (shared 3:2:1)	13,500	9,000	4,500	27,000

For tax purposes, each partner is now treated as a sole trader and is assessed on his or her share of the partnership profit. The position of each partner is as follows :

(a) Red began trading on 1 October 1997, preparing accounts to 30 September. Each accounting period is 12 months long. Profits are £10,500 for the year to 30/9/98, £12,000 for the year to 30/9/99 and £13,500 for the year to 30/9/00.

(b) White began trading on 1 October 1997, preparing accounts to 30 September. Each accounting period is 12 months long. Profits are £10,500 for the year to 30/9/98, £9,000 for the year to 30/9/99 and £9,000 for the year to 30/9/00.

(c) Blue began trading on 1 January 1999, preparing accounts to 30 September. The first accounts cover the 9-month period from 1/1/99 to 30/9/99 with profits of £3,000. Profits are £4,500 for the year to 30/9/00.

The assessments on each partner are as follows :

Red

Year	Basis period	Workings	Assessment £
1997/98	1/10/97 to 5/4/98	£10,500 x 6/12	5,250
1998/99	y/e 30/9/98		10,500
1999/00	y/e 30/9/99		12,000
2000/01	y/e 30/9/00		13,500

White

Year	Basis period	Workings	Assessment £
1997/98	1/10/97 to 5/4/98	£10,500 x 6/12	5,250
1998/99	y/e 30/9/98		10,500
1999/00	y/e 30/9/99		9,000
2000/01	y/e 30/9/00		9,000

Blue

Year	Basis period	Workings	Assessment £
1998/99	1/1/99 to 5/4/99	£3,000 x 3/9	1,000
1999/00	1/1/99 to 31/12/99	£3,000 + £4,500 x 3/12	4,125
2000/01	y/e 30/9/00		4,500

Note :

In the case of Red and White, the overlap period is from 1 October 1997 to 5 April 1998 and each partner has overlap profits of £5,250. In the case of Blue, there is an overlap period from 1 January 1999 to 5 April 1999 and another overlap period from 1 October 1999 to 31 December 1999. Blue's overlap profits are £1,000 + £4,500 x 3/12 = £2,125.

Non-trading income

A partnership which has trading income may also have non-trading income. For assessment purposes, non-trading income falls into two categories :

(a) **Taxed income**

For this purpose, "taxed income" is defined as income from which tax has been deducted at source (e.g. most types of bank interest) and Schedule F income (i.e. dividends). The amount of any taxed income arising in an accounting period is allocated between the partners in profit-sharing ratio and then each partner's share is apportioned between tax years and assessed on the actual basis.

(b) **Untaxed income**

For this purpose, "untaxed income" is defined as non-trading income which is not taxed income (e.g. income from property or interest received gross). The amount of any untaxed income arising in an accounting period is allocated between the partners in profit-sharing ratio and is then assessed using *the same basis periods as those used for the trading income.* The basis periods that would normally be applied if the income were received by an individual rather than a partnership are totally ignored. If this treatment results in non-trading income being taxed twice when a partner starts trading, overlap relief is available.

If a partnership does not carry on a trade or profession, the treatment described at (a) above applies to *all* of the partnership's non-trading income.

EXAMPLE 4

Hook, Line and Sinker begin trading as a partnership on 1 July 1998, sharing profits equally. The chosen accounting date is 30 June and the first accounts are made up for the year to 30 June 1999. In addition to its trading income, the partnership has non-trading income as follows :

	y/e 30/6/99	y/e 30/6/00
	£	£
Income from property	1,500	1,800
Net bank interest	2,400	3,600

(a) Compute each partner's Schedule A assessment for tax years 1998/99, 1999/00 and 2000/01.

(b) Compute the gross amount of bank interest assessed on each partner in tax years 1998/99 and 1999/00.

SOLUTION

(a)   Each partner is allocated property income of £500 in the year to 30 June 1999 and £600 in the year to 30 June 2000. The Schedule A assessments on each partner are as follows :

Year	Basis period	Workings	Assessment £
1998/99	1/7/98 to 5/4/99	£500 x 9/12	375
1999/00	y/e 30/6/99		500
2000/01	y/e 30/6/00		600

Each partner is entitled to overlap relief of £375.

(b)   Each partner is allocated net bank interest of £800 in the year to 30 June 1999 and £1,200 in the year to 30 June 2000. When grossed-up at 100/80, these figures become £1,000 and £1,500 respectively. The gross amount of bank interest assessed on each partner is as follows :

Year	Workings	Assessment £
1998/99	£1,000 x 9/12	750
1999/00	£1,000 x 3/12 + £1,500 x 9/12	1,375

The remaining 3/12th of the bank interest received during the year to 30 June 2000 will be assessed in 2000/01, along with the first 9/12th of any bank interest received in the year to 30 June 2001.

Trading losses

As explained above, a trading loss is allocated between the partners in the same way as a trading profit. Each partner is then entitled to precisely the same loss reliefs as a sole trader (see Chapter 11) with regard to his or her share of the loss.

EXAMPLE 5

Game, Set and Match begin trading in partnership on 1 August 1998, preparing accounts to 31 January each year and sharing profits equally. With effect from 1 March 1999, they agree to share profits in the ratio 1:2:2. The adjusted profits/(losses) of the partnership are as follows :

	£
period to 31/1/99	8,610
y/e 31/1/00	4,320
y/e 31/1/01	(7,420)

Compute each partner's Schedule D Case I assessment for tax years 1998/99, 1999/00 and 2000/01. Explain how the loss incurred in the year to 31 January 2001 will be treated.

SOLUTION

The allocation of profit for each accounting period is :

	Game £	Set £	Match £	Total £
period to 31/1/99 (shared equally)	2,870	2,870	2,870	8,610
y/e 31/1/00				
1/2/99 - 28/2/99				
£4,320 x 1/12 (shared equally)	120	120	120	360
1/3/99 - 31/1/00				
£4,320 x 11/12 (shared 1:2:2)	792	1,584	1,584	3,960
	912	1,704	1,704	4,320
y/e 31/1/01 (shared 1:2:2)	(1,484)	(2,968)	(2,968)	(7,420)

The assessments on each partner are as follows :

Game

Year	Basis period	Workings	Assessment £
1998/99	1/8/98 to 5/4/99	£2,870 + £912 x 2/12	3,022
1999/00	y/e 31/1/00		912
2000/01	y/e 31/1/01		nil

Set

Year	Basis period	Workings	Assessment £
1998/99	1/8/98 to 5/4/99	£2,870 + £1,704 x 2/12	3,154
1999/00	y/e 31/1/00		1,704
2000/01	y/e 31/1/01		nil

Match

Year	Basis period	Workings	Assessment £
1998/99	1/8/98 to 5/4/99	£2,870 + £1,704 x 2/12	3,154
1999/00	y/e 31/1/00		1,704
2000/01	y/e 31/1/01		nil

Notes :

(i) The basis period for 1998/99 for each partner includes 2 months out of the year to 31 January 2000. The profit for these 2 months is calculated by taking 2/12th of the partner's profit for that year. In the case of Game (for example) it would be wrong to take £120 + 1/11 x £792 as the profit of the period from 1/2/99 to 5/4/99.

(ii) Each partner has overlap profits, calculated in the usual way.

(iii) Each partner may choose individually how to relieve his or her share of the loss incurred in the basis period for 2000/01. Possibilities include carrying the loss forward under S385, a S380 claim for 2000/01 and/or 1999/00 and a S381 claim for 1997/98, 1998/99 and 1999/00.

Summary

► Under the partnership tax rules, Schedule D Case I assessments are raised on each partner individually and each partner is solely responsible for his or her tax liability.

► The trading income of a partnership is allocated between the partners according to the profit-sharing agreement for the accounting period in which the income arises. Notional profits and losses allocated to a partner are redistributed among the remaining partners.

► In effect, each partner is treated as a sole trader who begins trading when joining the partnership, has the same accounting dates as the partnership and ceases trading when leaving the partnership.

► The tax treatment of the non-trading income of a partnership depends upon whether the income ranks as taxed income or untaxed income and whether or not the partnership also has trading income.

► The trading losses of a partnership are allocated between the partners in the same way as trading profits. Each partner may then choose individually how to relieve his or her share of the loss.

Exercises

12.1   Nickleby, Copperfield and Drood have traded as equal partners for many years, making up accounts to 31 December each year. As from 1 April 2000 they agree to share profits in the ratio 1:2:2. The adjusted profit for the year to 31 December 2000 is £18,300. Show how this profit is allocated between the partners.

12.2   Pickwick, Snodgrass and Tupman are in partnership, making up accounts to 31 March annually. Each partner receives 6% interest on fixed capital, Pickwick and Tupman each receive an annual salary of £8,000 and remaining profits or losses are divided equally. Fixed capitals are Pickwick £12,000, Snodgrass £20,000 and Tupman £10,000. The adjusted trading profit for the year to 31 March 2001 is £14,500. Show how this profit is allocated between the partners.

12.3   Dodson and Fogg began trading in equal partnership on 1 July 1997. On 1 July 1998, they admitted Jackson as a partner and agreed to share profits in the ratio 5:4:1. The adjusted profits of the partnership are :

	£
year to 30 June 1998	17,000
year to 30 June 1999	22,000
year to 30 June 2000	29,000

Compute each partner's Schedule D Case I assessment for 1997/98 through to 2000/01.

12.4   Wardle, Jingle and Trotter began trading on 1 October 1998, preparing accounts to 30 September each year and sharing profits in the ratio 7:2:1. Results for the first two years of trading are as follows :

	y/e 30/9/99	y/e 30/9/00
	£	£
Trading profit	23,490	27,310
Interest received gross	2,000	2,200
Interest received net (net amount received)	1,000	1,088

(a)   Compute each partner's Schedule D Case I assessment for 1998/99, 1999/00 and 2000/01.

(b)   Compute each partner's Schedule D Case III assessment for 1998/99, 1999/00 and 2000/01.

(c)   Compute the gross amount of taxed interest assessed on each partner in 1999/00.

*12.5   Cluppins and Raddle form a partnership on 1 November 1996, preparing accounts to 31 May each year. Bardell is admitted as a partner on 1 January 1998. Cluppins leaves the partnership on 28 February 1999 and Winkle is admitted as a partner on 1 March 1999.

Profits and losses are shared as follows :

Cluppins and Raddle	1:2
Cluppins, Raddle and Bardell	7:8:5
Raddle, Bardell and Winkle	4:3:1

Adjusted trading profits are :

	£
1 November 1996 to 31 May 1997	6,000
year to 31 May 1998	12,000
year to 31 May 1999	3,000
year to 31 May 2000	8,000

Calculate each partner's Schedule D Case I assessments for 1996/97 through to 2000/01, identifying any overlap periods and profits.

Chapter 13
Pension schemes

Introduction

The most tax-efficient way of providing for a retirement pension is to make contributions into an approved pension scheme. Employees may join their employer's occupational pension scheme or may take out a personal pension plan. Self-employed people may have a personal pension plan or a retirement annuity contract. The main purpose of this chapter is to explain the tax reliefs available in relation to each of these types of pension scheme.

The introduction of "stakeholder pensions" as from 6 April 2001 will bring a number of changes to the tax treatment of pension schemes. These changes, which will affect tax year 2001/02 and subsequent years, are explained briefly at the end of this chapter.

Occupational pension schemes

An occupational pension scheme (or superannuation scheme) is a pension scheme set up by an employer for the benefit of employees. Employees normally contribute a percentage of their earnings each week or month into the scheme (though some employers operate non-contributory schemes) and the employer also makes contributions. In order for such a scheme to be approved by the Inland Revenue it is necessary that the following main conditions are satisfied:

(a) The sole purpose of the scheme must be to provide benefits on retirement (or death) to employees (or their widows, widowers and dependants).

(b) The employer must make contributions into the scheme.

(c) Any contributions made by employees must be non-returnable.

(d) Employees' pensions must normally start at some time between the ages of 60 and 75, with no distinction made between men and women.

(e) The maximum pension payable to an employee under the terms of the scheme must not exceed the product of:

(i) the number of years of service worked by the employee (up to a maximum of 40 years), and

(ii) 1/60th of the employee's final remuneration (i.e. the average annual remuneration of the employee over the final 3 years of service),

giving a maximum pension of 2/3rds of the employee's final remuneration.

(f) A lump sum may be payable on retirement of no greater than 3/80th of final remuneration for each year of service up to 40 years, giving a maximum lump sum of 1.5 x final remuneration.

If a scheme satisfies these criteria then :

(a) Any contributions made by an employee (up to a maximum of 15% of remuneration) are allowable against the employee's income from employment assessed under Schedule E (see Chapter 7).

(b) The contributions *actually paid* by the employer during an accounting period are allowable when computing the employer's profit assessed to income tax under Schedule D Case I or II (see Chapter 8) or to corporation tax (see Chapter 23).

(c) The employer's contributions on behalf of an employee are not treated as part of the employee's emoluments.

(d) Subject to further conditions, the scheme may enable employees to be "contracted-out" of the State Earnings-Related Pension Scheme (SERPS). In this case, both the employee's and the employer's National Insurance contributions are reduced (see Chapter 15).

For approved schemes established after 13 March 1989, or for employees joining older schemes on or after 1 June 1989, the employee's contributions and benefits are restricted by reference to an "earnings cap" of (for 2000/01) £91,800 per annum. Employees' contributions and benefits are calculated according to their actual remuneration or the earnings cap, whichever is the lower.

EXAMPLE 1

Gordon joined his employer's approved occupational pension scheme in 1992. Calculate the maximum pension contributions which he could make in 2000/01 if his earnings for the year were :

(a) £50,000

(b) £100,000.

SOLUTION

(a) Gordon could contribute no more than 15% of £50,000 = £7,500.

(b) Gordon could contribute no more than 15% of £91,800 = £13,770.

Retirement annuities and personal pensions

Subject to certain restrictions which are explained later in this chapter, tax relief is available in respect of premiums paid by an individual in relation to :

(a) a retirement annuity contract, or

(b) a personal pension plan.

Retirement annuity contracts

Retirement annuities were for many years the main means by which the self-employed and certain employees were able to provide for their retirement. The following persons were eligible to take out a retirement annuity contract :

(a) the self-employed

(b) employees in non-pensionable employment

(c) employees who chose to opt out of their employer's occupational pension scheme (if this was permitted by the employer).

Individuals taking out a retirement annuity contract agreed to pay regular premiums in order to provide for a pension (which would commence at some time between the ages of 60 and 75) and the premiums paid attracted tax relief.

  With effect from 1 July 1988 (the date on which personal pension plans were introduced) no new retirement annuity contracts can be taken out. However, there are many such contracts still in existence which were taken out on or before 30 June 1988 and the premiums paid in relation to such contracts continue to attract tax relief.

Personal pension plans

Personal pension plans were introduced on 1 July 1988 and are similar in many ways to retirement annuities. As before, premiums are paid by the self-employed or by employees in order to provide for a pension in later life and these premiums attract tax relief. The main differences between retirement annuities and personal pension plans are as follows :

(a) Benefits under a personal pension plan may be taken by the individual at any time from the age of 50.

(b) Employees are now legally entitled to opt out of their employer's occupational scheme if they so wish (whether or not the employer approves) and take out a personal pension plan instead.

(c) If a personal pension plan is taken out by an employee, the employer may also make contributions to the plan and these contributions do not rank as part of the employee's taxable emoluments. (It was not possible for employers to make contributions towards an employee's retirement annuity).

Relief for premiums paid

If a taxpayer pays premiums under an approved retirement annuity contract or personal pension plan, then :

(a) The premiums paid during a tax year are allowed against the taxpayer's "net relevant earnings" (see below) for that year.

(b) Self-employed taxpayers pay their premiums gross (whether for a retirement annuity or a personal pension) and obtain tax relief by the premiums being deducted in their Schedule D Case I or II assessment.

(c) Employees pay retirement annuity premiums gross and generally obtain tax relief by means of an adjustment to their tax code.

(d) Employees pay personal pension premiums net of basic rate tax. Further relief for employees who are higher rate taxpayers is given by adjusting the employee's tax code or by making a tax rebate at the end of the year. The basic rate tax deducted at source is not clawed back from those who do not pay tax at the basic rate.

Net relevant earnings

An employee's "net relevant earnings" (NRE) for a tax year are equal to the employee's earnings from non-pensionable employment for that year, including benefits in kind, less allowable expenses.

A self-employed taxpayer's net relevant earnings for a tax year are defined as the taxpayer's Schedule D Case I or II income for the year, plus any income arising from furnished holiday lettings (see Chapter 5), and less :

(a) loss reliefs claimed in the year and set against trading income

(b) trade charges paid in the year, to the extent that they cannot be set against the taxpayer's unearned income. An example of a trade charge would be patent royalties paid to an inventor by a self-employed person.

If, in a given tax year, a trading loss is relieved against non-trading income (e.g. by virtue of a Section 380 claim) then the amount relieved against non-trading income has no effect on that year's NRE but reduces the NRE of the following year instead. If the following year's earnings are insufficient to absorb the whole of the loss, any balance is carried forward to subsequent years.

EXAMPLE 2

Wesley is self-employed. His tax-adjusted profit for 2000/01 is £32,700. He has losses brought forward under Section 385 of £15,200 and pays trade charges during the year of £500. His only other income for 2000/01 is £200 of interest arising on a National Savings Bank investment account. Calculate his net relevant earnings for 2000/01.

SOLUTION

	£	£
Profits assessed under Sch. D Case I or II		32,700
<u>Less</u> : Loss relief	15,200	
Excess of trade charges over unearned income (£500 - £200)	300	15,500
Net relevant earnings for 2000/01		17,200

Maximum premiums allowable

There is an upper limit on the amount of personal pension or retirement annuity premiums which can attract tax relief in a given tax year. This upper limit depends upon the age of the taxpayer at the *start* of the tax year and is expressed as a percentage of NRE. The maximum allowable percentages are as follows :

Age at start of tax year	Personal Pensions	Retirement Annuities
Up to 35	17.5%	17.5%
36-45	20%	17.5%
46-50	25%	17.5%
51-55	30%	20%
56-60	35%	22.5%
61 or more	40%	27.5%

In the case of personal pension plans, the maximum NRE in 2000/01 to which the appropriate percentage can be applied is £91,800 (the earnings cap). There is no such maximum in the case of retirement annuity contracts.

EXAMPLE 3

Calculate the maximum relief available to each of the following taxpayers in respect of their retirement annuity or personal pension premiums in 2000/01 :

(a) Alana was born on 4 May 1964. She has a personal pension plan and her net relevant earnings for 2000/01 are £27,000.

(b) Bruce was born on 14 August 1942. He has a personal pension plan and his net relevant earnings for 2000/01 are £52,000.

(c) Charlotte was born on 24 December 1938. She has a personal pension plan and her net relevant earnings for 2000/01 are £95,000.

(d) Diane was born on 12 January 1948. She has a retirement annuity contract and her net relevant earnings for 2000/01 are £100,000.

SOLUTION

(a)   Alana is aged 35 at the start of tax year 2000/01. The maximum relief to which she is entitled is £4,725 (17.5% of £27,000).

(b)   Bruce is aged 57 at the start of tax year 2000/01. The maximum relief to which he is entitled is £18,200 (35% of £52,000).

(c)   Charlotte is aged 61 at the start of tax year 2000/01. Her net relevant earnings exceed the earnings cap, so the maximum relief to which she is entitled is £36,720 (40% of £91,800).

(d)   Diane is aged 52 at the start of tax year 2000/01. The earnings cap does not apply to retirement annuities so the maximum relief to which she is entitled is £20,000 (20% of £100,000).

Excess premiums carried back

If the retirement annuity or personal pension premiums paid by a taxpayer exceed the allowable maximum for the year, the excess premiums cannot be relieved in that year. However, the taxpayer may elect that excess premiums should be treated as if they had been paid in the previous tax year, or (if there are no net relevant earnings in that year) in the year before that. This "carry-back" election may be of use if the net relevant earnings of the previous tax year were higher than those of the current year and can absorb the current year's excess premiums.

EXAMPLE 4

Jill is self-employed, 29 years old and a member of a personal pension scheme into which she pays £1,000 per annum. Her net relevant earnings for 1999/00 were £12,400 but 2000/01 is a poor year and her net relevant earnings for that year are only £5,000. Can she use the carry-back election to obtain relief on her 2000/01 personal pension premiums ?

SOLUTION

In 1999/00 Jill's maximum allowable premiums were £2,170 (17.5% of £12,400) and so her premiums paid in that year of only £1,000 were allowable in full.

   But in 2000/01 her maximum allowable premiums drop to only £875 (17.5% of £5,000) and she has excess premiums of £125, which cannot be relieved in 2000/01. However, she can elect to treat the £125 as if it had been paid in 1999/00. This would give relief on £1,125 in 1999/00 (still within the maximum allowable for that year) and on £875 in 2000/01. In this way tax relief can be obtained on the entire £2,000 of premiums paid in 1999/00 and 2000/01.

In fact, all or part of *any* premium paid in a year (not just excess premiums) can be carried back in this way and the taxpayer would obviously elect to do this if a tax saving would result (e.g. if the taxpayer's marginal rate of tax was higher in the previous tax year than the current year).

The election to carry premiums back must be made by 31 January following the end of the tax year in which the premiums were paid.

EXAMPLE 5

Eric was born on 1 January 1967. He has net relevant earnings of £50,000 in 1999/00 and £18,000 in 2000/01. He pays £1,800 per annum into a personal pension plan. Show the alternative ways in which tax relief may be given on the premiums paid in 1999/00 and 2000/01.

SOLUTION

Eric's allowable percentage in both 1999/00 and 2000/01 is 17.5%. The maximum premiums allowable are therefore £8,750 in 1999/00 (17.5% of £50,000) and £3,150 in 2000/01 (17.5% of £18,000). The premiums of £1,800 paid in each year are beneath these maxima, so Eric could relieve each year's premiums in full against that year's NRE.

However, an alternative is to elect that the 2000/01 premiums should be treated as if they were paid in 1999/00 and to offset both the 1999/00 premiums and the 2000/01 premiums against the NRE of 1999/00. Since Eric is presumably a 40% taxpayer in 1999/00 (but not in 2000/01) this would provide a greater tax saving than relieving each year's premiums against the NRE of the year in which the premiums were paid.

Unused relief carried forward

If the retirement annuity or personal pension premiums paid by a taxpayer are less than the maximum allowed for the year, the premiums paid in the year are allowed in full and there is "unused relief" equal to the difference between the premiums actually paid and the maximum premiums that would have been allowed.

EXAMPLE 6

Freda is aged 30 and has net relevant earnings in 2000/01 of £15,000. She belongs to an approved personal pension scheme. Calculate the amount of Freda's unused relief in 2000/01 if the premiums paid in the year are :

(a) £1,500

(b) £2,625

(c) £3,000.

SOLUTION

Freda's allowable percentage in 2000/01 is 17.5%. The maximum premiums allowable in 2000/01 are therefore £2,625 (17.5% of £15,000).

(a) If Freda pays premiums of £1,500 then the entire £1,500 is allowable for tax purposes and she has unused relief of £1,125 (£2,625 - £1,500).

(b) If Freda pays premiums of £2,625 then she has paid precisely the maximum amount allowed. The entire £2,625 is allowable for tax purposes and she has no unused relief.

(c) If Freda pays premiums of £3,000 then she has paid more than the allowable maximum. Only £2,625 is allowable and she has no unused relief for the year. (She may elect to carry back the excess premiums of £375 to 1999/00).

Unused relief represents a wasted opportunity to obtain tax relief but it may not be lost irretrievably. Unused relief can be carried forward for up to 6 tax years and used to relieve excess premiums paid during those 6 years. It should be noted that :

(a) unused relief brought forward from previous years can only be used if the current year's maximum relief has already been used in full, and

(b) unused relief is used on a first-in, first-out basis i.e. unused relief brought forward from earlier years is used in preference to unused relief brought forward from later years.

EXAMPLE 7

Sharon is 32 years old and pays personal pension premiums of £1,900 in 2000/01. Her net relevant earnings for the year are £9,600. She has unused relief of £250 brought forward from 1994/95 and £400 brought forward from 1997/98. Compute the allowable premiums in 2000/01.

SOLUTION

Sharon's maximum allowable premiums would normally be £1,680 (17.5% of £9,600). Since the premiums paid exceed this maximum by £220 she would normally have excess premiums of £220 which would not attract tax relief (unless they could be carried back to the previous year).

However, £220 of the unused relief brought forward from 1994/95 (used in preference to the more recent unused relief from 1997/98) may be used to relieve this shortfall, so ensuring that the full £1,900 is allowed in 2000/01.

The remaining £30 of the 1994/95 unused relief is now too old to carry forward to 2001/02 and the opportunity to use this relief is lost forever. The £400 of unused relief arising in 1997/98 may carried forward for 3 further years before being lost.

Choice between carry-back and carry-forward

Sometimes, a taxpayer is confronted with a choice between :

(a) carrying excess premiums back to the previous year, or

(b) relieving excess premiums with unused relief brought forward from the previous 6 years.

In this situation it is necessary to consider the consequences of each choice and to select the most tax-effective alternative.

EXAMPLE 8

Stuart is aged 40 and has net relevant earnings of £46,000 in 1999/00 (he has no other income). He pays personal pension premiums of £2,350 in the year and he has no unused relief brought forward from previous years.

(a) How much unused relief does Stuart have in 1999/00 ?

(b) If his net relevant earnings for 2000/01 decrease to £7,200 and the premiums paid remain the same as in 1999/00, calculate his allowable premiums in that year (ignore for a moment the possibility of carrying back premiums from 2000/01 to 1999/00).

(c) Would the carry-back provisions described earlier be of any use to Stuart ?

SOLUTION

(a) Maximum allowable premiums for a taxpayer of Stuart's age are 20% of NRE i.e. £9,200. He has paid only £2,350 in 1999/00, so the full £2,350 is allowable and there is unused relief of £6,850. This unused relief may be carried forward for up to 6 tax years (i.e. up to and including 2005/06) and used to relieve excess premiums paid in those 6 years.

(b) 20% of Stuart's NRE in 2000/01 amounts to only £1,440, leaving excess premiums of £910. However, he has unused relief of £6,850 to bring forward from 1999/00 so £910 of this can be used to relieve the excess premiums. The remainder of the unused relief (£5,940) can be carried forward for a further 5 years. The situation in 1999/00 and 2000/01 is as follows :

	1999/00	2000/01
	£	£
NRE	46,000	7,200
Less : allowable premiums	2,350	2,350
Taxable earnings	43,650	4,850

(c) As an alternative to carrying forward unused relief from 1999/00 and using it to relieve excess premiums paid in 2000/01, Stuart could elect to treat £910 of his premiums paid in 2000/01 as if they had been paid in 1999/00. If he did this, the situation would be as follows :

	1999/00	*2000/01*
	£	£
NRE	46,000	7,200
Less : allowable premiums	3,260	1,440
Taxable earnings	42,740	5,760

As before, the total of the taxable earnings in the two years is £48,500. However, the way in which the £48,500 is split between the two years is different and, in particular, the carry-back alternative reduces Stuart's taxable earnings in 1999/00, a year in which he is probably a higher-rate taxpayer. In fact it would be beneficial for Stuart to carry back the whole of the £2,350 paid in 2000/01, not just the excess premium of £910.

Additional voluntary contributions

Employees who already belong to an occupational pension scheme can obtain tax relief on contributions made to a form of personal pension scheme known as a "free standing additional voluntary contributions" (FSAVC) scheme. An employee would contribute to such a scheme in order to provide for an extra pension, additional to the pension payable from the employer's scheme. Contributions are limited to a maximum of 15% of earnings up to the earnings cap (£91,800 for 2000/01), less any contributions made to the occupational pension scheme.

EXAMPLE 9

Darren belongs to his employer's superannuation scheme and contributes 6% of his gross pay into the scheme each month. In 2000/01 his total gross pay was £12,500. Calculate the maximum amount which Darren could pay into an FSAVC scheme in 2000/01 if he so wished.

SOLUTION

Darren has contributed 6% of his earnings to the occupational scheme and may therefore contribute a further 9% to an FSAVC scheme. His maximum contributions in 2000/01 are £1,125 (9% of £12,500).

Pension schemes as from 6 April 2001

The tax treatment of pension schemes will change in some ways with the introduction of *stakeholder pension schemes* as from 6 April 2001. Stakeholder pension schemes will be simple, low-cost schemes which will open up pension provision to those who have no access to an occupational pension scheme and which will allow individuals with low earnings to receive more tax relief on their contributions than they would in a personal pension plan.

Stakeholder pension schemes will be "defined contribution" (or "money purchase") schemes. The contributions made to a stakeholder scheme will be used to build up a fund which will then be used to buy a pension on retirement. The size of the pension will depend entirely upon the size of the fund and will not be based on the taxpayer's earnings before retirement. This is the way in which personal pension plans and retirement annuity contracts (and some occupational schemes) operate at present.

Stakeholder pensions will be available either through employers or directly from pension scheme providers. Employers with 5 or more employees who do not offer an occupational pension scheme will be required to facilitate access to stakeholder pensions by designating a scheme, passing details of that scheme to their employees and deducting pension contributions from pay if an employee so wishes.

Taxation implications

As from 6 April 2001 there will be a new integrated tax regime for nearly all defined contribution pension schemes, including personal pensions, stakeholder pensions and employers' money purchase occupational schemes (if an employer opts into the new regime). However, the changes will not apply to retirement annuity contracts. The main features of the new regime will be as follows :

(a) All contributions will be made net of basic rate tax. This tax will be recovered from the Inland Revenue by pension providers and will not be clawed back from non-taxpayers or from those who pay income tax at a rate which is lower than the basic rate. Higher-rate tax relief will be available to higher-rate taxpayers.

(b) Contributions (including any employer contributions) of up to £3,600 (gross) p.a. will be permitted *irrespective of earnings*. Higher contributions than this will be permitted subject to the age-related and earnings-related limits which apply at present to personal pension schemes. However, these higher contributions will be based upon the highest earnings of the previous 5 years and will be allowed to continue for up to 5 years after earnings have ceased.

(c) The rules which allow contributions to be carried back to the previous year will be simplified. Under the new arrangements, the carry-back provisions will apply only to contributions paid on or before 31 January in the current tax year (and only if a carry-back election was made at or before the time of payment).

(d) The rules which allow unused relief to be carried forward for up to 6 years will be abolished completely.

Summary

▶ Contributions of up to 15% of earnings made by an employee to an approved occupational pension scheme are allowable under Schedule E.

▶ Subject to certain conditions, tax relief is available on premiums paid by the self-employed and by certain employees in order to secure a retirement annuity or personal pension. The maximum allowable premium in any tax year depends upon the taxpayer's age at the start of the year and earnings during the year.

▶ A taxpayer may elect that retirement annuity or personal pension premiums paid in a tax year should be treated as if paid in the previous year.

▶ If retirement annuity or personal pension premiums paid in a tax year are less than the maximum amount that could have been relieved, the unused relief may be carried forward and used to relieve excess premiums for up to 6 years.

▶ An employee belonging to an occupational pension scheme may obtain tax relief on premiums paid to a free standing additional voluntary contributions scheme.

▶ Stakeholder pension schemes will be introduced as from 6 April 2001, together with a new integrated tax regime covering most defined contribution pension schemes other than retirement annuity contracts.

Exercises

13.1 List the main conditions which must be satisfied in order for an occupational pension scheme to be approved by the Inland Revenue and explain the taxation consequences of a scheme being approved.

13.2 Calculate the maximum contribution which could be made to an occupational pension scheme in 2000/01 by an employee with remuneration in the year of :

    (a) £20,000

    (b) £93,200.

13.3 Explain the meaning of the term "net relevant earnings" for a self-employed person and for an employee.

13.4   Karen is self-employed and was born on 7 April 1939. Her 2000/01 Schedule D Case I assessment is £22,450. She has losses brought forward under Section 385 of £1,200 and trade charges for the year of £250. She has no other income. Calculate the maximum allowable personal pension premium which Karen could pay in 2000/01.

13.5   Damon is self-employed and was born on 10 July 1963. He has net relevant earnings and personal pension premiums as follows :

	NRE	Premiums paid
	£	£
1998/99	17,200	2,500
1999/00	18,400	2,600
2000/01	5,600	2,600

He has unused relief brought forward from 1993/94 of £400. Assuming that no carry-back elections are made, show how relief would be given for Damon's personal pension premiums.

*13.6   Irma is self-employed. She was born in 1942. The following information relates to 2000/01 :

(a)   Irma's profits assessed under Schedule D Case I are £21,700. She has no other income.

(b)   She pays a trade charge on income of £300.

(c)   She pays personal pension premiums of £7,521 and has unused relief brought forward from 1994/95 of £220.

Calculate Irma's 2000/01 income tax liability.

*13.7   Tony is self-employed, aged 31 and has net relevant earnings of £67,200 in 1999/00 and £24,400 in 2000/01. He pays an annual premium of £5,000 into a personal pension scheme. Show how relief would be given for the personal pension premiums in 1999/00 and 2000/01 if :

(a)   Tony elects to carry back the 2000/01 premiums to 1999/00, or

(b)   Tony does not make a carry-back election.

Which of these alternatives is preferable ?

Chapter 14

Payment of income tax, surcharges, interest and penalties

Introduction

Interest is charged on income tax which is paid late. Conversely, interest may be added to repayments of income tax. The main purpose of this chapter is to identify the dates on which income tax is payable and to explain how the interest due on underpaid or overpaid tax is calculated. This chapter also considers financial penalties to which a taxpayer may become liable as a consequence of non-compliance with tax law.

Payment of income tax

Under the Self Assessment system (see Chapter 1) income tax which is not deducted at source is payable as follows :

(a) The taxpayer's liability in relation to all Schedules and Cases of income tax is aggregated into a single tax liability.

(b) Payments on account of this liability (POA's) are due on 31 January in the tax year and on 31 July following the end of the tax year. For example, the POA's for 2000/01 are due on 31 January 2001 and 31 July 2001. Each POA is normally equal to 50% of the taxpayer's income tax liability for the *previous* year (less any tax paid by deduction at source). For this purpose, the term "deduction at source" includes tax paid via the PAYE system and any tax satisfied by the set-off of tax credits, as well as tax deducted at source from bank interest etc. Note that :

    (i) POA's are not required at all if the taxpayer's total income tax liability for the preceding year (less tax deducted at source) was beneath a specified "de minimis" limit, currently set at £500.

    (ii) POA's are also not required if more than 80% of the taxpayer's income tax liability for the previous year was satisfied by deduction of tax at source.

(iii) The taxpayer may make a claim to reduce or cancel POA's by contacting the Inland Revenue and stating the grounds for the claim. Suitable grounds for a claim to reduce or cancel POA's would be the taxpayer's belief that the income tax liability for the year in question will be less than in the previous year. The Inland Revenue cannot reject such a claim but there are penalties for making a claim fraudulently or negligently (see below).

(c) A balancing payment (or repayment) is due on 31 January following the end of the tax year. For example, the balancing payment for 2000/01 is due on 31 January 2002. But note that :

(i) If a tax return is issued late (i.e. after 31 October following the end of the tax year to which it relates) and this has not been caused by the taxpayer's failure to notify his or her chargeability to tax, the balancing payment is due 3 months after the issue date of the return.

(ii) If a self-assessment is amended (either by the taxpayer or by the Inland Revenue) or if a discovery assessment is raised, any additional tax payable is due 30 days after the date of its notification to the taxpayer or on 31 January following the end of the tax year, whichever is the later.

It is important to note that POA's and balancing payments are automatically payable on the due dates and that interest and surcharges (see below) are charged in the case of late payment. At least once per year (usually in November or December) taxpayers are sent a statement showing the state of their account with the Inland Revenue and informing them of the payments which (according to Inland Revenue calculations) are due on the following 31 January and 31 July.

EXAMPLE 1

Warren's income tax liability for 1999/00 was £17,200, of which £14,500 was paid by deduction at source. His liability for 2000/01 is £19,300, of which £16,100 is paid by deduction at source. State the dates on which Warren is required to pay his 2000/01 income tax and compute the amount payable on each date.

SOLUTION

Over 80% of Warren's income tax liability for 1999/00 was paid by deduction at source and therefore no POA's are required for 2000/01. His liability of £3,200 (£19,300 - £16,100) is payable on 31 January 2002.

EXAMPLE 2

In 1999/00, Barbara paid income tax of £4,000 by deduction at source and £22,000 by self-assessment. Her total 2000/01 income tax liability is £34,000, of which £5,000 is paid by deduction at source. State the dates on which Barbara is required to pay her 2000/01 income tax and compute the amount payable on each date.

SOLUTION

(i)   31 January 2001, POA of £11,000 (50% of 1999/00 tax, excluding tax paid at source)

(ii)   31 July 2001, POA of £11,000

(iii) 31 January 2002, balancing payment of £7,000 (£34,000 - £5,000 - POA's £22,000).

Surcharges on income tax paid late

In addition to any interest due on income tax paid late (see below), the taxpayer may also be required to pay a "surcharge". The surcharges scheme operates as follows :

(a) If all or part of a balancing payment remains unpaid more than 28 days after the due date, a surcharge arises equal to 5% of the tax unpaid.

(b) If all or part of any additional tax payable because a self-assessment has been amended (or because a discovery assessment has been raised) remains unpaid more than 28 days after the due date, a surcharge arises equal to 5% of the tax unpaid.

(c) Any tax that remains unpaid more than 6 months after the due date is subject to a further 5% surcharge.

(d) Surcharges are payable 30 days after the date on which they are imposed.

The surcharges scheme does not apply to POA's. The scheme does apply, however, to any assessments for 1995/96 or earlier years (i.e. the years before the introduction of Self Assessment) which are raised on or after 6 April 1998.

EXAMPLE 3

Continuing the above example, Barbara paid income tax for 2000/01 as follows :

	£
31 January 2001	11,000
1 September 2001	11,000
31 January 2002	6,000
1 September 2002	1,000

Compute the surcharges (if any) which would be imposed.

SOLUTION

(i)   The first POA is paid in full and on time.

(ii) The second POA is paid in full but 32 days late. However, late POA's do not attract surcharges.

(iii) £1,000 of the balancing payment is paid over 6 months late. A first surcharge of £50 (£1,000 x 5%) will be imposed on 1 March 2002 (payable 31 March 2002) and a further surcharge of £50 will be imposed on 1 August 2002 (payable 31 August 2002).

Interest on income tax

Under the Self Assessment system, interest is charged on all late payments of income tax, surcharges and penalties. Conversely, interest is paid to the taxpayer when repayments of overpaid tax are made.

Interest on overdue income tax

Interest charged on overdue income tax is calculated as follows :

(a) In the case of late POA's and balancing payments, interest runs from the due date of payment up to the date on which the tax is actually paid.

(b) In the case of discovery assessments and amendments to self-assessments, interest normally runs from the *annual filing date* for the relevant tax year (i.e. 31 January following the tax year) even though the tax itself might not be due for payment until a later date.

(c) Interest on a surcharge runs from the due date of payment of the surcharge (i.e. 30 days after its imposition).

(d) If a taxpayer submits a tax return by the 30 September deadline (see Chapter 1) and asks the Inland Revenue to calculate the tax due, but the Inland Revenue fail to issue a statement of account in time for the first POA to be made on 31 January, then interest on this POA starts to run 30 days after the issue date of the statement of account.

These interest rules also apply to any assessments for 1995/96 or earlier years which are raised on or after 6 April 1998.

EXAMPLE 4

Again continuing the above example, calculate the total interest payable by Barbara for 2000/01, assuming that the two surcharges are both paid on 29 September 2002 and that interest is charged at 8.5% per annum.

SOLUTION

(i)   Interest on the second POA is £81.97 (£11,000 x 8.5% x 32/365).

(ii)   Interest on the final £1,000 of the balancing payment (paid 213 days late) is £49.60 (£1,000 x 8.5% x 213/365).

(iii)   Interest on the first surcharge (paid 182 days late) is £2.12 (£50 x 8.5% x 182/365).

(iv)   Interest on the second surcharge (paid 29 days late) is £0.34 (£50 x 8.5% x 29/365).

Total interest due is £134.03 (£81.97 + £49.60 + £2.12 + £0.34).

Interest on overpaid income tax

Repayments of overpaid income tax attract interest. This interest is calculated at a lower rate than the rate charged on overdue income tax but is itself exempt from income tax. Interest on overpaid income tax (sometimes referred to as "repayment supplement") runs from the "relevant time" to the date on which the tax is repaid to the taxpayer. The "relevant time" is :

(a)   as regards POA's and any other payments of income tax other than tax deducted at source, the date of payment

(b)   as regards income tax deducted at source, 31 January following the tax year for which the tax is deducted.

Interest is also payable if a surcharge or penalty is repaid to a taxpayer, running from the date of payment to the date of repayment.

Repayments of income tax for a year are attributed first to the balancing payment made for that year, secondly in two equal parts to the POA's for that year and finally to tax deducted at source for the year.

If a repayment of income tax is caused by a claim to carry back a loss or payment from a later year to an earlier year (e.g. if a trading loss is carried back under Section 380 or if a personal pension contribution is carried back) the repayment is regarded as a repayment of tax for the later year, *not* for the earlier year. This has the effect of reducing the amount of interest which is added on to the repayment.

Penalties

A taxpayer who fails to comply with statutory requirements may become liable to a number of financial penalties, the most important of which are listed below. Some of these penalties are fixed in amount but, in most cases, the law specifies only a *maximum* amount for the penalty and the Board of Inland Revenue has the power to "mitigate" (i.e. reduce) the amount charged if it sees fit to do so. Whether or not a penalty is mitigated will usually depend upon the seriousness of the taxpayer's offence and the degree to which the taxpayer has co-operated with the Inland Revenue.

(a) **Failure to notify chargeability to tax**. An individual must notify the Inland Revenue if he or she is liable to tax for a tax year, even if a return has not been issued for that year. Failure to do so within 6 months of the end of the tax year could render the individual liable to a maximum penalty equal in amount to the tax remaining unpaid on 31 January following the end of the tax year.

(b) **Late submission of a tax return**. A £100 fixed penalty is imposed if a tax return is submitted late and a further £100 fixed penalty is imposed if the return is more than 6 months late. If the return is more than 12 months late, an additional penalty may be imposed of up to 100% of the tax liability for the year.

Furthermore, the General or Special Commissioners may direct that a penalty of up to £60 per day should be imposed, running from the date of the Commissioners' direction to the date on which the tax return is finally submitted.

(c) **Submission of an incorrect tax return**. If a taxpayer, either negligently or fraudulently, submits an incorrect tax return (or submits incorrect information in support of a tax return) a penalty may be imposed of up to 100% of the amount of tax underpaid as a consequence of the incorrect return.

(d) **Fraud or negligence when claiming reduced POA's**. A taxpayer who makes a claim for reduced POA's and does so fraudulently or negligently may be subject to a maximum penalty equal to the difference between the POA's actually made and the POA's that would have been made if the claim had not been made.

(e) **Failure to keep required records**. A taxpayer who fails to maintain or retain adequate records in support of the year's tax return may be subject to a penalty of up to £3,000.

In every case, the penalty is *in addition* both to the tax itself and to any surcharges or interest charged in relation to that tax.

Summary

► Under the Self Assessment system, income tax not collected at source or via the PAYE system is usually payable by means of two payments on account, followed by a balancing payment.

► Surcharges may be levied if a balancing payment is paid late and interest is payable on any tax paid late. Interest usually runs from the due date of payment up the actual date of payment.

► Repayments of overpaid tax also attract interest, usually running from the date on which the tax was paid up to the date of repayment.

► Financial penalties may be imposed for various breaches of the tax law.

Exercises

14.1   For each of the following taxpayers, state the dates on which the taxpayer is due to pay his or her 2000/01 income tax and calculate the amount payable on each date.

(a)   Guy's 1999/00 income tax liability was £1,600, of which £1,150 was paid via the PAYE system and £50 was deducted at source from investment income. His 2000/01 liability is £1,750, of which £1,250 is paid via PAYE and £60 is deducted at source.

(b)   Marie's 1999/00 income tax liability was £6,730, of which £4,370 was paid via PAYE and £20 was deducted at source. Her 2000/01 liability is £6,580, of which £4,810 is paid via PAYE and £35 is deducted at source.

(c)   Majid's 1999/00 income tax liability was £14,850, of which £11,990 was paid via PAYE and £110 was deducted at source. His 2000/01 liability is £16,110, of which £12,370 is paid via PAYE and £140 is deducted at source.

14.2   Dorothy's 1999/00 income tax liability was £30,000, of which £6,000 was deducted at source. Her liability for 2000/01 is £35,000, of which £7,000 is deducted at source. She made a first POA for 2000/01 on 27 February 2001 and a second POA on 12 September 2001. She also made a balancing payment for the year on 21 February 2002. All of her payments were for the correct amount.

(a)   Calculate the amount of any surcharges payable by Dorothy in relation to 2000/01.

(b)   Assuming an interest rate of 8.5% per annum, calculate the amount of any interest payable by Dorothy in relation to 2000/01.

14.3   Jabran did not receive a tax return for 2000/01 but he was aware that he had income which had not been assessed to tax. He notified the Inland Revenue of this fact on 2 October 2001 and a return was issued to him on 15 November 2001. He completed the return and sent it back with the necessary payment on 7 April 2002.

Explain the penalties, surcharges and interest which Jabran might be required to pay.

*14.4   Frances paid income tax of £43,000 in 1999/00, of which £19,000 was deducted at source. Her liability for 2000/01 is £63,000, of which £21,000 is deducted at source. Her payments of income tax for 2000/01 are as follows :

	£
15 February 2001	12,000
14 September 2001	12,000
3 February 2002	14,000
15 December 2002	4,000

Calculate the surcharges and interest payable for the year, assuming that any surcharges are paid on 15 December 2002 and that interest is charged at 8.5% per annum.

Chapter 15

National Insurance contributions

Introduction

National Insurance contributions (NIC's) are payable by employees, by employers and by those who are self-employed. Contributions are collected by the National Insurance Contributions Office of the Inland Revenue and paid into a National Insurance Fund. This fund, supplemented by a grant from the Treasury, is then used to provide contributory social security benefits such as the state retirement pension. The purpose of this chapter is to explain the circumstances in which NIC's are payable and the way in which NIC's are calculated.

Class 1 National Insurance contributions

Class 1 NIC's are payable in relation to employees aged 16 or over. The employees themselves pay *primary* Class 1 NIC's whilst employers pay *secondary* Class 1 NIC's on their employees' behalf. Employees who continue to work after reaching state pension age (60 for women, 65 for men) pay no further primary contributions but employers must still pay secondary contributions for such employees.

The amount of Class 1 NIC's payable in relation to an employee depends upon the employee's earnings. For this purpose, an employee's earnings consist of his or her gross pay (including any profit related pay) *before* deducting contributions made to an occupational pension scheme, charitable donations made under the terms of a payroll giving scheme or any expenses borne by the employee. An employee's earnings for this purpose do *not* include :

(a) tips received directly from customers

(b) mileage allowances received from the employer (see Chapter 7) if calculated at a rate which is less than or equal to the FPCS rate for the first 4,000 miles, regardless of the number of miles actually driven by the employee (but any excess forms part of the employee's earnings chargeable to Class 1 NIC's)

(c) personal incidental expenses paid by the employer, if exempt from Schedule E income tax (see Chapter 7)

(d) relocation expenses paid by the employer, to the extent that these expenses are exempt from income tax

(e) business expenses paid for or reimbursed by the employer, including reasonable travel and subsistence expenses.

Apart from most non-cash vouchers, benefits in kind which are not convertible into cash are not subject to Class 1 NIC's. However, such benefits may give rise to a Class 1A liability (see below). If remuneration is paid in the form of non-cash assets such as gold bars, coffee beans, fine wines, assigned trade debts etc., a liability to Class 1 NIC's will arise if the assets are readily convertible into cash. Payments made in shares are also liable to Class 1 NIC's unless they are "own company" shares provided under an approved share scheme or share option scheme (see Chapter 7).

Contribution periods

The main principles of the Class 1 National Insurance system are as follows :

(a) Primary and secondary Class 1 NIC's are calculated according to the amount of an employee's earnings in a "contribution period". For those paid weekly or monthly, each week or month usually constitutes a contribution period (but see later in this chapter for special rules concerning company directors).

(b) The liability to Class 1 NIC's in a given contribution period is governed solely by the employee's earnings in that period and is totally unaffected by earnings in other periods. This is in contrast to the income tax PAYE system (see Chapter 7) which accumulates earnings over the year and calculates a tax liability each week or month based on the employee's total earnings for the tax year to date.

(c) If an employee has two or more employments in a contribution period, each of these employments is considered separately for the purposes of calculating the liability to Class 1 NIC's. Earnings from two or more employments are aggregated only if the employments are with the same employer or associated employers.

(d) The rate at which Class 1 NIC's are calculated depends upon whether or not the employee is contracted out of the State Earnings Related Pension Scheme (SERPS). Those who are not contracted out of SERPS pay higher Class 1 NIC's in return for an earnings-related increase in some of their social security benefits.

Most contracted-out employees are members of their employer's contracted-out salary-related (COSR) occupational pension scheme. Others belong to contracted-out money-purchase (COMP) schemes or pay contributions into an appropriate personal pension scheme. The primary and secondary Class 1 NIC's payable in relation to a contracted-out employee depend upon the type of scheme to which the employee belongs. Only members of COSR schemes are considered here.

The way in which primary and secondary Class 1 NIC's are calculated in tax year 2000/01 is explained below.

Primary Class 1 NIC's (2000/01)

The primary Class 1 NIC's payable by an employee for a contribution period falling during 2000/01 are calculated as follows :

(a) The employee's earnings in the period are compared with the *primary threshold* (also known as the "employee's earnings threshold"). This is £76 for weekly-paid employees and £329 for monthly-paid employees. No primary contributions are payable if earnings in a contribution period do not exceed this threshold.

(b) If earnings in the period exceed the primary threshold, primary Class 1 NIC's are payable on those earnings which lie between the primary threshold and the "upper earnings limit" (UEL). The UEL is £535 for weekly-paid employees and £2,319 for monthly-paid employees. No primary contributions are payable on the excess of an employee's earnings over the UEL.

(c) The rates at which primary Class 1 NIC's are calculated are as follows :

	Not contracted out	*Contracted out (COSR)*
Weekly-paid :		
On the first £76	nil	nil
On remaining earnings up to £535	10%	8.4%
Monthly-paid :		
On the first £329	nil	nil
On remaining earnings up to £2,319	10%	8.4%

EXAMPLE 1

(a) Compute the primary Class 1 NIC's payable by the following weekly-paid employees for the week ending 6 August 2000 :

    (i)   Employee A has earnings for the week of £73 and is not contracted out.

    (ii)   Employee B has earnings for the week of £206 and is not contracted out.

    (iii) Employee C has earnings for the week of £555 and is contracted out.

(b) Compute the primary Class 1 NIC's payable by the following monthly-paid employees for the month of August 2000 :

    (i)   Employee D has earnings for the month of £329 and is not contracted out.

    (ii)   Employee E has earnings for the month of £1,069 and is contracted out.

    (iii) Employee F has earnings for the month of £2,400 and is not contracted out.

SOLUTION

(a) (i)   £nil (earnings do not exceed the primary threshold).

    (ii)   10% x (£206 - £76) = £13.00.

    (iii) 8.4% x (£535 - £76) = £38.56. (In 2000/01, this is the maximum weekly contri-bution for a contracted-out employee, since earnings beyond the first £535 do not attract primary contributions).

(b) (i)   £nil (earnings do not exceed the primary threshold).

    (ii)   8.4% x (£1,069 - £329) = £62.16.

    (iii) 10% x (£2,319 - £329) = £199.00. (In 2000/01, this is the maximum monthly contribution for an employee who is not contracted-out, since earnings beyond the first £2,319 do not attract primary contributions.)

Secondary Class 1 NIC's (2000/01)

The secondary Class 1 NIC's payable by an employer in relation to an employee for a contribution period falling during 2000/01 are calculated as follows :

(a) The employee's earnings in the period are compared with the *secondary threshold* (also known as the "employer's earnings threshold"). This is set at the weekly or monthly equivalent of the income tax personal allowance for the year, rounded to the nearest pound. The secondary threshold for 2000/01 is therefore £84 (£4,385 x 1/52) for weekly-paid employees and £365 (£4,385 x 1/12) for monthly-paid employees. No secondary contributions are payable if an employee's earnings in a contribution period do not exceed this threshold.

(b) If earnings in the period exceed the secondary threshold, secondary Class 1 NIC's are payable on *all* of the earnings which lie above the threshold.

(c) The rates at which secondary Class 1 NIC's are calculated are as follows :

	Not contracted out	Contracted out (COSR)
Weekly-paid :		
On the first £84	nil	nil
On the next £451	12.2%	9.2%
On earnings above £535 (UEL)	12.2%	12.2%
Monthly-paid :		
On the first £365	nil	nil
On the next £1,954	12.2%	9.2%
On earnings above £2,319 (UEL)	12.2%	12.2%

Note that primary contributions are payable only on earnings up to the UEL whereas secondary contributions continue beyond the UEL.

EXAMPLE 2

Refer back to the previous example in this chapter and compute the secondary Class 1 NIC's payable in relation to each employee.

SOLUTION

(a) (i)   £nil (earnings do not exceed the secondary threshold).

     (ii)   12.2% x (£206 - £84) = £14.88.

     (iii) 9.2% x (£535 - £84) + 12.2% x (£555 - £535) = £43.93.

(b) (i)   £nil (earnings do not exceed the secondary threshold).

     (ii)   9.2% x (£1,069 - £365) = £64.77.

     (iii) 12.2% x (£2,400 - £365) = £248.27.

Directors' Class 1 NIC's

The fact that there is a maximum to the amount of primary contributions which an employee can pay in a contribution period means that employees with identical annual earnings may pay very different amounts of primary contributions in the year, depending upon the distribution of their earnings over the year. Consider the following (rather extreme) example :

EXAMPLE 3

During 2000/01, an employee (not contracted out) earns a total of £30,000, paid at the rate of £2,500 each month.

(a) Calculate the total primary Class 1 NIC's payable for the year.

(b) What would the total primary contributions be for the year if the employee received £30,000 in one month and nothing in the remaining 11 months ?

SOLUTION

(a) Primary contributions each month are 10% x (£2,319 - £329) = £199.00. This gives a total of £2,388.00 for the year.

(b) Primary contributions for the month in which the employee was paid £30,000 would be £199.00, with nothing payable for the rest of the year.

    Therefore the employee would save £2,189.00 in primary contributions (£2,388.00 - £199.00) if the entire year's salary were received in a single month.

Employees are not normally able to arrange for all their year's earnings to be paid in one contribution period so as to avoid primary Class 1 NIC's, but company directors may well have sufficient influence to make such an arrangement. To counter this, the Class 1 NIC's of company directors are always calculated on an *annual* basis, regardless of the distribution of their earnings over the tax year. For 2000/01, the calculation is as follows :

(a) The primary threshold and the upper earnings limit for the year are £3,952 and £27,820 respectively.

(b) The total primary contributions payable for the year by a director with earnings which exceed £3,952 are calculated as 10% of the earnings between £3,952 and £27,820 (or 8.4% for a director who is contracted out).

(c) The secondary threshold for the year is £4,385. The total secondary contributions payable for the year in relation to a director with earnings which exceed £4,385 are calculated according to the following table :

	Not contracted out	Contracted out (COSR)
Annual earnings :		
On the first £4,385	nil	nil
On the next £23,435	12.2%	9.2%
On earnings above £27,820 (UEL)	12.2%	12.2%

EXAMPLE 4

Rework the above example given that the employee in question is a company director.

SOLUTION

Regardless of the distribution of the director's earnings over the tax year, primary contributions would be 10% x (£27,820 - £3,952) = £2,386.80.

Class 1 NIC's (as from 2001/02)

The National Insurance contributions system has undergone a number of changes in recent years and further changes have been announced for 2001/02. The main changes which will take effect as from 6 April 2001 are as follows :

(a) The primary threshold will be increased so that it is the same as the secondary threshold. Both of these thresholds are expected to be £87 per week in 2001/02.

(b) The upper earnings limit will rise to an expected £575 per week in 2001/02.

(c) The main rate of secondary contributions will fall by 0.3% in 2001/02.

Class 1A National Insurance contributions

Benefits in kind which are not convertible into cash are generally exempt from Class 1 NIC's. However, these benefits give rise to a Class 1A contribution instead, *payable by the employer only* (not by the employee). For 2000/01, this contribution is calculated as 12.2% of the amount of the benefit in kind which is assessed on the employee under Schedule E (see Chapter 7). Until 6 April 2000, Class 1A applied only to cars and fuel provided for private use but this class of National Insurance has now been extended to cover benefits in kind generally. However, the provision of childcare (and childcare vouchers) by employers remains free of NIC's.

EXAMPLE 5

In 2000/01, George is provided with a 1,600cc petrol-engined car by his employer who pays for all fuel and other running costs. George's annual mileage is 20,000 of which 75% relates to business travel. The car had a list price of £11,700 when it was purchased new in late 1999. George's private medical insurance premium of £600 per annum is also paid by his employer.

Calculate the Class 1A contribution payable by George's employer for the year.

SOLUTION

The car benefit assessed under Schedule E is £2,925 (25% of £11,700). The assessable fuel benefit is £2,170. Therefore the Class 1A contribution payable by George's employer is 12.2% of (£2,925 + £2,170 + £600) = £694.79.

Class 2 National Insurance contributions

Class 2 NIC's are payable by self-employed people at a flat rate (for 2000/01) of £2.00 per week. A self-employed person whose earnings from self-employment in a tax year are less than the "small earnings exemption limit" (£3,825 for 2000/01) is not required to pay Class 2 NIC's for that year but may do so voluntarily in order to maintain a full contributions record. Note that :

(a) For Class 2 purposes, a self-employed person's earnings in a tax year are equal to the net profit, *before* adjustment for tax purposes, shown by the person's accounts for the year. The required figure is the actual net profit from 6 April to the following 5 April. Unless accounts are drawn up to 5 April, it will be necessary to apportion the net profits shown in two years' accounts to obtain this figure.

(b) If a self-employed person has two or more businesses, the profits of all of them are aggregated and a Class 2 liability arises unless the aggregate profits are less than the exemption limit.

EXAMPLE 6

(a) Alison is self-employed. Her accounts for the year to 5 April 2001 show a net profit of £3,775. Is she liable to pay Class 2 NIC's for 2000/01 ?

(b) Amanda is also self-employed. Her accounts for the year to 31 December 2000 show a net profit of £3,530 and her accounts for the year to 31 December 2001 show a net profit of £4,730. Is she liable to pay Class 2 NIC's for 2000/01 ?

SOLUTION

(a) Alison's accounts (which coincide with tax year 2000/01) show a net profit which is less than the small earnings exemption limit. Therefore she is not required to pay Class 2 NIC's for 2000/01.

(b) Amanda's accounts do not coincide with the tax year so some apportionment is necessary. Her actual net profit in 2000/01 is £3,830 (£3,530 x 9/12 + £4,730 x 3/12). This is not less than the small earnings exemption limit so she will be required to pay Class 2 NIC's for 2000/01.

Class 4 National Insurance contributions

In addition to the flat rate Class 2 liability described above, self-employed people may also be liable to pay earnings-related Class 4 NIC's. A self-employed person's Class 4 liability for a given tax year is based on the tax-adjusted profits assessed for that year under Schedule D Case I or II and is collected along with the income tax liability. Note the following points :

(a) The Class 4 liability is based on the Schedule D Case I or II assessment for the year, after deducting trade charges and loss reliefs but before deducting retirement annuity or personal pension premiums.

(b) If a self-employed person has more than one business, the earnings from all businesses for the year are aggregated.

(c) There is no Class 4 liability if profits do not exceed a specified lower limit (£4,385 for 2000/01).

(d) If profits do exceed the lower limit, Class 4 NIC's (for 2000/01) are payable at the rate of 7% on profits lying between the lower limit of £4,385 and an upper limit of £27,820.

EXAMPLE 7

Calculate the Class 4 NIC's payable for 2000/01 in each of the following cases :

(a)   Shawn has a 2000/01 Schedule D Case I assessment of £13,170.

(b)   Catherine has a 2000/01 Schedule D Case I assessment of £30,000.

(c)   Paul has a 2000/01 Schedule D Case I assessment of £4,220.

SOLUTION

(a)   7% x (£13,170 - £4,385) = £614.95.

(b)   7% x (£27,820 - £4,385) = £1,640.45. This is the maximum contribution since profits over the upper limit are not subject to Class 4 NIC's.

(c)   Paul's profits are less than the lower limit so his Class 4 liability for the year is nil.

Class 3 National Insurance contributions

Any individual (employed or self-employed) whose earnings are too low in a contribution period to require a National Insurance contribution may make a voluntary Class 3 contribution so as to maintain a full contributions record. For 2000/01, the amount of the Class 3 contribution is £6.55 per week.

Annual maximum contributions

An employee who has more than one employment will normally be required to make Class 1 contributions in respect of each employment. Similarly, an individual who is both employed and self-employed will normally be required to make Class 1 contributions in respect of the employment and Class 2 and Class 4 contributions in respect of the self-employment. In these circumstances, the total NIC's payable could become onerous but relief is available in the form of limits on the amount of NIC's payable by any one person in any one year. There are two limits to consider :

(a)   **Maximum Class 1 and 2 contributions**. The total of the Class 1 and Class 2 contributions payable by an individual in one year is limited to 53 primary Class 1 NIC's at the maximum weekly rate. For 2000/01 this is equal to £2,432.70 (53 x 10% x (£535 - £76)). If this limit is exceeded then the excess is refunded.

(b)   **Maximum Class 1, 2 and 4 contributions**. The total of the Classes 1, 2 and 4 contributions payable by an individual in one year is limited to 53 Class 2 contributions plus the maximum Class 4 contribution for the year. For 2000/01 this is £1,746.45 (53 @ £2.00 + 7% x (£27,820 - £4,385)). If this limit is exceeded, Class 4 contributions are refunded up to the amount of the excess.

EXAMPLE 8

(a)   Stephanie is employed at a monthly salary of £2,300. She is not contracted out of SERPS. She also has a small business and pays 53 weekly Class 2 NIC's in 2000/01. Calculate the refund of NIC's due for the year.

(b)   Stewart is self-employed and pays 53 weekly Class 2 NIC's in 2000/01. His business profits assessed in 2000/01 are £22,020. He also receives directors' fees of £10,000 in the year. He is not contracted out of SERPS. Calculate the refund of NIC's due for the year.

SOLUTION

(a)   Stephanie will have paid NIC's as follows :

	£
Class 1 (12 x 10% x (£2,300 - £329))	2,365.20
Class 2 (53 @ £2.00)	106.00
	2,471.20

This exceeds the maximum of £2,432.70, so Stephanie will be entitled to a refund of £38.50.

(b)   Stewart will have paid NIC's as follows :

	£
Class 1 (10% x (£10,000 - £3,952))	604.80
Class 2 (53 @ £2.00)	106.00
Class 4 (7% x (£22,020 - £4,385))	1,234.45
	1,945.25

His combined Class 1 and Class 2 contributions are within the allowed maximum of £2,432.70 but his combined Class 1, 2 and 4 contributions exceed the allowed maximum of £1,746.45. Therefore he is entitled to a refund of Class 4 contributions amounting to £198.80.

Summary

▶ Class 1 NIC's are payable by employees (primary contributions) and by their employers (secondary contributions).

▶ Class 1 NIC's are calculated with respect to earnings in a contribution period and each contribution period is considered independently.

▶ Both primary and secondary NIC's are reduced if the employee is contracted out of SERPS.

▶ The Class 1 NIC's of company directors are assessed on an annual basis and are unaffected by the distribution of the director's earnings over the year.

▶ Class 1A NIC's are payable by employers in relation to benefits in kind which are not convertible into cash.

▶ Class 2 NIC's are payable at a flat rate by self-employed people whose profits exceed the small earnings exemption limit.

▶ Class 4 NIC's are paid by self-employed people and are earnings-related.

▶ Class 3 NIC's are paid voluntarily in order to maintain a full contributions record.

▶ There are annual maximum limits on the amount of NIC's payable by an individual.

Exercises

15.1   Compute the primary and secondary Class 1 NIC's payable in relation to the following employees (none of whom are contracted out of SERPS) :

(a)   A earns £80 for the week ending 18 June 2000.

(b)   B earns £190 for the week ending 18 June 2000.

(c)   C earns £606 for the week ending 18 June 2000.

(d)   D earns £300 for the month of September 2000.

(e)   E earns £465 for the month of September 2000.

(f)   F earns £2,500 for the month of September 2000.

15.2   Rework your answer to Exercise 15.1, assuming now that each of the employees is a member of a COSR scheme.

15.3   Mark is self-employed and makes up his accounts annually to 30 November. His accounts for the year ended 30 November 2000 show a net profit of £6,890 and his accounts for the year ended 30 November 2001 show a net profit of £3,120. His 2000/01 Schedule D Case I assessment is £7,720. Calculate the NIC's payable by Mark for 2000/01.

*15.4 Brenda is a company director and earns a regular monthly salary of £2,000. In December 2000 she received a £5,000 bonus. She is provided with a one-year old 1,800cc diesel-engined company car which had a list price when new of £16,000 and she travels 10,000 miles a year of which 20% comprises business mileage. The company pays all the running costs of the car, including fuel. Her BUPA subscription of £650 per year is paid by the company.

Calculate the NIC's payable in respect of Brenda for 2000/01 (she is a member of a COSR scheme).

*15.5 Leonard is employed and receives a salary of £2,200 per month. He is not contracted out of SERPS. He also has a small business and pays 53 weekly Class 2 NIC's for 2000/01. His 2000/01 Schedule D Case I assessment is £7,670. Calculate the refund of NIC's due to Leonard for the year.

Review questions (Set A)

A 1   Tom Tulliver has been appointed sales director of Pembridge plc, a large company in the building industry. In addition to a basic salary of £50,000, he has been offered a comprehensive benefits package. The proposed deal is :

(i)   The company will provide him with a new 1,800 cc motor car which, together with accessories, will cost £19,500. Whilst the use would be primarily personal, he has carefully estimated that business mileage would be 2,400 miles per annum. Petrol for private use will be provided but Mr Tulliver must make a contribution of £400 per year towards its cost.

(ii)   An interest-free loan of £5,250 will be made to him on appointment and need only be repaid on his leaving the company. The loan will be used to purchase a stereo system and other household items.

(iii)   He has a choice of meals in the company canteen, which is open to all staff free of charge, or luncheon vouchers worth £5 per day, an amount equivalent to the normal cost of the meals. He has decided to accept the luncheon vouchers. The normal working year is 200 working days.

(iv)   His son, aged three, is presently attending a nursery group at a cost of £2,000 per year. Pembridge plc has offered to give his son a free place in their own day nursery but Mr Tulliver would like to continue the existing arrangement and for Pembridge to pay the fees to the existing nursery.

Mrs Tulliver's wife earns £14,000 per year. She pays pension contributions to her employer's pension scheme of 6% of her salary. Both Mr and Mrs Tulliver have building society accounts which will yield net interest of £6,400 and £2,240 respectively in 2000/01. Mr Tulliver receives UK preference dividends of £4,680 annually.

Mr Tulliver's appointment will begin on 1 April 2000 and he wishes to examine his and his wife's tax position before the start of fiscal year 2000/01.

Required :

(a)   Advise Mr Tulliver on the taxation implications of his employment package as it stands.

(b)   Advise him of any changes you consider that he should make to maximise the tax efficiency of the proposed package.

(c)   Using your answer in (a) as to the amount of Mr Tulliver's income, advise him of the likely income tax borne by him and his wife for 2000/01 and, again, suggest how the tax position might be improved. (*Note* : Assume that the official rate of interest is 6.25%). *(AAT)*

A 2   Jeremy, who is married, is 77 years old and receives a state retirement pension of £8,900 per annum. He also receives dividend income of £6,750 per annum. In 1998 Jeremy purchased a life annuity from which a monthly income of £325 (gross) is paid. The capital element of each payment was agreed with the Inland Revenue at £300. Income tax is being deducted from the income element.

Jeremy owns a furnished cottage which he rents to holidaymakers. In tax year 2000/01 it was let for 20 weeks at a weekly rental of £250.

The following expenditure was incurred :

	£
Insurance (see note)	400
Water rates	200
Council tax	300

Note : The £400 was paid on 1 January 2001. The insurance paid on 1 January 2000 was £360.

You are required :

To calculate the income tax payable by Jeremy for the year 2000/01.   *(ACCA)*

A 3   Sarah, who was born on 2 April 1956, is a self-employed computer consultant. Her agreed taxable profits were as follows :

	£
2000/01	50,000
1999/00	30,000
1998/99	10,000
1997/98	9,000
1996/97	8,000
1995/96	7,000
1994/95	6,000
1993/94	5,000
1992/93	4,000

On 1 June 2000, she tells you that she has never paid any personal pension premiums and that, in view of her recent high profits, she now wishes to make premium payments sufficient to utilise as much of the previous years' unused relief as possible.

You are required :

To calculate the amount of the premiums which Sarah should pay and to explain how these premiums should be applied.   *(ACCA)*

A 4 In each of the following situations, show the tax position assuming that the maximum potential reliefs are claimed as soon as possible. Then advise your client of any alternatives that might be available.

(i) Mr de Praet - a married man - begins trading on 1 January 1995, preparing accounts to 31 December annually. Recent results are :

	£	
Year to 31 December 1999	20,000	Profit
Year to 31 December 2000	(30,000)	Loss

He receives rents of £5,000 annually. His wife is employed part-time at a salary of £4,540 per year. It is estimated that the trading profits for the year to 31 December 2001 are likely to be £68,000.

(ii) Henry Percy began trading on 1 July 1996 and makes up accounts to 30 June annually. His adjusted trading results (before capital allowances) for the last two years have been :

	£	
Year to 30 June 1999	18,000	Profit
Year to 30 June 2000	(10,000)	Loss

Up to 31 December 1999 he always leased his plant and machinery but on 1 January 2000 he purchased a new machine for £18,400. He has no income other than his business profits. *(AAT)*

A 5 In May 2000 Bernard, a self-employed plumber, and his son Gerald, a self-employed electrician, purchased 1,000 empty barrels from a Scottish whisky distillery. The barrels were over 100 years old and of no further use to the distillery. Bernard and Gerald sawed the barrels into halves and sold them to several local garden centres for use as ornamental flower tubs. Bernard and Gerald paid £10 per barrel to the distillery and sold a half-barrel for £8. Three-quarters of the barrels were sold by Bernard and Gerald in the summer of 2000 and the remainder in the summer of 2001.

You are required :

To prepare a list of points for consideration prior to writing a report to Bernard and Gerald on the liability to income tax of the profit generated by the venture. *(ACCA)*

*A 6 Your directors are considering paying substantial cash bonuses to a number of senior employees, including some directors.

You are required :

To draft a report to the board setting out the regulations for taxing these bonuses, indicating when the tax and National Insurance contributions on them would be payable. *(CIMA)*

*A 7   Claud Chapperon is a self-employed wholesale clothing distributor who began trading on 1 July 1996. His summarised accounts for the year to 30 June 2000 are shown below (figures in brackets refer to notes).

	£	£
Sales (1)		400,000
Opening stock (2)	40,000	
Purchases	224,000	
	264,000	
Closing stock (2)	32,000	232,000
Gross profit		168,000
Wages and national insurance (3)	52,600	
Rent and rates	29,100	
Repairs and renewals (4)	3,490	
Miscellaneous expenses (5)	665	
Taxation (Claud's income tax)	17,555	
Bad debts (6)	820	
Legal expenses (7)	1,060	
Depreciation	570	
Lease rental on Claud's car (8)	8,400	
Loss on sale of office furniture	60	
Deeds of covenant (9)	195	
Transport costs	4,135	
Interest (10)	990	
Running expenses of Claud's car (11)	2,000	
Premium on lease (12)	6,000	
Lighting and heating	1,250	
Sundry expenses (all allowable)	710	
Relocation expenditure (13)	2,400	132,000
Net profit		36,000

Notes :

1. Sales include £500 reimbursed by Claud's family for clothing taken from stock. The reimbursement represented cost price.

2. The basis of both the opening and closing stock valuations was "lower of cost or market value", less a contingency reserve of 50%.

3. Included in wages are Claud's drawings of £50 per week, his NIC's of £285 for the year and his wife's wages and NIC's totalling £11,750. His wife works full-time in the business as a secretary.

4. The charge for repairs and renewals includes £2,945 for fitting protective covers over the factory windows and doors to prevent burglary.

5.   Miscellaneous expenses comprise :

	£
Theft of money by employee	65
Political donation to Green Party	100
Gifts of 100 "Chapperon" calendars	500
	665

6.   Bad debts comprise :

	£
Trade debt written off	720
Loan to former employee written off	250
Reduction in general provision	(150)
	820

7.   Legal expenses comprise :

	£
Defending action re alleged faulty goods	330
Costs re lease of new larger premises	250
Successful appeal against previous year's income tax assessment	200
Defending Claud in connection with speeding offence	190
Debt collection	90
	1,060

8.   Claud's leased car was a BMW costing £20,000.

9.   Deeds of covenant consist of £120 per annum paid to the local children's hospital and £75 per annum paid to Oxfam. Both payments were made on 30 April 2000.

10. Interest is as follows :

	£
Bank overdraft interest (business account)	1,020
Interest on overdue tax	130
Interest credited on NSB ordinary a/c (see note 14)	(160)
	990

11. The Inland Revenue have agreed that one-third of Claud's mileage is private. Included in the charge for motor running expenses is £65 for a speeding fine incurred by Claud whilst delivering goods to a customer.

12. The premium was for a lease of six years.

13. The relocation expenditure was incurred in transferring the business to new and larger premises.

14. The NSB ordinary account was opened on 1 March 1999 and interest was credited as follows :

	£
31 December 1999	160
31 December 2000	140

The following information is also provided :

(i) Capital allowances for the year to 30 June 2000 are £480.

(ii) Claud was born on 10 April 1944 and he always pays the maximum permitted personal pension contribution. His wife was also born in 1944.

You are required :

(a) To prepare a profit adjustment statement in respect of the accounting period to 30 June 2000, showing the 2000/01 Schedule D Case I assessment.

(b) To calculate the Class 4 NIC's payable by Claud for 2000/01.

(c) To prepare an estimate of Claud's income tax borne for 2000/01. *(ACCA)*

*A8 When submitting a business's annual accounts to the Inland Revenue, it is usual to send schedules under the following expenditure headings :

(i) Gifts and entertainment

(ii) Major repairs

(iii) Redundancy payments to employees.

You are required :

To state the information which should be included under each of the above headings, explaining why such information will be required. *(CIMA)*

*A9 Joseph Kent commenced in business on 1 October 1997 as a joiner making conservatories. His tax-adjusted profits (before deduction of capital allowances) were as follows :

	£
Period to 31 December 1998	35,000
Year ended 31 December 1999	24,000
Year ended 31 December 2000	42,000

Capital additions and disposals were as follows :

Additions

		£
1 October 1997	Car (at valuation)	12,200
1 October 1997	Trailer	2,000
1 October 1997	Plant and machinery	8,000
1 December 1999	Car	13,000
1 December 2000	Plant and machinery	6,000

	£
Disposals	
1 December 1999 Car acquired 1/10/97	7,000
1 January 2000 Plant and machinery (at less than cost)	2,000

Private use of both cars has been agreed with the Inland Revenue at 20%. No claim is made to treat any of the assets as short-life assets.

Joseph manufactured the conservatories in rented premises until 1 January 2000, when he purchased a new factory unit on an industrial estate for £20,000 (not in an enterprise zone). All assets were brought into use immediately upon acquisition.

Joseph's wife Sephora is a solicitor employed by a practising firm at a salary of £30,000 per annum. The following additional information is provided for 2000/01 :

(i)   A new 2,500cc petrol-engined car was provided for Sephora's use in August 1999. The list price at that time was £25,000. Of this amount, £4,000 was contributed by Sephora so that a better car could be provided. She was required to pay £25 per month towards the private use of the car but not towards the private fuel, all of which was provided by her employers. The business mileage in 2000/01 is 10,000 miles.

(ii)   Sephora has received a loan of £60,000 on the matrimonial home from her employers on which she pays interest at 3%.

(iii)   Sephora made a qualifying donation to the Oxfam charity on 1 July 2000 of £390 under the Gift Aid scheme.

(iv)   Both Joseph and Sephora are under 65 years old.

You are required :

(a)   To calculate Joseph's Schedule D Case I assessments for 1997/98 to 2000/01 inclusive.

(b)   To calculate Sephora's income tax liability for 2000/01 (assuming an official rate of interest of 6.25% per annum). *(ACCA)*

*A10   Thomas Pilkington bought an existing business, Marcus Fashionwear, a gentlemen's outfitters, on 1 December 1999. The summarised trading profit and loss account for the year to 30 November 2000 is set out below :

	£	£
Sales		201,600
Cost of sales		53,900
		147,700
Investment income		9,100
		156,800
Rent and rates	25,400	
Lighting and heating	3,200	
Wages and salaries	22,500	
Insurances	1,100	
Motor vehicle expenses	5,200	
Postage, stationery and telephone	800	
Repairs to premises	4,900	
Advertising	3,200	
Bad debts	2,100	
Subscriptions and donations	500	
Depreciation : Motor vehicles	3,900	
Fixtures and fittings	2,000	
Office machinery	3,000	
Legal and professional charges	3,300	81,100
Net profit		75,700

You are required :

To state what further information you would require to enable you to calculate the income assessable under the various Schedules.   *(ACCA)*

PART 2
CAPITAL GAINS TAX

Chapter 16

Introduction to capital gains tax

Introduction

The next seven chapters of this book deal with capital gains tax (CGT), which was introduced in 1965 with the aim of taxing gains arising on the disposal of capital assets. CGT has undergone many changes since its inception and the changes made between 1965 and 1992 were consolidated into the Taxation of Chargeable Gains Act 1992. This Act has since been amended by subsequent Finance Acts.

Chargeable persons

A liability to CGT may arise when a "chargeable person" makes a "chargeable disposal" of a "chargeable asset". The main categories of chargeable person are as follows :

(a) individuals who are resident or ordinarily resident in the UK (husbands and wives being assessed independently)

(b) partners, who are each responsible for their share of the CGT due on a partnership's capital gains

(c) trustees and personal representatives.

The following are *not* chargeable persons for CGT purposes and therefore cannot incur a CGT liability :

(a) companies, which pay corporation tax on their chargeable gains, not CGT

(b) registered charities and friendly societies, local authorities, approved superannuation funds, unit trusts, investment trusts and approved scientific research associations, all of which are exempt from CGT.

Chargeable assets

All assets are regarded as chargeable assets except for those which are specifically exempted from CGT. The main exemptions are as follows :

(a) a taxpayer's principal private residence (see Chapter 21)

(b) motor cars, including vintage and veteran motor cars

(c) items of tangible, movable property ("chattels") disposed of for £6,000 or less (see Chapter 18)

(d) chattels with a predictable useful life of 50 years or less ("wasting chattels") unless used in business and eligible for capital allowances (see Chapter 18)

(e) gilt-edged securities and qualifying corporate bonds (see Chapter 19)

(f) works of art and collections of scientific interest if donated for the benefit of the nation

(g) National Savings Certificates, Premium Bonds and British Savings Bonds

(h) foreign currency if acquired for private use

(i) winnings from pools, lotteries, betting etc.

(j) decorations for valour (unless acquired by purchase)

(k) compensation received for personal or professional injury and compensation for mis-sold personal pensions or (by concession) mis-sold free-standing additional voluntary contribution schemes taken out between certain dates

(l) life assurance policies (unless purchased from a third party)

(m) Personal Equity Plans, shares in a Venture Capital Trust and investments held in an Individual Savings Account (see Chapter 6).

If an asset is not a chargeable asset, then neither a chargeable gain nor an allowable loss can arise on its disposal.

Chargeable disposals

The main, and most obvious, instance of a chargeable disposal occurs when a chargeable asset is sold. However, the sale of an asset in the course of trade does *not* constitute a chargeable disposal for CGT purposes since trading profits are assessed instead to income tax under Schedule D Case I.

Before CGT was introduced in 1965 there was a great incentive for taxpayers to show that the gain arising on the sale of an asset was a capital gain (and so not taxable at all) rather than a trading profit (and so subject to income tax). With the introduction of CGT this incentive was diminished but it is still important to distinguish between capital gains and trading profits since the rules of computation for CGT and income tax are different.

As well as the sale of a chargeable asset, the following also rank as chargeable disposals :

(a) the sale of part of a chargeable asset

(b) the gift of all or part of a chargeable asset

(c) the loss or destruction of all or part of a chargeable asset.

The date on which a chargeable disposal is deemed to occur is the date on which ownership of the asset changes hands, regardless of the date on which payment (if any) takes place.

Non-chargeable disposals

The following types of disposal are *not* chargeable disposals and therefore any gains (or losses) arising on such disposals are exempt from CGT :

(a) gifts to charities, art galleries, museums etc.

(b) disposals caused by the death of the taxpayer.

Strictly speaking, disposals between a husband and wife who are living together *are* chargeable disposals. However, such disposals are deemed to occur at a disposal value such that neither a chargeable gain nor an allowable loss arises (see Chapter 17).

Basis of assessment

A person's CGT liability for a tax year is based upon the chargeable disposals made by that person during the tax year. For example, the 2000/01 CGT assessment is based upon chargeable disposals made between 6 April 2000 and 5 April 2001 inclusive. No liability to CGT arises until an asset is disposed of, so the mere fact that an asset has appreciated in value will not of itself trigger a CGT assessment. The amount of the CGT assessment for a tax year is calculated as follows :

(a) The gain or loss arising on each disposal made during the year is calculated separately (the method of calculation is described in great detail in subsequent chapters of this book).

(b) If total gains exceed total losses, the losses are subtracted from the gains to give the "net gains" for the year. If total losses exceed total gains, the gains are subtracted from the losses to give the "net losses" for the year.

(c) If there are net gains for the year, these are reduced first by any unrelieved losses brought forward from previous years or carried back on the death of the taxpayer (see below) and then by the total amount of "taper relief" available. Taper relief is calculated separately for each gain arising in the year, according to :

    (i)   the length of time for which the asset was held before disposal

    (ii) whether or not the asset qualifies as a "business asset"

    (iii) the extent to which the gain has been reduced by losses of the year or losses brought forward or carried back.

These results are then aggregated to give total taper relief for the year. (A much more detailed explanation of taper relief is given in Chapter 17).

(d)   The net gains left after deduction of taper relief are then further reduced by the amount of the "annual exemption" (£7,200 for 2000/01) and the remainder is the CGT assessment for the year. If net gains (after taper relief) are less than the annual exemption in any year, the CGT assessment for that year is £nil and the balance of the annual exemption is lost.

(e)   If there are net losses for the year, the CGT assessment for that year is £nil and the whole of the annual exemption is lost. The net losses may then be carried forward for relief in future years, as described later in this chapter.

Husbands and wives are each entitled to the full annual exemption. This exemption is also available to the trustees of a trust established for a mentally disabled person or for certain other infirm or disabled persons. For trustees of other settlements the annual exemption is lower (£3,600 for 2000/01). The personal representatives of a deceased person are entitled to the full annual exemption for the year of death and for the following two years.

EXAMPLE 1

Four taxpayers each make three chargeable disposals during 2000/01. Compute their CGT assessments for the year (assuming that there are no unrelieved losses brought forward or carried back and that no taper relief is available) if these disposals give rise to the following gains and losses :

(a)   Taxpayer A has gains of £2,000, £2,700 and £4,750.

(b)   Taxpayer B has gains of £3,500, £5,840 and a loss of £1,250.

(c)   Taxpayer C has gains of £450, £7,630 and a loss of £3,250.

(d)   Taxpayer D has a gain of £8,950 and losses of £9,500 and £800.

SOLUTION

(a)   Taxpayer A has total gains of £9,450 and no losses. Net gains are therefore £9,450. Subtracting the annual exemption of £7,200 gives a CGT assessment for the year of £2,250.

(b)   Taxpayer B has total gains of £9,340 and total losses of £1,250. Net gains are therefore £8,090. Subtracting the annual exemption of £7,200 gives a CGT assessment for the year of £890.

(c) Taxpayer C has total gains of £8,080 and total losses of £3,250. Net gains are therefore £4,830. This is less than the annual exemption of £7,200, so the CGT assessment for the year is £nil. The unused part of the annual exemption (£2,370) is lost.

(d) Taxpayer D has total gains of £8,950 and total losses of £10,300. Net losses are therefore £1,350. The CGT assessment for the year is £nil and the whole of the annual exemption is lost.

Rates of CGT

The rates of CGT for individuals are aligned with the rates of income tax payable on savings income (see Chapter 2). The rules for calculating the amount of capital gains tax due on an individual's CGT assessment for 2000/01 are as follows :

(a) If any part of the individual's income is charged to income tax at the higher rate (40%) or at the Schedule F upper rate (32.5%), the whole of the CGT assessment is charged to capital gains tax at the higher rate (40%).

(b) If none of the individual's income is charged to income tax at the higher rate or at the Schedule F upper rate, then :

    (i) capital gains of up to the amount of any unused part of the starting rate band are taxed at the starting rate (10%)

    (ii) remaining gains of up to the amount of any unused part of the basic rate band (which is extended if the taxpayer makes a Gift Aid donation in the year, as explained in Chapter 4) are taxed at the lower rate (20%)

    (iii) any further remaining gains are taxed at the higher rate (40%).

It is important to note that individuals with no income tax liability are *not* allowed to offset any unrelieved charges or unused personal allowances against their capital gains. Similarly, tax reducers may be used only to reduce a taxpayer's income tax liability, not his or her CGT liability.

The CGT rate applicable to trustees and personal representatives is equivalent to the special rate of income tax applicable to certain trusts, currently 34% (see Chapter 6).

EXAMPLE 2

Alan has a capital gains tax assessment of £7,400 in 2000/01. Calculate the amount of CGT payable for 2000/01 if his taxable income for the year (i.e. his total income after deduction of charges and the personal allowance) is :

(a) £20,000   (b) £25,000   (c) £30,000   (d) £300.

Assume that Alan makes no Gift Aid donations in 2000/01.

SOLUTION

(a) Taxable income uses the whole of the starting rate band and £18,480 (£20,000 - £1,520) of the basic rate band, leaving £8,400 (£26,880 - £18,480) of the basic rate band unused. Alan's CGT assessment is less than this. Therefore the amount of CGT payable is £7,400 @ 20% = £1,480.

(b) Taxable income uses the whole of the starting rate band and £23,480 (£25,000 - £1,520) of the basic rate band, leaving £3,400 (£26,880 - £23,480) of the basic rate band unused. Therefore the amount of CGT payable is £3,400 @ 20% + £4,000 @ 40% = £2,280.

(c) Alan's taxable income uses the whole of the starting rate and basic rate bands and he pays income tax at 40% on the last £1,600 of his income. Therefore the whole of his CGT assessment is charged to capital gains tax at 40%. The amount of CGT payable is £7,400 @ 40% = £2,960.

(d) The unused part of the starting rate band is £1,220 (£1,520 - £300) and the whole of the basic rate band (£26,880) is also unused. Therefore the amount of CGT payable is £1,220 @ 10% + £6,180 @ 20% = £1,358.

Relief for capital losses

If a taxpayer has net losses for a year, the CGT assessment for that year is £nil and the annual exemption is lost. The amount of the net losses may then be carried forward without time limit and set against the net gains of future years.

Losses carried forward must be offset against the first available net gains, but are offset only to the extent that untapered net gains exceed the annual exemption for the year in which they arise, so preventing the annual exemption from being wasted. Any losses remaining unrelieved are carried forward again to subsequent years. This method of preserving the annual exemption applies *only* to losses brought forward from a previous year. It is *not* possible to preserve the annual exemption by restricting the set-off of current year losses. Since married couples are taxed independently, the losses of one spouse cannot be offset against the gains of the other spouse.

EXAMPLE 3

Four taxpayers each have £3,000 of capital losses brought forward from previous years. Calculate their 2000/01 CGT assessments if their total gains and losses in 2000/01 are as follows (and no taper relief is available) :

(a) Taxpayer A has gains of £5,800 and losses of £1,100.

(b) Taxpayer B has gains of £7,800 and losses of £600.

(c) Taxpayer C has gains of £9,900 and losses of £1,000.

(d) Taxpayer D has gains of £13,300 and losses of £1,200.

SOLUTION

(a) Taxpayer A's net gains for the year are £4,700. This is less than the annual exemption of £7,200 so the CGT assessment for the year is £nil and the balance of the annual exemption is lost. There is no scope for relieving losses brought forward, so the entire £3,000 is carried forward to 2001/02.

(b) Taxpayer B's net gains for the year are £7,200. This is exactly equal to the annual exemption so the CGT assessment for the year is £nil. There is no scope for relieving losses brought forward, so the entire £3,000 is carried forward to 2001/02.

(c) Taxpayer C's net gains for the year are £8,900. This exceeds the annual exemption by £1,700 so £1,700 of the losses brought forward are relieved in 2000/01, giving a CGT assessment for the year of £nil. The remaining £1,300 of the losses are unrelieved and are therefore carried forward to 2001/02.

(d) Taxpayer D's net gains for the year are £12,100. This exceeds the annual exemption by £4,900 so the entire £3,000 of losses brought forward are relieved in 2000/01, giving a CGT assessment for the year of £1,900. There are no unrelieved losses to carry forward.

Losses in the year of death

As stated above, disposals caused by the death of a taxpayer are exempt from CGT, though such disposals may give rise to an inheritance tax liability. But disposals made in the year of death (i.e. from 6 April up to the date of death) are *not* exempt from CGT and are taxed in the usual way, with a full annual exemption given for the year.

If a taxpayer suffers net losses in the year of death, such losses cannot (for obvious reasons) be carried forward for relief in future years. However, a measure of relief is available in that net losses incurred in the year of death may be carried back and set off against the net gains of the previous 3 years (most recent years first). As is the case with losses carried forward, losses carried back are set against a year's net gains only to the extent that untapered net gains exceed the annual exemption for the year in which they arise.

EXAMPLE 4

Sarah dies on 16 December 2000, having made net capital losses of £7,300 between 6 April 2000 and the date of her death. Her net gains in the previous 3 years are :

	£
1997/98	7,650
1998/99	1,400
1999/00	11,450

Calculate her CGT assessments for 1997/98 to 2000/01 inclusive, given that the annual exemption was £6,500 in 1997/98, £6,800 in 1998/99 and £7,100 in 1999/00. (No taper relief is available in any year).

SOLUTION

Since losses in the year of death are carried back to the most recent year first, it is easier to begin with the year of death and then work backwards.

(a) In 2000/01, Sarah has net losses. Her CGT assessment for the year is therefore £nil and the annual exemption (available in full) is lost. The net losses of £7,300 may be carried back to 1999/00, 1998/99 and 1997/98, in that order.

(b) In 1999/00, Sarah's net gains of £11,450 exceed the annual exemption by £4,350 so £4,350 of the losses carried back are relieved in 1999/00, giving a CGT assessment for the year of £nil. The remaining £2,950 of the losses are carried back to 1998/99.

(c) In 1998/99, Sarah's net gains of £1,400 are less than the annual exemption of £6,800. Therefore the CGT assessment for the year is £nil and the balance of the annual exemption is lost. There is no scope for relieving losses carried back, so the £2,950 is now carried back to 1997/98.

(d) In 1997/98, Sarah's net gains of £7,650 exceed the annual exemption by £1,150 so £1,150 of the losses carried back are relieved in 1997/98, giving a CGT assessment for the year of £nil. The remaining £1,800 of the losses incurred in the year of death cannot be carried back any further and therefore cannot be relieved in any way.

Assuming that CGT assessments have already been issued for 1997/98 and 1999/00, it will be necessary to issue revised assessments to take into account the relief for losses carried back and to refund any CGT already paid for those years.

Losses on disposals to connected persons

A taxpayer is deemed to be "connected" with a number of persons, mainly relatives and business associates (a full list of "connected persons" is given in Chapter 17). As an anti-avoidance measure, the Taxation of Chargeable Gains Act 1992 states that losses incurred on a disposal to a connected person can be offset only against gains made on disposals to the *same connected person*, in the same or future years.

Relief for trading losses

Under Section 72 of the Finance Act 1991, a taxpayer's trading losses may in certain circumstances be offset against that taxpayer's net capital gains (the required circumstances are described in Chapter 11). If a Section 72 claim is made for a tax year, the amount of the claim must be for the *lower* of :

(a) the amount of the trading loss which is available for relief in that year, and

(b) the "maximum amount", which is the amount of the CGT assessment, *disregarding the annual exemption*, that would have been raised for that year if a Section 72 claim had not been made.

It is important to note that the "maximum amount" is calculated as if the annual exemption simply did not exist. Not only is the annual exemption itself ignored in this calculation but so is the fact that capital losses brought forward might be restricted so as to preserve the exemption.

When the amount of the Section 72 claim has been determined, it is treated as an allowable capital loss incurred in the year of the claim and is therefore relieved *before* giving relief for capital losses brought forward.

EXAMPLE 5

(a) Richard is a sole trader and is considering making a Section 72 claim for 2000/01. His net gains for the year are £11,400 and he has capital losses brought forward of £2,300. Calculate his CGT assessment for 2000/01 (ignoring any Section 72 claim).

(b) Richard's unrelieved trading losses (eligible for a Section 72 claim in 2000/01) amount to £12,500. Calculate his CGT assessment for 2000/01 if he decides to make a Section 72 claim for the year.

(c) Now calculate the CGT assessment for 2000/01 if Richard's capital losses brought forward are £5,300 instead of £2,300.

Assume in all cases that no taper relief is available in 2000/01.

SOLUTION

(a) If Richard does not make a Section 72 claim for 2000/01, his CGT assessment for the year will be :

	£
Net gains	11,400
Less : Capital losses b/f	2,300
	9,100
Less : Annual exemption	7,200
CGT assessment	1,900

There will be no unrelieved capital losses to carry forward.

(b) A Section 72 claim would have to be for the lower of :

(i) the trading loss (£12,500), and

(ii) the CGT assessment (disregarding the annual exemption) that would be raised if a Section 72 claim were not made (i.e. £9,100, as shown above).

Therefore the Section 72 claim would be for £9,100. This would be relieved in priority to capital losses brought forward and the CGT assessment would be :

	£
Net gains	11,400
<u>Less</u> : Section 72 claim	9,100
	2,300
<u>Less</u> : Annual exemption (restricted)	2,300
CGT assessment	nil

The remainder of the annual exemption (£4,900) would be lost. There would be no scope for relieving any of the capital losses brought forward, so the entire £2,300 would be carried forward to 2001/02.

(c)   In the absence of a Section 72 claim, Richard's CGT assessment would be calculated as follows :

	£
Net gains	11,400
<u>Less</u> : Capital losses b/f (restricted)	4,200
	7,200
<u>Less</u> : Annual exemption	7,200
CGT assessment	nil

There would be unrelieved capital losses of £1,100 carried forward. The maximum amount for Section 72 purposes is £6,100 (£11,400 - £5,300) so a Section 72 claim would have to be for £6,100 and the CGT assessment would be :

	£
Net gains	11,400
<u>Less</u> : Section 72 claim	6,100
	5,300
<u>Less</u> : Annual exemption (restricted)	5,300
CGT assessment	nil

The remainder of the annual exemption (£1,900) would be lost and the capital losses of £5,300 would be carried forward to 2001/02 in their entirety. The main effect of the claim would be to preserve all the capital losses at the expense of sacrificing trading losses of £6,100. This might be worthwhile if Richard believes that he will have more chance of relieving capital losses in future years than trading losses.

Administration of CGT

The administration system which was described in Chapter 1 applies to CGT as well as to income tax. Note that :

(a) Details of the chargeable disposals made by a taxpayer during a tax year need not be entered on the tax return for that year if:

    (i) total disposal proceeds for the year do not exceed twice the amount of the annual exemption (£14,400 for 2000/01), and

    (ii) total gains for the year do not exceed the amount of the annual exemption (£7,200 for 2000/01), and

    (iii) the taxpayer does not wish to notify the Inland Revenue that there are net losses for the year.

(b) Net losses cannot be carried forward and set against subsequent capital gains unless these losses have been notified to the Inland Revenue. If the taxpayer has received a tax return for the year in which the losses are incurred, then notification must be made in the tax return. Otherwise, notification may be made in a later year's tax return or by sending a separate notice to the Inland Revenue. Losses are not allowed unless notified to the Inland Revenue by 31 January in the sixth year of assessment following the year in which the losses are incurred. For example, the latest date by which capital losses incurred in 2000/01 must be notified to the Inland Revenue is 31 January 2007.

(c) Acquisitions of chargeable assets do not need to be entered on the tax return.

Payment of CGT

CGT is normally payable on 31 January following the end of the tax year to which the tax relates. For instance, the normal due date for the 2000/01 CGT liability is 31 January 2002. An important difference between the payment of CGT and the payment of income tax is that payments on account of the CGT liability are *not* required.

If the proceeds of a disposal are received by the taxpayer in instalments over a period of more than 18 months, the taxpayer may make a claim for the CGT due in relation to the disposal to be payable over the period of the instalments or over an 8-year period, whichever is the shorter.

Interest, surcharges and penalties

The regime of interest, surcharges and penalties which was described in Chapter 14 applies to both CGT and income tax.

Summary

▶ A liability to CGT may arise when a chargeable person makes a chargeable disposal of a chargeable asset. Individuals resident or ordinarily resident in the UK are chargeable persons. Companies are not chargeable persons.

▶ All assets are chargeable assets unless specifically exempted.

▶ A chargeable disposal occurs when all or part of a chargeable asset is sold (except in the course of trade), given away, lost or destroyed.

▶ An individual's CGT liability for a tax year is based upon the chargeable disposals made by that individual during the tax year. For 2000/01, the first £7,200 of net gains is exempt from CGT.

▶ Capital gains tax is payable at the same rates as the rates of income tax which apply to savings income.

▶ Net losses may be carried forward and set against the net gains of subsequent years. Net losses incurred in the year of death of a taxpayer may be carried back for up to 3 years. Losses incurred on a disposal to a connected person may be offset only against gains made on disposals to the same connected person.

▶ In certain circumstances, trading losses may be set against net gains.

▶ CGT is normally payable on 31 January following the end of the tax year.

Exercises

16.1 Which of the following disposals might give rise to a CGT liability ?

    (a)   the sale of freehold property by a UK company

    (b)   the gift of shares from husband to wife (assuming that the couple live together)

    (c)   the gift of an oil painting to a charity

    (d)   the sale of an oil painting by a charity

    (e)   the sale of an oil painting by an art dealer

    (f)   the sale of leasehold property by a partnership.

16.2 Which of the following are chargeable assets for CGT purposes ?

    (a)   shares in British Telecom plc   (b)   gilt-edged securities

    (c)   an antique table worth £20,000   (d)   an antique chair worth £5,000

    (e)   a taxpayer's home   (f)   a vintage Bentley.

16.3 A taxpayer has capital losses of £2,500 in 2000/01. Compute the CGT assessment for 2000/01 if capital gains for the year are as follows (assuming that there are no unrelieved losses brought forward or carried back and that no taper relief is available) :

either (a) £nil

   or (b) £1,500

   or (c) £5,050

   or (d) £11,350.

16.4 A single man's only income in 2000/01 consists of a salary of £29,060. His CGT assessment for the year is £5,400. Calculate his CGT liability, assuming that he makes no Gift Aid donations in the year.

16.5 A taxpayer has capital losses brought forward from previous years amounting to £4,800. Compute the CGT assessment for 2000/01 if total gains and losses for the year are as follows (and no taper relief is available) :

either (a) gains £8,000, losses £2,000

   or (b) gains £9,200, losses £1,400

   or (c) gains £13,400, losses £nil.

16.6 John dies on 3 March 2001. Between 6 April 2000 and 3 March 2001, he has total gains of £1,200 and total losses of £15,400. His net gains in recent years have been as follows :

	£
	£
1996/97	51,800
1997/98	13,000
1998/99	9,600
1999/00	250

Show how the losses incurred in the year of John's death may be relieved, given that the annual exemption was £6,300 in 1996/97, £6,500 in 1997/98, £6,800 in 1998/99 and £7,100 in 1999/00. (No taper relief is available in any year).

16.7 On what date is CGT for 2000/01 normally due for payment ?

*16.8 Rosemary has the following capital gains and losses :

	Gains	Losses
	£	£
1997/98	6,200	12,700
1998/99	6,700	2,350
1999/00	9,900	nil
2000/01	16,300	7,500

There were no unrelieved losses to bring forward from 1996/97 or earlier. Compute her CGT assessments for the years 1997/98 to 2000/01, given that the annual exemption was £6,500 in 1997/98, £6,800 in 1998/99 and £7,100 in 1999/00. (No taper relief is available in any year).

*16.9   In 1999/00, Ahmed (a UK resident) incurred a capital loss of £3,750 on the disposal of an asset to his father. He also had capital gains in that year of £10,500. In 2000/01, Ahmed has capital gains of £37,200 and no losses. The capital gains in 2000/01 include gains of £2,000 on a disposal to his father and £3,500 on a disposal to his mother.

Compute Ahmed's CGT assessments for the years 1999/00 and 2000/01 given that the annual exemption was £7,100 in 1999/00. (No taper relief is available in either year).

*16.10   Melissa is a sole trader. She has trading losses eligible for a Section 72 claim in 2000/01 of £9,500. Her capital gains and capital losses for 2000/01 are £24,000 and £1,300 respectively. She has capital losses brought forward from 1999/00 of £13,700.

Show Melissa's CGT assessment for 2000/01, assuming that :

(a)   the Section 72 claim is not made

(b)   the Section 72 claim is made.

No taper relief is available in 2000/01.

Chapter 17

Computation of gains and losses

Introduction

The computation of the gain arising on the disposal of a chargeable asset begins by subtracting the acquisition cost of the asset from its disposal value. It may then be necessary to adjust the gain to take account of inflation and it may also be necessary to deduct taper relief. The computation becomes more complex if the asset was acquired on or before 31 March 1982.

The main purpose of this chapter is to explain the basic method of computation and to show how this method is modified for disposals of older assets.

Layout of a CGT computation

The computation of the untapered gain or the allowable loss arising on a chargeable disposal is laid out as follows :

	£	£
Disposal value		x
<u>Less</u> : Incidental costs of disposal		x
		x
<u>Less</u> : *Allowable expenditure* :		
Acquisition cost of asset	x	
Incidental costs of acquisition	x	
Enhancement expenditure	x	
Cost of defending the owner's title to the asset	x	
Valuation fees	x	x
Unindexed gain (unindexed loss)		x
<u>Less</u> : Indexation allowance		x
Untapered gain (allowable loss)		x

Each of the terms used in this layout is explained below.

Disposal value

If a disposal consists of the sale of an asset, disposal value is generally taken to be the proceeds of the sale. But if the sale is to a "connected person", the sale proceeds are ignored and disposal value is taken to be the market value of the asset on the date of the sale. For CGT purposes, the main persons with whom a taxpayer is connected are his or her :

(a) spouse

(b) relatives (i.e. brothers, sisters, ancestors and direct descendants) and their spouses

(c) spouse's relatives and their spouses

(d) business partners and their spouses and relatives.

Market value is also used as disposal value if a disposal takes the form of a gift. But it is important to remember that disposals between a husband and wife who are living together are deemed to occur at a disposal value such that neither a gain nor a loss arises (see Chapter 16). This rule takes precedence over the usual rules concerning sales to connected persons and gifts.

In general, the market value of an asset is the amount which the asset would fetch if sold on the open market. Listed shares and securities are valued for CGT purposes in the same way as they are valued for inheritance tax purposes (see Chapter 31).

The incidental costs of disposal which may be deducted when calculating a gain or loss include legal fees, estate agents' and auctioneers' fees, advertising costs etc.

Allowable expenditure

The following expenditure may be set against disposal value when calculating the gain or loss arising on a disposal :

(a) the acquisition cost of the asset (or market value on the date of acquisition if the asset was acquired by gift or from a connected person)

(b) incidental costs of acquisition (e.g. legal fees)

(c) "enhancement expenditure", which is expenditure on making improvements to the asset, so long as that expenditure is still reflected in the state of the asset at the time of disposal (but the costs of mere repairs and maintenance are disallowed)

(d) costs incurred in defending the owner's title to the asset (generally legal costs)

(e) valuation fees necessarily incurred for CGT purposes.

If an asset is acquired as the result of a disposal between a husband and wife who are living together, the deemed acquisition cost of the spouse receiving the asset is equal to the deemed disposal value of the spouse who makes the disposal (see above).

Indexation allowance

The object of indexation allowance is to ensure that any gains which have been caused solely by the effects of inflation are not charged to tax. The allowance was originally introduced in 1982 but has now been "frozen" at April 1998. In consequence, no indexation allowance is available in relation to inflation occurring after April 1998.

Indexation allowance is calculated separately for each item of allowable expenditure shown in a computation. The indexation allowance available on an item of expenditure is equal to the amount of the expenditure multiplied by an *indexation factor*, which is computed according to the following formula and rounded to 3 decimal places :

$$\frac{RD - RI}{RI}$$

where : RD is the Retail Prices Index (RPI) for the month of disposal (or April 1998, if earlier)

RI is the RPI for the month in which the expenditure was incurred.

A table of RPI's is given at the end of this chapter. It is very important to note that :

(a) No indexation allowance is given in relation to allowable expenditure incurred on or after 1 April 1998.

(b) Special rules apply to expenditure incurred before 31 March 1982 (see below).

(c) Although companies are not chargeable persons for CGT purposes, their capital gains are computed in a similar way to those of individuals and are then charged to corporation tax. However, the freezing of indexation allowance at April 1998 does *not* apply to companies (see Chapter 23).

EXAMPLE 1

An asset was bought in June 1989 (RPI 115.4) for £1,200 and was sold in August 2000 (RPI 169.9) for £2,350. The RPI for April 1998 was 162.6. Compute the untapered gain.

SOLUTION

	£
Sale proceeds	2,350
<u>Less</u> : Acquisition cost	1,200
Unindexed gain	1,150
<u>Less</u> : Indexation allowance	
$\frac{162.6 - 115.4}{115.4} = 0.409 \times £1,200$	491
Untapered gain	659

(Note that the RPI for August 2000 was not used in this computation).

EXAMPLE 2

An asset was bought for £15,000 in August 1990 (RPI 128.1). Enhancement expenditure was £2,000 in January 1991 (RPI 130.2) and £3,000 in June 1998. The asset was sold in July 2000 for £28,000. The RPI for April 1998 was 162.6. Compute the untapered gain.

SOLUTION

			£	£
Sale proceeds				28,000
Less : Acquisition cost			15,000	
Enhancement expenditure (£2,000 + £3,000)			5,000	20,000
Unindexed gain				8,000
Less : Indexation allowance :				
(i)	on acquisition cost			
	$\dfrac{162.6 - 128.1}{128.1} = 0.269 \times £15,000$		4,035	
(ii)	on enhancement expenditure			
	$\dfrac{162.6 - 130.2}{130.2} = 0.249 \times £2,000$		498	4,533
Untapered gain				3,467

(Indexation allowance is not available on the expenditure incurred in June 1998).

Restrictions on indexation allowance

Note the following points about the indexation allowance :

(a) If RPI goes *down* between the month in which expenditure is incurred and the month of disposal (or April 1998), the indexation allowance available in relation to that expenditure is nil.

(b) No indexation allowance is available in respect of the incidental costs of disposal, even if they were incurred prior to the month of disposal.

(c) Indexation allowance cannot be used to convert a gain into a loss. Therefore, if the indexation allowance (calculated in the normal way) exceeds the unindexed gain, the indexation allowance is restricted so as to give neither a gain nor a loss.

(d) Indexation allowance cannot be used to increase an unindexed loss. If there is an unindexed loss on a disposal then the indexation allowance is nil.

EXAMPLE 3

An asset was acquired in February 1987 (RPI 100.4) at a cost of £5,000. The asset was sold in January 2001. The RPI for April 1998 was 162.6. Compute the untapered gain or allowable loss if the sale proceeds were :

(a) £9,000   (b) £6,500   (c) £4,800

SOLUTION

	(a) £	(b) £	(c) £
Sale proceeds	9,000	6,500	4,800
Less : Acquisition cost	5,000	5,000	5,000
Unindexed gain (unindexed loss)	4,000	1,500	(200)
Less : Indexation allowance			
$\frac{162.6 - 100.4}{100.4} = 0.620 \times £5,000$	3,100	1,500	nil
Untapered gain (allowable loss)	900	nil	(200)

Notes :

(i) In case (a), the indexation allowance can be given in full.

(ii) In case (b), the full indexation allowance would convert an unindexed gain of £1,500 into a loss of £1,600. Indexation allowance is restricted to £1,500 to prevent this.

(iii) In case (c) there is an unindexed loss, so indexation allowance is restricted to £nil.

Taper relief

To compensate for the withdrawal of indexation allowance for periods after April 1998, the gain arising on a disposal made on or after 6 April 1998 may be reduced by taper relief, which is calculated according to :

(a) the number of *complete* years after 5 April 1998 for which the asset has been held

(b) whether the asset is classed as a "business asset" or a "non-business asset"

(c) the extent to which the gain has been reduced by losses of the same year or losses brought forward or carried back (see below).

For disposals occurring on or after 6 April 2000, taper relief is calculated by reference to the following tables :

No. of years held after 5/4/98	% of gain chargeable (business assets)
0	100
1	87.5
2	75
3	50
4 or more	25

No. of years held after 5/4/98	% of gain chargeable (non-business assets)
0	100
1	100
2	100
3	95
4	90
5	85
6	80
7	75
8	70
9	65
10 or more	60

Note that :

(a) A *non-business* asset held on 17 March 1998 qualifies for an addition of one year to the "taper period" i.e. the period for which the asset is deemed to have been held after 5 April 1998. This extra year is often referred to as the "bonus year".

(b) If enhancement expenditure has been incurred in relation to an asset, the date of that expenditure is not relevant for taper relief purposes. Taper relief on the whole of the gain arising on disposal is calculated according to the period which has elapsed since the asset was originally acquired (or since April 1998, if later).

(c) If an asset is transferred between spouses who live together, taper relief on a subsequent disposal is based on the combined period of holding by both spouses.

(d) The taper relief available on the disposal of a business asset between 6 April 1998 and 5 April 2000 (inclusive) was calculated by reference to a different table of chargeable percentages than the one given above.

(e) Taper relief is *not* available to companies (which pay corporation tax on their chargeable gains).

EXAMPLE 4

Assuming that a gain arises on each of the following disposals (and that no losses are to be set against that gain), state the percentage of the gain which will be chargeable to capital gains tax in each case :

(a) A business asset is acquired on 1 January 2000 and disposed of on 17 March 2003.

(b) A non-business asset is acquired on 23 June 1995 and disposed of on 9 April 2000.

(c) A non-business asset is acquired on 12 May 1997 and disposed of on 30 May 2004.

(d) A business asset is acquired on 1 March 1998 and disposed of on 3 April 2001.

SOLUTION

(a) 50% (business asset held for 3 complete years after 5/4/98)

(b) 95% (non-business asset held for 2 complete years after 5/4/98 + bonus year)

(c) 75% (non-business asset held for 6 complete years after 5/4/98 + bonus year)

(d) 75% (business asset held for 2 complete years after 5/4/98).

Business assets and non-business assets

For taper relief purposes, a gain is a gain on the disposal of a business asset if the asset was a business asset throughout the "relevant period". This period is the shorter of :

(a) the period after 5 April 1998 for which the asset was held before disposal, and

(b) the period of 10 years ending on the date of disposal.

If an asset was a business asset for only *part* of the relevant period, then the gain is apportioned into two gains (a gain on a business asset and a gain on a non-business asset) according to the proportion of the relevant period for which the asset was a business asset. These two gains are then treated as if they had arisen on the disposal of two separate assets. A similar approach is adopted if an asset is used partly for business purposes and partly for private purposes throughout the relevant period. Business assets are defined broadly as follows :

(a) assets used for the purposes of a trade carried on by the taxpayer (either alone or in partnership) or by a qualifying company

(b) assets used for the purposes of any office or employment held by the taxpayer with a person carrying on a trade

(c) shares in a qualifying company.

A company is a qualifying company if it is a trading company and one or more of the following conditions is met :

(a) the company is unlisted, or

(b) the taxpayer is an officer or employee of the company, or

(c) the taxpayer has at least 5% of the voting rights in the company.

Interaction of taper relief and losses

Taper relief is applied only to those gains which remain after deducting :

(a) allowable losses for the year (including trading losses relieved under Section 72)

(b) allowable losses brought forward from previous years

(c) allowable losses carried back from the year of death.

The allocation of losses to gains for this purpose is to be done on the basis which produces the lowest charge to tax. This means that losses should be deducted from gains which have a high chargeable percentage in priority to gains which have a low chargeable percentage.

EXAMPLE 5

A taxpayer has the following untapered gains in a year of assessment :

(a) a gain of £12,000 on a business asset with a taper period of 3 years (Gain A)

(b) a gain of £10,000 on a non-business asset with a taper period of 4 years (Gain B)

(c) a gain of £3,000 on a non-business asset with a taper period of 2 years (Gain C).

The taxpayer also has a single allowable loss of £8,000 in the year. Compute the CGT assessment for the year, assuming an annual exemption of £7,200. (The year in question is not 1999/00 or earlier).

SOLUTION

	Total	Gain A (50%)	Gain B (90%)	Gain C (100%)
	£	£	£	£
Untapered gains	25,000	12,000	10,000	3,000
Less : Allowable losses	8,000		5,000	3,000
	17,000	12,000	5,000	nil
Less : Taper relief	6,500	6,000	500	nil
Tapered gains	10,500	6,000	4,500	nil
Less : Annual exemption	7,200			
CGT assessment	3,300			

The allowable loss is set first against Gain C (which attracts no taper relief) and then against Gain B (which attracts a lower rate of taper relief than Gain A). In this way, the gains which remain after deduction of taper relief are held to a minimum.

EXAMPLE 6

Charlie's only disposal in 2000/01 is a business asset disposed of in May 2000. The asset was purchased in 1993 and the untapered gain on the disposal is £20,000. Charlie also has trading losses of £18,000 which are available for relief under Section 72 of Finance Act 1991. Compute Charlie's CGT assessment for 2000/01, if :

(a) he has no capital losses b/f and does not make a Section 72 claim

(b) he has £15,000 of capital losses b/f and does not make a Section 72 claim

(c) he has £15,000 of capital losses b/f and makes a Section 72 claim

(d) he has £2,000 of capital losses b/f and does not make a Section 72 claim

(e) he has £2,000 of capital losses b/f and makes a Section 72 claim.

SOLUTION

	(a) £	(b) £	(c) £	(d) £	(e) £
Untapered gains	20,000	20,000	20,000	20,000	20,000
Less : Section 72 relief	-	-	3,750	-	13,500
	20,000	20,000	16,250	20,000	6,500
Less : Capital losses b/f	-	12,800	9,050	2,000	-
	20,000	7,200	7,200	18,000	6,500
Less : Taper relief	5,000	-	-	4,500	-
	15,000	7,200	7,200	13,500	6,500
Less : Annual exemption	7,200	7,200	7,200	7,200	6,500
CGT assessment	7,800	nil	nil	6,300	nil

Notes :

(i)   The asset disposed of is a business asset with a taper period of 2 years. The chargeable percentage is 75%.

(ii) In case (b), capital losses b/f must be used to the extent that untapered net gains exceed the annual exemption. There is no point in calculating taper relief since the remaining gains are covered by the exemption. In effect, taper relief of £5,000 is lost and capital losses b/f of £12,800 reduce the CGT assessment by only £7,800.

(iii) In case (c), the maximum amount of a Section 72 claim is (£20,000 - £15,000) x 75%, which is £3,750. This displaces £3,750 of capital losses b/f and therefore conserves capital losses at the expense of trading losses.

(iv) In case (e), the maximum amount of a Section 72 claim is £13,500. The effect of this claim is to conserve all £2,000 of capital losses b/f and to reduce the CGT assessment by £6,300. Taper relief of £4,500 is lost, as is £700 of the annual exemption.

Part disposals

The disposal of part of a chargeable asset is a chargeable disposal but since only part of the asset has been disposed of, only part of its cost can be allowed when computing the gain or loss. The allowable part cost is the full cost of the asset multiplied by the following fraction :

$$\frac{A}{A + B}$$

where :   A is the value of the part disposed of (i.e. the disposal value), and

B is the value of the part remaining in the taxpayer's ownership, and

A + B is the value of the entire asset on the day of disposal.

This part disposal fraction applies not only to the acquisition cost of the asset but also to any other items of allowable expenditure which relate to the whole asset. But any item of expenditure which relates only to the part of the asset which has been disposed of should be allowed in full.

EXAMPLE 7

Peter buys a piece of land for £26,000 in October 1985 (RPI 95.59). He sells one quarter of the land for £12,000 in August 2000, incurring incidental costs of disposal of £500. The value of the remaining three-quarters of the land in August 2000 is £40,000. The RPI for April 1998 was 162.6. Calculate the untapered gain.

SOLUTION

	£
Sale proceeds	12,000
<u>Less</u> : Incidental costs of disposal	500
	11,500
<u>Less</u> : Part cost :	
$\dfrac{£12,000}{£12,000 + £40,000}$ x £26,000	6,000
Unindexed gain	5,500
<u>Less</u> : Indexation allowance	
$\dfrac{162.6 - 95.59}{95.59}$ = 0.701 x £6,000	4,206
Untapered gain	1,294

Notes :

(i) The fact that Peter has sold one quarter of the area of the land is irrelevant. What is relevant is that he has sold £12,000 worth of land out of a holding currently worth £52,000, as indicated by the part disposal fraction. Since the allowable part cost (£6,000) is slightly less than a quarter of the acquisition cost (£26,000), it is probable that the land he has sold is of slightly lower quality than the land he has retained.

(ii) The incidental costs of disposal clearly relate only to the part of the land that has been disposed of, not to the whole holding. Therefore these costs are allowed in full.

(iii) If Peter disposes of the remainder of the land at some future time, then the remainder of the cost i.e. £20,000 (£26,000 - £6,000) will be allowable in the computation of the gain arising on that disposal.

Small part disposals of land

An exception to the usual part disposal rules occurs when a taxpayer makes a "small" part disposal of land. For this purpose a disposal of land is regarded as "small" so long as the following conditions are met :

(a) The land in question must be freehold or long leasehold (i.e. held on a lease with more than 50 years left to run).

(b) If the land is disposed of because of a compulsory purchase order by a public authority, the disposal proceeds must be no more than 5% of the value of the whole piece of land.

(c) If the disposal is not caused by a compulsory purchase order, the disposal proceeds must be no more than 20% of the value of the whole piece of land and the total proceeds of all disposals of land in the year of assessment (excluding small disposals caused by compulsory purchases) must be no more than £20,000.

In these circumstances, the taxpayer may claim that there should be no chargeable gain and that, instead, the disposal proceeds should be subtracted from the original cost of the land for CGT purposes. This has the effect of increasing the chargeable gain arising on a subsequent disposal of the remainder of the land and therefore, in effect, the gain arising on the small part disposal is deferred. Obviously, the taxpayer will not make such a claim if the gain arising on the small part disposal is covered by the annual exemption for the year.

On a subsequent disposal of the remainder of the land, it would be unfair to calculate indexation allowance on the reduced cost only. Instead, indexation allowance is first calculated on the full original cost of the land and is then reduced by a negative indexation allowance, calculated on the proceeds of the small part disposal.

It is very important to appreciate that these small part disposal rules apply only to land, whereas the more general part disposal rules explained earlier apply to all types of chargeable asset.

EXAMPLE 8

In July 1989 (RPI 115.5), Malcolm bought a piece of land for £40,000. In June 1993 (RPI 141.0) he sold part of the land for £11,000 (this being his only disposal of land in 1993/94). The value of the remainder of the land at the time of the part disposal was £50,000. Malcolm had substantial capital gains in 1993/94, sufficient to absorb his annual exemption for the year, and therefore decided to make the small part disposal claim.

Calculate the untapered gain arising in January 2001 when Malcolm sells the remainder of the land for £60,000. The RPI for April 1998 was 162.6.

SOLUTION

The small part disposal claim in 1993/94 was valid since the total value of the land immediately prior to the disposal was £61,000 (£11,000 + £50,000) and the disposal raised £11,000 which is less than 20% of £61,000. Also, the disposal proceeds of all land disposals in the year did not exceed £20,000. The gain on the January 2001 disposal is as follows :

			£
Sale proceeds			60,000
<u>Less</u> : Reduced cost (£40,000 - £11,000)			29,000
Unindexed gain			31,000
<u>Less</u> : Indexation allowance :			
(i) on full original cost			
$\dfrac{162.6 - 115.5}{115.5}$ = 0.408 x £40,000		16,320	
(ii) on proceeds of small part disposal			
$\dfrac{162.6 - 141.0}{141.0}$ = 0.153 x £11,000		(1,683)	14,637
Untapered gain			16,363

Assets with negligible value

If the value of a chargeable asset has become negligible, the owner of the asset may make a "negligible value" claim. If this claim is accepted, the asset is treated as if it had been disposed of at its current, negligible value (giving rise to an allowable loss) and then immediately re-acquired at that value.

Assets held on 31 March 1982

CGT was originally introduced in 1965 and applied to disposals made on or after 6 April 1965 (the "base date" for CGT). Gains accruing before 6 April 1965 were not taxable. Therefore, if an asset was acquired before 6 April 1965 and disposed of after that date, only the part of the gain accruing after 6 April 1965 was taxable. (The current treatment of assets held on 6 April 1965 is described later in this chapter).

The Finance Act 1988 changed the CGT base date to 31 March 1982. Therefore, if an asset is now disposed of which was acquired before 31 March 1982, only the part of the gain accruing since 31 March 1982 is taxable. The calculation of the taxable part of the gain is achieved by means of a technique known as "rebasing" whereby the market value of the asset at 31 March 1982 is substituted for its original acquisition cost in the CGT calculation. However, rebasing does *not* apply if the rebasing calculation results in a greater gain than the calculation based on original cost.

EXAMPLE 9

A chargeable asset was acquired in April 1976 for £2,000 and sold in January 2001 for £9,500. Compute the unindexed gain if the asset's market value at 31 March 1982 was :

(a) £4,200   (b) £1,500

SOLUTION

(a) The unindexed gain over the entire period of ownership, based on the original cost of the asset, is £7,500 (£9,500 - £2,000). But the rebasing calculation gives an unindexed gain of only £5,300 (£9,500 - £4,200). This is less than the gain based on original cost so rebasing applies and the unindexed gain is £5,300.

(b) The rebasing calculation gives an unindexed gain of £8,000 (£9,500 - £1,500). This is more than the gain based on original cost so rebasing does not apply and the unindexed gain is £7,500.

Indexation allowance for pre-31 March 1982 assets

The rules for calculating the indexation allowance available on the disposal of an asset held on 31 March 1982 are as follows :

(a) Indexation allowance is based on the change in RPI between March 1982 and the month of disposal (or April 1998, if earlier). No further indexation allowance is available to compensate for the effects of pre-March 1982 inflation (which is why the table of RPI's at the end of this chapter begins with the RPI for March 1982).

(b) In *both* the rebasing calculation and in the calculation based on original cost, indexation allowance is calculated with reference to the *greater* of original cost and market value at 31 March 1982 i.e. the same indexation allowance is given in both calculations.

EXAMPLE 10

Calculate the untapered gain arising on the disposal described in the above example. (RPI for March 1982 was 79.44 and RPI for April 1998 was 162.6).

SOLUTION

(a)

	Original cost £	Rebasing £
Sale proceeds	9,500	9,500
Less : Original cost	2,000	
Market value 31/3/82		4,200
Unindexed gain	7,500	5,300
Less : Indexation allowance		
$\frac{162.6 - 79.44}{79.44}$ = 1.047 x £4,200	4,397	4,397
Untapered gain	3,103	903

The rebasing calculation gives the lower gain, so rebasing applies and the untapered gain is £903.

(b)

	Original cost £	Rebasing £
Sale proceeds	9,500	9,500
Less : Original cost	2,000	
Market value 31/3/82		1,500
Unindexed gain	7,500	8,000
Less : Indexation allowance		
$\frac{162.6 - 79.44}{79.44}$ = 1.047 x £2,000	2,094	2,094
Untapered gain	5,406	5,906

The rebasing calculation gives the higher gain, so rebasing does not apply and the untapered gain is £5,406.

EXAMPLE 11

In May 1979, Margaret bought a chargeable asset for £10,000. Enhancement expenditure was incurred of £2,000 in June 1980 and £3,000 in June 1984 (RPI 89.20). The asset had a market value of £16,000 on 31 March 1982 (RPI 79.44) and was sold in July 2000 for £40,000. The RPI for April 1998 was 162.6. Compute the untapered gain.

SOLUTION

	£	Original cost £	Rebasing £
Sale proceeds		40,000	40,000
Less : Cost up to 31 March 1982 :			
Acquisition cost	10,000		
Enhancement expenditure June 1980	2,000	(12,000)	
Market value 31 March 1982			(16,000)
Enhancement expenditure June 1984		(3,000)	(3,000)
Unindexed gain		25,000	21,000
Less : Indexation allowance :			
(i) on MV at 31 March 1982			
$\dfrac{162.6 - 79.44}{79.44}$ = 1.047 x £16,000	16,752		
(ii) on enhancement June 1984			
$\dfrac{162.6 - 89.20}{89.20}$ = 0.823 x £3,000	2,469	19,221	19,221
Untapered gain		5,779	1,779

The rebasing calculation gives the lower gain, so rebasing applies and the untapered gain is £1,779.

Notes :

(i) Margaret has spent a total of £15,000 (£10,000 + £2,000 + £3,000) on buying and enhancing the asset. Therefore the calculation based on original cost takes into account total allowable expenditure of £15,000.

(ii) The market value at 31 March 1982 is the value of the asset as it stood on that date (i.e. the value of the asset including the June 1980 enhancement). But this valuation did not take into account the second enhancement, which did not occur until June 1984. Therefore the rebasing calculation takes into account both the market value at 31 March 1982 and the cost of the second enhancement.

(iii) Indexation allowance based on the change in RPI from March 1982 to April 1998 is given on *the greater of total cost up to 31 March 1982 and market value at 31 March 1982*. Indexation allowance is also given on the second enhancement, based on the change in RPI from June 1984 to April 1998.

Losses on disposal of pre-31 March 1982 assets

As shown above, if the rebasing calculation gives a gain and the original cost calculation also gives a gain, the untapered gain is the *smaller* of these two gains. Similarly, if the rebasing calculation gives a loss and the original cost calculation also gives a loss, the allowable loss is the *smaller* of these two losses. Finally, if the rebasing calculation gives a loss and the original cost calculation gives a gain (or vice-versa), or if either of the calculations gives a nil result, the situation is "no gain, no loss" i.e. there is no chargeable gain and no allowable loss.

EXAMPLE 12

Neil acquired a chargeable asset in 1978. The asset was sold in May 2000 for £2,200. The RPI for April 1998 was 162.6. Compute the untapered gain or allowable loss if the original cost of the asset and its market value on 31 March 1982 (RPI 79.44) were :

	Original cost £	MV 31 March 1982 £
(a)	750	850
(b)	3,500	4,000
(c)	10	2,050

SOLUTION

(a)

	Original cost £	Rebasing £
Sale proceeds	2,200	2,200
Less : Original cost	750	
Market value 31/3/82		850
Unindexed gain	1,450	1,350
Less : Indexation allowance		
$\dfrac{162.6 - 79.44}{79.44}$ = 1.047 x £850	890	890
Untapered gain	560	460

The rebasing calculation gives the lower gain, so rebasing applies and the untapered gain is £460.

(b)

	Original cost £	Rebasing £
Sale proceeds	2,200	2,200
Less : Original cost	3,500	
Market value 31/3/82		4,000
Allowable loss	(1,300)	(1,800)

The rebasing calculation gives the higher loss, so rebasing does not apply and the allowable loss is £1,300. Indexation allowance was £nil in both calculations, since indexation allowance cannot be used to increase an unindexed loss.

(c)	Original cost £	Rebasing £
Sale proceeds	2,200	2,200
Less : Original cost	10	
Market value 31/3/82		2,050
Unindexed gain	2,190	150
Less : Indexation allowance		
$\dfrac{162.6 - 79.44}{79.44}$ = 1.047 x £2,050	2,146	150
Untapered gain	44	nil

The rebasing calculation gives a nil result, whilst the calculation based on original cost gives a gain. Therefore the situation is "no gain, no loss". Indexation allowance was restricted to £150 in the rebasing calculation, since indexation allowance cannot be used to convert a gain into a loss.

Part disposals of pre-31 March 1982 assets

When a part disposal is made of an asset which was owned on 31 March 1982, the part disposal fraction which is applied to the original cost of the asset (see earlier in this chapter) is also applied to the market value at 31 March 1982 for the purposes of the rebasing calculation.

EXAMPLE 13

A chargeable asset was purchased in November 1976 for £2,000. The asset had a market value on 31 March 1982 (RPI 79.44) of £5,000. Part of the asset was disposed of for £8,000 in November 2000 at which time the remainder of the asset was valued at £12,000. The RPI for April 1998 was 162.6. Compute the untapered gain.

SOLUTION

The part disposal fraction to be used in this case is :

$$\frac{\pounds8,000}{\pounds8,000 + \pounds12,000}$$

The computation of the chargeable gain is therefore as follows :

	Original cost £	Rebasing £
Sale proceeds	8,000	8,000
Less : Part cost : $\frac{\pounds8,000}{\pounds8,000 + \pounds12,000}$ x £2,000	800	
Part market value 31/3/82 : $\frac{\pounds8,000}{\pounds8,000 + \pounds12,000}$ x £5,000		2,000
Unindexed gain	7,200	6,000
Less : Indexation allowance $\frac{162.6 - 79.44}{79.44} = 1.047$ x £2,000	2,094	2,094
Untapered gain	5,106	3,906

The rebasing calculation gives the lower gain, so rebasing applies and the untapered gain is £3,906.

The rebasing election

A taxpayer may make an *irrevocable* election to the effect that gains and losses arising on all future disposals of assets held on 31 March 1982 should be calculated by the rebasing method, with no reference whatsoever to the costs incurred before 31 March 1982. Such an election must be made on or before 31 January in the second tax year following the year in which the first disposal of a pre-31 March 1982 asset occurs after 5 April 1988. For example, if the first such disposal occurs during tax year 2000/01, the election must be made by 31 January 2003.

If this election is made, costs incurred before 31 March 1982 are completely ignored for all purposes, including calculation of the indexation allowance. Therefore indexation allowance will always be based upon market value at 31 March 1982, even if this is lower than the costs incurred before 31 March 1982.

Assets acquired before 6 April 1965

When CGT was first introduced, special rules were devised for the calculation of the gain arising on the disposal of an asset acquired before 6 April 1965 (since only the part of the gain accruing since 6 April 1965 was taxable).

However, from the perspective of disposals made in the 21st century, the disposal of an asset acquired before 6 April 1965 must also be the disposal of an asset held on 31 March 1982. Therefore rebasing is available in relation to such disposals. Rebasing will generally give a lower gain than the gain calculated according to the special rules referred to above but these rules will still be used if they give the lower gain.

In summary, the calculation of the untapered gain arising on the disposal of an asset acquired before 6 April 1965 is as follows :

(a) The gain is first calculated by the "time apportionment" method. This method calculates the total gain arising since the asset was acquired and then apportions the gain between the period before 6 April 1965 (which is not taxable) and the period after 6 April 1965 (which is taxable). For the purposes of this method, indexation allowance is based on the higher of original cost and market value at 31 March 1982. If the asset was acquired before 6 April 1945 it is assumed to have been acquired on that date for time apportionment purposes.

(b) Alternatively, the taxpayer may elect for the "6 April 1965 market value" method (and will presumably do so if this produces a lower gain). This method calculates the gain by comparing disposal proceeds with the market value of the asset on 6 April 1965. For the purposes of this method, indexation allowance is based on the higher of market value at 6 April 1965 and market value at 31 March 1982.

(c) Finally, the gain produced by the above rules is compared with the gain produced by the rebasing rules and the lower gain is taken as the chargeable gain. The indexation allowance used in the rebasing calculation is based on either :

    (i) the greater of original cost and market value at 31 March 1982 (if the time apportionment method is being used), or

    (ii) the greater of market value at 6 April 1965 and market value at 31 March 1982 (if the taxpayer has elected for the 6 April 1965 market value method).

EXAMPLE 14

A chargeable asset was purchased on 6 October 1953 for £50,000 and sold on 6 October 2000 for £250,000. The market value of the asset was £25,000 on 6 April 1965 and £75,000 on 31 March 1982 (RPI 79.44). The RPI for April 1998 was 162.6. Compute the untapered gain (performing apportionment calculations to the nearest month).

SOLUTION

	Time apportionment £	MV 6/4/65 £
Sale proceeds	250,000	250,000
Less : Original cost	50,000	
Market value 6/4/65		25,000
Unindexed gain	200,000	225,000
Less : Indexation allowance		
$\frac{162.6 - 79.44}{79.44} = 1.047 \times £75,000$	78,525	78,525
Untapered gain	121,475	146,475
Time apportioned $\frac{35.5}{47.0} \times £121,475$	91,752	

The gain produced by the time apportionment method is lower than the gain produced by the 6 April 1965 market value method. Therefore the taxpayer will not elect for the 6 April 1965 market value method and the gain (before considering rebasing) is £91,752. The gain produced by the rebasing calculation is £96,475 (£250,000 - £75,000 - £78,525). This is higher than the gain based on cost, so rebasing will not apply and the untapered gain is £91,752.

Notes :

(i) Indexation allowance was based on 31 March 1982 market value in each case, since this was greater than original cost or 6 April 1965 market value.

(ii) The asset was owned for 47 years and disposal took place 35 years and 6 months after 6 April 1965, hence the time apportionment fraction used above.

Losses on disposal of pre-6 April 1965 assets

If all three of the computations required on the disposal of an asset held on 6 April 1965 result in a gain (as in the above example), the untapered gain is the lowest of these three gains. But the situation is more complex if any of the computations result in a loss. If this happens then the following rules apply :

(a) If time apportionment gives a loss and market value at 6 April 1965 gives a gain (or a smaller loss), then the taxpayer will not elect (and cannot be forced to elect) for the 6 April 1965 market value method of calculation. The time apportioned loss is then compared with the outcome of the rebasing calculation in the usual way.

(b) If time apportionment gives a gain and market value at 6 April 1965 gives a loss then the situation is no gain, no loss and there is no point in performing a rebasing calculation.

(c) If time apportionment gives a loss and market value at 6 April 1965 gives a greater loss, the allowable loss is restricted to the amount of the loss based on original cost, *ignoring time apportionment*. This loss is then compared with the outcome of the rebasing calculation in the usual way.

EXAMPLE 15

A chargeable asset was purchased on 6 April 1963 for £24,000 and sold on 6 April 2000 for £18,000. RPI for April 1998 was 162.6. The market value of the asset was £26,000 on 6 April 1965 and £30,000 on 31 March 1982 (RPI 79.44). Compute the allowable loss.

SOLUTION

	Time apportionment £	MV 6/4/65 £
Sale proceeds	18,000	18,000
Less : Original cost	24,000	
Market value 6/4/65		26,000
Unindexed loss	(6,000)	(8,000)
Less : Indexation allowance		
$\dfrac{162.6 - 79.44}{79.44}$ = 1.047 x £30,000	nil	nil
Allowable loss	(6,000)	(8,000)
Time apportioned $\dfrac{35}{37}$ x £6,000	(5,676)	

Time apportionment gives a loss and market value at 6 April 1965 gives a greater loss, therefore the allowable loss is restricted to the amount of the loss based on original cost, ignoring time apportionment i.e. £6,000. This loss is then compared with the loss produced by the rebasing calculation, which is £12,000 (£18,000 - £30,000). The allowable loss is the lower of these figures i.e. £6,000.

Summary

▶ The disposal value of an asset is normally equal to the sale proceeds, but if an asset is given away or is sold to a connected person, the disposal value is deemed to be the market value of the asset on the date of the sale.

▶ Allowable costs include acquisition cost of the asset, costs of acquisition and disposal, enhancement expenditure, costs of defending the owner's title and valuation fees.

▶ Indexation allowance is calculated for each allowable cost (apart from the costs of disposal) and is based on the change in RPI between the month in which the cost was incurred and the month of the disposal (or April 1998, if earlier). Indexation allowance is not available for expenditure occurred on or after 1 April 1998.

▶ Indexation allowance cannot be used to create or increase a loss.

▶ Taper relief may be used to reduce a chargeable gain, depending upon the length of the taper period and the type of asset involved (business or non-business). This relief applies only to those gains remaining after losses have been relieved. Losses are allocated to gains on the basis which produces the lowest tax charge.

▶ On a part disposal, the allowable part cost is calculated by multiplying the full cost by the part disposal fraction.

▶ A taxpayer may claim that an asset has negligible value, so triggering a disposal which gives rise to an allowable loss.

▶ If an asset is disposed of which was owned on 31 March 1982, it is necessary to perform a calculation based on original cost and a "rebasing" calculation based on market value at 31 March 1982. The untapered gain (allowable loss) is the lower of the gains (losses) given by these two calculations. If one calculation gives a gain and the other gives a loss (or either calculation gives a nil result) the situation is no gain, no loss.

▶ A taxpayer may make a once-and-for-all election for the rebasing method to be used on all disposals of pre-31 March 1982 assets.

▶ Special rules apply to the disposal of assets owned on 6 April 1965.

Retail Prices Index (RPI)

(*Source* : Office for National Statistics)

	Jan	Feb	Mar	Apr	May	Jun	Jul	Aug	Sep	Oct	Nov	Dec
1982			79.44	81.04	81.62	81.85	81.88	81.90	81.85	82.26	82.66	82.51
1983	82.61	82.97	83.12	84.28	84.64	84.84	85.30	85.68	86.06	86.36	86.67	86.89
1984	86.84	87.20	87.48	88.64	88.97	89.20	89.10	89.94	90.11	90.67	90.95	90.87
1985	91.20	91.94	92.80	94.78	95.21	95.41	95.23	95.49	95.44	95.59	95.92	96.05
1986	96.25	96.60	96.73	97.67	97.85	97.79	97.52	97.82	98.30	98.45	99.29	99.62
1987	100.0	100.4	100.6	101.8	101.9	101.9	101.8	102.1	102.4	102.9	103.4	103.3
1988	103.3	103.7	104.1	105.8	106.2	106.6	106.7	107.9	108.4	109.5	110.0	110.3
1989	111.0	111.8	112.3	114.3	115.0	115.4	115.5	115.8	116.6	117.5	118.5	118.8
1990	119.5	120.2	121.4	125.1	126.2	126.7	126.8	128.1	129.3	130.3	130.0	129.9
1991	130.2	130.9	131.4	133.1	133.5	134.1	133.8	134.1	134.6	135.1	135.6	135.7
1992	135.6	136.3	136.7	138.8	139.3	139.3	138.8	138.9	139.4	139.9	139.7	139.2
1993	137.9	138.8	139.3	140.6	141.1	141.0	140.7	141.3	141.9	141.8	141.6	141.9
1994	141.3	142.1	142.5	144.2	144.7	144.7	144.0	144.7	145.0	145.2	145.3	146.0
1995	146.0	146.9	147.5	149.0	149.6	149.8	149.1	149.9	150.6	149.8	149.8	150.7
1996	150.2	150.9	151.5	152.6	152.9	153.0	152.4	153.1	153.8	153.8	153.9	154.4
1997	154.4	155.0	155.4	156.3	156.9	157.5	157.5	158.5	159.3	159.5	159.6	160.0
1998	159.5	160.3	160.8	162.6	163.5	163.4	163.0	163.7	164.4	164.5	164.4	164.4
1999	163.4	163.7	164.1	165.2	165.6	165.6	165.1	165.5	166.2	166.5	166.7	167.3
2000	166.6	167.5	168.4	*168.7*	*169.0*	*169.3*	*169.6*	*169.9*	*170.2*	*170.5*	*170.8*	*171.1*
2001	*171.4*	*171.7*	*172.0*									

Notes :

(i)   Indexation allowance is frozen at April 1998 for individuals. The RPI's for May 1998 onwards are used only when computing the chargeable gains of companies.

(ii) RPI's for April 2000 and later months have been estimated by the author.

Exercises

17.1   Carol purchased a holiday flat in December 1987 (RPI 103.3) for £35,000. She spent £3,000 on installing central heating in February 1988 (RPI 103.7) and a further £650 on repainting the interior of the flat in March 1992 (RPI 136.7). The flat was never Carol's main residence. She sold the flat at auction in February 2001 (RPI 171.7) for £72,000, paying a 5% fee to the auctioneer. The RPI for April 1998 was 162.6. Compute the untapered gain.

17.2   David was given a chargeable asset in November 1991 (RPI 135.6) at which time the asset had a market value of £4,500. He sold the asset in January 2001 (RPI 171.4). The RPI for April 1998 was 162.6. Compute the untapered gain or allowable loss if the sale proceeds were :

(a)   £4,950

(b)   £4,350

(c)   £5,780.

17.3   Brenda has the following untapered gains in a year of assessment :

(i)   a gain of £17,000 (Gain A) on a non-business asset with a taper period of 5 years

(ii)   a gain of £4,000 (Gain B) on a business asset with a taper period of 3 years

(iii)   a gain of £20,000 (Gain C) on an asset with a taper period of more than 10 years and a relevant period of exactly 10 years, during which time the asset has been used as a business asset for 3 years.

Brenda also has allowable losses for the year of £22,000. Compute her CGT assessment for the year, assuming an annual exemption of £7,200.

17.4   Edwina bought a chargeable asset in August 1991 (RPI 134.1) for £240,000, paying acquisition costs of £12,000. In June 2000 she sold a one-quarter interest in the asset for £100,000, incurring disposal costs of £5,000. The remaining three-quarter interest in the asset was valued at £500,000 in June 2000. RPI for April 1998 was 162.6. Compute the untapered gain.

In January 2001, Edwina sold her remaining three-quarter interest in the asset for £520,000. Compute the untapered gain.

17.5   Francis acquired an oil painting for £12,500 in March 1976. He sold the painting for £37,500 in March 2001. RPI for April 1998 was 162.6. Compute the untapered gain if the market value of the painting on 31 March 1982 (RPI 79.44) was :

(a)   £10,000

(b)   £15,000.

17.6 In April 1990 (RPI 125.1) Gillian was given a chargeable asset with a market value at that time of £6,000. In November 1997 (RPI 159.6) Gillian made a successful claim to the effect that the asset now had a negligible value of only £80.

(a) Compute the allowable loss.

(b) If Gillian sold the asset for £120 in March 2001, compute the untapered gain.

17.7 Henry acquired a chargeable asset in August 1970 at a cost of £100. The asset was sold in August 2000 for £8,450. The RPI for April 1998 was 162.6. Compute the untapered gain or allowable loss if the asset had a market value on 31 March 1982 (RPI 79.44) of :

(a) £7,000

(b) £12,500.

*17.8 Iris bought a chargeable asset on 6 April 1958 for £400. The asset had a market value of £600 on 6 April 1965 and £850 on 31 March 1982 (RPI 79.44). She sold the asset on 6 April 2000 for £4,200. The RPI for April 1998 was 162.6. Compute the untapered gain.

*17.9 Jon (who is self-employed) bought a chargeable asset in 1975 for £23,000. He incurred enhancement expenditure of £10,000 in 1979 and a further £4,000 in June 1998 (RPI 163.4). The asset was valued at £33,500 on 31 March 1982 (RPI 79.44) and was sold for £85,000 in February 2001 (RPI 171.7). RPI for April 1998 was 162.6.

(a) Compute the tapered gain, assuming that the asset was used for the purposes of Jon's trade throughout his period of ownership. Jon has no allowable losses in tax year 2000/01 and no allowable losses to bring forward from previous years.

(b) Now re-compute the gain, assuming that the person who bought the asset from Jon in February 2001 was his wife (who lives with him).

*17.10 Karen bought a house in 1979 for £30,000. The house was valued at £32,000 on 31 March 1982 (RPI 79.44). In November 1986 (RPI 99.29) she spent £18,000 on dividing the house into two self-contained flats and in May 2000 (RPI 169.0) she sold one of the flats for £95,000, at which time the other flat was valued at £105,000. In January 2001 (RPI 171.4) she sold the second flat for £110,000. Karen never lived in either of the flats. The RPI for April 1998 was 162.6.

Compute the tapered gains arising on the two disposals, given that the flats do not rank as business assets. (Karen has no allowable losses in 2000/01 and no allowable losses to bring forward from previous years).

Chapter 18

Chattels and wasting assets

Introduction

A "chattel" is an item of tangible, movable property. A "wasting asset" is one with an expected useful life not exceeding 50 years at the time of disposal. If an asset is both a chattel and a wasting asset (e.g. a TV set) it is a "wasting chattel". Special CGT rules apply to the disposal of chattels, wasting assets and wasting chattels. The purpose of this chapter is to explain these rules.

Please note that the RPI for April 1998 (which is used in many of the examples in this chapter) is 162.6.

The chattels exemption

If a chattel is disposed of for £6,000 or less, the disposal is exempt from CGT. This provision removes from charge a great many trivial disposals and ensures that CGT is levied only if the disposal is material. The following points relate to the chattels exemption :

(a) This exemption applies only to chattels, not to assets in general.

(b) The exemption means that gains arising on the disposal of a chattel for £6,000 or less are not chargeable to CGT. It also means that losses arising on such disposals are not generally allowable (but see later in this chapter for more information on chattels disposed of at a loss).

(c) The £6,000 figure relates to the *gross* disposal proceeds i.e. the proceeds before deducting incidental costs of disposal.

(d) If the gross disposal proceeds of a chattel exceed £6,000, the untapered gain cannot exceed five-thirds of the amount by which the proceeds exceed £6,000. This "marginal relief" ensures that taxpayers who dispose of chattels for slightly more than £6,000 are not unduly penalised by the tax system.

EXAMPLE 1

In 2000/01, a taxpayer makes a number of disposals, as listed below. Which of these disposals would be exempt from CGT ?

(a)   An antique table sold for £5,000.

(b)   A watercolour painting sold at auction, The auctioneer deducted his 10% commission from the selling price and sent the taxpayer a cheque for the remaining £5,670.

(c)   A holding of shares sold for £4,500.

SOLUTION

(a)   The antique table is a chattel disposed of for £6,000 or less. Therefore the disposal is exempt from CGT.

(b)   A watercolour painting is a chattel, but the gross disposal proceeds must have been £6,300 (since £6,300 less 10% = £5,670). The chattels exemption will not apply but the untapered gain cannot exceed five-thirds of £300 i.e. £500.

(c)   A shareholding is not a chattel. Therefore the £6,000 exemption does not apply and the disposal will be chargeable to CGT.

EXAMPLE 2

In December 2000, Michael sells a piece of antique furniture for £6,360. He pays incidental disposal costs of £320. He had acquired the furniture as a gift from his mother in January 1991 (RPI 130.2). Compute the untapered gain if the market value of the furniture in January 1991 was :

(a)   £4,800   (b)   £4,300

SOLUTION

	(a) £	(b) £
Sale proceeds	6,360	6,360
Less : Incidental costs of disposal	320	320
	6,040	6,040
Less : Deemed acquisition cost	4,800	4,300
Unindexed gain	1,240	1,740
Less : Indexation allowance		
$\dfrac{162.6 - 130.2}{130.2}$ = 0.249 x £4,800	1,195	
$\dfrac{162.6 - 130.2}{130.2}$ = 0.249 x £4,300		1,071
Untapered gain	45	669

Notes :

(a) £45 is less than the maximum untapered gain of £360 x 5/3 = £600, so the untapered gain is £45.

(b) £669 exceeds £600, so the untapered gain is restricted to £600.

Chattels disposed of at a loss

If a chattel is disposed of at a loss, there are two possibilities. Either :

(a) the disposal proceeds are more than £6,000, in which case the allowable loss is calculated in the usual way, or

(b) the disposal proceeds are £6,000 or less, in which case the chattels exemption applies and it appears that no allowable loss could arise.

However, if a chattel is acquired for more than £6,000 and then disposed of for less than £6,000, the chattels exemption is overruled and an allowable loss is given. But the amount of the loss is restricted to the amount that would arise if the disposal proceeds were exactly £6,000.

EXAMPLE 3

In March 2001, Naomi sells an oil painting which she had acquired some years previously for £10,000. Compute the allowable loss if she sells the painting for :

(a) £7,200   (b) £5,700

SOLUTION

(a) Naomi has disposed of a chattel for more than £6,000, so the disposal is not exempt from CGT. The allowable loss is calculated in the usual way as £10,000 - £7,200 = £2,800. There is of course no indexation allowance to consider, since indexation allowance cannot be used to increase a loss.

(b) Naomi has disposed of a chattel for less than £6,000 and normally this disposal would be exempt from CGT. However, since the asset was acquired for more than £6,000 a loss is allowed, calculated by substituting £6,000 for the disposal proceeds. The allowable loss is £10,000 - £6,000 = £4,000. Again, there is no point in calculating indexation allowance.

Part disposals of chattels

A part disposal of a chattel may be made in one of two ways. Either :

(a) a part interest in a chattel may be disposed of, or

(b) for chattels forming a set, one or more of the items in the set may be disposed of.

Each of these forms of part disposal is considered below.

Disposal of a part interest in a chattel

If a disposal is made of a part interest in a chattel, this part disposal will be exempt from CGT only if the value of the *whole* chattel immediately prior to the part disposal is £6,000 or less.

If the value of the whole chattel exceeds £6,000 the disposal is not exempt from CGT and the usual part disposal calculation is performed. However, the untapered gain on the part disposal is limited to five-thirds of the amount by which the value of the whole chattel exceeds £6,000, multiplied by the usual part disposal fraction.

EXAMPLE 4

In October 1989 (RPI 117.5) Jackie bought a statuette for £3,500. In October 2000 she sells a one-third interest in the statuette for £2,000. Compute the untapered gain if the value of the remaining two-thirds interest in October 2000 is :

(a) £4,000   (b) £5,000

SOLUTION

(a) The value of the whole chattel on the date of the part disposal is £6,000. Since this value does not exceed £6,000 the part disposal is exempt from CGT.

(b) The value of the whole chattel on the date of the part disposal is £7,000. Since this value exceeds £6,000 the part disposal is not exempt from CGT. The computation of the untapered gain is as follows :

	£
Sale proceeds	2,000
Less : Part cost :	
$\dfrac{£2,000}{£2,000 + £5,000}$ x £3,500	1,000
Unindexed gain	1,000
Less : Indexation allowance	
$\dfrac{162.6 - 117.5}{117.5}$ = 0.384 x £1,000	384
Untapered gain	616

The part disposal fraction cancels down to 2/7th, so the untapered gain is restricted to (£7,000 - £6,000) x 5/3 x 2/7 = £476.

Disposal of part of a set

If a taxpayer acquires a set of chattels (e.g. a set of dining chairs) and then disposes of them individually, each disposal is regarded as a part disposal and will in general be chargeable to CGT only if the disposal proceeds of an individual item exceed £6,000.

However, a taxpayer who wished to dispose of a set of chattels with a total value exceeding £6,000 could use this rule to avoid CGT by disposing of the items one by one (with each disposal raising less than £6,000). In order to prevent such avoidance, a series of disposals of chattels which form part of a set will be treated as a single transaction for the purposes of calculating the chattels exemption if all the disposals are *to the same person* or to persons connected with each other or acting together.

EXAMPLE 5

Andrew acquired a set of six dining chairs in January 1987 (RPI 100.0) for £4,300. In June 2000 he sold three of the chairs to a friend for £3,500 (the other 3 chairs also being valued at £3,500). In August 2000 he sold the remaining chairs to the friend's brother for £3,700. Compute the untapered gain on each disposal.

SOLUTION

If it were not for the rule introduced above, neither of these disposals would be chargeable to CGT since neither of them raises more than £6,000. However, the two disposals are made to connected persons and are therefore to be regarded as a single transaction for the purposes of calculating the chattels exemption. The total disposal proceeds are £7,200 (£3,500 + £3,700). This exceeds £6,000 so the disposals are chargeable. The computations are as follows :

	June 2000 £	August 2000 £
Sale proceeds	3,500	3,700
Less : Part cost :		
$\dfrac{£3,500}{£3,500 + £3,500}$ x £4,300	2,150	
Remainder of cost (£4,300 - £2,150)		2,150
Unindexed gain	1,350	1,550
Less : Indexation allowance		
$\dfrac{162.6 - 100.0}{100.0}$ = 0.626 x £2,150	1,346	
$\dfrac{162.6 - 100.0}{100.0}$ = 0.626 x £2,150		1,346
Untapered gain	4	204

This gives a total untapered gain of £208 (£4 + £204). The two transactions are also treated as one for the purpose of calculating the chattels marginal relief, so that the total untapered gain cannot exceed (£7,200 - £6,000) x 5/3 = £2,000. Since this exceeds £208, the untapered gain remains £208.

Wasting chattels

Wasting chattels (i.e. chattels with an expected useful life of 50 years or less at the time of disposal) are generally exempt from CGT. Therefore no chargeable gain or allowable loss can in general arise on the disposal of a wasting chattel.

The only exception to this rule relates to movable plant and machinery used in business and eligible for capital allowances. Plant and machinery is always regarded as a wasting asset for CGT purposes and therefore movable plant and machinery is a wasting chattel. Disposals of such plant and machinery are *not* exempt from CGT (unless disposal proceeds do not exceed £6,000 in which case the chattels exemption applies). One of two situations may arise on disposal :

(a) Disposal proceeds may be less than original cost. In this (the most likely) case, the unindexed loss is reduced by the total capital allowances which have been available on the asset. This will reduce the loss to £nil and since no indexation allowance is available on assets sold at a loss, the allowable loss will also be £nil.

(b) Disposal proceeds may be greater than original cost. In this case, the total of available capital allowances on the asset is £nil and therefore capital allowances have no effect on the computation which will proceed in the usual way.

In fact, these rules (other than the £6,000 exemption) also apply to immovable plant and machinery used in business and eligible for capital allowances.

EXAMPLE 6

An item of movable plant and machinery is bought in February 1992 (RPI 136.3) for £8,000 and used solely for trade purposes. Capital allowances are available in relation to this item. Compute the untapered gain arising if the item is sold in July 2000 and the sale proceeds are :

(a) £4,500   (b) £6,500   (c) £8,500   (d) £10,500.

SOLUTION

In case (a), sale proceeds do not exceed £6,000 so the disposal is exempt from CGT. In cases (b), (c) and (d), the sale proceeds exceed £6,000 so there is no exemption. The computations are as follows :

	(b) £	(c) £	(d) £
Sale proceeds	6,500	8,500	10,500
Less : Acquisition cost	8,000	8,000	8,000
	(1,500)	500	2,500
Less : Available capital allowances	1,500	0	0
Unindexed gain/(loss)	nil	500	2,500
Less : Indexation allowance	nil	500	1,544
Untapered gain	nil	nil	956

$$\frac{162.6 - 136.3}{136.3} = 0.193 \times £8,000 = £1,544$$

In case (d), the gain of £956 is less than the maximum untapered gain of £4,500 x 5/3 = £7,500, so the untapered gain is £956.

Wasting assets

A wasting asset which is not a chattel is *not* exempt from CGT. Typical examples of such wasting assets include :

(a) immovable plant and machinery (but see earlier in this chapter for a description of the CGT treatment if the plant is eligible for capital allowances)

(b) leases with less than 50 years' life remaining (to which special rules apply, as described later in this chapter)

(c) intangible assets such as copyrights, options etc. with less than 50 years' life remaining.

In general, the original cost of a wasting asset (less its scrap value, if any) is deemed to "waste away" on a straight line basis over the asset's predictable life. The computation of the gain or loss arising on the disposal of the asset is then achieved by comparing disposal proceeds with the unexpired portion of the asset's cost at the time of disposal.

EXAMPLE 7

In January 1992 (RPI 135.6), Fiona acquired a 20-year copyright at a cost of £30,000. In January 2001 she sold the copyright for £35,500. Compute the untapered gain.

SOLUTION

When the copyright was bought it had a 20-year life. When it was sold there were 11 years remaining. Therefore the computation is as follows :

	£
Sale proceeds	35,500
Less : Unexpired portion of cost	
$\frac{11}{20}$ x £30,000	16,500
Unindexed gain	19,000
Less : Indexation allowance	
$\frac{162.6 - 135.6}{135.6}$ = 0.199 x £16,500	3,284
Untapered gain	15,716

EXAMPLE 8

In March 1980, Philip acquired a 25-year copyright at a cost of £50,000. The copyright was valued at £63,000 on 31 March 1982 (RPI 79.44). In March 2001 Philip sold the copyright for £32,000. Compute the untapered gain.

SOLUTION

When the copyright was bought it had a 25-year life and when it was valued on 31 March 1982 it had a 23-year life. When it was sold there were 4 years remaining. Therefore the computation is as follows :

	Original cost £	Rebasing £
Sale proceeds	32,000	32,000
Less : Unexpired portion of cost		
$\frac{4}{25}$ x £50,000	8,000	
Unexpired portion of MV 31/3/82		
$\frac{4}{23}$ x £63,000		10,957
Unindexed gain	24,000	21,043
Less : Indexation allowance		
$\frac{162.6 - 79.44}{79.44}$ = 1.047 x £10,957	11,472	11,472
Untapered gain	12,528	9,571

The rebasing calculation gives the lower gain, so rebasing applies and the untapered gain is £9,571.

Leases

For CGT purposes, leases are classified into "long leases" (i.e. those with more than 50 years to run) and "short leases" (i.e. those with 50 years or less to run). A chargeable disposal may occur in connection with a lease in any of the following ways :

(a) A taxpayer who has a long lease on a piece of property assigns that long lease to someone else.

(b) A taxpayer who has a short lease on a piece of property assigns that short lease to someone else.

(c) A taxpayer who has the freehold (or a long head-lease) grants a long lease (or sub-lease) on the property to someone else, the property eventually reverting to the taxpayer.

(d) A taxpayer who has the freehold (or a long head-lease) grants a short lease (or sub-lease) on the property to someone else, the property eventually reverting to the taxpayer.

(e) A taxpayer who has a short head-lease grants a shorter sub-lease on the property to someone else, the property eventually reverting to the taxpayer.

Each of these cases is considered below. Note that if a property is or has been the taxpayer's main residence, the gain arising on the disposal of a lease on the property may be subject to the principal private residence exemption described in Chapter 21.

Assignment of a long lease

The assignment of a long lease is treated as a disposal of the whole asset and therefore causes no CGT difficulties at all. The computation proceeds in precisely the same way as the computation on the disposal of any other whole asset.

EXAMPLE 9

In 1988, Jim acquired a 99 year lease on a flat for £60,000. In 2001, he assigned the lease to a third party for £92,000. The flat was never Jim's residence. Compute the untapered gain, assuming an indexation factor of 50%.

SOLUTION

The unindexed gain is £32,000. Indexation allowance of £30,000 (50% x £60,000) reduces this to an untapered gain of £2,000.

Assignment of a short lease

A short lease is, by definition, a wasting asset. Therefore the computation of the gain arising on the disposal of a short lease should be achieved by comparing disposal proceeds with the unexpired portion of the lease's cost at the time of disposal.

However, unlike other wasting assets, the cost of a short lease is not deemed to waste away on a straight line basis. Instead, the cost of a short lease is deemed to waste away according to a table of percentages given in Schedule 8 of the Taxation of Chargeable Gains Act 1992. The effect of this table is to write off the cost of a short lease slowly in the early years and more quickly in the closing years. The table is reproduced at the end of this chapter.

The proportion of the cost of a short lease which is allowed in the CGT computation on its disposal is :

$$\frac{\% \text{ relating to number of years lease has left to run on disposal}}{\% \text{ relating to original length of lease}}$$

If the lease was originally a long lease but the taxpayer has occupied the property for some years so that the lease now being assigned is a short lease, the denominator in the above fraction is taken as 100%, corresponding to "50 or more" in the Schedule 8 table.

EXAMPLE 10

Jean acquired a 30-year lease on a property in July 1990 (RPI 126.8) for £32,000. In July 2000 she assigned the lease to a third party for £45,000. The property was never Jean's residence. Compute the untapered gain.

SOLUTION

When the lease was acquired it had a 30-year life (Sch 8 percentage 87.330%). When it was assigned there were 20 years remaining (Sch 8 percentage 72.770%). Therefore the computation is as follows :

	£
Sale proceeds	45,000
Less : Unexpired portion of cost	
$\frac{72.770}{87.330}$ x £32,000	26,665
Unindexed gain	18,335
Less : Indexation allowance	
$\frac{162.6 - 126.8}{126.8}$ = 0.282 x £26,665	7,520
Untapered gain	10,815

Schedule 8 gives percentages only for whole numbers of years. If the duration of a lease is not a whole number of years, then the appropriate percentage is calculated from the table on a pro rata basis.

EXAMPLE 11

A taxpayer assigns a lease of duration 12 years and 5 months. Calculate the appropriate percentage for use in the CGT computation on the disposal.

SOLUTION

The percentage for 12 years is 53.191%. The percentage for 13 years is 56.167%. The difference between these percentages is 2.976%. Therefore the appropriate percentage for a lease of duration 12 years and 5 months is 53.191 + 2.976 x 5/12 = 54.431%.

EXAMPLE 12

Joan acquired a 40-year lease on a property on 31 May 1981 for £38,000. The market value of the lease on 31 March 1982 (RPI 79.44) was £35,000. On 30 November 2000 she assigned the lease to a third party for £65,000. The property was never Joan's residence. Compute the untapered gain.

SOLUTION

When the lease was acquired it had a 40-year life (Sch 8 percentage 95.457%). On 31 March 1982 there were 39 years and 2 months remaining (Sch 8 percentage 94.842 + 0.615 x 2/12 = 94.945%). When it was assigned there were 20 years and 6 months remaining (Sch 8 percentage = 72.770 + 1.865 x 6/12 = 73.703%). The computation is as follows :

	Original cost £	Rebasing £
Sale proceeds	65,000	65,000
Less : Unexpired portion of cost		
$\dfrac{73.703}{95.457}$ x £38,000	29,340	
Unexpired portion of MV 31/3/82		
$\dfrac{73.703}{94.945}$ x £35,000		27,169
Unindexed gain	35,660	37,831
Less : Indexation allowance		
$\dfrac{162.6 - 79.44}{79.44}$ = 1.047 x £29,340	30,719	30,719
Untapered gain	4,941	7,112

The rebasing calculation gives the higher gain, so rebasing does not apply and the untapered gain is £4,941.

Grant of a long lease

The grant of a long lease (or sub-lease) out of a freehold (or a long head-lease) is treated as a part disposal for CGT purposes and the normal part disposal rules apply. The value of the part disposed of is clearly the proceeds of the disposal. The value of the part remaining takes into account both :

(a) the right of the taxpayer making the disposal to receive rents from the tenant, and

(b) the taxpayer's "reversionary interest" i.e. the right to take back the property when the lease (or sub-lease) finishes.

Grant of a short lease

The grant of a short lease (or sub-lease) out of a freehold (or a long head-lease) is also treated as a part disposal for CGT purposes and once again the part disposal rules apply. However, the premium received on the grant of a short lease (or sub-lease) will be assessable to Schedule A income tax (see Chapter 5) and therefore, in order to avoid double taxation, the disposal proceeds are reduced by the amount of the Schedule A assessment.

EXAMPLE 13

Jeffrey acquired a freehold property in 1992 for £117,000. In 2000 he granted Jill a lease on the property for £80,000. The market value of the freehold after the lease had been granted was £100,000. The property was never Jeffrey's residence. Compute the untapered gain, given that the lease granted to Jill was of duration :

(a)   99 years   (b)   40 years.

Assume an indexation factor of 18%.

SOLUTION

(a)   This is a part disposal with A = £80,000 and B = £100,000. The computation is as follows :

	£
Sale proceeds	80,000
<u>Less</u> : Part cost :	
$\dfrac{£80,000}{£80,000 + £100,000}$ x £117,000	52,000
Unindexed gain	28,000

	£
Unindexed gain	28,000
Less : Indexation allowance	
18% of £52,000	9,360
Untapered gain	18,640

(b) This is also a part disposal but the disposal proceeds will be subject to a Schedule A assessment of £17,600 (£80,000 - 2% x £80,000 x 39) and this must be taken into account in the CGT computation. The computation is as follows :

	£
Sale proceeds (£80,000 - £17,600)	62,400
Less : Part cost :	
$\dfrac{£62,400}{£80,000 + £100,000}$ x £117,000	40,560
Unindexed gain	21,840
Less : Indexation allowance	
18% of £40,560	7,301
Untapered gain	14,539

Note that the numerator of the part disposal fraction is taken as the disposal proceeds *after* deducting the Schedule A assessment, whilst the denominator takes into account the disposal proceeds *before* deducting the Schedule A assessment.

Grant of a short sub-lease out of a short head-lease

In essence, the grant of a short sub-lease out of a short head-lease is treated in a similar fashion to the assignment of a short lease, as discussed earlier in this chapter. Once again, the Schedule 8 table of percentages is called into use to determine the part cost that should be deducted in the CGT computation. But since the property will be returning to the original tenant when the sub-lease finishes, the proportion of the cost of the short head-lease which is allowed in the CGT computation on the granting of the sub-lease is equal to:

$$\frac{P1 - P2}{P3}$$

where :

P1 = % relating to the number of years left of the short head-lease when the sub-lease begins

P2 = % relating to the number of years left of the short head-lease when the sub-lease ends

P3 = % relating to original length of the short head-lease.

Since the premium received by the taxpayer on the grant of a short sub-lease will be assessable to Schedule A income tax, the gain arising is reduced by the amount of the Schedule A assessment. However, this reduction cannot be used to convert a gain into a loss or to increase a loss.

EXAMPLE 14

Joanna acquired a 15-year lease on a property in September 1994 (RPI 145.0) for £45,000. In September 2000 she granted a 4-year sub-lease to a third party for £20,000. The property was never Joanna's residence. Compute the untapered gain.

SOLUTION

The computation of the untapered gain is as follows :

	£
Sale proceeds	20,000
Less : Proportion of cost	
$\dfrac{43.154 - 26.722}{61.617}$ x £45,000	12,001
	———
Unindexed gain	7,999
Less : Indexation allowance	
$\dfrac{162.6 - 145.0}{145.0}$ = 0.121 x £12,001	1,452
	———
	6,547
Less : Schedule A assessment (£10,160)	6,547
	———
Untapered gain	nil
	———

Notes :

(i) P1 = 43.154 (9 years), P2 = 26.722 (5 years) and P3 = 61.617 (15 years)

(ii) The Schedule A assessment (see Chapter 5) is :

	£
Premium received	20,000
Less : £20,000 x (4 - 1) x 2%	1,200
	———
	18,800
Less : Relief for premium paid :	
$\dfrac{4}{15}$ x (£45,000 - £45,000 x (15 - 1) x 2%)	8,640
	———
	10,160

(iii) The relief given for the Schedule A assessment is restricted to £6,547 so as not to turn a gain into a loss.

Summary

► A chattel is an item of tangible, movable property. A wasting asset is one with an expected useful life of 50 years or less at the time of disposal. A wasting asset that is also a chattel is a wasting chattel.

► Chattels disposed of for £6,000 or less are exempt from CGT.

► The allowable loss on chattels acquired for more than £6,000 and disposed of for less than £6,000 is restricted by substituting £6,000 for the disposal proceeds.

► Disposals of a part interest in a chattel are exempt from CGT if the value of the whole chattel is £6,000 or less,

► A series of disposals of chattels forming a set will be treated as a single transaction for CGT purposes if the disposals are to connected persons.

► Wasting chattels are exempt from CGT apart from movable plant and machinery used in business on which capital allowances are available.

► Wasting assets are not exempt from CGT. In general, the original cost of a wasting asset is written off over its predictable life using the straight line method. However, special rules apply to plant and machinery used for trade purposes and to leases.

► An assignment of a long lease is regarded as the disposal of a whole asset.

► An assignment of a short lease is a disposal of a wasting asset. The original cost of a short lease is written off over its predictable life, using a table of percentages contained in Schedule 8, TCGA 1992.

► The grant of a long lease is treated as a part disposal.

► The grant of a short lease (or sub-lease) out of a freehold (or long head-lease) is treated as a part disposal. The Schedule A assessment raised on the premium received is deducted from disposal proceeds in the CGT computation.

► The grant of a short sub-lease out of a short head-lease is a part disposal of a wasting asset. The Schedule 8 table is used to determine the allowable cost used in the CGT computation. The Schedule A assessment raised on the premium received is deducted from the gain arising but cannot be used to convert a gain into a loss or to increase a loss.

Short lease amortisation table

(Schedule 8 of TCGA 1992)

Years	Percentage	Years	Percentage	Years	Percentage
50 or more	100	33	90.280	16	64.116
49	99.657	32	89.354	15	61.617
48	99.289	31	88.371	14	58.971
47	98.902	30	87.330	13	56.167
46	98.490	29	86.226	12	53.191
45	98.059	28	85.053	11	50.038
44	97.595	27	83.816	10	46.695
43	97.107	26	82.496	9	43.154
42	96.593	25	81.100	8	39.399
41	96.041	24	79.622	7	35.414
40	95.457	23	78.055	6	31.195
39	94.842	22	76.399	5	26.722
38	94.189	21	74.635	4	21.983
37	93.497	20	72.770	3	16.959
36	92.761	19	70.791	2	11.629
35	91.981	18	68.697	1	5.983
34	91.156	17	66.470	0	0

Exercises

Please note that the RPI for April 1998 is 162.6.

18.1 Classify each of the following assets as either chattels, wasting assets or wasting chattels :

(a) A domestic washing machine.

(b) A gold ring.

(c) A personal computer.

(d) A central heating system.

(e) A 20-year lease on a building.

(f) A suit of clothes.

(g) An antique vase.

18.2 In October 2000 Keith sells an antique cabinet for £7,200. He incurs incidental costs of disposal amounting to £200. The cabinet cost £2,000 in July 1989 (RPI 115.5). Compute the untapered gain.

18.3   In September 2000 Kevin sells a drawing for £2,000. He bought the drawing in February 1990 (RPI 120.2) for £50,000 when it was thought (incorrectly) to be by a famous artist. Compute the allowable loss.

18.4   In January 2001 Karl sells a one-quarter interest in a painting for £25,000. The remaining three-quarter interest is valued at £85,000. The painting had cost Karl £38,500 in January 1984 (RPI 86.84). Compute the untapered gain.

18.5   In January 1993 (RPI 137.9), Katrina buys an item of movable plant and machinery for use in her business. The plant costs her £50,000 and capital allowances are claimed. Compute the untapered gain in March 2001 when she sells the plant, assuming that sale proceeds are :

(a)   £65,000

(b)   £35,000.

18.6   In June 1998 (RPI 163.4), Katie acquired a 5-year option to buy a piece of land. The option cost her £10,000. In June 2000 she sold the option for £8,000. Compute the untapered gain.

18.7   Katherine acquired a 25-year lease on a property on 31 August 1980 for £12,500. The lease was valued at £15,000 on 31 March 1982 (RPI 79.44). On 31 August 2000 she assigned the lease to a third party for £20,000. The property was never Katherine's residence. Compute the untapered gain.

*18.8   In March 1987 (RPI 100.6), Sean acquired a pair of matching antique silver candlesticks at a cost of £4,000. In August 2000 he sold one of the candlesticks to James for £6,750. At that time the other candlestick was valued at £5,750. In September 2000 he sold the other candlestick to Julia for £5,800. Calculate the untapered gain on these two disposals if :

(a)   James and Julia are unconnected.

(b)   James and Julia are a married couple.

*18.9   On 31 March 1977, Estelle acquired a patent with a 30 year life at a cost of £21,000. The patent was valued at £18,000 on 31 March 1982 (RPI 79.44) and Estelle sold the patent on 31 March 2001 for £13,000. Compute the untapered gain.

*18.10   Edward bought a 20-year lease on a flat in May 1992 (RPI 139.3) at a cost of £35,000. In November 2000 he granted a 5-year sub-lease to a third party for £15,000. The flat was never Edward's principal private residence. Compute the untapered gain.

Chapter 19

Shares and securities (1)

Introduction

A disposal of shares or securities causes no CGT problems unless a taxpayer disposes of part of a shareholding which was originally acquired over a period of time in several separate transactions. If this happens, it is not possible to identify the shares which have been disposed of. But the calculation of the gain or loss arising on the disposal cannot proceed until the cost and acquisition date of the shares concerned have been established. It is necessary, therefore, to devise a set of *matching rules* which may be used to match disposals against acquisitions in these circumstances. The purpose of this chapter is to explain these matching rules and to show how they are used to calculate the gain or loss arising on a disposal of shares.

Please note that the RPI for April 1998 (which is used in many of the examples in this chapter) is 162.6.

The matching rules

With effect from 6 April 1998, disposals of shares or securities are matched for CGT purposes against acquisitions of *the same class of shares in the same company* in the following order :

(a) First, against any acquisitions made on the same day as the day of the disposal.

(b) Next, against any acquisitions made during the following 30 days, matching with shares acquired earlier rather than later within that 30-day period. (This rule is intended to counter the practice known as "bed and breakfasting", whereby shares are sold and then almost immediately re-acquired so as to trigger gains or losses for tax avoidance purposes).

(c) Next, against previous acquisitions made after 5 April 1998, matching the most recent acquisitions first (a last-in, first-out basis).

(d) Next, against shares forming the "Section 104 holding". This is a pool of shares acquired between 6 April 1982 and 5 April 1998 inclusive.

(e) Next, against shares forming the "1982 holding". This is a pool of shares acquired between 6 April 1965 and 5 April 1982 inclusive.

(f) Next, against shares acquired before 6 April 1965 (on a last-in, first-out basis).

(g) Finally, if the above rules fail to exhaust a disposal of shares, the remainder of the disposal is matched with subsequent acquisitions (beyond the 30-day period mentioned above in rule (b)).

These matching rules were introduced by Finance Act 1998 and replaced an older set of rules. However, it is important to note that the new rules do *not* apply to companies and that the gain or loss arising on a disposal of shares by a company is still computed in accordance with the old, pre-FA1998 matching rules (see Chapter 23).

EXAMPLE 1

Paul made the following acquisitions and disposals of ordinary shares in Crimson plc :

Date			Date		
11 May 1962	acquisition	1,000	1 October 1998	acquisition	100
15 January 1965	acquisition	100	1 October 1998	disposal	450
9 June 1979	acquisition	170	7 December 1998	acquisition	500
14 February 1990	acquisition	350	11 January 1999	disposal	750
4 July 1998	acquisition	200	18 February 1999	acquisition	400
31 August 1998	acquisition	300	28 March 2001	disposal	1,000

No further shares were acquired before the end of April 2001. Against which acquisitions will the disposals be matched ?

SOLUTION

(a) The 450 shares disposed of on 1 October 1998 are matched first against the 100 shares acquired on the same day, leaving 350 shares still to be matched. No shares were acquired in the next 30 days so the next step is to match against acquisitions made after 5 April 1998 on a LIFO basis. 300 of the shares disposed of are matched against those acquired on 31 August 1998 and the remaining 50 are matched against 50 of the shares acquired on 4 July 1998.

(b) The disposal of 750 shares on 11 January 1999 cannot be matched against any acquisitions on the same day or during the next 30 days. The only shares acquired after 5 April 1998 (on a LIFO basis) are the 500 acquired on 7 December 1998 and 150 acquired on 4 July 1998 (200, less 50 already matched with a disposal) so 650 of the shares disposed of on 11 January 1999 are matched with these acquisitions, leaving 100 shares still to be matched.

The next step is to match against the Section 104 holding i.e. the pool of shares acquired between 6 April 1982 and 5 April 1998 inclusive. This pool contains only the 350 shares acquired on 14 February 1990, so the remaining 100 shares in the disposal are matched against 100 of these shares.

(c) The disposal of 1,000 shares on 28 March 2001 cannot be matched against any acquisitions made on the same day or during the next 30 days. The disposal is matched first against the 400 shares acquired on 18 February 1999, leaving 600 shares still to be matched. The Section 104 holding now contains 250 of the shares which were acquired on 14 February 1990 (350, less 100 already matched) so 250 of the shares disposed of on 28 March 2001 are matched with this acquisition, leaving 350 shares still to be matched.

The next step is to match against the 1982 holding i.e. the pool of shares acquired between 6 April 1965 and 5 April 1982 inclusive. This pool contains only the 170 shares acquired on 9 June 1979 so 170 of the shares disposed of on 28 March 2001 are matched with this acquisition, leaving 180 shares still to be matched.

The remaining 180 shares are matched first against the 100 shares acquired on 15 January 1965 and finally against 80 of the 1,000 shares acquired on 11 May 1962.

The Section 104 holding

A taxpayer's "Section 104 holding" of shares of a certain class in a certain company consists of the pool of shares which were acquired between 6 April 1982 and 5 April 1998 inclusive. The pool's name is derived from Section 104 of TCGA 1992, which provides the legal basis for its existence, but it is important to note that this name was introduced fairly recently (by the Finance Act 1998) and that the pool might also be referred to as either :

(a) the "new holding", or

(b) the "Finance Act 1985 pool" (since share pooling was introduced by that Act).

The distinguishing characteristic of shares acquired between 6 April 1982 and 5 April 1998 is that the indexation factor used on their disposal will differ according to the date of acquisition. This is not true for shares acquired before 6 April 1982 (which all attract the same rate of indexation allowance, as explained later in this chapter) or for shares acquired after 5 April 1998 (which do not attract indexation allowance at all).

If it were not for the provisions of Section 104, it would be necessary to keep detailed records of the date and cost of each individual share acquisition made between 6 April 1982 and 5 April 1998, so that indexation allowance could be calculated correctly on a disposal. However, the pooling arrangement provided by Section 104 eliminates the need to keep these records. Instead, all that is required is a record of :

(a) the total number of shares in the pool, and

(b) their total cost, and

(c) their total *indexed cost*, which consists of total cost plus all indexation allowance due up to the date of the most recent "operative event". An operative event occurs whenever shares enter or leave the pool.

Shares acquired after 5 April 1998 cannot join this pool since it is necessary to retain the date and cost of each such acquisition for taper relief purposes.

EXAMPLE 2

Pauline makes the following purchases of preference shares in Violet plc :

Date	No of shares	Cost £
23 June 1990	1,000	1,100
14 May 1992	2,000	2,300
8 July 1997	3,000	3,150

Assuming an indexation factor of 10% between June 1990 and May 1992, and a further 13% between May 1992 and July 1997, calculate the cost and indexed cost of the S104 holding at :

(a) 14 May 1992   (b) 8 July 1997.

SOLUTION

(a) The S104 holding commences on 23 June 1990 with the purchase of 1,000 shares at a cost of £1,100. On 14 May 1992, an operative event occurs i.e. the purchase of a further 2,000 shares. Before adding these shares to the pool it is necessary to index the pool up to May 1992. The calculation is as follows :

	No of shares	Cost £	Indexed cost £
Bought 23 June 1990	1,000	1,100	1,100
Add : Indexation to May 1992			
10% x £1,100			110
			1,210
Bought 14 May 1992	2,000	2,300	2,300
S104 holding at 14 May 1992	3,000	3,400	3,510

The total of the indexed cost column represents the cost *in May 1992 terms* of the S104 holding and includes all indexation allowance due up to that date.

(b) The next operative event is the purchase of 3,000 shares in July 1997. Before adding these shares to the pool it is necessary to index the pool from May 1992 (when the previous indexation calculation took place) to July 1997. The calculation is :

	No of shares	Cost £	Indexed cost £
S104 holding b/f at 14 May 1992	3,000	3,400	3,510
Add : Indexation to July 1997			
13% x £3,510			456
			3,966
Bought 8 July 1997	3,000	3,150	3,150
S104 holding at 8 July 1997	6,000	6,550	7,116

The three acquisitions forming the S104 holding have now been combined into a single pool of 6,000 shares, costing £6,550 but with an indexed cost (including all indexation allowance due to July 1997) of £7,116. It is now necessary to carry forward only these three "bottom line" figures, rather than the details of each individual acquisition.

Calculation of the indexed cost of the S104 holding

The example given above was a slight simplification of the way in which the indexed cost of the S104 holding is actually calculated. The full method of calculation is as follows :

(a) The number of shares in the pool at 5 April 1985 (if any) is totalled and the cost of these shares is also totalled. The indexed cost of the pool at 5 April 1985 is calculated as total cost, plus an indexation allowance for each acquisition forming part of the pool, based on the change in RPI between the date of the acquisition and April 1985.

(b) On the occurrence of a subsequent operative event, the indexed cost of the pool is increased by reference to the change in RPI since the previous operative event (or since April 1985 if this is the first such event). The indexation factor used in this calculation is *not* rounded to 3 decimal places. No further indexation adjustments are required once the pool has been indexed up to April 1998. The pool is then adjusted to take account of the operative event as follows :

   (i) If the event is an acquisition, the number of shares acquired is added to the number of shares in the pool and their cost is added to the cost and to the indexed cost of the pool.

   (ii) If the event is a disposal, the number of shares disposed of is subtracted from the number of shares in the pool. It is then necessary to deduct a proportion of the cost and indexed cost of the pool. Strictly speaking, this proportion should be calculated using the part disposal fraction (see Chapter 17) which takes into account the value of the shares disposed of and the value of the shares remaining. In most cases, however, the value per share of the shares disposed of will be the same as the value per share of the shares remaining, so that the proportion to be deducted from the cost and indexed cost of the pool can be based upon the *number* of shares disposed of. This is assumed to be the case for the remainder of this book.

The unindexed gain (or loss) arising on a disposal from the pool is calculated as the difference between the disposal proceeds and the amount which has been subtracted from the cost of the pool as a consequence of the disposal. The indexation allowance due on the disposal is the difference between the amount subtracted from the cost of the pool and the amount subtracted from the indexed cost of the pool. As usual, indexation allowance cannot be used to create a loss or to increase a loss.

EXAMPLE 3

Paula makes the following acquisitions of ordinary shares in Indigo plc :

Date	No of shares	Cost £	RPI
1 July 1983	5,000	6,300	85.30
2 August 1984	2,000	2,500	89.94
3 February 1987	1,200	2,300	100.4
4 June 1993	1,800	3,400	141.0

She sells 500 shares on 8 July 2000. No shares are acquired within the next 30 days.

(a)   Calculate the cost and indexed cost of the S104 holding on 8 July 2000, just prior to and just after the above disposal (RPI for April 1985 is 94.78).

(b)   Compute the untapered gain or allowable loss on the disposal if the sale proceeds are :

(i)   £1,300   (ii)   £1,000   (iii)   £700

SOLUTION

(a)   The cost and indexed cost of the S104 holding on 8 July 2000 are calculated as follows :

	No of shares	Cost £	Indexed cost £
Bought 1 July 1983	5,000	6,300	6,300
Bought 2 August 1984	2,000	2,500	2,500

Add : Indexation to April 1985

$$\text{(a)} \quad \frac{94.78 - 85.30}{85.30} = 0.111$$

0.111 x £6,300   699

$$\text{(b)} \quad \frac{94.78 - 89.94}{89.94} = 0.054$$

0.054 x £2,500   135

	No of shares	Cost £	Indexed cost £
S104 holding at 5 April 1985	7,000	8,800	9,634

Add : Indexation to February 1987

$$\frac{100.4 - 94.78}{94.78} \times £9,634 \qquad 571$$

10,205

	No of shares	Cost £	Indexed cost £
Bought 3 February 1987	1,200	2,300	2,300
S104 holding at 3 February 1987	8,200	11,100	12,505

	No of shares	Cost £	Indexed cost £
S104 holding at 3 February 1987	8,200	11,100	12,505
Add : Indexation to June 1993			
$\dfrac{141.0 - 100.4}{100.4}$ x £12,505			5,057
			17,562
Bought 4 June 1993	1,800	3,400	3,400
S104 holding at 4 June 1993	10,000	14,500	20,962
Add : Indexation to April 1998			
$\dfrac{162.6 - 141.0}{141.0}$ x £20,962			3,211
			24,173
Sold 8 July 2000 (500/10,000th)	(500)	(725)	(1,209)
S104 holding at 8 July 2000	9,500	13,775	22,964

Notes :

1. The indexation allowance calculated on operative events occurring after 5 April 1985 has not been rounded off to 3 decimal places.

2. The disposal in July 2000 must have come from the S104 holding since it cannot be matched against shares acquired on the same day, during the next 30 days or after 5 April 1998.

3. The pool has been indexed up to April 1998 and no further, since indexation allowance is not available in relation to increases in the RPI after April 1998.

4. The disposal is of 500 shares out of a holding of 10,000. Therefore 500/10,000th or 1/20th of the pool has been sold and so 1/20th of the cost and indexed cost are subtracted from the pool.

5. The cost of the shares disposed of is £725. Since the equivalent indexed cost is £1,209, the maximum indexation allowance due on the disposal is £484 (£1,209 - £725).

(b)

	(i) £	(ii) £	(iii) £
Sale proceeds	1,300	1,000	700
Less : Cost	725	725	725
Unindexed gain (loss)	575	275	(25)
Less : Indexation allowance	484	275	nil
Untapered gain (allowable loss)	91	nil	(25)

The gain arising in case (i) has a taper period of two years (plus the bonus year if the shares do not rank as a business asset).

The 1982 holding

The 1982 holding is a pool of shares acquired between 6 April 1965 and 5 April 1982 inclusive. All of the shares in this pool (including those acquired during the first 5 days of April 1982) attract the same rate of indexation allowance, based on the change in RPI between March 1982 and the date of disposal (or April 1998, if earlier). This means that the calculation of this pool's value is much simpler than the calculation of the value of the Section 104 holding. All that is needed is a record of:

(a)   the number of shares in the pool

(b)   the total cost of these shares

(c)   their market value at 31 March 1982.

When a disposal occurs, the number of shares in the pool is reduced and proportionate amounts are deducted from the pool's cost and from its market value at 31 March 1982. The gain or loss arising on the disposal is then calculated in the usual way, as for any disposal of a pre-31 March 1982 asset.

EXAMPLE 4

Patrick made the following acquisitions of ordinary shares in Cornflower plc:

Date	No of shares	Cost
		£
1 June 1970	1,000	3,000
30 October 1975	800	2,500
15 August 1981	900	3,100

The shares had a market value of £3.10 per share on 31 March 1982 (RPI 79.44). Patrick sold 750 of the shares on 18 January 2001 for £6,500. No shares were acquired within the next 30 days. Compute the untapered gain.

SOLUTION

The sale of 750 shares on 18 January 2001 cannot be matched against any acquisitions on the same day, during the next 30 days, after 5 April 1998 or between 6 April 1982 and 5 April 1998. The next step is to match against the 1982 holding, as follows:

	No of shares	Cost	MV 31/3/82
		£	£
Acquired 1 June 1970	1,000	3,000	3,100
Acquired 30 October 1975	800	2,500	2,480
Acquired 15 August 1981	900	3,100	2,790
	2,700	8,600	8,370
Sold 18 January 2001 (750/2,700th)	(750)	(2,389)	(2,325)
1982 holding c/f	1,950	6,211	6,045

The sold shares are deemed to have cost £2,389 and their market value at 31 March 1982 was £2,325. The calculation of the untapered gain arising on the disposal is :

	Original cost £	Rebasing £
Sale proceeds	6,500	6,500
Less : Original cost	2,389	
Market value 31/3/82		2,325
Unindexed gain	4,111	4,175
Less : Indexation allowance		
$\dfrac{162.6 - 79.44}{79.44} = 1.047 \times £2,389$	2,501	2,501
Untapered gain	1,610	1,674

The rebasing calculation gives the higher gain, so rebasing does not apply and the untapered gain is £1,610. This gain has a taper period of two years (plus the bonus year if the shares do not rank as a business asset).

Shares acquired before 6 April 1965

The CGT treatment of shares acquired before 6 April 1965 depends upon whether the shares are listed or unlisted. Each of these classifications is considered below.

Listed shares - the pooling election

A taxpayer who owns listed shares acquired before 6 April 1965 may elect *irrevocably* for these shares to be incorporated into the 1982 holding at their market value on 6 April 1965. This is known as the "pooling election". If the election is made, the shares acquired before 6 April 1965 present no new difficulties and the gains or losses arising on subsequent disposals can be calculated as described earlier in this chapter.

The pooling election was first made available in 1968 and could be made either for equities or for fixed interest shares and securities (or for both). The election had to be made within two years of the end of the tax year in which the first disposal of such shares took place after 19 March 1968. Another opportunity to make the election is provided by TCGA 1992. This Act allows taxpayers to make the election (this time, for *all* types of listed shares and securities) by 31 January in the second year of assessment following the year in which the first disposal of such shares takes place after 5 April 1985.

EXAMPLE 5

Roseanne made the following acquisitions of ordinary shares in Magenta plc (a listed company) :

Date	No of shares	Cost	RPI
		£	
12 October 1960	100	1,100	
17 March 1963	120	1,400	
18 March 1979	80	800	
23 July 1988	150	1,800	106.7

The shares had a market value of £9 per share on 6 April 1965 and £11 per share on 31 March 1982 (RPI 79.44). Roseanne sold 200 shares on 9 October 2000 for £21 each. Compute the untapered gain, assuming that no shares were acquired within the next 30 days and that an election has been made to incorporate pre-6 April 1965 shares into the 1982 holding.

SOLUTION

The sale of 200 shares on 9 October 2000 cannot be matched against acquisitions made on the same day, during the next 30 days or after 5 April 1998. The next step is to match against the S104 holding. This pool consists only of the shares acquired in July 1988, so only 150 shares can be matched. The S104 holding is as follows :

	No of shares	Cost	Indexed cost
		£	£
Bought 23 July 1988	150	1,800	1,800
Add : Indexation to April 1998			
$\dfrac{162.6 - 106.7}{106.7} \times £1,800$			943
			2,743
Sold 9 October 2000	(150)	(1,800)	(2,743)
S104 holding c/f	nil	nil	nil

The untapered gain on the disposal of these 150 shares is :

	£
Sale proceeds (150 @ £21)	3,150
Less : Cost	1,800
Unindexed gain	1,350
Less : Indexation allowance (£2,743 - £1,800)	943
Untapered gain	407

The 50 remaining shares must be matched against the 1982 holding, which incorporates the pre-6 April 1965 shares (included at 6 April 1965 market value, *not* at original cost). The 1982 holding is :

	No of shares	Cost £	MV 31/3/82 £
Acquired 12 October 1960 (@ £9)	100	900	1,100
Acquired 17 March 1963 (@ £9)	120	1,080	1,320
Acquired 18 March 1979	80	800	880
	300	2,780	3,300
Sold 9 October 2000 (50/300th)	(50)	(463)	(550)
1982 holding c/f	250	2,317	2,750

The untapered gain on the disposal of these 50 shares is :

	Original cost £	Rebasing £
Sale proceeds (50 @ £21)	1,050	1,050
Less : Original cost	463	
Market value 31/3/82		550
Unindexed gain	587	500
Less : Indexation allowance $\frac{162.6 - 79.44}{79.44} = 1.047 \times £550$	576	500
Untapered gain	11	nil

The rebasing calculation gives a nil result, so this is a no-gain, no-loss situation. The total untapered gain on the disposal of the entire 200 shares is therefore £407.

Listed shares - no pooling election made

Without a pooling election, the disposal of listed shares acquired before 6 April 1965 is treated in a broadly similar way to the disposal of any other pre-6 April 1965 asset (see Chapter 17). Basically, the gain produced by a calculation based on original cost is compared with the gain produced by a calculation based on market value at 6 April 1965 and the lower of these two gains is then compared with the gain produced by a rebasing calculation. But there are some significant differences between a disposal of listed shares and a disposal of other types of asset. These differences are :

(a) The calculation based on original cost is performed *without* time apportionment.

(b) The comparison of the calculation based on original cost and the calculation based on market value at 6 April 1965 is mandatory, rather than depending on an election by the taxpayer.

(c) The treatment of losses is as follows :

    (i) If the calculation based on original cost gives a loss and the calculation based on market value at 6 April 1965 also gives a loss, then the lower of these two losses is compared with the outcome of the rebasing calculation in order to arrive at the allowable loss.

    (ii) If the calculation based on original cost gives a gain and the calculation based on market value at 6 April 1965 gives a loss (or vice-versa), then the situation is no gain, no loss. In these circumstances there is no need to perform a rebasing calculation.

EXAMPLE 6

In June 1964, Samuel acquired 1,000 shares in Purple plc (a listed company) at a cost of £500. The shares had a market value of £2 each on 6 April 1965 and £1 each on 31 March 1982. Samuel made no further acquisitions of shares in the company and no election was made to incorporate pre-6 April 1965 shares into the 1982 holding. He sold his entire shareholding in January 2001. Compute the untapered gain if sale proceeds were :

(a) £10 per share   (b) £1.80 per share.

SOLUTION

(a)

	Cost £	MV 6/4/65 £	MV 31/3/82 £
Sale proceeds	10,000	10,000	10,000
Less : Original cost	500		
Market value 6/4/65		2,000	
Market value 31/3/82			1,000
Unindexed gain	9,500	8,000	9,000
Less : Indexation allowance			
$\dfrac{162.6 - 79.44}{79.44}$ = 1.047 x £1,000	1,047		
$\dfrac{162.6 - 79.44}{79.44}$ = 1.047 x £2,000		2,094	2,094
Untapered gain	8,453	5,906	6,906

Comparing the gains based on cost and on market value at 6 April 1965 gives a gain of £5,906. This gain is lower than the gain produced by the rebasing calculation, so rebasing will not apply and the untapered gain is £5,906.

Notes :

(i)   The indexation allowance in the original cost calculation is based on the greater of original cost (£500) and market value at 31 March 1982 (£1,000).

(ii) The indexation allowance in the 6 April 1965 market value calculation is based on the greater of market value at 6 April 1965 (£2,000) and market value at 31 March 1982 (£1,000).

(iii) The indexation allowance in the rebasing calculation is also based on the greater of market value at 6 April 1965 (£2,000) and market value at 31 March 1982 (£1,000), since the rebasing calculation is being compared with the 6 April 1965 market value calculation (see Chapter 17).

(b)

	Cost £	MV 6/4/65 £
Sale proceeds	1,800	1,800
Less : Original cost	500	
Market value 6/4/65		2,000
Unindexed gain	1,300	(200)
Less : Indexation allowance	1,047	nil
Untapered gain	253	(200)

The situation is no gain, no loss. There is no need to perform a rebasing calculation.

Unlisted shares acquired before 6 April 1965

None of the rules described above for listed shares apply to unlisted shares. There is no pooling election available in respect of unlisted shares and the computation of the gain or loss arising on a disposal of unlisted shares acquired before 6 April 1965 is performed in the same way as for any other pre-6 April 1965 asset.

Gilts and qualifying corporate bonds

Gilt-edged securities and "qualifying corporate bonds" are not chargeable assets for CGT purposes. Therefore neither a chargeable gain nor an allowable loss can arise on their disposal. Note that :

(a) Gilt-edged securities are British Government securities such as Treasury Stock, Exchequer Stock, War Loan etc.

(b) "Qualifying corporate bonds" consist of company debentures and other fixed-interest securities which are expressed in sterling and which comprise a normal commercial loan.

(c) Gains and losses arising on the disposal of gilts or corporate bonds by a *company* are assessed under the "loan relationships" rules for corporation tax purposes (see Chapter 23).

Summary

▶ Special matching rules are used to match disposals of shares and securities against acquisitions.

▶ Disposals are matched first against shares acquired on the same day as the disposal, then against shares acquired in the next 30 days, then against shares acquired after 5 April 1998, then against the S104 holding, then against the 1982 holding and then against shares acquired before 6 April 1965.

▶ The S104 holding consists of a pool of shares acquired between 6 April 1982 and 5 April 1998 inclusive. It is necessary to keep a record of the number of shares in this pool, their total cost and their total indexed cost.

▶ The 1982 holding consists of a pool of shares acquired between 6 April 1965 and 5 April 1982 inclusive. It is necessary to keep a record of the number of shares in this pool, their total cost and their market value at 31 March 1982.

▶ Listed shares acquired before 6 April 1965 may join the 1982 holding at their 6 April 1965 market value if the taxpayer makes a pooling election to this effect.

▶ In the absence of a pooling election, disposals of listed shares acquired before 6 April 1965 are dealt with according to a special set of rules which differ in some respects from the usual rules for dealing with pre-6 April 1965 assets.

▶ Disposals of unlisted shares acquired before 6 April 1965 are dealt with according to the usual rules for dealing with pre-6 April 1965 assets.

▶ Gilt-edged securities and qualifying corporate bonds are not chargeable assets for CGT purposes.

Exercises

Please note that the RPI for April 1998 is 162.6.

19.1 A taxpayer makes the following acquisitions of preference shares in Mauve Ltd (an unlisted company) :

Date	No of shares purchased
1 August 1959	200
10 September 1962	500
4 August 1981	1,000
23 February 1990	250
17 October 2000	100
20 October 2000	200
1 December 2000	150

No further shares are acquired during 2000 or 2001. How will the following disposals be matched against these acquisitions?

(a)   250 shares sold on 20 October 2000

(b)   500 shares sold on 25 January 2001

(c)   1,200 shares sold on 1 February 2001.

19.2   Sandra acquired the following ordinary shares in Pink plc :

Date	No of shares	Cost	RPI
		£	
29 June 1982	1,000	3,000	81.85
5 May 1984	1,000	3,500	88.97
13 August 1987	1,350	6,500	102.1
7 September 1990	2,650	14,150	129.3
4 October 1995	2,000	22,500	149.8

Calculate the cost and indexed cost of the S104 holding at 4 October 1995 (RPI for April 1985 was 94.78).

19.3   In June 2000 Sandra (in question 19.2 above) sold 2,000 of her shares in Pink plc. She acquired no further shares in the company. Calculate the untapered gain (or allowable loss) if the sale proceeds are :

(a)   £14,000

(b)   £12,000

(c)   £17,000.

19.4   Dennis acquired the following ordinary shares in Bronze plc :

Date	No of shares	Cost
		£
5 August 1978	300	2,400
12 May 1980	200	1,700
11 July 1981	250	2,000

Dennis made no other acquisitions and the shares had a market value of £10 per share on 31 March 1982 (RPI 79.44). Calculate the untapered gain arising in August 2000 when Dennis sold 150 shares for £3,500.

19.5   Denise acquired the following ordinary shares in Turquoise plc :

Date	No of shares	Cost	RPI
		£	
28 December 1980	10,000	5,000	
21 June 1990	10,000	9,000	126.7
3 March 1993	10,000	11,000	139.3

The shares were valued at 60p each on 31 March 1982 (RPI 79.44). In December 2000, Denise sold 25,000 shares for £1.25 per share. She made no further acquisitions of the shares. Calculate the untapered gain arising in December 2000 and state the length of the taper period for this gain (assuming that the shares do not rank as a business asset).

19.6   Raymond acquired the following ordinary shares in Buff plc (which are listed on the Stock Exchange) :

Date	No of shares	Cost
		£
17 February 1963	500	4,000
8 January 1980	700	8,500

The shares were valued at £9 each on 6 April 1965 and £15 each on 31 March 1982. Raymond elected to incorporate pre 6-April 1965 shares into the 1982 holding and made no further acquisitions of the shares. In September 2000 he sold 1,000 shares for £40 each. Compute the untapered gain and state the length of the taper period for this gain (assuming that the shares do not rank as a business asset).

19.7   Rework exercise 19.6, assuming now that Raymond had *not* elected to incorporate pre 6-April 1965 shares into the 1982 holding.

*19.8   Suzanne acquired the following ordinary shares in Aquamarine plc :

Date	No of shares	Cost	RPI
		£	
2 October 1979	100	300	
10 January 1981	150	500	
5 December 1983	200	700	86.89
8 November 1984	250	1,000	90.95
4 July 1991	300	1,400	133.8
20 May 2000	400	2,500	169.0

She made no further acquisitions. The shares were valued at £3.25 each on 31 March 1982 (RPI 79.44). RPI for April 1985 was 94.78. On 5 October 2000 Suzanne sold 1,200 shares for £7 per share. Compute the untapered gains arising on this disposal and state the taper period for each gain (assuming that the shares do not rank as a business asset).

*19.9   Stephen acquired the following ordinary shares in Olive plc (a listed company) :

Date	No of shares	Cost
		£
1 June 1943	10	100
1 January 1960	90	9,000

The shares had a market value of £85 each on 6 April 1965 and £120 each on 31 March 1982 (RPI 79.44). Stephen acquired no further shares in the company and sold all his shares in January 2001 at £80 each. Compute the untapered gain (or allowable loss) given that no pooling election had been made (or will be made) in relation to shares acquired before 6 April 1965.

Chapter 20

Shares and securities (2)

Introduction

A company may reorganise its share capital by making bonus issues or rights issues or by repaying shareholders part of their share capital (to the extent that this is permitted by company law). This chapter considers the CGT impact of a reorganisation of share capital and also describes the treatment of disposals occurring on the takeover of one company by another.

Please note that the RPI for April 1998 (which is used in many of the examples in this chapter) is 162.6.

Bonus issues

A bonus issue occurs when a company issues free extra shares to its shareholders. The number of bonus shares received by a shareholder is generally in proportion to his or her existing shareholding. For instance, a "1 for 5" bonus issue would give each shareholder one free extra share for every five shares previously held.

For CGT purposes, the making of a bonus issue is regarded as a reorganisation of the company's share capital, rather than an issue of new shares. Accordingly, the CGT treatment of a bonus issue is as follows :

(a) Any bonus shares received by a taxpayer are *not* treated as an acquisition in the usual way. Instead, the bonus shares serve to increase the number of shares in each of the taxpayer's holdings as they stood immediately prior to the issue. The cost of those holdings is not affected, since bonus shares are issued free of charge.

(b) On a subsequent disposal, the qualifying period for taper relief purposes begins on the date that the taxpayer's original holdings were acquired and not on the date that the bonus shares were issued.

(c) If a bonus issue is made after 31 March 1982, the market value of the company's shares at 31 March 1982 is adjusted to reflect the issue.

EXAMPLE 1

Sherjeel made the following acquisitions of ordinary shares in Triangle plc :

Date	No of shares	Cost £	RPI
22 January 1978	1,000	2,000	
27 September 1981	200	500	
28 July 1986	800	2,800	97.52
3 February 1993	500	2,200	138.8
5 July 1998	300	1,500	

The market value of the company's shares on 31 March 1982 (RPI 79.44) was £3.19 per share. On 1 September 2000, the company made a 1 for 10 bonus issue. Show each of Sherjeel's holdings immediately after this bonus issue.

SOLUTION

Prior to the bonus issue, Sherjeel owned 2,800 shares in Triangle plc, of which 1,200 comprised the 1982 holding, 1,300 comprised the S104 holding and 300 were acquired on 5 July 1998 (and were not pooled). He received a further 280 shares as a consequence of the bonus issue. 120 of these shares join the 1982 holding, 130 shares join the S104 holding and 30 shares are attached to the acquisition made on 5 July 1998. The holdings immediately after the bonus issue are as follows :

The 1982 holding :

	No of shares	Cost £	MV 31/3/82 £
Acquired 22 January 1978	1,000	2,000	3,190
Acquired 27 September 1981	200	500	638
	1,200	2,500	3,828
Bonus issue 1 September 2000	120	nil	nil
1982 holding c/f	1,320	2,500	3,828

Notice that the market value of this holding at 31 March 1982 remains at £3,828 but the number of shares in the holding has increased to 1,320. In effect, the market value per share at 31 March 1982 has been reduced to £2.90 (£3,828 divided by 1,320) to reflect the fact that 11 shares now exist for every 10 that existed on 31 March 1982. The revised market value per share (£2.90) is 10/11th of the original market value (£3.19).

The S104 holding :

	No of shares	Cost £	Indexed cost £
Bought 28 July 1986	800	2,800	2,800
Add : Indexation to February 1993			
$\frac{138.8 - 97.52}{97.52} \times £2,800$			1,185
c/f	800	2,800	3,985

313

	No of shares	Cost	Indexed cost
		£	£
b/f	800	2,800	3,985
Bought 3 February 1993	500	2,200	2,200
S104 holding at 3 February 1993	1,300	5,000	6,185
Add : Indexation to April 1998			
$\dfrac{162.6 - 138.8}{138.8}$ x £6,185			1,061
			7,246
Bonus issue 1 September 2000	130	nil	nil
S104 holding at 1 September 2000	1,430	5,000	7,246

In summary, Sherjeel now has a 1982 holding containing 1320 shares, a S104 holding containing 1,430 shares and a holding of 330 shares acquired on 5 July 1998.

EXAMPLE 2

Calculate the untapered gain arising in March 2001 when Sherjeel (in the above example) sells 1,830 shares for £6 each, assuming that he makes no further acquisitions within the next 30 days.

SOLUTION

The disposal is matched first against the holding of 330 shares acquired on 5 July 1998. These shares were sold for £1,980 (330 x £6) and have a cost of £1,500 so the untapered gain is £480 (with a taper period of 2 years). The remainder of the disposal is matched against the S104 holding and the 1982 holding, as follows :

S104 holding (1,430 shares sold) :

	No of shares	Cost	Indexed cost
		£	£
S104 holding at 1 September 2000	1,430	5,000	7,246
Sold March 2001	(1,430)	(5,000)	(7,246)
S104 holding c/f	nil	nil	nil

The untapered gain on the disposal of the S104 holding is :

	£
Sale proceeds (1,430 @ £6)	8,580
Less : Cost	5,000
Unindexed gain	3,580
Less : Indexation allowance	
(£7,246 - £5,000)	2,246
Untapered gain	1,334

1982 holding (70 shares sold) :

	No of shares	Cost	MV 31/3/82
		£	£
b/f	1,320	2,500	3,828
Sold March 2001 (70/1,320th)	(70)	(133)	(203)
1982 holding c/f	1,250	2,367	3,625

The untapered gain on the disposal from the 1982 holding is :

	Original cost	Rebasing
	£	£
Sale proceeds (70 @ £6)	420	420
Less : Original cost	133	
Market value 31/3/82		203
Unindexed gain	287	217
Less : Indexation allowance		
$\dfrac{162.6 - 79.44}{79.44} = 1.047 \times £203$	213	213
Untapered gain	74	4

Rebasing applies and the untapered gain is £4. In summary, the untapered gains arising on the disposal are £480 with a taper period of 2 years and £1,338 (£1,334 + £4) with a taper period of 2 years plus the bonus year (if the shares are a non-business asset).

Rights issues

A rights issue occurs when a company offers its shareholders the right to buy extra shares. Rights issues are similar to bonus issues in that the number of shares offered to each shareholder is generally in proportion to his or her existing shareholding. But rights shares are not issued free of charge. Shareholders who are offered rights shares may either :

(a) ignore the rights issue (in which case there is no CGT impact)

(b) sell their "rights" (see later in this chapter)

(c) buy the shares which they are offered.

For CGT purposes, the making of a rights issue is regarded as a reorganisation of the company's share capital and therefore shares acquired as the result of such an issue are not treated as an acquisition in the usual way. The CGT treatment of a rights issue is as follows :

(a) Any rights shares acquired by a taxpayer serve to increase the number of shares in each of the taxpayer's holdings immediately prior to the rights issue. The cost of the rights shares increases the cost of these holdings.

(b) If rights shares join the 1982 holding after 31 March 1982, then :

    (i)   it is necessary (for indexation purposes) to keep a separate record of the original cost of the 1982 holding and the cost of the rights shares

    (ii) the cost of the rights shares is treated as enhancement expenditure incurred in relation to a pre-31 March 1982 asset (see Chapter 17).

(c) On a subsequent disposal, the qualifying period for taper relief purposes begins on the date that the taxpayer's original holdings were acquired and not on the date that the rights shares were acquired.

EXAMPLE 3

Tina made the following acquisitions of ordinary shares in Rhombus plc :

Date	No of shares	Cost £	RPI
15 August 1980	500	1,000	
23 January 1987	600	2,500	100.0

The market value of the company's shares on 31 March 1982 (RPI 79.44) was £2.50 per share. In June 1997 (RPI 157.5), the company made a 1 for 20 rights issue at £8 per share and Tina decided to buy the shares which she was offered. Show the S104 holding and the 1982 holding immediately after the rights issue.

SOLUTION

The 1982 holding :

	No of shares	Cost (original) £	Cost (rights) £	MV 31/3/82 £
Acquired 15 August 1980	500	1,000		1,250
Rights issue June 1997 (1 for 20)	25		200	
1982 holding c/f	525	1,000	200	1,250

The S104 holding :

	No of shares	Cost £	Indexed cost £
Bought 23 January 1987	600	2,500	2,500
Add : Indexation to June 1997 $\frac{157.5 - 100.0}{100.0}$ x £2,500			1,438
			3,938
Rights issue June 1997 (1 for 20)	30	240	240
S104 holding c/f	630	2,740	4,178

EXAMPLE 4

Calculate the untapered gain arising in November 2000 when Tina (in the above example) sells 840 shares for £7 each, assuming that she makes no further acquisitions within the next 30 days.

SOLUTION

S104 holding (630 shares sold) :

	No of shares	Cost £	Indexed cost £
b/f at June 1997	630	2,740	4,178
Add : Indexation to April 1998			
$\dfrac{162.6 - 157.5}{157.5}$ x £4,178			135
			4,313
Sold November 2000	(630)	(2,740)	(4,313)
S104 holding c/f	nil	nil	nil

The untapered gain on the disposal of the S104 holding is :

	£
Sale proceeds (630 @ £7)	4,410
Less : Cost	2,740
Unindexed gain	1,670
Less : Indexation allowance	
(£4,313 - £2,740)	1,573
Untapered gain	97

1982 holding (210 shares sold) :

	No of shares	Cost (original) £	Cost (rights) £	MV 31/3/82 £
b/f	525	1,000	200	1,250
Sold November 2000 (210/525th)	(210)	(400)	(80)	(500)
1982 holding c/f	315	600	120	750

The untapered gain arising on the disposal from the 1982 holding is :

	Original cost £	Rebasing £
Sale proceeds (210 @ £7)	1,470	1,470
Less : Cost up to 31 March 1982	(400)	
Market value 31/3/82		(500)
Cost June 1997	(80)	(80)
Unindexed gain	990	890
Less : Indexation allowance		
$\frac{162.6 - 79.44}{79.44}$ = 1.047 x £500	(524)	(524)
$\frac{162.6 - 157.5}{157.5}$ = 0.032 x £80	(3)	(3)
Untapered gain	463	363

The rebasing calculation gives the lower gain, so rebasing applies and the untapered gain is £363. The total untapered gain on the entire disposal of 840 shares is therefore £460 (£97 + £363) with a taper period of 2 years (plus the bonus year if the shares are a non-business asset).

Capital distributions

A capital distribution occurs when shareholders are repaid part of their share capital, usually when a company goes into liquidation. Unless the amount of the distribution is small (see later in this chapter) a capital distribution is regarded as a part disposal for CGT purposes.

EXAMPLE 5

In March 1990 (RPI 121.4), Vincent bought 10,000 ordinary shares in Trapezium plc for £44,000. In June 2000, the company went into liquidation and Vincent received a first distribution of £0.50 per share. The market value of an ordinary share in Trapezium plc just after this distribution was £0.75. Compute the allowable loss arising in June 2000.

SOLUTION

The value of the part disposed of is £5,000 (10,000 @ £0.50) and the value of the part remaining is £7,500 (10,000 @ £0.75). The part disposal fraction is 5,000/12,500 which is equivalent to 2/5ths.

S104 holding :

	No of shares	Cost	Indexed cost
		£	£
Bought March 1990	10,000	44,000	44,000
Add : Indexation to April 1998			
$\frac{162.6 - 121.4}{121.4}$ x £44,000			14,932
			58,932
Distribution June 2000 (2/5ths)	-	(17,600)	(23,573)
S104 holding c/f	10,000	26,400	35,359

The computation of the allowable loss is as follows :

	£
Disposal proceeds	5,000
Less : Part cost	(17,600)
Unindexed loss	(12,600)
Less : Indexation allowance (£23,573 - £17,600)	nil
Allowable loss	(12,600)

Sale of rights nil paid

Another example of a capital distribution occurs when a company makes a rights issue and a shareholder decides not to buy the shares concerned but instead to sell his or her rights to someone else (a "sale of rights nil paid"). When shareholders sell their rights they are *not* selling shares. What they are selling is the right to buy shares, often at an attractive price. The proceeds of such a sale are treated as a capital distribution. If the amount of money involved is small (see below) the amount received will be treated as a small capital distribution.

Small capital distributions

If the amount of a capital distribution is small when compared with the value of the shares concerned, the distribution is not treated as a disposal. Instead, the proceeds of the distribution are subtracted from the acquisition cost of the shares. The effect of this is that the gain which would have been chargeable on the distribution is deferred until a subsequent disposal takes place. This is very similar to the treatment of small part disposals of land (see Chapter 17). Note that :

(a) A capital distribution is generally regarded as small if it consists of no more than 5% of the value of the company's shares just before the distribution. It is also

Inland Revenue practice to regard an amount of £3,000 or less as small for this purpose, even if the 5% test is not satisfied.

(b) The Inland Revenue will usually allow a small capital distribution to be treated as a disposal if this is to the taxpayer's advantage (e.g. if the gain arising is covered by the annual exemption).

EXAMPLE 6

In April 1989 (RPI 114.3), Vanessa bought 100 shares in Pentagon plc at a cost of £5 per share. The company went into liquidation and Vanessa received a first distribution of 40p per share in July 2000. The shares had a market value of £9.75 immediately after the distribution.

(a) Show how the distribution will be dealt with for CGT purposes.

(b) Calculate the untapered gain arising in March 2001, when Vanessa received a second and final distribution of £9.82 per share.

SOLUTION

(a) The value of the shares immediately prior to the distribution must have been £10.15 (£9.75 + £0.40). 40p is 3.9% of £10.15 so the distribution ranks as a small capital distribution. The £40 received by Vanessa may be deducted from the £500 that she paid for her shares, reducing the allowable cost on a future disposal to £460.

(b) Assuming that the small capital distribution is not treated as a disposal, the S104 holding is :

	No of shares	Cost £	Indexed cost £
Bought April 1989	100	500	500
Add : Indexation to April 1998			
$\dfrac{162.6 - 114.3}{114.3} \times £500$			211
			711
Distribution July 2000	-	(40)	(40)
	100	460	671
Disposal March 2001	(100)	(460)	(671)
S104 holding c/f	nil	nil	nil

The untapered gain on the disposal is :

	£
Disposal proceeds (100 @ £9.82)	982
Less : Indexed cost	671
Untapered gain	311

Small capital distributions and the 1982 holding

If a small capital distribution which is not treated as a disposal is made after 31 March 1982 and the taxpayer has a 1982 holding, the part of the distribution which relates to the shares in that holding will be subtracted from its cost. Note that :

(a) It is necessary (for indexation purposes) to keep a separate record of the original cost of the 1982 holding and the amount of the small capital distribution

(b) In effect, the amount of the distribution is dealt with as *negative* enhancement expenditure incurred in relation to a pre-31 March 1982 asset.

EXAMPLE 7

In January 1980, Wendy bought 2,000 shares in Square plc for £2.50 per share. On 31 March 1982 (RPI 79.44) the shares had a market value of £3.00 each. In July 1997 (RPI 157.5) when the shares had a market value of £12 each, the company made a rights issue but Wendy decided to sell her rights, realising £100. Compute the untapered gain arising in December 2000, when Wendy sold all her shares for £25,000 (assuming that she made no further acquisitions within the next 30 days).

SOLUTION

The value of Wendy's shares immediately prior to the sale of rights was £24,000 (2,000 @ £12). Wendy realised £100, which is 0.4% of £24,000. Therefore the sale of rights ranks as a small capital distribution. Assuming that the distribution is not treated as a disposal, the 1982 holding is :

	No of shares	Cost (original) £	Small capital distribution £	MV 31/3/82 £
Bought January 1980	2,000	5,000		6,000
Distribution July 1997	-		(100)	
1982 holding c/f	2,000	5,000	(100)	6,000
Sold December 2000	(2,000)	(5,000)	100	(6,000)
1982 holding c/f	nil	nil	nil	nil

The computation of the untapered gain in December 2000 is as follows :

	Original cost £	Rebasing £
Sale proceeds	25,000	25,000
Less : Cost up to 31 March 1982	(5,000)	
Market value 31/3/82		(6,000)
Small capital distribution July 1997	100	100
Unindexed gain	20,100	19,100

	Original cost £	Rebasing £
Unindexed gain	20,100	19,100
Less : Indexation allowance :		
$\dfrac{162.6 - 79.44}{79.44}$ = 1.047 x £6,000	(6,282)	(6,282)
$\dfrac{162.6 - 157.5}{157.5}$ = 0.032 x £100	3	3
Untapered gain	13,821	12,821

The rebasing calculation gives the lower gain, so rebasing applies and the untapered gain is £12,821.

Takeovers

A takeover occurs when one company acquires the shares of another company. Shareholders of the "target" company exchange their shares in return for cash, or shares of the acquiring company, or a combination of both cash and shares. The CGT treatment of such disposals is as follows :

(a) If a takeover is entirely for cash, the shareholders of the target company have sold their shares and have made chargeable disposals. The fact that shares have been sold as a consequence of a takeover is irrelevant and the gain or loss is computed in the usual way.

(b) If a takeover is entirely for shares (a "paper for paper" takeover), no chargeable disposals have taken place. A shareholder's newly-acquired shares in the acquiring company replace the shares originally held in the target company and are deemed for all CGT purposes (including taper relief) to have been acquired on the same date and at the same cost as the original holding.

(c) If a takeover is partly for cash and partly for shares, a part disposal has taken place and a part disposal calculation is usually required. The value of the part disposed of is the amount of cash received and the value of the part remaining is the value of the shares received. However, if the amount of cash received by a taxpayer is no more than 5% of the total consideration (or no more than £3,000) the cash received may be treated as a small capital distribution.

EXAMPLE 8

In October 1992 (RPI 139.9), Winston bought 8,000 shares in Hexagon plc at a cost of £3 per share. In October 2000 Circle plc made a takeover bid for Hexagon plc, offering the Hexagon shareholders 3 Circle shares plus £1 in cash for every 2 Hexagon shares. The offer was accepted on 29 October 2000 when the market value of shares in Circle plc was £5 per share. Compute Winston's untapered gain.

SOLUTION

Winston received 12,000 shares in Circle plc, worth £60,000, plus £4,000 in cash, a total of £64,000. The amount received in cash is 6.25% of the total and exceeds £3,000, so this cannot be treated as a small capital distribution. The S104 holding is :

	No of shares	Cost £	Indexed cost £
Bought (Hexagon plc) October 1992	8,000	24,000	24,000
Add : Indexation to April 1998			
$\dfrac{162.6 - 139.9}{139.9}$ x £24,000			3,894
			27,894
Distribution October 2000 (6.25%)	-	(1,500)	(1,743)
S104 holding after distribution	8,000	22,500	26,151
S104 holding (Circle plc) c/f	12,000	22,500	26,151

The untapered gain on the disposal is :

	£
Disposal proceeds	4,000
Less : Cost	1,500
Unindexed gain	2,500
Less : Indexation allowance	
(£1,743 - £1,500)	243
Untapered gain	2,257

Summary

▶ The CGT effect of a bonus issue is to increase the number of shares in each of the taxpayer's holdings prior to the issue. The cost of the holdings is not affected.

▶ The CGT effect of a rights issue which is taken up is to increase both the number and the cost of the shares in each of the taxpayer's holdings prior to the issue.

▶ A sale of rights nil paid is regarded as a capital distribution.

▶ A capital distribution is treated for CGT purposes as a part disposal unless it ranks as a small capital distribution, in which case the amount of the distribution is deducted from the acquisition cost of the shares concerned.

▶ A small capital distribution is one which consists of no more than 5% of the value of the company's shares immediately prior to the distribution. A distribution which fails the 5% test is still regarded as small if the amount of money received by a taxpayer does not exceed £3,000.

▶ If a takeover is entirely for cash, the shareholders of the target company have made chargeable disposals.

▶ If a takeover is entirely for shares, no chargeable disposals have taken place.

▶ If a takeover is partly for cash and partly for shares, a part disposal has occurred unless the amount of cash can be treated as a small capital distribution.

Exercises

Please note that the RPI for April 1998 is 162.6.

20.1 William made the following acquisitions of preference shares in Heptagon plc :

Date	No of shares	Cost	RPI
		£	
17 February 1980	600	900	
13 November 1988	200	400	110.0
9 October 1999	100	300	

The market value of the shares at 31 March 1982 (RPI 79.44) was £1.70 per share. In January 2001 the company made a 1 for 4 bonus issue.

Show William's holdings as they stand immediately after this bonus issue.

20.2 In February 2001, William (in exercise 20.1) sells 425 shares for £4 per share. Calculate the untapered gain, assuming that he makes no acquisitions in the following 30 days.

20.3 Yvonne made the following acquisitions of ordinary shares in Rectangle plc :

Date	No of shares	Cost	RPI
		£	
30 September 1979	2,000	1,200	
1 December 1992	3,000	3,600	139.2

The market value of the shares on 31 March 1982 (RPI 79.44) was 75p each. In January 1998 (RPI 159.5), the company made a 1 for 8 rights issue at £1 per share and Yvonne decided to buy the shares which she was offered. Show the S104 holding and the 1982 holding as they stand immediately after the rights issue.

20.4 In March 2001, Yvonne (in exercise 20.3) sells all her shares in Rectangle plc for £1.80 per share. Calculate the untapered gain arising in March 2001, assuming that no further shares are acquired within the following 30 days.

20.5   In November 1989 (RPI 118.5), Yorick bought 6,000 ordinary shares in Octagon plc for £30,000. In May 2000, the company went into liquidation and Yorick received a first distribution of £1 per share. The market value of an ordinary share in Octagon plc just after this distribution was £2. Compute the allowable loss arising in May 2000.

20.6   In January 1990 (RPI 119.5), Yolande bought 300 ordinary shares in Ellipse plc at a cost of £1.20 per share. In March 1993 (RPI 139.3), when shares in Ellipse plc had a market value of £2 each, the company made a rights issue. Yolande sold her rights, realising £25. Compute the untapered gain arising in November 2000, when Yolande sold all her shares for £780 (assuming that no further shares are acquired within the following 30 days).

20.7   In April 1993 (RPI 140.6), Walter bought 12,000 shares in Oval plc at a cost of £5.85 per share. In September 2000, Round plc made a takeover bid for Oval plc, offering the Oval shareholders 8 Round shares plus £2.50 in cash for every 5 Oval shares. The offer was accepted on 2 September 2000 when the market value of shares in Round plc was £4.30 per share. Compute Walter's untapered gain.

*20.8   Saeed made the following purchases of ordinary shares in Hyperbola plc :

Date	No of shares	Cost	RPI
		£	
24 August 1975	800	800	
25 November 1980	1,200	1,350	
26 February 1985	1,600	2,400	91.94
11 October 1993	400	800	141.8

The company's shares had a market value of £1.20 each on 31 March 1982 (RPI 79.44). In March 1994 (RPI 142.5), the company made a 1 for 40 rights issue at £1.50 per share and Saeed took up the shares which he was offered.

Calculate the untapered gain in November 2000, when Saeed sold 2,870 shares at £3 each. Assume that no further shares were acquired within the following 30 days. (RPI for April 1985 was 94.78).

*20.9   Susan made the following purchases of ordinary shares in Semicircle plc :

Date	No of shares	Cost
		£
11 January 1981	1,500	4,800
20 January 1982	1,140	5,700

The market value of the company's shares on 31 March 1982 (RPI 79.44) was £4. In January 2001, the company went into liquidation and Susan received a first distribution of £2 per share. The market value of an ordinary share in Semicircle plc just after this distribution was £1. Compute the allowable loss arising in January 2001.

*20.10   Steven made the following purchases of ordinary shares in Convex plc :

Date	No of shares	Cost
		£
9 May 1977	2,000	8,000
28 November 1981	500	2,500

The market value of the company's shares on 31 March 1982 (RPI 79.44) was £5 per share. In June 2000, Concave plc made a takeover bid for Convex plc, offering the Convex shareholders 2 Concave shares plus £2 in cash for every Convex share. The offer was accepted on 21 June 2000 when the market value of shares in Concave plc was £4 per share. Compute Steven's untapered gain or allowable loss.

Chapter 21

Principal private residences

Introduction

This chapter examines the CGT consequences of the disposal of a taxpayer's principal private residence. Although a principal private residence is not a chargeable asset for CGT purposes, a CGT liability may arise when a property is disposed of which has been used as a residence for only part of the period of ownership or which has been used partly as a residence and partly for other purposes.

Please note that the RPI for April 1998 (which is used in many of the examples in this chapter) is 162.6.

Principal private residence

A dwelling which is a taxpayer's only or main residence is known as that taxpayer's principal private residence (PPR). A taxpayer's PPR is not a chargeable asset for CGT purposes. Therefore any gain which arises on the disposal of a PPR is not chargeable to tax and any loss which arises is not allowable. For a property to be regarded as a PPR, the taxpayer must actually occupy the property as a residence. Mere ownership is not sufficient. Furthermore, the term "residence" implies a degree of permanency and it is unlikely that the PPR exemption will apply to a property which has been used only as temporary accommodation. In *Goodwin* v *Curtis* (1998) a property which had been occupied by the taxpayer for only 32 days did not qualify as a residence.

The large majority of taxpayers own (at most) a single property and reside in that property, so that it is obvious that the property is the taxpayer's PPR. However, the following points may be relevant in more complex cases :

(a) A taxpayer may have only one PPR at any given time.

(b) If a taxpayer owns and lives in two (or more) properties, the taxpayer may elect which property is to be regarded as the PPR. Such an election must be made within two years of the date from which it is to take effect.

(c) A married couple may have only one PPR between them.

(d) The PPR exemption covers the residence itself together with grounds or gardens of up to half a hectare (5,000 square metres) in area. Larger areas of grounds or gardens may be included in the exemption if they are warranted by the size of the residence.

(e) The requirement that there must be actual residence in the property is relaxed if the taxpayer is required to live in job-related accommodation (see Chapter 7). In these circumstances, the PPR exemption is extended to any property which the taxpayer owns so long as he or she intends to occupy the property in the future.

Partial exemption

If a property has been occupied as a PPR for only a part of the period of ownership, only a part of the gain realised on disposal will be exempt from CGT. The exempt part of the gain is equal to :

$$\frac{\text{length of period of residence}}{\text{length of period of ownership}} \times \text{whole gain}$$

The lengths of the periods of residence and ownership are usually calculated to the nearest month. Note the following important points :

(a) If the property was acquired before 31 March 1982, the period of ownership and any period of residence prior to that date are ignored in the calculation of the exempt part of the gain.

(b) If a property has been the taxpayer's PPR at some time, the last 36 months of ownership always count as a period of residence, whether or not the taxpayer was actually resident then (so helping taxpayers who move house and have difficulty in selling their previous residence). This rule applies even if the taxpayer claims another property to be his or her PPR during the 36 months.

EXAMPLE 1

Allan bought a house in January 1979 for £20,000. The market value of the house on 31 March 1982 (RPI 79.44) was £29,000. Allan lived in the house until 1 May 1997 on which date he bought another house and made this his principal private residence. The house which he had bought in January 1979 was sold on 31 January 2001 for £75,000. Compute the untapered gain.

SOLUTION

In examples of this type it is necessary first to calculate the gain arising (ignoring any PPR exemption) and then to consider the PPR exemption as a second stage. The gain arising is as follows :

	Original cost	Rebasing
	£	£
Sale proceeds	75,000	75,000
Less : Original cost	20,000	
Market value 31/3/82		29,000
	──────	──────
Unindexed gain	55,000	46,000
Less : Indexation allowance		
$\dfrac{162.6 - 79.44}{79.44} = 1.047 \times £29,000$	30,363	30,363
	──────	──────
Untapered gain before PPR exemption	24,637	15,637
	══════	══════

The rebasing calculation gives the lower gain, so rebasing applies and the untapered gain arising (before considering the PPR exemption) is £15,637.

After 31 March 1982, Allan owned the house for 18 years and 10 months (226 months). He was actually resident for 15 years and 1 month (181 months) and the last 36 months of ownership also count as a period of residence, making a total of 217 months during which the PPR exemption applies. The untapered gain is therefore as follows :

	£
Total gain (as above)	15,637
Less : $\dfrac{217}{226} \times £15,637$	15,014
	──────
Untapered gain	623
	══════

Deemed residence

The period of residence in a property is deemed to include certain periods when the taxpayer was not actually resident, so long as :

(a) there is a period of actual residence both at some time before the period of absence and at some time after the period of absence, and

(b) the taxpayer claims no other property to be a PPR during the period of absence.

These periods of "deemed residence" are as follows :

(a) any period or periods of absence during which the taxpayer is working abroad

(b) a total of up to 4 years of absence during which the taxpayer is working elsewhere in the UK

(c) a total of up to 3 years of absence for any reason.

By concession, the requirement that the taxpayer must reside in the property at some time after the period of absence is waived if the absence is work-related and the terms of the taxpayer's employment prevent him or her from returning to the residence.

EXAMPLE 2

On 1 June 1985 (RPI 95.41), Alice bought a house in Derby for £35,000. She occupied the house as her PPR until 1 May 1987 when she left to work in Exeter, living in rented accommodation. She returned to the house in Derby on 1 November 1988 and stayed until 1 July 1991 when she left to take up a post in the USA, again living in rented accommodation. She returned to Derby on 1 February 1994 and stayed until 1 December 1997 when she bought another house in Nottingham and made this her principal private residence. She had trouble in selling the Derby house but eventually managed to sell it for £84,000 on 1 February 2001. Compute the untapered gain.

SOLUTION

	£
Sale proceeds	84,000
Less : Acquisition cost	35,000
Unindexed gain	49,000
Less : Indexation allowance	
$\dfrac{162.6 - 95.41}{95.41}$ = 0.704 x £35,000	24,640
Untapered gain before PPR exemption	24,360

Alice's period of ownership of the house in Derby (a total of 188 months) can be broken down into the following periods :

(i)	1 June 1985 to 30 April 1987	23 months	Actual residence
(ii)	1 May 1987 to 31 October 1988	18 months	Working in UK
(iii)	1 November 1988 to 30 June 1991	32 months	Actual residence
(iv)	1 July 1991 to 31 January 1994	31 months	Working abroad
(v)	1 February 1994 to 30 November 1997	46 months	Actual residence
(vi)	1 December 1997 to 31 January 2001	38 months	Living in new PPR

Periods (i), (iii) and (v) are exempt since Alice was actually resident in the property during those periods. Period (ii) is exempt since Alice was working elsewhere in the UK, the 4-year time limit has not been exceeded and she was resident in the property both before and after the absence. Similarly, period (iv) is exempt. The last 36 months of ownership are always exempt, which leaves the first 2 months of period (vi) to consider. During these 2 months Alice was claiming another property to be her PPR, so the period cannot count as a period of deemed residence and the gain arising during these 2 months is chargeable. The remaining 186 months benefit from the PPR exemption. The untapered gain is therefore as follows :

	£
Total gain (as above)	24,360
Less : $\dfrac{186}{188}$ x £24,360	24,101
Untapered gain	259

Letting relief

An extension to the PPR exemption, known as "letting relief", applies if a PPR has been let to tenants as residential accommodation. There are two situations to consider :

(a) A property might have been used entirely as a residence for part of the period of ownership but let to tenants during periods of absence by the owner. A chargeable gain will arise if the periods of absence are not entirely covered by the exemptions already described in this chapter, but letting relief will then be available in relation to this gain.

(b) Part of a property might have been used as a residence whilst the other part has been let. In this case, the PPR exemption will cover :

    (i) the gain arising on the whole property during the last 36 months of ownership, and

    (ii) the remainder of the gain, to the extent that this is attributable to the part of the property which was occupied by the owner.

The balance of the gain will be chargeable to CGT, but letting relief may then be available. In general, letting relief will *not* be granted if the part that has been let forms a dwelling which is entirely separate from the accommodation which forms the owner's residence (e.g. a self-contained flat with its own access from the road). Relief *will* normally be granted if the let accommodation forms part of the owner's dwelling and the owner previously resided in the entire premises.

Letting relief is calculated as the *lowest* of :

(a) the part of the gain which relates to the let part of the property or to the letting period

(b) the part of the gain which is exempt because of the PPR exemptions

(c) £40,000.

EXAMPLE 3

In relation to the previous example in this chapter, assume now that Alice always let her Derby house when she was not resident there. Compute the untapered gain.

SOLUTION

The only chargeable period was a period of 2 months during which a gain of £259 arose and during which the property was let. Letting relief is available as the lowest of :

(a) The part of the gain which relates to the letting period (£259)

(b) The part of the gain which is exempt because of the PPR exemptions (£24,101)

(c) £40,000.

The lowest of these is £259. Therefore letting relief of £259 is available and the untapered gain is reduced to £nil.

EXAMPLE 4

Alistair bought a house in 1978 for £97,500 and occupied the entire house until 1 May 1992 when he rented the top floor (comprising one-half of the house) to tenants, retaining the ground floor as his own residence. This arrangement continued until 1 October 2000 when he sold the house for £615,000. The house had a market value of £125,000 on 31 March 1982 (RPI 79.44). Compute the untapered gain.

SOLUTION

	Original cost £	Rebasing £
Sale proceeds	615,000	615,000
Less : Original cost	97,500	
Market value 31/3/82		125,000
Unindexed gain	517,500	490,000
Less : Indexation allowance		
$\dfrac{162.6 - 79.44}{79.44}$ = 1.047 x £125,000	130,875	130,875
Untapered gain before PPR exemption	386,625	359,125

The rebasing calculation gives the lower gain, so rebasing applies and the untapered gain arising (before considering exemptions) is £359,125.

After 31 March 1982, Alistair owned the house for 18 years and 6 months (222 months). Exemption is available for the 121 months during which he occupied the whole property and for the last 36 months (a total of 157 months). He was resident in half of the property for the remaining 65 months, so 50% of the gain arising during these 65 months is also exempt. The other 50% is chargeable but letting relief is available. The untapered gain is calculated as follows :

	£	£
Total gain (as above)		359,125
Less : PPR exemption :		
£359,125 x 157/222	253,976	
£359,125 x 65/222 x 1/2	52,575	306,551
		52,574
Less : Letting relief, lowest of :		
(a) £52,574		
(b) £306,551		
(c) £40,000		40,000
Untapered gain		12,574

Business use

If a property is used partly as a residence and partly for business purposes, the gain which is attributable to the part used for business purposes is chargeable to CGT. No reliefs are available in relation to this gain. The usual exemption for the last 36 months of ownership does not apply to the part of the property which has been used for business purposes.

EXAMPLE 5

Ava bought a house on 1 July 1987 (RPI 101.8) for £32,000. She occupied the entire property as her PPR until 1 August 1992 when she began using one-quarter of the house for business purposes. This continued until 1 November 2000 when she sold the house for £87,000. Compute the untapered gain.

SOLUTION

	£
Sale proceeds	87,000
<u>Less</u> : Acquisition cost	32,000
Unindexed gain	55,000
<u>Less</u> : Indexation allowance	
$\dfrac{162.6 - 101.8}{101.8}$ = 0.597 x £32,000	19,104
Untapered gain before PPR exemption	35,896

Ava owned the house for 13 years and 4 months (160 months). For the first 5 years and 1 month (61 months) she occupied the entire house as her PPR but for the remaining 99 months she occupied only three-quarters of the house. The untapered gain is as follows :

	£	£
Total gain (as above)		35,896
<u>Less</u> : PPR exemption :		
£35,896 x 61/160	13,685	
£35,896 x 99/160 x 3/4	16,658	30,343
Untapered gain		5,553

Summary

▶ A taxpayer's principal private residence (PPR) is exempt from CGT.

▶ Taxpayers with two or more residences may elect which property is to be regarded as the PPR.

▶ A married couple may have only one PPR between them.

▶ If a property has been occupied as a PPR for only a part of the period of ownership, only a part of the gain realised on disposal will be exempt from CGT.

▶ The last 36 months of ownership of a PPR always count as a period of residence.

▶ Certain periods of absence are deemed to be periods of residence.

▶ Letting relief may be available if a residence has been let to tenants as residential accommodation.

▶ If a residence is used partly for business purposes, the gain relating to the part used for business purposes is chargeable to CGT.

Exercises

Please note that the RPI for April 1998 is 162.6.

21.1 Mohammed owns two properties - a flat in Central London and a country cottage in Sussex. In general he lives in his London flat during the week and spends the weekends in his Sussex cottage. Which of his two properties will be regarded as his principal private residence ?

21.2 Melanie bought a house in November 1979 for £18,000. The house had a market value of £21,000 on 31 March 1982 (RPI 79.44) and was sold on 31 October 2000 for £63,000. Compute the untapered gain in each of the following cases :

(a) Melanie occupied the house as her principal private residence throughout the period of ownership.

(b) Melanie occupied the house throughout her period of ownership with the exception of the period between 1 June 1985 and 31 May 1989 when she lived with a friend. During this time the house stood empty.

(c) As (b) except that the house was let as residential accommodation during Melanie's absence.

21.3 Rupert bought a house in Manchester on 1 November 1985 (RPI 95.92) for £55,000. He occupied the house until 1 November 1989 when he left to work abroad for a year, moving back into the house on 1 November 1990. He stayed until 1 February 1992 when he left again, this time to work in Aberdeen, where he stayed until his return on 1 May 1996. This time he stayed for only a month, leaving on 1 June 1996 to go to live with a friend. He never returned to the house and it was sold on 1 March 2001 for

£172,000. During his absences, Rupert always let his house and he claimed no other property to be his principal private residence. Compute the untapered gain arising on the disposal.

21.4 Samantha bought a house for £37,500 on 1 August 1986 (RPI 97.82) and occupied the house as her principal private residence. On 1 June 1988 she began to use one-fifth of the house for business purposes. Unfortunately her business eventually failed and on 1 June 1994 she ceased trading. From that date onwards she resided in the entire house until it was sold on 1 August 2000 for £85,000. Compute the untapered gain.

*21.5 Terry bought a house for £65,000 on 1 June 1986 (RPI 97.79) and occupied the house as his principal private residence. He lived in the house until 1 June 1990 when he went to stay with relatives in Australia, letting the house in his absence. He did not return until 1 June 1994, when he began using one-quarter of the house for business purposes and the other three-quarters as his residence. This arrangement continued until 1 June 2000 when he sold the house for £190,000. Compute the untapered gain.

Chapter 22
CGT reliefs

Introduction

A taxpayer's capital gains tax liability may sometimes be reduced or deferred by taking advantage of various CGT reliefs. The purpose of this chapter is to explain, for each of these reliefs, the circumstances in which the relief is available and the way in which the amount of relief is calculated.

Please note that the RPI for April 1998 (which is used in many of the examples in this chapter) is 162.6.

Damaged assets

If an asset has been damaged and insurance money or other compensation is received in consequence, the situation is usually treated as a part disposal. The value of the part disposed of (A) is the amount of money received and the value of the part remaining (B) is the value of the asset on the date that the money is received. Any money spent on restoration is treated as enhancement expenditure.

However, in certain circumstances, the taxpayer may elect that the situation should *not* be treated as a part disposal and that the amount of money received should instead be deducted from the allowable expenditure relating to the asset. This has the effect of increasing the gain arising on a subsequent disposal and is very similar to the CGT treatment of small capital distributions (see Chapter 20). The circumstances in which a part disposal may be avoided are as follows :

(a) All of the money received is applied to restoring the asset, or

(b) The asset is not a wasting asset and all the money received is applied to restoring the asset except for an amount which is "small" in comparison with the amount received and which is not reasonably required for restoration purposes, or

(c) The asset is not a wasting asset and the amount of money received is "small" in comparison with the value of the asset.

For this purpose, a sum is regarded as "small" if it does not exceed £3,000 or 5% of the amount with which it is being compared, whichever is the higher.

A part disposal calculation is unavoidable if only part of the money received is spent on restoring the asset and neither of the "small" tests is satisfied. However, the taxpayer may elect that the calculation should relate only to the amount which is received but not spent on restoration. If this election is made, the remainder of the money received is deducted from the allowable expenditure relating to the asset (so increasing the gain arising on a subsequent disposal).

EXAMPLE 1

In July 1987 (RPI 101.8), Laura bought an oil painting for £80,000. In October 2000, the painting was damaged by fire. In February 2001, Laura received compensation from her insurance company of £30,000. Compute the untapered gain or allowable loss arising in each of the following circumstances :

(a) Laura spent none of the insurance money on restoration and the damaged painting was valued at £170,000 in February 2001.

(b) Laura spent £30,000 on restoring the painting in November 2000 and elected that the situation should not be treated as a part disposal.

(c) Laura spent £29,000 on restoring the painting in November 2000 and elected that the situation should not be treated as a part disposal.

(d) Laura spent £20,000 on restoring the painting in November 2000 and elected that the part disposal should relate only to the retained £10,000. The restored painting was valued at £200,000 in February 2001.

SOLUTION

(a) This is a part disposal, with A = £30,000 and B = £170,000. The computation is :

	£
Disposal proceeds	30,000
Less : Part cost :	
$\dfrac{£30,000}{£30,000 + £170,000} \times £80,000$	12,000
Unindexed gain	18,000
Less : Indexation allowance	
$\dfrac{162.6 - 101.8}{101.8} = 0.597 \times £12,000$	7,164
Untapered gain	10,836

The balance of allowable expenditure carried forward and used in the calculation of the gain arising on a subsequent disposal of the painting is £68,000 (£80,000 - £12,000).

(b) The entire amount received is spent on restoration so the election to avoid a part disposal is valid. The balance of allowable expenditure carried forward is :

	£
Incurred July 1987	80,000
Incurred November 2000	30,000
	110,000
Less : Received February 2001 (and not treated as a disposal)	30,000
	80,000

(c) The £1,000 retained is small in comparison with the amount received and therefore the election to avoid a part disposal is valid (so long as the £1,000 is not required for restoration purposes). The balance of allowable expenditure carried forward is :

	£
Incurred July 1987	80,000
Incurred November 2000	29,000
	109,000
Less : Received February 2001 (and not treated as a disposal)	30,000
	79,000

(d) The amount retained is not small in comparison with the amount received and so a part disposal is unavoidable. However, by virtue of Laura's election, this will relate only to the retained £10,000, not to the entire £30,000 received. The computation is :

	£	£
Disposal proceeds		10,000
Less : Part original expenditure :		
$\dfrac{£10,000}{£10,000 + £200,000}$ x £80,000	3,810	
Part restoration expenditure :		
$\dfrac{£10,000}{£10,000 + £200,000}$ x £20,000	952	4,762
Unindexed gain		5,238
Less : Indexation allowance		
$\dfrac{162.6 - 101.8}{101.8}$ = 0.597 x £3,810		2,275
Untapered gain		2,963

The balance of allowable expenditure carried forward in this case is :

	£
Incurred July 1987 (£80,000 - £3,810)	76,190
Incurred November 2000 (£20,000 - £952)	19,048
	95,238
Less : Received February 2001 (and not treated as a disposal)	20,000
	75,238

Destroyed assets

The loss or destruction of an asset is a chargeable disposal and usually results in a CGT computation in which disposal value is equal to the amount of any insurance money or other compensation received. However, if *all* of the money received is spent (within 12 months) on the purchase of a replacement asset, the taxpayer may claim that the disposal of the original asset should give rise to neither a gain nor a loss. The cost of the replacement asset is then reduced by the untapered gain which would have been chargeable on the disposal of the original asset if this claim had not been made.

If only *part* of the money received is spent on the purchase of a replacement asset, the taxpayer may claim that the untapered gain on the disposal of the original asset should be restricted to the amount of money retained (so long as this is less than the gain). The cost of the replacement asset is then reduced by the balance of the gain that would have been chargeable if the claim had not been made.

Taper relief

Taper relief is available only if gains are chargeable to tax. This means that the effect of making the first of the claims described above is that any taper relief which might have been available in connection with the original asset is lost. The effect of making the other claim is that taper relief is available only in relation to the restricted amount of the gain which remains chargeable to tax. In both cases, taper relief on the disposal of the replacement asset is calculated according to the qualifying holding period of that asset only (i.e. the holding period of the original asset is ignored).

EXAMPLE 2

Maurice bought an item of jewellery in November 1990 (RPI 130.0) for £125,000. In 1993 the jewellery was stolen. As a result, Maurice's insurance company paid him £141,500 in October 1993 (RPI 141.8). In December 1993 (RPI 141.9) he spent £150,000 on the purchase of replacement jewellery and claimed that neither a gain nor a loss should arise on the disposal of the original jewellery.

(a) Compute the untapered gain arising in March 2001 when the replacement jewellery was sold for £180,000.

(b) How would this computation alter if the jewellery bought in December 1993 had cost only £140,000 and Maurice had made an appropriate claim ?

SOLUTION

(a) Without a claim, the gain arising on the loss of the original jewellery would be :

	£
Disposal proceeds	141,500
Less : Acquisition cost	125,000
Unindexed gain	16,500
Less : Indexation allowance	
$\dfrac{141.8 - 130.0}{130.0} = 0.091 \times £125,000$	11,375
Chargeable gain	5,125

The entire proceeds were spent on a replacement asset within 12 months so Maurice is entitled to make the claim. This reduces the acquisition cost of the new jewellery to £144,875 (£150,000 - £5,125). The gain arising on the subsequent sale of this jewellery is as follows :

	£
Disposal proceeds	180,000
Less : Deemed acquisition cost	144,875
Unindexed gain	35,125
Less : Indexation allowance	
$\dfrac{162.6 - 141.9}{141.9} = 0.146 \times £144,875$	21,152
Untapered gain	13,973

Since the replacement jewellery was acquired before 17 March 1998 and disposed of in March 2001, this gain has a taper period of 3 years (2 years plus the bonus year).

(b) £1,500 of the insurance money was retained and so £1,500 of the gain arising on the stolen jewellery is immediately chargeable. The remaining £3,625 of the gain may be deducted from the acquisition cost of the new jewellery, reducing this cost to £136,375 (£140,000 - £3,625). The untapered gain arising on the March 2001 disposal becomes £23,714 (£180,000 - £136,375 - 0.146 x £136,375).

Replacement of business assets

Subject to certain conditions, a taxpayer may claim that the gain arising on the disposal of a business asset (the "old asset") may be "rolled-over" against the cost of acquiring a replacement business asset (the "new asset"). The main effects of a claim for roll-over relief are as follows :

(a) The disposal of the old asset is deemed to give rise to neither a gain nor a loss.

(b) The cost of the new asset is reduced by the untapered gain which would have been chargeable on the disposal of the old asset if the claim for roll-over relief had not been made.

Full relief is available only if the disposal proceeds of the old asset are *wholly* applied in acquiring the new asset. If only *part* of the disposal proceeds are used to acquire the new asset, the effect of a claim for roll-over relief is that the untapered gain on the disposal of the old asset is restricted to the amount of money retained (so long as this is less than the gain). The cost of the new asset is then reduced by the balance of the gain that would have been chargeable if the claim had not been made. The conditions which must be satisfied if a roll-over claim is to be accepted are :

(a) Both the old asset and the new asset must be drawn from the following list (though they need not both be the same type of asset) :

    (i)   land and buildings

    (ii) fixed plant and machinery

    (iii) ships, aircraft and hovercraft

    (iv) goodwill

    (v) satellites, space stations and spacecraft

    (vi) milk, potato and fish quotas and certain EU agricultural quotas.

(b) The old asset must have been used for trade purposes only throughout the period of ownership and the new asset must be used for trade purposes only.

(c) The new asset must be acquired during a period beginning one year before and ending three years after the date of disposal of the old asset.

(d) The taxpayer must claim the relief by 31 January in the sixth year of assessment following the *later* of the year in which the old asset is disposed of and the year in which the new asset is acquired.

Taper relief

As mentioned earlier in this chapter, taper relief is available only if gains become chargeable to tax. Therefore one effect of making a roll-over claim is that any taper relief which might have been available on the disposal of the old asset is either lost completely or restricted according to the amount of the gain which remains chargeable after the claim has been made. Taper relief on the eventual disposal of the new asset is calculated according to the qualifying holding period of that asset only (i.e. the holding period of the old asset is ignored).

EXAMPLE 3

Janine bought a building for use in her business in May 1982 (RPI 81.62) for £75,000. In July 2000 she sold the building for £160,000 and, in the same month, bought another building for use in her business. Assuming that Janine claims roll-over relief, calculate the untapered gain arising on the July 2000 disposal if the replacement building has a cost of :

(a) £170,000   (b) £155,000   (c) £140,000.

SOLUTION

The gain on the disposal of the original building is computed as follows :

	£
Sale proceeds	160,000
Less : Acquisition cost	75,000
Unindexed gain	85,000
Less : Indexation allowance	
$\dfrac{162.6 - 81.62}{81.62} = 0.992 \times £75,000$	74,400
Untapered gain	10,600

(a) The entire sale proceeds have been spent on a replacement building. Therefore none of the gain is immediately chargeable and the entire gain may be rolled-over against the cost of the new building, reducing its allowable cost to £159,400 (£170,000 - £10,600).

(b) £5,000 of the sale proceeds have been retained. Therefore £5,000 of the gain is immediately chargeable. The remaining £5,600 may be rolled-over against the cost of the new building, reducing its allowable cost to £149,400 (£155,000 - £5,600).

(c) £20,000 of the sale proceeds have been retained. This exceeds the amount of the gain. Therefore the whole gain is immediately chargeable and no part of the gain may be rolled-over. The allowable cost of the new building is the full £140,000.

Replacement with a depreciating asset

If the new asset is a "depreciating asset" (defined as one which has an expected life of 60 years or less at the time of acquisition) the gain arising on the disposal of the old asset cannot be permanently rolled-over and is *not* deducted from the cost of the new asset. Instead, the gain is temporarily deferred or "held-over" until it crystallises (i.e. becomes chargeable) on the *earliest* of the following three dates :

(a) the date on which the new asset is disposed of

(b) the date on which the new asset ceases to be used for trade purposes

(c) the 10th anniversary of the acquisition of the new asset.

Clearly, a gain which is held-over in these circumstances will become chargeable no more than 10 years after the date of acquisition of the depreciating asset. However, if a suitable non-depreciating asset is acquired at any time before the end of this 10-year period, the held-over gain may be transferred to this new asset, so converting a temporarily held-over gain into a permanently rolled-over gain.

Taper relief

Taper relief in relation to a held-over gain which has become chargeable is calculated according to the qualifying holding period of the old asset on which the held-over gain arose. The period of up to 13 years which may have passed since that asset was disposed of (i.e. up to 3 years until the replacement depreciating asset was acquired, then a further 10 years until crystallisation) is ignored.

EXAMPLE 4

In June 2000, Ian sells a freehold building for £100,000, realising an untapered gain of £25,000. (The building was acquired in 1989 and used only for trade purposes). In the same month he acquires fixed plant and machinery costing £120,000 and elects to hold-over the gain on the freehold property against the plant and machinery. Explain the way in which the held-over gain will be treated in each of the following situations :

(a) Ian sells the plant and machinery in July 2004.

(b) Ian sells the plant and machinery in March 2013.

SOLUTION

(a) The replacement asset is sold before the 10th anniversary of its acquisition and so the deferred gain becomes chargeable in 2004/05.

(b) The replacement asset is still in Ian's possession 10 years after its acquisition, so the held-over gain of £25,000 crystallises in June 2010 and forms part of Ian's chargeable gains in 2010/11.

In both cases, taper relief will be calculated with reference to a taper period of 2 years.

EXAMPLE 5

Imagine now that Ian (in the above example) buys another freehold building for business use in November 2003 and elects to transfer the held-over gain on the plant and machinery to the new freehold building. Explain the treatment of the held-over gain if the new building costs :

(a) £150,000   (b) £90,000.

SOLUTION

(a)　The entire proceeds of the sale of the original building have been invested in a new building so the whole held-over gain of £25,000 can be converted into a rolled-over gain, reducing the allowable cost of the new building to £125,000.

(b)　£10,000 out of the sale proceeds of the original building have not been invested in the new building and therefore cannot be rolled-over against its cost. This £10,000 will continue to be held-over against the plant and machinery and will become chargeable no later than June 2010. However, the remaining £15,000 is converted into a rolled-over gain, reducing the allowable cost of the new building to £75,000.

Gains rolled over between 1 April 1982 and 5 April 1988

Special provisions apply to a claim for roll-over relief on the replacement of a business asset which was originally acquired before 31 March 1982 and replaced between 1 April 1982 and 5 April 1988. In these circumstances, some part of the rolled-over gain relates to the period before 31 March 1982 and it would now be unfair to bring such gains to charge when the replacement asset is sold (since gains arising before 31 March 1982 have been exempt from CGT since 6 April 1988).

So as to avoid detailed calculations of the amount of the rolled-over gain which relates to the period before 31 March 1982, the Finance Act 1988 provides that such rolled-over gains are to be reduced by a flat-rate 50%.

Gift of business assets

The gift of an asset is a chargeable disposal and this is the case whether or not the asset is used in business. However, subject to certain conditions, a claim may be made for the gain arising on a gift of business assets to be held-over until the transferee disposes of the assets concerned. If such a claim is made, the transferor's gain on the disposal is reduced to zero and the transferee's deemed acquisition cost is reduced by the amount of the untapered gain that would have been chargeable on the transferor if the claim had not been made. The conditions which must be satisfied are as follows :

(a)　Both the transferor and the transferee must elect for the gain arising on the gift to be held-over. This election must be made by 31 January in the sixth year of assessment following the year in which the gift is made.

(b)　The gifted assets must consist of either :

　(i)　assets used in a business carried on by the transferor or by the transferor's personal company (i.e. a company in which the transferor has at least 5% of the voting rights), or

　(ii)　shares in an unlisted trading company or shares in the transferor's personal company (so long as the transferee is not a company).

If the gift is of shares, rather than of individual business assets, the gain arising on the disposal is apportioned between the amount which relates to chargeable business assets owned by the company on the date of the gift and the amount which relates to other chargeable assets (e.g. investments). Only the part of the gain relating to chargeable business assets is eligible for hold-over relief.

Taper relief

Any taper relief to which the transferor might have been entitled is lost if a hold-over claim is made. Taper relief available to the transferee on a subsequent disposal of the gifted assets is calculated according to the qualifying holding period of the transferee only. The holding period of the transferor is completely ignored.

EXAMPLE 6

Kathy is the managing director of Kathy Ltd (an unlisted trading company). She bought 90% of the voting share capital of the company for £70,000 in July 1985 (RPI 95.23). In August 1993 (RPI 141.3) she gave all her shares to her son and both Kathy and her son elected that the gain arising on this gift should (as far as possible) be held-over. The net assets of the company on the date of the gift (at market value) were as follows :

	£
Goodwill	100,000
Freehold building (used only for business purposes)	150,000
Listed investments	50,000
Net current assets (none of which are chargeable)	40,000
Total net assets	340,000

(a) Compute the gain arising on the gift and the amount which may be held-over.

(b) Compute the gain arising in December 2000 when Kathy's son sold the shares for £350,000.

SOLUTION

(a) Presumably, the value of the shares on the date of the gift was 90% of £340,000 = £306,000. The gain arising on the gift is therefore as follows :

	£
Deemed disposal proceeds	306,000
Less : Acquisition cost	70,000
Unindexed gain	236,000
Less : Indexation allowance	
$\dfrac{141.3 - 95.23}{95.23} = 0.484 \times £70,000$	33,880
Chargeable gain	202,120

The chargeable assets of the company on the date of the gift are £300,000 of which £250,000 are chargeable business assets. Therefore £202,120 x 250,000/300,000 = £168,433 of the gain may be held-over whilst the remaining £33,687 is chargeable.

(b) The gain arising in December 2000 is as follows :

	£
Sale proceeds	350,000
Less : Deemed acquisition cost	
(£306,000 - £168,433)	137,567
Unindexed gain	212,433
Less : Indexation allowance	
$\frac{162.6 - 141.3}{141.3}$ = 0.151 x £137,567	20,773
Untapered gain	191,660

This gain has a taper period of 2 years.

Gifts between 1 April 1982 and 5 April 1988

Special provisions apply to a claim for hold-over relief on the gift of a business asset which was originally acquired before 31 March 1982 and gifted between 1 April 1982 and 5 April 1988. These special provisions are identical to those described above for roll-over relief on the replacement of business assets (i.e. the held-over gain is reduced by a flat-rate 50%).

Transfer of a business to a limited company

Subject to certain conditions, the gain arising on the transfer of a business to a limited company in return for shares in that company is held-over until the transferor disposes of the shares. If this relief applies, the untapered gain arising on the disposal of the business is deducted from the deemed acquisition cost of the shares. The conditions which must be satisfied are as follows :

(a) The business is transferred as a going concern.

(b) All of the assets of the business (other than cash) are transferred to the company.

(c) The consideration received by the transferor consists wholly or partly of shares in the company.

The relief is applied automatically and so there is no need for the transferor to claim that the gain should be held-over. If the consideration for the transfer consists only partly of shares, then only part of the untapered gain is held-over. The held-over gain is calculated as follows :

$$\frac{\text{value of the shares received}}{\text{total consideration received}} \times \text{whole gain}$$

If a transfer of this type was made between 1 April 1982 and 5 April 1988 and at least some of the assets transferred were acquired before 31 March 1982, the held-over gain is reduced by a flat-rate 50%.

Taper relief

Taper relief is not available in relation to the held-over gain. On a subsequent disposal of the shares, taper relief is calculated according to the qualifying holding period of the shares only. The holding period of the assets which were transferred to the company is ignored.

EXAMPLE 7

In July 2000, Leroy transferred his business to a limited company in exchange for £5,000 in cash and shares valued at £60,000. The untapered gain arising on the transfer was £26,000. Calculate the amount of the gain which is immediately chargeable and the amount which is held-over.

SOLUTION

The held-over gain is £26,000 x 60,000/65,000 = £24,000. The remaining £2,000 of the gain is immediately chargeable and is eligible for taper relief. The acquisition cost of the shares is reduced to £36,000 (£60,000 - £24,000).

Retirement relief

Subject to certain conditions, a relief known as "retirement relief" is granted when a taxpayer makes a material disposal of business assets. This may occur on the disposal of business assets by a sole trader, the disposal of a partnership share or the disposal of shares in a personal company. The conditions which must be satisfied are :

(a) There is a *material* disposal of business assets, comprising a whole business or a distinct part of a business.

(b) The taxpayer is at least 50 years old or is making the disposal because ill-health renders him or her permanently unable to continue in business. Despite the name of the relief, there is no requirement that the taxpayer should actually retire unless relief is given on the grounds of ill-health.

(c) For sole traders and partnerships, the business has been owned by the taxpayer for at least 10 years. A proportionate relief is available if the business has been owned for at least one year but less than 10 years.

(d) For disposals of shares in a personal company, the company has been the taxpayer's personal company for the 10-year period leading up to the disposal and the taxpayer has been a full-time working director or full-time employee of the company for those 10 years. Again, a proportionate relief is available if either of the 10-year requirements is not satisfied.

Retirement relief is deducted from the untapered gain arising on the disposal and is granted automatically. Taper relief is calculated by reference to the amount of the gain which remains *after* retirement relief has been deducted. For disposals made in tax year 2000/01, the amount of retirement relief is calculated as follows :

(a) 100% of the gains up to £150,000, plus

(b) 50% of the gains between £150,000 and £600,000 (i.e. the next £450,000).

The limits of £150,000 and £600,000 are scaled down proportionately if the taxpayer has a qualifying period of at least one year but less than 10 years.

Phasing out of retirement relief

With the introduction of taper relief in 1998/99, retirement relief is being phased out by progressively reducing the limits for 100% relief and 50% relief. These limits are as follows in tax years 1998/99 through to 2002/03 :

Year	100% relief on gains up to	50% relief on remaining gains between
1998/99	£250,000	£250,000 - £1,000,000
1999/00	£200,000	£200,000 - £800,000
2000/01	£150,000	£150,000 - £600,000
2001/02	£100,000	£100,000 - £400,000
2002/03	£50,000	£50,000 - £200,000

Retirement relief will altogether cease to be available as from 6 April 2003.

EXAMPLE 8

Compute the amount of retirement relief available to the following taxpayers, each of whom is a sole trader (in good health) making a material disposal of business assets in 2000/01 :

	Age	No of years trading	Amount of untapered gains
(a)	65	12	£130,000
(b)	68	27	£490,000
(c)	67	20	£2,115,000
(d)	48	12	£26,000
(e)	58	8	£210,000
(f)	62	7	£750,000

SOLUTION

(a) The taxpayer is fully eligible for retirement relief. The total gains of £130,000 are less than £150,000, so retirement relief of £130,000 will be given, reducing the untapered gain to £nil.

(b) The taxpayer is fully eligible for retirement relief. The first £150,000 is fully exempt and half of the remaining £340,000 is also exempt. Total retirement relief is £320,000, leaving an untapered gain of £170,000.

(c) The taxpayer is fully eligible for retirement relief. The first £150,000 is fully exempt and 50% relief will be granted on the gains lying between £150,000 and £600,000 (i.e. the next £450,000). Total retirement relief is £375,000, leaving an untapered gain of £1,740,000.

(d) The taxpayer (who is in good health) is too young for retirement relief and so none is available.

(e) The taxpayer is entitled to a proportionate relief based on 8 years of trading. The lower and upper limits are scaled down to £120,000 and £480,000 respectively, so the first £120,000 is fully exempt and half of the remaining £90,000 is also exempt. Total retirement relief is £165,000, leaving an untapered gain of £45,000.

(f) The taxpayer is entitled to a proportionate relief based on 7 years of trading. The lower and upper limits are scaled down to £105,000 and £420,000 respectively, so the first £105,000 is fully exempt and 50% relief will be granted on the gains lying between £105,000 and £420,000 (i.e. the next £315,000). Total retirement relief is £262,500, leaving an untapered gain of £487,500.

Disposals of shares in a personal company

As stated above, retirement relief may be granted when a taxpayer disposes of shares in a personal company. In this case, the gain arising on the disposal is apportioned between the amount which relates to chargeable business assets owned by the company on the date of the disposal and the amount relating to other chargeable assets (e.g.

investments). Only the part of the gain which relates to chargeable business assets is eligible for retirement relief. This is identical to the way in which hold-over relief is given on a gift of shares (see earlier in this chapter).

EXAMPLE 9

Gloria (who was born in 1943) acquired a 50% shareholding in G Ltd in 1976. She has been a full-time working director of the company ever since. In January 2001 she sold her entire shareholding. The untapered gain arising on this disposal (before deduction of retirement relief) was £650,000. On the day that Gloria sold her shares the company had chargeable assets of £3.2 million, of which £2.8 million comprised chargeable business assets. Compute Gloria's untapered gain after deduction of retirement relief.

SOLUTION

Gloria is fully eligible for retirement relief but relief is available only in relation to the part of her gain which relates to chargeable business assets. This part of the gain is £650,000 x 2.8/3.2 = £568,750. The remaining £81,250 (which relates to non-business chargeable assets) does not attract retirement relief. The computation is :

	£
Gain eligible for retirement relief	568,750
Less : Retirement relief :	
(£150,000 + 50% x £418,750)	359,375
	209,375
Add : Gain not eligible for retirement relief	81,250
Untapered gain	290,625

Relationship between retirement relief and gift relief

If a taxpayer makes a gift of business assets on retirement it is quite possible that both retirement relief and hold-over relief might be available in relation to the gift. In this situation, retirement relief (which is mandatory) is first subtracted from the gain arising on the disposal. Hold-over relief may then be claimed in relation to the balance of the gain (if both the transferor and the transferee agree to do so).

Reinvestment into EIS or VCT shares

The gain arising on the disposal of *any* asset may be deferred if an amount of money equal to the gain is used to subscribe for shares which are eligible under the rules of the Enterprise Investment Scheme (see Chapter 6). Note the following points :

(a) The shares must be subscribed for during the period starting one year before and finishing three years after the disposal concerned.

(b) The entire gain arising on a disposal may be deferred if an amount equal to the gain is invested in eligible shares. It is *not* necessary to invest the entire disposal proceeds.

(c) There is no requirement that income tax relief should be available in relation to the investment. It follows that the taxpayer does not have to be unconnected with the company concerned and that the amount of a deferred gain can exceed the maximum amount on which income tax relief is granted (currently £150,000).

(d) A taxpayer claiming this relief may restrict the amount of relief claimed so as to avoid wasting the annual exemption.

(e) The deferred gain becomes chargeable when a "chargeable event" occurs. The most common example of such an event is the disposal of the shares concerned.

(f) When the deferred gain becomes chargeable, taper relief on that gain is calculated by reference to the qualifying holding period of the asset on which the deferred gain arose.

A similar relief is available if the amount of a gain is used to subscribe for shares in a Venture Capital Trust (see Chapter 6). In this case, it *is* necessary that income tax relief should be available in relation to the investment. The VCT shares must be subscribed for during the period starting one year before and finishing one year after the disposal which gave rise to the gain.

Serial EIS investment

If a chargeable gain arises on the disposal of EIS shares (perhaps because the shares were not retained for at least 3 years) this gain, like any other gain, can be deferred by reinvesting it in new EIS shares. The gain on the disposal of the original EIS shares will then become chargeable when the new EIS shares are disposed of.

If the usual EIS reinvestment rules applied, taper relief on the deferred gain would be calculated by reference to the holding period of the original EIS shares. However, in order to encourage investors to move from one EIS investment to another, taper relief on this type of deferred gain will instead be calculated *as though the holding period of the original EIS shares began when they were acquired and ended when the second EIS shares were disposed of.*

Loans to traders

If a taxpayer lends money to a trader and then finds that all or part of the loan is irrecoverable, the loss incurred may be treated as a capital loss and set against the taxpayer's capital gains. This relief is subject to the following conditions :

(a) the trader who has borrowed the money must be resident in the UK

(b) the money must have been borrowed for trade purposes (but not for the trade of money-lending)

(c) the debt must be unsecured.

Subject to these conditions, the amount lost is treated as a capital loss of the year in which the taxpayer makes the claim for relief, though a claim may be backdated for up to two years if it can be shown that the debt was irrecoverable then. If relief is given and then all or part of the loan is recovered, the amount recovered is treated as a capital gain of the year in which recovery takes place.

Summary

▶ If the compensation received on the loss or destruction of an asset is spent on the purchase of a replacement, the taxpayer may claim that the disposal should give rise to neither a gain nor a loss. The gain which would have been chargeable is then subtracted from the cost of the replacement asset.

▶ The gain arising on the disposal of a business asset may be rolled-over against the cost of acquiring a replacement.

▶ If a business asset is replaced by a depreciating asset, the gain arising cannot be permanently rolled-over but may be temporarily held-over instead. This gain will become chargeable no later than 10 years after the replacement asset was acquired (unless the gain can be transferred to a non-depreciating asset in the meantime).

▶ The gain arising on the gift of a business asset may be held-over until the transferee disposes of the asset.

▶ The gain arising on the transfer of a business to a limited company is held-over until the transferor disposes of the shares which were received in exchange for the assets of the business.

▶ Until 6 April 2003, retirement relief may be available when a taxpayer makes a material disposal of business assets.

▶ The gain arising on the disposal of any asset may be deferred if the amount of the gain is used to subscribe for shares eligible under the rules of the EIS. A similar relief applies if the gain is used to subscribe for shares in a VCT.

Exercises

Please note that the RPI for April 1998 is 162.6.

22.1 Matthew bought a piece of antique porcelain in March 1986 (RPI 96.73) for £10,000. The porcelain was damaged in early 1992 and Matthew spent £3,850 on restoration work in March of that year (RPI 136.7). In July 1992 (RPI 138.8) Matthew's insurance company paid him £4,000 and Matthew successfully claimed that this should not be treated as a part disposal. In March 2001 he sold the porcelain for £23,500. Compute the untapered gain.

22.2 Maria bought a diamond necklace in February 1988 (RPI 103.7) for £13,500. In 1993 the necklace was stolen and, as a result, an insurance payment of £19,000 was received in February 1994 (RPI 142.1). In the same month, Maria spent £19,500 on the purchase of a replacement necklace and claimed that the disposal of the original necklace should give rise to neither a gain nor a loss. Compute the untapered gain arising in January 2001 when the replacement necklace was sold for £22,000.

22.3 Pamela bought a building for business use in September 1990 (RPI 129.3) at a cost of £50,000. In September 2000 she sold the building for £74,300 and immediately bought another building, again for business use. Assuming that Pamela claims roll-over relief, calculate the untapered gain arising in September 2000 if the cost of the new building is :

(a) £71,800

(b) £62,700

(c) £76,800.

22.4 Phillip is a sole trader. In July 2000 he gives his entire business to his grandson. Both Phillip and his grandson elect that the gains arising on this gift should be held-over. The untapered gains arising are as follows :

	£
Freehold buildings	23,500
Goodwill	40,000
Listed investments	10,600

State the amount of the untapered gains which may be held-over and the amount which is immediately chargeable.

22.5 Compute the amount of retirement relief available to each of the following taxpayers, each of whom is a sole trader (in good health) making a material disposal of business assets in 2000/01 :

	Age	No of years trading	Amount of untapered gains
(a)	57	35	£500,000
(b)	69	9	£1,200,000
(c)	56	2	£120,000

*22.6   In January 1981, Norman bought a freehold building for use in his business at a cost of £120,000. The building had a market value on 31 March 1982 (RPI 79.44) of £125,000. In June 1990 (RPI 126.7) he sold the building for £275,000 and in August 1990 (RPI 128.1) he spent £270,000 on buying another building for use in his business. This building was sold in December 2000 for £330,000. Compute the gains arising on the disposal of each building (assuming that Norman claims roll-over relief).

*22.7   In May 2000, Ruth sold a freehold building which she had used exclusively for business purposes. The building was sold for £120,000, realising an untapered gain of £42,500. In the following month, Ruth acquired fixed plant for £120,000 and elected to hold-over the gain on the freehold property against this plant and machinery. In August 2004, she acquired another freehold building for £105,000 and elected to transfer the held-over gain to this new building. Explain the treatment of the £42,500 gain.

*22.8   In October 2000, Roger sold the goodwill of his business for £100,000. He had acquired the goodwill in the form of a gift from his brother in January 1986 (RPI 96.25) when it was valued at £50,000. Roger's brother had purchased the goodwill in 1980 and the gain arising on the gift to Roger was £37,350. Both Roger and his brother elected that this gain should be held-over. Compute the untapered gain arising in October 2000.

*22.9   Susannah has reached her 60th birthday and decides to retire after over 20 years of owning her own business. In June 2000 she gives her entire business to her daughter, realising untapered gains (all relating to chargeable business assets) of £270,000. Calculate the amount of retirement relief which is available and the amount of the gain which may be held-over (if Susannah and her daughter so elect).

*22.10   For the last 15 years, Shaun has been a full-time working director of an unlisted trading company in which he has a 10% stake. He has now reached the age of 59 and has decided to retire, so in January 2001 he sells his entire shareholding for £250,000. He bought the shares in 1981 for £80,000 and they had a market value of £75,000 in March 1982 (RPI 79.44). In January 2001, the company's assets are valued as follows :

	£
Freehold land and buildings	1,700,000
Goodwill	500,000
Investments	100,000
Motor cars	40,000
Plant and machinery	60,000
Net current assets	100,000

The plant and machinery consist entirely of small movable items costing less than £6,000 each and with a current value of less than £6,000 each. Calculate the untapered gain.

Review questions (Set B)

B 1 Olivia purchased her home on 1 March 1975 for £20,000 and sold it on 31 August 2000 (RPI 169.9) for £180,000. An extension was added in July 1984 (RPI 89.10) costing £8,000. From 1 January 1992 until 30 April 1995, one-half of the house had been let for residential purposes. On 1 May 1995 Olivia went to live with her daughter and let the whole house for residential purposes until it was sold. The value of the house on 31 March 1982 (RPI 79.44) was £50,000. The RPI for April 1998 was 162.6.

Gaynor purchased an antique wardrobe for £3,000 in July 1987 (RPI 101.8) and sold it at auction for £7,500 in September 2000 (RPI 170.2). She paid the auctioneer 10% of the sale proceeds of £7,500. The RPI for April 1998 was 162.6.

You are required to :

(i) Calculate Olivia's tapered gain, assuming no other disposals in 2000/01 and no losses brought forward from previous years. No election has been made to re-base the cost of all assets held on 31 March 1982 to their value on that date.

(ii) Calculate Gaynor's tapered gain, assuming no other disposals in 2000/01 and no losses brought forward from previous years. *(ACCA)*

B 2 Victor had the following transactions in the ordinary shares of Victorious Vulcanising plc, a listed company :

		No of shares	Total amount £	RPI
1/8/78	Bought	600	7,200	
1/4/87	Bought	1,000	11,000	101.8
1/9/89	(1 for 2 rights) Bought	800	4,800	116.6
1/8/00	Sold	2,100	42,000	

The value per share on 31 March 1982 (RPI 79.44) was £8. RPI April 1998 was 162.6.

You are required to :

Calculate the untapered gain arising on the August 2000 disposal, assuming that Victor acquired no further shares in the company within the next 30 days. *(ACCA)*

B 3   Ranek sold a factory in November 2000 for £250,000 and moved his business into rented premises. The factory was purchased in April 1984 (RPI 88.64) for £100,000. Ranek purchased fixed plant in December 1999 costing £240,000 and elected to "hold-over" any gain on the sale of the building against the cost of the plant.

You are required to :

(i)   Calculate the untapered gain on the sale of the factory and the effect of the "hold-over" claim on that gain. (RPI April 1998 was 162.6).

(ii)   State the earliest time that the "hold-over" would cease to be effective.   *(ACCA)*

B 4   Consider each of the following situations :

(a)   Marlene has untapered gains for the year 2000/01 of £12,000 and capital losses for the year 2000/01 of £8,000.

(b)   Moira has untapered gains for the year 2000/01 of £12,000 and capital losses brought forward of £8,000.

(c)   Marina has untapered gains for the year 2000/01 of £3,000 and capital losses brought forward of £8,000.

(d)   Melissa has untapered gains for the year 2000/01 of £12,000, capital losses for the year 2000/01 of £8,000 and capital losses brought forward of £4,000.

You are required to :

For each situation, calculate the capital gains assessable for 2000/01 (assuming that no taper relief is available) and state the amount of any losses carried forward.   *(ACCA)*

B 5   In the year to 5 April 2001, Thomas More, who was born on 1 October 1951, made the following disposals :

(i)   A flat in a house that he had purchased on 1 December 1981 for £29,000. It had never been occupied as the main residence and had been consistently let during his period of ownership. The property had been converted into two flats in September 1984 at a cost of £18,000. The flat was sold for £71,000 on 1 December 2000 and out of this legal fees of £2,000 were paid. It was agreed that the value of the other flat was £65,000 in December 2000 and that the entire house was valued at £40,000 in March 1982.

(ii)   20,000 shares in ICI plc which cost £60,000 in December 1983 and which were sold for £150,000 in December 2000. (No shares were acquired within the next 30 days).

Thomas also received an offer to sell his 10,000 shares in Hampton Ltd on 30 June 2001. An estimated balance sheet at that date is as follows :

	£	£
Freehold land and buildings - cost		200,000
Plant and machinery (all small items)		
cost less depreciation		60,000
Investment in shares of a major supplier - cost		100,000
		360,000
Current Assets :		
Stock	360,000	
Debtors	140,000	
	500,000	
Less : Bank overdraft	130,000	370,000
		730,000
Share Capital - 30,000 shares of £1		30,000
Reserves		700,000
		730,000

On 30 June 2001, it was agreed that the freehold land and buildings, which were all used in the trade, would have a market value of £800,000 and that the investments would be worth £300,000. The offer made to Thomas is that his shares would be bought at asset value less 10%. The purchaser is also willing to buy them in December 2001 at the same asset values as indicated above but less a discount of 15%. The shares cost Thomas £40,000 on 31 March 1982 when he joined the Board as the production director of the company. Goodwill has been valued at £280,000 in June 2001.

Assume that the Retail Prices Index has the following values :

March 1982	79.44	December 1983	86.89
September 1984	90.11	April 1985	94.78
April 1998	162.6		

Required :

(a) Calculate the capital gains tax payable on the sale of the flat and the shares in ICI plc (neither of which are business assets) assuming that Thomas is married and has taxable income of £20,000 after the personal allowance for 2000/01. There were no other chargeable disposals in the year and no capital losses brought forward from previous years. Thomas made no Gift Aid donations in the year.

(b) If you were told that Mrs More had capital losses of £32,000 brought forward and had made no capital disposals in 2000/01, would there be any advice that you should consider giving to Thomas ?

(c) What will be the untapered gain arising if Thomas sells his shares in Hampton Ltd on 30 June 2001 ? Again, is there any advice that you should consider giving to him ? Illustrate your answer with appropriate computations.   *(AAT)*

357

*B6   Mrs Laura Stapleton, a widow, has decided to dispose of her residence and retire to Canada, where she will live with her son, Danny.

She acquired her house on 1 June 1986 and lived there until 31 March 1987 when she left the UK in order to care for Danny and his wife who had been injured in a serious car accident in Canada. Liking it there, she extended her stay and on 1 November 1987 she took a job at a local hospital until 31 December 1988 when she returned to the UK and resumed residence in her property.

Having incorporated a company, which commenced to operate a nursing agency on 1 February 1989, she remained living in her house until 31 December 1995, when she left it permanently in order to live in a flat over the company's offices. Contracts were exchanged for the sale of the house on 31 May 2000.

The house originally cost £50,000 and an extension was completed in December 1991 at a cost of £20,000. The agreed sale proceeds are £300,000 and the expenses of sale are £5,200. Throughout the periods of Mrs Stapleton's absence, the property was let at a market rent.

Assume that the Retail Prices Index has the following values :

June 1986	97.79	December 1991	135.7
April 1998	162.6		

Required :

Calculate the untapered gain arising on the disposal of Mrs Stapleton's residence. *(AAT)*

*B7   You have been consulted by Mr Christopher Rodrigues on two matters relating to capital gains tax. Extracts from his letter to you are :

"On 31 January 2001, I sold my shares in Fledgeby plc, a listed company. I had acquired them as follows :

1 January 1983	1,000	shares cost £4,200
19 June 1984	700	shares cost £2,950
31 December 1986	1,200	shares cost £5,620
11 August 1988	400	shares cost £2,100

I also took up a 1 for 4 rights issue at £3.50 per share on 31 May 1987. The shares were all sold for £38,000 on 31 January 2001 and I do not intend to buy any shares in the company in the future.

Also on 31 January 2001, I sold for £100,000 a plot of land that I acquired in January 1970 for £10,000. A friend has told me that the gain might be either a capital gain or a trading gain but, as capital gains are broadly charged at income tax rates, it doesn't really matter which way it is dealt with".

Assume that the Retail Prices Index has the following values :

January 1983	82.61	June 1984	89.20
April 1985	94.78	December 1986	99.62
May 1987	101.9	August 1988	107.9
April 1998	162.6		

Required :

(a)   Calculate the untapered gain or allowable loss arising on the sale of the shares in Fledgeby plc.

(b)   Do you agree with the statement of the other taxation practitioner ? Draft brief notes that will form the basis of the letter that you will write to Mr Rodrigues.

(AAT)

*B8   On 1 May 1987 (RPI 101.9), Nigel acquired a 30-year lease for £20,000. He assigned the lease on 1 November 2000 for £75,000. The RPI for April 1998 was 162.6.

Kay purchased 20 acres of land in February 1995 (RPI 146.9) for £40,000. She sold part of the land for £18,000 in March 2001 when the value of the remainder of the land was £60,000. The RPI for April 1998 was 162.6. Kay made no other capital disposals in 2000/01.

You are required to :

(i)   Calculate Nigel's untapered gain.

(ii)   Calculate Kay's tapered gain, assuming no losses brought forward from previous years. The land is a business asset for taper relief purposes.   *(ACCA)*

*B9   In October 2000 Kathleen had her 57th birthday and decided to retire immediately from her personal company. She had two children, Corinne and Stephen, to whom she gave all her shares in the company in equal shares. In October 2000 the total value of the shares was £750,000. The shares had cost £250,000 in September 1981 and were valued at £200,000 in March 1982 (RPI 79.44). Kathleen had been a full-time working director in the company since October 1995. The company did not own any "non-business" chargeable assets.

No election has been made, or will be made, to have all pre-31 March 1982 acquisitions re-based to 31 March 1982 (S35(5) TCGA 1992). RPI April 1998 was 162.6.

You are required to :

(i)   Calculate the untapered gain assessable on Kathleen for 2000/01.

(ii)   Explain the present and future consequences of a joint election made by Kathleen, Corinne and Stephen to "hold-over" any capital gain.   *(ACCA)*

*B10   Gillian purchased 10,000 ordinary shares in Downtown plc in January 1995 (RPI 146.0) for £20,000. In October 2000, Upmarket plc acquired the whole of the share capital of Downtown plc following a take-over bid. The terms of the take-over offer were :

> One ordinary share in Upmarket plc, and
>
> Two preference shares in Upmarket plc, and
>
> £3 cash

for every five shares held in Downtown plc. The share prices of Upmarket plc immediately after the take-over were :

> Ordinary shares £10 each, and
>
> Preference shares £3 each.

The RPI for April 1998 was 162.6.

You are required to :

Calculate the untapered gain arising in 2000/01.   *(ACCA)*

PART 3
CORPORATION TAX

Chapter 23

Introduction to corporation tax

Introduction

The next six chapters of this book deal with corporation tax, which was introduced in 1965 as the tax payable on the profits of companies. Prior to 1965, companies paid income tax on their profits. The purpose of this first chapter is to provide an introduction to the basic principles of corporation tax. Corporation tax legislation is to be found in the Income and Corporation Taxes Act 1988 and in the Taxation of Chargeable Gains Act 1992, as amended by subsequent Finance Acts.

Scope of corporation tax

UK resident companies are liable to corporation tax on their "chargeable profits", no matter where in the world those profits arise. Companies which are not UK resident but which operate in the UK through a branch or agency are liable to corporation tax on the chargeable profits of that branch or agency (see Chapter 32).

A company's "chargeable profits" consist of its income plus capital gains, less charges on income. The system of Schedules and Cases used for income tax purposes also applies to corporation tax, but there are some important distinctions between the assessment of an individual's income and the assessment of a company's income. These distinctions are explained later in this chapter.

For corporation tax purposes, the word "company" is taken to mean any corporate body or unincorporated association, excluding partnerships, local authorities and local authority associations. As well as limited companies, some of the main types of organisation which are liable to corporation tax include clubs and societies, political associations, building societies and nationalised corporations.

Charities are generally exempt from corporation tax, as are agricultural societies, scientific research associations, friendly societies, trade unions (subject to certain conditions) and approved pension schemes.

Accounting periods

Corporation tax is charged in respect of "accounting periods". It is very important to distinguish between an *accounting period* (i.e. a period for which corporation tax is charged) and a *period of account* (i.e. a period for which a company prepares a set of accounts). Although accounting periods and periods of account are often the same thing, this is not always the case. An accounting period *begins* when :

(a) the company starts to trade, or otherwise comes within the charge to corporation tax, or

(b) when the previous accounting period ends, so long as the company remains within the charge to corporation tax.

An accounting period *ends* on the *earliest* occurrence of any of the following events:

(a) the expiration of 12 months from the beginning of the accounting period

(b) the end of a period of account

(c) the commencement of winding-up proceedings

(d) the company ceasing to be UK resident

(e) the company ceasing to be within the charge to corporation tax.

These rules have the following consequences :

(a) The length of an accounting period can never exceed 12 months.

(b) If a set of accounts covers a period of 12 months or less, the period covered by the accounts is regarded as an accounting period in its own right and a corporation tax assessment is raised for this period.

(c) If a set of accounts covers a period exceeding 12 months, the period covered by the accounts is broken down into two or more accounting periods, each giving rise to a separate corporation tax assessment. The first accounting period consists of the first 12 months of the period of account. The second accounting period consists of the next 12 months and so forth. If the period covered by the accounts is not an exact multiple of 12 months, the final accounting period will be of less than 12 months' duration.

EXAMPLE 1

Identify the accounting periods which relate to the following periods of account :

(a) A Ltd prepares accounts for the year to 31 December 2000.

(b) B Ltd prepares accounts for the six months to 31 October 2000.

(c) C Ltd prepares accounts for the sixteen months to 31 December 2000.

(d) D Ltd prepares accounts for the thirty months to 31 March 2001.

SOLUTION

(a)   The year to 31 December 2000 is an accounting period in its own right.

(b)   The six months to 31 October 2000 is an accounting period in its own right.

(c)   The sixteen months to 31 December 2000 is divided into two accounting periods - the 12 months to 31 August 2000 and the 4 months to 31 December 2000.

(d)   The thirty months to 31 March 2001 is divided into three accounting periods. These are the 12 months to 30 September 1999, the 12 months to 30 September 2000 and the 6 months to 31 March 2001.

Chargeable profits

A company's chargeable profits for an accounting period are calculated as follows :

	£
Schedule D Case I (trading income, less capital allowances)	x
Schedule D Case III (principally net credits on "non-trading loan relationships")	x
Schedule D Case V (income from foreign possessions)	x
Schedule D Case VI (miscellaneous income)	x
Schedule A (income from property)	x
Unfranked investment income	x
Chargeable gains	x
	x
Less : Charges on income	x
Profits chargeable to corporation tax (PCTCT)	x

Notes :

(i)   A company cannot be assessed under Schedule E, since Schedule E relates to income from employment and a company cannot be an employee. Similarly, a company cannot exercise a profession or a vocation and therefore cannot be assessed under Schedule D Case II.

(ii)   Schedule D Case IV (income from foreign securities) no longer applies to companies. The tax treatment of a company's foreign income is described in Chapter 32 of this book.

(iii)   In general, a company's income under each Schedule and Case is computed in accordance with income tax principles and its chargeable gains are computed in accordance with CGT principles. However, this general rule is over-ridden by special corporation tax provisions in some instances (see below).

(iv)   A company is not a "person" and is not entitled to claim personal allowances.

Schedule D Case I

A company's Schedule D Case I assessment for an accounting period is always based on its actual trading income for that period, adjusted for tax purposes in the usual way. There are no special rules relating to the commencement of trade, cessation of trade or a change of accounting date. Note that :

(a) In a company's capital allowances computation there will be no restriction relating to the private use of assets. This is because a company cannot make private use of its own assets and any private use by employees is assessed as a benefit in kind under Schedule E.

(b) The provisions whereby farmers may average their profits (see Chapter 9) do not apply to companies.

(c) As from 1 April 2000, a small or medium-sized company which incurs research and development expenditure may, subject to certain conditions, claim tax relief on 150% of the amount of that expenditure. The main conditions which must be satisfied are :

(i) The expenditure must not be of a capital nature and must be relevant to the company's trade, consisting of staffing costs, consumable stores or payments made to subcontractors.

(ii) The company must have incurred at least £25,000 of qualifying research and development expenditure in the accounting period (or proportionately less if the accounting period is less than 12 months in length).

For this purpose, the definition of a "small or medium-sized company" is the same as that given by European Union recommendations. Currently, companies with an annual turnover of up to £25 million qualify as small or medium-sized.

In general, tax relief is given by deducting 150% of the qualifying expenditure when computing the company's Schedule D Case I income. However, a company which has a trading loss may (subject to certain conditions) claim payment from the Inland Revenue of a "research and development tax credit" equal to 24% of the qualifying expenditure.

Schedule D Case III

The main classes of income assessed under Schedule D Case III for a company are as follows :

(a) profits and gains arising from "non-trading loan relationships"

(b) any annuity or other annual payment which is not chargeable under Schedule A and which does not fall within the loan relationships regime.

Broadly, income from non-trading loan relationships consists of bank interest, building society interest and other interest receivable by a company. Such interest is assessed on the *accruals* basis. (The loan relationships rules are explained in detail later in this chapter). Note that :

(a) Unlike individuals, companies receive all bank and building society interest gross.

(b) The first £70 p.a. of National Savings Bank ordinary account interest received by a company is *not* exempt from corporation tax.

Schedule A

A company's property income is assessed in much the same way as an individual's property income (see Chapter 5). However, the following important distinctions should be noted :

(a) Interest payable on a loan taken out by a company for the purpose of buying or improving let property is dealt with under the loan relationships rules and is therefore disallowed in the company's Schedule A computation.

(b) The loss reliefs available to a company which suffers a Schedule A loss are different from the loss reliefs available to an individual (see Chapter 26).

Unfranked investment income

The term "unfranked investment income" (UFII) refers to income which is received by a company net of *basic rate* income tax. A company receiving such income is able to reclaim the income tax deducted at source (see Chapter 25) but the grossed-up amount of the income is then assessed to corporation tax *on the receipts basis*. Patent royalties are now the main example of this form of income.

Before the introduction of the provisions relating to loan relationships (see below) interest received net of lower rate income tax was also classed as UFII but this is now assessed instead under Schedule D Case I or Case III.

Franked investment income

Dividends received from other UK companies are paid out of profits which have already been subject to corporation tax once in the hands of the paying company and are therefore not subjected to corporation tax for a second time in the hands of the receiving company. The term "franked investment income" (FII) is used to refer to the UK dividends received by a company, together with the attached tax credits. For example, a company which receives a UK dividend of £9,000 after 5 April 1999 has FII of £10,000 (£9,000 + tax credits £1,000). FII does *not* form part of a company's chargeable profits.

Chargeable gains

A company's chargeable profits for an accounting period include any chargeable gains arising in respect of disposals made in that period. The chargeable gains of a company are computed in a similar way to those of an individual but the following important distinctions should be noted :

(a) The CGT reforms which were introduced by the Finance Act 1998 do *not* apply when computing the chargeable gains of companies. Therefore, for the purposes of corporation tax :

    (i) Indexation allowance is not frozen at April 1998.

    (ii) Taper relief does not apply.

    (iii) The matching rules used on a disposal of shares or securities are the old, pre-FA98 rules (see below).

(b) When a company makes a disposal of shares or securities, the disposal is matched against acquisitions in the following order :

    (i) first, against acquisitions made on the same day

    (ii) next, against acquisitions made in the previous 9 days (on a FIFO basis)

    (iii) next, against shares taken from the S104 holding (which is the pool of shares acquired on or after 1 April 1982 and which is *not* frozen at April 1998)

    (iv) next, against the 1982 holding (which is the pool of shares acquired between 6 April 1965 and 31 March 1982 inclusive)

    (v) finally, against shares acquired before 6 April 1965 (on a LIFO basis).

(c) Companies are not entitled to the annual exemption.

Charges on income

For corporation tax purposes, the main types of payment which are classed as charges on income are :

(a) qualifying donations under the Gift Aid scheme (see Chapter 4)

(b) patent royalties

(c) any annuity or other annual payment which is not chargeable under Schedule A and which does not fall within the loan relationships regime.

In general, a company's charges on income are paid net of *basic rate* income tax. But as from 1 April 2000, Gift Aid payments made by a company (including covenanted payments) are paid gross. Note the following important points :

(a) The amount of charges deducted when computing a company's chargeable profits for an accounting period is the amount of the charges actually *paid* during the period (grossed-up if necessary). Accruals and prepayments are ignored.

(b) A company which pays a charge net of income tax must account to the Inland Revenue for the income tax deducted at source (see Chapter 25).

(c) Companies may obtain tax relief on their charitable donations as follows :

(i) Payments made under the Gift Aid scheme (including payments made under the terms of a deed of covenant) are relieved as a charge on income.

(ii) Charitable donations incurred for trade purposes are deductible under the rules of Schedule D Case I and are not treated as a charge on income.

(iii) From 1 April 2000, a gift of listed shares or securities to a charity is treated as a charge on income. The amount of the charge is taken as the market value of the shares on the date of the gift.

Before the introduction of the provisions relating to loan relationships (see below) interest paid net of lower rate income tax was regarded as a charge on income, but this is no longer the case. Such interest is now deductible when computing the company's income under Schedule D Case I or Case III.

Loan relationships

The Finance Act 1996 introduced a new tax regime for the treatment of company "loan relationships". A company has a loan relationship if it is a debtor or creditor with regard to any debt which is a loan under general law. The main classes of debt to which the term "loan relationship" refers are bank and building society deposits, bank overdrafts, Government securities (gilts), corporate bonds (e.g. debentures) and other corporate debt. The tax treatment of income and expenditure relating to a loan relationship depends upon whether the relationship has been entered into for trade purposes :

(a) **Trading loan relationships**. If a company has entered into a loan relationship for trade purposes, then :

(i) Any interest payable (and any other cost relating to the debt) is allowable as a trading expense and is deducted when computing the company's Schedule D Case I income.

(ii) Any interest receivable (and other income relating to the debt) is regarded as a trading receipt and is treated as Schedule D Case I income. This will usually apply only if the company's trade is that of lending money.

(b) **Non-trading loan relationships**. If a company has entered into one or more loan relationships for non-trading purposes, then all of the "debits" and "credits" (costs and income) relating to such relationships are aggregated. Then :

(i) If total credits exceed total debits, the net credits are assessable under Schedule D Case III.

(ii) If total debits exceed total credits, the net debits may be relieved in a variety of ways (see Chapter 26).

Interest payable on underpaid corporation tax for accounting periods ending on or after 1 July 1999 is treated as a non-trading debit. Similarly, interest receivable on a repayment of overpaid corporation tax for such a period is treated as a non-trading credit (see Chapter 24).

It is important to appreciate that the above treatment of costs and income relating to loan relationships applies to all such costs and income, *whether of a revenue or capital nature*. This means that the profit (or loss) arising on a disposal of Government securities or corporate bonds by a company is taxable (or allowable) even though such assets would not be chargeable assets for CGT purposes if held by individuals.

Accounting methods for loan relationships

In most cases, the amount of income and expenditure brought into account for a loan relationship is calculated on the *accruals basis*. If receipts or payments are made net of income tax (at the lower rate) they must be grossed-up. Any income tax deducted from the income received in an accounting period may be reclaimed from the Inland Revenue and any income tax deducted from the payments made in an accounting period must be accounted for to the Inland Revenue (see Chapter 25).

An alternative accounting method which is authorised by the Finance Act 1996 is the *mark to market* basis. If this method is used, the fair value of the loan relationship must be determined at the end of each accounting period. The income or expenditure which is brought into account for an accounting period then comprises the receipts and payments of that period, together with the change in the fair value of the loan relationship between the start and end of the period.

EXAMPLE 2

A manufacturing company has the following results for the year to 31 March 2001 :

	£
Trading income	875,000
Income from property	14,200
Bank interest (gross amount received)	6,200
Patent royalties (net amount received)	6,240
Interest on Government securities (gross amount received)	28,000
Dividends from UK companies	18,450
Chargeable gains	123,000
Charitable covenant (gross amount paid)	24,000

The following information is also relevant :

(a) Bank interest of £2,100 and net royalties of £3,120 were owing to the company at the end of the year. The corresponding amounts at the start of the year were both zero.

(b) The patent royalties were all received on or after 6 April 2000.

(c) The Government securities were acquired on 1 July 2000. Interest of £28,000 (gross) is payable to the company on 30 June and 31 December each year.

(d) The charitable covenant began on 1 January 2001 and, on that date, the company made the first annual payment of £24,000 (gross).

Compute the company's chargeable profits for the year to 31 March 2001.

SOLUTION

	£
Schedule D Case I	875,000
Schedule A	14,200
Schedule D Case III (£8,300 + £42,000)	50,300
Unfranked Investment Income	8,000
Chargeable gains	123,000
	1,070,500
Less : Charges on income	24,000
Chargeable profits	1,046,500

Notes :

(i) The bank interest is income from a non-trading loan relationship and is assessed under Schedule D Case III on the accruals basis. The amount assessable for the year is £8,300 (£6,200 received + £2,100 accrued).

(ii) The patent royalties are unfranked investment income and have been received net of 22% income tax (the basic rate for 2000/01). The company may reclaim the £1,760 (£6,240 x 22/78) income tax suffered by deduction at source but the gross income of £8,000 (£6,240 x 100/78) forms part of the company's chargeable profits for corporation tax purposes. Since UFII is assessed on the receipts basis, the amount owing to the company at the end of the year is irrelevant.

(iii) The interest on Government securities is income from a non-trading loan relationship and is assessed under Schedule D Case III on the accruals basis. The gross income accrued in the year of £42,000 (£28,000 + £14,000) forms part of the company's chargeable profits for corporation tax purposes.

(iv) The dividends received from UK companies are franked investment income and do not form part of the company's chargeable profits for corporation tax purposes.

(v) The covenanted payment of £24,000 is a charge on income and is deducted when computing the company's chargeable profits. Since charges are dealt with on a payments basis, the whole of the £24,000 is deductible in the year to 31 March 2001.

(vi) In this example, the UFII was stated net. However, it is standard accounting practice for a company's profit and loss account to show the grossed-up figures for items paid or received net of income tax.

EXAMPLE 3

A company produces the following profit and loss account for the year to 31 March 2001 :

	£	£
Gross profit brought down from trading account		758,950
Add : Rental income (Note 1)	5,000	
Loan interest receivable (Note 2)	2,600	
Dividends received (Note 3)	18,750	
Bank interest receivable (Note 4)	4,789	
Patent royalties receivable (Note 5)	6,500	
Profit on sale of building (Note 6)	6,000	43,639
		802,589
Less : Operating expenses (Note 7)		568,912
Net profit for the year		233,677

Notes :

1. The property was let on 1 January 2001 at a rent of £20,000 per annum, payable annually in advance. The figure shown in the profit and loss account represents the rent for the period 1 January 2001 to 31 March 2001. No allowable expenditure has been incurred in relation to the let property.

2. Net loan interest of £1,560 was received during the year and a further £520 (net) was owing to the company at the end of the year. None was owed to the company at the start of the year. The profit and loss account shows the gross equivalent figure (i.e. £2,080 x 100/80 = £2,600).

3. Dividends of £18,750 were received from other UK companies during the year.

4. Bank interest received in the year was £4,684. Of this, £1,000 was owed to the company at the start of the year. A further £1,105 was owing to the company at the end of the year but was not received until April 2001.

5. Net patent royalties of £4,680 were received in the year (all after 5 April 2000) and a further £390 (net) was owing to the company at the end of the year. None was owed to the company at the start of the year. The profit and loss account shows the gross equivalent figure (i.e. £5,070 x 100/78 = £6,500).

6. The chargeable gain on the sale of the building is £2,350.

7. Operating expenses include :

	£
Directors' fees	100,000
Debenture interest (grossed-up amounts) :	
Paid 1 January 2001	4,000
Accrued at 31 March 2001	2,000
Depreciation	102,500
Entertaining expenses	2,400
Charitable covenant (paid gross) :	
Paid during the year	500
Accrued at 31 March 2001	250

All of the remaining operating expenses are allowable under the rules of Schedule D Case I. The debentures were issued on 1 July 2000 for trade purposes. The company claims capital allowances for the year of £87,450.

Required :

(a) Compute the company's trading profit assessable under Schedule D Case I for the year to 31 March 2001.

(b) Compute the company's chargeable profit for the year to 31 March 2001.

SOLUTION

(a) The Schedule D Case I assessment is as follows :

	£	£
Net profit per accounts		233,677
Less : *Non-trading income* :		
Income from property	5,000	
Loan interest receivable	2,600	
Dividends received	18,750	
Bank interest receivable	4,789	
Patent royalties receivable	6,500	
Profit on sale of building	6,000	43,639
		190,038
Add : *Disallowed expenses* :		
Depreciation	102,500	
Entertaining	2,400	
Charitable covenant	750	105,650
		295,688
Less : Capital allowances		87,450
Schedule D Case I assessment		208,238

(b) The chargeable profits for the year are :

	£
Schedule D Case I	208,238
Schedule A	5,000
Schedule D Case III (£2,600 + £4,789)	7,389
UFII	6,000
Chargeable gain	2,350
	228,977
Less : Charges on income (charitable covenant)	500
Chargeable profits	228,477

Notes :

(i) The computation of the Schedule D Case I assessment is performed in the same way as that of an individual. The starting point is the net profit shown by the accounts. Non-trading income included in this net profit is subtracted and disallowed expenses are added back. The aim is to separate out the company's trading profit from the total net profit shown in the accounts. (Note that debenture interest payable for the year is an allowable expense since the debentures were issued for trade purposes).

It is extremely important to classify the company's profits correctly and to arrive at a separate figure for each category of profit (e.g. trading income, rents, interest, chargeable gains etc.). This analysis is necessary because different rules of assessment apply to each category of profit and is especially vital if the company has incurred any losses (see Chapter 26).

(ii) The Schedule A assessment is made on the accruals basis.

(iii) The gross amount of the loan interest accrued for the year forms part of the Schedule D Case III assessment (assuming that the loan was not made for trade purposes). The remainder of the Schedule D Case III figure is bank interest, which is received gross and assessed on the accruals basis.

(iv) UFII consists of patent royalties which are assessed on the receipts basis (£4,680 x 100/78 = £6,000).

(v) FII is not chargeable to corporation tax and does not form part of the chargeable profit.

(vi) The chargeable gain on the sale of the building is fully chargeable to corporation tax since the company is not entitled to the annual exemption.

(vii) The amount actually paid under the terms of the deed of covenant (£500) is treated as a charge on income when computing chargeable profits.

Long periods of account

As stated above, a period of account exceeding 12 months must be divided into two or more accounting periods, each of which will give rise to a separate corporation tax assessment. A company's profit for a long period of account is allocated between accounting periods as follows :

(a) Trading profits assessable under Schedule D Case I (before deduction of capital allowances) are usually time-apportioned. Capital allowances are then computed separately for each accounting period.

(b) Schedule D Case VI income and the profits of a Schedule A business are also usually time-apportioned.

(c) A net credit on non-trading loan relationships is allocated between accounting periods on the accruals basis.

(d) Capital gains are allocated to the accounting period in which the disposals occur.

(e) Patent royalties are allocated to the accounting period in which they are received.

(f) Charges on income are allocated to the accounting period in which they are paid.

(g) Dividends received from other UK companies are allocated to the accounting period in which they are received. Although a company's FII does not form part of its chargeable profits, this allocation may be important when determining the rate of corporation tax which must be paid by the company (see Chapter 24).

In practice, the time-apportionment method which is normally used for Schedule D Cases I and VI and for Schedule A may be replaced by a more accurate method of allocation if one is available. For instance, if trading profits have been earned as a result of a small number of transactions and the profit arising on each transaction can be calculated individually, the company's Schedule D Case I income may be allocated between accounting periods according to the transactions occurring in each period.

Strictly speaking, all time-apportionments should be made exactly, according to the number of days in the period concerned. However, the Inland Revenue will accept any other reasonable time-based apportionment so long as it is applied consistently. In practice, calculations are usually made to the nearest month and this is the approach adopted in this book. However, *some examining bodies may require exact apportionments*. Therefore the reader is advised to find out whether his or her examining body requires apportionments to be made in days or months and to proceed accordingly when answering examination questions.

EXAMPLE 4

A company makes up accounts for the 21 months to 30 September 2000. The company's results for this period of account are as follows (all figures are shown gross) :

	£
Trading income (before capital allowances)	630,000
Non-trade loan interest receivable :	
Received 31 October 1999	600
Received 30 April 2000	600
Accrued to 30 September 2000	500
Chargeable gains :	
Disposal on 25 May 1999	2,300
Disposal on 12 December 1999	700
Disposal on 15 February 2000	10,500
Charges on income :	
Paid 31 December 1999	4,000
Accrued to 30 September 2000	3,000

The loan interest receivable relates to a £12,000 loan made on 1 May 1999 at an interest rate of 10% p.a. Show how the period of account will be divided into accounting periods and compute the company's chargeable profits for each accounting period (ignoring capital allowances).

SOLUTION

The period of account is divided into two accounting periods i.e. the 12 months to 31 December 1999 and the 9 months to 30 September 2000. The chargeable profits for each accounting period are as follows :

	12 months to 31/12/99 £	9 months to 30/9/00 £
Trading income (12/21th, 9/21th)	360,000	270,000
Loan interest receivable	800	900
Chargeable gains	3,000	10,500
	363,800	281,400
Less : Charges on income	4,000	nil
Chargeable profits	359,800	281,400

Notes :

(i) The loan interest is allocated on the accruals basis. Interest on the loan accrues at £100 per month so the interest for the period from 1 May 1999 to 31 December 1999 (eight months) is £800 and the interest for the period from 1 January 2000 to 30 September 2000 (nine months) is £900.

(ii) The chargeable gains are allocated according to the date of disposal and the charges on income are allocated according to the date of payment. The charges accrued at 30 September 2000 are ignored for now but will be taken into account when computing the chargeable profits of the subsequent accounting period in which they are paid.

Summary

▶ Corporation tax is charged on the profits of UK resident companies. The term "company" includes clubs, societies and other unincorporated associations.

▶ Corporation tax is charged in respect of accounting periods. An accounting period can never be more than 12 months in length. Accounts covering a period exceeding 12 months are divided into two or more accounting periods.

▶ A company's chargeable profits consist of its income and capital gains, less charges on income.

▶ A company's Schedule D Case III income consists mainly of net credits on non-trading loan relationships. Income and expenditure relating to loan relationships entered into for trade purposes is taken into account when computing Schedule D Case I income.

▶ A company's property income is assessed in a similar way to the property income of an individual. However, interest payable on a loan for the purchase or improvement of property is dealt with under the loan relationships rules. Schedule A loss reliefs available to a company are different from those available to an individual.

▶ Income received net of basic rate income tax is known as "unfranked investment income" (UFII). The gross equivalent of the UFII received in an accounting period forms part of the chargeable profits for that period.

▶ Dividends received from other UK companies (plus the attached tax credits) are known as "franked investment income" (FII) and do not form part of the chargeable profits of the receiving company.

▶ The CGT reforms which were introduced by the Finance Act 1998 do not apply to corporation tax.

▶ A company's charges on income consist mainly of qualifying donations under the Gift Aid scheme (paid gross as from 1 April 2000) and patent royalties (paid net of basic rate income tax). Charges are relieved on the payments basis.

Exercises

23.1 Identify the accounting periods relating to the following periods of account :

(a) year to 30 November 2000

(b) 1 October 1999 to 31 July 2000

(c) 1 January 2001 to 31 January 2001

(d) 33 months to 31 August 2000

(e) 1 April 1999 to 30 September 2000.

23.2 On 1 January 2001, a company receives debenture interest of £1,280 (net of income tax) and pays debenture interest of £8,640 (net of income tax).

(a) Outline the corporation tax treatment of each of these items.

(b) Explain how each of these items would appear in the company's accounts.

23.3 During the year to 31 March 2001, a company receives gross interest of £1,500 on its holding of Government securities. Describe the corporation tax treatment of this item.

23.4 A company's accounts for the 17 months to 30 June 2000 include :

	£
Trading income	425,000
Debenture interest (gross amounts) :	
Received 31 October 1999	2,400
Received 30 April 2000	2,400
Accrued to 30 June 2000	800
Income from property (let in 1996)	9,010
Chargeable gains :	
Disposal on 31 January 2000	28,700
Disposal on 1 February 2000	49,760
Dividend received from UK company	10,000
Patent royalties paid net (gross amounts) :	
Paid 31 July 1999	6,000
Paid 31 January 2000	6,000
Accrued to 30 June 2000	5,000

The debentures were acquired (not for trade purposes) on 1 May 1999. Interest is payable half-yearly on 30 April and 31 October. Show how the company's period of account will be divided into accounting periods and compute the chargeable profits for each accounting period.

23.5 A company has the following results for the year to 31 March 2001 :

	£	£
Trading profits, after capital allowances		1,549,400
Bank deposit interest (account opened 1/4/00) :		
Received 30 June 2000		19,820
Received 31 December 2000		44,670
Accrued to 31 March 2001		23,980
Chargeable gain on sale of factory		531,000
Dividends received from UK companies		132,000
Patent royalties receivable (net amounts) :		
Accrued to 31 March 2000		924
Received 28 February 2001		9,360
Accrued to 31 March 2001		1,404
Deed of covenant payable to charity (gross amounts)		
Paid 1 October 2000, for year to 30 September 2001	9,000	
<u>Less</u> : Prepayment	4,500	4,500

Compute the company's chargeable profits for the year.

*23.6 A company's profit and loss account for the year to 31 March 2001 is as follows :

	£	£
Gross trading profit		373,870
Receivable from other UK companies :		
Dividends		4,000
Debenture interest (Notes 1,8)		6,000
Bank interest receivable (Note 2)		12,600
Income from property (Note 3)		4,000
Profit on sale of investments (Note 4)		22,490
		422,960
Less :		
Distribution costs (all allowable)	97,500	
Administrative expenses (all allowable)	101,150	
Directors' fees	50,000	
Interest on bank overdraft	23,780	
Debenture interest payable (Notes 5,8)	50,000	
Patent royalties payable (Notes 6,8)	7,500	
Depreciation	108,300	438,230
Net loss for the year		15,270

Notes :

1. The company acquired £240,000 of 10% debentures (for non-trade purposes) on 1 January 2001. Interest is receivable half-yearly on 30 June and 31 December. No interest was received during the year to 31 March 2001.

2. Bank interest receivable includes interest of £1,450 which had accrued at 31 March 2001 but which was not received until April 2001. There was no accrued interest at 31 March 2000.

3. The property was let on 1 December 2000 at a rent of £1,000 per month payable quarterly in advance on 1 December, 1 March, 1 June and 1 September. There were no allowable expenses in the year to 31 March 2001.

4. The agreed chargeable gain on the sale of the investments was £8,450.

5. £500,000 of 10% debentures were issued (for trade purposes) on 1 April 2000. The interest is payable annually on 1 January.

6. As from 1 July 2000, the company is required to pay patent royalties of £10,000 per annum. The net amount actually paid in the year to 31 March 2001 (all after 5 April 2000) was £3,900.

7. Capital allowances of £32,700 are claimed for the year.

8. Debenture interest and patent royalties were received or paid net of income tax. The figures given above are gross.

Compute the company's chargeable profits for the year.

Chapter 24

Computation and payment of the corporation tax liability

Introduction

Having ascertained a company's chargeable profits for an accounting period, the next step is to compute the corporation tax liability arising in that period. The purpose of this chapter is to describe the way in which the corporation tax liability is computed and to explain the system by means of which the tax is collected.

Corporation tax financial years

A corporation tax financial year (FY) runs from 1 April to the following 31 March and is identified by the year in which it *begins*. For example, FY1999 ran from 1 April 1999 to 31 March 2000 and FY2000 runs from 1 April 2000 to 31 March 2001. The income tax year (6 April to the following 5 April) is largely irrelevant when dealing with corporation tax matters.

The rates of corporation tax are fixed for each financial year, so if an accounting period coincides with an FY (the year to 31 March) or is entirely contained within an FY (e.g. the 6 months to 31 October) the computation of the tax liability for the period is very straightforward. The appropriate rate of corporation tax for the FY in question is applied to the chargeable profits for the accounting period, giving the corporation tax liability.

If an accounting period straddles 31 March, the chargeable profits for the period have to be time-apportioned between the two FY's involved and then charged to tax at the rates applicable to each FY. It may seem obvious that this apportionment will be required only if corporation tax rates have changed from one FY to the next. However, the amount of tax payable for each FY has to be calculated separately in order to ascertain the figures required for the company's tax return (see later in this chapter). It is important to note that a simple time-apportionment is always made in these circumstances. This differs from the method described in Chapter 23 for the apportionment between accounting periods of the income, gains and charges of long periods of account.

EXAMPLE 1

A company has chargeable profits of £5,000,000 for an accounting period. Explain how the corporation tax liability for this period will be calculated if :

(a) the accounting period is the 12 months to 31 March 2001

(b) the accounting period is the 9 months to 31 January 2001

(c) the accounting period is the 10 months to 31 October 2000.

SOLUTION

(a) The 12 months to 31 March 2001 coincide with FY2000, so the chargeable profits of £5,000,000 will be charged to corporation tax at the rates applicable to FY2000.

(b) The 9 months to 31 January 2001 are entirely contained within FY2000, so the chargeable profits of £5,000,000 will be charged to corporation tax at the rates applicable to FY2000.

(c) The 10 months to 31 October 2000 are contained partly within FY1999 (3 months) and partly within FY2000 (7 months). The chargeable profits of £5,000,000 will be apportioned between FY's as follows :

FY1999	1 Jan 2000 to 31 March 2000	£5,000,000 x 3/10	= £1,500,000
FY2000	1 April 2000 to 31 Oct 2000	£5,000,000 x 7/10	= £3,500,000

The profits of £1,500,000 falling into FY1999 will be taxed at FY1999 rates whilst the profits of £3,500,000 falling into FY2000 will be taxed at FY2000 rates.

Rates of corporation tax

There are currently three rates of corporation tax, known as the *starting rate*, the *small companies rate* and the *full rate*. For FY2000, these rates are 10%, 20% and 30%. The rate which applies to a company for an accounting period depends upon the amount of the company's profits for that period and is determined as follows :

(a) The starting rate applies to companies with profits not exceeding the *starting rate lower limit* (£10,000 for FY2000).

(b) The small companies rate applies to companies with profits which lie between the *starting rate lower limit* and the *small companies rate lower limit* (£300,000 for FY2000). But the tax liability is reduced by an amount known as "marginal relief" if profits do not exceed the *starting rate upper limit* (£50,000 for FY2000). The marginal relief calculation is explained later in this chapter.

(c) The full rate applies to companies with profits which exceed the *small companies rate lower limit*. But the tax liability is reduced by marginal relief if profits do not exceed the *small companies rate upper limit* (£1,500,000 for FY2000).

It is important to appreciate that the applicable rate of corporation tax is applied to the *whole* of a company's chargeable profits. This differs from the income tax system, in which each band of an individual's income is taxed at a different rate.

In FY1999 and earlier years, the starting rate (and limits) did not exist. In those years, companies with profits not exceeding the small companies rate lower limit were simply charged to tax at the small companies rate. Recent corporation tax rates and limits have been as follows :

	Starting rate	*Small companies rate*	*Full rate*	*Starting rate limits*		*Small companies rate limits*	
				Lower	*Upper*	*Lower*	*Upper*
				£	£	£	£
FY1994	-	25%	33%	-	-	300,000	1,500,000
FY1995	-	25%	33%	-	-	300,000	1,500,000
FY1996	-	24%	33%	-	-	300,000	1,500,000
FY1997	-	21%	31%	-	-	300,000	1,500,000
FY1998	-	21%	31%	-	-	300,000	1,500,000
FY1999	-	20%	30%	-	-	300,000	1,500,000
FY2000	10%	20%	30%	10,000	50,000	300,000	1,500,000

Note that :

(a) The upper and lower limits are reduced pro rata if the accounting period (or the part of the period that falls into the FY) is of less than 12 months' duration.

(b) It has been announced that the full rate of corporation tax will remain at 30% for FY2001.

Profits and chargeable profits

The profits which are compared with the upper and lower limits in order to determine the applicable rate of corporation tax are *not* the company's chargeable profits. For this purpose alone, the term "profits" is defined as the company's chargeable profits plus its franked investment income. Even though FII is not charged to corporation tax, the FII received by a company *is* taken into account when determining the rate of tax which the company should pay. The process of calculating a company's corporation tax liability for an accounting period involves the following steps :

(a) The chargeable profits (or "basic profits") for the period are calculated.

(b) The "profits" figure is calculated by adding on any FII for the period.

(c) The profits figure calculated at (b) is used to determine the applicable rate of corporation tax. That rate is then applied to the company's chargeable profits.

(d) If the accounting period straddles 31 March, chargeable profits and profits are both time-apportioned between the two FY's involved and a separate computation is performed for each FY. The results of these two tax computations are then aggregated to give the corporation tax liability for the period.

EXAMPLE 2

Four companies each prepare a set of accounts for the year to 31 March 2001. Calculate the corporation tax liability of each company, given that :

(a) A Ltd has chargeable profits of £2,000,000 and has received no UK dividends
(b) B Ltd has chargeable profits of £143,000 and UK dividends of £9,000
(c) C Ltd has chargeable profits of £282,500 and UK dividends of £1,125,000
(d) D Ltd has chargeable profits of £7,500 and UK dividends of £270.

SOLUTION

	(a) £	(b) £	(c) £	(d) £
Chargeable profits	2,000,000	143,000	282,500	7,500
FII (UK dividends + tax credits)	0	10,000	1,250,000	300
Profits	2,000,000	153,000	1,532,500	7,800
Applicable rate of corporation tax	30%	20%	30%	10%
Corporation tax liability :				
£2,000,000 @ 30%	£600,000			
£143,000 @ 20%		£28,600		
£282,500 @ 30%			£84,750	
£7,500 @ 10%				£750

Notes :

(i) Each company's accounting period coincides with FY2000. Therefore the limits and rates of tax used are those for FY2000.
(ii) All of the dividends have an attached tax credit of 1/9th (see Chapter 2).
(iii) In each case, the profits figure is used to determine the applicable rate of tax but this rate is then applied to the chargeable profits.

EXAMPLE 3

D Ltd has chargeable profits of £7,040 for the 11 months to 30 November 2000 and received a UK dividend of £99 on 30 June 2000. Calculate the corporation tax liability for this period.

SOLUTION

The company has chargeable profits of £7,040. FII is £110 (£99 + tax credit £11) so profits are £7,150 for the 11-month accounting period. 3 months of this period fall into FY1999 and the remaining 8 months fall into FY2000. Chargeable profits, profits, the lower limits and the upper limits are apportioned between the two FY's as follows :

	FY1999 (1/1/00 to 31/3/00)	*FY2000 (1/4/00 to 30/11/00)*
Chargeable	£7,040 x 3/11 = £1,920	£7,040 x 8/11 = £5,120
Profits	£7,150 x 3/11 = £1,950	£7,150 x 8/11 = £5,200
SR limits:		
Lower limit	-	£10,000 x 8/12 = £6,667
Upper limit	-	£50,000 x 8/12 = £33,333
SCR limits:		
Lower limit	£300,000 x 3/12 = £75,000	£300,000 x 8/12 = £200,000
Upper limit	£1,500,000 x 3/12 = £375,000	£1,500,000 x 8/12 = £1,000,000

Notes :

(i)   The date on which the FII was received is irrelevant to the apportionment process.

(ii) Profits are less than the small companies rate lower limit in FY1999 and less than the starting rate lower limit in FY2000.

(iii) The corporation tax liability for the period is 20% x £1,920 + 10% x £5,120 = £896.00.

(iv) Given the modest size of the company's profits for the 11 months, it was fairly obvious in this case that the small companies rate would apply in FY1999 and that the starting rate would apply in FY2000. Realising this would have saved the effort of apportioning the lower and upper limits between the two FY's.

Marginal relief

As explained earlier, a company's tax liability is reduced by an amount known as the "marginal relief" if either :

(a) the company's profits fall between the starting rate lower limit and the starting rate upper limit (in which case the tax liability is calculated at the small companies rate, less marginal relief), or

(b) the company's profits fall between the small companies rate lower limit and the small companies rate upper limit (in which case the tax liability is calculated at the full rate, less marginal relief).

In each case, the marginal relief (or "taper relief") is calculated according to the following formula :

$$\text{fraction} \ \text{x} \ (M - P) \ \text{x} \ \frac{I}{P}$$

where : M = the relevant upper limit
P   = profits
I   = chargeable profits.

The fraction used in this formula (the "marginal relief fraction") is set for each FY and is 1/40 for FY2000. The fraction was also 1/40 in FY1997, FY1998 and FY1999. It was 9/400 in FY1996 and was 1/50 in FY1991 through to FY1995.

EXAMPLE 4

(a) A company makes up accounts annually to 31 March. In the year to 31 March 2001, the company has chargeable profits of £30,000 and no FII. Compute the corporation tax liability for the year.

(b) Another company has chargeable profits of £975,000 for the year to 31 March 2001 and FII of £50,000. Compute the corporation tax liability for the year.

SOLUTION

(a) The company's profits are £30,000, a figure which lies between the starting rate lower limit and the starting rate upper limit for FY2000. Therefore the chargeable profits (also £30,000) are taxed at the small companies rate and marginal relief is available. The computation is as follows :

	£
Corporation tax on £30,000 @ 20%	6,000.00
<u>Less</u> : Marginal relief :	
$\frac{1}{40}$ x (£50,000 - £30,000) x $\frac{£30,000}{£30,000}$	500.00
Corporation tax liability	5,500.00

(b) The company's profits are £1,025,000 (£975,000 + £50,000), which lie between the small companies rate lower and upper limits for FY2000. The chargeable profits (£975,000) are taxed at the full rate and marginal relief is available. The computation is as follows :

	£
Corporation tax on £975,000 @ 30%	292,500.00
<u>Less</u> : Marginal relief :	
$\frac{1}{40}$ x (£1,500,000 - £1,025,000) x $\frac{£975,000}{£1,025,000}$	11,295.73
Corporation tax liability	281,204.27

Marginal rate

The above example shows that the marginal relief formula seems to be achieving its object. This is to set a corporation tax rate (in FY2000) of somewhere between 10% and 20% for companies whose profits lie between the starting rate lower and upper limits and somewhere between 20% and 30% for companies whose profits lie between the small companies rate lower and upper limits. In the first part of the example, tax of £5,500 on chargeable profits of £30,000 gives a tax rate of 18.33%. In the second part, tax of £281,204.27 on chargeable profits of £975,000 gives a tax rate of 28.84%.

However, if a company's profits lie between the starting rate lower and upper limits, each extra £1 of chargeable profits gives rise to an extra 22.5p of corporation tax. For instance, if the first company in the above example had a further £2 of chargeable profits, its tax liability would increase by 45p (the calculation is left to the reader). So a *marginal rate* of 22.5% applies in these circumstances, higher than the small companies rate of 20%. Similarly, a company with profits which lie between the small companies rate lower and upper limits is subject to a marginal rate of 32.5%, which is higher than the full rate of 30%.

Marginal relief when accounting period straddles 31 March

If an accounting period straddles 31 March it is necessary to apportion profits and chargeable profits between the two FY's involved and calculate the corporation tax liability separately for each FY. Marginal relief creates no new problems in these circumstances, as illustrated by the following example.

EXAMPLE 5

In the year ended 31 December 2000, a company has chargeable profits of £37,500 and FII of £2,500. Compute the corporation tax liability for the year.

SOLUTION

The company has chargeable profits for the accounting period of £37,500 and profits of £40,000 (£37,500 + £2,500). Apportionment between the two FY's is as follows :

	FY1999 (1/1/00 to 31/3/00)	FY2000 (1/4/00 to 31/12/00)
Chargeable	£37,500 x 3/12 = £9,375	£37,500 x 9/12 = £28,125
Profits	£40,000 x 3/12 = £10,000	£40,000 x 9/12 = £30,000
SR limits:		
Lower limit	-	£10,000 x 9/12 = £7,500
Upper limit	-	£50,000 x 9/12 = £37,500
SCR limits:		
Lower limit	£300,000 x 3/12 = £75,000	£300,000 x 9/12 = £225,000
Upper limit	£1,500,000 x 3/12 = £375,000	£1,500,000 x 9/12 = £1,125,000

In FY1999, profits are beneath the small companies rate lower limit. In FY2000, profits are between the starting rate lower and upper limits. The computation is as follows :

	£	£
FY1999		
Corporation tax on £9,375 @ 20%		1,875.00
FY2000		
Corporation tax on £28,125 @ 20%	5,625.00	
Less : Marginal relief :		
$\frac{1}{40}$ x (£37,500 - £30,000) x $\frac{£28,125}{£30,000}$	175.78	5,449.22
		_____
Corporation tax liability		7,324.22

Corporate Venturing Scheme

As from 1 April 2000, one way in which a company might reduce its corporation tax liability is by making an investment under the Corporate Venturing Scheme. Under the terms of this scheme, which applies for FY2000 onwards, a company (the "investing company") which subscribes for new ordinary shares in a small unlisted trading company (the "issuing company") may qualify for a number of tax reliefs. These are :

(a) relief against corporation tax ("investment relief") equal to 20% of the amount invested, so long as the shares are held for at least 3 years

(b) deferral of the tax due on any gain made on a subsequent disposal of the shares, so long as the amount of the gain is re-invested in another shareholding which qualifies under the scheme

(c) relief against income for any capital loss which arises on a disposal of the shares.

For these tax reliefs to be available, the issuing company must satisfy certain criteria. These are similar to those which apply for the purposes of the Enterprise Investment Scheme (see Chapter 6). Basically, the gross assets of the issuing company must be no more than £15 million immediately before the investment is made and no more than £16 million immediately afterwards. Also, the issuing company must carry on a "qualifying trade". This term excludes certain activities such as share dealing, banking and property development. Finally, at least 20% of the issuing company's ordinary shares must be held by individuals and the investing company's stake in the issuing company must not exceed 30%.

Due date of payment

A company's corporation tax liability for an accounting period is generally payable by means of a single payment which is due nine months and one day after the end of that period. But for accounting periods ending on or after 1 July 1999, large companies are required to pay their corporation tax by instalments. The instalments system is outlined below.

EXAMPLE 6

(a) A company's period of account is the year to 31 July 2000. When is the corporation tax liability for this period due for payment ?

(b) A company's period of account is the 18 months to 31 December 2000. When is the corporation tax liability for this period due for payment ?

Assume in both cases that the company is not required to pay by instalments.

SOLUTION

(a) The year to 31 July 2000 is a single accounting period. Tax is payable on 1 May 2001.

(b) This period of account breaks down into two accounting periods. The corporation tax for the year to 30 June 2000 is due on 1 April 2001. The corporation tax for the 6 months to 31 December 2000 is due on 1 October 2001.

Payment by instalments

Large companies are required to pay corporation tax by instalments for accounting periods ending on or after 1 July 1999. The main features of the instalments system are as follows :

(a) A "large company" for this purpose is generally defined as one which pays corporation tax at the full rate, without deduction of marginal relief. However, a company does *not* have to pay tax by instalments for an accounting period if :

    (i) it has a tax liability of less than £10,000 for the period (£5,000 for periods ending before 1 July 2000) but pays tax at the full rate, either because it has substantial amounts of dividend income or because it has a number of associated companies (see Chapter 28), or

    (ii) it has chargeable profits of £10 million or less for the accounting period and was not a large company in the 12 months preceding that period.

(b) Instalment payments are based on the company's own estimate of its corporation tax liability for the accounting period. When the tax liability for the year is finalised, the company is charged interest on any underpaid instalments and is paid interest on any overpaid instalments.

(c) For a 12-month accounting period there are four equal instalments. The first instalment falls due on the 14th day of the 7th month of the accounting period. The remaining three instalments then fall due at quarterly intervals. For instance, if the accounting period is the year to 31 December 2000, instalments fall due on 14 July 2000, 14 October 2000, 14 January 2001 and 14 April 2001.

If an accounting period is of less than 12 months' duration, there are as many quarterly instalments as can be fitted in, starting with the date which is 6 months and 13 days after the start of the period and ending with the date which is 3 months and 14 days after the end of the period. For instance, if the accounting period is the 6 months to 30 September 2000, corporation tax is payable in two equal instalments on 14 October 2000 and 14 January 2001.

(d) Payment by instalments is being phased-in over a four-year period, as indicated by the following table :

Last day of accounting period	% of liability payable by instalments
1 July 1999 - 30 June 2000	60%
1 July 2000 - 30 June 2001	72%
1 July 2001 - 30 June 2002	88%
1 July 2002 onwards	100%

Any tax not payable by instalments is payable nine months and one day after the end of the accounting period.

Self Assessment

Self Assessment for companies was announced in 1998 and took effect for accounting periods ending on or after 1 July 1999. The new system built upon the "Pay and File" system which it replaced and is similar in many ways to Self Assessment for individuals (see Chapter 1). The main features of Self Assessment for companies are as follows :

(a) On the issue of a notice (form CT603) by the Inland Revenue, a company must file a corporation tax return (form CT600) for the period specified in the notice, together with supporting accounts and computations. The return is made up of a basic 12-page form, together with any necessary supplementary pages. There are supplementary pages for such matters as loans to participators by close companies (see Chapter 27), group relief claims (see Chapter 28) and controlled foreign companies (see Chapter 32). This return must normally be filed by the *latest* of the following dates :

(i) 12 months after the end of the period specified in the notice

(ii) 12 months after the end of the period of account in which the last day of the specified period falls (but periods of account which last for more than 18 months are treated for this purpose as ending after 18 months)

(iii) 3 months after issue of the notice.

Most companies prepare their accounts to the same date each year and notices are usually issued within a few weeks of the end of each period of account, so that the required filing date is normally 12 months after the end of the period of account. There is nothing to prevent a company from submitting an early return.

(b) The CT600 return includes a formal self-assessment of the company's tax liability for the accounting period covered by the return. Unlike individuals, a company is *not* able to ask the Inland Revenue to calculate the tax liability.

(c) The Inland Revenue has the right to repair a company's self-assessment (i.e. to correct any obvious errors or omissions) within 9 months of the date on which the company files the return. Similarly, the company has the right to amend its return and self-assessment within 12 months of the required filing date for that return. A company which detects an error in its tax return after these 12 months have expired may make an "error or mistake" claim to recover any overpaid tax within six years of the end of the relevant accounting period.

(d) A company which is chargeable to corporation tax for an accounting period but has not received a notice requiring submission of a return must notify the Inland Revenue of its chargeability to tax within 12 months of the end of the period.

(e) Unless the Inland Revenue makes an enquiry into a company's tax return, the company's tax position for the accounting period may usually be regarded as finalised 12 months after the required filing date for that return. However, the Inland Revenue may raise a "discovery assessment" after these 12 months have elapsed if it discovers that insufficient tax has been assessed. In general, no such assessment can be made later than 6 years after the end of the accounting period to which it relates, but this period is extended to 21 years in the case of fraud or negligence on the part of the company or a person acting for the company.

(f) If a company fails to file a return by the required date, the Inland Revenue may make a determination of the amount of tax due. A determination can be displaced only if the company delivers the required return. (There is no right of appeal against a determination).

(g) A company is required to keep and preserve adequate records to substantiate the information entered on its tax return. These records must be retained for at least six years after the end of the accounting period concerned.

(h) Appeals are heard by the General or Special Commissioners (see Chapter 1) and may then progress to the courts.

Interest and penalties

Interest on underpaid corporation tax runs from the date on which the tax should have been paid until the date on which it is actually paid. The rate at which the interest is calculated rises and falls in line with base rates. Interest on overpaid corporation tax is calculated at a lower rate than interest on underpaid tax and runs from the "material date" until the date of the repayment. The material date is the date on which the tax was originally paid or (if later) the date on which it was due to be paid. For accounting periods ending on or after 1 July 1999 :

(a) Interest receivable on a repayment of overpaid corporation tax is taxable as a credit arising from a non-trading loan relationship. Similarly, interest payable on underpaid corporation tax is deductible as a non-trading debit.

(b) The gap between the interest rates applicable to underpaid corporation tax and overpaid corporation tax is reduced for the period between the due date of the first instalment for a large company and the date which falls nine months and one day after the end of the accounting period concerned.

(c) If a company makes instalment payments on the assumption that it is a large company and this assumption later proves to be false, interest on any repaid instalments runs from the date on which a truly large company would have paid those instalments (or from the actual date of payment, if later).

(d) If a repayment of *income tax* is made to a company for an accounting period (see Chapter 25), interest on this repayment runs from the end of the accounting period concerned. (For accounting periods ending before 1 July 1999, interest on a repayment of income tax ran from the date which fell nine months after the end of the period).

EXAMPLE 7

(a) Hay Ltd calculates its corporation tax liability for the year to 30 September 2000 as £250,000 and pays this amount on the due date. The correct liability for the year eventually turns out to be £274,000 and the company pays a further £24,000 on 12 September 2001. Calculate the interest payable by Hay Ltd (assuming an interest rate of 8.5% per annum).

(b) Bee Ltd also calculates its corporation tax liability for the year to 30 September 2000 as £250,000 and also pays this amount on the due date. The correct liability for the year eventually turns out to be only £193,000. The necessary repayment is made on 18 December 2001. Calculate the interest payable to Bee Ltd (assuming an interest rate of 5% per annum).

Neither company is a large company for the purposes of payment by instalments.

SOLUTION

(a) The due date is 1 July 2001 (9 months and 1 day after 30 September 2000). Most of the corporation tax was paid on this date but the final £24,000 was paid on 12 September 2001, 73 days late. The interest payable by the company is :

$$£24,000 \times 8.5\% \times \frac{73}{365} = £408.00.$$

(b) The overpaid tax of £57,000 was paid on the due date of 1 July 2001 and repaid on 18 December 2001, 170 days later. The interest payable to the company is :

$$£57,000 \times 5\% \times \frac{170}{365} = £1,327.40.$$

Penalties

Penalties are charged if a company does not file its CT600 tax return (together with the supporting accounts and computations) by the required date, normally 12 months after the end of the accounting period. These penalties are as follows :

(a) If the return is up to 3 months late, a fixed penalty of £100 is charged, increased to £500 for a third consecutive late return.

(b) If the return is over 3 months late, a fixed penalty of £200 is charged, increased to £1,000 for a third consecutive late return.

(c) In addition to the above penalties, a further tax-geared penalty is charged if the return is submitted more than 6 months late. In these circumstances the penalty is expressed as a percentage of the amount of tax outstanding at the end of the 6 months, as follows :

   (i) If the return is made between 6 and 12 months late, the penalty is 10% of the tax outstanding 6 months after the return was due.

   (ii) If the return is made more than 12 months late, the penalty rises to 20% of the tax outstanding 6 months after the return was due.

Penalties may also arise in the following circumstances :

(d) If a company which has neither filed a return nor been issued with a notice fails to notify the Inland Revenue of its chargeability to corporation tax within 12 months of the end of the accounting period, a penalty may be charged of up to 100% of the tax which remains unpaid 12 months after the end of the period.

(e) If a company fraudulently or negligently submits an incorrect return (or fails to rectify an error which it has detected in a return) a penalty may be charged of up to 100% of the tax lost.

(f) A company which fails to keep and preserve adequate records is liable to a penalty of up to £3,000.

EXAMPLE 8

A company makes up accounts to 31 July. It calculates its corporation tax liability for the year to 31 July 1999 at £180,000 and pays this sum on 1 May 2000. Despite being issued with a notice by the Inland Revenue in August 1999, the company fails to submit its return for the year to 31 July 1999 until 31 March 2001. The corporation tax liability for the year was finally assessed at £206,000. Calculate the penalties that would be charged.

SOLUTION

The return was made 8 months late and tax of £26,000 was still outstanding 6 months after the return was due. Assuming that the company is not a persistent offender, a fixed penalty of £200 would be charged, together with a tax-geared penalty of £2,600 (10% of £26,000). Interest would also be charged on the unpaid tax.

Summary

▶ A corporation tax financial year runs from 1 April to the following 31 March.

▶ There are currently three rates of corporation tax. These are the starting rate, the small companies rate and the full rate.

▶ The rate of corporation tax which applies to a company for a given accounting period depends upon the company's profits (including FII) for that period.

▶ Marginal relief eases the transition from the starting rate to the small companies rate and from the small companies rate to the full rate.

▶ A company which subscribes for new ordinary shares in a small unlisted trading company under the terms of the Corporate Venturing Scheme may qualify for a reduction in its corporation tax liability.

▶ The due date of payment for corporation tax is normally nine months and one day after the end of the accounting period. Large companies are required to pay their tax by instalments. Interest is charged on underpaid tax and is paid on refunds of overpaid tax.

▶ Self Assessment for companies was introduced for accounting periods ending on or after 1 July 1999. The system is similar in many ways to Self Assessment for individuals.

▶ Companies are usually required to file a CT600 return within 12 months of the end of each period of account. Late submission results in a penalty fine and there are penalties for various other infringements of the Self Assessment regulations.

Exercises

24.1   A company has chargeable profits of £30,000 for the year to 30 June 2000. Show how these profits will be apportioned between corporation tax financial years.

24.2   Four companies each have an accounting year ending on 31 March 2001. Compute the corporation tax liability of each company, given the following information :

(a)   Company A has chargeable profits of £267,000 and UK dividends of £18,450.

(b)   Company B has chargeable profits of £1,450,000 and UK dividends of £49,500.

(c)   Company C has chargeable profits of £10,000,000 and no UK dividends.

(d)   Company D has chargeable profits of £1,000 and no UK dividends.

24.3   A company has chargeable profits of £536,000 for the year to 31 March 2001 and UK dividends of £36,900 received in June 2000. Compute the corporation tax liability.

24.4   Compute the corporation tax liability of each of the following companies for the year to 28 February 2001 :

(a)   Company X has chargeable profits of £875,983 and FII of £32,800.

(b)   Company Y has chargeable profits of £25,000 and no FII.

24.5   A company calculates its corporation tax liability for the year to 31 August 1999 as £120,000 and pays this amount on 1 June 2000. The company's CT600 return is submitted during August 2000 and the tax liability for the year is finalised at £124,650. The balance of £4,650 is paid on 3 October 2000. The company is not a large company for the purposes of payment by instalments. Calculate the interest payable (assuming an interest rate of 8.5% per annum).

*24.6   A company has the following results for the year to 31 March 2001 :

	£
Trading profits, less capital allowances	349,782
Bank deposit interest :	
Received 31 December 2000	9,957
Accrued to 31 March 2001	3,000
Patent royalties received in June 2000 (net amount)	8,190
UK dividend received in January 2001	24,300
Chargeable gains	295,327
Patent royalties payable (net amounts) :	
Paid 30 November 2000	19,188
Accrued to 31 March 2001	6,396

Compute the company's corporation tax liability for the year.

*24.7   A company has the following results for the 14 months to 31 December 2000 :

	£
Trading profits, before deduction of capital allowances	1,413,508
Capital allowances claimed :	
Year to 31 October 2000	222,650
2 months to 31 December 2000	37,210
Capital gains :	
Disposal 12 May 2000	16,575
Disposal 6 November 2000	17,492
Building society interest :	
Received 31 December 1999	3,500
Received 31 December 2000	4,300
UK dividend received on 25 September 2000	3,150

Accrued building society interest was £3,000 on 31 October 1999, £4,000 on 31 October 2000 and £4,200 on 31 December 2000.

Compute the company's total corporation tax liability for the 14-month period.

Chapter 25

Income tax and advance corporation tax

Introduction

Companies are liable to corporation tax, not income tax. Therefore, companies which suffer income tax by deduction at source from any of their income are entitled to a repayment of the income tax suffered. Similarly, companies which deduct income tax at source from any of their payments must account for this income tax to the Inland Revenue. The first purpose of this chapter is to explain how the necessary repayments and payments of income tax are made.

Until 6 April 1999, companies were required to pay Advance Corporation Tax (ACT) when paying dividends or making other qualifying distributions. Subject to certain conditions, the ACT paid for an accounting period was generally treated as an advance payment of the corporation tax liability for that period, so reducing the amount of tax payable on the normal due date. ACT has been abolished with effect from 6 April 1999 but some aspects of the ACT system will linger on for many years to come. The second purpose of this chapter is to provide a brief description of the way in which the ACT system operated before abolition and then to explain the situation which applies as from 6 April 1999.

Income received net of income tax

As explained in Chapter 23, certain types of income received by a company are received net of income tax. A company receiving such income is able to reclaim the income tax deducted at source but the grossed-up amount of the income is then liable to corporation tax. The main sources of taxed income are as follows :

Type of income	Rate of income tax deducted at source
Patent royalties	basic rate
Debenture and other loan interest	lower rate
Gilt interest (if company opts to receive net interest)	lower rate

Patent royalties are assessed as UFII on the receipts basis. Debenture interest, loan interest and interest on gilt-edged securities are all assessed under the loan relationships system, usually on the accruals basis. But in all cases, the income tax which may be reclaimed for an accounting period is the amount of income tax suffered on the taxed income actually *received* during that period. Remember that companies (unlike individuals) receive their bank deposit interest and building society interest gross.

Gilt-edged securities

In general, the holders of gilt-edged securities receive their interest gross. But as from 6 April 1998, anyone receiving such interest may choose whether to receive the interest gross or net (see Chapter 2). Before 1 April 1999, companies receiving gross gilt interest were required to account to the Inland Revenue at quarterly intervals for the amount of income tax that would have been deducted if the interest had been received net. Many companies decided to opt for net interest so as to avoid involvement in this system. However, the abolition of quarterly accounting for gilt interest (QAGI) now makes it much more likely that a company will choose to receive its gilt interest gross.

Payments made net of income tax

Certain types of payment made by a company are made net of income tax. A company making such a payment must account to the Inland Revenue for the income tax deducted at source but the grossed-up amount of the payment is then granted relief in the company's corporation tax computation. The main types of payment made net of income tax are :

Type of payment	Rate of income tax deducted at source
Patent royalties	basic rate
Deeds of covenant to charities (until 1 April 2000)	basic rate
Other Gift Aid donations (until 1 April 2000)	basic rate
Debenture and other loan interest	lower rate

Patent royalties, covenanted payments to charities and other Gift Aid donations are all relieved as charges on income on the payments basis. Debenture and other loan interest is relieved under the loan relationships system, usually on the accruals basis. But in all cases, the income tax which must be accounted for to the Inland Revenue for an accounting period is the income tax deducted from the amounts actually *paid* during that period. The Gift Aid scheme now includes covenanted payments to charities and, as from 1 April 2000, companies making Gift Aid donations do so without deduction of tax at source.

The quarterly accounting system

Companies are required to make periodic (usually quarterly) returns to the Inland Revenue of the income tax deducted from payments and the income tax suffered on taxed income. A return, on form CT61, is required for :

(a) each of the four quarters ending on 31 March, 30 June, 30 September and 31 December which fall completely into an accounting period, and

(b) each part of an accounting period which does not comprise a complete quarter.

A company with an annual accounting date which coincides with one of the above four dates will make four returns each year but companies with any other accounting date will need to submit a fifth return each year. Each return must be submitted (and any tax due must be paid) within 14 days of the end of the period to which the return relates. Nil returns are not required.

EXAMPLE 1

(a) A company prepares accounts to 30 June each year. Identify the income tax return periods for the year to 30 June 2000.

(b) A company prepares accounts to 31 January each year. Identify the income tax return periods for the year to 31 January 2001.

SOLUTION

(a) The company's accounting date coincides with one of the four standard dates, so there will be four return periods each year. The return periods for the year to 30 June 2000 are 1/7/99 to 30/9/99, 1/10/99 to 31/12/99, 1/1/00 to 31/3/00 and 1/4/00 to 30/6/00.

(b) The company's accounting date does not coincide with one of the four standard dates, so there will be five return periods each year. The five return periods for the year to 31 January 2001 are 1/2/00 to 31/3/00, 1/4/00 to 30/6/00, 1/7/00 to 30/9/00, 1/10/00 to 31/12/00 and 1/1/01 to 31/1/01.

The quarterly procedure

The procedure adopted for each return period is as follows :

(a) The income tax suffered on taxed income received during the return period is subtracted from the income tax deducted from payments made during the return period. The result of this calculation is the excess of income tax deducted over income tax suffered (or vice-versa).

(b) The cumulative excess of income tax deducted over income tax suffered (or vice-versa) for the accounting period to date is then calculated.

(c) If there is a cumulative excess of income tax deducted over income tax suffered, this excess is compared with the total of the income tax payments made to the Inland Revenue in previous return periods during the same accounting period (if any) and the difference is payable by the company or repayable to the company.

(d) If there is a cumulative excess of income tax suffered over income tax deducted, then no income tax payment is required for the current return period and any payments made to the Inland Revenue in previous return periods during the same accounting period may be reclaimed. However, the excess itself is *not* repayable to the company but is carried forward to the next return period.

EXAMPLE 2

A company has the following payments made net of income tax and income received net of income tax for the year to 31 March 2001 (amounts are stated net) :

		Payments £	Income £
1 May 2000	Debenture interest paid	4,000	
5 July 2000	Patent royalties paid	780	
1 September 2000	Debenture interest received		6,000
1 November 2000	Debenture interest paid	4,000	
12 January 2001	Patent royalties paid	9,360	
31 March 2001	Loan interest received		1,600

Compute the amounts of income tax payable or repayable in each return period.

SOLUTION

Return period	Tax deducted £	Tax suffered £	Tax deducted less tax suffered £	Cumulative £	Income tax payable (repayable) £
1/4/00 - 30/6/00	1,000		1,000	1,000	1,000
1/7/00 - 30/9/00	220	1,500	(1,280)	(280)	(1,000)
1/10/00 - 31/12/00	1,000		1,000	720	720
1/1/01 - 31/3/01	2,640	400	2,240	2,960	2,240
	4,860	1,900	2,960		2,960

Notes :

(i) The net payments and the net income in each return period are grossed up at the appropriate rate to give the amounts of income tax deducted and suffered, as shown in the first two columns of the table. For each return period, the excess of tax deducted over tax suffered is shown in the third column. If tax suffered exceeds tax deducted, the figure is shown in parentheses. The cumulative total of tax deducted less tax suffered is shown in the fourth column.

(ii) At the end of the first return period, tax deducted exceeds tax suffered by £1,000, so £1,000 is due for payment on 14 July 2000.

(iii) At the end of the second return period, there is a cumulative excess of tax suffered over tax deducted of £280. The company now has no income tax liability for the accounting period to date and may reclaim the £1,000 paid in the previous return period. The excess tax suffered of £280 is *not* repayable to the company but the cumulative nature of the system ensures that this excess will automatically be taken into account in future return periods.

(iv) At the end of the third return period, there is a cumulative excess of tax deducted over tax suffered of £720. Since the tax paid in previous return periods is £nil (£1,000 paid less £1,000 reclaimed), income tax of £720 is due for payment on 14 January 2001.

(v) At the end of the fourth return period, there is a cumulative excess of tax deducted over tax suffered of £2,960. Since the tax paid in previous return periods is £720, income tax of £2,240 is due for payment on 14 April 2001.

(vi) Strictly speaking, calculations of income tax due and suffered should be made to the nearest penny. However, in the interests of clarity, pence have been omitted from the above table.

Tax suffered in excess of tax deducted

At the end of an accounting period, one of two possible situations will apply :

(a) The income tax deducted from payments made in the accounting period exceeds the income tax suffered on income received during that period. In this case, the excess will have been paid over to the Inland Revenue by virtue of the system described above and no further action is required.

(b) The income tax suffered on income received during the accounting period exceeds the income tax deducted from payments made in that period. In this case the quarterly system will not have provided the necessary income tax repayment.

EXAMPLE 3

A company has the following net payments and net income for the year to 31 March 2001 (amounts are stated net) :

		Payments £	Income £
1 April 2000	Debenture interest paid	8,000	
1 July 2000	Loan interest received		9,600
1 October 2000	Debenture interest paid	8,000	
1 January 2001	Loan interest received		9,600

Compute the amounts of income tax payable or repayable in each return period.

SOLUTION

Return period	Tax deducted	Tax suffered	Tax deducted less tax suffered	Cumulative	Income tax payable (repayable)
	£	£	£	£	£
1/4/00 - 30/6/00	2,000		2,000	2,000	2,000
1/7/00 - 30/9/00		2,400	(2,400)	(400)	(2,000)
1/10/00 - 31/12/00	2,000		2,000	1,600	1,600
1/1/01 - 31/3/01		2,400	(2,400)	(800)	(1,600)
	4,000	4,800	(800)		0

Note :

The income tax suffered exceeds the income tax deducted by £800 but the operation of the quarterly accounting system has not resulted in repayment of this income tax.

Set-off against corporation tax liability

If the amount of income tax suffered during an accounting period exceeds the amount of income tax deducted from payments, the required repayment of income tax is made by means of a reduction in the company's corporation tax liability for the accounting period in which the surplus arises. If this liability is less than the required repayment, the balance is repaid in cash.

EXAMPLE 4

In the year to 31 March 2001, a company receives net debenture interest of £40,000 and makes no payments net of income tax. Calculate the required income tax repayment and show how this repayment will be made if the company's corporation tax liability for the year is :

(a) £100,000

(b) £7,000.

The company is not a large company for the purposes of payment by instalments.

SOLUTION

(a) The required repayment is £40,000 x 20/80 = £10,000. This will be offset against the company's corporation tax liability payable on 1 January 2002, reducing this liability from £100,000 to £90,000.

(b) If the company's corporation tax liability for the year is only £7,000, this liability will be reduced to £nil and the remaining £3,000 will be repaid to the company in cash.

ACT before 6 April 1999

A company which made a "qualifying distribution" before 6 April 1999 was required to make a payment of ACT, calculated as a specified fraction of the amount of that distribution. By far the most common example of a qualifying distribution was the payment of a dividend, but other qualifying distributions included :

(a) any distribution in respect of shares in the company (other than a repayment of share capital) if the cost of the distribution was borne by the company

(b) any issue of redeemable share capital, unless the new issue was paid for otherwise than out of the assets of the company

(c) any payments of interest over and above interest calculated at a reasonable commercial rate

(d) certain bonus issues of shares

(e) the transfer of assets or liabilities between a company and its members at less than full market value.

For the remainder of this chapter, all references to "dividends" also refer to the other types of qualifying distribution.

The ACT fraction

The ACT payable in relation to a dividend paid before 6 April 1999 was calculated as a fraction of the amount of the dividend. For FY1994 (after 5 April 1994) through to FY1999 (up to 6 April 1999) the *ACT fraction* was linked to the lower rate of income tax and was set at 20/80. In other words, the amount of ACT payable was equal to one-quarter of the amount of the dividend. The amount of a dividend, plus the attributable ACT, was known as a "franked payment". For dividends paid between 6 April 1994 and 5 April 1999 :

(a) The franked payment was equal to the dividend paid multiplied by 100/80.

(b) The ACT attributable to a dividend could be expressed as 20% of the franked payment. Thus the *rate of ACT* was 20%.

EXAMPLE 5

On 3 April 1999, a company with an issued share capital of ten million £1 ordinary shares paid a dividend of 40p per share.

(a) Compute the amount of ACT payable in relation to this dividend.

(b) Compute the amount of the franked payment.

SOLUTION

(a) The amount of the dividend was £4,000,000. The ACT fraction for FY1999 (before 6 April 1999) was 20/80. Therefore the ACT payable in relation to the dividend was £4,000,000 x 20/80 = £1,000,000.

(b) The franked payment was £5,000,000 (i.e. the dividend plus the attributable ACT). The ACT payable could be expressed as 20% of £5,000,000 = £1,000,000.

Franked investment income

As explained in Chapter 23, the term "franked investment income" (FII) refers to the UK dividends received by a company, together with the attached tax credits. These tax credits cannot be paid to the company but, before 6 April 1999, they *could* be used to reduce the amount of ACT payable by the company. In essence, the FII for an accounting period was set against the franked payments made in that period and ACT was then payable only on the excess. Note the following points :

(a) The tax credit attached to a dividend received before 6 April 1999 was linked to the rate of ACT and was *not* equal to one-ninth of the amount of the dividend (as is now the case). For instance, the tax credit attached to a dividend received between 6 April 1994 and 5 April 1999 was equal to *one-quarter* of the amount of the dividend.

(b) The use of FII to reduce a company's ACT liability provided only a temporary form of tax relief. A reduction in the amount of ACT payable in the short term would result in a correspondingly greater payment on the normal due date.

(c) If there was an excess of FII over franked payments for an accounting period then the company had "surplus FII". There was no ACT liability in such an accounting period. Surplus FII was carried forward to the next accounting period and treated as if it were FII received on the first day of that period.

(d) Dividends received from foreign companies are not FII and could not be used to reduce the receiving company's ACT liability.

EXAMPLE 6

In the year to 31 March 1999, a company paid dividends totalling £6,000 and received UK dividends totalling £5,300. Compute the amount of ACT payable for the year.

SOLUTION

(i) Dividends paid were £6,000, so franked payments were £7,500 (£6,000 x 100/80).

(ii) Dividends received were £5,300, so FII was £6,625 (£5,300 + £1,325).

(iii) The excess of franked payments over FII was £875. Therefore the amount of ACT payable for the year was £175 (20% x £875).

EXAMPLE 7

In the year to 31 March 1998, a company paid dividends of £5,000 and received dividends (all from UK companies) of £9,000. In the year to 31 March 1999, the company paid dividends of £4,800 and received none. Compute the amounts of ACT payable for each year.

SOLUTION

In the year to 31 March 1998, franked payments were £6,250 (£5,000 x 100/80) and FII was £11,250 (£9,000 + £2,250). Therefore there was surplus FII of £5,000. There was no ACT liability for the year and surplus FII of £5,000 was carried forward to the following year.

In the year to 31 March 1999, the surplus FII brought forward was treated as if received on the first day of the year. Therefore FII for the year was £5,000. Franked payments were £6,000 (£4,800 x 100/80). The excess of franked payments over FII was £1,000, so ACT of £200 (20% x £1,000) was payable for the year.

Set-off of ACT

In general, the ACT paid for an accounting period ending before 6 April 1999 was treated as a payment on account of the company's tax liability for the period. However, there was an upper limit on the amount of ACT which could be set against the company's corporation tax liability. The *maximum ACT set-off* was equal to the amount of ACT which would be attributable to a franked payment equal in size to the company's entire chargeable profits. If the amount of ACT paid by a company in relation to an accounting period exceeded the maximum set-off allowed, the company had "surplus ACT" equal to the excess.

The corporation tax due to be paid on the normal due date (after deducting ACT) was known as "mainstream corporation tax" (MCT).

EXAMPLE 8

A company had chargeable profits of £100,000 for the year to 31 March 1999 and paid a dividend of £28,000 on 1 January 1999. No other dividends were paid or received during the year.

(a) Calculate the ACT payable for the year and the amount of any surplus ACT.

(b) Repeat the calculation, now assuming that the amount of the dividend was £88,000 rather than £28,000.

SOLUTION

(a) ACT payable for the year was £7,000 (£28,000 x 20/80). This is within the maximum ACT set-off of £20,000 (20% of £100,000) so there was no surplus ACT. The whole of the £7,000 could be set against the corporation tax liability for the year.

402

(b) ACT payable for the year was £22,000 (£88,000 x 20/80), exceeding the maximum ACT set-off. Only £20,000 of the £22,000 could be set against the corporation tax liability for the year and there was surplus ACT of £2,000.

Relief of surplus ACT

Surplus ACT arising in accounting periods ending before 6 April 1999 could be relieved in two main ways :

(a) Surplus ACT could be *carried back* and relieved against the corporation tax liability of accounting periods beginning in the six years prior to the period in which the surplus ACT arose. Relief was given in more recent years first.

(b) If no carry-back election was made (or if surplus ACT still remained after a carry-back election had been made) surplus ACT was *carried forward* and relieved against the corporation tax liability of the next accounting period. To the extent that it could not be relieved in that accounting period it could be carried forward again, without time limit, until it could eventually be relieved.

It is important to note that the total amount of ACT relieved in any accounting period (including any surplus ACT carried back from subsequent years or carried forward from previous years) could not exceed the maximum ACT set-off for that accounting period, calculated as described above.

Surplus ACT on a change of ownership

A company which incurred losses (or made fairly low profits) over a number of years prior to 6 April 1999 and yet managed to maintain dividend payments during those years may have accumulated a substantial amount of surplus ACT. Such a company could be a desirable acquisition, since a new owner could :

(a) use the company to operate a profitable business (perhaps very different in nature from the company's business before the acquisition), and then

(b) set the pre-acquisition surplus ACT against the tax payable on the post-acquisition profits, so avoiding liability to corporation tax.

Before 6 April 1999, this manoeuvre was prevented from succeeding by anti-avoidance legislation. If there was a change in the ownership of a company and certain conditions were satisfied, surplus ACT arising before the change in ownership could not be set against a corporation tax liability arising after the change. Nor could surplus ACT arising after the change be set against a corporation tax liability arising before it. The required conditions were that :

(a) a change in ownership and a major change in the nature or conduct of the company's business had both occurred within the same three-year period, or

(b) a change in ownership had occurred at a time when the company's business had become negligible and then (at any time after the change) there had been a revival of the company's business.

For this purpose, a change in ownership was deemed to occur if over half of the company's ordinary share capital was acquired either by one person or by a group of people, each acquiring at least a 5% shareholding.

This anti-avoidance legislation was repealed with effect from 6 April 1999 when ACT was abolished. However, the substance of the legislation is preserved in the "shadow ACT" regulations which apply as from 6 April 1999 (see below).

Abolition of ACT

As was stated at the beginning of this chapter, ACT has been abolished with effect from 6 April 1999. The main consequences of this abolition are as follows :

(a) No ACT is payable on a dividend (or other qualifying distribution) which is paid after 5 April 1999 and therefore no ACT liability can arise in connection with accounting periods which begin after that date.

(b) When calculating the ACT due on dividends paid before 6 April 1999, any FII received on or after that date cannot be taken into account.

(c) If an accounting period straddles 5 April 1999, it is divided into two "notional" accounting periods for ACT purposes and the company's chargeable profits are apportioned between these two periods. The maximum ACT set-off for the notional period to 5 April 1999 is 20% of the chargeable profits of that period.

(d) If a company has unrelieved surplus ACT at 6 April 1999, the extent to which the surplus may be relieved against future corporation tax liabilities is determined by the "shadow ACT" regulations (see below).

Shadow ACT

The legislation which allows surplus ACT to be carried forward and then set against the corporation tax liabilities of subsequent accounting periods has been repealed with effect from 6 April 1999. However, unrelieved surplus ACT existing on that date is dealt with by the "shadow ACT" system, which substantially preserves previous rights with regard to the carry-forward of surplus ACT. The main features of this system are as follows :

(a) The previous limit on the set-off of ACT is retained, so that a company may use ACT of up to 20% of chargeable profits to satisfy its corporation tax liability for an accounting period.

(b) The capacity for relieving ACT in an accounting period must first be filled by "shadow ACT", which is calculated in the way that real ACT would have been calculated on the dividends paid in the period if ACT had not been abolished but had continued at the rate of 20%. However, *shadow ACT does not result in any reduction in the corporation tax liability* for the period. All that it does is to reduce the scope for set-off of surplus ACT brought forward.

(c) When calculating the shadow ACT arising in an accounting period, the FII for that period must be multiplied by nine-eighths before being used in the computation. This is because the rate of tax credits on dividends was reduced from one-quarter to one-ninth as from 6 April 1999. For example, a UK dividend of £720 received before 6 April 1999 was equivalent to FII of £900. The same dividend received on or after that date is equivalent to FII of only £800. Therefore it is necessary to multiply the post-6/4/99 FII by nine-eighths to convert the FII figure to a pre-6/4/99 equivalent (£800 x 9/8 = £900).

(d) If there is still capacity for relieving ACT in an accounting period after shadow ACT has been deducted, this capacity may be used to relieve surplus ACT brought forward from before 6 April 1999. Subtracting surplus ACT results in an actual reduction in the corporation tax liability for the period.

(e) If the amount of shadow ACT for an accounting period exceeds the maximum ACT set-off for that period, then the company has "surplus shadow ACT". The consequences of this are as follows :

   (i) There is no scope for relieving real surplus ACT in such a period

   (ii) The surplus shadow ACT is first carried back to any accounting periods beginning in the previous six years (but not before 6 April 1999) in which shadow ACT has not filled the capacity available for relieving it. The carry-back is to more recent years in priority to earlier years.

   (iii) Carried-back surplus shadow ACT displaces any real surplus ACT relieved in periods beginning in the 24 months before the end of the period in which the surplus shadow ACT arose. Any real surplus ACT which is displaced by surplus shadow ACT in this way is payable to the Inland Revenue.

   (iv) Any remaining surplus shadow ACT is carried forward and regarded as shadow ACT of the next accounting period.

(f) The process continues (for as many accounting periods as required) until all of the surplus ACT brought forward from before 6 April 1999 is relieved. However, companies may opt out of the shadow ACT system if they wish (so avoiding all of the computations involved) and simply write off their surplus ACT instead.

(g) The shadow ACT regulations contain certain anti-avoidance provisions. These are very similar to the surplus ACT anti-avoidance legislation which was repealed as from 6 April 1999 (see above).

EXAMPLE 9

A company has unrelieved surplus ACT of £70,000 brought forward from before 6 April 1999. In the year to 31 March 2001, the company has chargeable profits of £200,000, pays dividends of £80,000 and receives UK dividends of £36,000. Calculate the amount of surplus ACT which will be relieved in the year.

SOLUTION

The maximum ACT set-off for the year is £40,000 (20% x £200,000). If ACT had not been abolished on 6 April 1999, franked payments for the year would have been £100,000 (£80,000 x 100/80). The company has FII of £40,000 (£36,000 + £4,000) so the amount of FII taken into account in ACT calculations is £45,000 (£40,000 x 9/8).

The excess of franked payments over uplifted FII is £55,000 so there is shadow ACT of £11,000 (20% x £55,000). This reduces the scope for relieving surplus ACT brought forward to £29,000 (£40,000 - £11,000). Therefore the company's corporation tax liability for the year is reduced by £29,000 and the remaining £41,000 of surplus ACT is carried forward.

Summary

▶ Companies receive certain types of income net of income tax at either the basic rate or the lower rate, depending upon the type of income.

▶ Companies make certain types of payment net of income tax at either the basic rate or the lower rate, depending upon the type of payment.

▶ Companies must submit quarterly returns of the income tax suffered on taxed income and deducted from relevant payments. From the information given in these returns, the amount of income tax payable/repayable for each return period can be calculated.

▶ If the income tax suffered in an accounting period exceeds the income tax deducted from payments made in that period, the income tax suffered on the excess is deducted from the company's corporation tax liability.

▶ Until 6 April 1999 (when ACT was abolished) ACT was payable when a company made a qualifying distribution. The most common example of a qualifying distribution was the payment of a dividend.

▶ The amount of a dividend paid, plus its associated ACT, was known as a franked payment. The ACT liability for an accounting period was based upon the excess of franked payments over franked investment income for the period.

▶ Surplus FII could be carried forward to subsequent accounting periods and used to reduce the company's ACT liability in those accounting periods.

▶ The maximum ACT set-off for an accounting period was the ACT which would be attributable to a franked payment equal to the entire chargeable profits for that accounting period.

▶ Unrelieved surplus ACT on 6 April 1999 is dealt with by the shadow ACT system.

Exercises

25.1 Classify each of the following as either a payment made net of income tax, income received net of income tax or neither :

(a) debenture interest paid
(b) debenture interest received
(c) dividends paid
(d) UK dividends received
(e) Gift Aid donations
(f) interest received from a UK bank.

Also specify the rate at which income tax (if any) is deducted or suffered in each case.

25.2 A company has the following payments made net of income tax and income received net of income tax for the year to 31 March 2001 (amounts are stated net) :

		Payments £	Income £
1 May 2000	Debenture interest paid	16,000	
30 June 2000	Patent royalties received		7,800
1 November 2000	Debenture interest paid	16,000	
1 January 2001	Loan interest received		5,200

Compute the amounts of income tax payable or repayable in each return period.

25.3 A company has chargeable profits of £240,000 for the year to 31 March 2001. No dividends were paid or received during the year and there was no surplus ACT brought forward on 1 April 2000. Payments made net of income tax and income received net of income tax during the year (net amounts) were as follows :

		Payments £	Income £
30 June 2000	Loan interest received		28,000
17 August 2000	Debenture interest paid	36,000	
1 January 2001	Loan interest received		28,000

Compute the corporation tax payable on 1 January 2002.

25.4   In the year to 30 November 1999, a company paid dividends and received dividends (all from UK companies) as follows :

	Paid £	*Received* £
15 December 1998	16,800	
5 April 1999	9,200	
6 April 1999		24,000
21 August 1999	10,000	

Surplus FII brought forward on 1 December 1998 was £4,000. Compute the amount of ACT which was payable for the year.

*25.5   A company's profit and loss account for the year to 31 March 2001 is as follows :

	£	£
Sales		254,628
Less : Cost of sales		112,876
Gross profit		141,752
Add : Profit on sale of fixed asset	542	
Income from investments	16,000	16,542
		158,294
Less : Distribution costs	32,189	
Administrative expenses	42,974	
Interest payable	22,876	98,039
Net profit		60,255

Notes :

(i)   The sale of the fixed asset gave rise to a chargeable gain of £212.

(ii)   Income from investments consists of :

	£
UK dividends (including tax credit)	10,000
Debenture interest received (gross amount)	4,000
Debenture interest accrued (gross amount)	2,000
	16,000

(iii)   Administrative expenses include :

	£
Directors' fees	20,000
Depreciation	5,764
Audit fee	1,000

(iv)   Interest payable consists of :

	£
Debenture interest paid (gross amount)	2,000
Debenture interest accrued (gross amount)	1,000
Bank overdraft interest	19,876
	22,876

(v) The debentures on which the company receives interest were not acquired for trade purposes. The debentures on which the company pays interest were issued for trade purposes.

(vi) Capital allowances of £5,318 are claimed for the year.

(vii) There was no surplus ACT brought forward on 1 April 2000.

Calculate the corporation tax payable on 1 January 2002.

*25.6   On 1 October 1998, a company had surplus ACT brought forward of £10,000. The company's chargeable profits for the years to 30 September 1999 and 2000 were £80,000 and £32,000 respectively. In these two years, the company paid dividends and received dividends (all from UK companies) as follows :

	Paid	Received
	£	£
31 March 1999	20,000	
30 September 1999	12,000	
31 July 2000		9,000
30 September 2000	30,000	

Assuming that no election was made to carry surplus ACT back to previous accounting periods, calculate the amount of ACT set against the company's corporation tax liability for each year and state the amount of any surplus ACT carried forward at the end of each year.

Chapter 26

Corporation tax losses

Introduction

The loss reliefs which are available to a company incurring a trading loss are similar to those available to individuals (see Chapter 11) and generally involve either carrying the loss forward against future trading profits or setting the loss against the company's total profits for a specified period. The main purpose of this chapter is to describe these loss reliefs and to explain the factors which might influence a company when choosing between them. The tax treatment of a company's non-trading losses is also considered in this chapter.

Relief for trading losses

A company's trading losses may be relieved in any of the following ways :

(a) Under Section 393(1) of ICTA 1988, trading losses may be carried forward and relieved against future trading profits.

(b) Under Section 393A(1)(a) of ICTA 1988, trading losses may be relieved against the total profits of the accounting period in which the loss arises.

(c) Under Section 393A(1)(b) of ICTA 1988, trading losses may be relieved against the total profits of the 12 months prior to the accounting period in which the loss arises.

(d) Under Section 242 of ICTA 1988, trading losses may be relieved against surplus FII. However, this relief applies only to trading losses incurred in an accounting period beginning before 2 July 1997 and is considered no further here.

Each of these forms of loss relief (other than Section 242) is described below. The loss reliefs are usually referred to by their section numbers in the Income and Corporation Taxes Act 1988 and this practice is followed for the remainder of this chapter.

Section 393(1) relief

Unless a company claims any other form of loss relief, trading losses are carried forward under S393(1) and relieved against the company's future trading profits. It is important to note the following points :

(a) Relief under S393(1) is given only against future *trading* profits, not against any other form of profits.

(b) Furthermore, relief is given only against future trading profits arising from *the same trade* as that in which the loss was incurred. If a company ceases one trade and commences another, the losses of the old trade cannot be carried forward and relieved against the future profits of the new trade. Similarly, if a company carries on two trades simultaneously, a loss incurred in one of the trades cannot be carried forward and relieved against the future profits of the other trade.

(c) Relief must be given against the *first available* trading profits of future accounting periods.

(d) There are restrictions on the carry-forward of trading losses when there is a change in the ownership of a company (see later in this chapter).

EXAMPLE 1

In the year to 31 March 1999, a company incurred a trading loss of £240,000 which was carried forward under S393(1). The company's results for the next two years were :

	y/e 31 March 2000 £	y/e 31 March 2001 £
Trading profits	210,000	1,850,000
Bank interest receivable	50,000	60,000
Chargeable gains	125,000	572,000
Franked investment income	nil	nil

Compute the company's chargeable profits for the years to 31 March 2000 and 2001.

SOLUTION

	y/e 31 March 2000 £	y/e 31 March 2001 £
Schedule D Case I	210,000	1,850,000
Less : S393(1) relief	210,000	30,000
	0	1,820,000
Schedule D Case III	50,000	60,000
Chargeable gains	125,000	572,000
Chargeable profits	175,000	2,452,000

411

Notes :

(i)   In the year to 31 March 2000, the trading losses brought forward are relieved to the fullest possible extent against the trading profits of the year. The trading losses of £30,000 which remain unrelieved cannot be offset against the bank interest or chargeable gains but must instead be carried forward and relieved against the trading profits of the following year.

(ii) In the year to 31 March 2000 the company pays corporation tax at only 20% (the small companies rate for FY1999). But in the year to 31 March 2001 it pays corporation tax at 30% (the full rate for FY2000). If the company were able to defer the whole £240,000 of S393(1) relief until the year to 31 March 2001 it would make a tax saving. However, relief under S393(1) must be given at the first available opportunity and therefore the company cannot prevent relief being given to the fullest possible extent in the year to 31 March 2000.

Unrelieved charges on income

Charges on income fall into two categories :

(a)   *Trade charges* are those charges which are incurred wholly and exclusively for trade purposes (e.g. patent royalties).

(b)   *Non-trade charges* are charges not incurred for trade purposes (e.g. covenanted payments to charity and other Gift Aid donations).

As explained in Chapter 23, total charges are deducted when calculating a company's chargeable profits and if charges can be fully relieved in this way the distinction between trade and non-trade charges is not important. However, if a company's total profits are insufficient to cover its charges (perhaps because the company has incurred a trading loss) some or all of the charges will be unrelieved. Unrelieved charges are dealt with as follows :

(a)   Under Section 393(9) of ICTA 1988, unrelieved *trade* charges are carried forward in the same way as trading losses and set against future trading profits. But non-trade charges cannot be carried forward in this way and will remain permanently unrelieved to the extent that they cannot be relieved in the accounting period in which they are incurred. (In practice, unrelieved trade charges are often added onto trading losses carried forward rather than being treated as a separate item).

(b)   In an accounting period in which charges exceed total profits, non-trade charges are relieved in priority to trade charges, so giving non-trade charges the greatest possible chance of relief.

There are restrictions on the carry-forward of trade charges when there is a change in the ownership of a company (see later in this chapter).

EXAMPLE 2

A company has the following results for the three years to 30 June 2000 :

	y/e 30/6/98	y/e 30/6/99	y/e 30/6/00
	£	£	£
Trading profits/(losses)	(17,600)	8,700	14,900
Bank interest receivable	1,000	-	-
Patent royalties paid (gross amount)	2,000	2,400	2,800
Deed of covenant to charity (gross amount)	300	300	300

Assuming that the trading loss of £17,600 is to be carried forward under S393(1), calculate the company's chargeable profits for each of the three years.

SOLUTION

	y/e 30/6/98	y/e 30/6/99	y/e 30/6/00
	£	£	£
Schedule D Case I	-	8,700	14,900
Less : S393(1)/(9) relief	-	8,700	12,600
	-	0	2,300
Schedule D Case III	1,000	-	-
Less : Non-trade charges	300	-	300
	700	0	2,000
Less : Trade charges	700	-	2,000
Chargeable profits	0	0	0
Trading losses and trade charges c/f	18,900	12,600	800
Non-trade charges unrelieved	-	300	-

Notes :

(i)   In the year to 30 June 1998, the £300 of non-trade charges and £700 of the trade charges can be relieved against the bank interest receivable. This leaves £1,300 of unrelieved trade charges to be carried forward together with the £17,600 of trading losses, giving a total of £18,900.

(ii)   In the year to 30 June 1999, the trading profit of £8,700 is used to relieve part of the losses brought forward, leaving £10,200 unrelieved. This is increased by the trade charges for the year of £2,400, giving a total of £12,600 to carry forward. The non-trade charges for the year are completely unrelieved.

(iii)   In the year to 30 June 2000, the losses brought forward are fully relieved. The remaining profits of £2,300 are used to relieve the non-trade charges and £2,000 of the trade charges, leaving £800 of unrelieved trade charges to carry forward to the following year.

Section 393A(1) relief

As indicated earlier in this chapter, Section 393A(1) relief is available in two parts :

(a) Under S393A(1)(a), a company may claim that a trading loss incurred during an accounting period should be relieved against the total profits of that accounting period. For this purpose, the term "total profits" means the income and gains of the company, *before* deducting any charges on income.

(b) Under S393A(1)(b), the company may further claim that any part of the trading loss which remains unrelieved after a claim has been made under S393A(1)(a) should be relieved against the total profits of accounting periods falling wholly or partly within a specified prior period. For losses incurred after 1 July 1997, this specified prior period is the *12 months* prior to the loss-making period. Note the following points :

  (i) For S393A(1)(b) purposes, "total profits" means the company's income and gains *after* deducting trade charges but *before* deducting non-trade charges.

  (ii) If more than one accounting period falls wholly or partly into the 12 months preceding a loss-making period, S393A(1)(b) relief is given in later accounting periods in priority to earlier accounting periods.

  (iii) If an accounting period falls only partly into the 12 months preceding a loss-making period, the profits of that accounting period are time-apportioned and S393A(1)(b) relief is available against only the profits which fall into the specified 12 months.

For trading losses incurred before 2 July 1997, the specified prior period was the *3 years* prior to the loss-making accounting period.

S393A(1) relief is voluntary in its operation and a company wishing to relieve a trading loss in this way must make the appropriate claim within two years of the end of the accounting period in which the trading loss arises. A claim may be made under S393A(1)(a) without a further S393A(1)(b) claim but a claim under S393A(1)(b) cannot be made without a prior S393A(1)(a) claim.

A company may not specify how much of its trading loss should be relieved under S393A(1). The effect of a claim is to relieve trading losses to the fullest possible extent in each affected accounting period. Any part of the trading loss which remains unrelieved after a S393A(1) claim has been made is automatically carried forward under S393(1). If no claim at all is made under S393A(1) then the entire trading loss is carried forward under S393(1).

EXAMPLE 3

A company has the following results for the year to 31 December 2000 :

	£
Trading loss	(22,500)
Building society interest receivable	4,000
Unfranked investment income (gross amount)	23,000
Patent royalties paid (gross amount)	7,500
Deed of covenant to charity (gross amount)	1,200

Assuming that a claim is made for the trading loss to be relieved under S393A(1)(a), compute the company's chargeable profits for the year.

SOLUTION

	£
Schedule D Case I	-
Schedule D Case III	4,000
Unfranked investment income	23,000
	27,000
Less : S393A(1)(a) relief	22,500
	4,500
Less : Non-trade charges	1,200
	3,300
Less : Trade charges	3,300
Chargeable profits	0

Note :

All of the non-trade charges are relieved but only £3,300 of the trade charges can be relieved. The balance of £4,200 must be carried forward under S393(9).

EXAMPLE 4

A company has the following results for the three years to 31 March 2001 :

	y/e 31/3/99 £	y/e 31/3/00 £	y/e 31/3/01 £
Trading profits/(losses)	12,500	10,700	(36,500)
Income from property	3,300	8,400	8,800
Trade charges	1,500	1,500	1,500
Non-trade charges	500	500	500

Assuming that a claim is made under both S393A(1)(a) and S393A(1)(b) in relation to the trading loss incurred in the year to 31 March 2001, calculate the company's chargeable profits for each of the three years.

SOLUTION

	y/e 31/3/99	y/e 31/3/00	y/e 31/3/01
	£	£	£
Schedule D Case I	12,500	10,700	-
Schedule A	3,300	8,400	8,800
	15,800	19,100	8,800
Less : S393A(1)(a) relief	-	-	8,800
	15,800	19,100	0
Less : Trade charges	1,500	1,500	-
	14,300	17,600	0
Less : S393A(1)(b) relief	-	17,600	-
	14,300	0	0
Less : Non-trade charges	500	-	-
Chargeable profits	13,800	0	0
Trading loss c/f	-	-	10,100
Trade charges c/f	-	-	1,500
Non-trade charges unrelieved	-	500	500

Notes :

(i)   In the year to 31 March 2001, the claim under S393A(1)(a) must be for the maximum possible amount of £8,800, leaving nothing against which to relieve charges. The trade charges may be carried forward under S393(9) but the non-trade charges are permanently unrelieved.

(ii)   The remaining £27,700 of the trading loss is eligible for S393A(1)(b) relief in the year to 31 March 2000. The relief is given after trade charges have been relieved and must be for the maximum possible amount of £17,600. This leaves nothing against which to relieve the non-trade charges.

(iii) None of the loss-making accounting period fell before 2 July 1997, so none of the loss may be carried back any further. The computation for the year to 31 March 1999 is therefore completely unaffected by loss reliefs.

(iv)   A total of £26,400 (£8,800 + £17,600) of the trading loss has been relieved under S393A(1)(a) and S393A(1)(b). The remaining loss of £10,100 is carried forward under S393(1).

EXAMPLE 5

A company has the following results for the three accounting periods to 31 March 2001 :

	y/e 30/6/99	9 months to 31/3/00	y/e 31/3/01
	£	£	£
Trading profits/(losses)	13,400	19,900	(42,800)
Chargeable gains	1,200	3,500	8,600

Assuming that a claim is made under both S393A(1)(a) and S393A(1)(b) in relation to the trading loss incurred in the year to 31 March 2001, calculate the company's chargeable profits for each of the three accounting periods.

SOLUTION

		y/e 30/6/99	9 months to 31/3/00	y/e 31/3/01
		£	£	£
Schedule D Case I		13,400	19,900	-
Chargeable gains		1,200	3,500	8,600
		14,600	23,400	8,600
Less : S393A(1)(a) relief		-	-	8,600
		14,600	23,400	0
Less : S393A(1)(b) relief	(1)		23,400	
	(2)	3,650		
Chargeable profits		10,950	0	0
Trading losses c/f		-	-	7,150

Notes :

(i)   £8,600 of the trading losses incurred in the year to 31 March 2001 are relieved under S393A(1)(a). This leaves losses of £34,200 which are eligible for S393A(1)(b) relief in the previous 12 months.

(ii) The 9-month accounting period to 31 March 2000 is entirely contained within the specified 12 months and so losses of £23,400 are relieved under S393A(1)(b). Losses relieved so far now total £32,000, leaving £10,800 still to be relieved.

(iii) Only 3 months of the year to 30 June 1999 falls into the specified 12-month period (i.e. 1 April 1999 to 30 June 1999). The maximum S393A(1)(b) relief available is therefore £3,650 (£14,600 x 3/12). The remaining £7,150 of the trading loss is carried forward under S393(1).

Further points relating to S393A(1) relief

(a)   A trading loss can be carried back under S393A(1)(b) only to accounting periods in which the loss-making trade was being carried on.

(b) If more than one loss is eligible for relief against the profits of a given accounting period, earlier losses are relieved before later losses.

(c) Trading losses incurred by a company in the 12 months before the loss-making trade ceases (together with any unrelieved trade charges of the final 12 months) may be carried back and set against the company's profits for the preceding 3 years. This 3-year carry-back remains, despite the fact that trading losses incurred other than on a cessation may now be carried back for only 12 months.

(d) Relief under S393A(1) is available only if the loss-making trade is being carried on on a commercial basis with a view to profit. In the case of companies which carry on the trade of farming or market gardening, a loss is not normally eligible for relief under S393A(1) if losses have also been incurred in each of the previous 5 years.

(e) There are restrictions on the carry-back of trading losses under S393A(1)(b) when there is a change in the ownership of a company (see below).

Anti-avoidance legislation

Specific anti-avoidance legislation exists to prevent the following manoeuvre, which would otherwise be very tax-efficient :

(a) Acquire a company with substantial amounts of unrelieved trading losses and/or unrelieved trade charges.

(b) Revive the loss-making trade.

(c) Use S393(1) and S393(9) relief to set the company's pre-acquisition trading losses and charges against its post-acquisition trading profits, so avoiding liability to corporation tax.

The legislation referred to above provides that if there is a change in the ownership of a company and certain conditions are satisfied, trading losses and trade charges arising before the change cannot be set against trading profits arising after the change. Nor can trading losses arising after the change be set (by virtue of S393A) against profits arising before it. The required conditions are that :

(a) a change in ownership has occurred at a time when the company's business has become negligible and then (at any time after the change) there has been a revival of the company's business, or

(b) a change in ownership and a major change in the nature or conduct of the company's business have both occurred within the same three-year period.

For this purpose, a change in ownership is deemed to occur if over half of the company's ordinary share capital is acquired either by one person or by a group of people, each acquiring at least a 5% shareholding.

Losses and surplus ACT

If a trading loss is set against the profits of an accounting period under S393A(1)(a) or S393A(1)(b), the chargeable profits of that period are reduced. This also reduces the maximum ACT set-off allowed in that period (see Chapter 25). For accounting periods starting before 6 April 1999, this might create surplus ACT which could be difficult to relieve. For more recent accounting periods, the effect is to reduce the scope for relieving surplus ACT brought forward from before 6 April 1999. In either case, the expected beneficial effects of the S393A(1) claim might be diminished or even eliminated and it is evident that the potential ACT consequences of making S393A(1) claims should be considered before such claims are made.

Repayments of corporation tax

If a claim under S393A(1)(b) results in a repayment of corporation tax for an earlier accounting period, this repayment will attract interest. The interest is calculated in the usual way (see Chapter 24) unless the accounting period for which repayment is being made began more than 12 months before the loss-making accounting period. In these circumstances, the interest is calculated as if the repayment were a repayment of tax for the loss-making accounting period itself.

EXAMPLE 6

A company has the following results for the three accounting periods to 31 March 2002 :

	y/e 30/9/00	6 months to 31/3/01	y/e 31/3/02
	£	£	£
Chargeable profits	182,500	120,000	nil
Franked investment income	nil	nil	nil

A claim is made under S393A(1)(b) in relation to trading losses of £250,000 incurred in the year to 31 March 2002. All corporation tax was originally paid on the due date and the necessary repayment of corporation tax is made on 1 February 2003. Calculate the amount of the repayment and the amount of interest which will accompany this repayment, assuming an interest rate of 5% per annum.

SOLUTION

The trading loss for the year to 31 March 2002 may be relieved against the company's profits of the previous 12 months. The whole of the profit for the 6 months to 31 March 2001 is available, together with the profit of the 6-month period from 1 April 2000 to 30 September 2000. The S393A(1)(b) claim will generate the following repayment :

			£
6 months to 31 March 2001	120,000 @ 20%		24,000
y/e 30 September 2000	182,500 x 6/12 @ 20%		18,250
Total repayment			42,250

(i) The 6 months to 31 March 2001 did not begin more than 12 months before the loss-making period so interest on the £24,000 will run from 1 January 2002 (i.e. the due date of payment for the 6 months to 31 March 2001).

(ii) The year to 30 September 2000 began more than 12 months before the loss-making period so interest on the £18,250 will run only from 1 January 2003 (i.e. the due date of payment for the loss-making period itself).

(iii) The repayment takes place on 1 February 2003, which is 396 days after 1 January 2002 and 31 days after 1 January 2003. Therefore the interest due is :

$$£24,000 \times 5\% \times \frac{396}{365} + £18,250 \times 5\% \times \frac{31}{365} = £1,379.42.$$

Choice of loss relief

A company which incurs a trading loss must choose between carrying the loss forward against future trading profits or relieving the loss against the total profits of the current period and (possibly) the total profits of the previous 12 months. Some of the main criteria which will influence this choice are as follows :

(a) the likelihood and expected amount of future profits arising from the same trade as that in which the loss was incurred

(b) the company's cash flow situation (a cash shortage may dictate that loss relief should be obtained as soon as possible)

(c) the possibility of reducing the scope for relieving surplus ACT brought forward from before 6 April 1999

(d) the possibility that non-trade charges might become unrelieved

(e) the rates of corporation tax in earlier accounting periods and the expected rates in future periods

(f) the possibility that relief for trading losses may reduce the chargeable profits of an accounting period to such an extent that the rate of corporation tax payable for that period is reduced (e.g. from the full rate to the small companies rate) or that marginal relief becomes available

(g) the desire to maximise the amount of tax saved as a result of loss relief claims.

Non-trading losses

A company may incur non-trading losses in any of the following ways :

(a) **Schedule A losses**. As from 1 April 1998, a Schedule A loss which is incurred by a company in an accounting period is set against the total profits of the company for that accounting period. To the extent that the loss cannot be relieved in this way, it is either :

    (i) carried forward and set against the total profits of succeeding accounting periods (so long as the Schedule A business is still being carried on in those accounting periods), or

    (ii) relieved by means of group relief (see Chapter 28).

These reliefs are much more generous than their income tax equivalents (see Chapter 5). Note that there are restrictions on the carry-forward of Schedule A losses when there is a change in the ownership of a company. These restrictions are similar to those relating to trading losses (see earlier in this chapter).

(b) **Schedule D Case VI losses**. A Schedule D Case VI loss is relieved first against any other Schedule D Case VI income of the same accounting period and then against the Schedule D Case VI income of subsequent accounting periods.

(c) **Net debits on non-trading loan relationships**. If a company incurs a deficit on its non-trading loan relationships (see Chapter 23), a claim may be made for the deficit to be relieved in any of the following ways :

    (i) by set-off against the company's total profits for the accounting period in which the deficit occurs

    (ii) by group relief (see Chapter 28)

    (iii) by set-off against the company's income from non-trading loan relationships in the previous 12 months (or 3 years in the case of deficits occurring before 2 July 1997)

    (iv) by set-off against non-trading profits of the next accounting period.

Part of the deficit may be relieved in one way and part in another, if the company so wishes. Claims must be made within two years of the end of the accounting period in which the deficit occurs. Any part of the deficit which is not subject to such a claim is carried forward automatically and regarded as a non-trading debit of the next accounting period.

(d) **Capital losses**. A company's capital losses are treated in a similar way to those of an individual (see Chapter 16). Capital losses are relieved first against capital gains of the same accounting period and then against the capital gains of subsequent accounting periods. Since companies are not entitled to the annual exemption, there is no need to restrict capital losses brought forward so as to conserve the exemption. Capital losses cannot be relieved against any other form of income.

Summary

▶ A company's trading losses are carried forward under S393(1) and relieved against the first available profits of the same trade, unless the company makes a claim under S393A(1).

▶ Unrelieved trade charges may be carried forward under S393(9) but unrelieved non-trade charges are lost.

▶ Under S393A(1)(a), a trading loss may be relieved against the total profits of the loss making accounting period.

▶ Under S393A(1)(b), a trading loss may be further relieved against the total profits of a specified period prior to the loss making accounting period. The specified prior period is 12 months in the case of losses incurred after 1 July 1997 and 3 years in the case of losses incurred before 2 July 1997.

▶ Trading losses relieved in an accounting period under S393A(1) may reduce the scope in that period for relieving surplus ACT brought forward from before 6 April 1999.

▶ If a claim under S393A(1)(b) results in a repayment of corporation tax for an earlier accounting period, this repayment will attract interest.

▶ Loss reliefs are also available in relation to Schedule A losses, Schedule D Case VI losses, net debits on non-trading loan relationships and capital losses.

Exercises

26.1   A Ltd has the following results for the three years to 31 May 2000 :

	y/e 31/5/98	y/e 31/5/99	y/e 31/5/00
	£	£	£
Trading profits/(losses)	(31,200)	23,800	11,500
Trade charges	1,000	1,200	1,400
Non-trade charges	400	500	600

Assuming that the trading loss is to be carried forward under S393(1), calculate the company's chargeable profits for each of the three years, showing the amount of the losses carried forward at the end of each year.

26.2   B Ltd has the following results for the year to 31 October 2000 :

	£
Trading loss	(7,300)
Income from property	10,200
Capital gains	540
Patent royalties paid (gross amount)	9,000
Deed of covenant to charity (gross amount)	4,000

Assuming that a loss relief claim is made under S393A(1)(a), calculate the chargeable profits for the year.

26.3   Which of the following statements is true ?

(a)   Capital losses may be carried forward and relieved against future trading profits.

(b)   Trading losses may be carried forward and relieved against future capital gains.

(c)   Trading losses may be relieved against capital gains of the same period.

(d)   Capital losses may be relieved against trading profits of the same period.

26.4   C Ltd has the following results for the three years to 31 January 2001 :

	y/e 31/1/99	y/e 31/1/00	y/e 31/1/01
	£	£	£
Trading profits/(losses)	22,700	28,600	(65,700)
Capital gains	-	-	8,700
Trade charges	5,000	5,000	5,000
Non-trade charges	1,000	1,000	1,000

Assuming that a claim is made under both S393A(1)(a) and S393A(1)(b) in relation to the trading loss incurred in the year to 31 January 2001, calculate the company's chargeable profits for each of the three years.

26.5 In the year to 31 March 2001, D Ltd has chargeable profits of £800,000. In the nine months to 31 December 2001, the company incurs a trading loss of £600,000 and has no other income or gains. There is no franked investment income and there are no charges on income in either period.

Describe the corporation tax effects of a claim under S393A(1)(b) in relation to the trading loss (detailed computations are not required).

*26.6 E Ltd has the following results for the four years to 31 March 2001 :

	y/e 31/3/98 £	y/e 31/3/99 £	y/e 31/3/00 £	y/e 31/3/01 £
Trading profits/(losses)	61,900	27,400	24,200	(72,500)
Capital gains/(losses)	(7,500)	4,300	2,700	5,700
Trade charges	2,500	2,500	2,500	2,500
Non-trade charges	900	900	900	900

Calculate the total repayment of corporation tax (together with interest) to which the company is entitled, assuming that :

(a) claims under S393A(1)(a) and S393A(1)(b) are made in relation to the trading loss for the year to 31 March 2001

(b) any repayment of corporation tax which is generated by these claims is made on 15 January 2002

(c) corporation tax for each of the three years to 31 March 2000 was paid on the due date

(d) the company has neither paid not received any dividends in any of the four years

(e) the rate of interest paid on repayments of corporation tax is 5%.

Chapter 27

Close companies and investment companies

Introduction

In general terms, a "close company" is one which is controlled by a small number of people and an "investment company" is one whose principal activity is the making of investments. Special corporation tax rules apply to each of these types of company and the main purpose of this chapter is to explain the nature of these special rules. The tax implications of incorporation are also considered in this chapter.

Close companies

The essence of a close company is that its affairs can be controlled and manipulated by a small group of people, possibly for tax-avoidance purposes. (In fact, most UK companies are close companies). A body of anti-avoidance legislation has grown up over the years in relation to close companies and the main points of this legislation are explained later in this chapter. The first step, however, is to provide a precise definition of the term "close company".

Definition of a close company

A close company is defined as a UK resident company which is under the *control* of either :

(a) five or fewer *participators*, or

(b) any number of participators who are also *directors* of the company.

The rights of a participator's *associates* are aggregated with that participator's own rights for the purpose of determining whether a company is a close company. Some important terms used in this definition are explained below.

Control

Persons are deemed to have "control" over a company if, taken together, they :

(a) own over 50% of the company's issued share capital, or

(b) have over 50% of the company's voting power, or

(c) would receive over 50% of the company's income, if all of that income were to be distributed, or

(d) would receive over 50% of the company's assets, if the company were wound up.

Participators

A "participator" is defined as someone who has a share or interest in the capital or income of the company. In most cases, a company's only participators are its shareholders, but other persons (e.g. option holders) might also rank as participators.

Directors

A "director", for this purpose, is any person :

(a) who occupies the position of director (whether called a director or not), or

(b) whose directions or instructions are normally obeyed by the directors, or

(c) who is a manager of the company and (possibly together with associates) controls at least 20% of the company's ordinary share capital.

Associates

The "associates" of a participator are defined as :

(a) the participator's business partners

(b) the participator's relatives (which, for this purpose, consist of spouses, parents or remoter ancestors, children or remoter issue, brothers and sisters)

(c) the trustee(s) of any settlement established by the participator or by any of the participator's relatives.

EXAMPLE 1

A company's issued share capital consists of 1,000 £1 ordinary shares, held as follows :

	No of shares		No of shares
David	200	Helen	50
Emma	50	Ian	30
Frederick	100	Jacqueline	40
George	50	Others (1 share each)	480

None of the shareholders are associated in any way and no shareholder is also a director.

(a)   Is the company a close company ?

(b)   Would the company be a close company :

    (i)   if David were Jacqueline's brother, or

    (ii)   if Emma married Ian, or

    (iii) if David were Jacqueline's brother and Emma married Ian ?

SOLUTION

(a)   The five largest shareholders own 45% of the share capital, so the company is not under the control of five or fewer participators. The company is also not under the control of its directors. Therefore the company is not a close company.

(b)   (i)   If David were Jacqueline's brother, her 4% holding would be aggregated with his and the five largest shareholders would control 49% (45% + 4%) of the share capital. The company would not be a close company.

    (ii)   If Emma married Ian, his 3% would be aggregated with hers and the five largest shareholders would control 48% (45% + 3%) of the share capital. The company would still not be a close company.

    (iii) If David were Jacqueline's brother and Emma married Ian, the five largest shareholders would control 52% (45% + 4% + 3%) of the share capital. The company would then be a close company.

EXAMPLE 2

A company's issued share capital consists entirely of ordinary shares, held as follows :

	% holding	Director
Keith	7	Yes
Leonora	7	Yes
Martin	7	Yes
Norma	7	Yes
Oliver	7	Yes
Penny	16	No
Richard	4	No
Others (all non-directors owning under 1%)	45	
Total	100	

None of the shareholders are associated in any way.

(a)   Is the company a close company ?

(b)   Would the company be a close company :

    (i)   if Penny were a manager, or

    (ii)   if Penny were Richard's daughter, or

    (iii) if Penny were both a manager and Richard's daughter ?

SOLUTION

(a) The five largest shareholders own 44% of the share capital, so the company is not under the control of five or fewer participators. The company is also not under the control of its directors, who own 35% of the share capital. Therefore the company is not a close company.

(b) (i) If Penny were a manager, she would not rank as a director since her shareholding is less than 20%. The situation would be unaltered and the company would not be a close company.

   (ii) If Penny were Richard's daughter, then his 4% holding would be aggregated with hers and the five largest shareholders would control 48% (44% + 4%) of the share capital. The company would still not be a close company.

   (iii) If Penny were both a manager and Richard's daughter, then her deemed 20% holding (16% + 4%) would make her a director. The six directors would control 55% of the share capital and the company would then be a close company.

Exceptions

Certain types of company are statutorily excepted from close company status, even if controlled by five or fewer participators (or by the participator-directors). The main exception consists of listed companies with a substantial public interest. In order for this exception to apply, a company must satisfy all of the following conditions :

(a) The company's voting shares must have been both dealt in and listed on a recognised stock exchange within the 12 months prior to the date on which the company's status is being determined.

(b) The total voting power possessed by the *principal members* of the company must not exceed 85% of the total voting power.

(c) At least 35% of the company's voting power must be in the hands of the public.

For this purpose, a "principal member" is a shareholder who (possibly with associates) has more than 5% of the voting power of the company and is also one of the top five shareholders. If two or more shareholders, each holding more than 5%, tie for fifth place, there will be more than five principal members.

   The "public" excludes the company's directors, their associates and most principal members. However, principal members which are themselves either :

(a) non-close companies, or

(b) occupational pension schemes (other than schemes established for the benefit of the company's own employees or directors)

are included within the definition of the public.

EXAMPLE 3

The issued share capital of XYZ plc consists entirely of ordinary shares. For many years, these shares have been listed on the London Stock Exchange and there have been frequent dealings in these shares within the last 12 months. The company's shares are owned as follows :

	% holding	Director
ABC Ltd (a non-close company)	13	-
DEF Ltd (a close company)	7	-
Terry	8	Yes
Ursula	10	Yes
Vincent (a manager)	33	No
Wendy	4	No
Others (all non-directors owning under 1%)	25	
Total	100	

None of the shareholders are associated in any way. Is the company a close company ?

SOLUTION

At first sight, XYZ plc seems to be a close company. It is under the control of its directors (since Vincent ranks as a director) and it is also under the control of five or fewer participators. However, the company is listed on a recognised stock exchange and its shares have been dealt in within the past 12 months. Furthermore, its principal members (the top five shareholders, each owning more than 5% of the voting shares) hold only 71% of the company's voting power and the public (ABC Ltd, Wendy and the others) hold 42%. Therefore the company is excepted from being a close company.

Consequences of close company status

There are two main tax consequences of being a close company. These are :

(a) Benefits in kind provided by the company to participators or their associates are generally treated as distributions.

(b) Loans made to participators or their associates are assessed to tax.

Benefits in kind provided to participators

Benefits in kind provided by a close company to its participators (or to their associates) are generally regarded as distributions. The taxation effects of this are as follows :

(a) The cost to the company of the benefit in kind is disallowed when computing its corporation tax liability.

(b) The company is deemed to have made a distribution equal to the amount which would be assessed on a director or employee earning at least £8,500 per annum if the benefit in kind had been received by such a employee (see Chapter 7).

(c) The person receiving the benefit is taxed as if he or she had received a dividend of the same amount as the deemed distribution.

(d) Until 6 April 1999 (when ACT was abolished) ACT was due on the amount of the deemed distribution, exactly as if a dividend of the same amount had been paid. This ACT could then be set against the company's corporation tax liability in accordance with the usual rules.

Note that a benefit in kind provided to a participator is *not* treated as a distribution if it is already assessable under Schedule E because the participator receiving the benefit is a director or an employee earning at least £8,500 per annum (see Chapter 7).

EXAMPLE 4

On 31 August 2000, a close company which prepares accounts to 31 March each year provides the brother of one of its major shareholders with a free holiday abroad. The cost of the holiday is £3,600 and this amount is charged to the profit and loss account for the year to 31 March 2001. Explain the tax treatment of this item.

SOLUTION

The £3,600 is disallowed in the company's tax computation for the year to 31 March 2001. The company is deemed to have made a distribution of £3,600 and the shareholder's brother is taxed as if he had received a UK dividend of £3,600 (tax credit £400).

Loans made to participators

If a close company makes a loan to a participator (or associate), the tax consequences are as follows :

(a) For loans made on or after 6 April 1999, the company must pay an amount of tax calculated at 25% of the amount of the loan. For loans made before 6 April 1999, the company was required to pay an amount of tax equal to the ACT which would have been payable if the loan had been a dividend. Although often referred to as "notional ACT", this tax was actually not ACT at all and could not be set against the company's corporation tax liability.

(b) The tax due is payable nine months and one day after the end of the accounting period in which the loan is made. However, no tax is payable in relation to any part of a loan which is repaid to the company before the date on which the tax falls due.

(c) The tax paid when the loan was made is repaid to the company if the participator repays the loan. This tax repayment is made nine months and one day after the end of the accounting period in which the loan is repaid.

(d) If a loan to a participator is wholly or partly written-off, the participator is deemed to have received net income equal to the amount written-off. For loans written-off on or after 6 April 1999, this income is grossed-up at the Schedule F ordinary rate (currently 10%).

The tax which is deemed to have been deducted at source from this income is not repayable to the participator, even if he or she is a non-taxpayer. However, further tax at the Schedule F upper rate (currently 32.5%) is payable on any part of the grossed-up income which, when added to the participator's other income, falls beyond the basic rate limit.

From the company's point of view, the tax which was paid when a loan was made is repaid if the loan is written-off on or after 6 April 1999. But if a loan was written-off before 6 April 1999, this tax was *not* refunded.

(e) Certain loans are excluded from the treatment described above. These include loans made to a participator in the normal course of the company's business and loans not exceeding £15,000 made to a participator who is a full-time employee or director of the company, so long as that participator (with associates) has no more than a 5% interest in the company.

EXAMPLE 5

On 1 May 2000, a close company which prepares accounts to 30 June each year lends £30,000 to Ravi, who is one of its directors. No interest is charged on this loan. Ravi owns 25% of the company's ordinary share capital. Explain the tax treatment of the loan if :

(a) it is repaid in full on 30 April 2001

(b) £12,000 is repaid on 30 April 2001 and the remainder of the loan is written off on the same day.

SOLUTION

Tax of £7,500 (25% of £30,000) is payable by the company on 1 April 2001. Since the loan is made interest-free, it is treated as a beneficial loan and Ravi is subject to Schedule E income tax on the related benefit in kind. As regards the eventual repayment or write-off of the loan :

(a) The tax of £7,500 is repaid to the company on 1 April 2002.

(b) The tax of £7,500 is repaid to the company on 1 April 2002. Ravi is taxed as if he had received net income in 2001/02 of £18,000 (tax deducted at source £2,000).

Investment companies

An investment company is defined by ICTA 1988 as "any company whose business consists wholly or mainly in the making of investments and the principal part of whose income is derived therefrom". The chargeable income of such a company will normally consist of :

(a) income from property

(b) net credits on non-trading loan relationships

(c) chargeable gains.

The company may also receive franked investment income, but (as explained in Chapter 23) this is not chargeable to corporation tax. The expenses incurred by an investment company fall into two categories :

(a) expenses which are directly related to one of the company's sources of income and which may be set against that income (e.g. property expenses offset against property income, debits on non-trading loan relationships set against credits), and

(b) general management expenses, which are not related to any particular source of income but which may be set against the company's total income.

Note that only genuine management expenses are allowed. For example, in *L G Berry Investments Ltd* v *Attwooll* (1964), excessive directors' remuneration included in general management expenses was disallowed.

To the extent that management expenses cannot be relieved in the accounting period in which they are incurred they may be carried forward (without time limit) to future accounting periods. Unrelieved charges paid wholly and exclusively for the purposes of the company's business may also be carried forward. There are restrictions on the carry-forward of management expenses and charges when there is a change in the ownership of a company. These restrictions are similar to those relating to the carry-forward of trading losses (see Chapter 26).

Close investment-holding companies

A close company is also a close investment-holding company unless it exists wholly or mainly for one or more of a number of purposes defined by statute. The main purposes which except a company from close investment-holding company status are :

(a) the carrying on of a trade on a commercial basis, or

(b) the letting of property (other than to connected persons).

Therefore a close company which is also an investment company will probably be a close investment-holding company, unless its main purpose is the letting of property.

A close investment-holding company is subject to all of the close company rules described above, but is also subject to further provisions. The main provisions affecting close investment-holding companies (CIC's) are as follows :

(a) A CIC is not entitled to the starting rate or the small companies rate of corporation tax, no matter how small its chargeable profits. Nor can it benefit from marginal relief. A CIC always pays corporation tax at the full rate (30% for FY2000).

(b) Before 6 April 1999, the Inland Revenue had the right to restrict the payment of tax credits to a person who received a distribution from a CIC. This power was exercised only if the Revenue believed that the purpose of making the distribution was to gain a tax advantage. This provision became redundant on 6 April 1999, when the payment of tax credits was generally abolished.

Unincorporated business vs close company

An individual who starts trading is faced with a choice between two alternatives :

(a) To trade as an unincorporated business, either as a sole trader or in partnership with others. In this case the individual is self-employed and the business profits are assessed under Schedule D Case I.

(b) To trade as a limited company (almost certainly a close company), with the individual concerned being a director and/or shareholder of the company. In this case, the company's profits are assessed to corporation tax and the individual's emoluments and dividends from the company are assessed to income tax.

The choice between these two alternatives will be determined partly (though not solely) by taxation considerations. A full analysis of these considerations is beyond the scope of this book but some of the main factors which should be taken into account when deciding whether to trade as an unincorporated business or as a company include :

(a) the rates of income tax and corporation tax

(b) the NI contributions which are payable by the self-employed and by employees

(c) the tax effects of distributing profits to the owner of the business

(d) the tax reliefs available on pension contributions

(e) the dates on which tax and NI contributions are due for payment

(f) the tax reliefs available in relation to trading losses

(g) the taxation of chargeable gains

(h) the tax treatment of loans made to the owner of the business.

Each of these factors is discussed below.

Rates of tax

The entire profits of an unincorporated business are charged to income tax, regardless of whether or not the profits are drawn out of the business. The rate of tax in 2000/01 is 10%, 22% or 40%, depending upon the owner's taxable income. A marginal rate of 40% applies if the owner's taxable income exceeds £28,400 (a relatively small sum).

By contrast, the profits of a company for FY2000 are charged to corporation tax at 10%, 20% or 30% with marginal rates of 22.5% and 32.5% if profits lie between the starting rate limits or the small companies rate limits (see Chapter 24). The marginal rate of 32.5% does not apply until profits reach £300,000 and the full rate of 30% does not apply until profits reach £1,500,000. Furthermore, the owners of a company can decide on the amount of profits (if any) which should be paid out in the form of directors' remuneration and can therefore control the extent to which the profits are assessed to personal income tax rather than corporation tax.

Note, however, that retaining profits in a company so as to minimise the tax liability in the short term will serve to increase the value of the company's shares. This may result in an increased CGT liability in the longer term when shareholders dispose of their shares (though the gains made on disposal might be eligible for business assets taper relief and/or other CGT reliefs).

National Insurance

In 2000/01, a self-employed person pays flat-rate Class 2 NIC's of £2 per week. Profits-related Class 4 contributions are also payable, with a maximum contribution for the year of £1,640.45.

The Class 1 NIC's payable in respect of a director's emoluments can be much higher than this. The director pays primary contributions (maximum £2,386.80 in 2000/01) and the company pays unlimited secondary contributions, calculated as 12.2% of all emoluments in excess of £4,385. However, the secondary contributions are deductible in the company's corporation tax computation.

Distribution of profits

The amount of income tax payable on the profits of an unincorporated business is entirely unaffected by the level of the owner's drawings. But the distribution of profits by a company (either as directors' emoluments or as dividends) has tax implications :

(a) The payment of directors' emoluments reduces the company's corporation tax liability at the expense of increasing the income tax liability of the directors concerned and creating a liability to both primary and secondary NIC's.

(b) The payment of a dividend avoids the NI liability and a dividend has an attached tax credit. But dividends are an appropriation of profit and are not allowed in the company's corporation tax computation, so the company's tax liability will be higher than if the payment took the form of directors' emoluments.

The decision as to whether to pay out a company's profits as directors' emoluments or dividends (or a mixture of both) is a complex one and should take into account the personal circumstances of the shareholders and directors as well as all of the factors listed above. A constraint which should be borne in mind is the need to pay sufficient directors' emoluments to comply with National Minimum Wage regulations.

EXAMPLE 6

A close company which prepares accounts to 31 March each year is owned and managed by a single shareholder/director who is paid a salary of £5,000 per month. In addition to this salary, the company's owner intends to withdraw £20,000 from the company on 31 March 2001. Two approaches are being considered :

(a) that the company should make an extra salary payment to the owner, such that the total of this payment and the related secondary NIC's will equal £20,000

(b) that the company should pay a dividend to the owner, such that the total of this dividend and the company's extra corporation tax liability (when compared with the other approach) will equal £20,000.

Consider the tax-effectiveness of each of these two approaches. For the approach which involves the payment of a dividend, show separately the situation which will apply if the company's marginal rate of corporation tax for the year is 20%, 30% or 32.5%. (Perform all calculations to the nearest £).

SOLUTION

	Extra Salary £	Dividend (20%) £	Dividend (30%) £	Dividend (32.5%) £
Payments made by company :				
Salary	17,825			
Secondary Class 1 NIC's @ 12.2%	2,175			
Corporation tax on £20,000		4,000	6,000	6,500
Dividend		16,000	14,000	13,500
Total payments	20,000	20,000	20,000	20,000
Amount received by owner :				
Gross salary	17,825			
Dividend + tax credit (1/9th)		17,778	15,556	15,000
Income tax @ 40%	7,130			
Income tax @ 32.5%		5,778	5,056	4,875
Income remaining after tax	10,695	12,000	10,500	10,125

Notes :

(i)   The owner's regular salary is sufficient to ensure that maximum primary Class 1 NIC's have already been paid and that any further income is taxed at the higher rate or at the Schedule F upper rate.

(ii) If the company's marginal rate of corporation tax is 20%, payment of a dividend seems to be more tax-effective than payment of extra salary. The situation is reversed if the company's marginal rate is 30% or 32.5%.

Pension contributions

A self-employed person may contribute up to 17.5% of net relevant earnings (more for older taxpayers) into a personal pension scheme and obtain tax relief on these contributions. A company director may obtain tax relief on payments into an occupational pension scheme of up to 15% of emoluments and the company may make further substantial contributions on the director's behalf, these payments being deductible in the company's corporation tax computation.

In general, the total of the tax-deductible contributions which may be made is greater for a company director than for a self-employed person but this depends upon profits being paid out in the form of emoluments (which are earned income and so relevant for pension contributions relief purposes) rather than as dividends (which are unearned income).

Dates of payment of tax and NIC's

A self-employed person must make payments on account of his or her liability to income tax and Class 4 NIC's. These payments are due on 31 January in the tax year and on the following 31 July. The balance of the liability (if any) is payable on the following 31 January. Note that :

(a)   Choosing an accounting date early in the tax year (e.g. 30 April) maximises the delay between earning profits and paying tax on them. For example, the tax on profits for the year to 30 April 2000 (basis period for 2000/01) is payable on 31 January 2001 and 31 July 2001 with a balancing payment on 31 January 2002.

(b)   However, choosing an accounting date early in the tax year has the adverse effect of maximising the amount of overlap profits which are assessed twice on the commencement of trade.

(c)   Class 2 NIC's of £2 per week are payable throughout the tax year.

In general, close companies will pay their corporation tax 9 months and 1 day after the end of the accounting period. Income tax and Class 1 NIC's in relation to directors' emoluments must be accounted for via the PAYE system.

Relief for trading losses

For both individuals (Section 385) and companies (Section 393(1)) trading losses may be carried forward and set against future trading profits. The main distinctions between trading loss reliefs for individuals and companies are concerned with the opportunities to set such losses against total income :

(a) Section 380 of ICTA 1988 allows the trading losses of a self-employed person to be set against that person's total income for the year of the loss, the previous year or both of these years.

In the case of a company, a Section 393A(1)(b) claim to set trading losses against profits of the previous year cannot be made unless a Section 393A(1)(a) claim has already been made, to set losses against profits of the current accounting period.

(b) Section 72 of FA1991 allows the trading losses of an individual to be set against capital gains. A company receives a similar relief by virtue of the fact that a company's capital gains are automatically included in its total income.

(c) Trading losses of an individual incurred in the opening years of a business may be relieved against total income of the previous three years. There is no equivalent relief for companies.

Note that a company's losses can be relieved only against the company's own income and gains, not against the income and gains of individual shareholders.

Chargeable gains

If an unincorporated business disposes of a chargeable asset, the resulting gain is calculated in accordance with the reformed rules of computation introduced by the Finance Act 1998 and is assessed to CGT on the owner of the business. The rates of CGT (for 2000/01) are 10%, 20% and 40% and the annual exemption is available.

If a company makes a chargeable disposal, the gain is calculated in accordance with the rules of computation which applied before FA1998 and is subject to corporation tax (in FY2000) at either 10%, 20%, 22.5%, 30% or 32.5%. No annual exemption is available. Gains retained in the company increase the value of the company's shares, so resulting in an increased CGT liability when shareholders eventually dispose of their shares. In effect a gain may be taxed twice, first to corporation tax and then to CGT.

Close company loans to participators

As explained earlier in this chapter, close companies must pay tax when making loans to participators. A tax charge of this type can sometimes be triggered accidentally if a director overdraws his or her current account with the company. These provisions have no relevance to unincorporated businesses.

Incorporation

If the initial choice is to trade as an unincorporated business, the trader may still consider incorporation at some future time. Some of the main consequences of incorporation are as follows :

(a) The transfer of the assets of a business to a company might give rise to a CGT liability. However, subject to certain conditions, the gains arising may be held-over until the shares which were acquired in exchange for the business assets are disposed of (see Chapter 22).

(b) If the company is under the control of the person who was previously the owner of the unincorporated business, assets which are eligible for capital allowances can be transferred at their written down values for capital allowances purposes, so avoiding the need for balancing adjustments (see Chapter 10).

(c) The transfer of assets to the company will not be treated as a supply for VAT purposes so long as the business is transferred as a going concern and the company is a taxable person at the time of the transfer (see Chapter 29).

(d) If the proprietor of the unincorporated business has unrelieved trade losses, these cannot be carried forward and used by the company but may, subject to certain conditions, be relieved against the proprietor's income from the company (see Chapter 11).

Summary

▶ A close company is one which is under the control of five or fewer participators or any number of participator-directors. The rights of the associates of a participator are aggregated with that participator's own rights when determining whether or not a company is a close company.

▶ Certain types of company (mainly listed companies with a substantial public interest) are excepted from close company status.

▶ Benefits in kind provided to the participators of a close company are treated as distributions. Loans to the participators are charged to tax.

▶ An investment company is one whose main purpose is the making of investments.

▶ A close company is also a close investment-holding company unless it exists wholly or mainly for the purposes of trading or the letting of property. A close investment-holding company always pays corporation tax at the full rate.

Exercises

27.1   Andrew Pearson is a shareholder of A Pearson (Nottingham) Ltd. Which of the following (if any) are his associates for the purposes of deciding whether the company is a close company ?

(a)   his married sister, Angela Birt   (b)   his brother-in-law, Eric Birt

(c)   his nephew, Michael Birt   (d)   his father, Bill Pearson

(e)   his partner in a firm of practising accountants, Alan Johnson.

27.2   The share capital of Romans Ltd consists of 5,000 ordinary shares, held as follows :

	Number of shares
Sejanus (a manager)	900
Claudius (a director)	400
Agrippa (a director)	300
Cleopatra (a director)	300
Tiberius (a director)	200
Gaius (a director)	200
Ptolemy	190
Livia (the grandmother of Claudius)	190
Apicata (the wife of Sejanus)	120
Others (all non-directors owning 10 shares or less)	2,200
Total	5,000

Is the company a close company ?

27.3   On 31 October 2000, a close company which prepares accounts to 31 March each year provides one of its full-time working directors with :

(a)   an interest-free loan of £12,000 (the company does not provide loans in the ordinary course of its business), and

(b)   a season ticket for the opera, costing the company £1,800.

Explain the tax treatment of these two items, assuming that the director in question owns 10% of the company's ordinary share capital.

*27.4   On 19 April 2000, a close company (which makes up accounts to 31 March annually) lends £100,000 to Siobhan, who is a director of the company and who owns 30% of its ordinary share capital. The company does not provide loans in the ordinary course of its business. Siobhan pays a commercial rate of interest on this loan until 1 October 2001, when she repays £55,000. She then continues to pay a commercial rate of interest on the remainder of the loan until it is written-off by the company on 31 March 2002. Explain the tax implications of these transactions.

*27.5   A close company has the following results for the year to 31 March 2001 :

	£
Income from letting property	89,000
Chargeable gains	600
Franked investment income	1,200

(a)   Compute the corporation tax payable for the year.

(b)   Would it make any difference if the property income were trading income instead ?

(c)   Would it make any difference if the property income were a net credit on non-trading loan relationships instead ?

Chapter 28

Groups of companies and reorganisations

Introduction

For corporation tax purposes, group of companies are divided into a number of categories and each category enjoys certain tax advantages. These advantages may include :

(a) the payment of charges and annual interest from one group member to another without accounting for income tax

(b) until 6 April 1999, the payment of intra-group dividends without accounting for ACT and the "surrender" of ACT from one group member to another

(c) the transfer of trading losses from one group member to another

(d) the transfer of chargeable assets from one group member to another in such a way that no chargeable gain arises on the transfer.

However, group companies also incur certain tax disadvantages, principally a reduction in the starting rate and small companies rate upper and lower limits. The main purpose of this chapter is to describe the categories of group which exist and the extent to which these advantages and disadvantages apply to each category. The tax implications of company reorganisations are also briefly considered in this chapter.

Associated companies

For taxation purposes, two companies are "associated" if one of the companies is under the control of the other, or if they are both under the control of a third party (which may be an individual, a partnership or a company). In this context, the word "control" means the same as it does with regard to close companies (see Chapter 27). Control over a company is deemed to accompany :

(a) ownership of over 50% of the company's issued share capital, or

(b) ownership of over 50% of the company's voting power, or

(c) entitlement to over 50% of the company's income, if all of that income were to be distributed, or

(d) entitlement to over 50% of the company's assets, if the company were wound up.

The main consequence of two or more companies being associated with one another is that the starting rate and small companies rate upper and lower limits are divided equally between the companies concerned. This is an anti-avoidance measure, designed to block the practice of breaking large companies into several smaller ones in order to take advantage of the starting rate or the small companies rate. The following points should be noted :

(a) Companies which are associated for only part of an accounting period are deemed for this purpose to be associated for the entire period.

(b) But if a company's accounting period straddles two FY's and the upper and lower limits have changed between the two FY's, the accounting period is treated as two separate "notional accounting periods" for this purpose.

(c) Associated companies which are dormant are ignored.

EXAMPLE 1

S Ltd has chargeable profits of £120,000 for the 6 months to 30 September 2000 and no franked investment income. Until 1 July 2000 the company had no associated companies but, on that date, its entire share capital was acquired by H Ltd. H Ltd has five other wholly-owned subsidiaries, two of which are dormant. Compute S Ltd's corporation tax liability for the period.

SOLUTION

S Ltd is deemed to have had four associated companies (i.e. H Ltd and its three active subsidiaries) throughout the entire accounting period. Therefore the small companies rate lower and upper limits are reduced to £60,000 and £300,000 respectively (one-fifth of their usual values). These are annual figures, which are multiplied by 6/12 for a 6-month accounting period, giving £30,000 and £150,000. Profits of £120,000 fall between these limits, so marginal relief is available. The corporation tax computation is :

	£
FY2000	
£120,000 @ 30%	36,000.00
Less : Marginal relief :	
$\frac{1}{40}$ x (£150,000 - £120,000) x $\frac{£120,000}{£120,000}$	750.00
Corporation tax liability	35,250.00

Of course, the starting rate limits are also reduced to one-fifth of their usual values but the company's profits are too high for this to be relevant.

51% groups

Company B is said to be a "51% subsidiary" of Company A if all of the following conditions are satisfied :

(a) Company A owns, either directly or indirectly, more than 50% of Company B's ordinary share capital (ignoring any shares held indirectly through a non-UK resident company), and

(c) Company A is entitled to more than 50% of the profits available to the ordinary shareholders of Company B, and

(d) Company A would be entitled to more than 50% of the assets available to the ordinary shareholders of Company B if Company B were to be wound-up.

Two companies are said to be members of a "51% group" if they are both UK resident and either :

(a) one company is a 51% subsidiary of the other, or

(b) they are both 51% subsidiaries of a third UK resident company.

EXAMPLE 2

P Ltd owns 80% of the ordinary share capital of Q Ltd, which owns 70% of the ordinary share capital of R Ltd and 60% of the ordinary share capital of S Ltd. All the companies are UK resident. Describe the relationship which exists between the following pairs of companies.

(a) P Ltd and Q Ltd	(b) Q Ltd and R Ltd	(c) Q Ltd and S Ltd	
(d) P Ltd and R Ltd	(e) P Ltd and S Ltd.	(f) R Ltd and S Ltd	

SOLUTION

(a) P Ltd owns more than 50% of the ordinary share capital of Q Ltd, so Q Ltd is a 51% subsidiary of P Ltd.

(b) Q Ltd owns more than 50% of the ordinary share capital of R Ltd, so R Ltd is a 51% subsidiary of Q Ltd.

(c) Q Ltd owns more than 50% of the ordinary share capital of S Ltd, so S Ltd is a 51% subsidiary of Q Ltd.

(d) P Ltd owns (indirectly) 80% x 70% = 56% of the ordinary share capital of R Ltd, so R Ltd is a 51% subsidiary of P Ltd.

(e) P Ltd owns (indirectly) 80% x 60% = 48% of the ordinary share capital of S Ltd, so S Ltd is not a 51% subsidiary of P Ltd.

(f) R Ltd and S Ltd are both 51% subsidiaries of the same parent company (Q Ltd).

By definition, members of a 51% group are also associated companies. Therefore such companies suffer from the reductions in the starting rate limits and small companies rate limits which were described above. On the other hand, 51% groups enjoy certain tax advantages. The main advantages are :

(a) the payment of charges and annual interest from one group member to another without accounting for income tax, and

(b) until 6 April 1999 (when ACT was abolished) the payment of dividends from one group member to another without accounting for ACT and the "surrender" of ACT from one group member to another.

These advantages are described below.

Intra-group charges and interest

The principal tax advantage enjoyed by a 51% group is concerned with the payment of charges and annual interest between a 51% subsidiary and its parent (in either direction) or between fellow 51% subsidiaries. The advantage lies in the fact that such payments may be made without accounting for income tax. Note that :

(a) The paying company and the receiving company must elect jointly that charges and interest should be paid in this way. The Inland Revenue then has 3 months in which to accept or reject the election. If accepted, the election comes into force on the *earlier* of the date of acceptance and the date falling 3 months after the date of the election.

(b) The election may be revoked at any time but cannot be set aside for individual payments.

EXAMPLE 3

Hold Ltd owns 60% of the ordinary share capital of Sub Ltd and all £2,000,000 of the 7.5% debentures issued by Sub Ltd. Both companies are UK resident and prepare accounts to 31 March each year. The debenture interest is payable annually on 31 May and the two companies have elected jointly that charges and annual interest should be paid between them without accounting for income tax. Hold Ltd pays patent royalties of £500,000 (gross amount) on 1 March each year.

(a) Assuming that neither company receives any income net of income tax and that the only payments made net of income tax are those mentioned above, compute the amounts of income tax for which each company must account to the Inland Revenue in the year to 31 March 2001.

(b) Show how this would differ if the election had not been made.

SOLUTION

(a)   Sub Ltd deducts no income tax from payments and so has no income tax to account for to the Inland Revenue.

Hold Ltd deducts income tax of £110,000 (22% x £500,000) when paying the patent royalties and must account for this to the Inland Revenue by 14 April 2001.

(b)   Without the election, Sub Ltd deducts income tax of £30,000 (20% x £150,000) from the debenture interest, payable to the Inland Revenue by 14 July 2000.

Hold Ltd sets this £30,000 against the income tax deducted from the royalties and accounts to the Inland Revenue for income tax of £80,000 by 14 April 2001.

The total income tax payable to the Inland Revenue is £110,000 in both cases, but the group obtains a cashflow benefit from making the election.

Intra-group dividends and ACT surrender

Until 6 April 1999, 51% groups enjoyed two further tax advantages, both of which ceased to exist when ACT was abolished. Briefly, these advantages were as follows :

(a)   Dividends paid by a 51% subsidiary to its parent company or to a fellow 51% subsidiary could be paid without accounting for ACT. From the point of view of the receiving company, such dividends were known as *group income* and were not included when computing that company's profits for the purposes of determining the applicable rate of corporation tax (see Chapter 24).

(b)   A parent company which had paid ACT in relation to an accounting period could "surrender" all or part of that ACT to a 51% subsidiary. The effect of this was that the surrendered ACT was treated as if it had been paid not by the parent company but by the subsidiary company instead.

Note, however, that dividends received on or after 6 April 1999 from a 51% subsidiary or from a fellow 51% subsidiary continue to be disregarded when calculating the "profits" of the receiving company.

Shadow ACT and 51% groups

Any surplus ACT existing on 6 April 1999 is dealt with by means of the shadow ACT system (see Chapter 25). The shadow ACT regulations contain the following special provisions relating to 51% groups :

(a)   If a member of a 51% group has surplus shadow ACT in an accounting period and that surplus cannot be carried back to accounting periods beginning on or after 6 April 1999 and during the previous six years, the surplus *must* be allocated (so far as is possible) to other companies in the group. This reduces the capacity of those other companies to relieve surplus ACT.

(b)   The allocation should be performed by the parent company of the group. Failing this, the allocation will be done by the Inland Revenue.

(c) If the surplus to be allocated exceeds the total amount which can be utilised by all of the companies in the group, the excess is retained by the company in which the surplus arose and is carried forward to the next accounting period.

(d) Intra-group dividends are not treated as distributions when computing the shadow ACT of the paying company. Similarly, such dividends are not treated as FII when computing the shadow ACT of the receiving company.

(e) If a group company receives FII from outside the group, it may elect to pay an intra-group dividend of up to the amount of this FII (multiplied by 9/8ths) and treat this dividend as a distribution. This election has the effect of transferring FII from one group company to another and allows the company which receives the intra-group dividend to reduce the shadow ACT arising on its own dividends.

75% groups

Company B is said to be a "75% subsidiary" of Company A if all of the following conditions are satisfied :

(a) Company A owns, either directly or indirectly, at least 75% of the ordinary share capital of Company B, and

(b) Company A is entitled to at least 75% of the profits available to the ordinary shareholders of Company B, and

(c) Company A would be entitled to at least 75% of the assets available to the ordinary shareholders of Company B if Company B were to be wound-up.

Two companies are said to be members of a "75% group" if they are both UK resident and either :

(a) one company is a 75% subsidiary of the other, or

(b) they are both 75% subsidiaries of a third company (which might or might not be UK resident).

The members of a 75% group benefit from two main tax reliefs. These are the right to transfer trading losses and certain other items between group members ("group relief") and the transfer of chargeable assets between group members in such a way that no chargeable gain arises on the transfer. These reliefs are described below.

Group relief

Group relief consists of the surrender of trading losses and/or certain other items by one member of a 75% group (the "surrendering company") to another member of the group (the "claimant company"). The items which may be surrendered are :

(a) trading losses and deficits on non-trading loan relationships

(b) charges on income, Schedule A losses and management expenses.

The surrender may be in whole or in part as best meets the requirements of the surrendering company and the claimant company. Trading losses and deficits on non-trading loan relationships may be surrendered even if they could instead be set against the profits of the accounting period in which they are incurred. The remaining items are available for surrender only to the extent that (in aggregate) they exceed the surrendering company's gross profits for the accounting period in which they are incurred. For this purpose, a company's "gross profits" for an accounting period are its profits for that period without any deduction for either :

(a) losses and other amounts incurred in the period and eligible for group relief, or

(b) losses and other amounts incurred in any other period (e.g. trading losses brought forward or carried back).

Capital losses cannot be surrendered under the group relief rules, but a capital loss can in effect be transferred from one group company to another by a different means (see later in this chapter). Note the following points with regard to group relief :

(a) A surrender may be made from subsidiary to parent, from parent to subsidiary or from subsidiary to fellow subsidiary.

(b) Only current-period losses etc. are eligible for group relief and these must be set against the claimant company's profits for a *corresponding* accounting period. If the accounting periods of the surrendering company and the claimant company do not correspond exactly, group relief is available only in respect of the period of overlap between the two periods. The losses etc. of the surrendering company and the profits of the claimant company are time-apportioned so as to determine the amounts which fall into the overlap period.

(c) The amount surrendered to any one claimant company cannot exceed that company's profits for the corresponding accounting period, *before* deduction of any reliefs derived from a subsequent accounting period but *after* deduction of any other relief from tax, including :

(i) trading losses brought forward under Section 393(1), together with trade charges brought forward under Section 393(9)

(ii) current-period trading losses which are relieved (or which could have been relieved) under S393A(1)(a)

(iii) Schedule A losses of the current period or previous periods

(iv) deficits on non-trading loan relationships set against profits of the current period or brought forward from previous periods

(v) charges for the accounting period.

The above reference to "reliefs derived from a subsequent accounting period" means that group relief is given before relief for trading losses carried back and before relief for deficits on non-trading loan relationships carried back.

(d) A group relief claim must normally be made within 2 years of the end of the claimant company's accounting period.

(e) Any amount of money paid to the surrendering company by the claimant company as consideration for the surrendered items is ignored for tax purposes so long as the payment does not exceed the amount of the surrendered items.

EXAMPLE 4

Low Ltd is a wholly-owned subsidiary of High Ltd. Both companies are UK resident and prepare accounts to 31 March each year. Results for the year to 31 March 2001 are :

	High Ltd £	Low Ltd £
Trading profit/(loss)	100,000	(180,000)
Chargeable gains	5,000	10,000
Trade charges	12,000	-

Show how the trading loss sustained by Low Ltd may be relieved.

SOLUTION

High Ltd has chargeable profits of £93,000 (£100,000 + £5,000 - £12,000). This sets an upper limit on the amount of group relief which may be claimed. The trading loss sustained by Low Ltd may be relieved in a number of ways. For example :

(a) The entire loss could be carried forward under S393(1).

(b) £10,000 of the loss could be relieved against the company's chargeable gains under S393A(1)(a) and the balance of £170,000 carried forward.

(c) The claim under S393A(1)(a) could be supplemented by a further claim under S393A(1)(b) to set the remaining £170,000 of the loss against the profits of Low Ltd for the previous 12 months.

(d) Group relief of anything up to £93,000 could be claimed and the balance of the loss then dealt with as above.

EXAMPLE 5

L Ltd prepares accounts annually to 31 March and is a 75% subsidiary of H Ltd, which prepares accounts annually to 31 December. Both companies are UK resident. Recent results are as follows :

	H Ltd	L Ltd
	£	£
Trading loss for year to 31 March 2000		(40,000)
Chargeable profits year to 31 December 1999	35,000	
Chargeable profits year to 31 December 2000	56,000	

Compute the amount of group relief that may be claimed.

SOLUTION

The accounting periods of H Ltd and L Ltd do not correspond, so it is necessary to time-apportion profits and losses, as follows :

		1/4/99 - 31/12/99 (9 months)	1/1/00 - 31/3/00 (3 months)
		£	£
(i)	H Ltd profit	26,250	14,000
(ii)	L Ltd loss	(30,000)	(10,000)

The group relief available in each period is the lower of (i) and (ii). Therefore, H Ltd may claim that group relief of £26,250 should be set against its 1999 profits and that group relief of £10,000 should be set against its 2000 profits. The remaining £3,750 of the loss is not eligible for group relief.

Using group relief effectively

Group relief should be used to ensure that trading losses are relieved as tax-effectively as possible and that the group's overall tax liability is minimised. Points to bear in mind are :

(a) Surrendering companies should surrender trading losses first to claimant companies which pay corporation tax at the marginal rate of 32.5% and then to those companies paying tax at 30%, 22.5%, 20% and 10% (in that order)

(b) Claimant companies should consider claiming less than the full amount of capital allowances available for an accounting period, so maximising the profits available for group relief set-off.

(c) A company with a trading loss should use the loss itself in a claim under S393A(1)(a) and S393A(1)(b), if this would save more tax than surrendering the loss to another group company.

Transfer of chargeable assets within a group

If a chargeable asset is transferred from one member of a 75% group to another, the transfer is deemed to have occurred at a value giving rise to neither a gain nor a loss. When an asset which has been transferred between group members in this way is finally disposed of outside the group, the chargeable gain arising on the disposal is then (in effect) calculated with reference to the original cost of the asset to the group.

The definition of a 75% group for this purpose is less rigorous than the definition given above in relation to group relief. A *capital gains group* consists of a principal company plus its 75% subsidiaries (as previously defined) plus the subsidiaries' 75% subsidiaries and so forth, subject to the overriding requirement that the principal company must have more than a 50% interest in each member of the group.

EXAMPLE 6

J Ltd owns 80% of the ordinary share capital of K Ltd, which owns 80% of the share capital of L Ltd, which owns 80% of the share capital of M Ltd, which owns 80% of the share capital of N Ltd. All of these companies are UK resident. Which of the companies belongs to a capital gains group with J Ltd as the principal company ?

SOLUTION

At first sight, all five companies seem to belong to the capital gains group which has J Ltd at its head. However, J Ltd must have more than a 50% interest in each member of the group. J Ltd's actual interests in each member are as follows :

K Ltd	80%
L Ltd	80% x 80% = 64%
M Ltd	80% x 80% x 80% = 51.2%
N Ltd	80% x 80% x 80% x 80% = 40.96%

Therefore, N Ltd is not a member of this capital gains group.

A chargeable gain may arise in relation to an intra-group transfer if a company has a chargeable asset transferred to it from another group member and then leaves the group within 6 years of the date of the transfer. The company leaving the group is deemed :

(a) to have sold the asset on the date of the intra-group transfer for its market value on that date (perhaps giving rise to a chargeable gain), and then

(b) to have immediately re-acquired the asset on the same date and for the same amount.

Any chargeable gain arising from this treatment is chargeable in the accounting period in which the company leaves the group.

EXAMPLE 7

SubOne Ltd and SubTwo Ltd are members of a capital gains group. In January 1997, SubOne Ltd transferred a chargeable asset to SubTwo Ltd. The asset had originally cost £10,000 and its market value in January 1997 was £25,000. If the asset had been sold outside the group in January 1997, indexation allowance of £1,350 would have been available. In March 2000, SubTwo Ltd (which prepares accounts to 31 December each year) leaves the group. Calculate the chargeable gain arising on SubTwo Ltd's departure.

SOLUTION

SubTwo Ltd is deemed to have sold the asset for £25,000 in January 1997. This would have given rise to a chargeable gain of £13,650 (£25,000 - £10,000 - £1,350) so a chargeable gain of £13,650 arises in SubTwo Ltd's accounting period for the year to 31 December 2000.

Roll-over relief for capital gains groups

For the purposes of roll-over relief on the replacement of a business asset (see Chapter 22), all the companies in a capital gains group are treated as a single company. This means that a gain arising on the disposal of a business asset by one member of a group can be rolled-over against the cost of a qualifying business asset acquired by any other member of that group.

It is important to note that the qualifying business asset against which a gain is rolled-over must be an asset which has been newly acquired *by the group as a whole*. It is not possible to roll-over a gain against an asset which has been acquired by one group member from another.

Capital losses

Capital losses cannot be surrendered to another group member. This is in contrast to the treatment of trading losses and certain other items which can be surrendered (see above). Until 1 April 2000, the only way around this problem was to transfer assets between group members in such a way that capital gains and capital losses arose in the same company. Imagine that Company L and Company G were both members of a capital gains group, that Company L had capital losses and that Company G was about to dispose of an asset and realise a capital gain. Company L's capital losses could be set against this gain in the following way :

(a) Company G could transfer its asset to Company L (on a no gain/no loss basis).

(b) Company L could then dispose of the asset. The gain arising would in this way be realised by Company L rather than Company G, so allowing Company L's losses to be set against it.

However a simpler procedure is now available. As from 1 April 2000, two members of a 75% group may jointly elect that an asset which has been disposed of outside the group by one of them should be treated as if it had been transferred between them immediately before that disposal. This election allows gains and losses to be brought together in the same company without having to transfer assets between group members. The election must be made within 2 years of the end of the accounting period in which the disposal outside the group takes place.

Pre-entry capital losses

A group which anticipates making disposals which will give rise to substantial capital gains might seek to shelter those gains by first acquiring a "capital loss company" i.e. a company which has substantial capital losses brought forward, or has assets which would realise substantial capital losses on disposal. The intention of such an acquisition would be to set these capital losses against the group's capital gains (by means of the procedure outlined above) and so reduce the group's overall corporation tax liability.

This tax-avoidance manoeuvre is prevented by TCGA 1992, which allows a group company's *pre-entry capital losses* to be set only against gains arising on the following types of disposal :

(a) disposals of assets which the company owned before it became a member of the group, and

(b) disposals of assets acquired by the company *from outside the group* since becoming a group member.

The pre-entry capital losses of a company are defined as :

(a) any capital losses incurred by the company before joining the group, and

(b) the pre-entry part of any capital losses incurred by the company after joining the group on the disposal of pre-entry assets.

When a company joins a group and subsequently disposes of a pre-entry asset at a loss, the pre-entry part of that loss is obtained by applying a formula to each item of allowable expenditure in the computation and then aggregating the results. The formula used is :

$$A \times \frac{B}{C} \times \frac{D}{E}$$

where : A = the total amount of the allowable loss

B = the amount of the item of allowable expenditure

C = the sum of the amounts of all the items of allowable expenditure

D = the length of time between the date of acquiring the asset (or 1 April 1982 if later) and the date of joining the group

E = the length of time between the date of acquiring the asset (or 1 April 1982 if later) and the date of disposal.

EXAMPLE 8

A company acquired a chargeable asset on 1 January 1991 at a cost of £200,000 and incurred enhancement expenditure of a further £50,000 on 1 January 1995. The company joined a capital gains group on 1 April 2000 and the asset was sold on 1 September 2000 for £130,000. Calculate the total loss arising on this disposal and the amount of the pre-entry loss (working to the nearest whole month).

SOLUTION

	£	£
Sale proceeds		130,000
Less : Cost	200,000	
Enhancement	50,000	250,000
Allowable loss		(120,000)

Notes :

(i) Indexation allowance is £nil, since indexation allowance cannot be used to increase a loss.

(ii) The asset was originally acquired 111 months before joining the group and 116 months before disposal. The enhancement expenditure was incurred 63 months before joining the group and 68 months before disposal.

(iii) The pre-entry loss is :

$$\text{£120,000} \times \frac{\text{£200,000}}{\text{£250,000}} \times \frac{111}{116} + \text{£120,000} \times \frac{\text{£50,000}}{\text{£250,000}} \times \frac{63}{68} = \text{£114,097.}$$

Pre-entry capital gains

Anti-avoidance legislation applies when a company joins a group part-way through an accounting period and has realised capital gains between the start of its accounting period and the date of joining the group. In these circumstances, the only losses which may be set against those earlier gains are losses which arose before the company joined the group and losses which arose after that date on assets which the company owned before it joined the group.

Pre-entry surplus ACT

In Chapter 25, it was stated that there are restrictions on the carry-forward of a company's surplus ACT when the ownership of the company changes and there is a major change in the nature of the company's business. Another restriction on the relief of surplus ACT arises when a company joins a group, but this time there is no need for there to be a major change in the nature of the company's business. The restriction is that the company's *pre-entry surplus ACT* cannot be set against the corporation tax due in relation to disposals of chargeable assets which :

(a) are acquired from other group members (on a no-gain, no-loss basis), and

(b) are then disposed of within 3 years of the company joining the group.

This provision is intended to prevent groups from acquiring companies with the sole intention of using their surplus ACT (arising from before 6 April 1999) to avoid paying corporation tax on the group's capital gains.

Consortia

A company is owned by a consortium (and is known as a *consortium company*) if at least 75% of its ordinary share capital is owned by other companies (who are known as *consortium members*) each of which :

(a) owns at least 5% but less than 75% of the consortium company's ordinary share capital, and

(b) is entitled to at least 5% of the profits available to the consortium company's ordinary shareholders, and

(c) would be entitled to at least 5% of the assets available to the consortium company's ordinary shareholders on a winding-up.

A 90% subsidiary of a consortium company is also a consortium company.

Group relief for a consortium

Group relief (see above) is available in either direction between a consortium member and a consortium company, so long as both companies are UK resident and the consortium company is either :

(a) a trading company, or

(b) a holding company, which (for this purpose) is one whose business consists wholly or mainly of holding shares in trading companies which are its 90% subsidiaries.

Note the following points :

(a) The relief available is restricted in proportion to the consortium member's shareholding in the consortium company. For instance, if CC Ltd is a consortium company and CM Ltd is a consortium member which owns x% of CC Ltd, CM Ltd may claim up to x% of CC Ltd's losses. Alternatively, CM Ltd may surrender to CC Ltd losses of up to x% of CC Ltd's profits.

(b) A group relief claim must be agreed by all the consortium members.

(c) The amount of a consortium company's trading loss which is available for group relief is the amount of the loss less any potential claim for loss relief under S393A(1)(a), whether or not such a claim is actually made.

EXAMPLE 9

The ordinary share capital of W Ltd (a UK trading company) is owned 30% by X Ltd, 25% by Y Ltd and 45% by Z Ltd. All companies are UK resident and prepare accounts to 31 March annually. Results for the year to 31 March 2001 are as follows :

	W Ltd £	X Ltd £	Y Ltd £	Z Ltd £
Trading profit/(loss)	(62,000)	41,000	11,000	38,000
Chargeable gains	10,000	-	-	-

What are the maximum possible group relief claims which may be made ?

SOLUTION

The amount of W Ltd's loss which is available for group relief is £52,000 i.e. £62,000 less a potential S393A(1)(a) claim of £10,000 (whether or not that claim is actually made). This is shared between the consortium members in proportion to their shares in the consortium, as follows :

	X Ltd £	Y Ltd £	Z Ltd £
Share of W Ltd's available loss	15,600	13,000	23,400
Chargeable profits	41,000	11,000	38,000
Maximum group relief claim	15,600	11,000	23,400

Charges and annual interest for a consortium

Charges and interest payable by a consortium company to a consortium member may (on election) be paid without accounting for income tax. Similarly, dividends paid by a consortium company to a consortium member before 6 April 1999 (when ACT was still in force) could be paid without accounting for ACT.

Reorganisations

If a company transfers a trade to another company, this ranks as a cessation of that trade and any unrelieved trading losses incurred before the date of the transfer cannot normally be carried forward under S393(1) and set against the subsequent profits of the transferred trade. But if a trade is transferred between two companies (both within the charge to UK corporation tax in respect of that trade) and at least 75% of the trade is effectively owned by the same persons both :

(a) at some time within the year before the date of the transfer, and

(b) at some time within the two years after the date of the transfer

then the unrelieved trading losses of the transferor company may be carried forward and set against subsequent trading profits (from that same trade) of the transferee company. This "succession of trade" relief is applicable if, for instance, a company creates a new wholly-owned subsidiary and then transfers a trade to that subsidiary. Note the following points in relation to such a transfer :

(a) For capital allowances purposes, assets are transferred at their tax-written down values, with no balancing adjustments.

(b) Chargeable business assets are transferred to the transferee company on a no-gain, no-loss basis, so long as the transferor company receives no consideration for the assets and the assets remain within the scope of UK corporation tax.

(c) Only trading losses may be carried forward as described above. The relief does not extend to non-trading losses, capital losses, surplus ACT or surplus FII, none of which can be carried forward.

Summary

► Two companies are associated if one of the companies is under the control of the other, or if they are both under the control of a third party.

► The starting rate and small companies rate upper and lower limits are shared equally between associated companies.

► Charges and annual interest payable between a 51% subsidiary and its parent (in either direction) or from one 51% subsidiary to a fellow 51% subsidiary may be paid without accounting for income tax.

► Trading losses and certain other items may be surrendered between members of a 75% group. This is known as "group relief".

► Chargeable assets may be transferred between members of a capital gains group without giving rise to a chargeable gain.

► Subject to certain conditions, group relief is available between consortium members and consortium companies.

► If a trade is transferred between two companies, the unrelieved trading losses of the transferor company may, if certain conditions are satisfied, be carried forward and set against the subsequent trading profits of the transferee company.

Exercises

28.1 Arm Ltd and Foot Ltd are both 100% subsidiaries of Head Ltd, which has no other subsidiaries. They are all UK resident. How will the relationship of the three companies affect the way in which they are taxed ?

28.2 Alpha Ltd is a wholly-owned subsidiary of Beta Ltd, which has two other wholly-owned subsidiaries (one of which is dormant). In the year to 31 March 2001, Alpha Ltd has the following results :

	£
Trading profits	220,000
Bank deposit interest	6,000
UFII (gross amount)	4,000
UK dividend received from non-group company on 1 May 2000	27,000
Patent royalties paid (gross amount)	17,000

Compute the corporation tax liability for the year.

28.3 Gamma Ltd owns 85% of the ordinary share capital of Delta Ltd and £300,000 of the £500,000 of 8% debentures issued by Delta Ltd. Both companies are UK resident. The debenture interest is payable half-yearly on 30 June and 31 December and an election has been made for charges and annual interest payable between the two companies to be paid without accounting for income tax. Both companies prepare accounts annually to 31 December and neither is required to pay corporation tax by instalments.

(a) Compute the amounts of income tax payable by or repayable to each company for the year to 31 December 2000, assuming that neither company receives any income net of income tax and that the only payments made net of income tax are those mentioned above.

(b) How would this differ if the election had not been made ?

28.4 Base Ltd is a wholly-owned subsidiary of Apex Ltd. Both companies are UK resident and prepare accounts annually to 31 March. The results for the year to 31 March 2001 are as follows :

	Apex Ltd £	Base Ltd £
Trading profit/(loss)	120,000	(90,000)
Trading losses b/f under S393(1)	(42,000)	(19,000)
Schedule A income	7,000	3,000
Trade charges	12,000	4,000

Calculate the maximum group relief that may be claimed for the year by Apex Ltd.

28.5 A1 Ltd owns 90% of the ordinary share capital of A2 Ltd. A2 Ltd owns 80% of the ordinary share capital of A3 Ltd and 70% of the ordinary share capital of A4 Ltd. Which of these companies (all UK resident) form a capital gains group with A1 Ltd as its principal company ?

28.6 The ordinary share capital of PP Ltd (a UK trading company) is owned 32% by QQ Ltd, 35% by RR Ltd, 23% by SS Ltd. The remaining 10% is owned by various individuals, none of whom own more than 1%. All companies are UK resident and prepare accounts to 31 July annually. Results for the year to 31 July 2000 are as follows :

	PP Ltd £	QQ Ltd £	RR Ltd £	SS Ltd £
Trading profit/(loss)	(96,000)	41,000	38,000	11,000
Chargeable gains	-	15,000	-	-
Schedule D Case III income	12,000	6,000	11,000	4,000
Trade charges	-	(3,000)	(2,000)	(1,000)

Compute the maximum possible group relief claims.

*28.7 T Ltd owns 90% of the ordinary share capital of B Ltd. Both are UK resident. Recent results for the two companies are as follows :

	T Ltd y/e 31/3/00 £	T Ltd y/e 31/3/01 £	B Ltd y/e 30/11/00 £
Trading profit(loss)	190,000	130,000	(174,000)
Chargeable gains	25,000	13,000	8,000
Patent royalties paid (gross)	5,000	5,000	4,000

No dividends have been paid or received by either company in any of these accounting periods and maximum group relief is claimed. Calculate the corporation tax payable by each company for each accounting period, making and stating any necessary assumptions.

Review questions (Set C)

C 1   Tolbooth Ltd is a small manufacturing company. It commenced trading on 1 April 1999 and prepared its first set of accounts for the 18 month period to 30 September 2000. As the accounting technician responsible for preparing the tax computation, you have extracted the following information from the audit file :

		£
(i)	Trading profits (before capital allowances)	390,000

(ii) Rental income :
    £20,000 per year from property rented on 1 April 1999.
    Rent received annually in advance on 1 April.

(iii) Bank deposit interest :

Received 30 June 1999	2,000
Received 31 December 1999	2,000
Accrued to 31 March 2000	1,000
Received 30 June 2000	12,000
Accrued to 30 September 2000	4,000

(iv)	Plant and machinery was purchased on 30 June 1999, costing	100,000

(v) Patent royalties (gross amounts) :

Paid 31 December 1999	5,000
Accrued to 31 March 2000	2,500
Paid 30 June 2000	5,000
Accrued to 30 September 2000	2,500

(vi)	Chargeable gain on disposal 1 August 2000	10,000

Required :

(a) State how the first period of account to 30 September 2000 will be divided into accounting periods.

(b) Calculate the corporation tax liability for each accounting period.   *(AAT)*

C2   P Ltd is a company with various shareholdings in other UK companies. It is in receipt of periodic payments in respect of patent royalties and it pays debenture interest twice in each accounting period. The following is a list, in date order, of the various transactions of these types during the year to 31 March 2001 (amounts are shown net) :

		£
10/5/00	Patent royalties received	24,960
12/7/00	Debenture interest paid	36,000
30/8/00	Patent royalties received	15,600
24/11/00	Debenture interest paid	41,600
15/1/01	Patent royalties received	21,840

The directors wish to have information on the cash inflows and outflows arising from the taxation associated with each transaction.

You are required :

To calculate, by means of quarterly settlement statements for income tax, the amounts which became payable and/or recoverable in each case, stating the date (or approximate date) concerned. *(CIMA)*

C3   Poynton Producers Ltd, who make up annual accounts to 30 September, purchased a new industrial building for £150,000 on 1 April 1993. The building was not in an enterprise zone and was bought into industrial use immediately. On 31 August 1995, production ceased and the building was leased to a national charity as a collection centre. Production in the factory re-commenced on 1 February 1997. On 1 April 2000 the building was sold to Sale Switches Ltd, who make up annual accounts to 31 December, for £140,000. It was brought into industrial use immediately.

You are required to calculate :

(a)   the Industrial Buildings Allowances for all accounting periods when the building was owned by Poynton Producers Ltd (initial allowance was not claimed)

(b)   the balancing adjustment on the sale of the building in 2000

(c)   the Industrial Buildings Allowances claimable by Sale Switches Ltd in respect of the building in future years. *(ACCA)*

C4   Unusual Urns Limited is a UK resident company. It has no associated companies. Recent results are as follows:

	Year to 31 July 1999 £	6 months to 31 January 2000 £
Schedule D Case I profit/(loss)	200,000	(150,000)
Charges on income:		
Patent royalties paid (gross)	7,500	10,000
Charitable covenant paid (gross)	1,500	750

The company's chargeable profits for the year to 31 January 2001 are expected to be approximately £700,000, derived mostly from trading income. The company receives no dividends.

You are required :

(a)   to state the alternative methods by which the company can obtain relief for the loss of £150,000 sustained in the period to 31 January 2000, and

(b)   to state, with your reasons, which of these alternatives you would choose so as to obtain the maximum tax advantage when claiming relief in respect of the £150,000 loss. You should also state the effect that your proposed treatment will have on the charges on income paid by the company.   *(ACCA)*

C5   Antietam Ltd makes up accounts to 31 March annually. Results for the 12 months to 31 March 2001 are as follows :

	£
Trading profits (before capital allowances)	170,000
Capital allowances	32,000
Rental income	18,000
Patent royalties received June 2000 (net amount)	21,840
Capital gains	6,400

The company has capital losses brought forward from previous accounting periods of £1,400 and paid a charitable covenant (gross) on 31 March 2001 of £20,000. It also received a dividend from ICI plc on 16 December 2000 of £14,400.

Required :

(a)   Calculate the corporation tax liability of Antietam Ltd for the year to 31 March 2001.

(b)   Recalculate the liability if you are told that the company has one subsidiary company.   *(AAT)*

*C6   Undulating Uplands Ltd is a UK resident manufacturing company with no associated companies. It had always made up accounts to 30 November but decided to change the year end from November to February. The company's results for the period from 1 December 1999 to 28 February 2001 are as follows :

	Notes	£
Adjusted trading profit		750,000
Dividends received from UK companies	1	43,000
Bank interest received	2,6	13,500
Building society interest received	3,6	8,400
Patent royalties received (gross amount)	4,7	20,000
Charitable covenant paid (gross amount)	5	16,000
Capital allowances on plant and machinery	12	85,000

The following additional information is available :

1.   Dividends were received from UK companies as follows :

	£
30/12/99	7,200
30/3/00	10,800
30/9/00	9,000
30/1/01	18,000

2.   Bank interest was credited by Natland Bank plc as follows :

	£
21/12/99	4,900
20/6/00	3,800
21/12/00	4,800

Accrued interest amounted to £4,500 on 30/11/99, £4,300 on 30/11/00 and £4,000 on 28/2/01.

3.   Building society interest was credited by Northshires Building Society as follows :

	£
31/3/00	4,000
30/9/00	4,400

The account was opened on 1/12/99 and closed on 30/9/00.

4.   Patent royalties were received as follows :

	£
28/2/00	4,000
31/5/00	4,000
31/8/00	4,000
30/11/00	4,000
28/2/01	4,000

5.   The charitable covenant was paid as follows :

	£
15/5/00	8,000
15/11/00	8,000

6. The amounts shown for bank and building society interest received are the actual amounts received.

7. Income tax has been deducted from the patent royalties received.

8. The company had trading losses brought forward of £400,000 on 1 December 1999.

9. The company had capital losses brought forward of £15,000 on 1 December 1999.

10. On 1 September 2000, the company bought a factory which qualifies for Industrial Buildings Allowance from the original owner for £450,000. The factory was first brought into qualifying use by the original owner on 1 September 1984. It had then cost £250,000 and a 50% initial allowance had been claimed. It was not in an Enterprise Zone. There had been no non-qualifying use before 1 September 2000.

11. The company had purchased a new factory, which qualified for Industrial Buildings Allowance, on 1 January 1995 for £150,000. It was brought into use immediately. The factory was sold on 1 January 2001 for £350,000. An appropriate claim to minimise the chargeable capital gain was made. The building was not in an Enterprise Zone. (Assume RPI's of 146.0 in January 1995 and 171.4 in January 2001).

12. The capital allowances figure of £85,000 comprised :

	£
12 months to 30/11/00	55,000
3 months to 28/2/01	30,000

You are required :

To calculate the corporation tax payable for the accounting periods ended 28 February 2001 and to state when this is payable.   *(ACCA)*

*C7   R Ltd is a small company engaged in the manufacture and distribution of plumbing equipment. Following a period of poor trading results, its taxable income in recent years has been approximately £180,000. Early in 1999 the directors estimated that the taxable profits would be £220,000 for each of the two years to 31 March 2000 and 2001.

In March 1999, the directors were considering the possibility of R Ltd acquiring a controlling interest in two other small companies in the same trade - S Ltd and T Ltd. The taxable profits of each of these companies for the two years above were estimated at £20,000 per annum.

You are required :

To advise the directors of the differing aggregate corporation tax liabilities which will arise if :

(i)   the above plan is adopted

(ii) R Ltd acquires the businesses of S Ltd and T Ltd - taking over their assets, trades and workforces, but not acquiring a shareholding. S Ltd and T Ltd would be wound up.   *(CIMA)*

*C8   On 1 August 1997 X Ltd granted a 20-year lease to Y Ltd on the following terms :

- An annual rental of £20,000, payable quarterly in advance on 1 August, 1 November, 1 February and 1 May each year.
- A premium of £80,000 payable by Y Ltd on 1 August 1997.

On 1 April 2000, Y Ltd intends sub-letting the premises to Z Ltd on the following terms :

- A term of 5 years, at the end of which Y Ltd will resume occupancy.
- An annual rental of £28,000, payable in advance each year on 1 April.
- A premium of £45,000 payable by Z Ltd on 1 April 2000.

You are required :

(a)   To compute, for the year ended 31 March 1998, the amount assessed to corporation tax under Schedule A on X Ltd and the amount of the premium which Y Ltd may deduct in arriving at its trading profits chargeable to corporation tax. (Assume that both companies make up accounts annually to 31 March).

(b)   To compute the amount assessed to corporation tax under Schedule A on Y Ltd for its year ended 31 March 2001.

(c)   To comment briefly on the capital gains implications of the above transactions.

(CIMA)

*C9   Mr B has been production manager in a large engineering firm for several years, earning approximately £40,000 p.a. He has recently decided to start up his own business and seeks your advice on all of the differences, from a taxation point of view, between trading as a sole trader or as a limited company. It is possible that his wife will become involved in the running of the business.

He has estimated that during the first year, while the business is developing, it is unlikely that any profit will result. Indeed, it is possible that a loss will arise. Thereafter he anticipates that profits will rise rapidly to approximately £70,000 p.a. His living expenses amount to about £20,000 per year and initially this will be provided from his savings.

You are required :

To prepare a list of headings which would be contained in a report designed to highlight these differences. Under each heading, you should give a brief description of the difference between trading as a sole trader or as a company. You are not required to write the complete report.   *(CIMA)*

*C10   HD Ltd owns 80% of the ordinary share capital of SD Ltd. These shares were acquired during 1986. Both companies are UK resident for tax purposes and neither has any other associated companies. Their most recent results have been :

	HD Ltd y/e 31/12/00 £	SD Ltd 9 months to 31/3/01 £
INCOME		
Trading profit	890,000	-
Trading loss	-	102,000
Bank interest	6,000	4,000
Schedule A	2,000	8,000
Capital gains	-	20,000
Capital losses	15,000	-
Dividend from SD Ltd	27,000	
Dividends from UK companies		32,000
CHARGES PAID		
Trade charge (gross amount)	4,000	5,000
DIVIDEND PAID	327,000	33,750

You are required :

(a)   To compute the corporation tax payable by each company for the above accounting periods, assuming that maximum group relief is claimed by HD Ltd.

(b)   To suggest a more tax-efficient way in which HD Ltd might have arranged the sales of the assets which gave rise to the capital gains and losses shown above.

(CIMA)

PART 4
MISCELLANEOUS

Chapter 29

Value added tax (1)

Introduction

This is the first of two chapters concerned with value added tax (VAT), which is an indirect tax charged on the supply of a wide variety of goods and services. The tax was introduced in 1973 but current legislation is to be found in the VAT Act 1994, as amended by subsequent Finance Acts. As stated in Chapter 1, VAT is administered by the Customs and Excise, not by the Inland Revenue.

The principle of VAT

The basic principle of VAT is that tax should be charged at each stage of the production and distribution process but that the total tax due should be borne by the final consumer of the product. This is achieved as follows :

(a) Traders who are registered for VAT (see below) are required to charge VAT on their sales and must account for this "output tax" to Customs and Excise, but

(b) such traders are allowed to recover from Customs and Excise the "input tax" which they pay to their own suppliers, so that

(c) in effect, registered traders suffer no VAT and the total VAT is borne by the consumer at the end of the distribution chain.

EXAMPLE 1

A Ltd owns a quarry. It extracts stone from this quarry and sells the stone to B Ltd for £10,000 plus VAT. B Ltd converts all the stone into paving slabs and sells these slabs to C Ltd for £18,000, plus VAT. C Ltd owns and runs a garden centre, where the slabs are sold to the general public for a total of £32,000, plus VAT. Show how VAT is charged and collected at each stage of this process. (Assume that VAT is to be calculated at 17.5% throughout).

SOLUTION

	Cost price before VAT £	Input tax £	Selling price before VAT £	Output tax £	Paid to C & E £
A Ltd	-	-	10,000	1,750	1,750
B Ltd	10,000	1,750	18,000	3,150	1,400
C Ltd	18,000	3,150	32,000	5,600	2,450
Total VAT charged					5,600

Note :

None of the three companies involved suffers any net VAT. In each case, the total of input tax paid to suppliers and the amount due to Customs and Excise is precisely equal to the output tax received from customers. The final consumers, who are unable to reclaim the VAT which they pay, bear the total VAT of £5,600.

Taxable persons

Formally, VAT is chargeable when a *taxable supply* of goods or services is made in the UK by a *taxable person* in the course of business. For VAT purposes, the term "person" can refer to an individual, a partnership or a company, as well as to any other body which is supplying goods or services in the course of business. There is no requirement that a profit motive should exist, merely that goods or services are supplied for a consideration, so the term "person" can also refer to a charity, club etc.

A *taxable person* is a person making taxable supplies who is, or who should be, registered for VAT. Persons must register if their turnover of taxable items exceeds a prescribed threshold and might register voluntarily even if their turnover is below the threshold (see later in this chapter).

A taxable person charges VAT to customers when supplying them with taxable items, must account for this output tax to the Customs and Excise and may reclaim the tax suffered on inputs. A person who is not a taxable person can neither charge VAT to customers nor reclaim input tax.

Taxable supplies

A *taxable supply* is any supply of goods or services in the UK other than a supply which is specifically exempted from VAT. VAT is charged on a taxable supply at the standard rate (17.5%) unless the supply attracts VAT at the lower rate (5%) or at the zero rate (0%). The lower rate (also known as the "reduced rate") applies to :

(a) fuel and power supplied for domestic or charity use

(b) the installation of energy-saving materials in all homes

(c) the grant-funded installation, repair or maintenance of central heating systems in the homes of qualifying pensioners

(d) qualifying security goods installed in the homes of qualifying pensioners at the same time as energy saving materials or central heating systems

(e) the grant-funded installation of heating system measures in the homes of the less well-off

(f) women's sanitary products (as from 1 January 2001).

The types of supply which are taxable at the zero rate and the types of supply which are exempted from VAT altogether are described later in this chapter.

Supply of goods

A supply of goods is deemed to occur when the ownership of goods passes from one person to another. In general, a supply of goods will fall within the scope of VAT only if it is made for a consideration (i.e. in return for money or payment in kind) but the following are also deemed to be supplies of goods for VAT purposes :

(a) gifts of business assets other than :

    (i) gifts costing no more than £15 which are not part of a series or succession of gifts to the same person

    (ii) gifts consisting of samples (but if two or more identical samples are given to the same person, only one of these samples is deemed not to be a supply).

(b) goods permanently taken out of a business for private use by the owner or an employee of the business, in respect of which input tax has been paid.

The sale of goods on hire purchase is deemed to be a supply of goods even though, strictly speaking, ownership of the goods does not transfer until the end of the HP contract. VAT is charged on the cash price of the goods, not the HP price.

Supply of services

Any supply which is made for a consideration but which is not a supply of goods is deemed to be a supply of services. However, a gift of services is not a taxable supply. The hiring of goods to a customer is a supply of services, not a supply of goods, since the ownership of the goods does not pass to the customer. A supply of services is also deemed to occur if the owner or an employee of a business :

(a) temporarily makes private use of goods owned by the business, in respect of which input tax has been paid, or

(b) makes private use of services which have been supplied to the business, in respect of which input tax has been paid.

By concession, the private use of a business motor car does not rank as a taxable supply.

Exempt supplies

A supply of goods or services is an exempt supply if it falls within one of thirteen exemption groups. In summary, these exemption groups are as follows :

Group 1   The sale or lease of land and buildings, other than :

    (i)   the sale (or lease for more than 21 years) of new and certain second-hand buildings to be used for residential or charitable purposes (zero-rated)

    (ii)   the sale of new or uncompleted commercial buildings or of land to be used for their construction (standard-rated)

    (iii)   the supply of used commercial buildings, if the vendor has elected to treat the supply as taxable at the standard rate (the "option to tax", see below)

    (iv)   the grant of gaming or fishing rights; the provision of hotel or holiday accommodation or seasonal caravan and camping pitches; the grant of timber rights; the provision of parking facilities or facilities for the storage or mooring of aircraft, ships etc; the grant of the right to occupy a box or a seat at a theatre, sports ground etc; the letting of sports facilities (all standard-rated).

Group 2   Insurance

Group 3   Postal services provided by the Post Office

Group 4   Betting, gaming and lotteries

Group 5   Financial services (e.g. bank charges, stockbroking, underwriting)

Group 6   Education provided by schools, universities and further education colleges

Group 7   Health and welfare services

Group 8   Burial and cremation services

Group 9   Supplies made to members of trade unions and professional bodies in return for a membership subscription

Group 10   Entry fees paid to non-profit-making bodies for the right to enter sports competitions

Group 11   Disposals of works of art to approved bodies (e.g. the National Gallery)

Group 12   Certain fund-raising events organised by charities.

Group 13   Cultural services (i.e. charges made by public and other eligible bodies for admission to museums, galleries, exhibitions, zoos or performances of a cultural nature).

As from 1 January 2000, the supply of investment gold is also an exempt supply. The tax implications of a supply of goods or services being exempt are as follows :

(a)   VAT cannot be charged on an exempt supply.

(b) A person who makes only exempt supplies cannot register for VAT, charges no output tax, is not a taxable person and, most importantly, cannot reclaim input tax.

(c) In effect, a person making only exempt supplies is in the same position as the final consumer at the end of a distribution chain.

It is this inability to reclaim input tax which might lead the vendor of a used commercial building to elect for the "option to tax" (see above). If the election is made, the vendor charges output tax on the sale or rent of the building, becomes a taxable person and may reclaim input tax. Of course, the buyer of the building will have to pay VAT, but if the buyer is also a taxable person then he or she will be able to reclaim the tax paid and therefore may not object to the arrangement.

Zero-rated supplies

Supplies which are made by a taxable person and which are not specifically exempted from VAT are taxed at the standard rate of 17.5% (or at the lower rate of 5%) unless they fall within one of sixteen zero-rated groups. These are listed below.

Group 1   Food, but certain luxury foods (e.g. chocolates) and food supplied in the course of catering are standard-rated

Group 2   Sewerage services and water (other than for industrial use)

Group 3   Books, newspapers, journals etc. (but stationery is standard-rated)

Group 4   Talking books, radios etc. for the blind

Group 5   The sale by builders of new buildings to be used for residential or charitable purposes and second-hand buildings which were previously non-residential but which have been converted for residential use. Zero-rating also applies to the amount payable by a tenant on the grant of a lease of more than 21 years on such a building.

Group 6   The sale by builders of substantially reconstructed "protected buildings" (i.e. listed buildings) to be used for residential or charitable purposes. As for Group 5, zero-rating also applies to leases of more than 21 years on such buildings.

Group 7   International services (e.g. making arrangements for services which are to be performed outside the European Union)

Group 8   Passenger transport, but pleasure transport and transport in vehicles seating less than 12 people (e.g. taxis) are standard-rated

Group 9   Certain caravans and houseboats

Group 10 Gold supplied by a central bank to another central bank or to a member of the London Gold Market

Group 11   Bank notes

Group 12   Drugs, medicines etc. prescribed by a medical practitioner

Group 13   Certain exports (see later in this chapter)

Group 14   Sales in tax-free shops

Group 15   The sale by a charity of donated goods and certain types of supply made to a charity (e.g. advertising)

Group 16   Children's clothing and footwear and certain protective clothing (e.g. crash helmets).

The implications of a supply of goods or services being zero-rated are as follows :

(a) The supply is a taxable supply but the VAT due is calculated at 0% so, in effect, no tax is charged.

(b) A person who makes only zero-rated supplies is nonetheless making taxable supplies and must register as a taxable person if taxable turnover exceeds the prescribed threshold. Having registered (and this may be done voluntarily, even if taxable turnover is less than the threshold, as explained below) the person will then be able to reclaim all input tax paid.

The value of a supply

The "value" of a taxable supply is the amount on which the VAT charge is based and this is normally equal to the price (before VAT) charged by the supplier. For example, if a standard-rated supply is made at a price of £1,000, plus VAT at 17.5%, then the value of the supply is £1,000 and the total consideration given for the supply is £1,175.

The VAT component of the consideration (for standard-rated supplies) can be found by multiplying the consideration by the "VAT fraction" which is currently 17.5/117.5 = 7/47. Note the following points regarding the value of a supply :

(a) If a supply consists of a gift of business assets, the value of the supply is deemed to be the price (excluding VAT) which the person receiving the gift would have to pay to purchase goods identical in every respect to the goods concerned. This rule also applies if assets are taken permanently out of a business for private use by the owner or an employee of the business.

(b) If the owner or an employee temporarily makes private use of business assets, the value of the resulting supply of services is the cost of providing the services. This cost is based on the amount by which the assets have depreciated whilst being used for private purposes.

(c) If private use is made of services which have been supplied to the business, the value of the resulting supply of services is equal to an appropriate proportion of the value of the supply which was made to the business.

(d) If the consideration for a supply is paid in kind or if the supply is made to a connected person for less than market value, the value of the supply is taken to be the market value of the goods or services supplied.

EXAMPLE 2

(a) A standard-rated supply is made with a value of £180. Calculate the VAT charged and the total consideration for the supply.

(b) A standard-rated supply is made for a total consideration of £1,739. Calculate the VAT element and the value of the supply.

SOLUTION

(a) The VAT charged is £31.50 (£180 x 17.5%) and the total consideration is £211.50.

(b) The VAT element is £259 (£1,739 x 7/47) and the value of the supply is £1,480.

Cash discounts

If a customer is offered a cash discount in return for prompt payment, the value of the supply is the price charged by the supplier (before VAT), less the maximum cash discount which the customer might receive. This is the case whether or not the customer actually takes advantage of the discount.

Note that the VAT fraction cannot be used to calculate the VAT component of the consideration if a cash discount is offered but not taken.

EXAMPLE 3

A standard-rated supply is made at a price of £4,000, plus VAT. The customer is offered a 3% discount if payment is made within 30 days. Calculate the value of the supply and the VAT charged on the supply.

SOLUTION

The value of the supply is £3,880 (£4,000, less 3%) and the VAT charged is £679 (£3,880 x 17.5%). If the customer pays within 30 days, the consideration will be £4,559. If the customer pays after 30 days, the consideration will be £4,679 (£4,000 + £679).

Mixed supplies

A "mixed supply" occurs if a mixture of goods and/or services is invoiced together at a single inclusive price. If all of the items in the mixture are chargeable to VAT at the same rate, the value of the supply and the related output tax can be calculated in the usual way. Otherwise, it will be necessary to apportion the price charged between the various elements of the mixture in order to calculate the output tax due. There is no standard way of achieving this apportionment but the method used must be fair and justifiable.

EXAMPLE 4

A VAT-exclusive price of £320 is charged for a mixed supply of goods. The goods concerned consist of standard-rated goods which cost the supplier £141 (excluding VAT) and zero-rated goods which cost the supplier £19. Calculate the output tax due.

SOLUTION

From the information given, the only way of apportioning the price of the mixed supply into the standard-rated element and the zero-rated element is to split the price according to the cost of each element to the supplier. On this basis, the value of the supply represented by standard-rated goods is £320 x 141/160 i.e. £282. VAT at 17.5% of this figure gives £49.35. Therefore the total price charged should be £369.35.

Composite supplies

A "composite supply" occurs if a mixture of goods and/or services is supplied together in such a way that it is not possible to split the supply into its component parts. In this case, the supply as a whole must be considered in order to determine the rate of tax due (if any). For example, in the case of *Mander Laundries Ltd* (1973) it was held that the services of a launderette consist of a single, standard-rated supply of services, not a mixed supply of water, heat, hire of washing machines etc.

Self-supply

A "self-supply" occurs when a person makes a supply to himself or herself. For example, a self-supply of stationery takes place if a business sets up its own printing works to provide the business with necessary stationery and other printed matter. The Treasury is empowered to order that, for VAT purposes, self-supplied goods or services are regarded as both :

(a)   a taxable supply made *by* the business, and

(b)   a taxable supply made *to* the business.

The effect of such an order is that output tax must be accounted for in relation to the supply but that an equal amount of input tax is deemed to have been suffered. This input tax will be irrecoverable if the person concerned makes wholly exempt supplies.

Imports and exports

The VAT treatment of imports and exports depends upon two main factors:

(a) whether the transactions involve goods or services, and

(b) whether the transactions are between the UK and a country which is not a member of the European Union (EU) or between the UK and another EU member.

A brief summary of this complex area is given below.

Imports of goods to the UK from non-EU countries

VAT is charged on the import of goods to the UK from outside the EU (at the same rate as if the goods had been supplied in the UK) and must be paid by the person to whom the goods are supplied, whether or not that person is a taxable person. Note the following points:

(a) The VAT on imported goods is normally payable at the point of entry to the UK, but importers who are taxable persons may defer immediate payment and pay by direct debit once a month. Customs and Excise require a guarantee from an approved bank or insurance company before allowing importers to defer payments in this way.

(b) For importers who are taxable persons, the VAT due on postal imports with a value not exceeding £2,000 may be deferred until the VAT return is submitted for the tax period which includes the date of importation.

(c) The VAT suffered by taxable persons on imported goods may be treated as input tax.

Exports of goods from the UK to non-EU countries

Exports of goods from the UK to non-EU countries are zero-rated.

Goods traded between EU countries

If a registered person in one EU country supplies goods to a registered person in another EU country (and the customer's VAT registration number is obtained and shown on the sales invoice) then:

(a) The supply is zero-rated in the country of origin, so the supplier does not have to account for any output tax in relation to the supply.

(b) The customer must account for VAT on the "acquisition" (the term "import" is not used in this context) at whatever rate is applicable to those goods in the destination country.

(c) The VAT suffered by the customer may then be treated as input tax.

If the purchaser's VAT registration number is not known, or if the purchaser is not a registered person, the supplier will charge VAT at the rate applicable in the country of origin.

International services

If certain services are supplied in the UK by an overseas supplier then the person *receiving* the services is treated as if he or she were the supplier and is required to account for output tax in relation to them. This is known as the "reverse charge" procedure. The VAT suffered by taxable persons on imported services as a result of this procedure may be treated as input tax. The reverse charge procedure applies to the following types of services (excluding any services which are exempt from VAT) :

(a) certain advertising, professional, financial, insurance etc. services which are used by the recipient for business purposes (whether or not the recipient is a registered person)

(b) services of any kind which are supplied to a registered person and which are used for business purposes.

Subject to the normal registration rules, an overseas supplier may register in the UK and charge UK VAT on the supply of services in the UK. In this case, the reverse charge procedure does not apply.

Exports of services are largely outside the scope of UK VAT, but those which are taxable are zero-rated.

Registration

The total value of the taxable supplies made by a person in a year is known as that person's "taxable turnover". A person whose taxable turnover exceeds the registration threshold (£52,000 as from 1 April 2000) *must* register with Customs and Excise. Form VAT1 is used for this purpose, though Customs and Excise have indicated that it will eventually be possible to register via the Internet. A VAT registration number is issued, which must be quoted on the person's tax invoices (see next chapter).

A person who is liable to register but who fails to do so is still a taxable person and is personally responsible for the output tax due in relation to supplies made since the date on which registration should have occurred.

When deciding whether or not the registration threshold has been exceeded, it is necessary to aggregate the taxable turnover from all of a person's business activities. The registration relates to the person, *not* to an individual business. It is important to bear in mind the definition of the word "person" for VAT purposes (see above) and to aggregate taxable supplies only if they are made by the same person.

EXAMPLE 5

(a) Jim is a sole trader with a taxable turnover of £46,000 p.a. Is he required to register with Customs & Excise ?

(b) Pearl and Dean are in partnership, operating a business with a taxable turnover of £60,000 p.a. Is anyone required to register ?

(c) Julia is a sole trader with a taxable turnover of £21,000 p.a. She is also in partnership with Julie, operating a business with a taxable turnover of £45,000 p.a. Is anyone required to register ?

SOLUTION

(a) No. Jim's taxable turnover does not exceed the registration threshold.

(b) Yes. The partnership of Pearl and Dean is one "person" for VAT purposes and has a taxable turnover exceeding the registration threshold. Therefore the partnership must register.

(c) No. Julia as a sole trader is one "person", whilst the partnership of Julia and Julie is another, quite separate, "person". Neither of these persons has a taxable turnover exceeding the registration threshold so neither of them is required to register.

Business splitting

"Business splitting" or "disaggregation" occurs when a business with a taxable turnover exceeding the registration threshold is divided into two or more smaller businesses, each operated by a different person and each with a taxable turnover not exceeding the registration threshold, in the hope of avoiding registration.

If this type of manoeuvre were successful, supplies could be made to customers without charging VAT and the administrative costs associated with making VAT returns and maintaining VAT records (see next chapter) could be avoided. The only disadvantage would be that input tax could not be reclaimed but in the case of a business with mainly exempt or zero-rated inputs this disadvantage would be slight.

However, if a business has been split artificially, Customs and Excise have the power to direct that the persons conducting the split businesses should be treated as a single taxable person for VAT purposes. This direction may be made even if the split businesses have never been operated as a single unit, so long as Customs and Excise are satisfied that only one business really exists.

When to register

In general, a person is required to register for VAT if, at the end of any month, the value of that person's taxable supplies for the year ended on the last day of the month exceeds the registration threshold (£52,000 as from 1 April 2000). Customs and Excise must be notified within 30 days of the end of the relevant month. Registration will then usually take effect after the end of the month following the relevant month. However, registration will not be required if Customs & Excise are satisfied that taxable turnover during the next 12 months will not exceed the deregistration threshold (£50,000 as from 1 April 2000).

Registration is also required if, at any time, there are reasonable grounds for believing that taxable turnover during the next 30 days will exceed the registration threshold. In this case, Customs & Excise must be notified no later than the end of the 30-day period and registration takes effect from the beginning of that period.

For the purpose of deciding whether the registration threshold has been or will be exceeded, supplies consisting of the capital assets of a business are not included in taxable turnover. (But note that such supplies normally receive no special treatment, so that the sale of a fixed asset will be a taxable supply unless the asset falls into one of the exemption groups).

EXAMPLE 6

Kevin begins trading on 1 January 1999. Taxable turnover during the first 18 months of trading is as follows :

1999	£	*2000*	£
January	1,800	January	4,400
February	2,100	February	4,000
March	2,800	March	3,500
April	2,600	April	4,500
May	2,400	May	5,500
June	2,900	June	5,300
July	3,300		
August	3,500		
September	4,200		
October	5,500		
November	6,900		
December	6,200		

The turnover in January 2000 includes £2,000 relating to the sale of plant and machinery previously used in the trade. State the date on which Kevin must register for VAT. (The VAT registration threshold was £50,000 until 1 April 1999 and £51,000 until 1 April 2000).

SOLUTION

At the end of each month, cumulative taxable turnover during the previous 12 months (or since the start of trade, if less) are as follows :

1999	£	2000	£
January	1,800	January	44,800
February	3,900	February	46,700
March	6,700	March	47,400
April	9,300	April	49,300
May	11,700	May	52,400
June	14,600	June	54,800
July	17,900		
August	21,400		
September	25,600		
October	31,100		
November	38,000		
December	44,200		

Notes :

(i) The cumulative figure at the end of January 2000 consists of the turnover for the months of February 1999 to January 2000 inclusive, less the £2,000 relating to the sale of plant and machinery.

(ii) The registration threshold is passed at the end of May 2000. Kevin must notify Customs & Excise of this fact by 30 June 2000 and registration will probably take effect as from 1 July 2000.

If a registered person transfers a business as a going concern to an unregistered person then (for the purpose of deciding whether or not the transferee should register for VAT) supplies made by the transferred business before the transfer are deemed to have been made by the transferee. So if the transferred business, together with any other business operated by the transferee, had a taxable turnover exceeding the registration threshold in the 12 months prior to the transfer, the transferee must register for VAT immediately.

Voluntary registration

A person making taxable supplies which do not exceed the registration threshold may nonetheless register for VAT voluntarily. This enables the person concerned to recover input tax but means that output tax must be charged when taxable supplies are made to customers. However, if the supplies are all zero-rated, or consist of standard-rated supplies made wholly or mainly to customers who are themselves taxable persons, the fact that output tax must be charged will probably not deter customers.

Being registered for VAT will add to the administrative costs of running the business but this consideration may be outweighed by the benefit of being able to recover input tax.

EXAMPLE 7

Lindsey is not registered for VAT. In the year to 31 December 2000, she has inputs costing £10,000 plus VAT at 17.5%. Her outputs total £32,000.

(a) How much profit does she make for the year ?

(b) If she had registered for VAT voluntarily, how much profit would she have made for the year ?

(c) Does it matter whether the supplies that she makes are all :

   (i) zero-rated ?

   (ii) standard-rated supplies made to VAT-registered businesses ?

   (iii) standard-rated supplies made to the general public ?

SOLUTION

(a) Her profit is £20,250 (£32,000 - £11,750).

(b) If she had registered for VAT (and her outputs had remained at £32,000) she would have been able to reclaim her input tax, giving her a profit of £22,000 (£32,000 - £10,000).

(c) (i) If she makes only zero-rated supplies, voluntary registration has no effect on her selling prices and, therefore, no effect on her sales.

   (ii) If she makes only standard-rated supplies to VAT-registered businesses, her prices will increase by 17.5% but her customers will be able to reclaim the extra tax paid and so there will be no effect on her sales.

   (iii) If she makes only standard-rated supplies to the general public, increasing her prices by 17.5% may well entail a loss of custom. In these circumstances she may prefer not to register.

Exemption from registration

Customs and Excise may grant exemption from registration to a person making supplies which exceed the registration threshold, so long as these supplies are all zero-rated. Such an application might be made if the amount of input tax which could be reclaimed if the person concerned were registered is small when contrasted with the increased administrative costs associated with VAT registration.

Pre-registration input tax

VAT incurred before registration is not input tax. Nonetheless, it can be treated as input tax so long as certain conditions are satisfied. These conditions vary according to whether the VAT is incurred on a supply of goods or a supply of services :

(a) **Goods**. VAT suffered on a pre-registration supply of goods may be treated as input tax so long as the goods were supplied to the taxable person for business purposes and were not sold or consumed before the date of registration.

(b) **Services**. VAT suffered on a pre-registration supply of services may be treated as input tax so long as the services were supplied to the taxable person for business purposes no more than six months before the date of registration.

Group registration

A group of associated companies (see Chapter 28) may apply for the group to be registered as a single taxable person, rather than each company in the group being registered individually. Group registration has the following consequences :

(a) The input tax suffered by the group as a whole is set against the output tax charged by the group as a whole.

(b) One of the companies in the group is nominated as the "representative member" and this company takes responsibility for submitting VAT returns and accounting for VAT on behalf of the entire group. However, if the representative member fails to pay any VAT which is due to Customs and Excise, any other company in the group can be held liable for the debt.

(c) Supplies between group members are not regarded as taxable supplies and are ignored for VAT purposes.

Individual group companies may register separately if they wish and choose not to join the VAT group. This may improve the cash flow position of a company which makes mainly zero-rated supplies and which has chosen to make monthly VAT returns (see next chapter). It is also possible for a group of associated companies to form two or more VAT groups, with some of the companies belonging to one VAT group and some belonging to another.

It is worth noting that the group registration rules offer tax avoidance opportunities to certain companies and that Customs and Excise are empowered to remove a company from a VAT group if they suspect avoidance.

Deregistration

Deregistration may be either voluntary or compulsory :

(a) A registered person may deregister voluntarily if the Customs and Excise are satisfied that taxable turnover excluding supplies of capital assets will not exceed the deregistration threshold (£50,000 from 1 April 2000) in the next 12 months.

(b) Compulsory deregistration is triggered when a registered person entirely ceases to make taxable supplies. The person must notify Customs and Excise within 30 days that this has occurred and deregistration will normally take effect as from the date on which taxable supplies ceased.

(c) Deregistration is also compulsory on a change of legal status (e.g. when a sole trader admits a partner or when the business of a partnership is taken over by a company).

On deregistration, the person concerned is deemed to make a supply of all the tangible assets of the business and output tax is charged accordingly. However, assets on which no input tax was incurred are excluded from this deemed supply and the output tax due is not collected if it does not exceed £1,000 in total. The deemed supply does *not* take place if the business is sold as a going concern to another taxable person.

Summary

► VAT is chargeable when a taxable person makes a taxable supply of goods or services in the course of business.

► A taxable supply is any supply of goods or services other than an exempt supply and may be charged to value added tax at either the standard rate, the lower rate or the zero rate.

► A taxable person is a person who is making taxable supplies and who is (or should be) VAT registered. A taxable person may be an individual, a partnership, a company, a charity, a club or an association.

► A person making taxable supplies which exceed the registration threshold must register with Customs and Excise. A person making taxable supplies which do not exceed the threshold may register voluntarily.

► A taxable person must account to Customs and Excise for the output tax charged to customers but may recover some or all of the input tax paid to suppliers.

► A person making only exempt supplies cannot charge VAT to customers and is unable to recover input tax.

Exercises

29.1 A standard-rated supply is made at a price of £340, plus VAT. Calculate the VAT chargeable and the consideration for the supply if :

(a) no discount is offered

(b) a 2% discount is offered for prompt payment and the customer takes advantage of this discount

(c) a 2% discount is offered for prompt payment and the customer does not take advantage of this discount.

29.2 In each of the following cases, is anyone required to register with Customs and Excise ? If so, who ?

(a) Lorna is a sole trader, making taxable supplies of £53,000 p.a.

(b) Mike owns two distinct businesses. One has a taxable turnover of £28,000 p.a. and the other has a taxable turnover of £35,000 p.a.

(c) Pat and Phil are in partnership. The taxable turnover of their business is £42,000. Phil also owns another business with a taxable turnover of £38,000 p.a.

(d) JS Ltd has a taxable turnover of £250,000 p.a. The company's shares are owned entirely by John Smith and his wife.

29.3 Rosemary owns a business which has an annual turnover (excluding any VAT) of £55,000. Describe her VAT position if :

(a) she makes wholly exempt supplies

(b) she makes wholly standard-rated supplies

(c) she makes wholly zero-rated supplies.

29.4 Explain the VAT consequences of making a "self-supply".

*29.5 Answer the following questions :

(a) who should register for VAT ?

(b) when should registration occur ?

(c) what are the consequences of failing to register ?

(d) when may a taxable person deregister ?

(e) why might someone choose to register voluntarily ?

Chapter 30

Value added tax (2)

Introduction

The previous chapter outlined the main principles of value added tax and explained the processes of registration and deregistration. This second VAT chapter is concerned with the procedures used to account for VAT to HM Customs and Excise and the way in which the tax is administered. Other matters considered in this chapter include non-recoverable input tax and the VAT position of persons who supply a mixture of exempt and taxable goods or services.

Accounting for VAT

At regular intervals (usually quarterly) registered persons must submit a return to Customs and Excise, showing the input tax and output tax for the period covered by the return. Any excess of output tax over input tax is payable to Customs and Excise, whilst any excess of input tax over output tax is repayable by Customs and Excise. The return is made on form VAT100 and must be submitted within one month of the end of the "tax period" to which it relates, together with any tax due.

During tax year 2000/01, Customs and Excise intend to introduce services which will allow VAT returns to be submitted via the Internet. Small businesses which file their VAT returns in this way in 2001/02 (and pay any tax due electronically) will receive a one-off discount of £50.

Monthly accounting

A registered person making supplies which are wholly or mainly zero-rated will be entitled to a VAT repayment in most tax periods. Such a person may opt to submit VAT returns monthly rather than quarterly, so speeding up tax repayments at the expense of making twelve returns per year rather than four.

Annual accounting

A registered person making supplies which are wholly or mainly standard-rated will be required to make a payment of VAT in most tax periods. So long as taxable turnover does not exceed £300,000 p.a., such a person may opt to join the "annual accounting scheme" and submit only one VAT return per year. The scheme operates as follows :

(a) At the beginning of each year, Customs and Excise estimate the total VAT liability for the year (based on past experience).

(b) During the year the person makes nine interim payments to Customs and Excise, each equal to 10% of the estimated liability for the year. These payments must be made by direct debit and begin in the fourth month of the year.

(c) At the end of the year the annual return is submitted together with a tenth payment consisting of the balance of the VAT due for the year. The return and payment must be made within 2 months of the end of the year.

The scheme operates differently for businesses with a taxable turnover which does not exceed £100,000 p.a. Such businesses are not required to make any interim payments at all unless their estimated VAT liability for the year is £2,000 or more, in which case three quarterly interim payments are required, each equal to 20% of the estimated liability for the year.

Monthly payments on account

A registered person who makes quarterly returns and whose annual VAT liability exceeds £2,000,000 is obliged to make monthly payments on account (POA's) to Customs and Excise. The first payment is due one month before the end of the quarter, the second payment is due at the end of the quarter and a balancing payment is due one month after the end of the quarter. All of these payments must be made electronically (e.g. through the Bankers Automated Clearing System (BACS)).

Each of the two payments on account is usually calculated as 1/24th of the person's total VAT liability for the previous year. However, the person concerned may choose to pay his or her actual VAT liability for each month rather than the set POA's.

The tax point

The date on which a supply is deemed to occur is known as the "tax point" of that supply. The tax point of a supply determines :

(a) for outputs, the tax period in which the output tax relating to that supply must be accounted for

(b) for inputs, the tax period in which the input tax relating to that supply may be reclaimed

(c) the rate of VAT applicable to the supply (if VAT rates change).

For a supply of goods the "basic tax point" is the date on which the goods are removed or made available to the customer. For a supply of services the basic tax point is the date on which the services are performed. However, the actual tax point of a supply will differ from the basic tax point in the following circumstances :

(a) If the supplier issues a tax invoice or receives payment on a date which is earlier than the basic tax point, then that date becomes the actual tax point.

(b) If the supplier issues a tax invoice within 14 days after the basic tax point, then the invoice date becomes the actual tax point.

Customs and Excise may extend the 14-day rule mentioned above if asked to do so by a registered person. For example, a person who normally issues invoices at the end of each month might request that the invoice date should always be used as the tax point, even though this date will be more than 14 days after the basic tax point for supplies made in the first half of the month.

Cash accounting

A registered person whose taxable turnover does not exceed £350,000 p.a., may opt to join the "cash accounting scheme". Registered persons who belong to this scheme account for output tax in the tax period in which *payment is received* from the customer and reclaim input tax in the tax period in which *payment is made* to the supplier. (The tax point is ignored when allocating inputs and outputs to tax periods).

Joining this scheme allows a registered person to delay the payment of output tax to Customs & Excise until the tax has actually been received from customers, which is of benefit if customers are given extended credit. The scheme also provides automatic relief for bad debts (see below). On the other hand, input tax cannot be reclaimed until that input tax has actually been paid to suppliers. A registered person may not join the cash accounting scheme unless :

(a) the person's taxable turnover (excluding sales of capital items) is not expected to exceed £350,000 in the next 12 months, and

(b) the person's VAT returns are up to date, and

(c) all amounts of VAT due to be paid to Customs and Excise (including any penalties and interest) have in fact been paid, or the person has come to an arrangement for such payments to be made by instalments, and

(d) within the previous 12 months, the person has not been convicted of a VAT offence or assessed to a penalty for VAT evasion involving dishonest conduct.

A person operating the cash accounting scheme must withdraw from the scheme at the end of a tax period if the value of his or her taxable turnover for the last 12 months has exceeded £437,500. Customs and Excise will allow such a person to remain in the scheme only if it can be demonstrated that the high turnover was caused by a large "one-off" sale which is not expected to recur and that the expected value of taxable turnover for the next 12 months will be no more than £350,000.

The cash accounting scheme cannot be used for supplies of goods and services which are invoiced before the supply is made, or for supplies where payment is not due for more than six months after the date of the invoice.

Tax invoices

If a taxable person makes a taxable supply to another taxable person, then a "tax invoice" must be issued. The purpose of this invoice is to provide documentary evidence of the transaction, so allowing the person receiving the supply to reclaim the input tax related to that supply. The required contents of a valid tax invoice are :

(a) the invoice number, date and tax point

(b) the name, address and VAT registration number of the supplier

(c) the name and address of the customer

(d) the type of supply (e.g. sale, HP sale, hire etc.)

(e) for each invoice item, a description of the goods or services supplied

(f) for each description, the quantity of the goods or the extent of the services, the amount payable (before VAT) and the rate of VAT applicable.

(g) the total amount due, before VAT

(h) the rate of any cash discount available

(i) the total amount of VAT chargeable at each rate and the total VAT chargeable.

The issue of a tax invoice is optional if a supply is made to a customer who is not a taxable person. Retailers are not required to issue a tax invoice unless asked for one by the customer and may then issue a less detailed tax invoice (so long as the consideration for the supply does not exceed £100). A less detailed tax invoice need show only the following information :

(a) the name, address and VAT registration number of the retailer

(b) the tax point

(c) a description of the goods or services supplied

(d) the total amount payable by the customer, including VAT

(e) the rate of tax applicable to the supply.

Accounting records

Every taxable person must keep such records as are required by Customs and Excise. The main records which must be kept are as follows :

(a) the usual business and accounting records (e.g. cashbooks, till rolls, paying-in slips, bank statements, purchases and sales books, orders and delivery notes, business correspondence, annual accounts etc.)

(b) a VAT account

(c) a copy of each tax invoice issued

(d) all tax invoices received (though tax invoices are not required for payments of £25 or less relating to telephone calls, parking fees or purchases made through coin-operated machines)

(e) documentation relating to imports and exports.

These records must be retained for at least 6 years and are open to inspection by Customs and Excise, who make regular "control visits" to all registered persons.

Bad debts

If a taxable person makes use of the cash accounting scheme, the output tax relating to a supply is not accounted for until the consideration for that supply has been received, and so automatic relief is given for bad debts.

But persons who do not use the cash accounting scheme might account for the output tax relating to a supply before the consideration for that supply is received and then find that a bad debt has occurred. In these circumstances, a claim may be made for a refund of the VAT lost, so long as :

(a) goods or services have been supplied for a consideration in money, and the related output tax has been accounted for to Customs and Excise

(b) the value of the supply was no more than its open market value

(c) the debt has been written off in the books of account

(d) at least 6 months have elapsed since both the date of the supply and the date that payment was due

(e) the claim for bad debt relief is made within 3 years and 6 months from the later of the date of the supply and the date that payment was due.

Non-deductible input tax

In general, a taxable person can reclaim the input tax relating to a supply so long as the supply is evidenced by a tax invoice and the goods or services involved are for use in the person's business. However, input tax is not reclaimable on certain types of supply, even though the supply is received in the course of business. The main examples of such "non-deductible input tax" are :

(a) VAT on business entertaining, if the entertaining is not allowable under the rules of Schedule D Case I

(b) VAT on costs incurred by a company in relation to the provision of domestic accommodation for a director of the company.

(c) VAT on the purchase of motor cars, apart from :

    (i)   cars acquired by a car dealer, as stock in trade, or

    (ii) cars acquired for use by a driving school, self-drive car rental business or taxi business

    (iii) cars acquired *wholly* for business use (primarily for leasing purposes).

If the input tax on the purchase of a car cannot be reclaimed, the subsequent sale of that car should be treated as an exempt supply. However, taxable persons may choose instead to charge output tax on the excess (if any) of the selling price over the purchase price.

(d) VAT on second-hand goods bought from a dealer operating the margin scheme (see later in this chapter).

The VAT on goods or services which are not used at all for business purposes cannot be reclaimed. If goods or services are used partly for business purposes and partly for private purposes, then there are two possible treatments. Either :

(a) the input tax on the supply is apportioned and the business element of the tax is then reclaimed, or

(b) the whole of the input tax on the supply is reclaimed, but output tax is then accounted for in relation to the element of private use.

The first treatment may be applied to a supply of either goods or services. The second treatment may be applied only to a supply of goods.

Fuel for private motoring

If the owner or an employee of a business is provided with fuel for private motoring, then all of the input tax relating to purchases of fuel by the business is reclaimable, but output tax (in accordance with set scale charges) must be accounted for in relation to the supply of fuel for private use. The quarterly scale charges (from 6 April 2000) are as follows :

	Petrol engines £	*Diesel engines* £
up to 1,400 cc	38.12	34.55
up to 2,000 cc	48.40	34.55
2,001 cc or more	71.19	43.93

Note the following points :

(a) These charges can be avoided if no input tax is reclaimed in relation to car fuel.

(b) The input tax suffered in relation to car repairs and maintenance is reclaimable in full (without any adjustment for private use) so long as the car is used for business purposes.

(c) Only 50% of the input tax relating to car leasing charges is reclaimable if there is any private use of the car.

EXAMPLE 1

Malcolm is self-employed and owns a 1,300 cc petrol-engined car which he uses for both business and private use. During the year to 5 April 2001, the total cost of the fuel used by the car (all paid for out of Malcolm's business bank account) is £1,200. Should Malcolm reclaim the input tax paid in relation to this fuel ?

SOLUTION

The input tax in question is £1,200 x 7/47 = £178.72. If this is reclaimed, Malcolm will have to account for output tax amounting to 4 x £38.12 = £152.48. This is less than £178.72 and so Malcolm should reclaim the input tax.

Partial exemption

As explained in the previous chapter, a taxable person making wholly taxable supplies may reclaim all input tax suffered (with the exceptions listed above). A person making wholly exempt supplies is not a taxable person and may reclaim no input tax at all.

A taxable person making partly taxable and partly exempt supplies is "partially exempt" and may reclaim only part of the input tax suffered. The amount of input tax which may be reclaimed for a tax period is the amount which is "attributed to taxable supplies". This amount is usually calculated as follows :

(a) Input tax suffered in the period on goods and services which are used exclusively for the purpose of making taxable supplies is attributed to taxable supplies and is reclaimable in full.

(b) Input tax suffered in the period on goods and services which are used exclusively for the purpose of making exempt supplies is not attributed to taxable supplies and cannot be reclaimed at all.

(c) A proportion of any remaining input tax suffered in the period (on goods and services used for making both taxable and exempt supplies) is attributed to taxable supplies and may be reclaimed. This proportion is calculated as follows :

$$\text{Remaining input tax} \quad x \quad \frac{\text{Value of taxable supplies}}{\text{Value of all supplies}}$$

The ratio of taxable supplies to all supplies is expressed as a percentage rounded up to the nearest whole number. When computing this ratio, certain supplies made by the taxable person are omitted from the calculation, including self-supplies and supplies consisting of the capital assets of the business.

(d) If the total amount of input tax not attributed to taxable supplies for a tax period does not exceed a "de minimis" limit of £625 per month (on average) and is also no more than 50% of all the input tax for the period, then it is treated as being attributed to taxable supplies and is reclaimable in full.

It is important to note that the calculation of reclaimable input tax for a tax period is only provisional. The calculation is performed again at the end of each year, taking into account input tax for the whole year and using a de minimis limit of £7,500 (12 x £625). Any difference between the amount of reclaimable input tax for the year and the total of the amounts which were calculated provisionally is an underpayment or overpayment of VAT and this must be accounted for to Customs and Excise. Note also that (subject to Customs and Excise approval) alternative methods may be used to calculate the amount of input tax which is reclaimable by a partially exempt taxable person.

EXAMPLE 2

During the quarter to 31 March 2001, Nancy makes supplies as follows :

	£
Standard-rated supplies (excluding VAT)	120,000
Zero-rated supplies	80,000
Exempt supplies	50,000

She suffers input tax as follows :

	£
Attributed to taxable supplies	7,500
Attributed to exempt supplies	8,500
Unattributed	12,000

Compute the VAT provisionally payable to Customs and Excise for the quarter.

SOLUTION

	£	£
Output tax		
Standard-rated supplies £120,000 @ 17.5%		21,000
Zero-rated supplies £80,000 @ 0%		0
		21,000
Input tax		
Attributed to taxable supplies	7,500	
Unattributed :		
$\dfrac{£120,000 + £80,000}{£120,000 + £80,000 + £50,000} = 80\% \times £12,000$	9,600	17,100
Payable to Customs and Excise		3,900

The input tax not attributed to taxable supplies for the quarter is £10,900 (£8,500 + 20% x £12,000). This is more than £625 per month on average and so cannot be reclaimed.

VAT schemes

VAT "schemes" exist in order to simplify the workings of the VAT system. The annual accounting scheme and the cash accounting scheme have already been described (see above). Other schemes include :

(a) the retail schemes

(b) the margin scheme for second-hand goods

(c) the flat-rate scheme for farmers.

Retail schemes

Retailers are those who supply goods and services directly to the public. A retailer's sales will often consist of a very large number of relatively small transactions and in these circumstances it would sometimes be difficult and expensive to keep detailed records of each transaction for VAT purposes. In response to this problem, retail schemes have been devised which enable retailers to calculate their output tax in a fairly straightforward way. The standard retail schemes (*which are available only to retailers with a taxable turnover of up to £100 million a year*) are as follows :

(a) **Point of Sale Scheme**. This scheme is the only standard retail scheme available to retailers who make supplies at just one positive rate of tax (i.e. all standard-rated or all lower-rated). The scheme is also available to retailers who make supplies at two or more rates, so long as they can distinguish at the point of sale between supplies made at each rate (usually by having a till which can accumulate separate daily totals for supplies at each rate or by having separate tills).

Retailers operating this scheme keep a record of their daily gross takings (DGT) for supplies at each rate. Output tax is then calculated by multiplying DGT by 7/47 (standard rate) or 1/21 (lower rate).

(b) **Apportionment Scheme 1**. This scheme is available to retailers with an annual taxable turnover of £1 million or less who make supplies at more than one rate of tax. The scheme covers only the supply of goods bought for resale. It cannot be used in relation to supplies of services or supplies of self-made or self-grown goods. For a retailer operating this scheme, the computation of output tax for a tax period involves the following steps :

Step 1 Calculate total DGT for the period.

Step 2 Calculate the VAT-inclusive cost (S) of goods bought in the period for resale at the standard rate.

Step 3 Calculate the VAT-inclusive cost (L) of goods bought in the period for resale at the lower rate.

Step 4 Calculate the VAT-inclusive cost (A) of all goods bought in the period for resale (at any rate).

Step 5   Output tax on sales at the standard rate = Total DGT x S/A x 7/47.

Step 6   Output tax on sales at the lower rate = Total DGT x L/A x 1/21.

This computation is performed again at the end of each year, taking into account takings and purchases for the whole year. Any difference between the result of this computation and the total of the amounts which were computed during the year must be accounted for to Customs and Excise.

(c)   **Apportionment Scheme 2**. This scheme is available to retailers who make supplies at more than one rate of tax. It can be used for supplies of goods bought for resale and for supplies of self-made or self-grown goods. It cannot be used for supplies of services. The computation of output tax for a tax period (for retailers making quarterly returns) normally proceeds as follows :

Step 1   Calculate total DGT for the period.

Step 2   Calculate the total (S) of the expected selling prices, including VAT, of standard-rated goods received, made or grown for retail sale in the current tax period and in the three previous periods.

Step 3   Calculate the total (L) of the expected selling prices, including VAT, of lower-rated goods received, made or grown for retail sale in the current tax period and in the three previous periods.

Step 4   Calculate the total (A) of the expected selling prices, including VAT, of all goods (standard, lower and zero-rated) received, made or grown for retail sale in the current tax period and in the three previous periods.

Step 5   Output tax on sales at the standard rate = Total DGT x S/A x 7/47.

Step 6   Output tax on sales at the lower rate = Total DGT x L/A x 1/21.

The computation for the first three tax periods in which the scheme is used is slightly more complex, since an adjustment is required for the expected selling prices of opening stock on the date that the retailer started using the scheme.

For a retailer making monthly returns, each monthly computation will involve the expected selling prices of the previous eleven tax periods (rather than the previous three) and the computation for the first eleven tax periods in which the scheme is used will involve a stock adjustment.

(d)   **Direct Calculation Scheme 1**. This scheme is available to retailers with an annual taxable turnover of £1 million or less who make supplies at more than one rate of tax. The scheme works by calculating the expected selling prices of the retailer's "minority goods". These are defined as those goods which are supplied at the rate (or rates) of tax which :

(i)   forms the smallest proportion of retail supplies (where goods are supplied at two rates of VAT) or

(ii)   form the two smaller proportions of retail supplies (where goods are supplied at three rates of VAT).

The scheme can be used for supplies of goods bought for resale and for supplies of self-made or self-grown goods. Supplies of services cannot be included unless they are taxable at a different rate from the minority goods. If a retailer's minority goods are zero rated and/or lower-rated, the computation of output tax for a tax period involves the following steps :

Step 1   Calculate total DGT for the period.

Step 2   Calculate the total (Z) of the expected selling prices of zero-rated goods received, made or grown for retail sale in the period.

Step 3   Calculate the total (L) of the expected selling prices of lower-rated goods received, made or grown for retail sale in the period.

Step 4   The standard-rated element of takings (S) = Total DGT - Z - L.

Step 5   Output tax on sales at the standard rate = S x 7/47.

Step 6   Output tax on sales at the lower rate = L x 1/21.

If, on the other hand, a retailer's minority goods are standard rated and/or lower-rated, the computation of output tax for a tax period is as follows :

Step 1   Calculate total DGT for the period. (Although this figure is not used in the calculation it must still be calculated and entered on the retailer's VAT return).

Step 2   Calculate the total (S) of the expected selling prices of standard-rated goods received, made or grown for retail sale in the period.

Step 3   Calculate the total (L) of the expected selling prices of lower-rated goods received, made or grown for retail sale in the period.

Step 4   Output tax on sales at the standard rate = S x 7/47.

Step 5   Output tax on sales at the lower rate = L x 1/21.

(e) **Direct Calculation Scheme 2**. This scheme works in a very similar way to Direct Calculation Scheme 1 but requires an annual stock adjustment. The £1 million turnover limit does not apply to this scheme.

Retailers with an annual taxable turnover exceeding £100 million cannot use any of the standard schemes listed above. If such retailers wish to use a retail scheme they must negotiate an individual "bespoke retail scheme" with Customs and Excise.

It should be noted that the growing use of information technology by large retailers (and by many small retailers) means that it is now much easier to record individual sales than it was when VAT was introduced in 1973. This means that the original rationale for the retail schemes has been diminished over the years. Accordingly, retailers may not use any of these schemes unless permitted to do so by Customs and Excise. Permission will be granted only if a retailer cannot reasonably be expected to account for VAT in the normal way, so that the use of a retail scheme is strictly necessary.

Margin scheme for second-hand goods

In general, VAT is charged on the full value of goods sold by a taxable person, regardless of whether those goods are new or second-hand. However, subject to certain conditions, a taxable person selling second-hand goods may choose to sell them through the "margin scheme" and charge VAT only on his or her profit margin. The scheme operates as follows :

(a) VAT is charged only on the seller's profit margin (i.e. the difference between the purchase price and the selling price).

(b) The seller's profit margin is deemed to be VAT-inclusive, so that the amount of tax due is calculated by multiplying this margin by the VAT fraction.

(c) Any expenses incurred by the seller (e.g. the costs of restoration, repairs, spare parts etc.) are ignored when establishing the amount of the profit margin.

(d) No tax invoice is issued.

(e) The buyer of the goods cannot reclaim the input tax suffered, even if he or she is a taxable person.

The margin scheme is intended mainly for use by those who deal in second-hand goods. The main conditions which must be satisfied for the scheme to be used are that the goods concerned are second-hand and that they were acquired either :

(a) on a supply on which no tax was chargeable (e.g. the goods were acquired from a non-taxable person), or

(b) on a supply from someone who also sold the goods under the margin scheme.

EXAMPLE 3

A dealer in second-hand antiques buys an antique table from a member of the public for £2,000, spends a further £500 on restoration work and then sells the table for £5,000. Compute the output tax which must be accounted for on the sale.

SOLUTION

The dealer's margin is £3,000, ignoring the restoration costs. The output tax due is therefore £3,000 x 7/47 = £446.81.

Flat-rate scheme for farmers

In general, a farmer making taxable supplies which exceed the registration threshold is liable to register for VAT in the normal way. Similarly, a farmer whose taxable supplies are below the threshold may register voluntarily. Since farmers make mainly zero-rated supplies, a farmer who is registered will usually receive regular repayments of input tax, at the expense of maintaining the necessary VAT records.

An alternative to registration is the "flat-rate scheme", which is available to farmers regardless of the size of their taxable turnover and which is intended to reduce the administrative costs associated with VAT registration. This scheme operates as follows :

(a) A farmer who is a member of the scheme does not register for VAT. This reduces administrative costs but deprives the farmer of the opportunity to reclaim input tax.

(b) In compensation, the farmer is allowed to add a flat-rate addition of 4% to his or her selling prices and to retain this addition.

(c) From the point of view of a taxable person buying goods from a flat-rate farmer, the flat-rate addition is treated as input tax and may be reclaimed, subject to the usual rules.

A farmer may not join this scheme if the total of the flat-rate additions which would be charged if the farmer were a member of the scheme exceeds the total amount of input tax which the farmer would otherwise be entitled to reclaim by £3,000 p.a. or more.

Administration of VAT

Overall responsibility for the VAT system rests with the Board of Commissioners of Customs and Excise. There is an administration directorate in London but the collection of VAT is dealt with by the VAT Central Unit in Southend. The main functions of the VAT Central Unit are :

(a) to maintain registration records

(b) to issue VAT return forms to registered persons and to receive the completed returns

(c) to collect the VAT due from registered persons and to make repayments of tax where necessary.

There is also a network of local VAT offices which deal with local VAT administration and make regular "control visits" to registered persons in their area. The purpose of a control visit is to check the accuracy of the registered person's VAT returns and to ensure that the VAT system is being operated correctly.

VAT assessments

VAT is very largely a self-assessed tax and, in the normal course of events, it is not necessary to raise formal tax assessments. However, the Commissioners may issue such assessments if they believe that a taxable person has either failed to make a VAT return or has made an incorrect or incomplete return.

In normal circumstances, assessments may not be raised any later than 3 years after the end of the tax period to which they relate, but this time limit is extended to 20 years if the taxable person has behaved dishonestly or fraudulently. Any claim for a refund of overpaid tax must also be made within 3 years.

Appeals

A person who disagrees with a Customs & Excise decision may, within 30 days of the date of the document containing the disputed decision, either appeal to a VAT tribunal or ask a local VAT office to reconsider the decision. Note that :

(a) Appeals to a tribunal are permitted in relation to a wide variety of matters, but certain matters may not be the subject of an appeal.

(b) A VAT tribunal may award costs to the successful party.

(c) If either the Customs and Excise or the person concerned is dissatisfied with a tribunal decision, a dispute on a point of law may be referred to the High Court and beyond.

(d) If the local VAT office is asked to reconsider a decision, it may either confirm the decision (in which case the person concerned has 21 days in which to lodge an appeal with a VAT tribunal) or revise the decision (in which case the person concerned may still wish to appeal to a tribunal and may do so within 30 days).

Penalties, surcharges and interest

A wide variety of penalties may be exacted for non-compliance with VAT regulations. The main penalties are as follows :

(a) **Criminal fraud**. A person who attempts to evade tax in such a way that his or her conduct amounts to criminal fraud may, on a "summary" conviction obtained before a magistrate, be imprisoned for up to 6 months and/or fined up to £5,000 or three times the amount of tax evaded, whichever is the greater. If the conviction is "on indictment" (i.e. obtained before a jury), the maximum term of imprisonment is 7 years and there is no limit to the size of any fine.

(b) **Conduct involving dishonesty**. A person who attempts to evade tax in such a way that his or her conduct involves dishonesty is liable to a maximum penalty equal to 100% of the amount of tax evaded.

(c) **Misdeclaration**. If a VAT return is made which understates the VAT payable (or overstates the VAT repayable) and the amount of tax which would have been lost if the inaccuracy had not been detected is at least :

(i) 30% of the "gross amount of tax" (i.e. the total of input tax and output tax) for the period concerned, or

(ii) £1,000,000

whichever is the lower, a penalty may be exacted of up to 15% of the tax which would have been lost.

(d) **Material inaccuracies**. Customs and Excise may issue a "penalty liability notice" to a taxable person if that person has made a "material inaccuracy" in a VAT return. A material inaccuracy is defined as one which, if undiscovered, would have resulted in a loss of tax equal to at least 10% of the gross amount of tax for the period in question, or £500,000, whichever is the lower. If the person concerned then makes at least two further material inaccuracies during the "penalty period" specified in the notice, a penalty may be exacted of up to 15% of the tax which would have been lost.

(e) **Late registration**. A taxable person who fails to notify Customs and Excise of liability to register, or makes late notification, is liable to a penalty. The penalty is calculated as a percentage of the amount of tax due between the date on which registration should have occurred and the date on which notification is eventually made. The percentage is 5% for a delay of up to 9 months, 10% for a delay of between 9 and 18 months and 15% for a delay of over 18 months. The minimum penalty is £50 in all cases.

(f) **Breaches of regulations**. A taxable person who fails to comply with sundry VAT regulations will receive a written warning from Customs and Excise. If non-compliance is continued, the person is liable on a first offence to a penalty of £5 per day until the breach is remedied. The penalty rises to £10 per day on a second offence within a period of two years and to £15 per day on a third or subsequent offence. The maximum penalty which may be exacted is equal to 100 times the daily rate and the minimum penalty is £50.

(g) **Default surcharge**. If a taxable person submits a late VAT return, or submits a return on time but makes late payment of the VAT due, then a default has occurred and Customs and Excise may issue a "surcharge liability notice", specifying a "surcharge period". If within this period the person concerned makes a further default, a default surcharge is levied, calculated as the greater of £30 and a percentage of the tax paid late. The surcharge percentage is 2% for the first default within the surcharge period, 5% for the second default, 10% for the third default and 15% for the fourth and any subsequent default. A surcharge period comes to an end only when no defaults have occurred for a continuous 12-month period.

In general, penalties may be mitigated (i.e. reduced or not charged at all) if the taxable person has a reasonable excuse for his or her conduct. Penalties may also be mitigated if the person concerned has voluntarily disclosed any non-compliance and has co-operated fully with Customs and Excise.

Interest

"Default interest" is charged on VAT which has been assessed (see above) or which could have been assessed but for the fact that payment was made before an assessment was raised. Such interest normally runs from the "reckonable date" to the date of payment, where the reckonable date is the date on which the tax should originally have been paid. Conversely, if a taxable person makes an overpayment of VAT as a result of an error on the part of Customs and Excise, that person is paid interest on the amount of tax which is subsequently refunded.

Repayment supplement

If a taxable person is entitled to a repayment of VAT for a tax period, this repayment is increased by a "repayment supplement" of 5% (or £50, if greater) so long as :

(a) the return for the relevant tax period is submitted on time, and

(b) the amount stated to be repayable in the return is correct (or differs from the correct figure by no more than 5% or £250, whichever is the greater), and

(c) Customs and Excise fail to issue written instructions for the repayment to be made within 30 days from the *later* of the date on which the return was received and the end of the tax period to which it relates.

Summary

▶ VAT is normally accounted for quarterly to HM Customs and Excise but monthly and annual accounting schemes exist.

▶ The date on which a supply is deemed to occur is known as the "tax point".

▶ A taxable person may join the cash accounting scheme if certain conditions are satisfied. Members of this scheme account for VAT according to the dates on which payments are received from customers and made to suppliers.

▶ The input tax suffered in relation to certain types of supply (e.g. business entertaining) is not recoverable.

▶ A person making a mixture of taxable supplies and exempt supplies is "partially exempt" and may reclaim only part of the input tax suffered.

▶ Special VAT schemes exist in relation to retailers, small businesses, farmers and second-hand goods.

▶ The VAT system is administered by Customs and Excise and various penalties may be exacted for non-compliance with VAT regulations.

Exercises

30.1 List the required contents of a valid VAT invoice.

30.2 Describe the main features of :

(a) the cash accounting scheme

(b) the annual accounting scheme.

30.3 Calculate the output tax which must be accounted for or the input tax which may be reclaimed by a taxable person in respect of each of the transactions below. All of the amounts shown exclude any VAT which may be applicable.

(a) the purchase of a book for £18.95

(b) the sale for £3,000 of a motor car which had been bought originally for £4,000 (the input tax paid when acquiring the car could not be reclaimed)

(c) the sale of a used commercial building for £200,000.

30.4 Sebastian is self-employed. He drives a 3,000 cc petrol-engined car and charges the cost of all the petrol used to his business bank account. In the quarter to 31 March 2001 he drives 3,800 miles on business and 1,400 miles for private purposes. The VAT-inclusive cost of all the petrol bought in the quarter is £692. How should Sebastian deal with petrol in his VAT return for the quarter ?

*30.5 During the quarter to 31 August 2000, a taxable person makes the following supplies :

	£
Standard-rated supplies (including VAT)	319,600
Zero-rated supplies	88,000
Exempt supplies	440,000

Input tax for the quarter is £118,000, attributed as follows :

	%
Attributed to taxable supplies	35
Attributed to exempt supplies	40
Unattributed	25

Compute the VAT provisionally payable to or reclaimable from Customs and Excise for the quarter.

*30.6   Tracey is a sole trader. She has the following transactions during the quarter to 30
         November 2000 (all amounts shown are VAT-exclusive) :

	£
Sales to UK customers :	
Standard-rated	39,400
Zero-rated	12,600
Exports :	
To non-EU members	8,600
To EU members (all customers are VAT registered)	17,300
Purchases :	
Standard-rated	25,800
Zero-rated	6,200
Expenses :	
Wages and salaries	22,450
Car repairs	120
Insurances	260
Entertaining foreign customers	420
Other expenses (all standard-rated)	9,700
Capital transactions :	
Purchase of new plant and machinery	8,000
Purchase of motor van	12,000

Tracey drives a 1,800 cc diesel-engined car and charges the cost of all the petrol used,
whether for business or private motoring, to her business bank account. Calculate the
amount of VAT due for the quarter.

Chapter 31

Inheritance tax

Introduction

This chapter provides a basic introduction to Inheritance tax (IHT). An IHT liability can arise in a number of ways but the events which most commonly trigger such a liability are the transfer of assets on the death of their owner and the gift of assets during the lifetime of their owner.

IHT was introduced in 1986 but was firmly based on its predecessor, Capital Transfer Tax. Current legislation is to be found in the Inheritance Tax Act 1984, originally the Capital Transfer Tax Act 1984, as amended by subsequent Finance Acts.

Chargeable transfers of value

The main situation in which a charge to IHT may arise is when a *transfer of value* of *chargeable property* is made by a *chargeable person*.

Transfers of value

A "transfer of value" occurs when a person (known as the "transferor") makes a "disposition" such that his or her estate is lower in value than it was before the disposition occurred. The value of a transfer is equal to the reduction in the value of the transferor's estate. If the transferor also pays the IHT in relation to the transfer, this further reduces the value of the estate, so that the total value of the transfer is then equal to the amount of the disposition plus the associated IHT.

A "disposition" is any disposal of property or an interest in property. The term includes disposals made during the lifetime of the transferor ("lifetime transfers") as well as disposals caused by the death of the transferor. However, certain dispositions are *not* regarded as transfers of value for IHT purposes. The most important exemptions are :

(a) dispositions without gratuitous intent (e.g. genuine commercial transactions which give rise to a loss and therefore a reduction in the value of the transferor's estate)

(b) dispositions made for the maintenance of the transferor's family, including spouses, children and dependant relatives

(c) gratuitous dispositions which constitute allowable expenditure for the purposes of income tax and corporation tax (e.g. payments made by an employer into a pension fund for the benefit of employees)

(d) dispositions caused by the fact that the transferor has been killed whilst on active service.

Chargeable property

All property is chargeable property unless specifically excluded from charge. The main exclusions are :

(a) property which is situated outside the UK and owned by a person who is "domiciled" outside the UK (see Chapter 32)

(b) reversionary interests in a trust or settlement (see later in this chapter) unless acquired for a consideration.

Chargeable persons

An individual who is domiciled in the UK is a chargeable person and is liable to IHT in relation to all of his or her chargeable property, wherever in the world that property is situated. An individual who is not domiciled in the UK is liable to IHT only in relation to property situated in the UK. Note the following points :

(a) Husbands and wives are assessed to IHT independently.

(b) A partnership is not a chargeable person. The assets of a partnership are owned by the partners and each partner is liable to IHT in relation to his or her share of those assets.

(c) A company is not a chargeable person and cannot incur an IHT liability. In certain circumstances, however, the participators of a close company (see Chapter 27) may incur an IHT liability in relation to transfers of value made by the company.

(d) The life tenants of an interest in possession trust (see later in this chapter) are regarded for IHT purposes as owning the assets of the trust, divided between them in proportion to their interests. The trust itself is not a chargeable person.

Exempt transfers

Certain transfers are wholly exempt from IHT. In other cases, an exemption may serve to reduce the value of a transfer for IHT purposes. The main exemptions are of three types :

(a) business and agricultural property reliefs (see later in this chapter)

(b) exemptions for transfers made to certain transferees (see below)

(c) exemptions available to the transferor (see below).

If more than one type of exemption applies to a given transfer, then the exemptions should be applied in the order given above.

Exemptions for transfers made to certain transferees

The following transfers are wholly exempt from IHT whether made on death or during the lifetime of the transferor :

(a) transfers to the transferor's spouse

(b) transfers to charities

(c) transfers to political parties

(d) transfers made for national purposes to certain national bodies (museums, libraries, art galleries etc.)

(e) transfers of eligible property made for the public benefit to a non-profit making body, so long as the body receiving the property undertakes to maintain and preserve it and provide reasonable public access to it.

Exemptions available to the transferor

The following exemptions are available in relation to lifetime transfers only :

(a) **Small gifts**. Gifts to individuals with a value of up to £250 per transferee per tax year (6 April to 5 April) are wholly exempt from IHT. This exemption cannot be used to exempt part of a gift which has a value exceeding £250.

(b) **Normal expenditure out of income**. Transfers which consist of "normal expenditure out of income" (e.g. birthday and Christmas presents) are wholly exempt from IHT. In order that a transfer should benefit from this exemption, the Inland Revenue must believe that the transfer :

    (i) is part of the normal expenditure of the transferor, and

    (ii) is made out of income rather than capital, and

    (iii) leaves the transferor sufficient income to maintain his or her usual standard of living.

(c) **Gifts in consideration of marriage**. Gifts made by a transferor to a bride or bridegroom in consideration of their marriage are exempt from IHT up to the following limits :

(i) £5,000 if made by a parent of the bride or groom

(ii) £2,500 if made by the grandparent or remoter ancestor of the bride or groom

(iii) £2,500 if made by the bride to the groom or vice-versa

(iv) £1,000 in any other case.

The above exemptions are per transferor per marriage and can be used to exempt part of the value of larger gifts.

(d) **Annual exemption**. The first £3,000 of lifetime transfers made in any tax year is exempt from IHT. Note that :

(i) If the total of the lifetime transfers made in a tax year exceeds £3,000 the exemption is set against the year's transfers in chronological order.

(ii) Any unused part of the annual exemption may be carried forward to the following tax year (but no further) and set against the excess of that year's lifetime transfers over that year's annual exemption.

(iii) It is Inland Revenue practice to set the annual exemption against potentially exempt transfers (see below) as well as chargeable lifetime transfers, even though potentially exempt transfers may never become chargeable to inheritance tax. There is some doubt as to whether this practice is statutorily correct but it has been followed in this book.

EXAMPLE 1

Tania makes no transfers during 1998/99. Her only transfers during 1999/00 and 2000/01 are as follows :

		£
1999/00		
June 1999	Gift to her son on his marriage	6,000
October 1999	Gift to her granddaughter	4,500
January 2000	Gift to Oxfam	10,000
March 2000	Gift to a friend	100
2000/01		
July 2000	Gift to her nephew	1,000
August 2000	Gift to her cousin	3,500

Calculate the value of each of the above transfers after deduction of all the relevant exemptions. (None of the gifts are regarded as normal expenditure out of income).

SOLUTION

(AE = Annual exemption)

	Value before AE £	AE for current year £	AE for previous year £	Value after AE £
1999/00				
Gift to son on marriage (£6,000 - £5,000)	1,000	1,000	-	-
Gift to granddaughter	4,500	2,000	2,500	-
Gift to charity (exempt)	-	-	-	-
Gift to friend (exempt as a small gift)	-	-	-	-
	5,500	3,000	2,500	-
2000/01				
Gift to nephew	1,000	1,000		-
Gift to cousin	3,500	2,000		1,500
	4,500	3,000		1,500

Note :

£500 of the 1998/99 annual exemption remains unused but cannot be carried forward beyond 1999/00. The 1999/00 and 2000/01 annual exemptions are fully utilised.

Potentially exempt transfers (PET's)

If a lifetime transfer has not been wholly exempted from IHT as a result of the various exemptions described above, then the transfer will be either a "chargeable lifetime transfer" or a "potentially exempt transfer". A chargeable lifetime transfer is charged to IHT immediately. A potentially exempt transfer (PET) is subject to IHT only if the transferor dies within seven years of the date of the transfer.

A potentially exempt transfer is a lifetime transfer which is made by an individual to either :

(a) another individual, or

(b) a trust with an interest in possession, or

(c) an accumulation and maintenance trust, or

(d) a trust which is for the benefit of a person who is physically or mentally handicapped.

Most lifetime transfers are in fact PET's. The main example of a chargeable lifetime transfer is a transfer made to a discretionary trust.

Types of trust

The above definition of a PET makes reference to various types of trust. These were introduced briefly in Chapter 6 but are explained again below :

(a) A trust (or settlement) is an arrangement whereby property is held by persons known as trustees for the benefit of other persons known as beneficiaries.

(b) If one or more persons are entitled to the lifetime use of the trust property or to the income generated by the trust property, those persons are "life tenants" and the trust is a "trust with an interest in possession". A person whose interest will not take effect until some future event occurs (e.g. the death of a life tenant) is said to have a "reversionary interest".

(c) A trust with no interest in possession is known as a "discretionary trust". The trustees of such a trust have the discretion to distribute as much or as little of the trust income to the beneficiaries as they see fit.

(d) An accumulation and maintenance trust is a special instance of a discretionary trust, where the trustees may choose whether to accumulate the trust income or to pay it out for the maintenance of the beneficiaries, who must be under 25 years old.

EXAMPLE 2

Consider each of the following transfers (assuming in each case that the annual exemption for both the current year and the previous year have been set against earlier transfers) and classify each one as either an exempt transfer, a PET or a chargeable lifetime transfer.

(a) a gift of £10,000 made by a husband to his wife

(b) a gift of £20,000 made by a mother to her son on his marriage

(c) a gift of £50,000 made to a trust with an interest in possession

(d) a gift of £100,000 made to a discretionary trust.

SOLUTION

(a) wholly exempt (transfers between spouses are not chargeable)

(b) exempt £5,000 (made in consideration of marriage); PET £15,000

(c) PET

(d) chargeable lifetime transfer.

IHT payable on chargeable lifetime transfers

The amount of IHT payable on a chargeable lifetime transfer depends upon :

(a) the value of the transfer (less any relevant exemptions), which must be grossed up if the tax is paid by the transferor

(b) the rates of IHT in force on the date of the transfer

(c) the total (including the current transfer) of the gross chargeable lifetime transfers made during the seven years ending on the date of the current transfer.

Grossing up

IHT is chargeable on the *gross* value of a transfer i.e. the reduction in the value of the transferor's estate which the transfer has caused. If the transferee pays the tax due on a transfer, the gross value of the transfer is simply the amount received by the transferee (less any exemptions). However, if the tax due is paid by the transferor, the amount received by the transferee (less exemptions) is only the net value of the transfer, and this must be grossed up at the appropriate rate or rates to find the gross value.

In general, any capital gains tax payable by the transferor in relation to the transfer is ignored when calculating the reduction in value of the transferor's estate.

Rates of IHT applicable to chargeable lifetime transfers

The rates of IHT applicable to chargeable lifetime transfers made on or after 6 April 2000 are as follows :

Gross chargeable lifetime transfers for the 7 years to date	Rate of tax	Grossing up fraction
first £234,000	0%	nil
remainder after the first £234,000	20%	100/80

The rates of tax have remained at 0% and 20% for many years, but the threshold beyond which 20% tax is payable has changed from time to time. Recent values of the threshold have been :

Date of transfer	£
10 March 1992 to 5 April 1995	150,000
6 April 1995 to 5 April 1996	154,000
6 April 1996 to 5 April 1997	200,000
6 April 1997 to 5 April 1998	215,000
6 April 1998 to 5 April 1999	223,000
6 April 1999 to 5 April 2000	231,000

For each transfer, the calculation of the tax due involves the following steps :

(a) The total gross value of chargeable lifetime transfers made in the preceding seven years is brought forward.

(b) If the total brought forward has utilised the whole of the 0% band, tax is due at 20% on the gross value of the current transfer.

(c) If the total brought forward has not utilised the whole of the 0% band, the balance of the 0% band is set against the current transfer. If this does not absorb the whole of the transfer, tax is due at 20% on the gross value of the remainder.

EXAMPLE 3

On 1 July 2000, Violet makes a chargeable lifetime transfer (after deduction of relevant exemptions) of £40,000. Her only previous chargeable lifetime transfer was made in 1995 and had a gross value (i.e. the value after exemptions, grossed up if necessary) of £200,000. Calculate the IHT due if :

(a) the transferee agrees to pay the tax due

(b) the tax due is paid by Violet.

SOLUTION

The total of transfers brought forward is £200,000, leaving £34,000 of the nil band to set against the current transfer.

(a) If the transferee pays the tax, the gross value of the transfer is £40,000 and the IHT due is £34,000 @ 0% + £6,000 @ 20% = £1,200.

(b) If Violet pays the tax, the net value of the transfer is £40,000. The gross value and the tax due are calculated as follows :

	Net £	Gross £	Tax £
£34,000 grossed up @ 0%	34,000	34,000	0
£6,000 grossed up @ 20%	6,000	7,500	1,500
Totals	40,000	41,500	1,500

The gross value of the transfer is £41,500 and the tax due is £1,500. The total of gross transfers for the seven years to 1 July 2000 is now £241,500.

IHT payable on death

The IHT payable on death consists of :

(a) additional tax on any chargeable lifetime transfers made by the deceased person during the previous seven years

(b) tax on any PET's made by the deceased person during the previous seven years (these PET's have now become chargeable by virtue of the death of the transferor)

(c) tax on the estate of the deceased person as at the date of death (to the extent that the transfers made on death are not exempt from IHT).

Tax on chargeable lifetime transfers and PET's

The tax payable on death in respect of the chargeable lifetime transfers and PET's made in the seven years prior to the date of death is calculated as follows :

(a) The transfers are considered in chronological order, with no distinction made between chargeable lifetime transfers and PET's.

(b) The gross value of each chargeable lifetime transfer remains as previously calculated. The gross value of a PET is simply the amount received by the transferee, less any relevant exemptions (since the tax due is always paid by the transferee).

(c) Tax is recalculated on the gross value of each transfer using the IHT bands and rates in force *on the date of death* and taking into account any other chargeable transfers made in the seven years preceding the transfer. The tax rates used are those applicable to transfers on death, *not* those used for chargeable lifetime transfers. For deaths occurring on or after 6 April 2000 the applicable rates are as follows :

Gross chargeable transfers for the 7 years to date	Rate of tax
first £234,000	0%
remainder after the first £234,000	40%

(d) The tax calculated at (c) for each transfer may then be reduced by *taper relief*, depending upon the number of years which have elapsed between the date of the transfer and the date of death. Taper relief is given as follows :

Period between transfer and death	Percentage tax reduction
3 years or less	0%
Over 3 but not more than 4 years	20%
Over 4 but not more than 5 years	40%
Over 5 but not more than 6 years	60%
Over 6 but not more than 7 years	80%

(e) Finally, for each transfer, any tax paid during the lifetime of the transferor is subtracted, leaving a balance of tax due on that transfer. This tax liability is the responsibility of the transferee. If the lifetime tax paid in relation to a transfer exceeds the liability on death, no further tax is due on that transfer but no repayment is given.

EXAMPLE 4

Wilson dies on 20 December 2000, having made only the following transfers during his lifetime :

		£
6 June 1990	Gift to daughter	50,000
4 May 1996	Gift to discretionary trust	404,000
11 June 1997	Gift to son on marriage	50,000

Calculate the IHT payable during Wilson's lifetime (if any) in relation to each of the above transfers, assuming that Wilson paid this tax himself. Also calculate the further IHT payable (if any) on Wilson's death.

SOLUTION

The value of each gift after deduction of exemptions is as follows :

		Value before AE	AE for current year	AE for previous year	Value after AE
		£	£	£	£
1990/91	Daughter	50,000	3,000	3,000	44,000
1996/97	Discretionary trust	404,000	3,000	3,000	398,000
1997/98	Son (£50,000 - £5,000)	45,000	3,000	-	42,000

Lifetime tax liability

The gifts to Wilson's son and daughter were PET's and gave rise to no immediate tax liability but the gift to the discretionary trust was a chargeable lifetime transfer. There were no such transfers during the preceding 7 years so the whole of the 0% band (£200,000 at that time) was set against the gift. The tax due was £49,500, calculated as follows :

	Net	Gross	Tax
	£	£	£
£200,000 grossed up @ 0%	200,000	200,000	0
£198,000 grossed up @ 20%	198,000	247,500	49,500
Totals	398,000	447,500	49,500

Tax liability on death

The June 1990 PET is more than 7 years old at the time of Wilson's death. This PET is exempt from tax and can be completely ignored for IHT purposes. The tax due on the other two transfers is calculated as follows :

(i)   *Transfer made on 4 May 1996*

The gross value of this transfer is £447,500 and there were no chargeable transfers in the previous 7 years (5/5/89 - 3/5/96). The tax due at the death rates applicable on 20/12/00 is :

	£
£234,000 @ 0%	0
£213,500 @ 40%	85,400
	85,400
<u>Less</u> : Taper relief (4-5 years) @ 40%	34,160
	51,240
<u>Less</u> : Lifetime tax paid	49,500
IHT payable by transferee	1,740

(ii)   *Transfer made on 11 June 1997*

The gross value of this transfer is £42,000. Gross chargeable transfers in the previous 7 years (12/6/90 - 10/6/97) were £447,500, completely absorbing the 0% band. The tax due at the death rates applicable on 20/12/00 is :

	£
£42,000 @ 40%	16,800
<u>Less</u> : Taper relief (3-4 years) @ 20%	3,360
	13,440
<u>Less</u> : Lifetime tax paid	0
IHT payable by transferee	13,440

Tax on the deceased person's estate

IHT on the deceased's person's estate (to the extent that the transfers made on death are not exempt from IHT) is calculated using the rates of tax applicable on death. The calculation proceeds as follows :

(a)   First, the 0% band is reduced by the total of gross chargeable transfers made in the preceding seven years, including any PET's made during that period.

(b)   The remainder of the 0% band (if any) is then set against the value of the estate and tax at 40% is calculated on the balance.

(c)   The tax due is divided by the value of the estate and the result (expressed as a percentage) is the "estate rate" i.e. the average rate of tax borne by the estate.

EXAMPLE 5

Toby dies on 2 March 2001, leaving an estate valued at £284,000. None of the transfers made on death are exempt from IHT. Calculate the IHT due on the estate if the total of the gross chargeable transfers made by Toby in the seven years prior to his death was :

(a)   Nil   (b)   £70,000   (c)   £240,000.

SOLUTION

(a) £234,000 @ 0% + £50,000 @ 40% = £20,000. (Estate rate 7.04%).

(b) £164,000 @ 0% + £120,000 @ 40% = £48,000. (Estate rate 16.9%).

(c) £284,000 @ 40% = £113,600. (Estate rate 40%).

Quick succession relief

Quick succession relief (QSR) is available when property which is transferred on death was transferred to the deceased person within the previous 5 years and was charged to IHT at that time. The tax (if any) payable in relation to the transfer made on death is reduced by an amount which depends upon the value of the earlier transfer and the amount of IHT paid on that transfer. The relief is calculated as :

$$\frac{\text{net value of earlier transfer}}{\text{gross value of earlier transfer}} \text{ x IHT paid on earlier transfer x QSR\%}$$

The QSR percentage depends upon the date of the earlier transfer, as follows :

Period between earlier transfer and death	QSR percentage
1 year or less	100%
Over 1 but not more than 2 years	80%
Over 2 but not more than 3 years	60%
Over 3 but not more than 4 years	40%
Over 4 but not more than 5 years	20%

Valuation

As stated at the beginning of this chapter, the value of a transfer for IHT purposes is equal to the reduction in value of the transferor's estate as a result of that transfer. In general, this is equivalent to the open market value of the transferred assets on the date of the transfer but it should not be assumed that this will always be the case. For instance, if the transferor disposes of :

(a) a single item from a matching set of such items, or

(b) a small number of shares in a company, sufficient to convert a majority shareholding into a minority shareholding

it is likely that the true reduction in value of the transferor's estate (and therefore the value of the transfer for IHT purposes) will exceed the market value of the transferred assets. This caveat aside, determining the market value of the transferred assets may in itself cause difficulty and special valuation rules are sometimes required. The most important of these rules are described below.

Listed shares

Shares which are listed on the Stock Exchange are valued at the *lower* of :

(a) the lower of the two prices quoted for those shares on the day of the transfer, plus one-quarter of the difference between the lower price and the higher price (the "quarter-up" rule) and,

(b) the average of the highest and lowest prices at which bargains have been marked on that day (if any).

If listed shares are transferred on a non-working day (for which no prices are available) the shares are valued as if transferred on the last working day before the date of the transfer or the first working day after it, whichever gives the lower figure.

Units in a unit trust are valued at the bid price (i.e. the buying price quoted by the trust manager) for the day of the transfer. If this is a non-working day the bid price for the last working day before the date of the transfer is used.

EXAMPLE 6

On 1 June 2000, Shirley gives 5,000 shares in Listed plc to her daughter. The shares are quoted at 189 - 197 on that day, with bargains marked at 190, 192 and 196 (all quoted prices are in pence). Calculate the market value of the shares for IHT purposes.

SOLUTION

The quarter-up rule gives 189 + 1/4 x (197 - 189) = 191. The average of the highest and lowest marked bargains is 193, so the shares are valued at 191p and the transfer has a market value of 5,000 x £1.91 = £9,550.

Overseas property

Property situated outside the UK is valued in the appropriate foreign currency. This value is then converted into sterling, using the exchange rate for the day of the transfer which gives the lowest sterling value.

Related property

When calculating the value of a transfer for IHT purposes, the existence of any "related property" may be taken into account. Related property consists of property which :

(a) is owned by the transferor's spouse, or

(b) is owned by a charity, political party etc. (or has been within the previous 5 years) as a result of an exempt transfer made by either spouse.

Under the related property rules, the property being transferred and the related property are valued together, as a whole, and then part of that value is apportioned to the property being transferred. These rules are intended to prevent taxpayers from avoiding IHT by fragmenting the ownership of an asset and will only be used if the valuation given by the related property rules is greater than the valuation that would have been calculated normally.

EXAMPLE 7

Roy owns 3,500 ordinary shares in R Ltd, an unlisted company which has an issued share capital of 10,000 ordinary shares. Roy's wife owns a further 1,600 shares. Shareholdings in R Ltd are valued as follows :

	£
500 shares	5,000
3,000 shares	33,000
3,500 shares	43,750
4,600 shares	64,400
5,100 shares	96,900

Roy now transfers 500 of his shares to a discretionary trust. Calculate the value of this transfer for IHT purposes.

SOLUTION

Ignoring related property, Roy's estate has reduced in value by £10,750 (£43,750 - £33,000) and this would normally be the value of the transfer. But taking related property into account, the value of the transfer is calculated as follows :

	£
Value of Roy's holding before the transfer (£96,900 x 3,500/5,100)	66,500
Value of Roy's holding after the transfer (£64,400 x 3,000/4,600)	42,000
Value of the transfer	24,500

Since £24,500 exceeds £10,750, the value of the transfer is £24,500.

Business property relief

Business property relief of either 100% or 50% is available in relation to a transfer which meets all of the following conditions :

(a) the property transferred consists of "relevant business property", and

(b) the business concerned is a "qualifying business" (non-profit making businesses and investment businesses do not qualify), and

(c) the property has been owned by the transferor for at least two years, or has replaced other relevant business property, such that the combined period of ownership of both the original and replacement property is at least two years out of the five years preceding the date of the transfer.

The main categories of "relevant business property", together with the applicable rates of relief are as follows :

		Rate of relief
(a)	Property consisting of a business or an interest in a business (e.g. a share in a partnership)	100%
(b)	Securities in an unlisted company which (either by themselves or with other such securities or unlisted shares) gave the transferor control of the company immediately before the transfer	100%
(c)	Shares in an unlisted company	100%
(d)	Shares transferred from a controlling holding in a listed company	50%
(e)	Land, buildings, plant and machinery owned by the transferor and used for business purposes by a partnership in which he/she was a partner or by a company of which he/she had control immediately before the transfer	50%
(f)	Land, buildings, plant and machinery used in the transferor's business and owned by a trust of which the transferor is a life tenant.	50%

No relief is given in relation to "excepted assets" i.e. assets which have not been used for business purposes throughout the two years prior to the transfer (or since they were acquired, if within the last two years) and which are not required for the future use of the business.

Agricultural property relief

Agricultural property relief of either 100% or 50% is available in relation to a transfer of "agricultural property" so long as that property has been either :

(a) occupied by the transferor and used for agricultural purposes throughout the two years preceding the transfer, or

(b) owned by the transferor throughout the seven years preceding the transfer and occupied by the transferor or someone else for agricultural purposes throughout those seven years.

For this purpose, "agricultural property" consists mainly of agricultural land and pasture, woodlands and associated buildings. Land managed according to the terms of certain wildlife habitat schemes (together with associated buildings) is also eligible for agricultural property relief. The rates of relief are :

(a) 100% if, immediately before the transfer, the transferor enjoys vacant possession of the property or the right to obtain it within the following 12 months (extended by extra-statutory concession to 24 months in certain cases)

(b) Otherwise 100% if the property is let on a tenancy starting after 31 August 1995 and 50% if the property is let on a tenancy starting before 1 September 1995.

These rates apply only to the "agricultural value" of the property i.e. the value that the property would have if it could only ever be used for agricultural purposes. No relief is available in respect of any extra value that the property might have by virtue of its development potential. If a property qualifies for both business property relief and agricultural property relief, then agricultural property relief is given first.

Administration of IHT

Inheritance tax is administered by the Capital Taxes Office (CTO) of the Inland Revenue. For chargeable lifetime transfers and transfers caused by the death of the transferor, an "account" must be delivered to this office, giving details of the transfers made and their value. Details of this procedure are as follows :

(a) **Chargeable lifetime transfers**. The transferor must deliver an account to the CTO within 12 months of the end of the month in which the transfer occurred. There is no requirement to deliver an account if the transfer is exempt or potentially exempt, or if the total value of transfers for the tax year to date does not exceed £10,000 and the total for the 7 years to date does not exceed £40,000.

(b) **Death**. The personal representatives of a deceased person must deliver an account to the CTO within 12 months of the end of the month in which the death occurred. However, there is no requirement to deliver an account if :

(i) the deceased person was domiciled in the UK, and

(ii) the gross value of the estate does not exceed £210,000, and

(iii) no more than £50,000 of the estate is situated outside the UK, and

(iv) there have been no chargeable lifetime transfers (or PET's) made within the previous 7 years, other than transfers consisting of cash, listed shares or listed securities with a total gross value not exceeding £75,000.

Assessments and appeals

When a transfer gives rise to an IHT liability, the CTO issues a "notice of determination", showing the value of the transfer for IHT purposes and the amount of IHT payable. Appeals in writing, stating the grounds for the appeal, may be lodged within 30 days of the date of the notice. Such appeals are normally heard in the first instance by the Special Commissioners but may progress to the courts.

Payment of IHT

The IHT relating to a transfer is usually payable 6 months after the end of the month in which the transfer (or death) occurred. However, the tax on chargeable lifetime transfers made in roughly the first half of the tax year (6 April to 30 September) is not payable until 30 April in the following tax year.

It is notable that the tax on a transfer is usually due for payment well before the end of the 12-month period within which an account of the transfer must be delivered to the CTO. Since interest is charged on tax paid late, there is an incentive to deliver the account (and pay the tax due) on or before the due date of payment.

Summary

► The main occasion on which IHT is charged is when a transfer of value of chargeable property is made by a chargeable person. A transfer may be a lifetime transfer or a transfer made on death.

► The value of a transfer is equal to the reduction in value of the transferor's estate as a result of the transfer.

► Transfers made to certain transferees (e.g. spouses, charities, political parties) are exempt from IHT.

► Lifetime transfers comprising small gifts, gifts made out of income and gifts made on consideration of marriage are wholly or partly exempt from IHT. The first £3,000 of lifetime transfers made in any tax year is exempt from IHT.

► A potentially exempt transfer (PET) is not chargeable to IHT unless the transferor dies within 7 years.

► The value of a transfer for IHT purposes may be reduced by business property relief and/or agricultural property relief.

► The IHT on a transfer is normally payable six months after the end of the month in which the transfer took place.

Exercises

31.1   Phoebe made the following transfers during 2000/01 :

		£
12 April 2000	Gift to grandson	50
17 May 2000	Gift to her nephew on his marriage	3,000
3 August 2000	Gift to her husband	25,000
31 October 2000	Gift to a discretionary trust	10,000
1 January 2001	Gift to the Labour Party	5,000

None of the gifts are regarded as normal expenditure out of income. Phoebe made no transfers at all during 1999/00. Calculate the value of each of her 2000/01 transfers after deduction of all the available exemptions.

31.2 Classify each of the following lifetime transfers as either exempt, potentially exempt, or chargeable :

    (a)   a gift to an accumulation and maintenance trust

    (b)   a gift to the transferor's favourite charity

    (c)   a gift to a discretionary trust

    (d)   a gift to the transferor's grandfather

    (e)   a gift to a trust with an interest in possession.

31.3 On 5 December 2000, Nicholas makes a gift of £80,000 to a discretionary trust. His only previous chargeable lifetime transfers were in June 1991 (gross chargeable value £200,000) and July 1995 (gross chargeable value £190,000). Calculate the IHT payable and state the due date of payment :

    (a)   if the trustees pay the tax   (b)   if Nicholas pays the tax.

31.4 On 31 August 1995, Martha gave £500,000 to her daughter as a wedding present. On 1 June 1999 she gave a further £500,000 to a discretionary trust. Martha died on 1 January 2001, having made only these two transfers during her life.

    (a)   Calculate any lifetime tax due on each of the above transfers and state the due date of payment, assuming that Martha paid this tax herself.

    (b)   Calculate any further tax due on Martha's death in relation to these transfers and state the due date of payment.

31.5 On 29 June 2000, Hyacinth makes a transfer consisting of 1,000 shares in a listed company. The shares are quoted at 572 - 588 on that day, with bargains marked at 572, 577 and 578. Calculate the market value of the transfer for IHT purposes.

*31.6 On 12 November 1990, Hazel made a gross chargeable transfer to a discretionary trust of £180,000. On 1 April 1996 she gave £300,000 to her grandson. These were her only transfers. She died on 17 December 2000. Calculate the tax payable by her grandson as a result of Hazel's death.

*31.7 Tony died on 11 July 2000, leaving an estate valued at £500,000. None of the transfers made on his death were exempt from IHT. He had made the following transfers during his lifetime :

		£
3/5/92	Gift to discretionary trust (tax paid by trustees)	100,000
1/7/93	Gift to daughter	250,000
1/8/93	Gift to son	250,000
10/6/97	Gift to discretionary trust (tax paid by Tony)	450,000

Calculate the tax payable as a result of Tony's death.

Chapter 32

Overseas aspects of taxation

Introduction

The main purpose of this final chapter is to consider the way in which the UK tax system deals with the overseas income and gains of UK resident individuals and companies. The treatment of non-residents with income or gains arising in the UK is also briefly considered.

The chapter begins by explaining the factors which affect an individual's UK tax status and then continues with a brief review of the overseas aspects of income tax, capital gains tax and inheritance tax. The UK tax status of companies and overseas aspects of corporation tax are dealt with towards the end of the chapter.

Residence, ordinary residence and domicile

The extent to which an individual is chargeable to UK tax depends entirely upon that individual's *residence*, *ordinary residence* and *domicile*. These key concepts are explained below. It should be noted that an individual's nationality is usually *not* an important factor when determining that individual's UK tax status.

Residence

The term "residence" is not clearly defined in statute law and therefore the meaning of the term has had to evolve from case law. Although most individuals are very obviously resident in one country, it is possible (for UK tax purposes at least) to be resident in more than one country for a given tax year or even to be resident in no country at all. The main circumstances in which an individual is normally deemed to be UK resident are as follows :

(a) An individual who is physically present in the UK for at least 183 days during a given tax year (excluding days of arrival or departure) is deemed to be resident in the UK for the whole of that tax year.

(b) An individual who is in the habit of making regular visits to the UK (averaging at least 91 days per tax year, excluding days spent in the UK because of circumstances beyond the individual's control e.g. illness) is usually regarded as UK resident. Two situations are possible :

   (i) An ex-resident who has now left the UK but who makes regular visits as described above is deemed to be UK resident for the whole of each tax year during which the visits continue.

   (ii) An individual who was not previously a UK resident but who begins making regular visits as described above is normally deemed to be UK resident with effect from the fifth year of the visits. However, if it is clear from the outset that the visits are going to be regular, the individual may be regarded as UK resident with effect from the first year of the visits.

Note that the concept of UK residence normally applies to whole tax years. An individual is deemed to be UK resident for the whole of a tax year or for none of it and it is not usually possible to apportion a tax year into periods of residence and non-residence. (The significance of this will become clear when the tax implications of residence and non-residence are described below). However, by concession, such apportionment is permitted in the following cases :

(a) in the year of arrival, if an individual takes up permanent residence in the UK or comes to stay in the UK for at least 2 years

(b) in the year of departure, if an individual leaves the UK in order to take up permanent residence abroad or to live abroad for at least 3 years

(c) in the years of departure and return, if an individual leaves the UK in order to take up employment abroad under a contract of employment for at least a whole tax year (in which case the individual concerned is normally regarded as being non-resident throughout the period of the contract, so long as UK visits during that period do not exceed 183 days in any one tax year or 91 days per year on average).

If a tax year is apportioned into periods of residence and non-residence, personal allowances are available in full for that year.

Ordinary residence

The term "ordinary residence" is also without a statutory definition. In general terms, an individual is ordinarily resident in the UK if he or she is habitually UK resident i.e. resident year after year. In a given tax year, it is quite possible to be resident but not ordinarily resident, or vice-versa.

An individual who is ordinarily resident in the UK but who is temporarily abroad during a given tax year (i.e. not present for at least 183 days but not absent for the entire tax year either) is deemed to be resident in the UK for the whole of that tax year.

EXAMPLE 1

(a) Pierre, who has lived in France for the whole of his life, arrives in the UK on 1 May 2000 and remains until 31 March 2001, when he returns permanently to France. What is his UK residence status for 2000/01 ?

(b) Peter, who has lived in the UK for the whole of his life, leaves the UK on 1 May 2000 and returns permanently on 31 March 2001. What is his UK residence status for 2000/01 ?

(c) Petra, who has lived in the UK for the whole of her life, leaves the UK on 1 April 2000 and returns permanently on 30 April 2001. What is her UK residence status for 2000/01 ?

SOLUTION

(a) Pierre is *resident* in 2000/01 (spending at least 183 days in the UK during the year) but he is *not ordinarily resident*.

(b) Peter does not spend at least 183 days in the UK during 2000/01. However, he does spend at least some time in the UK during the year and he is *ordinarily resident*. Therefore he is also *resident* for the year.

(c) Petra is *ordinarily resident*. However, she is absent from the UK for the whole of 2000/01 and therefore she is *not resident* for that year.

Domicile

An individual's domicile is the country in which the individual has his or her permanent home. Whilst it is possible to be resident in more than one country at a time, it is not possible to have more than one domicile at a time.

Individuals acquire a "domicile of origin" on birth. This is usually the domicile of the father or other person on whom the individual is dependent and is not necessarily the country of birth. Having reached the age of 16, an individual may then change domicile and acquire a "domicile of choice", but such a domicile can only be acquired by settling in the chosen country.

If an individual acquires a domicile of choice, that domicile is also acquired by anyone under the age of 16 who is dependent on that individual. A domicile acquired in this way is known as a "domicile of dependency".

Income tax - general rules

The general rules governing an individual's liability to UK income tax are as follows :

(a) Individuals who are *resident* in the UK for a tax year are liable to pay UK income tax on all of their income for that year, including both UK income and overseas income. Note that :

    (i) Income from an overseas employment is taxed under Schedule E, income from an overseas trade, profession or vocation is usually taxed under Schedule D Case I or II and other overseas income is taxed under Schedule D Cases IV and V.

    (ii) Personal allowances may be claimed by UK residents.

    (iii) The overseas income of a UK resident who is not domiciled in the UK is only subject to UK income tax to the extent that the income is remitted to the UK. This is known as the "remittance basis".

(b) Individuals who are *not resident* in the UK are liable to pay UK income tax on their UK income only. Note that :

    (i) The property income of non-residents is usually payable after deduction of basic rate income tax by the letting agent or tenant.

    (ii) Personal allowances may be claimed by certain non-residents, principally those who are citizens of either the European Economic Area or the Commonwealth (see Chapter 3).

(c) Interest on UK Government securities is generally exempt from UK income tax if the recipient is *not ordinarily resident* in the UK.

(d) If a tax year is apportioned into a period of residence and a period of non-residence (see above) then the above rules apply to the two periods as if they were separate tax years.

These general rules are subject to a number of exceptions, depending on the type of income involved (as explained later in this chapter).

Double taxation relief (DTR)

The rules given above are likely to lead to a number of situations in which income is taxed twice. For example, the overseas income of a UK resident will be taxed in the UK and might also be taxed in the country in which the income arises (depending upon that country's taxation laws). Similarly, the UK income of a non-resident will be taxed in the UK and might also be taxed overseas. In order to avoid this situation, the UK has made "double taxation agreements" with many overseas countries. A full description of double taxation agreements is beyond the scope of this book but, typically, the outcome of such an agreement might be that :

(a) Country X agrees to give relief for any tax paid to Country Y when computing tax payable to itself (and vice-versa), or

(b) Country X agrees to exempt the residents of Country Y from paying tax on income arising in Country X (and vice-versa).

Unilateral double tax relief

In the absence of a double taxation agreement with the country from which a UK resident receives income, the UK tax system provides "unilateral double tax relief" for the foreign tax which has been suffered. The foreign income received net of foreign tax is grossed up and charged to UK income tax but the taxpayer is then given tax relief equal to the *lower* of :

(a) the amount of foreign tax suffered (the "withholding tax") and

(b) the amount of UK tax due on the foreign income.

The UK tax due on the foreign income is the difference between the tax due on the taxpayer's total income (including foreign income) and the tax which would be due if the foreign income were ignored. If the foreign tax suffered exceeds the UK tax due, part of the foreign tax suffered will be unrelieved.

Unilateral relief is available only if the UK resident concerned has taken all reasonable steps to minimise the amount of the foreign tax liability.

EXAMPLE 2

Vicky has the following income in 2000/01 :

	£
Salary from UK employment	33,640
Rents from foreign property (net of 30% withholding tax)	3,500

Vicky is UK resident in 2000/01. Calculate her UK income tax liability for the year.

SOLUTION

	£
Schedule E	33,640
Schedule D Case V (£3,500 x 100/70)	5,000
	38,640
<u>Less</u> : Personal allowance	4,385
Taxable income	34,255

		£
Income tax		
1,520	@ 10%	152.00
26,880	@ 22%	5,913.60
5,855	@ 40%	2,342.00
34,255		8,407.60

<u>Less</u> : Double tax relief, lower of :
     (a) foreign tax (£1,500)   1,500.00
     (b) UK tax on foreign income (40% x £5,000)

UK tax liability   6,907.60

Income from employment

Schedule E is divided into three Cases (Cases I, II and III) and the extent to which an individual's income from employment is charged to UK income tax depends upon which of these three Cases is applicable. The circumstances in which each Case applies are as follows :

Residence status	*Duties performed wholly or partly in the UK*		*Duties performed wholly outside the UK*
	UK duties	*Non-UK duties*	
Resident and ordinarily resident	Case I	Case I	Case I or III (see below)
Resident but not ordinarily resident	Case II	Case III	Case III
Not resident	Case II	Not taxable	Not taxable

If an individual is both resident and ordinarily resident in the UK, emoluments earned for duties performed wholly outside the UK are assessed under Case I unless they are "foreign emoluments" assessed under Case III. Foreign emoluments are those earned from a non-resident employer by an individual who is not domiciled in the UK.

Schedule E basis of assessment

Schedule E Case I and II assessments are made on the receipts basis. Case III assessments are made on the remittance basis. Therefore any emoluments which fall within the scope of Case III but are not remitted to the UK escape UK income tax altogether.

The 100% deduction for seafarers

Individuals who are both resident and ordinarily resident in the UK are normally assessed under Schedule E Case I on all of their emoluments, whether their duties are performed in the UK or abroad. However, in the case of individuals *who are employed as seafarers,* if the duties are performed wholly or partly outside the UK throughout a continuous "qualifying period" of 365 days or more, a 100% deduction is given against all of the emoluments earned during this period (including the emoluments relating to any work performed in the UK). In effect, the emoluments attributable to such a qualifying period are entirely exempt from UK income tax. Note that :

(a) The emoluments which are attributable to a qualifying period are those which are *earned* in that period, not necessarily those which are received in that period.

(b) A "qualifying period" begins when an individual leaves the UK to work abroad as a seafarer and the period is treated as continuous even if the individual returns to the UK from time to time, so long as :

   (i) no visit in the UK during the period lasts for more than 183 days, and

   (ii) on each day of return to the UK, the total number of days present in the UK since the qualifying period began is no more than one-half of the total length of the period so far.

   If condition (i) is broken, the qualifying period ends immediately before the start of the offending UK visit. If condition (ii) is broken, the qualifying period ends immediately before the start of the most recent UK visit.

(c) An individual is deemed to be present in the UK on a given day if he or she is in the UK at midnight on that day. Therefore, a day of arrival in the UK counts as a day present in the UK, but a day of departure from the UK does not.

EXAMPLE 3

Robin is domiciled in the UK and has lived in the UK all his life. On 1 June 2000 he leaves to work as a seafarer and does not visit the UK again until he returns on 31 July 2001.

(a) What is his residence status in 2000/01 ?

(b) To what extent are his earnings as a seafarer subject to UK income tax ?

SOLUTION

(a) Robin is ordinarily resident in the UK and spends some time in the UK during 2000/01. Therefore he is resident for the year.

(b) As Robin is domiciled, resident and ordinarily resident in the UK he is normally taxed under Schedule E Case I on all of his earnings from employment, no matter where in the world his duties are performed. But the period from 1 June 2000 to 31 July 2001 is a qualifying period of at least 365 days. Therefore Robin's earnings as a seafarer are not subject to UK tax.

Travelling and subsistence expenses

If the duties of an employment are performed abroad and the employee is resident and ordinarily resident in the UK then, so long as the emoluments concerned are not "foreign emoluments" (see above), the following expenses are allowable deductions under Schedule E :

(a) where duties are performed wholly abroad :

    (i) the costs of travelling abroad at the start of the employment and travelling back to the UK at the end of it

    (ii) the costs of overseas board and lodging paid for or reimbursed by the employer (and assessable as emoluments)

(b) where duties are performed partly in the UK and partly abroad, travelling and subsistence expenses paid for or reimbursed by the employer (and assessable as emoluments) relating to :

    (i) travel by the employee between the UK and the overseas place of work

    (ii) travel by the employee's spouse and minor children, if the employee is working abroad for a continuous period of 60 days or more, but limited to two return journeys per person per tax year.

Similar deductions to those described at (b) above are available to non-UK domiciled individuals who are working in the UK but these deductions are available for only five years, beginning with the date of arrival in the UK.

Income from overseas businesses

The profits of a business carried on in the UK are taxed under Schedule D Case I (or Case II), whilst the profits of a business carried on overseas are taxed under Schedule D Case V. Note that :

(a) A business is "carried on" in the country from which it is controlled, no matter where in the world the business activities actually take place. Therefore a business owned by a UK resident is usually deemed to be carried on in the UK and is taxed under Schedule D Case I, even if the business is conducted entirely overseas.

(b) In the case of a partnership, it is possible for a given partner to be UK resident whilst control of the partnership is located abroad. In this case, the UK resident partner would be assessed under Schedule D Case V.

(c) A business which is exercised in the UK by a non-resident is also assessed under Schedule D Case I, even though the business is controlled from abroad.

If the profits of a business are assessed under Schedule D Case V, the assessable profits are computed using the rules of Schedule D Case I. However, there are two significant differences between Case I and Case V :

(a) Case V trading losses may be relieved under Sections 385 and 388 in the same way as Case I losses, but relief under Sections 380 and 381 is available only against overseas trading income, overseas pensions and foreign emoluments.

(b) Case I income is UK income (always assessed in full) whilst Case V income is overseas income and is assessed only on the remittance basis for non-UK domiciled individuals.

Travelling and subsistence expenses

So long as the profits of an overseas business are not taxed on the remittance basis, the following expenses are allowable deductions :

(a) expenses incurred by the proprietor of the business in travelling between the UK and the location of the overseas business (if wholly and exclusively for business purposes), and

(b) expenses relating to travel by the proprietor's spouse and minor children, if the proprietor is abroad for a continuous period of 60 days or more, but limited to two return journeys per person per tax year.

Income from overseas investments/possessions

Income from foreign *securities* (i.e. investments which yield interest, but not stocks and shares) is assessed under Schedule D Case IV. Income from foreign *possessions* is assessed under Schedule D Case V. Income assessed under Case V includes rents from overseas property, dividends from overseas companies, overseas pensions or annuities and the profits of overseas trades (see above). Note the following points :

(a) The basis of assessment for both Case IV and Case V is normally the same as that of Case III (see Chapter 6). However, as stated above, the profits of an overseas trade assessed under Case V are computed using the rules of Case I.

(b) As stated earlier in this chapter, the overseas income of a UK resident who is not domiciled in the UK is assessed on the remittance basis.

(c) Savings income arising abroad is generally taxed at the lower rate of 20% in the basic rate band. Overseas dividends charged under Schedule D Case V are usually taxed at the Schedule F ordinary rate (10%) in the starting rate and basic rate bands and at the Schedule F upper rate (32.5%) otherwise. If the remittance basis applies, however, overseas savings income and dividends are treated as if they were non-savings income and are taxed at 10%, 22% or 40%.

(d) The tax due on foreign pensions and annuities is calculated on only 90% of the amount assessable in the tax year (unless the remittance basis applies, in which case the income is fully taxable).

Capital gains tax - general rules

The general rules which govern an individual's liability to UK capital gains tax (CGT) are as follows :

(a) Individuals who are resident or ordinarily resident in the UK for a tax year are liable to CGT on all disposals of chargeable assets occurring in that year, no matter where in the world the assets are situated. Double taxation relief (as described above for income tax) may be available.

(b) Individuals who are neither resident nor ordinarily resident in the UK are not liable to CGT at all, even in relation to disposals of assets situated in the UK.

There are three main exceptions to these general rules :

(a) A non-UK domiciled individual who is resident or ordinarily resident in the UK is fully liable to CGT on the disposal of assets situated in the UK but is liable to CGT on the remittance basis only in relation to disposals abroad.

(b) An individual who is neither resident nor ordinarily resident in the UK but who carries on a business in the UK is chargeable to CGT in relation to disposals of business assets situated in the UK.

(c) Individuals who acquire assets before temporarily leaving the UK (for up to five years) and then dispose of those assets whilst abroad remain chargeable to CGT in relation to these disposals. Gains arising in the tax year of departure are taxed in that year. Later gains are taxed in the year in which residence resumes.

A claim may be made to defer a CGT assessment relating to a disposal of overseas assets if it can be shown that the gain in question cannot be remitted to the UK because of either :

(a) the laws of the country in which the gain arises, or

(b) the actions of the government of that country, or

(c) the impossibility of obtaining foreign currency in that country.

Such a claim must be made by 31 January in the sixth year of assessment following the year in which the gain arises. If the conditions preventing remittance of the gain to the UK subsequently cease to exist, the gain becomes chargeable in the year in which this occurs.

Inheritance tax - general rules

An individual who is domiciled in the UK is liable to inheritance tax (IHT) in relation to all of his or her chargeable property, wherever in the world that property is situated. An individual who is not domiciled in the UK is liable to IHT only in relation to property situated in the UK.

The definition of "domicile" for IHT purposes is broader than the general definition given earlier in this chapter. An individual is treated as domiciled in the UK on the date of a transfer if that individual :

(a) was domiciled in the UK at any time within the previous 3 years, or

(b) was UK resident for at least 17 of the 20 tax years ending with the tax year in which the transfer takes place.

Corporation tax - general rules

A company's liability to UK corporation tax depends upon whether or not it is resident in the UK. A company is regarded as resident in the UK if it is incorporated in the UK or if its central management and control is situated in the UK. The general rules which govern a company's liability to UK corporation tax are as follows :

(a) A UK resident company is chargeable to UK corporation tax on all of its profits, no matter where in the world those profits are earned. The overseas income and gains of UK resident companies are taxed as follows :

(i) The profits of a trade conducted through an overseas branch or agency but controlled in the UK are taxed under Schedule D Case I. Trading losses may be relieved as usual and group relief is generally available. However, as from 1 April 2000, the losses of an overseas branch may be surrendered to another UK resident company in the same group only to the extent that those losses are not relievable in the overseas country.

(ii) The profits of a trade conducted through an overseas branch or agency which is controlled abroad are taxed under Schedule D Case V. Trading losses may be relieved only against other overseas trading income.

(iii) Income from foreign investments is taxed under either Schedule D Case III (foreign securities) or Schedule D Case V (foreign possessions). Schedule D Case IV does not apply to companies. Dividends received from non-UK resident companies are not franked investment income.

(iv) The gains arising on the disposal of overseas assets are chargeable gains and form part of the company's chargeable profits.

(b) A non-UK resident company is chargeable to UK corporation tax only if it carries on a trade in the UK through a branch or agency, and then only on the following profits :

(i) the trading profits of the UK branch

(ii) income from property in the possession of the UK branch

(iii) chargeable gains arising from the disposal of assets used by the UK branch.

The trading losses of a UK branch of a non-UK resident company may generally be set against any other profits of the branch or may be carried forward against the branch's future trading profits. As from 1 April 2000, the branch may also surrender its losses to UK resident companies in the same group, so long as those losses are not relievable in the overseas country. Similarly, the branch may claim losses surrendered by other UK resident group companies. Also as from 1 April 2000, assets transferred between such a branch and a UK resident group company are transferred on a no-gain, no-loss basis (so long as the assets remain within the charge to UK corporation tax).

A non-UK resident company is not generally entitled to the starting rate or small companies rate of corporation tax or to marginal relief. However, this rule will not apply if it is overridden by the double taxation agreement (if any) between the UK and the country in which the non-UK company is resident.

Overseas subsidiaries

The profits of a non-UK resident subsidiary of a UK resident parent company may be subject to overseas tax but are not generally subject to UK tax unless the subsidiary is treated as a controlled foreign company (see later in this chapter). The UK resident parent company is of course liable to corporation tax on any income received from the overseas subsidiary. As explained in Chapter 28, groups of companies usually enjoy a number of corporation tax reliefs, including (subject to certain conditions) :

(a) the payment of charges and annual interest between group members without accounting for income tax

(b) the transfer of trading losses and certain other items between group members

(c) the transfer of chargeable assets between group members on a no-gain, no-loss basis.

However, these reliefs are generally available only to UK resident companies and do not apply to an overseas subsidiary. An overseas subsidiary *does* count as an associated company for small company relief purposes.

Company migration

A UK resident company may wish to "migrate" overseas in order to escape paying UK corporation tax on its worldwide profits. This is only possible for companies which are incorporated outside the UK and involves moving the central management and control of the company from the UK to an overseas location. A company wishing to take this step must :

(a) notify the Inland Revenue of its intentions, specifying the date on which it intends to become non-resident, and

(b) give the Inland Revenue a statement of all the tax payable up to that date, specifying the arrangements which will be made to ensure that this tax is paid.

On the date that a company becomes non-resident it is deemed to make a disposal of all its assets at their market value on that date. This deemed disposal is likely to result in a sizeable chargeable gain, which is sometimes referred to as the "exit charge". However, this charge is not made in full in the following circumstances :

(a) If a company retains a branch or agency in the UK, the deemed disposal does not include assets which are situated in the UK and which are used for trade purposes by the branch or agency.

(b) If the company in question is, immediately on becoming non-resident, a 75% subsidiary of a UK resident company (the "principal company"), the gains arising in connection with the deemed disposal of the company's *foreign* assets may be postponed, so long as both companies make an election in writing to that effect. The postponed gains will crystallise if :

(i) within the following 6 years, any of the foreign assets are disposed of, or

(ii) at any time, the company concerned ceases to be a 75% subsidiary of the principal company, or

(iii) at any time, the principal company ceases to be UK resident.

Any gains which crystallise are chargeable on the principal company.

Controlled foreign companies (CFC'S)

A UK resident company which wishes to operate overseas may either :

(a) operate through an overseas branch or agency, or

(b) operate through a separate non-UK resident company which is under the control of the UK company.

Since the profits of a non-UK resident company are not generally chargeable to UK corporation tax, it would seem to be beneficial for a UK company to adopt the second of these alternatives, especially if the operation is carried on in a country with low tax rates. The overseas profits would not be subject to UK tax at all and could be accumulated in the overseas company. Admittedly, any dividends paid to the UK company would be taxed under Schedule D Case V but such dividends might be put off indefinitely or at least paid some time after the accounting year to which they relate, so delaying the Case V liability. As an anti-avoidance measure, the profits of a *controlled foreign company* (CFC) are apportioned between its shareholders and the profits which are apportioned to UK resident companies are charged to corporation tax. However, no assessment is raised on a UK company to which less than 25% of a CFC's profits are apportioned. A CFC is a company which :

(a) is resident overseas but is under UK control, and

(b) is subject to a level of taxation in the country in which it is resident which is less than 75% of the corresponding UK tax which would be due if the company were UK resident, or

(c) is resident in one of a number of countries which (in effect) allow companies to choose their own "designer rate" of tax as a means of side-stepping the CFC rules.

The definition of "control" for this purpose normally means that the overseas company must be more than 50% controlled from the UK. However, an overseas company will also be treated as a CFC if it is at least 40% controlled by a UK company and at least 40% controlled by a foreign company. The profits of a CFC for an accounting period are *not* apportioned between its shareholders if any of the following conditions are satisfied for that period :

(a) The CFC adopts an "acceptable distribution policy", which means that it has distributed at least 90% of its taxable profits within 18 months of the end of the accounting period.

(b) The profits of the CFC for the period do not exceed £50,000 per annum.

(c) The CFC has a public quotation, at least 35% of its ordinary share capital is held by the public and its shares have been dealt in on a recognised stock exchange.

(d) The CFC is engaged in certain exempt activities.

(e) The Inland Revenue are convinced that the main reason for setting up the CFC was not to achieve a reduction in UK tax.

Double taxation relief for companies

A UK resident company which receives income from a foreign country which has no double taxation agreement with the UK is given unilateral double tax relief. This relief usually takes the form of a tax credit equal to the lower of :

(a) the amount of foreign tax suffered, and

(b) the amount of UK tax due on the foreign income.

Any excess foreign tax is unrelieved, but it may be possible to carry the excess back or forward to other accounting periods (see below).

EXAMPLE 4

In the year to 31 March 2001, a UK resident company had UK trading profits of £5,200,000 and received overseas dividends (net of 35% withholding tax) of £130,000. Compute the corporation tax liability for the year.

SOLUTION

	UK £	Overseas £	Total £
Sch D Case I	5,200,000		5,200,000
Sch D Case V £130,000 x 100/65		200,000	200,000
Chargeable profits	5,200,000	200,000	5,400,000
Corporation tax @ 30%	1,560,000	60,000	1,620,000
Less : Unilateral DTR		(60,000)	(60,000)
Corporation tax due	1,560,000	-	1,560,000

Note :

The unilateral relief given is restricted to the UK tax due on the overseas income. The remaining £10,000 (£70,000 - £60,000) of foreign tax paid is unrelieved.

Unrelieved foreign tax

Any unrelieved foreign tax arising in accounting periods ending before 1 April 2000 is simply lost. However, unrelieved foreign tax arising in accounting periods ending on or after 1 April 2000 may in general be carried back to the immediately preceding accounting period or carried forward without time limit. Note the following points :

(a) If unrelieved foreign tax arising in respect of a source of income is carried back or carried forward, it is treated as if it were foreign tax paid in respect of that same source of income in the accounting period to which it is carried back or forward.

(b) The carry back and carry forward rules relate only to foreign tax on the profits of an overseas branch or agency and to foreign tax on dividends. In the case of dividends, the rules extend to underlying tax (see below) as well as to direct tax.

(c) In the case of overseas branch profits, these rules apply to unrelieved foreign tax arising in any accounting period ending on or after 1 April 2000, but unrelieved tax cannot be carried back to periods ending before 1 April 2000.

(d) In the case of foreign dividends, these rules apply to dividends arising on or after 1 July 2000, but unrelieved tax cannot be carried back for set-off against UK tax payable on dividends arising before 1 July 2000.

Underlying DTR

If a UK resident company owns at least 10% of the voting power of an overseas company from which it receives a dividend, then an additional form of unilateral relief, known as "underlying double tax relief", is available. The idea of underlying DTR is to give relief for the foreign tax suffered on the profits out of which the dividend has been paid. Underlying relief is calculated by the formula :

$$\frac{D}{P} \times T$$

where : D = the gross dividend received

P = the profit available for distribution as shown in the accounts for the accounting period to which the dividend relates

T = the overseas tax actually paid on the profits of that period.

EXAMPLE 5

A UK resident company receives a dividend from an overseas company (in which it holds 15% of the voting power) of £10,500, net of 30% withholding tax. The profit and loss account of the overseas company for the year to which the dividend relates is as follows :

	£
Profit before tax	400,000
Less : Provision for taxation liability	150,000
Profits after tax	250,000
Dividends	100,000
Retained profits c/f	150,000

The actual tax liability of the overseas company for the year is finally agreed at £160,000. Compute the maximum unilateral double tax relief available in respect of the £10,500 dividend received.

SOLUTION

(i) D = £10,500 x 100/70 = £15,000. P = £250,000. T = £160,000

(ii) Withholding tax = £4,500

(iii) Underlying tax $= \dfrac{D}{P} \times T = \dfrac{£15,000}{£250,000} \times £160,000 = £9,600$

(iv) Maximum unilateral DTR = £4,500 + £9,600 = £14,100. The gross dividend is £24,600 (net £10,500 + tax £14,100).

It is worth noting that Finance Act 2000 introduced some controversial changes to the rules relating to underlying double tax relief. These changes were intended to take effect as from 1 July 2000 but have now been delayed until 31 March 2001. The main consequence of these changes is to restrict the amount of underlying DTR available to a UK resident parent company which channels dividends from a number of overseas subsidiaries through a single overseas "mixer company". This practice allows dividends received from low-tax countries to be mixed in with dividends received from high-tax countries, so generating an average rate of underlying tax more or less equal to the UK corporation tax rate. In this way (until 31 March 2001) dividends from low-tax countries can be paid to the UK without incurring a UK corporation tax liability.

Unilateral expense relief

A company may waive the right to claim unilateral "credit relief" (where the double tax relief takes the form of a tax credit) and opt instead for unilateral "expense relief". In this case, the company is assessed on the *net* foreign income, so that the foreign tax is treated as if it were an expense. Expense relief may be attractive if (for example) a company makes a claim under Section 393A(1)(a) to set a trading loss against its total profits, so that it has no corporation tax liability on the foreign income and so cannot obtain any credit relief.

EXAMPLE 6

A UK resident company has a trading loss for the year to 31 March 2001 of £50,000. During the year, the company received a dividend from an overseas company of £12,000, net of 40% withholding tax. Show the corporation tax computation for the year if :

(a) unilateral credit relief is claimed (underlying relief is not available), or

(b) unilateral expense relief is claimed.

Note : The company will be claiming loss relief under S393A(1)(a).

SOLUTION

		Credit relief £	Expense relief £
Schedule D Case I		0	0
Schedule D Case V :			
Gross dividend	20,000	20,000	
Less : Foreign tax	8,000		12,000
		20,000	12,000
Less : S393A(1)(a) relief		(20,000)	(12,000)
Chargeable profits		0	0
Corporation tax liability		0	0
Losses available for carry-back or carry-forward		30,000	38,000
Unrelieved foreign tax available for carry-forward		8,000	nil

Notes :

(i) No unilateral credit relief is available since the overseas dividend is absorbed by the S393A(1)(a) claim, leaving a UK tax liability of £nil.

(ii) The choice of credit relief gives £8,000 of unrelieved foreign tax. This can be carried forward and treated as foreign tax paid in respect of dividends received from the same foreign company in future years. However, if dividends from that company continue to be received net of 40% tax (and UK tax rates remain at no more than 30%) it is unlikely that there will be any scope for relieving the £8,000 in future years.

(iii) The choice of expense relief increases by £8,000 the trading losses available for carry-back under S393A(1)(b) or carry-forward under S393(1).

Interaction of charges, loss reliefs and DTR

As explained in Chapters 23 and 26, a company's chargeable profits are reduced by the amount of any charges paid in the accounting period and by the amount of any loss relief claimed under S393A(1). Normally, it is sufficient simply to subtract the charges and loss reliefs from total income without allocating these deductions to particular sources of income. However, if unilateral double tax relief is claimed, such an allocation must be made so that the amount of UK tax payable on the foreign income can then be computed.

Clearly, if any charges or losses are deemed to be set against the foreign income, this will have the effect of reducing the UK tax due on that foreign income and so reducing the maximum unilateral DTR available. Therefore charges and losses should be set first against UK income, then against foreign income. If a company has more than one source of foreign income, charges and losses should be set against foreign income which has suffered low rates of foreign tax in preference to foreign income which has suffered high rates of foreign tax.

DTR and relief of surplus ACT

If a company has surplus ACT brought forward from before 6 April 1999, the amount of that ACT which can be relieved in an accounting period is governed by the shadow ACT regulations (see Chapter 25). These regulations stipulate that the maximum ACT set-off for an accounting period is equal to the ACT which would be payable on a franked payment equal to the chargeable profits for that period. If double tax relief is claimed, the maximum offset is further restricted to the amount of corporation tax payable on each source of income after DTR has been deducted.

EXAMPLE 7

In the year to 31 March 2001, a UK resident company has UK trading profits of £4,800,000 and receives overseas dividends (net of 45% withholding tax) of £2,750,000. Charges of £1,000,000 (gross) are paid in the year. The company also has unrelieved surplus ACT brought forward from before 6 April 1999. Compute the corporation tax liability for the year and the maximum ACT set-off.

SOLUTION

	UK £	Overseas £	Total £
Schedule D Case I	4,800,000		4,800,000
Schedule D Case V			
£2,750,000 x 100/55		5,000,000	5,000,000
	4,800,000	5,000,000	9,800,000
Less : Charges	1,000,000	-	1,000,000
Chargeable profits	3,800,000	5,000,000	8,800,000
Corporation tax @ 30%	1,140,000	1,500,000	2,640,000
Less : Unilateral DTR		(1,500,000)	(1,500,000)
Corporation tax liability	1,140,000	-	1,140,000
Maximum ACT set-off	760,000	-	760,000

Notes :

(i) The charges are set against the UK income so as to maximise double tax relief on the overseas income.

(ii) DTR is limited to the UK tax due on the overseas income. Foreign tax paid is £2,250,000, of which £750,000 is unrelieved.

(iii) ACT set-off is restricted in the usual way but is also restricted to the corporation tax liability on each source of income after deduction of DTR. For the UK income, the first of these restrictions gives a maximum set-off of £760,000 (20% of £3,800,000). For the overseas income, the second restriction gives a maximum set-off of £nil.

(iv) As usual, the shadow ACT arising on any dividends paid in the year will use up some or all of the maximum ACT set-off and so reduce the scope for relieving surplus ACT brought forward from before 6 April 1999.

Summary

► An individual's liability to UK tax depends upon that individual's residence, ordinary residence and domicile.

► Individuals who are resident in the UK for a tax year are liable to UK income tax on their worldwide income for that year.

► Double taxation relief may be available if income is subject to both UK tax and overseas tax.

► Income from employment is taxed under the three Cases of Schedule E. Case III assessments are made on the remittance basis only.

► Income from an overseas trade which is controlled from the UK is assessed under Schedule D Case I.

► Individuals who are resident or ordinarily resident in the UK for a tax year are liable to UK CGT on their disposals throughout the world in that year.

► Individuals who are domiciled in the UK are liable to UK IHT. The definition of "domicile" for IHT purposes is broader than the general definition.

► UK resident companies are liable to UK corporation tax on their worldwide profits. Non-resident companies are chargeable only on the profits of a trade carried on in the UK through a branch or agency.

► The profits of a controlled foreign company may be apportioned between the controlling UK companies and assessed to UK corporation tax.

► In the absence of a double tax agreement, double tax relief for companies may take the form of credit relief, underlying tax relief or expense relief.

Exercises

32.1 Jean-Paul is a Canadian citizen. He owns a house in Canada and regards Canada as his home but he lives in London for nearly all of tax year 2000/01. His income for the year is derived from the following sources :

(a) a part-time employment with a UK company (the duties of which are performed entirely in London)

(b) a second part-time employment with a Belgian company (the duties of which are performed entirely in Brussels, which he visits on one day each month)

(c) dividends from stocks and shares held in Canada

(d) interest on UK Government securities.

To what extent is any of his income chargeable to UK income tax ?

32.2 Amy is domiciled in the UK and has lived in the UK all her life. On 1 January 1999 she leaves to work in Australia for three years. Explain her UK income tax status for tax years 1998/99 to 2001/02 inclusive.

32.3 Cara is a UK resident. She receives a pension of £10,000 per annum from the Italian company for whom she used to work when she lived in Italy. Explain how the UK income tax system will treat this pension if Cara is :

(a) domiciled in the UK

(b) domiciled in Italy.

32.4 How would a UK resident company proceed if it wished to "migrate" overseas ? Why might this be a desirable step ?

32.5 Explain the term "controlled foreign company" (CFC). In what circumstances are the profits of a CFC chargeable to UK corporation tax ?

32.6 Brits Ltd is a UK resident company and has a trading profit of £2,120,000 for the year ended 31 March 2001. During the year, the company received a dividend from a wholly-owned overseas subsidiary of £57,400 (net of 18% withholding tax). The overseas company is liable to 50% overseas tax on all of its profits. Compute the corporation tax liability of Brits Ltd for the year.

*32.7   Donald is domiciled, resident and ordinarily resident in the UK. He has the following income in 2000/01 :

	£
UK trading profits	27,085
UK bank interest (net amount)	1,600
Income from foreign property (net of 45% withholding tax)	2,200

Donald claims only the personal allowance. Compute his income tax payable for 2000/01.

*32.8   X Ltd is a UK resident company with nineteen subsidiaries, one of which is situated abroad. In the year to 31 March 2001, X Ltd had the following results :

	£
UK trading profits	720,000
UK dividends received	40,000
UK chargeable gains	120,000
Dividend from overseas subsidiary (net of 30% withholding tax)	8,400
Charges paid (gross amount)	80,000

X Ltd owns 60% of the ordinary share capital of the overseas subsidiary (which does not rank as a controlled foreign company). The summarised profit and loss account of this subsidiary for the year to 31 March 2001 is as follows :

	£
Profit before tax	75,000
Less : Provision for taxation liability	25,000
Profits after tax	50,000
Dividends	20,000
Retained profits c/f	30,000

Calculate the corporation tax liability of X Ltd for the year. Also (given that X Ltd has a substantial amount of surplus ACT brought forward from before 6 April 1999) calculate the maximum ACT set-off for the year.

Review questions (Set D)

D 1   You have received a letter from the managing director of Wakem & Co. Ltd, a company making wholly standard rated supplies. Extracts from the letter are as follows :

"During the course of the last quarter, sales have been very good. In particular, we sold £30,000 worth of goods to St. Oggs Inc, an American company, and we also sold £20,000 worth of goods to Rappit Ltd in Scotland. Mr Jakin, the managing director of Rappit Ltd, drove a hard bargain and to secure the order we had to allow a 5% discount for prompt settlement. As we closed down the box manufacturing line, we sold off the machinery and made a useful £15,000. The electrical equipment remaining has been hired to Mudport Ltd for £1,000 per month. One piece of bad news is that Garum Furs plc has gone into liquidation owing us £14,000, though there is a possibility of recovering part of that amount in the liquidation."

Required :

Explain the significance for VAT purposes of the events described in this letter.   *(AAT)*

D 2   A Ltd is the holding company for a group of five companies. The relationships between the companies in the group are shown in the diagram below :

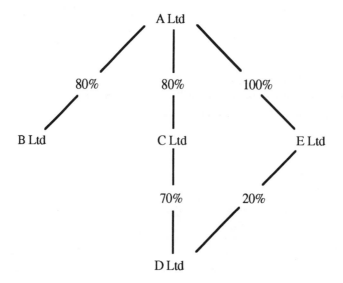

All of the companies are UK resident except for E Ltd which is resident in a country where the rate of tax is 5%. For the purposes of this question, E Ltd can be regarded as a

Controlled Foreign Company. All of the companies have an accounting year ended 31 March 2001 and their incomes/(losses) for the year were as follows :

	Schedule D Case I	Bank interest
	£	£
A Ltd	90,000	-
B Ltd	100,000	15,000
C Ltd	(90,000)	12,000
D Ltd	(5,000)	-
E Ltd	15,000	-

You are required :

(a)   To identify the companies which are treated as associated companies.

(b)   To identify the companies which form a group (or groups) for group relief purposes.

(c)   To compute the corporation tax liability of each company, assuming that the most efficient use is made by the group of any trading losses.

(d)   To advise the board of any steps it should take to minimise next year's corporation tax liabilities, given that E Ltd will have chargeable profits of £60,000.   *(CIMA)*

D 3   Your company has a number of branches and subsidiaries trading outside the UK. The board is about to offer contracts to employees resident in the UK and working in UK locations which will allow them to transfer to foreign locations on a temporary basis, with all of their duties being performed outside the UK. There are two contracts being offered - one lasting nine months and one lasting eighteen months.

You are required :

To draft a report to the board on the taxation implications, for the employees, of each of the possible contracts.   *(CIMA)*

D 4   M Ltd, a UK resident trading company, owns 6% of the share capital of Z Inc and 8% of the share capital of X S.A. Neither of these companies is resident in the UK for tax purposes. In addition, M Ltd has a controlling interest in two UK resident companies - N Ltd and O Ltd. The following information relates to M Ltd's 12-month accounting period ended 31 March 2001 :

	£	£
INCOME		
Schedule D Case I trading profits		500,000
Schedule D Case V :		
Dividend from Z Inc, after deduction of 30% withholding tax	35,000	
Dividend from X S.A., after deduction of 5% withholding tax	38,000	73,000
CHARGE PAID		
Patent royalties (gross amount)		10,000

M Ltd also has a substantial amount of unrelieved surplus ACT brought forward from before 6 April 1999.

You are required :

To compute the corporation tax liability of M Ltd for the above period, showing clearly the relief for double taxation. Also calculate the maximum ACT set-off for the period.

(CIMA)

*D5 David Deans started trading as a painter and decorator on 1 July 2000. He has notified you of his turnover each month which, up to November 2000, has been as follows :

	£
July 2000	5,000
August 2000	6,000
September 2000	7,000
October 2000	8,200
November 2000	9,000

In anticipation of a meeting with Mr Deans, you have received a letter from him, of which the following is an extract :

"In preparation for our meeting, I have some further information for you and some questions which I hope you will be able to answer for me. I anticipate that my turnover is likely to be £10,000 in December 2000 and £8,500 in January 2001. It must be reaching the time at which I need to be registered for VAT. Could you give me some idea of when this might be and whether I could delay it in order to improve my cash flow ?

Since starting business I have purchased substantial quantities of stock. Will I be able to recover any of the VAT I have paid ?

In June next year, I intend to buy a new van and a new car for the business. Their cost, including VAT, will be £14,000 and £8,000 respectively. I assume that I will be able to recover the VAT on both items. The van will be used wholly for business and the car both for business and private use. The firm will pay for all the petrol used by both vehicles.

As yet, I have not suffered any bad debts but as the business expands there is always the risk that they might arise. Are there any special VAT arrangements to deal with them ?"

Required :

Draft notes in preparation for the meeting with Mr Deans, responding to the queries which he has raised.

(AAT)

*D6 Mrs Lammle, who is registered for VAT, has traded as a manufacturer of standard-rated items since 1 January 1991. She has decided to retire on 31 May 2000, her 65th birthday, and you are asked to finalise her tax position up to that date. You are provided with the following information :

(i)   Mrs Lammle's first accounts covered the period to 31 May 1992. Since then, she has prepared accounts annually to 31 May. Recent profits, adjusted for tax purposes, have been agreed as :

	£
Year to 31 May 1997	45,000
Year to 31 May 1998	48,000
Year to 31 May 1999	51,000

(ii)   The last accounts will be for the year to 31 May 2000. Interim accounts have been prepared to 28 February 2000, revealing the following :

	£
Sales	100,200
Cost of sales	24,700
Gross profit	75,500
Expenses	29,000
Net profit	46,500

All of the above figures are net of VAT and contain no disallowable items for income tax purposes.

(iii)   For the last three months to 31 May 2000 (which is also the last VAT quarter), you have extracted the following figures from the accounting records :

	£
Sales :	
To UK customers	30,652
To overseas customers	8,000
Materials purchased :	
Standard-rated	4,087
Zero-rated	2,000
Exempt	800
Expenses :	
General (all standard-rated)	6,130
Wages	7,000
Hire of machinery	613
Business bank charges	500
Entertaining overseas clients	400

All of the above include VAT if appropriate. All of Mrs Lammle's sales are made to order so there is no outstanding stock left at the date of cessation. All the general expenses are allowable for income tax purposes.

(iv)   The tax written down value of the plant and machinery carried forward after capital allowances had been calculated for the year to 31 May 1999 was :

	£
Plant and machinery pool	12,375
Expensive car (with no private use)	5,250

No plant and machinery was acquired during the year to 31 May 2000.

(v) The business was sold as a going concern to a major competitor on 31 May 2000 (RPI 169.0). The items sold were :

	£
Freehold shop	200,000
Freehold workshop	130,000
Goodwill	180,000
Plant (no item worth more than £6,000)	25,000
Car	6,000

The shop and workshop were acquired on 1 January 1991 (RPI 130.2) for £30,000 and £27,000 respectively. The RPI for April 1998 was 162.6.

Required :

(a) Calculate the VAT due for the quarter to 31 May 2000.

(b) Calculate the final adjusted profit for the year to 31 May 2000, after deduction of capital allowances.

(c) Calculate Mrs Lammle's Schedule D Case I assessment for 2000/01.

(d) Calculate the untapered gain on the disposal of the business. *(AAT)*

*D7 The group structure below shows holdings in ordinary shares in other companies. All of the companies are UK resident except for O Inc which is foreign resident.

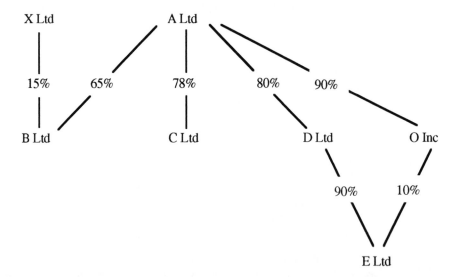

The results for each of the above companies for the accounting year ended 31 March 2001 are as follows :

		£				£
X Ltd	Loss	(40,000)		D Ltd	Profit	35,000
B Ltd	Profit	60,000		O Inc	Loss	(30,000)
A Ltd	Profit	103,000		E Ltd	Loss	(2,000)
C Ltd	Loss	(70,000)				

You are required :

(a) To identify the associated companies for starting rate and small company rate purposes and to state the upper and lower thresholds for each of the companies shown.

(b) To identify any groups and consortia in the above structure qualifying for group relief.

(c) To compute the corporation tax liability of each company, assuming that loss relief has been claimed in the most efficient manner.

(d) To advise the directors of A Ltd on the weakness, from a tax point of view, of the existing structure. *(CIMA)*

*D8 You are the chief accountant of Z Ltd, a UK resident company, whose activities to date have been confined wholly to the UK. The company is about to acquire three UK resident subsidiaries and the members of the newly-formed group will engage, for the first time, in import and export activities (all with non-EU countries).

You are required :

To draft a brief report to the board on the VAT implications of the above changes.

(CIMA)

PART 5
ANSWERS

Answers to exercises

Chapter 2

2.1

(a)   1,520 @ 10% + 10,600 @ 22% = £2,484.00.

(b)   1,520 @ 10% + 26,880 @ 22% + 7,700 @ 40% = £9,145.60.

(c)   1,520 @ 10% + 26,880 @ 22% + 33,703 @ 40% = £19,546.80.

2.2

(a)

			Total £	Non-savings £	Savings £
Schedule D Case I/II			19,280	19,280	
Bank interest £720 x 100/80			900		900
Statutory total income			20,180	19,280	900
Less : Personal allowance			4,385	4,385	
Taxable income			15,795	14,895	900
Income tax due					
Starting rate band : Non-savings		1,520	@ 10%	152.00	
Basic rate band : Non-savings		13,375	@ 22%	2,942.50	
: Savings		900	@ 20%	180.00	
		15,795			
Tax borne				3,274.50	
Less : Tax deducted at source				180.00	
Tax payable				3,094.50	

(b)

	Total £	Non-savings £	Savings £
Schedule D Case I/II	20,520	20,520	
Building society interest £8,000 x 100/80	10,000		10,000
Bank interest £2,300 x 100/80	2,875		2,875
Statutory total income	33,395	20,520	12,875
Less : Personal allowance	4,385	4,385	
Taxable income	29,010	16,135	12,875

Income tax due

Starting rate band	: Non-savings	1,520	@ 10%	152.00
Basic rate band	: Non-savings	14,615	@ 22%	3,215.30
	: Savings	12,265	@ 20%	2,453.00
Higher rate	: Savings	610	@ 40%	244.00
		29,010		

Tax borne	6,064.30
Less : Tax deducted at source	2,575.00
Tax payable	3,489.30

(c)

Total (all savings income)

£

Building society interest £26,912 x 100/80	33,640
Statutory total income	33,640
Less : Personal allowance	4,385
Taxable income	29,255

Income tax due

Starting rate band	: Savings	1,520	@ 10%	152.00
Basic rate band	: Savings	26,880	@ 20%	5,376.00
Higher rate	: Savings	855	@ 40%	342.00
		29,255		

Tax borne	5,870.00
Less : Tax deducted at source	6,728.00
Tax refund due	(858.00)

2.3

(a) Income from employment is assessed under Schedule E. Rents received are assessed under Schedule A. NSB interest would normally be assessed under Schedule D Case III but ordinary account interest of less than £70 is exempt from income tax. UK dividends are Schedule F income. Bank interest taxed at source is not directly assessed under a Schedule or Case.

(b)

	Total £	Non-savings £	Savings £	Dividends £
Schedule E	19,395	19,395		
Schedule A	13,000	13,000		
Bank interest £160 x 100/80	200		200	
Schedule F £225 + tax credit £25	250			250
Statutory total income	32,845	32,395	200	250
Less : Personal allowance	4,385	4,385		
Taxable income	28,460	28,010	200	250

Income tax due

Starting rate band	: Non-savings	1,520	@ 10%	152.00
Basic rate band	: Non-savings	26,490	@ 22%	5,827.80
	: Savings	200	@ 20%	40.00
	: Dividends	190	@ 10%	19.00
Higher rate	: Dividends	60	@ 32.5%	19.50
		28,460		

Tax borne	6,058.30
Less : Tax credits on dividends	25.00
Tax payable	6,033.30
Less : Tax deducted at source	40.00
Tax payable	5,993.30

Note : Stephanie would also be given credit for any PAYE tax paid.

2.4

	Total	Non-savings	Savings
	£	£	£
Schedule E	3,375	3,375	
Bank interest £416 x 100/80	520		520
Statutory total income	3,895	3,375	520
Less : Personal allowance	3,895	3,375	520
Taxable income	0	0	0

£490 of the personal allowance (£4,385 - £3,895) is unused. Tax borne is £nil and Ernest is entitled to repayment of the £104.00 of tax deducted at source. If he received dividends of £468, Schedule F income of £520 (£468 + £52) would replace the bank interest. Tax borne would still be £nil but he would not be able to claim payment of the £52 tax credit.

Chapter 3

3.1

(a) This taxpayer is in the 65-74 age group and is entitled to a PA of £5,790 for the year.

(b) This taxpayer is over 75 and has an STI which exceeds the limit by £1,000, giving a PA of £5,550 (£6,050 - 1/2 x £1,000).

(c) This taxpayer reaches the age of 65 during tax year 2000/01 and has an STI which exceeds the income limit by £3,600. This would give a PA of £3,990 (£5,790 - 1/2 x £3,600) but the allowance is never reduced to less than the PA for those aged under 65 so the taxpayer will claim £4,385.

3.2

(a) The husband is over 75 and therefore receives a PA of £6,050. His wife is over 65 but her STI exceeds the limit by £300, giving her a PA of £5,640 (£5,790 - 1/2 x £300). The MCA is £5,255 (which is not reduced at all, since the husband's STI does not exceed the income limit).

(b) The husband is over 65 but his STI exceeds the limit by £700, giving him a PA of £5,440 (£5,790 - 1/2 x £700). His wife is over 65 and is entitled to a PA of £5,790 (of which £590 is unused). An MCA of £5,185 is also available. This is not reduced at all since the reduction required because of the husband's STI has already been made in full against his PA.

(c) The husband is over 65 but his STI exceeds the limit by £4,560. Therefore he must lose a total of £2,280 in allowances. His own PA is first reduced from £5,790 to the minimum of £4,385 (a reduction of £1,405). The remaining £875 is deducted from the MCA of £5,185 giving an MCA of £4,310. His wife is under 65 and is therefore entitled to a PA of £4,385.

3.3

	(a) £	(b) £	(c) £
HUSBAND			
Statutory total income	11,980	5,000	6,385
Less : Personal allowance	6,050	5,000	6,050
Taxable income	5,930	0	335

Income tax

(a)	(b)	(c)				
1,520	0	335	@ 10%	152.00	0.00	33.50
4,410	0	0	@ 22%	970.20	0.00	0.00
5,930	0	335		1,122.20	0.00	33.50

Less : MCA £5,255 @ 10%	525.50		
MCA £5,255 x 8/12 @ 10% = £350.33		0.00	
(all transferred to wife)			
MCA £5,255 @ 10% = £525.50			33.50
(£492.00 transferred to wife)			
Tax borne	596.70	0.00	0.00

	(a)	(b)	(c)
WIFE			
Statutory total income	13,280	10,705	13,145
Less : Personal allowance	6,050	6,050	6,050
Taxable income	7,230	4,655	7,095

Income tax

(a)	(b)	(c)				
1,520	1,520	1,520	@ 10%	152.00	152.00	152.00
5,710	3,135	5,575	@ 22%	1,256.20	689.70	1,226.50
7,230	4,655	7,095		1,408.20	841.70	1,378.50

Less : MCA transferred from husband		(350.33)	(492.00)
Tax borne	1,408.20	491.37	886.50

3.4

(a) No MCA is available if both taxpayers were born on or after 6 April 1935.

(b)   The MCA is reduced to £5,185 x 2/12 = £864.

(c)   The husband's income is £1,100 over the limit. He is not able to claim age-related PA so the MCA of £5,185 is reduced by £550 (1/2 x £1,100), giving £4,635. This is further reduced to £4,635 x 4/12 = £1,545.

3.5

	Total £	Non-savings £	Savings £
Pension (Schedule E)	5,030	5,030	
Bank interest £912 x 100/80	1,140		1,140
Statutory total income	6,170	5,030	1,140
Less : Personal allowance	6,050	5,030	1,020
Taxable income	120	0	120

Income tax due

120 @ 10%	12.00
Less : Tax deducted at source	228.00
Refund due	(216.00)

3.6

(a)   PA £4,385, Blind person's allowance £1,400.

(b)   PA £4,385, WBA £2,000 (unless she remarries before 6/4/2000). CTC not yet available.

(c)   PA £4,385 (which is mostly unused).

(d)   PA £4,385 (better than £5,790 - 1/2 x £8,800). There is no widower's bereavement allowance.

3.7

	Richard £	Patricia £
Schedule D Case I/II	18,040	
Schedule F £1,800 + £200		2,000
Less : Personal allowance	4,385	2,000
Taxable income	13,655	0

Income tax

Richard	Patricia			
1,520	0	@ 10%	152.00	0.00
12,135	0	@ 22%	2,669.70	0.00
13,655	0		2,821.70	0.00
Less : MCA £4,665 @ 10%			466.50	
Tax borne			2,355.20	0.00
Less : Tax credits on dividends				0.00
Tax payable			2,355.20	0.00

Notes :

(i)   Patricia was born before 6 April 1935. MCA is £4,665 (£5,185 - 1/2 x £1,040).

(ii)   Patricia is entitled to a PA of £5,790 but can use only £2,000 of this. The remainder is lost and she cannot claim payment of the tax credits on dividends of £200.

Chapter 4

4.1

	£
Income	18,380
<u>Less</u> : Charges £195 x 100/78	250
Statutory total income	18,130
<u>Less</u> : Personal allowance	4,385
Taxable income	13,745

Income tax

			£
1,520	@ 10%		152.00
12,225	@ 22%		2,689.50
13,745			

	£
Tax borne	2,841.50
<u>Add</u> : Tax deducted from charge	55.00
Tax liability	2,896.50

4.2

	(a) £	(b) £
Income	36,890	36,890
<u>Less</u> : Charges £1,248 x 100/78	1,600	
Statutory total income	35,290	36,890
<u>Less</u> : Personal allowance	4,385	4,385
Taxable income	30,905	32,505

Income tax

(a)	(b)		(a)	(b)
1,520	1,520	@ 10%	152.00	152.00
26,880	26,880	@ 22%	5,913.60	5,913.60
2,505	4,105	@ 40%	1,002.00	1,642.00
30,905	32,505			

	(a)	(b)
Tax borne	7,067.60	7,707.60
<u>Add</u> : Tax deducted from charge	352.00	
Tax liability	7,419.60	7,707.60

Paul's tax liability is reduced by £288 if he pays the charge. The cost of the charge to him is therefore only £960 (payment £1,248 less reduction in tax liability £288). In effect, the gross charge of £1,600 is reduced by tax relief at 40% (£640), leaving £960 as the cost to Paul.

4.3

	£
Income	4,375
Less : Charges £19.50 x 100/78	25
Statutory total income	4,350
Less : Personal allowance (restricted)	4,350
Taxable income	nil

Income tax	
Tax borne	0.00
Add : Tax deducted from charge	5.50
Tax liability	5.50

4.4

(a) 23% (b) marginal rate (c) 10% (d) marginal rate.

4.5

(a) The donation is deemed to be made net of 22% income tax. Charities are not liable to income tax so the charity concerned recovers a further £264 (£936 x 22/78) from the Inland Revenue, making the donation worth £1,200 in total.

(b) If the taxpayer does not pay income tax for 2000/01 of at least £264, his or her income tax liability for the year will be increased to exactly £264.

(c) The taxpayer's basic rate band for 2000/01 is extended by £1,200. If the taxpayer pays income tax at the higher rate, this extension will have the effect of moving up to £1,200 of income from the higher rate to the basic rate, resulting in a tax saving of up to £216 (18% x £1,200).

4.6

	£
Schedule D Case I/II	18,000
Less : Personal allowance	5,465
Taxable income	12,535

Income tax	
1,520 @ 10%	152.00
11,015 @ 22%	2,423.30
12,535	
Tax liability	2,575.30

Notes :

(i) The grossed-up donation is £350 (£253 x 100/78) and tax deemed to have been deducted is £77.

(ii) For the purpose of computing age-related allowances, STI is reduced by £350 to £17,650. This is £650 over the income limit, so the personal allowance is £5,465 (£5,790 - 1/2 x £650).

(iii) Raj pays income tax of far more than £77 so there is nothing more to be done.

4.7

	Total £	Non-savings £	Dividends £
Schedule E	31,365	31,365	
Schedule F £2,700 + tax credit £300	3,000		3,000
Statutory total income	34,365	31,365	3,000
Less : Personal allowance	4,385	4,385	
Taxable income	29,980	26,980	3,000

Income tax due

Starting rate band	: Non-savings	1,520	@ 10%	152.00
Basic rate band	: Non-savings	25,460	@ 22%	5,601.20
	: Dividends	1,820	@ 10%	182.00
Higher rate	: Dividends	1,180	@ 32.5%	383.50
		29,980		

Tax liability	6,318.70
Less : Tax credits on dividends	300.00
Tax payable	6,018.70

Notes :

(i) The basic rate band is extended by the grossed-up donation of £400 (£312 x 100/78) to £27,280 (£26,880 + £400).

(ii) Geoffrey is not entitled to MCA (he and his wife are too young). Nor is he yet entitled to the children's tax credit, which does not begin until 2001/02.

(iii) Tax paid under PAYE would also be deducted.

Chapter 5

5.1

The income assessable in 2000/01 (i.e. the income accrued for the year) is £4,100 (£4,000 x 9/12 + £4,400 x 3/12). The amount actually received is not relevant.

5.2

	£	£	£
Rents received £120 x 48			5,760
Less : Expenses allowed in full :			
Accountant's fee		35	
Repairs to furniture		50	
Apportioned expenses :			
Council tax	400		
Gardener's wages	520		
Insurance	230		
$\frac{48}{52}$ x 1,150		1,062	
Wear and tear (see below)		539	1,686
Schedule A assessment			4,074

Note :

The wear and tear allowance is 10% of (£5,760 - (£400 x 48/52)) = £539.

5.3

(a) Premiums received in relation to the granting of long leases (i.e. leases of more than 50 years) are not assessable to income tax.

(b) £12,000 less (49 x 2% of £12,000) = £240.

(c) £12,000 less (19 x 2% of £12,000) = £7,440.

5.4

The premium assessed on Jasper's landlord is £12,300 i.e. £15,000 less (9 x 2% of £15,000). Therefore Jasper will be allowed an annual deduction from his trading profits of £1,230 for each of the 10 years of the lease.

5.5

All three flats pass the 140-day test. However, Flat 1 does not pass the 70-day test and so will not be regarded as a furnished holiday let unless it can be averaged with one or more of the other flats. Possible averaging claims are :

(a) Average Flat 1 with Flat 2. This is no use since the average number of days let is only 68.

(b) Average Flat 1 with Flat 3. This is no use since the average number of days let is only 69.

(c) Average Flat 1 with Flat 2 and Flat 3. This is beneficial since the average number of days let is 70.

Chapter 6

6.1

	Total £	Savings £	Dividends £
BSI £6,900 x 100/80	8,625	8,625	
Schedule F £27,468 + tax credit £3,052	30,520		30,520
Statutory total income	39,145	8,625	30,520
Less : Personal allowance	4,385	4,385	
Taxable income	34,760	4,240	30,520

Income tax due

Starting rate band	: Savings	1,520	@ 10%	152.00	
Basic rate band	: Savings	2,720	@ 20%	544.00	
	: Dividends	24,160	@ 10%	2,416.00	
Higher rate	: Dividends	6,360	@ 32.5%	2,067.00	
		34,760			

Tax borne		5,179.00
Less : Tax deducted at source and tax credits		4,777.00
Tax payable		402.00

6.2

	Total £	Non-savings £	Savings £	Dividends £
Schedule E	5,436	5,436		
Bank interest £384 x 100/80	480		480	
Schedule F £585 + tax credit £65	650			650
Statutory total income	6,566	5,436	480	650
Less : Personal allowance	6,050	5,436	480	134
Taxable income	516	0	0	516

Income tax is due of £51.60 (£516 @ 10%), less tax credit on dividends of £51.60, leaving a tax liability of zero. Anne cannot claim payment of the remaining £13.40 of the tax credits but she is entitled to a refund of the £96 tax deducted at source from her bank interest.

Note :

The TESSA interest is not taxable since no capital has been withdrawn from the account. The ISA interest is also exempt from tax.

6.3

See text.

6.4

See text.

6.5

	Total £	Non-savings £	Savings £
Schedule E	12,470	12,470	
Schedule D Case III (£8 + £52)	60		60
BSI £3,784 x 100/80	4,730		4,730
Statutory total income	17,260	12,470	4,790
Less : Personal allowance	5,660	5,660	
Taxable income	11,600	6,810	4,790

Income tax due

Starting rate band	: Non-savings	1,520	@ 10%	152.00
Basic rate band	: Non-savings	5,290	@ 22%	1,163.80
	: Savings	4,790	@ 20%	958.00
		11,600		
				2,273.80
Less : WBA £2,000 @ 10%				200.00
Tax borne				2,073.80
Less : Tax deducted at source				946.00
Tax payable				1,127.80

Notes :

(a) The first £70 of the NSB ordinary account interest is exempt from income tax.

(b) Bernice reaches her 65th birthday during 2000/01 and is therefore entitled to the personal allowance of £5,790 for the year. However, her STI exceeds the income limit by £260, so the allowance is reduced by £130 to £5,660.

(c) Bernice is entitled to the WBA since her husband died in 1999/00.

(d) Any PAYE tax deducted from the pension will be subtracted when calculating tax payable.

Chapter 7

7.1

See text.

7.2

The basis of assessment for Schedule E is the receipts basis. The assessable income for 2000/01 is therefore £19,850 (£17,500 + £2,350).

7.3

(a) 15p per day would be exempt. The remaining £1.85 per day would be taxable.

(b) Free meals in the company canteen are exempt if available to all employees.

(c) Removal expenses of up to £8,000 are exempt if reasonable and incurred on first taking up an appointment or transferring to a new location.

(d)   Long-service awards made in cash are taxable.

(e)   A gift on marriage is exempt so long as reasonable in amount.

(f)   The mileage allowance is exempt since it is less than the standard figure of 35p per mile for the first 4,000 miles in a car with this engine size. The employee has an allowable expense of £250 (2,500 @ 10p).

7.4

(a)   Not generally allowable since not incurred in performing the duties of the employment. (But see the text of Chapter 7 for exceptions to this rule in the case of site-based employees, employees undertaking business journeys from home and employees who are seconded to a temporary place of work).

(b)   Allowable so long as necessarily incurred.

(c)   Allowable if relevant to the employment.

(d)   Allowable.

(e)   Not allowable, even if worn only at the office. A suit provides warmth and decency and is therefore not purchased exclusively for the purposes of the employment.

(f)   Not allowable unless reimbursed or paid out of a specific entertaining allowance. The expenses must also be wholly, exclusively and necessarily incurred.

7.5

For the purpose of deciding Kim's classification it is necessary to take into account all emoluments (valued as if she were a P11D employee) and to ignore expenses other than superannuation contributions. This gives total emoluments of £9,450 (95% of £7,000 + £1,000 + £1,800) which exceeds £8,500 so Kim is a P11D employee.

7.6

Car benefit is £2,115 (15% of £18,800, less a one-quarter reduction for a car over 4 years old at the end of the tax year). There is a further assessable fuel benefit of £3,200.

7.7

The SRP of £1,750 is exempt from income tax but reduces the usual £30,000 exemption for partially exempt payments to £28,250.

(a)   £12,000 is less than £28,250 and therefore exempt from income tax.

(b)   £29,000 exceeds £28,250 so the excess of £750 is taxable.

Chapter 8

8.1

Subject matter; length of ownership; frequency of transactions; supplementary work; reason for sale; motive.

8.2

Expenditure must be incurred wholly and exclusively for the purposes of the trade.

8.3

(a)   allowable so long as the salary is commensurate with the work done

(b)   not allowable under Schedule D Case I, but given relief in the overall tax computation

(c)   not allowable (capital expenditure)

(d)   allowable so long as the diaries carry a prominent advertisement for the business

(e)   allowable

(f)   not allowable (fails the duality test)

(g)   not allowable (related to capital expenditure)

(h)   probably allowable as a trade subscription

(i)   not allowable (food, drink or tobacco)

(j)   allowable (relates directly to trading).

8.4

(a)   add £45   (b)   add £15   (c)   no adjustment required.

8.5

(a)   The allowable amount each year is given by :

$$£5,670 \ \times \ \frac{£12,000 + 1/2(£21,000 - £12,000)}{£21,000} = £4,455$$

The amount to be added back each year is therefore £1,215 (£5,670 - £4,455).

(b)   The allowable amount each year is given by :

$$\frac{£15,000 - 14 \times 2\% \times £15,000}{15} = £720.$$

The amount to be added back each year is therefore £280 (£1,000 - £720).

8.6

	£	£
Net profit for the year		6,960
Add : *Disallowed expenditure* :		
Proprietor's salary	10,400	
Cost of new heating system	3,800	
Telephone (1/4th of £880)	220	
Motor expenses (1/5th of £3,250)	650	
Entertaining	520	
General provision for bad debts	200	
Loss on sale of fixed asset	70	
Depreciation	2,500	18,360
		25,320
Less : *Non-trading income* :		
Rents receivable	1,200	
Bank interest receivable	80	
Profit on sale of fixed assets	310	1,590
Schedule D Case I adjusted profit (before capital allowances)		23,730

Chapter 9

9.1

(a) 2000/01   (b) 2000/01   (c) 2002/03   (d) 2001/02

9.2

(a)

1999/00	Actual	1/7/99 to 5/4/00
2000/01	12 months to a/c date in year 2	1/7/99 to 30/6/00
2001/02	CYB	y/e 30/6/01
2002/03	CYB	y/e 30/6/02

There is an overlap period between 1 July 1999 and 5 April 2000.

(b)

1999/00	Actual	1/7/99 to 5/4/00
2000/01	Actual	6/4/00 to 5/4/01
2001/02	12 months to a/c date in year 3	1/5/00 to 30/4/01
2002/03	CYB	y/e 30/4/02

There is an overlap period between 1 May 2000 and 5 April 2001.

(c)

1999/00	Actual	1/7/99 to 5/4/00
2000/01	First 12 months	1/7/99 to 30/6/00
2001/02	CYB	y/e 30/4/01
2002/03	CYB	y/e 30/4/02

There is an overlap period between 1 July 1999 and 5 April 2000. There is another overlap period between 1 May 2000 and 30 June 2000.

9.3

				£
1999/00	Actual	1/1/00 to 5/4/00	£27,300 x 3/18	4,550
2000/01	Actual	6/4/00 to 5/4/01	£27,300 x 12/18	18,200
2001/02	12 months to a/c date in year 3	1/7/00 to 30/6/01	£27,300 x 12/18	18,200

Overlap period is 1/7/00 to 5/4/01 (9 months). Overlap profits are 9/18 x £27,300 = £13,650.

9.4

(a)

1999/00	CYB	y/e 31/1/00
2000/01	CYB	y/e 31/1/01
2001/02	End of previous basis period to date of cessation	1/2/01 to 31/5/01

(b)

1999/00	CYB	y/e 31/1/00
2000/01	CYB	y/e 31/1/01
2001/02	End of previous basis period to date of cessation	1/2/01 to 31/3/02

(c)

2000/01	CYB	y/e 31/1/01
2001/02	12 months to normal a/c date	1/2/01 to 31/1/02
2002/03	End of previous basis period to date of cessation	1/2/02 to 30/4/02

9.5

The assessment for 1996/97 (the transitional year) would be based upon the 24 months to 31 July 1996. Therefore transitional overlap relief relates to the period from 1 August 1996 to 5 April 1997 (8 months). The relief is £15,900 x 8/12 = £10,600.

The basis period for 2000/01 is the year to 31 July 2000, so the 2000/01 assessment is £600 (£11,200 - £10,600).

Chapter 10

10.1

	Pool £	Expensive car £	Allowances £
1/6/99 - 30/6/00			
Additions not qualifying for FYA		15,000	
WDA (restricted, £3,000 x 13/12)		3,250 x 60% =	1,950
Additions qualifying for 40% FYA	18,000		
FYA @ 40%	7,200 10,800		7,200
WDV c/f	10,800	11,750	
Total allowances			9,150

The adjusted profit is now £32,630 (£41,780 - £9,150). Schedule D Case I assessments are :

Year	Basis period	Workings	Assessment £
1999/00	1/6/99 to 5/4/00	£32,630 x 10/13	25,100
2000/01	1/7/99 to 30/6/00	£32,630 x 12/13	30,120

Overlap period is 9 months from 1/7/99 to 5/4/00. Overlap profits = £32,630 x 9/13 = £22,590.

10.2

	Main Pool £	Cars pool £	Allowances £
y/e 31/3/01			
WDV b/f	2,700	7,600	
Transfer to main pool	7,600	(7,600)	
	10,300	0	
Additions not qualifying for FYA	8,000		
	18,300		
Disposals (£3,000 + £4,000)	(7,000)		
	11,300		
WDA @ 25%	2,825		2,825
	8,475		
Additions qualifying for 40% FYA	1,000		
FYA @ 40%	400 600		400
WDV c/f	9,075		
Total allowances			3,225

10.3

Norma's first accounting period covers 20 months and must be divided into two chargeable periods for capital allowances purposes. These are 1 November 1997 to 31 October 1998 and 1 November 1998 to 30 June 1999. The capital allowances computation is as follows :

	Main Pool	Cars Pool	Car bought 12/10/98 (40% private)	Car bought 31/3/00 (40% private)	Allowances
	£	£	£	£	£
1/11/97 - 31/10/98					
Additions (no FYA)			8,800		
WDA @ 25%			2,200 x 60%		1,320
Additions 27,400					
FYA @ 50% 13,700	13,700				13,700
	13,700		6,600		
1/11/98 - 30/6/99					
Additions (no FYA)		7,200			
Disposals	(1,750)				
	11,950				
WDA @ 25% x 8/12	1,992	1,200	1,100 x 60%		3,852
	9,958				
Additions 4,600					
FYA @ 40% 1,840	2,760				1,840
	12,718	6,000	5,500		
Total allowances					20,712
y/e 30/6/00					
Transfer to main pool	6,000	(6,000)			
	18,718	0			
Additions (no FYA)				14,100	
Disposals	(1,500)		(6,300)		
	17,218				
Balancing charge			(800) x 60%		(480)
WDA @ 25%	4,305				4,305
	12,913				
WDA (restricted)				3,000 x 60%	1,800
Additions 11,500					
FYA @ 40% 4,600	6,900				4,600
WDV c/f	19,813			11,100	
Total allowances					10,225

Profits after deduction of capital allowances are £35,488 (£56,200 - £20,712) for the period from 1/11/97 to 30/6/99 and £49,675 (£59,900 - £10,225) for the year to 30 June 2000. The first four Schedule D Case I assessments are as follows :

Year	Basis period	Workings	Assessment
			£
1997/98	1/11/97 to 5/4/98	£35,488 x 5/20	8,872
1998/99	6/4/98 to 5/4/99	£35,488 x 12/20	21,293
1999/00	1/7/98 to 30/6/99	£35,488 x 12/20	21,293
2000/01	y/e 30/6/00		49,675

The overlap period is the 9 months from 1/7/98 to 5/4/99. Overlap profits are 9/20 x £35,488 = £15,970.

10.4

	Factory	Allowances
	£	£
y/e 30/6/99		
Cost	57,500	
WDA @ 4% of £57,500	2,300	2,300
WDV c/f	55,200	
y/e 30/6/00		
WDA @ 4% of £57,500	2,300	2,300
WDV c/f	52,900	

Note :

Subtracting the cost of the land (which does not attract IBA's) from the total cost of the factory leaves £80,000. The cost of the offices is more than 25% of £80,000 and so IBA's are available only on the cost excluding offices i.e. £57,500.

10.5

(a)

	Building	Allowances
	£	£
y/e 31/12/97,98,99,00,01,02 & 03		
Cost	45,000	
WDA @ 4% of £45,000 for 7 years	12,600	12,600
WDV c/f	32,400	
y/e 31/12/04		
Disposal value	30,000	
Balancing allowance	2,400	2,400

Note :

The building was not in use on 31/12/96 and therefore no IBA's are available for the year to 31/12/96. The tax life of the building begins on 1 January 1997.

(b) The residue of expenditure is £30,000 (£32,400 - £2,400). The tax life of the building ends on 31 December 2021, giving an unexpired life of 17 years 6 months on the date of the second-hand purchase by Maria. Maria may claim an annual WDA of £30,000/17.5 = £1,714.

Note that Maria's first accounting period (1/5/04 - 30/11/04) is only 7 months long, so she will receive IBA's for that period of only £1,714 x 7/12 = £1,000.

10.6

(a) Giles' allowances are :

		£
year to 31/3/00	£30,000 x 4%	1,200
year to 31/3/01	£30,000 x 4% x 6/12	600

Pam's allowances are :

1/5/00 to 31/12/00	£30,000 x 4% x 3/12	300
y/e 31/12/01 etc.	£30,000 x 4%	1,200

Note :

Pam will continue to receive WDA's of £1,200 per annum until the barn's WDV reaches zero.

(b) Giles' allowances in y/e 31/3/00 are £1,200, reducing the WDV of the building to £28,800. The building is sold for £35,000, but the disposal value is restricted to the original cost of £30,000, giving a balancing charge of £1,200 in y/e 31/3/01.

The tax life of the building began on 1 April 1999 (the first day of the chargeable period in which ABA's were first given) and ends on 31 March 2024, giving an unexpired life of 23 years and 6 months on the date of the second-hand purchase by Pam (23.5 years). The residue of expenditure is £30,000 (£28,800 + £1,200). Therefore Pam's annual WDA is calculated at £30,000/23.5 = £1,277. But Pam's first accounting period is only 8 months long, so she will receive ABA's for that period of only £1,277 x 8/12 = £851.

Chapter 11

11.1

(a) £nil.

(b) The loss will be carried forward indefinitely under S385 and set against the first available profits of the same trade.

(c) The loss may be set against the STI of 2000/01 and/or 1999/00.

11.2

	1998/99	*1999/00*	*2000/01*	*2001/02*
	£	£	£	£
Adjusted profits	-	4,710	6,210	14,810
<u>Less</u> : S385 relief	-	(4,710)	(6,210)	(7,940)
	-	-	-	6,870
Other income	5,000	5,000	5,000	5,000
Total income	5,000	5,000	5,000	11,870

11.3

(a) The Schedule D Case I assessments are :

Year	Basis period	Workings	Assessment
			£
1998/99	1/1/99 to 5/4/99	(£12,720 - £2,460) x 3/12	2,565
1999/00	1/1/99 to 31/12/99	£12,720 - £2,460	10,260
2000/01	y/e 31/12/00		nil

(b)   The trading loss of 2000/01 is £9,800 (£8,480 + £1,320). A Section 380 claim could be made for 2000/01 or for 1999/00 or for both of these years :

   (i)   A claim for 2000/01 is pointless since there is no income in that year.

   (ii)   A claim for 1999/00 would reduce total income for that year to £460 (£10,260 - £9,800) and so eliminate the income tax liability for the year. The personal allowance would be largely wasted.

   (iii) A claim for both years is pointless since a claim in 2000/01 is pointless.

   The 1999/00 claim would be less wasteful if Marcus declined to claim any capital allowances in either of the first two years of trading. The 1999/00 assessment would become £12,720 and the 2000/01 loss would become £8,480. Claiming Section 380 relief in 1999/00 would then leave income of £4,240 for the year, which would absorb most of the personal allowance.

11.4

The losses eligible for Section 381 relief are :

Year	Basis period	Workings	Loss £	Years for S381 claim
1998/99	1/10/98 to 5/4/99	£(11,850) x 6/15	(4,740)	95/96-97/98
1999/00	1/1/99 to 31/12/99	£(11,850) x 12/15 - overlap £(11,850) x 3/15	(7,110)	96/97-98/99
2000/01	y/e 31/12/00		(9,660)	97/98-99/00

If all possible Section 381 claims are made, total income is :

		1995/96 £	1996/97 £	1997/98 £	1998/99 £
Schedule D Case I		-	-	-	nil
Other income		6,100	6,250	6,400	3,450
		6,100	6,250	6,400	3,450
Less : Section 381 relief :	1998/99 loss	(4,740)			
	1999/00 loss		(6,250)	(860)	
	2000/01 loss			(5,540)	(3,450)
Total income (after loss reliefs)		1,360	-	-	-

Notes :

(a)   Personal allowances are totally wasted in 1996/97 to 1998/99 and partly wasted in 1995/96.

(b)   The loss incurred in 2000/01 has been only partly relieved. The remaining £670 of the loss (£9,660 - £5,540 - £3,450) is eligible for S381 relief in 1999/00 but there is no income in this year against which to set the loss. The loss will be carried forward under S385.

Chapter 12

12.1

	Nickleby £	Copperfield £	Drood £	Total £
1/1/00 - 31/3/00 (£18,300 x 3/12 = £4,575)	1,525	1,525	1,525	4,575
1/4/00 - 31/12/00 (£18,300 x 9/12 = £13,725)	2,745	5,490	5,490	13,725
Allocation of profit for the year	4,270	7,015	7,015	18,300

12.2

	Pickwick £	Snodgrass £	Tupman £	Total £
Interest on capital	720	1,200	600	2,520
Salaries	8,000	-	8,000	16,000
Remainder (shared equally)	(1,340)	(1,340)	(1,340)	(4,020)
	7,380	(140)	7,260	14,500
Notional loss divided 7,380:7,260	(71)	140	(69)	-
Allocation of profit for the year	7,309	-	7,191	14,500

12.3

The allocation of profit for each accounting period is :

	Dodson £	Fogg £	Jackson £	Total £
y/e 30/6/98 (shared equally)	8,500	8,500	-	17,000
y/e 30/6/99 (shared 5:4:1)	11,000	8,800	2,200	22,000
y/e 30/6/00 (shared 5:4:1)	14,500	11,600	2,900	29,000

The assessments on each partner are :

Dodson

Year	Basis period	Workings	Assessment £
1997/98	1/7/97 to 5/4/98	£8,500 x 9/12	6,375
1998/99	y/e 30/6/98		8,500
1999/00	y/e 30/6/99		11,000
2000/01	y/e 30/6/00		14,500

Fogg

Year	Basis period	Workings	Assessment £
1997/98	1/7/97 to 5/4/98	£8,500 x 9/12	6,375
1998/99	y/e 30/6/98		8,500
1999/00	y/e 30/6/99		8,800
2000/01	y/e 30/6/00		11,600

Jackson

Year	Basis period	Workings	Assessment
			£
1998/99	1/7/98 to 5/4/99	£2,200 x 9/12	1,650
1999/00	y/e 30/6/99		2,200
2000/01	y/e 30/6/00		2,900

Note

Dodson and Fogg each have overlap profits of £6,375. Jackson has overlap profits of £1,650.

12.4

(a) The trading profit of £23,490 for the year to 30 September 1999 is allocated Wardle £16,443, Jingle £4,698, Trotter £2,349. The trading profit of £27,310 for the year to 30 September 2000 is allocated Wardle £19,117, Jingle £5,462, Trotter £2,731. The Schedule D Case I assessments on each partner are :

	Wardle	Jingle	Trotter
	£	£	£
1998/99 (6/12 x y/e 30/9/99)	8,222	2,349	1,174
1999/00 (y/e 30/9/99)	16,443	4,698	2,349
2000/01 (y/e 30/9/00)	19,117	5,462	2,731

(b) The untaxed interest of £2,000 for the year to 30 September 1999 is allocated Wardle £1,400, Jingle £400, Trotter £200. The untaxed interest of £2,200 for the year to 30 September 2000 is allocated Wardle £1,540, Jingle £440, Trotter £220. The Schedule D Case III assessments on each partner are :

	Wardle	Jingle	Trotter
	£	£	£
1998/99 (6/12 x y/e 30/9/99)	700	200	100
1999/00 (y/e 30/9/99)	1,400	400	200
2000/01 (y/e 30/9/00)	1,540	440	220

(c) The taxed interest of £1,250 (gross) for the year to 30 September 1999 is allocated Wardle £875, Jingle £250, Trotter £125. The taxed interest of £1,360 (gross) for the year to 30 September 2000 is allocated Wardle £952, Jingle £272, Trotter £136. The amount assessed on each partner in 1999/00 is:

	£
Wardle (£875 x 6/12 + £952 x 6/12)	914
Jingle (£250 x 6/12 + £272 x 6/12)	261
Trotter (£125 x 6/12 + £136 x 6/12)	131

Chapter 13

13.1

See text.

13.2

(a) 15% of £20,000 = £3,000.

(b) 15% of £91,800 = £13,770.

13.3

See text.

13.4

	£	£
Profits assessed under Schedule D Case I or II		22,450
<u>Less</u> : Loss relief	1,200	
Excess of trade charges over unearned income (£250 - £0)	250	1,450
Net relevant earnings for 2000/01		21,000

Karen was aged 60 at the start of 2000/01 so her allowable percentage is 35%. The maximum allowable personal pension premium which Karen could pay in 2000/01 is £7,350 (35% of £21,000).

13.5

Damon reaches his 36th birthday on 10 July 1999, so the allowable percentage of NRE is 17.5% in 1998/99 and 1999/00 and 20% in 2000/01.

In 1998/99, 17.5% of NRE is £3,010. The premiums paid of £2,500 are allowed in full and there is £510 of unused relief to carry forward (up to 2004/05).

In 1999/00, 17.5% of NRE is £3,220. The premiums paid of £2,600 are allowed in full and there is £620 of unused relief to carry forward (up to 2005/06).

In 2000/01, 20% of NRE is £1,120, so there are excess premiums of £1,480 in the year. The unused relief of £400 from 1993/94 is now too old to be used but £1,130 of the excess premiums can be relieved by using the unused relief from 1998/99 and 1999/00 (£510 + £620). The remaining £350 of excess premiums (£1,480 - £1,130) cannot be relieved in any way.

Chapter 14

14.1

(a) No POA's are required because the 1999/00 liability (less tax deducted at source) is less than £500. A balancing payment of £440 (£1,750 - £1,250 - £60) is payable on 31 January 2002.

(b) The amount paid by deduction at source in 1999/00 (£4,390) is less than 80% of the total liability for 1999/00 and the remainder of the liability (£2,340) exceeds £500, so POA's are required for 2000/01. A first POA of £1,170 (one-half of £2,340) is due on 31 January 2001 and a second POA of £1,170 is due on 31 July 2001. A balancing *repayment* of £605 (£6,580 - £4,810 - £35 - £2,340) will be made on 31 January 2002. Marie could have made a claim to pay reduced POA's for 2000/01 if she had known that the POA's based on her 1999/00 liability were likely to be excessive.

(c) No POA's are required because more than 80% of the 1999/00 liability was satisfied by deduction at source. A balancing payment of £3,600 (£16,110 - £12,370 - £140) is payable on 31 January 2002.

14.2

(a) Dorothy's balancing payment was not more than 28 days late so no surcharges are payable.

(b) The first POA of £12,000 was paid 27 days late, the second POA of £12,000 was paid 43 days late and the balancing payment of £4,000 was paid 21 days late. The interest payable is as follows :

	£
£12,000 x 8.5% x 27/365	75.45
£12,000 x 8.5% x 43/365	120.16
£4,000 x 8.5% x 21/365	19.56
	215.17

14.3

(a) Jabran notified the Inland Revenue of his chargeability to tax within the permitted six months and so incurs no penalty in relation to this notification.

(b) His completed tax return was due to be submitted to the Inland Revenue within 3 months of the issue date. He submitted the return late (but not more than 6 months late) and so incurs a fixed penalty of £100.

(c) The balancing payment was due 3 months after the issue date of the tax return. His payment was more than 28 days late and therefore he incurs a 5% surcharge.

(d) Interest is payable on the tax paid late and interest is payable on the surcharge if it is not paid within 30 days of the date of its imposition.

Chapter 15

15.1

(a) Primary : 10% x (£80 - £76) = £0.40
Secondary : £nil (earnings do not exceed the secondary threshold)

(b) Primary : 10% x (£190 - £76) = £11.40
Secondary : 12.2% x (£190 - £84) = £12.93

(c) Primary : 10% x (£535 - £76) = £45.90
Secondary : 12.2% x (£606 - £84) = £63.68

(d) Primary : nil (earnings do not exceed the primary threshold)
Secondary : nil (earnings do not exceed the secondary threshold)

(e) Primary : 10% x (£465 - £329) = £13.60
Secondary : 12.2% x (£465 - £365) = £12.20

(f) Primary : 10% x (£2,319 - £329) = £199.00
Secondary : 12.2% x (£2,500 - £365) = £260.47.

15.2

(a) Primary : 8.4% x (£80 - £76) = £0.34
Secondary : £nil (earnings do not exceed the secondary threshold)

(b) Primary : 8.4% x (£190 - £76) = £9.58
Secondary : 9.2% x (£190 - £84) = £9.75

(c) Primary : 8.4% x (£535 - £76) = £38.56
Secondary : 9.2% x (£535 - £84) + 12.2% x (£606 - £535) = £50.15

(d)   Primary   : nil (earnings do not exceed the primary threshold)

        Secondary   : nil (earnings do not exceed the secondary threshold)

(e)   Primary   : 8.4% x (£465 - £329) = £11.42

        Secondary   : 9.2% x (£465 - £365) = £9.20

(f)   Primary   : 8.4% x (£2,319 - £329) = £167.16

        Secondary   : 9.2% x (£2,319 - £365) + 12.2% x (£2,500 - £2,319) = £201.85.

15.3

Mark's profit for Class 2 purposes in 2000/01 is £5,633 (£6,890 x 8/12 + £3,120 x 4/12). This exceeds the small earnings exemption limit so Mark is liable to pay Class 2 contributions of £2.00 per week. His profit for Class 4 purposes in 2000/01 is £7,720 so Class 4 contributions of £233.45 are payable (7% x (£7,720 - £4,385)).

Chapter 16

16.1

(a)   Companies are not chargeable persons, so the sale will not give rise to a CGT liability.

(b)   Disposals between husband and wife who are living together are deemed to occur at a disposal value such that neither a gain nor a loss arises, therefore there will be no CGT liability on the gift.

(c)   Gifts to charities are exempt from CGT.

(d)   Charities are not chargeable persons, therefore disposals by charities do not give rise to a CGT liability.

(e)   The sale is made in the course of trade. Therefore the profit arising will be subject not to CGT but to income tax under Schedule D Case I.

(f)   The partnership is not a chargeable person but the partners are. Any CGT liability arising on the disposal of the leasehold property will be divided between them.

16.2

(a)   Shares and securities are chargeable assets (apart from gilt-edged securities and certain corporate bonds).

(b)   Gilt-edged securities are not chargeable assets.

(c)   A table is a chattel. Chattels disposed of for more than £6,000 are chargeable assets.

(d)   A chair is a chattel. Chattels disposed of for £6,000 or less are not chargeable assets.

(e)   A taxpayer's principal private residence is not a chargeable asset.

(f)   Motor cars are not chargeable assets.

16.3

(a)   Net losses are £2,500. The annual exemption is lost and the CGT assessment is £nil.

(b)   Net losses are £1,000. The annual exemption is lost and the CGT assessment is £nil.

(c)   Net gains are £2,550. The unused part of the annual exemption (£4,650) is lost and the CGT assessment is £nil.

(d)   Net gains are £8,850. The annual exemption of £7,200 is fully used and the CGT assessment is £1,650.

16.4

Taxable income is £24,675 (£29,060 - £4,385), using the whole of the 10% band and £23,155 of the 22% band. This leaves £3,725 (£26,880 - £23,155) of the 22% band remaining. Therefore CGT is payable at 20% on the first £3,725 and 40% on the remaining £1,675, giving a CGT liability of £1,415.

16.5

(a) Net gains are £6,000. £1,200 of the annual exemption is lost and the CGT assessment is £nil. The losses brought forward of £4,800 remain unrelieved and are carried forward to 2001/02.

(b) Net gains are £7,800. This exceeds the annual exemption by £600, so £600 of the losses brought forward are relieved and the CGT assessment is £nil. The remaining £4,200 of the losses brought forward are carried forward to 2001/02.

(c) Net gains are £13,400. This exceeds the annual exemption by £6,200, so all of the losses brought forward are relieved and the CGT assessment is £1,400 (£13,400 - £4,800 - £7,200). There are no unrelieved losses to carry forward.

16.6

Net losses in 2000/01 are £14,200. The annual exemption is lost and the CGT assessment for the year is £nil. The net losses may be offset against the net gains of 1999/00, 1998/99 and 1997/98, in that order, to the extent that those net gains exceed the annual exemption. Relief available is £nil in 1999/00, £2,800 (£9,600 - £6,800) in 1998/99 and £6,500 (£13,000 - £6,500) in 1997/98. Total relief is £9,300. The remaining £4,900 of net losses in 2000/01 cannot be relieved at all.

16.7

31 January 2002.

Chapter 17

17.1

		£
Sale proceeds		72,000
<u>Less</u> : Incidental costs of disposal		3,600
		68,400
<u>Less</u> : Acquisition cost	35,000	
Enhancement expenditure	3,000	38,000
Unindexed gain		30,400
<u>Less</u> : Indexation allowance :		
(i) on acquisition cost		
$\dfrac{162.6 - 103.3}{103.3} = 0.574 \times £35{,}000$	20,090	
(ii) on enhancement expenditure		
$\dfrac{162.6 - 103.7}{103.7} = 0.568 \times £3{,}000$	1,704	21,794
Untapered gain		8,606

(The repainting costs do not rank as enhancement expenditure).

17.2

	(a) £	(b) £	(c) £
Sale proceeds	4,950	4,350	5,780
Less : Deemed acquisition cost	4,500	4,500	4,500
Unindexed gain (loss)	450	(150)	1,280
Less : Indexation allowance			
$\frac{162.6 - 135.6}{135.6} = 0.199 \times £4,500 = £896$	450	nil	896
Untapered gain (allowable loss)	nil	(150)	384

Notes :

(i)   In case (a) indexation allowance is restricted to £450 to avoid converting a gain into a loss.

(ii) In case (b) there is an unindexed loss. Therefore the indexation allowance is restricted to £nil.

(iii) In case (c) the indexation allowance can be given in full.

17.3

	Total £	Gain A (85%) £	Gain B (50%) £	Gain C (25%) £	Gain C (60%) £
Untapered gains	41,000	17,000	4,000	6,000	14,000
Less : Allowable losses	22,000	17,000			5,000
	19,000	nil	4,000	6,000	9,000
Less : Taper relief	10,100	nil	2,000	4,500	3,600
Tapered gains	8,900	nil	2,000	1,500	5,400
Less : Annual exemption	7,200				
CGT assessment	1,700				

Gain C has been divided into a business gain of £6,000 (3/10th of £20,000) and a non-business gain of £14,000 (7/10th of £20,000). Both of these gains have a taper period of 10 or more years.

17.4

	£
Sale proceeds (June 2000)	100,000
Less : Incidental costs of disposal	5,000
	95,000
Less : Part cost :	
$\frac{£100,000}{£100,000 + £500,000} \times £240,000$	(40,000)
Part incidental costs of acquisition :	
$\frac{£100,000}{£100,000 + £500,000} \times £12,000$	(2,000)
Unindexed gain c/f	53,000

	£
Unindexed gain b/f	53,000
Less : Indexation allowance	
$\frac{162.6 - 134.1}{134.1} = 0.213 \times £42,000$	8,946
Untapered gain	44,054

	£
Sale proceeds (January 2001)	520,000
Less : Remainder of cost (£240,000 - £40,000)	(200,000)
Remainder of costs of acquisition (£12,000 - £2,000)	(10,000)
Unindexed gain	310,000
Less : Indexation allowance	
$\frac{162.6 - 134.1}{134.1} = 0.213 \times £210,000$	44,730
Untapered gain	265,270

17.5

(a)

	Original cost £	Rebasing £
Sale proceeds	37,500	37,500
Less : Original cost	12,500	
Market value 31/3/82		10,000
Unindexed gain	25,000	27,500
Less : Indexation allowance		
$\frac{162.6 - 79.44}{79.44} = 1.047 \times £12,500$	13,088	13,088
Untapered gain	11,912	14,412

The rebasing calculation gives the higher gain, so rebasing does not apply and the untapered gain is £11,912.

(b)

	Original cost £	Rebasing £
Sale proceeds	37,500	37,500
Less : Original cost	12,500	
Market value 31/3/82		15,000
Unindexed gain	25,000	22,500
Less : Indexation allowance		
$\frac{162.6 - 79.44}{79.44} = 1.047 \times £15,000$	15,705	15,705
Untapered gain	9,295	6,795

The rebasing calculation gives the lower gain, so rebasing applies and the untapered gain is £6,795.

17.6

(a)

	£
Deemed disposal proceeds	80
Less : Acquisition cost	6,000
Unindexed loss	(5,920)
Less : Indexation allowance	nil
Allowable loss	(5,920)

(b)

	£
Disposal proceeds	120
Less : Deemed acquisition cost (Nov. 1997)	80
Unindexed gain	40
Less : Indexation allowance	
$\dfrac{162.6 - 159.6}{159.6} = 0.019 \times £80$	2
Untapered gain	38

17.7

(a)

	Original cost £	Rebasing £
Sale proceeds	8,450	8,450
Less : Original cost	100	
Market value 31/3/82		7,000
Unindexed gain (loss)	8,350	1,450
Less : Indexation allowance		
$\dfrac{162.6 - 79.44}{79.44} = 1.047 \times £7,000$	7,329	1,450
Untapered gain	1,021	nil

One calculation gives a gain and the other gives a nil result. So the situation is "no gain, no loss".

(b)

	Original cost £	Rebasing £
Sale proceeds	8,450	8,450
Less : Original cost	100	
Market value 31/3/82		12,500
Unindexed gain (loss)	8,350	(4,050)
Less : Indexation allowance		
$\dfrac{162.6 - 79.44}{79.44} = 1.047 \times £12,500 = £13,088$	8,350	nil
Allowable loss	nil	(4,050)

One calculation gives a loss and the other gives a nil result. So the situation is "no gain, no loss".

Chapter 18

18.1

(a) Wasting chattel. (b) Chattel. (c) Wasting chattel.
(d) Wasting asset. (e) Wasting asset. (f) Wasting chattel.
(g) Chattel.

18.2

	£
Sale proceeds	7,200
<u>Less</u> : Incidental disposal costs	200
	7,000
<u>Less</u> : Acquisition cost	2,000
Unindexed gain	5,000
<u>Less</u> : Indexation allowance	
$\dfrac{162.6 - 115.5}{115.5} = 0.408 \times £2,000$	816
Untapered gain	4,184

However, the untapered gain is restricted to (£7,200 - £6,000) x 5/3 = £2,000.

18.3

	£
Deemed sale proceeds	6,000
<u>Less</u> : Acquisition cost	50,000
Unindexed loss	(44,000)
<u>Less</u> : Indexation allowance	nil
Allowable loss	(44,000)

18.4

	£
Sale proceeds	25,000
<u>Less</u> : Part cost :	
$\dfrac{£25,000}{£25,000 + £85,000} \times 38,500$	8,750
Unindexed gain	16,250
<u>Less</u> : Indexation allowance	
$\dfrac{162.6 - 86.84}{86.84} = 0.872 \times £8,750$	7,630
Untapered gain	8,620

The maximum untapered gain is (£110,000 - £6,000) x 5/3 x 25/110 = £39,394. The actual gain is far less than this so the untapered gain is £8,620.

18.5

	(a) £	(b) £
Sale proceeds	65,000	35,000
Less : Acquisition cost	50,000	50,000
	15,000	(15,000)
Less : Available capital allowances	0	15,000
Unindexed gain/(loss)	15,000	0
Less : Indexation allowance		
$\dfrac{162.6 - 137.9}{137.9}$ = 0.179 x £50,000	8,950	0
Untapered gain	6,050	nil

18.6

	£
Sale proceeds	8,000
Less : Unexpired portion of cost $\dfrac{3}{5}$ x £10,000	6,000
Untapered gain	2,000

Note :

Indexation allowance is not available in relation to expenditure incurred on or after 1 April 1998.

18.7

When the lease was acquired it had a 25-year life (Sch 8 percentage 81.100%). On 31 March 1982 there were 23 years and 5 months remaining (Sch 8 percentage 78.055 + 1.567 x 5/12 = 78.708%). When it was assigned there were 5 years remaining (Sch 8 percentage = 26.722%). Therefore the computation is as follows :

	Original cost £	*Rebasing* £
Sale proceeds	20,000	20,000
Less : Unexpired portion of cost		
$\dfrac{26.722}{81.100}$ x £12,500	4,119	
Unexpired portion of MV 31/3/82		
$\dfrac{26.722}{78.708}$ x £15,000		5,093
Unindexed gain	15,881	14,907

	Original cost £	Rebasing £
Unindexed gain	15,881	14,907
<u>Less</u> : Indexation allowance		
$\frac{162.6 - 79.44}{79.44} = 1.047$ x £5,093	5,332	5,332
Untapered gain	10,549	9,575

The rebasing calculation gives the lower gain, so rebasing applies and the untapered gain is £9,575.

Chapter 19

19.1

(a)	20 October 2000	200	(bought on same day)
	17 October 2000	50	(bought after 5 April 1998)
(b)	1 December 2000	150	(bought after 5 April 1998)
	17 October 2000	50	(bought after 5 April 1998)
	23 February 1990	250	(S104 holding)
	4 August 1981	50	(1982 holding)
(c)	4 August 1981	950	(1982 holding)
	10 September 1962	250	(pre-6 April 1965)

19.2

	No of shares	Cost £	Indexed cost £
Bought 29 June 1982	1,000	3,000	3,000
Bought 5 May 1984	1,000	3,500	3,500
<u>Add</u> : Indexation to April 1985			
(a) $\frac{94.78 - 81.85}{81.85} = 0.158$			
0.158 x £3,000			474
(b) $\frac{94.78 - 88.97}{88.97} = 0.065$			
0.065 x £3,500			228
S104 holding at 5 April 1985	2,000	6,500	7,202
<u>Add</u> : Indexation to August 1987			
$\frac{102.1 - 94.78}{94.78}$ x £7,202			556
			7,758
Bought 13 August 1987	1,350	6,500	6,500
S104 holding at 13 August 1987	3,350	13,000	14,258
<u>Add</u> : Indexation to September 1990			
$\frac{129.3 - 102.1}{102.1}$ x £14,258			3,798
c/f	3,350	13,000	18,056

	No of shares	Cost £	Indexed cost £
b/f	3,350	13,000	18,056
Bought 7 September 1990	2,650	14,150	14,150
S104 holding at 7 September 1990	6,000	27,150	32,206
Add : Indexation to October 1995			
$\frac{149.8 - 129.3}{129.3}$ x £32,206			5,106
Bought 4 October 1995	2,000	22,500	22,500
S104 holding at 4 October 1995	8,000	49,650	59,812

19.3

	No of shares	Cost £	Indexed cost £
S104 holding at 4 October 1995	8,000	49,650	59,812
Add : Indexation to April 1998			
$\frac{162.6 - 149.8}{149.8}$ x £59,812			5,111
			64,923
Sold June 2000 (2,000/8,000th)	(2,000)	(12,413)	(16,231)
S104 holding c/f	6,000	37,237	48,692

	(a) £	(b) £	(c) £
Sale proceeds	14,000	12,000	17,000
Less : Cost	12,413	12,413	12,413
Unindexed gain (loss)	1,587	(413)	4,587
Less : Indexation allowance			
(£16,231 - £12,413 = £3,818)	1,587	nil	3,818
Untapered gain (allowable loss)	nil	(413)	769

19.4

The 1982 holding is as follows :

	No of shares	Cost £	MV 31/3/82 £
Acquired 5 August 1978	300	2,400	3,000
Acquired 12 May 1980	200	1,700	2,000
Acquired 11 July 1981	250	2,000	2,500
	750	6,100	7,500
Sold August 2000 (150/750th)	(150)	(1,220)	(1,500)
1982 holding c/f	600	4,880	6,000

The calculation of the untapered gain arising on the disposal is as follows :

	Original cost	Rebasing
	£	£
Sale proceeds	3,500	3,500
Less : Original cost	1,220	
Market value 31/3/82		1,500
Unindexed gain	2,280	2,000
Less : Indexation allowance		
$\frac{162.6 - 79.44}{79.44}$ = 1.047 x £1,500	1,571	1,571
Untapered gain	709	429

The rebasing calculation gives the lower gain, so rebasing applies and the untapered gain is £429.

19.5

S104 holding :

	No of shares	Cost	Indexed cost
		£	£
Bought 21 June 1990	10,000	9,000	9,000
Add : Indexation to March 1993			
$\frac{139.3 - 126.7}{126.7}$ x £9,000			895
			9,895
Bought 3 March 1993	10,000	11,000	11,000
S104 holding at 3 March 1993	20,000	20,000	20,895
Add : Indexation to April 1998			
$\frac{162.6 - 139.3}{139.3}$ x £20,895			3,495
			24,390
Sold December 2000	(20,000)	(20,000)	(24,390)
S104 holding c/f	nil	nil	nil

The untapered gain on the disposal of the S104 holding is :

	£
Sale proceeds (20,000 @ £1.25)	25,000
Less : Cost	20,000
Unindexed gain	5,000
Less : Indexation allowance	
(£24,390 - £20,000)	4,390
Untapered gain	610

1982 holding :

	No of shares	Cost	MV 31/3/82
		£	£
Bought 28 December 1980	10,000	5,000	6,000
Sold December 2000 (5,000/10,000th)	(5,000)	(2,500)	(3,000)
1982 holding c/f	5,000	2,500	3,000

The untapered gain on the disposal from the 1982 holding is :

	Original cost	Rebasing
	£	£
Sale proceeds (5,000 @ £1.25)	6,250	6,250
Less : Original cost	2,500	
Market value 31/3/82		3,000
Unindexed gain	3,750	3,250
Less : Indexation allowance		
$\dfrac{162.6 - 79.44}{79.44} = 1.047 \times £3,000$	3,141	3,141
Untapered gain	609	109

The untapered gain is £109. The total untapered gain (taper period 3 years) is £719 (£610 + £109).

19.6

The 1982 holding is as follows :

	No of shares	Cost	MV 31/3/82
		£	£
Acquired 17 February 1963 (@ £9)	500	4,500	7,500
Acquired 8 January 1980	700	8,500	10,500
	1,200	13,000	18,000
Sold September 2000 (1,000/1,200th)	(1,000)	(10,833)	(15,000)
1982 holding c/f	200	2,167	3,000

The untapered gain on the disposal is :

	Original cost	Rebasing
	£	£
Sale proceeds (1,000 @ £40)	40,000	40,000
Less : Original cost	10,833	
Market value 31/3/82 (1,000 @ £15)		15,000
Unindexed gain	29,167	25,000
Less : Indexation allowance		
$\dfrac{162.6 - 79.44}{79.44} = 1.047 \times £15,000$	15,705	15,705
Untapered gain	13,462	9,295

The untapered gain is £9,295 (with a taper period of 3 years).

19.7

1982 holding :

	No of shares	Cost £	MV 31/3/82 £
Acquired 8 January 1980	700	8,500	10,500
Sold September 2000	(700)	(8,500)	(10,500)
1982 holding c/f	nil	nil	nil

The gain on the disposal of the 1982 holding is :

	Original cost £	Rebasing £
Sale proceeds (700 @ £40)	28,000	28,000
Less : Original cost	8,500	
Market value 31/3/82 (700 @ £15)		10,500
Unindexed gain	19,500	17,500
Less : Indexation allowance		
$\frac{162.6 - 79.44}{79.44} = 1.047 \times £10,500$	10,994	10,994
Untapered gain	8,506	6,506

The rebasing calculation gives the lower gain, so rebasing applies and the untapered gain is £6,506.

Pre-6 April 1965 shares :

	Original cost £	MV 6/4/65 £
Sale proceeds (300 @ £40)	12,000	12,000
Less : Original cost (£4,000 x 300/500)	2,400	
Market value 6/4/65 (300 @ £9)		2,700
Unindexed gain	9,600	9,300
Less : Indexation allowance		
$\frac{162.6 - 79.44}{79.44} = 1.047 \times £4,500$ (300 @ £15)	4,712	4,712
Untapered gain	4,888	4,588

The lower gain is £4,588, which is then compared with the gain produced by rebasing i.e. :

	Rebasing £
Sale proceeds	12,000
Less : Market value 31/3/82 (300 @ £15)	4,500
Unindexed gain	7,500
Less : Indexation allowance	4,712
Untapered gain	2,788

This is lower than £4,588 so rebasing applies and the gain is £2,788. The total untapered gain (all with a taper period of 3 years) is £6,506 + £2,788 = £9,294.

Chapter 20

20.1

25 bonus shares are attached to the 100 shares acquired on 9 October 1999 (which do not join any pool). The remaining 200 bonus shares join the 1982 holding and the S104 holding, as follows :

1982 holding :

	No of shares	Cost	MV 31/3/82
		£	£
Acquired 17 February 1980	600	900	1,020
Bonus issue January 2001 (1 for 4)	150	nil	nil
1982 holding c/f	750	900	1,020

In effect, the market value at 31/3/82 is now reduced to 4/5th of £1.70 = £1.36 per share.

S104 holding :

	No of shares	Cost	Indexed cost
		£	£
Acquired 13 November 1988	200	400	400
Add : Indexation to April 1998			
$\dfrac{162.6 - 110.0}{110.0}$ x £400			191
			591
Bonus issue January 2001 (1 for 4)	50	nil	nil
S104 holding c/f	250	400	591

20.2

The first 125 shares out of the disposal are matched with the shares acquired on 9 October 1999. The cost of these shares is £300 and they are sold for £500, giving an untapered gain of £200. The remaining 300 shares are matched with the S104 holding and the 1982 holding, as follows :

S104 holding (250 shares sold) :

	No of shares	Cost	Indexed cost
		£	£
S104 holding b/f	250	400	591
Sold February 2001	(250)	(400)	(591)
S104 holding c/f	nil	nil	nil

The untapered gain on the disposal of the S104 holding is :

	£
Sale proceeds (250 @ £4)	1,000
Less : Cost + indexation allowance	591
Untapered gain	409

1982 holding (50 shares sold) :

	No of shares	Cost £	MV 31/3/82 £
b/f	750	900	1,020
Sold February 2001 (50/750th)	(50)	(60)	(68)
1982 holding c/f	700	840	952

The untapered gain on the disposal from the 1982 holding is :

	Original cost £	Rebasing £
Sale proceeds (50 @ £4)	200	200
Less : Original cost	60	
MV 31/3/82		68
Unindexed gain	140	132
Less : Indexation allowance		
$\dfrac{162.6 - 79.44}{79.44} = 1.047 \times £68$	71	71
Untapered gain	69	61

The rebasing calculation gives the lower gain, so rebasing applies and the untapered gain is £61. In summary, William has an untapered gain of £200 with a taper period of 1 year and untapered gains of £470 (£409 + £61) with a taper period of 2 years plus the bonus year (if the shares are a non-business asset).

20.3

1982 holding :

	No of shares	Cost (original) £	Cost (rights) £	MV 31/3/82 £
Acquired 30 September 1979	2,000	1,200		1,500
Rights issue January 1998 (1 for 8)	250		250	
1982 holding c/f	2,250	1,200	250	1,500

S104 holding :

	No of shares	Cost £	Indexed cost £
Acquired 1 December 1992	3,000	3,600	3,600
Add : Indexation to January 1998			
$\dfrac{159.5 - 139.2}{139.2} \times £3,600$			525
			4,125
Rights issue January 1998 (1 for 8)	375	375	375
S104 holding c/f	3,375	3,975	4,500

20.4

S104 holding :

	No of shares	Cost £	Indexed cost £
b/f at January 1998	3,375	3,975	4,500
Add : Indexation to April 1998			
$\frac{162.6 - 159.5}{159.5}$ x £4,500			87
			4,587
Sold March 2001	(3,375)	(3,975)	(4,587)
S104 holding c/f	nil	nil	nil

The untapered gain on the disposal of the S104 holding is :

	£
Sale proceeds (3,375 @ £1.80)	6,075
Less : Cost	3,975
Unindexed gain	2,100
Less : Indexation allowance (£4,587 - £3,975)	612
Untapered gain	1,488

1982 holding :

	No of shares	Cost (original) £	Cost (rights) £	M V 31/3/82 £
b/f	2,250	1,200	250	1,500
Sold March 2001	(2,250)	(1,200)	(250)	(1,500)
1982 holding c/f	nil	nil	nil	nil

The untapered gain on the disposal of the 1982 holding is :

	Original cost £	Rebasing £
Sale proceeds (2,250 @ £1.80)	4,050	4,050
Less : Cost up to 31/3/82	(1,200)	
Market value 31/3/82		(1,500)
Cost January 1998	(250)	(250)
Unindexed gain c/f	2,600	2,300

	Original cost £	Rebasing £
Unindexed gain c/f	2,600	2,300
Less : Indexation allowance :		
$\dfrac{162.6 - 79.44}{79.44}$ = 1.047 x £1,500	(1,571)	(1,571)
$\dfrac{162.6 - 159.5}{159.5}$ = 0.019 x £250	(5)	(5)
Untapered gain	1,024	724

Rebasing gives the lower gain, so the untapered gain is £724. The total untapered gain on the entire disposal is £2,212 (£1,488 + £724) with a taper period of 2 years (plus the bonus year if the shares are a non-business asset).

20.5

The value of the part disposed of is £6,000 (6,000 @ £1) and the value of the part remaining is £12,000 (6,000 @ £2) so there has been a 6,000/18,000th (1/3rd) part disposal. The S104 holding is as follows :

	No of shares	Cost £	Indexed cost £
Bought November 1989	6,000	30,000	30,000
Add : Indexation to April 1998			
$\dfrac{162.6 - 118.5}{118.5}$ x £30,000			11,165
			41,165
Distribution May 2000 (1/3rd)	-	(10,000)	(13,722)
S104 holding c/f	6,000	20,000	27,443

The computation of the allowable loss is :

	£
Disposal proceeds	6,000
Less : Part cost	(10,000)
Unindexed loss	(4,000)
Less : Indexation allowance (£13,722 - £10,000)	nil
Allowable loss	(4,000)

20.6

The value of Yolande's shares immediately prior to the sale of rights was £600. £25 is less than 5% of £600, so the sale of rights ranks as a small capital distribution. Assuming that this distribution is not treated as a disposal, the S104 holding is as follows :

	No of shares	Cost	Indexed cost
		£	£
Bought January 1990	300	360	360
Add : Indexation to March 1993			
$\dfrac{139.3 - 119.5}{119.5}$ x £360			60
			420
Distribution March 1993	-	(25)	(25)
	300	335	395
Add : Indexation to April 1998			
$\dfrac{162.6 - 139.3}{139.3}$ x £395			66
			461
Sold November 2000	(300)	(335)	(461)
S104 holding c/f	nil	nil	nil

The untapered gain on the disposal is :

	£
Sale proceeds	780
Less : Cost	335
Unindexed gain	445
Less : Indexation allowance (£461 - £335)	126
Untapered gain	319

20.7

Walter received 19,200 shares worth £82,560, plus £6,000 in cash, a total of £88,560. The amount received in cash is more than 5% of the total and exceeds £3,000 so this does not rank as a small capital distribution. The S104 holding is :

	No of shares	Cost	Indexed cost
		£	£
Bought (Oval plc) April 1993	12,000	70,200	70,200
Add : Indexation to April 1998			
$\dfrac{162.6 - 140.6}{140.6}$ x £70,200			10,984
			81,184
Disposal September 2000 (6,000/88,560th)	-	(4,756)	(5,500)
S104 holding after disposal	12,000	65,444	75,684
S104 holding (Round plc) c/f	19,200	65,444	75,684

The untapered gain on the disposal is :

	£
Disposal proceeds	6,000
<u>Less</u> : Cost	4,756
Unindexed gain	1,244
<u>Less</u> : Indexation allowance (£5,500 - £4,756)	744
Untapered gain	500

Chapter 21

21.1

So long as Mohammed actually resides in both properties he may choose which is to be regarded as his PPR. Whichever property he bought and lived in first was automatically regarded as his PPR. After he bought the second property (and began residing in it) he could, if he wished, elect that this property should become his PPR for CGT purposes. He would do this if he thought that the gain arising on the disposal of the second property would exceed the gain arising on the disposal of the first property. The election would have to be made within 2 years of the date from which it is to take effect.

21.2

	Original cost £	Rebasing £
Sale proceeds	63,000	63,000
<u>Less</u> : Original cost	18,000	
Market value 31/3/82		21,000
Unindexed gain	45,000	42,000
<u>Less</u> : Indexation allowance		
$\dfrac{162.6 - 79.44}{79.44}$ = 1.047 x £21,000	21,987	21,987
Untapered gain before PPR exemption	23,013	20,013

The rebasing calculation gives the lower gain, so rebasing applies and the untapered gain (before considering the PPR exemption) is £20,013. Considering each of the three cases individually :

(a) The house is not a chargeable asset and therefore the disposal is exempt from CGT. The gain is £nil.

(b) After 31 March 1982, Melanie owned the house for 18 years and 7 months (223 months) and was absent for 48 months. There is no indication that the absence was work-related and this absence exceeds the permissible maximum "absence for any reason" by 12 months. Therefore the PPR exemption is £20,013 x 211/223 = £18,936 and the untapered gain is £20,013 x 12/223 = £1,077.

(c) Letting relief is available equal to the lowest of £1,077, £18,936 and £40,000 i.e. £1,077. This reduces the untapered gain to £nil.

21.3

	£
Sale proceeds	172,000
Less : Acquisition cost	55,000
Unindexed gain	117,000
Less : Indexation allowance	
$\frac{162.6 - 95.92}{95.92} = 0.695 \times £55,000$	38,225
Untapered gain before PPR exemption	78,775

Rupert's period of ownership (a total of 184 months) is broken down as follows :

(i)	1 November 1985 to 31 October 1989	48 months	Actual residence
(ii)	1 November 1989 to 31 October 1990	12 months	Working abroad
(iii)	1 November 1990 to 31 January 1992	15 months	Actual residence
(iv)	1 February 1992 to 30 April 1996	51 months	Working in UK
(v)	1 May 1996 to 31 May 1996	1 month	Actual residence
(vi)	1 June 1996 to 1 March 2001	57 months	Living with friend

Periods (i), (iii) and (v) are exempt (actual residence) and period (ii) is exempt (working abroad). Period (iv) exceeds the 4-year maximum allowable for working in the UK but the remaining 3 months of this period are exempt as part of the 36 months allowed for any reason. The last 36 months of ownership are exempt but the remaining 21 months of period (vi) cannot be exempt since they are not followed by a period of actual residence. The untapered gain is :

	£
Total gain (as above)	78,775
Less : PPR exemption :	
£78,775 x 163/184	69,784
	8,991
Less : Letting relief (lowest of £8,991, £69,784	
and £40,000)	8,991
Untapered gain	nil

21.4

	£
Sale proceeds	85,000
Less : Acquisition cost	37,500
Unindexed gain	47,500
Less : Indexation allowance	
$\frac{162.6 - 97.82}{97.82} = 0.662 \times £37,500$	24,825
Untapered gain before PPR exemption	22,675

Samantha owned the house for a total of 14 years (168 months). For 6 years (72 months) the house was used partly for business purposes. The computation of the untapered gain is as follows :

	£	£
Total gain (as above)		22,675
Less : PPR exemption :		
£22,675 x 96/168	12,957	
£22,675 x 72/168 x 4/5	7,774	20,731
Untapered gain		1,944

Chapter 22

22.1

The allowable expenditure in relation to the porcelain is £9,850 (£10,000 incurred March 1986, plus £3,850 incurred March 1992, less £4,000 received July 1992). The computation of the gain arising in March 2001 is :

		£	£
Sale proceeds			23,500
Less : Allowable expenditure			9,850
Unindexed gain			13,650
Less : Indexation allowance :			
(i)	on original cost		
	$\frac{162.6 - 96.73}{96.73} = 0.681$ x £10,000	6,810	
(ii)	on restoration costs		
	$\frac{162.6 - 136.7}{136.7} = 0.189$ x £3,850	728	
(iii)	on compensation received		
	$\frac{162.6 - 138.8}{138.8} = 0.171$ x £4,000	(684)	6,854
Untapered gain			6,796

22.2

The gain arising on the loss of the original necklace would have been:

	£
Disposal proceeds	19,000
Less : Acquisition cost	13,500
Unindexed gain	5,500
Less : Indexation allowance	
$\frac{142.1 - 103.7}{103.7} = 0.370$ x £13,500	4,995
Chargeable gain	505

The allowable cost of the new necklace is reduced to £18,995 (£19,500 - £505). The gain arising on its disposal is as follows :

	£
Disposal proceeds	22,000
Less : Deemed acquisition cost	18,995
Unindexed gain	3,005
Less : Indexation allowance	
$\frac{162.6 - 142.1}{142.1}$ = 0.144 x £18,995	2,735
Untapered gain	270

22.3

The gain on the disposal of the original building is computed as follows :

	£
Sale proceeds	74,300
Less : Acquisition cost	50,000
Unindexed gain	24,300
Less : Indexation allowance	
$\frac{162.6 - 129.3}{129.3}$ = 0.258 x £50,000	12,900
Untapered gain	11,400

(a) £2,500 of the sale proceeds have been retained. Therefore £2,500 of the gain is immediately chargeable. The remaining £8,900 may be rolled-over against the cost of the new building, reducing its allowable cost to £62,900 (£71,800 - £8,900).

(b) £11,600 of the sale proceeds have been retained. This exceeds the gain. Therefore the whole gain is immediately chargeable and no part of the gain may be rolled-over. The allowable cost of the new building is the full £62,700.

(c) The entire sale proceeds have been spent on a replacement building. Therefore none of the gain is immediately chargeable and the entire gain may be rolled-over against the cost of the new building, reducing its allowable cost to £65,400 (£76,800 - £11,400).

22.4

The gains which may be held-over are those relating to chargeable business assets i.e. the freehold (£23,500) and the goodwill (£40,000), totalling £63,500. Listed investments do not rank as a chargeable business asset, so the gain of £10,600 is immediately chargeable.

22.5

(a) The taxpayer is fully eligible for retirement relief. The first £150,000 is fully exempt and half of the remaining £350,000 is also exempt. Total retirement relief is £325,000, leaving an untapered gain of £175,000.

(b) The taxpayer is entitled to a proportionate retirement relief based on 9 years of trading. The lower and upper limits are scaled down to £135,000 and £540,000 respectively. The first £135,000 is fully exempt and 50% relief will be granted on the gains lying between £135,000 and £540,000 (i.e. the next £405,000). Total retirement relief is £337,500 (£135,000 + £202,500), leaving an untapered gain of £862,500.

(c) The taxpayer is entitled to a proportionate retirement relief based on 2 years of trading. The lower and upper limits are scaled down to £30,000 and £120,000 respectively. The first £30,000 is fully exempt and half of the remaining £90,000 is also exempt. Total retirement relief is £75,000, leaving an untapered gain of £45,000.

Chapter 23

23.1

(a) The year to 30 November 2000 is an accounting period.

(b) The period from 1 October 1999 to 31 July 2000 does not exceed 12 months and is an accounting period.

(c) The period from 1 January 2001 to 31 January 2001 does not exceed 12 months and is an accounting period.

(d) The 33 months to 31 August 2000 is divided into 3 accounting periods. These are the 12 months to 30 November 1998, the 12 months to 30 November 1999 and the 9 months to 31 August 2000.

(e) The 18 months to 30 September 2000 is divided into 2 accounting periods. These are the 12 months to 31 March 2000 and the 6 months to 30 September 2000.

23.2

(a) (i) The debenture interest received is Schedule D Case III income (assuming that the debentures were acquired for non-trading purposes). The income tax of £320 (£1,280 x 20/80) suffered by deduction may be reclaimed, but the gross debenture interest accrued during the accounting period is chargeable to corporation tax.

(ii) The income tax of £2,160 (£8,640 x 20/80) deducted at source from the debenture interest paid must be accounted for to the Inland Revenue, but the gross interest accrued during the accounting period is allowed either as a trading expense in the company's Schedule D Case I computation or as a debit when computing the net credit or debit arising from non-trading loan relationships (depending on whether or not the loan is for trade purposes).

(b) Both items would normally be shown gross in the company's profit and loss account.

23.3

The gross amount of interest accrued for the accounting period is a credit on a non-trading loan relationship (assuming that the securities were acquired for non-trading purposes) and will be aggregated with other debits and credits arising on non-trading loan relationships. Net credits are assessed under Schedule D Case III. Net debits may be relieved in various ways (see text).

23.4

The 17 months to 30 June 2000 will be divided into two accounting periods. These are the 12 months to 31 January 2000 and the 5 months to 30 June 2000. The chargeable profits for each accounting period are as follows :

	12 months to 31/1/00	5 months to 30/6/00
	£	£
Trading income (time apportioned)	300,000	125,000
Debenture interest receivable	3,600	2,000
Income from property (time apportioned)	6,360	2,650
Chargeable gains	28,700	49,760
	338,660	179,410
Less : Charges on income	12,000	-
Chargeable profits	326,660	179,410

Notes :

(a) The debenture interest receivable is allocated on the accruals basis. Interest accrues at £400 per month. In the first accounting period, interest is due for the 9 months from 1/5/99 to 31/1/00. In the second accounting period, interest is due for the 5 months from 1/2/00 to 30/6/00.

(b) The chargeable gains are allocated according to the dates of the disposals. Even though the two disposals are on consecutive days, they fall into different accounting periods.

(c) The charges on income are allocated according to the date of payment. Accruals are ignored.

23.5

The chargeable profits for the year to 31 March 2001 are as follows :

	£
Schedule D Case I	1,549,400
Schedule D Case III	
Bank deposit interest (£19,820 + £44,670 + £23,980)	88,470
Chargeable gains	531,000
UFII (£9,360 x 100/78)	12,000
	2,180,870
Less : Charges on income	9,000
Chargeable profits	2,171,870

Chapter 24

24.1

FY1999	1 July 1999 to 31 March 2000	£30,000 x 9/12 = £22,500
FY2000	1 April 2000 to 30 June 2000	£30,000 x 3/12 = £7,500

24.2

(a) Profits are £287,500 (£267,000 + (£18,450 + £2,050)). This is less than the small companies rate lower limit of £300,000 but greater than the starting rate upper limit of £50,000. The small company rate applies and the corporation tax liability is £53,400 (20% x £267,000).

(b) Profits are £1,505,000 (£1,450,000 + (£49,500 + £5,500)). This exceeds the FY2000 small companies rate upper limit of £1,500,000. Therefore the full rate applies and the corporation tax liability is £435,000 (30% x £1,450,000).

(c)   Profits and chargeable profits are both £10,000,000. Profits exceed the small companies rate upper limit for FY2000 so the full rate applies and the corporation tax liability is £3,000,000 (30% x £10,000,000).

(d)   Profits and chargeable profits are both £1,000. Profits do not exceed the FY2000 starting rate lower limit of £10,000. Therefore the starting rate applies and the corporation tax liability is £100 (10% x £1,000).

24.3

The company's profits are £577,000 (£536,000 + (£36,900 + £4,100)), a figure which lies between the small companies rate lower and upper limits for FY2000. The chargeable profits (£536,000) are taxed at the full rate and marginal relief is available. The computation is as follows :

	£
Corporation tax on £536,000 @ 30%	160,800.00
Less : Marginal relief :	
$\frac{1}{40}$ x (£1,500,000 - £577,000) x $\frac{£536,000}{£577,000}$	21,435.35
Corporation tax liability	139,364.65

24.4

(a)   Company X has chargeable profits of £875,983 and profits of £908,783 (£875,983 + £32,800) for this accounting period which falls partly into FY1999 and partly into FY2000. Chargeable profits, profits, lower limits and upper limits are apportioned between the two FY's as follows :

	FY1999 (1/3/00 to 31/3/00)	FY2000 (1/4/00 to 28/2/01)
Chargeable	£875,983 x 1/12 = £72,999	£875,983 x 11/12 = £802,984
Profits	£908,783 x 1/12 = £75,732	£908,783 x 11/12 = £833,051
SR limits :		
Lower limit	-	£10,000 x 11/12 = £9,167
Upper limit	-	£50,000 x 11/12 = £45,833
SCR limits :		
Lower limit	£300,000 x 1/12 = £25,000	£300,000 x 11/12 = £275,000
Upper limit	£1,500,000 x 1/12 = £125,000	£1,500,000 x 11/12 = £1,375,000

In both FY's, profits are between the small companies rate lower and upper limits so tax is charged at the full rate, less marginal relief. The computation is :

FY1999	£	£
Corporation tax on £72,999 @ 30%	21,899.70	
Less : Marginal relief :		
$\frac{1}{40}$ x (£125,000 - £75,732) x $\frac{£72,999}{£75,732}$	1,187.25	20,712.45
FY2000		
Corporation tax on £802,984 @ 30%	240,895.20	
Less : Marginal relief :		
$\frac{1}{40}$ x (£1,375,000 - £833,051) x $\frac{£802,984}{£833,051}$	13,059.65	227,835.55
Corporation tax liability		248,548.00

Since the tax rates and limits which affect this company did not change between FY1999 and FY2000, the same total result could have been obtained more easily without splitting the liability between the two financial years. However, this split is required so as to ascertain the figures required for the company's tax return.

(b) Company Y has chargeable profits and profits of £25,000. The apportionment between FY's is as follows :

	FY1999 (1/3/00 to 31/3/00)	FY2000 (1/4/00 to 28/2/01)
Chargeable	£25,000 x 1/12 = £2,083	£25,000 x 11/12 = £22,917
Profits	£25,000 x 1/12 = £2,083	£25,000 x 11/12 = £22,917
SR limits :		
Lower limit	-	£10,000 x 11/12 = £9,167
Upper limit	-	£50,000 x 11/12 = £45,833
SCR limits :		
Lower limit	£300,000 x 1/12 = £25,000	£300,000 x 11/12 = £275,000
Upper limit	£1,500,000 x 1/12 = £125,000	£1,500,000 x 11/12 = £1,375,000

In FY1999, profits do not exceed the small companies rate lower limit. In FY2000, profits are between the starting rate lower and upper limits. The computation is as follows :

	£	£
FY1999		
Corporation tax on £2,083 @ 20%		416.60
FY2000		
Corporation tax on £22,917 @ 20%	4,583.40	
Less : Marginal relief :		
$\frac{1}{40}$ x (£45,833 - £22,917) x $\frac{£22,917}{£22,917}$	572.90	4,010.50
Corporation tax liability		4,427.10

24.5

The due date of payment is 1 June 2000 (9 months and one day after 31 August 1999). The final payment of £4,650 was made on 3 October 2000, i.e. 124 days late. The interest due is :

$$£4,650 \text{ x } 8.5\% \text{ x } \frac{124}{365} = £134.28.$$

Chapter 25

25.1

(a) payment made net of lower rate income tax

(b) income received net of lower rate income tax

(c) neither (dividends paid before 6 April 1999 trigger payments of ACT)

(d) neither (UK dividends received are franked investment income)

(e) payments made before 1 April 2000 were paid net of basic rate income tax

(f) neither (interest from a UK bank is received by companies gross).

25.2

Return period	Tax deducted	Tax suffered	Tax deducted less tax suffered	Cumulative	Income tax payable (repayable)
	£	£	£	£	£
1/4/00 - 30/6/00	4,000	2,200	1,800	1,800	1,800
1/10/00 - 31/12/00	4,000		4,000	5,800	4,000
1/1/01 - 31/3/01		1,300	(1,300)	4,500	(1,300)
	8,000	3,500	4,500		4,500

25.3

The income tax returns for the year are as follows :

Return period	Tax deducted	Tax suffered	Tax deducted less tax suffered	Cumulative	Income tax payable (repayable)
	£	£	£	£	£
1/4/00 - 30/6/00		7,000	(7,000)	(7,000)	0
1/7/00 - 30/9/00	9,000		9,000	2,000	2,000
1/1/01 - 31/3/01		7,000	(7,000)	(5,000)	(2,000)
	9,000	14,000	(5,000)		0

The company requires an income tax repayment of £5,000. This is made by means of a reduction in the corporation tax liability for the year, as follows :

	£
Corporation tax liability for the year (20% of £240,000)	48,000
Less : Income tax repayable	5,000
Corporation tax payable 1 January 2002	43,000

25.4

Before 6 April 1999, the company paid dividends of £26,000 (£16,800 + £9,200), giving franked payments of £32,500 (£26,000 x 100/80).

There was no FII before 6 April 1999 but there was surplus FII brought forward of £4,000. The surplus of franked payments over FII was therefore £28,500 (£32,500 - £4,000). Notice that the FII received on 6 April 1999 was received one day too late to be taken into account when computing the company's ACT liability for the year.

ACT payable was £5,700 (20% x £28,500).

Chapter 26

26.1

	y/e 31/5/98 £	y/e 31/5/99 £	y/e 31/5/00 £
Schedule D Case I	-	23,800	11,500
<u>Less</u> : S393(1)/(9) relief	-	23,800	9,600
	-	0	1,900
<u>Less</u> : Non-trade charges	-	-	600
	-	0	1,300
<u>Less</u> : Trade charges	-	-	1,300
Chargeable profits	0	0	0
Trading losses and trade charges c/f	32,200	9,600	100
Non-trade charges unrelieved	400	500	-

26.2

	£
Schedule D Case I	-
Schedule A	10,200
Chargeable gains	540
	10,740
<u>Less</u> : S393A(1)(a) relief	7,300
	3,440
<u>Less</u> : Non-trade charges	3,440
	0
<u>Less</u> : Trade charges	0
Chargeable profits	0
Trade charges c/f	9,000
Non-trade charges unrelieved	560

26.3

The correct answer is (c). Under S393A(1)(a), trading losses may be relieved against total profits (including capital gains) of the accounting period in which the loss was incurred.

26.4

	y/e 31/1/99	y/e 31/1/00	y/e 31/1/01
	£	£	£
Schedule D Case I	22,700	28,600	-
Capital gains	-	-	8,700
	22,700	28,600	8,700
Less : S393A(1)(a) relief	-	-	8,700
	22,700	28,600	0
Less : Trade charges	5,000	5,000	-
	17,700	23,600	0
Less : S393A(1)(b) relief	-	23,600	-
	17,700	0	0
Less : Non-trade charges	1,000	-	-
Chargeable profits	16,700	0	0
Trade losses c/f	-	-	33,400
Trade charges c/f	-	-	5,000
Non-trade charges unrelieved	-	1,000	1,000

Notes :

(i) None of the loss-making accounting period falls before 2 July 1997 so losses may be carried back for only 12 months.

(ii) Losses totalling £32,300 (£8,700 + £23,600) are relieved, leaving losses of £33,400 to carry forward.

26.5

The main effects of a S393A(1)(b) claim are as follows :

(a) Chargeable profits for the year to 31 March 2001 are reduced to £200,000 and the company pays corporation tax at the small companies rate of 20%. Without the claim, the company would pay corporation tax at the full rate, less marginal relief.

(b) The maximum ACT set-off for the year to 31 March 2001 is reduced to 20% of £200,000 = £40,000. This reduces the scope for relief of any surplus ACT brought forward from before 6 April 1999.

(c) The corporation tax refund due for the year to 31 March 2001 carries interest dating from 1 January 2002 (or the date on which the tax was originally paid, if later).

Chapter 27

27.1

(a), (d) and (e) are associates, (b) and (c) are not.

27.2

The top five shareholders are Sejanus (with Apicata) 1020 shares, Claudius (with Livia) 590 shares, Agrippa 300 shares, Cleopatra 300 shares and Tiberius 200 shares, totalling 2410 shares. So the company is not under the control of five or fewer shareholders.

Sejanus is ranked as a director (since he is a manager and, with his wife, owns 20.4% of the share capital). So the directors are Sejanus (with Apicata) 1020 shares, Claudius (with Livia) 590 shares, Agrippa 300 shares, Cleopatra 300 shares, Tiberius 200 shares and Gaius 200 shares, totalling 2610 shares. The company is under the control of its participator-directors and is therefore a close company.

27.3

(a) The director owns more than 5% of the company's share capital so the loan is taxable. The company must pay tax of £3,000 (25% of £12,000) by 1 January 2002 (unless the loan is repaid before then). Once paid, this tax is not refundable until 9 months and one day after the end of the accounting period in which the loan is repaid or written off. The director will be subject to Schedule E income tax on loan interest calculated at the official rate. If the loan is eventually written-off (wholly or partly) the director will be taxed on the amount written-off.

(b) The director will be subject to Schedule E income tax on a benefit in kind of £1,800. But if the ticket had been given to a shareholder who was *not* a director or other employee earning at least £8,500 per annum, it would have been treated as a distribution. The cost of the ticket would have been disallowed in the company's accounts and the shareholder would have been charged to income tax as if he or she had received a dividend of £1,800 (tax credit £200).

Chapter 28

28.1

(a) They are associated companies and therefore they share the starting rate and small companies rate upper and lower limits.

(b) They form a 51% group so charges and annual interest may be paid between any of the group members without accounting for income tax.

(c) Until 6 April 1999, Arm Ltd and Foot Ltd could pay dividends to Head Ltd without accounting for ACT and Head Ltd could surrender ACT to Arm Ltd and/or Leg Ltd.

(d) They also form a 75% group so trading losses and other items may be surrendered by a group member to any other group member.

(e) Chargeable assets are transferred between the three companies on a no-gain, no-loss basis.

28.2

	£
Trading profits	220,000
Bank deposit interest	6,000
UFII	4,000
Patent royalties	(17,000)
Chargeable profits	213,000
FII (£27,000 + £3,000)	30,000
Profits	243,000
Small companies rate lower limit (£300,000 x 1/3)	100,000
Small companies rate upper limit (£1,500,000 x 1/3)	500,000

	£
Corporation tax on £213,000 @ 30%	63,900.00
Less : Marginal relief :	
$\frac{1}{40}$ x (£500,000 - £243,000) x $\frac{£213,000}{£243,000}$	5,631.79
Corporation tax due	58,268.21

Note :

Small companies rate limits are shared between Alpha Ltd, Beta Ltd and the other active subsidiary.

28.3

(a) (i) Delta Ltd will pay income tax of £1,600 (£200,000 x 4% x 20%) on 14 July 2000 and on 14 January 2001.

(ii) Gamma Ltd will neither pay nor be repaid any income tax.

(b) (i) Delta Ltd would pay income tax of £4,000 (£500,000 x 4% x 20%) on 14 July 2000 and 14 January 2001.

(ii) Gamma Ltd would suffer income tax of £4,800 (£300,000 x 8% x 20%) during the year. This would be repaid by deduction from the corporation tax due on 1 October 2001.

28.4

Base Ltd has current year trading losses of £90,000 and excess charges of £1,000, giving a total of £91,000. But Apex Ltd has chargeable profits of only £73,000 (£120,000 - £42,000 + £7,000 - £12,000), so the maximum group relief that may be claimed is £73,000.

28.5

A1 Ltd owns at least 75% of A2 Ltd and A2 Ltd owns at least 75% of A3 Ltd, of which A1 Ltd (indirectly) owns more than 50%. Therefore A1 Ltd, A2 Ltd and A3 Ltd form a capital gains group. A2 Ltd does not own at least 75% of A4 Ltd, so A4 Ltd is not a member of the group, even though A1 Ltd does (indirectly) own more than 50% of its ordinary share capital.

28.6

The amount of PP Ltd's loss which is available for group relief is £84,000 (£96,000 less a potential S393A(1)(a) claim of £12,000). This is shared between the consortium members as follows :

	QQ Ltd £	RR Ltd £	SS Ltd £
Share of PP Ltd's available loss	26,880	29,400	19,320
Chargeable profits	59,000	47,000	14,000
Maximum group relief claim	26,880	29,400	14,000

Chapter 29

29.1

(a) The value of the supply is £340, VAT charged is 17.5% x £340 = £59.50 and the consideration for the supply is £399.50.

(b) The value of the supply is £333.20 (£340, less 2%), VAT charged is 17.5% x £333.20 = £58.31 and the consideration for the supply is £391.51.

(c) VAT chargeable remains at £58.31 but the consideration for the supply is £398.31.

29.2

(a) Lorna must register since her taxable turnover exceeds the registration threshold.

(b) Mike must register since his aggregate taxable turnover exceeds the registration threshold.

(c) No-one need register. The partnership of "Pat and Phil" is not the same person as "Phil" so the turnover of the two businesses is not aggregated.

(d) The taxable "person" in this case is the company (not the shareholders) and therefore the company must register.

29.3

(a) She is not a taxable person, may not register for VAT and cannot reclaim input tax.

(b) She is a taxable person and must register for VAT. She must account for output tax and may reclaim input tax.

(c) She is a taxable person and must register for VAT unless granted an exemption by Customs and Excise. If she registers she may reclaim input tax. If she is granted exemption she will not be able to reclaim input tax but she will avoid the administrative burden associated with VAT registration.

29.4

See text.

Chapter 30

30.1/2 See text.

30.3

(a) Books are zero-rated. No input tax has been paid and so none may be reclaimed.

(b) No output tax is chargeable if a second-hand car is sold for less than its original purchase price, so long as input tax paid when acquiring the car was not deductible.

(c) The supply of a used commercial building is exempt unless the seller elects for the "option to tax". If this is the case, output tax of £200,000 @ 17.5% = £35,000 must be accounted for.

30.4

Input tax reclaimed is £692 x 7/47 = £103.06. Output tax must be accounted for of £71.19 (scale figure).

Chapter 31

31.1

	Value before AE	AE for 2000/01	AE for 1999/00	Value after AE
	£	£	£	£
Gift to grandson (exempt as a small gift)	-	-	-	-
Gift on marriage (£3,000 - £1,000)	2,000	2,000	-	-
Gift to husband (spouse exemption)	-	-	-	-
Gift to discretionary trust	10,000	1,000	3,000	6,000
Gift to Labour Party (exempt)	-	-	-	-
	12,000	3,000	3,000	6,000

31.2

(a) PET   (b) exempt   (c) chargeable   (d) PET   (e) PET.

31.3

The total of transfers brought forward in the last 7 years is £190,000, leaving £44,000 of the nil band to set against the current transfer.

(a) If the trustees pay the tax, the gross value of the transfer is £80,000 and the IHT due is £44,000 x 0% + £36,000 @ 20% = £7,200, payable on 30 June 2001.

(b) If Nicholas pays the tax, the net value of the transfer is £80,000. The gross value and the tax due are as follows :

	Net £	Gross £	Tax £
£44,000 grossed up @ 0%	44,000	44,000	0
£36,000 grossed up @ 20%	36,000	45,000	9,000
Totals	80,000	89,000	9,000

The tax due is £9,000, payable on 30 June 2001.

31.4

The value of each gift after deduction of exemptions is as follows :

		Value before AE	AE for current year	AE for previous year	Value after AE
		£	£	£	£
1995/96	Daughter (£500,000 - £5,000)	495,000	3,000	3,000	489,000
1999/00	Discretionary trust	500,000	3,000	3,000	494,000

Lifetime tax liability

The gift to Martha's daughter was a PET, so no lifetime tax was payable. The lifetime tax on the gift to the discretionary trust was £65,750, payable on 30 April 2000 and calculated as follows :

	Net	Gross	Tax
	£	£	£
£231,000 grossed up @ 0%	231,000	231,000	0
£263,000 grossed up @ 20%	263,000	328,750	65,750
Totals	494,000	559,750	65,750

Tax liability on death

(i) *Transfer made on 31 August 1995*

The gross value of this transfer is £489,000 and there were no chargeable transfers in the previous 7 years. Tax due at death rates applicable on 1/1/01 :

	£
£234,000 @ 0%	0
£255,000 @ 40%	102,000
	102,000
Less : Taper relief (5-6 years) @ 60%	61,200
	40,800
Less : Lifetime tax paid	0
IHT payable by daughter on 31 July 2001	40,800

(ii) *Transfer made on 1 June 1999*

The gross value of this transfer is £559,750 and gross chargeable transfers in the previous 7 years (2/6/92 - 31/5/99) were £489,000, which used the whole of the 0% band. Tax due at death rates applicable on 1/1/01 :

	£
£559,750 @ 40%	223,900
Less : Taper relief (0-3 years) @ 0%	0
	223,900
Less : Lifetime tax paid	65,750
IHT payable by trustees on 31 July 2001	158,150

31.5

The quarter-up rule gives 572 + 1/4 x (588 - 572) = 576. The average of the highest and lowest marked bargains is 575, so the shares are valued at 575p and the transfer has a market value of 1,000 x £5.75 = £5,750.

Chapter 32

32.1

Jean-Paul is a UK resident during 2000/01 but he is neither ordinarily resident nor domiciled in the UK. His UK income tax position is as follows :

(a) The emoluments of his UK employment are fully taxable under Schedule E Case II.

(b) The emoluments of his Belgian employment are assessed under Schedule E Case III but only on the remittance basis. This would be the case even if he were ordinarily resident in the UK (the "foreign emoluments" rule).

(c) The dividends on the Canadian shares are assessed under Schedule D Case V but only on the remittance basis.

(d) The interest on UK Government securities is exempt from UK income tax since Jean-Paul is not ordinarily resident in the UK.

(e) He may claim personal allowances for 2000/01.

32.2

Normally, a person is regarded as being either resident for the whole of a tax year or non-resident for the whole of that year, but a person who leaves the UK to take up employment abroad for at least an entire tax year (as Amy has done) is regarded as resident for the part of the tax year before the date of departure and non-resident thereafter. Amy's situation is therefore as follows :

(a) In 1998/99 she is resident until 31/12/98 and non-resident from 1/1/99. She will receive full personal allowances for 1998/99 to set against her income for that year. Her income for UK tax purposes after 31/12/98 will consist only of any income arising in the UK (e.g. rents from letting her house whilst away). Her Australian salary will not be subject to UK tax.

(b) In 1999/00 and 2000/01 she is non-resident. Her Australian salary will not be subject to UK tax and she will be taxed only on her UK income, if any. As a citizen of the European Economic Area, she is entitled to personal allowances.

(c) In 2001/02 she is resident from 1/1/02. She will receive full personal allowances for 2001/02 to set against her income for the year. Her income for UK tax purposes before 1/1/02 consists only of her UK income. Once again, her Australian salary will not be subject to UK tax.

However, if Amy visits the UK for 183 days or more in any one tax year she will be resident for that year and her worldwide income will be subject to UK income tax. Similarly, she will be regarded as resident if she visits the UK for 91 days or more per annum.

32.3

(a) 90% of the pension is subject to UK income tax under Schedule D Case V.

(b) 100% of the amount of the pension remitted to the UK is subject to UK income tax under Schedule D Case V.

32.4

See text.

32.5

See text.

32.6

	UK	Overseas	Total
	£	£	£
Schedule D Case I	2,120,000		2,120,000
Schedule D Case V			
(£57,400 x 100/82 x 100/50)		140,000	140,000
Chargeable profits	2,120,000	140,000	2,260,000
Corporation tax @ 30%	636,000	42,000	678,000
Less : Unilateral DTR		(42,000)	(42,000)
Corporation tax due	636,000	-	636,000

Notes :

(i) Underlying tax relief is available since Brits Ltd owns at least 10% of the voting power of the overseas company.

(ii) The unilateral relief given is restricted to the UK tax due on the foreign income. The remaining £40,600 (£82,600 - £42,000) of foreign tax paid is unrelieved.

Answers to review questions

Set A

Question A1

(a)

	£
Car (35% of £19,500)	6,825
Fuel scale charge	2,170
Loan (6.25% of £5,250)	328
LV's (200 @ £4.85)	970
Nursery fees	2,000
	12,293

(b) (i)   Drive an extra 100 miles per year on business and reduce the taxable car benefit to 25% of the car's list price, a reduction of £1,950.

     (ii)   If the £400 contribution is made towards running costs of the car such as maintenance, insurance etc. (not towards private fuel) it will reduce the taxable car benefit.

     (iii) Reduce the loan to £5,000, so that no taxable benefit arises.

     (iv) Take the canteen meals instead of LV's. No taxable benefit will arise.

     (v)   Transfer the son to the in-house nursery. No taxable benefit will arise.

These combined measures would reduce the taxable benefits by £5,648 (£1,950 + £400 + £328 + £970 + £2,000).

(c)

	Mr Tulliver Total	Non-savings	Savings	Divs	Mrs Tulliver Total	Non-savings	Savings
	£	£	£	£	£	£	£
Salary	50,000	50,000			14,000	14,000	
Less : Pension cont.					840	840	
					13,160	13,160	
Benefit package	12,293	12,293					
BSI (x 100/80)	8,000		8,000		2,800		2,800
Sch. F £4,680 + £520	5,200			5,200			
	75,493	62,293	8,000	5,200	15,960	13,160	2,800
Less : PA	4,385	4,385			4,385	4,385	
Taxable income	71,108	57,908	8,000	5,200	11,575	8,775	2,800

Income tax

Mr T	Mrs T			
1,520	1,520	@ 10%	152.00	152.00
26,880	7,255	@ 22%	5,913.60	1,596.10
	2,800	@ 20%		560.00
37,508		@ 40%	15,003.20	
5,200		@ 32.5%	1,690.00	
71,108	11,575			
Tax borne			22,758.80	2,308.10

Tax could be saved by switching investments from Mr T to Mrs T, using the rest of her basic rate band (where savings income would be taxed at only 20% and dividends at only 10%).

Question A2

	Total £	Non-savings £	Savings £	Dividends £
Schedule E	8,900	8,900		
Schedule A	3,680	3,680		
Annuity £25 x 12	300		300	
Schedule F £6,750 + tax credit £750	7,500			7,500
Statutory total income	20,380	12,580	300	7,500
Less : Personal allowance	4,385	4,385		
Taxable income	15,995	8,195	300	7,500

Income tax due

Starting rate band	: Non-savings	1,520	@ 10%	152.00
Basic rate band	: Non-savings	6,675	@ 22%	1,468.50
	: Savings	300	@ 20%	60.00
	: Dividends	7,500	@ 10%	750.00
		15,995		
				2,430.50
Less : MCA £5,230 @ 10%				523.00
Tax borne				1,907.50
Less : Tax credits on dividends				750.00
Tax payable				1,157.50
Less : Tax deducted at source (£300 @ 20%)				60.00
Tax payable				1,097.50

Notes :

1. Rents received are £5,000. Insurance is £370 (9/12 x £360 + 3/12 x £400). The wear and tear allowance is £450 (10% x (£5,000 - £200 - £300)) so total expenses are £1,320 (£370 + £200 + £300 + £450). The Schedule A assessment is £3,680 (£5,000 - £1,320).

2. STI exceeds the limit for age-related allowances by £3,380 so allowances are reduced by £1,690 (£3,380 x 1/2). £1,665 is deducted from the personal allowance of £6,050, bringing it down to the lowest possible figure of £4,385. The remaining £25 is deducted from the MCA of £5,255, giving £5,230.

Question A3

Sarah was 36 years old at the start of 1992/93 and 44 years old at the start of 2000/01, so the applicable percentage in all years is 20%. Unused relief is therefore :

	£		£
2000/01	10,000	1995/96	1,400
1999/00	6,000	1994/95	1,200
1998/99	2,000	1993/94	1,000
1997/98	1,800	1992/93	800
1996/97	1,600		

(i)   Sarah should pay a premium in 2000/01 for 2000/01 of £10,000.

(ii) She should also pay a premium of £6,000 in 2000/01 and elect for this to be carried back to 1999/00, so using the 1999/00 relief. This election must be made by 31 January 2002.

(iii) Unused relief in the six years prior to 1999/00 (1993/94 to 1998/99) totals £9,000. Sarah should therefore pay a premium of £9,000 in 2000/01 and elect (by 31 January 2002) for this to be carried back to 1999/00, where it will be covered by the unused relief brought forward from the previous six years.

(iv) The total premium to be paid in 2000/01 is £25,000 (£10,000 + £6,000 + £9,000).

Question A4

(i) *Mr de Praet*

	1999/00	2000/01
	£	£
Schedule D Case I	20,000	nil
Schedule A	5,000	5,000
	25,000	5,000
Less : S380 relief	25,000	5,000
Statutory total income	nil	nil

Mr de Praet's own personal allowance is lost in both years. If either he or his wife are over 65 so that MCA is available, a small part of the tax reduction relating to this could be used by his wife but most of this is lost as well. Tax savings are achieved at starting rate and basic rate. If the loss had been carried forward under S385, there would have been much less loss of personal allowances and tax savings would have been achieved at the higher rate.

(ii) An FYA of £7,360 (40% x £18,400) is available in the year to 30 June 2000. This increases the loss to £17,360. A Section 380 claim for 1999/00 will reduce total income to £640 (£18,000 - £17,360), so wasting personal allowances.

It would be better to restrict the capital allowances claim to £3,665. This reduces the S380 claim to £13,665, leaving total income of £4,335 which exactly absorbs the 1999/00 personal allowance. The unclaimed capital allowances increase the WDV carried forward and so result in higher capital allowances in future years.

Question A5

If the transactions are of a trading nature, then the profits made by the partnership of Bernard and Gerald will be charged to income tax in years 2000/01 and 2001/02 under Schedule D Case I. The "badges of trade" will be used to decide whether they are trading, as follows :

(a) *Subject matter*. It appears that the subject matter of the transaction is of a type normally associated with a trading venture, rather than of a type more normally associated with investments or personal consumption.

(b) *Frequency of transactions*. There was only one purchase but there were several sales. The fact that sales were made to a number of different garden centres gives the impression of trading.

(c) *Length of ownership*. This was a fairly short-term venture. Most of the barrels had been sold within 6 months and this again gives the impression of trading.

(d) *Supplementary work*. The barrels were sawn in half and Bernard and Gerald canvassed garden centres in the hope of finding customers. These activities constitute supplementary work and support the view that they were trading.

(e) *Motive*. It seems clear that the barrels were bought with only one view in mind - resale at a profit. This is a clear indicator of trading.

(f) *Acquisition*. The barrels were not inherited or gifted. They were purchased by Bernard and Gerald. This and all the other badges of trade combine to support the view that they were trading and are liable under Schedule D Case I.

Set B

Question B1

(i)

	Original cost £	Rebasing £
Sale proceeds	180,000	180,000
Less : Cost up to 31/3/82	(20,000)	
Market value 31/3/82		(50,000)
Cost July 1984	(8,000)	(8,000)
Unindexed gain	152,000	122,000
Less : Indexation allowance :		
$\dfrac{162.6 - 79.44}{79.44} = 1.047 \times £50,000$	(52,350)	(52,350)
$\dfrac{162.6 - 89.10}{89.10} = 0.825 \times £8,000$	(6,600)	(6,600)
Untapered gain (before PPR exemption)	93,050	63,050

The lower gain is £63,050.

		£
Capital gain as calculated		63,050

Less : PPR exemption :

   (i)   Full exemption 1/4/82 to 31/12/91 + final
         36 months = 153/221 x £63,050   43,650

   (ii)   Partial exemption 1/1/92 to 30/4/95 (half
         let) = 50% x 40/221 x £63,050   5,706   49,356

         13,694

Less : Letting relief, lowest of :

   (i)   £49,356   (ii) £13,694   (iii) £40,000   13,694

Chargeable gain   nil

(ii)

	£
Sale proceeds	7,500
Less : Auctioneer's commission	750
	6,750
Less : Acquisition cost	3,000
Unindexed gain	3,750

Less : Indexation allowance

$$\frac{162.6 - 101.8}{101.8} = 0.597 \times £3,000 \qquad 1,791$$

Untapered gain	1,959

The maximum gain is 5/3 x £1,500 = £2,500, so the untapered gain is £1,959. This is a non-business asset with a taper period of 3 years (2 years plus the bonus year). The tapered gain is 95% x £1,959 = £1,861.

Question B2

S104 holding :	No of shares	Cost £	Indexed cost £
Bought 1 April 1987	1,000	11,000	11,000
Add : Indexation to Sept. 1989			
$\frac{116.6 - 101.8}{101.8}$ x £11,000			1,599
			12,599
Rights issue Sept. 1989 (1 for 2)	500	3,000	3,000
	1,500	14,000	15,599
Add : Indexation to April 1998			
$\frac{162.6 - 116.6}{116.6}$ x £15,599			6,154
All sold 1 August 2000	1,500	14,000	21,753

Sale proceeds are £30,000 (£42,000 x 1,500/2,100), and therefore the untapered gain is £8,247 (£30,000 - £21,753).

1982 holding :

	No of shares	Cost (original) £	Cost (rights) £	M V 31/3/82 £
Acquired 1 August 1978	600	7,200		4,800
Rights issue Sept. 1989 (1 for 2)	300		1,800	
	900	7,200	1,800	4,800
Sold 1 August 2000 (600/900th)	600	4,800	1,200	3,200
1982 holding c/f	300	2,400	600	1,600

The gain arising on the disposal from the 1982 holding is :

	Original cost £	Rebasing £
Sale proceeds (£42,000 x 600/2,100)	12,000	12,000
Less : Cost up to 31/3/82	(4,800)	
Market value 31/3/82		(3,200)
Cost Sept. 1989	(1,200)	(1,200)
Unindexed gain	6,000	7,600
Less : Indexation allowance :		
$\dfrac{162.6 - 79.44}{79.44} = 1.047 \times £4,800$	(5,026)	(5,026)
$\dfrac{162.6 - 116.6}{116.6} = 0.395 \times £1,200$	(474)	(474)
Untapered gain	500	2,100

The lower gain is £500. Total untapered gain on the entire disposal = £8,247 + £500 = £8,747. The taper period is 2 years plus the bonus year (if the shares are a non-business asset).

Question B3

(i) The gain on the disposal of the building is :

	£
Sale proceeds	250,000
Less : Acquisition cost	100,000
Unindexed gain	150,000
Less : Indexation allowance	
$\dfrac{162.6 - 88.64}{88.64} = 0.834 \times £100,000$	83,400
	66,600
Less : "Held-over" gain	56,600
Untapered gain	10,000

The immediately chargeable gain is the amount not re-invested (£250,000 - £240,000).

(ii) The "held-over" gain of £56,600 is deferred until the earliest of :

    a.   disposal of the plant

    b.   the date that the plant ceases to be used in Ranek's business

    c.   December 2009 (10 years after the acquisition of the plant).

Question B4

(a) Marlene has net gains of £4,000. These are covered by £4,000 of the annual exemption, leaving a CGT assessment of £nil. The remaining £3,200 of the annual exemption is wasted. There are no losses carried forward.

(b) Moira has net gains of £12,000. Losses brought forward of £4,800 are subtracted from these gains, leaving £7,200. This is covered by the annual exemption, leaving a CGT assessment of £nil. Losses carried forward are £3,200 (£8,000 - £4,800).

(c) Marina has net gains of £3,000. These are covered by £3,000 of the annual exemption, leaving a CGT assessment of £nil. The remaining £4,200 of the annual exemption is wasted. The losses brought forward of £8,000 are carried forward to next year.

(d) Melissa has net gains of £4,000. These are covered by £4,000 of the annual exemption, leaving a CGT assessment of £nil. The remaining £3,200 of the annual exemption is wasted. The losses brought forward of £4,000 are carried forward to next year.

Question B5

(a) *Disposal of flat*

	Original cost £	Rebasing £
Sale proceeds	71,000	71,000
Less : Incidental costs of disposal	2,000	2,000
	69,000	69,000
Less : Part cost :		
$\dfrac{£71,000}{£71,000 + £65,000} \times £29,000$	(15,140)	
Part market value 31/3/82 :		
$\dfrac{£71,000}{£71,000 + £65,000} \times £40,000$		(20,882)
Part conversion costs :		
$\dfrac{£71,000}{£71,000 + £65,000} \times £18,000$	(9,397)	(9,397)
Unindexed gain	44,463	38,721
Less : Indexation allowance		
$\dfrac{162.6 - 79.44}{79.44} = 1.047 \times £20,882$	(21,863)	(21,863)
$\dfrac{162.6 - 90.11}{90.11} = 0.804 \times £9,397$	(7,555)	(7,555)
Untapered gain	15,045	9,303

The untapered gain is £9,303. The taper period is 3 years (2 years plus the bonus year) so that the tapered gain is 95% x £9,303 = £8,838.

Disposal of ICI shares

S104 holding :

	No of shares	Cost £	Indexed cost £
Bought December 1983	20,000	60,000	60,000
Add : Indexation to April 1985			
$\frac{94.78 - 86.89}{86.89} = 0.091 \times £60,000$			5,460
			65,460
Add : Indexation to April 1998			
$\frac{162.6 - 94.78}{94.78} \times £65,460$			46,840
All sold December 2000	20,000	60,000	112,300

The untapered gain is £37,700 (£150,000 - £112,300) and the tapered gain is 95% x £37,700 = £35,815. The total tapered gains are £44,653 (£8,838 + £35,815). After deducting the 2000/01 annual exemption of £7,200, chargeable gains for the year are £37,453. CGT due is (£28,400 - £20,000) @ 20% + £29,053 @ 40% = £13,301.20.

(b) Mr More should transfer the shares to Mrs More (at no gain, no loss). If she then disposes of them and realises the gain of £37,700, this will be entirely covered by her annual exemption and losses brought forward, so saving a substantial amount of CGT.

(c) *Disposal of shares in Hampton Ltd :*

	£		£
Sale proceeds :			
Freehold land	800,000		
Plant and machinery	60,000		
Investments	300,000		
Goodwill	280,000		
Net current assets	370,000		
	1,810,000		
Less : 10% discount	181,000		
	1,629,000	x 1/3 =	543,000
Less : Cost			40,000
			503,000
Less : Indexation allowance			
$\frac{162.6 - 79.44}{79.44} = 1.047 \times £40,000$			41,880
Untapered gain			461,120

If the shares are sold in December 2001, Mr More will be over 50 and entitled to retirement relief, reducing the gain considerably. The computation is :

	£
Sale proceeds £1,810,000, less 15% x 1/3	512,833
<u>Less</u> : Cost	40,000
	472,833
<u>Less</u> : Indexation allowance	
$\dfrac{162.6 - 79.44}{79.44}$ = 1.047 x £40,000	41,880
Gain before retirement relief	430,953
Gain eligible for retirement relief :	
$\dfrac{£800,000 + £280,000}{£800,000 + £280,000 + £300,000}$ x £430,953	337,268
<u>Less</u> : Retirement relief :	
(£100,000 + 50% x £237,268)	218,634
	118,634
<u>Add</u> : Gain not eligible for retirement relief	93,685
Untapered gain	212,319

Set C

Question C1

(a) The accounting periods are the year to 31/3/00 and the 6 months to 30/9/00.

(b)

	y/e 31/3/00	*6 months to 30/9/00*
	£	£
Trading profits (time apportioned)	260,000	130,000
<u>Less</u> : Capital allowances :		
25% x £100,000	25,000	
25% x £75,000 x 6/12		9,375
Schedule D Case I	235,000	120,625
Schedule A	20,000	10,000
Schedule D Case III :		
£2,000 + £2,000 + £1,000	5,000	
£12,000 - £1,000 + £4,000		15,000
Chargeable gains		10,000
	260,000	155,625
<u>Less</u> : Charges on income	5,000	5,000
Chargeable profits	255,000	150,625
Corporation tax @ 20%	51,000.00	
Corporation tax @ 30%		45,187.50
<u>Less</u> : 1/40 x (£750,000 - £150,625)		14,984.38
Corporation tax liability	51,000.00	30,203.12

SCR lower and upper limits for 2nd accounting period are £150,000 (£300,000 x 6/12) and £750,000 (£1,500,000 x 6/12) respectively.

Question C2

Quarterly accounting for income tax

Return period	Tax deducted	Tax suffered	Tax deducted less tax suffered	Cumulative	Income tax payable (repayable)
	£	£	£	£	£
1/4/00 - 30/6/00	-	7,040	(7,040)	(7,040)	-
1/7/00 - 30/9/00	9,000	4,400	4,600	(2,440)	-
1/10/00 - 31/12/00	10,400	-	10,400	7,960	7,960
1/1/01 - 31/3/01	-	6,160	(6,160)	1,800	(6,160)
	19,400	17,600	1,800		1,800

£7,960 is payable on 14 January 2001, but £6,160 of this is repaid in (approximately) April 2001.

Question C3

(a) *Poynton Producers Ltd*

	£
Cost 1 April 1993	150,000
WDA for accounting period to 30/9/93 (4%)	6,000
	144,000
WDA for accounting period to 30/9/94	6,000
	138,000
Notional WDA's for 2 accounting periods to 30/9/96	12,000
	126,000
WDA for accounting periods to 30/9/97, 98 & 99	18,000
WDV at 30/9/99	108,000

(b) The net cost of the building is £10,000 (£150,000 - £140,000). The period of ownership is 7 years and the period of industrial use is 5 years and 7 months (5.583 years), so the adjusted net cost is £7,976 (£10,000 x 5.583/7). The allowances actually given are £30,000, so the balancing charge is £22,024 (£30,000 - £7,976).

(c) The residue of expenditure after the sale is £130,024 (£108,000 + £22,024) and the remaining tax life of the building is 18 years. Sale Switches Ltd may claim an annual WDA of £7,224 (£130,024 x 1/18) for each of its 18 accounting periods to 31 December 2017.